# Atlas of American History

# Atlas of American History

by Gary B. Nash and Carter Smith

## Facts On File
*An imprint of Infobase Publishing*

**Atlas of American History**

Copyright © 2007 by Media Projects Inc.

**Media Projects, Inc.**
Principal Writer and Project Editor: Carter Smith
Associate Editor: James Burmester
Production Editor: Laura Smyth
Indexer: Marilyn Flaig

Facts On File, Inc.
An imprint of Infobase Publishing
132 West 31st Street
New York NY 10001

Library of Congress Cataloging-in-Publication Data

Nash, Gary B.
  Atlas of American history / Gary B. Nash and Carter Smith.—1st ed.
      p. cm.
  Includes bibliographical references and index.
  ISBN 0-8160-5952-7 (hardcover : alk. paper)  1.  United
States—Historical geography. 2.  United States—Historical
geography—Maps. 3.  United States—History. 4.  United
States—History—Pictorial works.  I. Smith, Carter, 1962- II. Title.
  E179.5.N37 2006
  911'.73—dc22
                              2006015915

Facts On File books are available at special discounts when purchased in bulk quantities for businesses, associations, institutions, or sales promotions.  Please call our Special Sales Department in New York at (212) 967-8800 or (800) 322-8755.

You can find Facts On File on the World Wide Web at http://www.factsonfile.com

Printed in China

CP MPI 10 9 8 7 6 5 4 3 2 1


(pbk) 10 9 8 7 6 5 4 3 2 1

This book is printed on acid-free paper.

# TABLE OF CONTENTS

INTRODUCTION                                    1

## PART ONE

### THREE WORLDS MEET, Beginnings to 1607

1    NATIVE AMERICA                             2
2    EUROPE TRANSFORMED                        10
3    THE AFRICAN HERITAGE                      14

## PART TWO

### COLONIZATION AND SETTLEMENT, 1492–1760

4    THE ARRIVAL OF THE EUROPEANS              22
5    THE CONQUISTADORS                         28
6    COLONISTS IN THE AMERICAS                 32
7    POLITICS, RELIGION, AND ECONOMICS         42
8    SLAVERY AND THE COLONIAL ECONOMY          50

## PART THREE

### REVOLUTION AND NEW NATION, 1761–1812

9    THE AMERICAN REVOLUTION                   60
10   THIRTEEN INDEPENDENT STATES               74
11   THE U.S. CONSTITUTION                     80

## PART FOUR

### EXPANSION AND REFORM, 1790–1855

12   WESTWARD EXPANSION AND MANIFEST DESTINY   88
13   A CHANGING NATION                        114
14   DEMOCRACY AND DISCONTENT                 124

## PART FIVE

### CIVIL WAR AND RECONSTRUCTION, 1856–1869

15   THE ROAD TO WAR                          138
16   THE AMERICAN CIVIL WAR                   144
17   RECONSTRUCTION                           160

## PART SIX

### THE DEVELOPMENT OF THE INDUSTRIAL UNITED STATES, 1870–1899

18   THE INDUSTRIAL ERA                       172
19   IMMIGRATION, EQUALITY
     AND VICTORIAN AMERICA                    180
20   THE AMERICAN WORKER                      188
21   THE CLOSING FRONTIER AND
     OVERSEAS EXPANSION                       198

## PART SEVEN

### THE EMERGENCE OF MODERN AMERICA, 1900–1928

22   THE PROGRESSIVE MOVEMENT                 210
23   WORLD WAR I                              218
24   THE ROARING '20s                         230

## PART EIGHT

### THE GREAT DEPRESSION AND WORLD WAR II, 1929–1945

25   THE GREAT DEPRESSION                     238
26   THE NEW DEAL                             244
27   WORLD WAR II                             250

## PART NINE

### POSTWAR UNITED STATES, 1946–1968

28   THE POSTWAR BOOM                         258
29   COLD WAR AND HOT WARS                    266
30   THE CIVIL RIGHTS MOVEMENT                274

## PART TEN

### THE CONTEMPORARY UNITED STATES, 1969–Present

31   DOMESTIC AND FOREIGN POLICY SINCE 1968   290
32   ECONOMIC, SOCIAL AND CULTURAL CHANGES    308

Bibliography and Selected Sources            319

Index                                        321

# Introduction

When the 27-year-old soldier-adventurer John Smith reached the Chesapeake Bay in 1607 as part of the first wave of English colonists settling at Jamestown, he was a man who knew the use of maps, understood how to draw them, and appreciated their use in promoting exploration and settlement in the Americas. He spent most of his first year in Virginia exploring the Chesapeake Bay and the Algonquian Indian country of the region. Back in England, one of the main sources of information on the struggling colony was his *A Map of Virginia,* soon to be followed by *The Proceedings of the English Colonie in Virginia,* both published in 1612. Thus, history and geography, as he understood, must be joined at the hip. "As geography without history seems a carcass without motion," Smith wrote, "so history without geography wandereth as a vagrant without a certain habitation."

Maps are not only useful for the study of American history; they are indispensable. The work of geographers and mapmakers today help historians visualize for readers where societies are located; assist readers in understanding the physical extent of them; aid the student in comprehending human and environmental interaction; and bring alive the movement of people, goods, ideas, and even fads. Without maps—often accompanied by charts and graphs—we are hobbled in understanding some of the most important aspects of history in the United States: exploration and territorial expansion, cultural diffusion, trade, immigration and migration, the role of climate and natural resources in shaping regional societies, urban and suburban development, and human interaction with the environment.

This new atlas has provided an engaging and concise history of the American people from the earliest peoples inhabiting the North American continent to the present day. Particular care has been taken to design and explain maps that go beyond those usually found in history books that accompany accounts of military, diplomatic, and political history. In this atlas readers will find less familiar maps and charts that illuminate the history of women, Native Americans, African Americans, laboring people, and other groups that have captured the attention of social historians in the last few decades. Also, the reader will find intriguing charts and maps, not usually found in atlases, that trace such phenomena as the effect of disease, the role of technology, the spread of public education, changes in family size, 9/11 hijacked plane routes, and the rise of global internet connectivity.

GARY B. NASH
University of California, Los Angeles

**A MAP OF VIRGINIA** John Smith's 1612 map of Jamestown Colony and the surrounding area.

# Chapter 1: Native America

**FIRST PEOPLES** Warrior (Virginia) 1587, From John White's images

According to the Apache people of the American Southwest, the sky was once dark and the earth was covered with water. Then the Hactin—the four great spirits—created four mountains, one each to the north, south, east and west.

The Hactin then built a ladder, woven from the rays of the sun. They placed it on top of the tallest mountain so that it could reach a hole in the sky. From out of that hole came the first man and woman.

According to their tradition, today's Apache are the children of the Sky-Father and Earth-Mother who climbed down from the sky. The mountains of Colorado and New Mexico where many Apache still live today are believed to be the same mountains where their earliest ancestors were born.

## The Origins of Native America

Archeologists and most historians tell a different story. According the most prevelant theories, the roots of Native America lie in Asia. Evidence suggests that during the Paleolithic age, nomadic peoples crossed the Bering Strait between Siberia and Alaska along a land bridge known as Beringia.

Beringia had been created during the last stage of the long period of global cooling known as the Ice Age. As vast amounts of the earth's water supply were frozen in glaciers, sea levels fell as much as 300 feet. In the north, falling water levels caused the Bering Sea to recede, leaving the land bridge and allowing Asiatic peoples to cross in the hunt for game.

Exactly when this crossing began is in dispute: most estimates range from about 8,000 to 50,000 years ago. Some Native American historians have placed the date at 100,000 years ago, basing their arguments on tools thought to be 100,000 years old, found at Calico Mountain in northern California. This view is discounted by archeologists who argue that human bones were different 100,000 years ago, and no human bones from that era have ever been found in the Americas.

Some have also argued that these first peoples traveled routes other than the Bering Strait route from Asia. Arguments have been made in favor of trans-Pacific ocean routes as well as for alternate routes along the Alaskan coast.

Regardless of when and where the nomadic migration began, it is known that after 15,000 BCE, rising global temperatures eventually melted the glaciers along the eastern slopes of the Rocky Mountains, opening a ice-free trail to the Great Plains of the present-day United States.

The journey from Siberia to the Great Plains and further south was a gradual one, lasting hundreds, if not thousands of years. Yet as early as 14,000 BCE, nomadic

*"There was a time when our people covered the land as the waves of a wind-ruffled sea cover its shell-paved floor."*

—Seattle (Sealth), Duwamish-Suquamish chief, 1855

**SPEARHEADS** propelled by bow and arrow, were among the first hunting and fighting tools used by Native Americans. Blunt spearheads were used for stunning the target and sharp, smooth spearheads were used for hunting since they could be easily removed. Sharp, rough spearheads were used in battle.

## Prehistoric Routes from Asia to the Americas

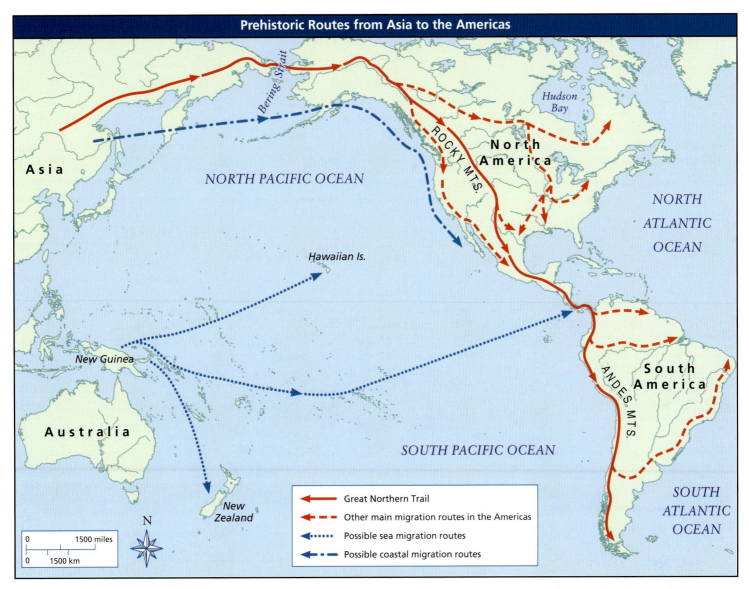

**Legend:**
- → Great Northern Trail
- - → Other main migration routes in the Americas
- ◄····· Possible sea migration routes
- ◄-·- Possible coastal migration routes

**FIRST AMERICANS** Many historians believe Native Americans first crossed the Bering Strait to reach the Americas from Asia. Some moved east to present day Quebec and the eastern United States while others headed as far south as present-day Argentina.

big-game hunters had begun to spread out across the American continent.

Scholars refer to the period beginning in about 14,000 BCE as the Lithic, or Stone, Age. The name refers to the stone tools used by the era's nomadic peoples to track game, as they moved from place to place sheltering in caves, makeshift lean-tos and under rock outcroppings.

Among the early evidence of these early Lithic era peoples comes from a settlement in southwest Pennsylvania, known as "Meadowcroft Rock Shelter." The site was continually inhabited until about 1300 CE, just two centuries prior to Columbus' landing in the Bahamas.

Little is known about the people who settled at Meadowcroft Rock Shelter. Yet the use of stone tools by 12,000 B.C.E is well-documented. The people of the Clovis culture, for example, inserted fluted spearpoints made of obsidian and other hard rock into the wooden shaft of a spear, and secured the point with twine.

These spearpoints—first uncovered near Clovis, New Mexico—have been found throughout present-day America. Scientists have uncovered human remains as well as distinctive bone tools and fluted spearpoints carved from obsidian and other hard rock. These spearpoints were inserted into a slot in the wooden shaft of the spear and secured with twine.

Other cultures , such as the Sandia of the Southwest (before 12,000 BCE), the Folsom of the Southwest and Great Plains (11,000–9000 BCE) and the Plano of the Great Plains (9500–4500 BCE) have likewise been identified through their unique spearpoints.

**SEMINOLE FISHERMEN** Seminole hunt fish and gather them into a canoe. A long fence or weir stretches across the river to channel more fish into a cage.

# Moundbuilders and Cliff Dwellers

By 5000 BCE, North America looked much as it does today. The great woolly mammoths and other big game had died off, possibly due to over-hunting. Early American Indians were forced to adapt to their new environment. Big-game hunting gave way to foraging and hunting for smaller game. Native Americans of the period also developed fishing skills and a knowledge of edible wild plants. Although they remained nomads, they generally moved within a region rather than long, cross-continental distances. Thanks to this more sedentary lifestyle, Native Americans of the Archaic era created tools out of wood, bone, shell, animal skins, plant fibers and even copper. Archaic peoples built boats, and wove baskets and clothing.

By 1000 BCE, many Native American peoples had settled into the small village life that would characterize much of Native American culture for the next 2,500 years that led up to contact with Europeans. During this period, known as the Formative Period, small scale agriculture, domestication of animals, the construction of permanent homes and other buildings, and other advances took place. More advanced tools and practices, such as the bow and arrow, weaving, pottery, and highly developed religious rituals came into being. In the Mississippi River Valley and the American Southwest in particular, highly developed, complex civilizations were born.

## The Moundbuilders

On top of a ridge in Adams County, Ohio sits an enormous earth mound, shaped like a partly coiled serpent. At the serpent's head is an oval embankment with a heap of stones in the center. Scholars believe the site, known as the Great Serpent Mound, was built between 1300 and 3000 years ago by a people known as the Adena Culture.

The people of the Adena Culture, who first emerged in about 1000 BCE near Adena, Ohio, survived by fishing and by gathering wild plants. Although no evidence exists that the Adena culture was agricultural, it was sophisticated nonetheless—advanced pottery, ornate art, jewelry and stone smoking pipes have all been found buried within earth mounds. Although the Serpent Mound appears to have had strictly ceremonial purposes, most other Adena earth mounds were built as gravesites to honor the dead. The size of many of these mounds suggests that the Adena culture contained an upper class that was able to command the participation of a large labor force.

By about 300 BCE, another mound building culture displaced the Adena culture. Also named for an Ohio archeological site, the Hopewell Mound Culture had a vast cultural reach, stretching from its core in the Ohio river valley east along Lake Ontario and west along the Mississippi and Illinois river valleys. The Hopewell lived in wigwam structures, and unlike the Adena, grew crops like corn and squash. Objects made a wide array of materials, such as obsidian, mica, shells, and alligator teeth suggest that the Hopewell participated in a trading network with other peoples.

Adena and Hopewell influence is visible in the sites left by the last of the major mound building cultures. The Mississippian Culture emerged after 700 CE along the middle Mississippi River, and in time

**LEADING MOUNDBUILDER CULTURES** The influence of the Adena-Hopewell and the Mississippian cultures was felt from the Carolina sea coast to Minnesota and Wisconsin.

**MOUND CULTURE** Cultures in the Mississippi and Ohio River valleys used earth mounds as temples or tombs. Most are small, but the Great Serpent Mound in Ohio stretches for almost a quarter of a mile.

**CLIFF DWELLERS** Remains of cliff dwellings in the Canyon de Chelley, Arizona, home to the Anasazi people in approximately 1200 CE.

spread as far north as Minnesota, south to the Gulf Coast of Louisiana and Red River Valley of Texas, and northeast through the Ohio River heartland and southeast to the present day Georgia-Florida border. Mississippian earth mounds were temple mounds—massive mounds with sloping sides and flat tops, on which wood thatched temples stood. Mounds were usually located around a large central plaza, with smaller villages located on outskirts of the central plaza. The prime example is at Cahokia, Illinois, where the central temple mound rises 100 feet and has a base that covers 16 acres. Cahokia may have been home to 40,000—making the settlement the largest single Native American settlement in all North America when it reached its apex in the 12th century.

Although there is no direct evidence for the link, the structure of Mississippian sites strongly resembles those of the great Mesoamerican civilizations such as the Maya. So too do many of the artifacts found at Cahokia and elsewhere—sophisticated tools, pottery and ceremonial objects—many of which have a strong similarity to Mesoamerican artifacts. Yet by the time that the first Europeans were arriving in the Americas, the Mississippian culture had begun to collapse, perhaps from famine or drought, perhaps from disease.

## The Cliff Dwellers

At about the same time that the Hopewell Culture was emerging in the Ohio Valley, three major groups of people were appearing in the desert Southwest. Flourishing from about 300 BCE to 1300 CE, the Mogollan people used primitive tools to grow crops like corn, beans, and squash in southern New Mexico and Arizona.

Settling along the sandy river valleys of southern Arizona, the Hohokam people (100 BCE–1500 CE) built long irrigation canals and diverted water with valves of woven mat. But it was the third southwestern culture, the Anasazi of the four-corners region of Colorado, Utah, Arizona and New Mexico that was most extraordinary.

The Anasazi divide their history into two periods. The first is known as the Basket Maker period (100 BCE to 750 CE). During this era, the Anasazi mastered weaving objects from straw and rushes and began the transition from hunting and gathering to settled farming.

It is the following era, known as the Pueblo era (c. 750–1300 CE) for which the Anasazi are best remembered. A pueblo is a multistoried structure of stone and adobe mortar or brick. Different stories were connected by ladders. Spaniards in the 16th century were the first to refer to these settlements and the Indians who lived in them as Pueblos, as "pueblo" means "village" in Spanish.

Early Anasazi pueblos were built on the tops of mesas. Chaco Canyon in New Mexico, was home to Pueblo Bonito, a five-story semi-circular structure with 800 rooms. To support such massive settlements, the Anasazi developed sophisticated agriculture, using irrigation techniques and terraced fields. Gifted Anasazi artisans crafted ornate pottery, mosaics, turquoise jewelry and clothing of cotton and feathers.

Then, in about 1300, the Anasazi moved from atop the mesas, building terraced cliff dwellings along the ledges of canyon walls. Presumably, the move to such inaccessabile locations was done for defense against raids by outsiders such as the nomadic Apache, who had arrived in the region in about 850 CE. A major drought in 1275 may also have forced the Anasazi from their cliffside homes in search of food. Today, their ancestors can be found among the Hopi, Tewa, Zuni and other Pueblo-dwelling people of the region.

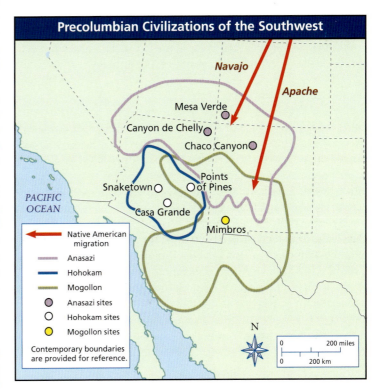

**Precolumbian Civilizations of the Southwest**

Navajo

Apache

Mesa Verde

Canyon de Chelley

Chaco Canyon

Snaketown

Points of Pines

PACIFIC OCEAN

Casa Grande

Mimbros

Native American migration

Anasazi

Hohokam

Mogollon

Anasazi sites

Hohokam sites

Mogollon sites

Contemporary boundaries are provided for reference.

N

0        200 miles
0        200 km

**NORTHERN INVADERS:** The nomadic Apache arrived in the Southwest from Canada in about 850 CE.

# From Nomads to Nations

Although mound builders and cliff dwellers are among the earliest and most dramatic examples of the transition from hunting and gathering to sophisticated large scale settlement, the changes unleashed by this shift were not isolated to a few groups. The domesticated agriculture that allowed for permanent settlement also led to more advanced social organizations, since not everyone needed to help with the hunt for food. Where hunter-gatherers typically organized themselves as loose affiliations of families, known as bands. As more Native Americans settled into small villages, groups of bands joined together into larger units known as tribes, or as they are more frequently referred to today, nations. Each nation consisted of a number of villages or bands, sharing common histories, territory, and traditions.

At the time of contact with Europeans, there may have been as many as 1,000 or 2,000 such nations. Some shared similar languages and cultural traits but more often each nation maintained its own unique way of life.

## Culture Areas

Early Native American tribes had no formal political institutions, yet each tribe functioned on the basis of hereditary family custom. Tribes within similar geographic regions shared many of the same customs and cultural traits. For this reason, anthropologists divide Native American tribes into geographical "culture areas" to provide a broader framework for understanding the wide variety of cultural and settlement patterns of Native American peoples before the arrival of Columbus. Although there are a number ways to divide the Native American population, one common breakdown consists of 10 unique culture areas in the territory that stretches from the Arctic Circle in the north to northern Mexico in the south.

Geographic regions—Arctic, Subarctic, Northeast, Southeast, California, Great Basin, Great Plains, Northwest Coast, Plateau, and Southwest — not only lent their names to culture areas but also shaped the ways of life of the people living in them.

## Trade Between Nations

As diverse as the pre-Columbian Native American culture areas were, the nations of North America had considerable contact with each other, often across great distances. The waterways of North America, especially the great Mississippi River basin, connected peoples from the Rocky Mountains to the Appalachians and from Canada to the Gulf of Mexico. Traders traveled hundreds of miles to attend regularly scheduled trade gatherings at great centers like Cahokia on the Mississippi or the Dalles along the Columbia River in Washington, where plentiful food sources—whether northwestern salmon or whitefish from the Great Lakes—allowed for the feeding of thousands of visitors. Regional trade alliances allowed the Mandan Indians of the Upper Missouri to trade excess corn with the Cree of Canada in exchange for skins and furs. Long distance trade brought exotic feathers north from Mexico and animal pelts from the Pacific Northwest were exchanged for cotton cloth from the Southwest.

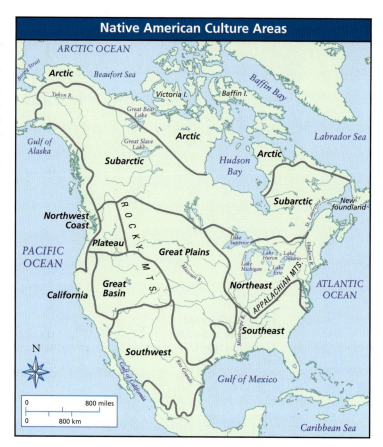

**CULTURE AREAS** Anthropologists call regions that share similar geography and peoples "culture areas." The map above shows one of the most common culture area breakdowns.

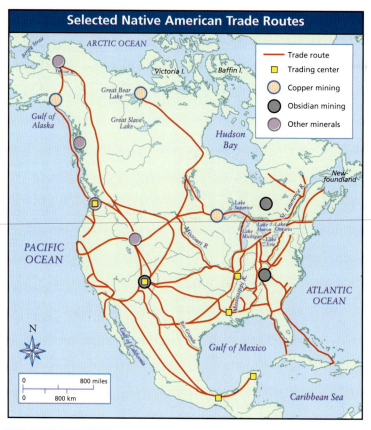

**TRADING CENTERS** The Dalles in the Northwest, Chaco Canyon in the Southwest, Cahokia and Poverty Point in the Mississippi valley, and several Mayan cities in Central America were centers of trade.

## Characteristics of Native American Culture Areas

| CULTURE AREA | LOCATION AND TOPOGRAPHY | SAMPLE NATIONS | LANGUAGE FAMILIES | CLOTHING AND DWELLINGS | WAY OF LIFE |
|---|---|---|---|---|---|
| California | Most of modern California and Baja California. Coastal mountains, forests, rivers. | Chumash, Maidu, Pomo, Wailaki, Yahi, Yurok | Algonquian, Athapascan, Chumashan, Maidu, Pomo, Uto-Aztecan, Wintun; more than 100 dialects | Simple skin loincloths (or no clothes) for men; skin skirts and cloaks for women. Moccasins and leggings in cooler weather. Cone-shaped houses, pithouses, plank houses. | Dense populations of individual nations. Most subsisted on plants, nuts, small game, shellfish. Families were important social units; formed permanent settlements. Ostentation and ceremonial rites in many nations. |
| Great Basin | Parts of Utah, Nevada, Colorado, Idaho, Oregon, California, Arizona, New Mexico, Wyoming. Largely desert. | Bannock, Paiute, Shoshone, Ute | Uto-Aztecan, with several dialects | Occasionally skins, but usually no clothing worn. Wickiups (pole frames usually covered with reeds). | Small-game hunter-gatherers; no agriculture. Reliance on roots, berries and nuts. Small, separate family units with some communal activities. |
| Great Plains | Mississippi River valley to Rocky Mountains and parts of Canada down to southern Texas. Mostly treeless grasslands, prairies; some plateaus, mountains. | Arapaho, Blackfeet, Cheyenne, Comanche, Crow, Pawnee, Mandan, Sioux | Algonquian, Athapascan, Caddoan, Siouian, Uto-Aztecan | Elaborate skin fashions, often trimmed with feathers. Largely portable tipis; some earth lodges, grass houses. | Before contact, mostly farmers. After introduction of horses, increasingly nomadic, with buffalo main source of food, clothing, shelter, trade. Women farmed while men hunted. |
| Northeast | Atlantic seaboard to the Mississippi Valley, Great Lakes to Tidewater region of Virginia-North Carolina. Dense forests, lakes, rivers. | Abenaki, Algonkin, Delaware, Huron, Iroquois, Mohegan, Powhatan, Shawnee. | Algonquian, Iroquoian, Siouian. | Men: skin breechcloths, shirts, leggings, moccasins; women: skin skirts, jackets, robes. Longhouses, wigwams. | Hunters-gatherers, farmers, fishers. Deer a primary source of food and clothing. Nations usually composed of family clans. Many formed alliances—i.e., the Iroquois, Abenaki, and Powhatan confederacies. |
| Northwest Coast | Pacific Coast from Alaskan panhandle to northern California. Mountains, forests, rivers, coastline with inlets, islands. | Chinook, Clatsop, Haida, Squamish, Tillamook, Tlingit, Umpqua | Athapascan, Chinookian, Kalapuyan, Salishian, Wakashan, Yakonan | Men: Usually naked. Women: skirts of plant fibers. Breechcloths, furs, and hides in cooler weather. Plank houses. | Fishers, game hunters, traders. Villages and family groups formed social cores. Rank determined by material possessions (given away in a custom called potlatch). |
| Plateau | Sections of Washington, Oregon, British Columbia, Idaho, Montana, and northern California. Columbia Plateau and rivers surrounded by mountains, forests, desert. | Cayuse, Flathead, Modoc, Nez Perce, Palouse, Walla Walla, Yakima | Athapascan, Chinookian, Sahaptian, Salishian | Minimal clothing. Earth-covered pithouses; pole dwellings in warm weather. | Primarily fishers, some hunters. Salmon primary food source; sustenance also drawn from wild roots, berries, and vegetation. Villages were main social unit, politically separate from other villages. |
| Southeast | Atlantic Ocean to eastern Texas and Gulf of Mexico northward. Rich farmland, milder climates. | Cherokee, Chicasaw, Creek, Natchez, Seminole | Caddoan, Iroquoian, Muskogean, Siouian, Timucuan, Tunican | Hides, furs, feathers; often nudity in hot weather. Wattle and daub houses; chickees (stilt houses). | Farmers; diet supplemented by hunting and fishing. Some nations thought to descend from ancient Mississippian mound builders. |
| Southwest | Southern Utah and Colorado into Mexico. Arid; mountains, canyons, mesas, plateaus, and desert. | Apache, Hopi, Navajo, Pueblo, Zuni. | Athapascan, Kiowa-Tanoan, Uto-Aztecan, Yuman, Zunian | Pueblo cultures: cotton clothing; other nations wore skins. Pueblo: adobe houses. Others: hogans, brush huts, wick-iups. | Skilled farmers (despite arid conditions) and nomadic hunter-gatherers. Reliance on native roots, seeds, nuts, berries. Autonomous settlements. Sophisticated art. |

# The Native American Worldview

To the earliest European explorers and settlers who came to America in the sixteenth and seventeenth centuries, the land they found was a "New World." In that land some sought freedom to practice their religious ideals without harassment; others sought to spread their religion at the point of a sword to the "heathens" they found there; many others came in search of riches—either by charting swift passage through this New World to the even wealthier East Indies of Asia, or by reaping riches from the virgin soil. In either, the early Europeans saw the American landscape as a wilderness to be tamed.

## The Web of Life

To the roughly 4 million Native Americans who lived north of the Rio Grande at the time Europeans first arrived, nature was not an inanimate object to conquer. Instead, it was a sacred gift, imbued with spirits in every rock, every tree, and every animal. Together all nature—including humankind—was linked inextricably, and the fate of one sphere of the natural world impacted the whole. Harming nature risked angering the spirits that protected it. Where Europeans understood land as something to be possessed by individuals, Native Americans saw the land as something to be shared by all. While Native Americans did recognize both personal possessions and territorial boundaries, the land itself was shared by all.

This view of human relations had a profound impact on everyday life. According to historian Gary Nash, the concept of communal ownership made Native American societies far less class-conscious than their European counterparts. While some stratified Native American societies, such as the Inca, Aztec and Natchez did exist, but they were an exception to the egalitarian rule.

Political structure reflected this view. Unlike many sixteenth and seventeenth century European monarchs, most Native American tribal chiefs derived their authority from the larger group rather than a supposed divine right to rule. Important decisions were usually made in consultation with other village leaders.

## Women in Native America

In many Native American societies, family organization was determined through the female line, rather than the male. Among the Iroquois, for example, families included an elderly woman, and her daughters and their husbands and children. When a son married, he left his home to live with his wife's family. Clans were made of several kinship groups, tied through blood on the mother's side. Clan matriarchs selected the village chief, and could remove them if he strayed too far from the will of the women who chose them.

While men were responsible for the hunt, women controlled the harvest and distribution of food, and ran the villages when men were away on the hunt.

The Native American view of the natural world, their communal practices, and power of women in Native American societies were all viewed by Europeans with alarm—and as proof that the peoples of the New World were godless heathens. In the centuries following Columbus' landing in the Bahama Islands, this deep misunderstanding of Native American culture would prove fatal to original inhabitants of the continent.

**THE FIRST PEOPLES** By the time Columbus arrived in 1492, North America was home to hundreds of different nations, speaking hundreds of different languages and practicing wide-ranging customs.

Native American Nations Prior to European Colonization

## Native American, West European and West African Societies

| SUBJECT | NATIVE AMERICAN | WEST EUROPEAN | WEST AFRICAN |
|---|---|---|---|
| Architecture | Location dictated building materials, resulting in immense variety. Dwellings included wigwams, longhouses, plank houses, sod houses, wickiups, earth lodges, stilt houses, hogans, and tipis. | Timber, brick, and stone were the basis of virtually all public buildings. | Location determined building materials. Styles ranged from earthen roundhouses, houses of mud wall with thatched roofs, wooden-rimmed houses, and in some regions, styles influenced by Islamic architecture. |
| Clothing | Simple apparel made of animal skins was most common; some southern nations wore cotton. In warmer climates, people went naked or semi-naked; feathers, bones and furs were worn for ornamentation. | According to climate, bodies were fully covered in clothes that indicated social status. Fabrics ranged from silk to wool. Upper classes wore jewelry and fine ornamentation. | Generally warm climates throughout West Africa allowed some people to go naked or semi-naked. Clothing materials included animal hide and fur, pounded and dyed bark fiber, woven grass and ornately detailed linen fabrics produced by specialized artisans. |
| Economies | Most nations engaged in simple exchanges and barter. Wampum (a crude form of coinage) was used among the more developed nations of the Northeast. Most nations depended on small-scale hunting and farming. | A capitalist monetary economy had been established. Trade, banking, and national coinage were accepted across Europe. Economic activities included small and large scale agriculture, mining and manufacturing. | An economic system closely tied to agriculture, long-distance trade, and iron production. |
| Language | An estimated 2,000 dissimilar languages had developed in the Americas by the time of contact. Due to linguistic differences, neighboring peoples were often unable to communicate with each other. | Relatively few languages, with most of them in western Europe descended from Latin or Germanic, both of which had a common root in Indo-European. Everyone with in a nation could communicate, and educated people throughout western Europe could communicate in Latin | At least several thousand languages in sub-Saharan, generally classified as part of the Niger-Congo language family is usually divided into ten sub-groups. Nearly half of them are made up of different Bantu languages. |
| Medicine | With experience and accumulation of empirical knowledge over generations, Native Americans had developed medical systems using natural herbal medicines and crude but effective surgery methods. | The Rennaisance spawned remarkable advances in scientific research and medicine, although many old practices such as bloodletting were still in use. | Traditional medicine included herbs and plants. Illness was believed to be connected to spiritual forces exacting punishment. Healers, were called upon to administer treatment and intervene with the gods on behalf of the patient |
| Political Organization and Government | Nations tended to be small, self-contained, family oriented units that generally did not form attachments to larger groups. The Iroquois in the Northeast and the Aztec in Mexico were exceptions. | By 1492, most European nations had developed into large, centralized nation-states. They shares the same organization as a monarch ruling with more or less absolute power | Well before European contact, a number of powerful empires had risen in West Africa, including Ghana, Mali, and later, Congo, Songhai, and Benin. Each had detailed legal codes and complex political systems. |
| Religion | Nations formed their own religious beliefs and practices. Reverence for nature played a large role, as did a belief in a benign god to whom prayers were addressed. | Although Protestantism became an important factor in Europe in the 16th century, Roman Catholicism remained the predominant religion, as it had been for more than a thousand years. | West Africans believed in a supreme being as well as a number of lesser nature gods, all of whom were honored in elaborate ritual. Ancestor worship also played a key role. After the 11th century, Islam also played a growing role. |
| Social Organization | Aztec society was highly stratified and came closer to the European model than other Native American nations, who generally had fewer class distinctions | Distinct social classes were the norm, including royalty, aristocracy, small landowners and merchants, and peasants. | Society was highly stratified, with nobles and priests at the top of society, followed by commoners. At the bottom rung were slaves. Unlike slaves of the transatlantic trade, their status did not automatically transfer to their children. |
| Technology | The wheel, guns, horses, cows, and (for most) ironworking were unknown. Other technologies were highly developed, including the weaving of baskets fine and strong enough they could contain boiling water. Certain nations perfected highly successful farming techniques. | Technology included wheeled vehicles, iron tools, and guns and gunpowder, which gave Europeans a distinct advantage over Native Americans. Europeans also raised livestock, such as horses and cows. | Technology included wheeled vehicles, iron, weaving, ceramics, and sophisticated architecture. |
| Warfare | War involved disputes between small forces over food or to capture women or slaves. Before Europeans introduced guns and horses, Natives Americans fought guerilla-style wars with clubs, axes, lances, and bows and arrows. | Uniforms, armor, and strict discipline among large armies was standard. Wars generally stemmed from claims for land or a monarch's desire for power. | Wars were traditionally limited, fought to capture slaves rather than conquer lands. However, large empires were also subject to invasion from the outside. In many tribes, warriors masked their faces in battle as a form of protection. |

# Chapter 2: Europe Transformed

*"To God I speak Spanish, to women Italian, to men French, and to my horse—German."*

—Holy Roman Emperor Charles V

**ARTFUL COMMERCE** *The Money-lender and His Wife*, painted in 1514 by Dutch artist Quentin Metsys, highlights the rise of mercantilism at the dawn of the Renaissance.

I n 986 CE, a small group of adventurous Norsemen led by Eric the Red founded three settlements on the southern coast of Greenland. There they found new pastures for their sheep and traded with the local Inuit. They gathered wood in what is thought to be Labrador, Canada and in about 1000 founded the first European settlement on the mainland of North America at Vineland, or Newfoundland. The remains of a Norse settlement, built at this time, have been found at L'Anse Aux Meadows, Newfoundland.

The Norse settlement of North America would not last. L'Anse Aux Meadows would be abandoned within 20 years. Over the next several centuries, changing climate and resistance by the Inuit would doom the Greenland settlements as well. In 1540, when a European ship arrived at a village called Eastern Settlement, the ship's crew found it deserted. They also found burial sites for the dead—save for the last man to die, who was discovered wearing clothing dating from the late fifteenth century, on the floor of his farmhouse.

The Norsemen had come to southern Greenland and eastern Canada in the 10th century to find land that could support their agricultural way of life. By the time Christopher Columbus reached the Bahama Islands under a Spanish flag in 1492, however, the modus operandi behind the journey reflected the enormous cultural, political, and technological changes that had swept Europe in the intervening years. Columbus and his successors were not looking for pastureland. Instead they sought gold, spices and other riches. And they wanted souls to save in the name of God.

## The Growth of Medieval Trade

When Eric the Red and his men arrived in Greenland just before 1000 CE, northern and western Europe were far from the era's major economic, political and cultural centers. Most Europeans were desperately poor peasants, tied to lands owned by remote feudal lords. The two centers of the European and Western Asian world were far away—Christian Byzantium in southeastern Europe and Asia Minor and the Islamic world, which stretched from southwest Asia across north Africa and into southern Spain.

Yet between 1000 and 1600, Western Europe underwent an unparalleled period of economic, political and technological transformation that helped spur overseas exploration. The spark that ignited this rebirth was in Italy.

Especially after about 1200, traders from Venice, Genoa, Pisa and elsewhere plied the waters of the Mediterranean, Baltic, and even the Atlantic's North Sea on long-distance trade missions. With Italians working as intermediaries, raw materials and necessities such as cloth from northern Europe were exchanged for imported luxuries like Asian spices or African ivory. Contacts with faraway peoples brought wealth, knowledge and prestige to the merchants who commissioned these voyages, in time rivaling that of the feudal lords that controlled the surrounding countryside.

The breakdown of the old feudal system was also spurred by a renewed interest in classical art and literature, again centered in Italy. This movement, known as the Renaissance, celebrated secular human achievement, education and the search for knowledge. The drive for new knowledge spread through Europe just as the age of exploration was set to begin.

## The Rise of Nation States

During the fifteenth century, European merchants faced a major challenge. Land route access to Asia and Africa was tightly controlled by Muslim traders. Since 1291, when Venetian merchant Marco Polo returned from China with stories of vast wealth, European merchants had dreamed of circumventing the Muslim world by finding a sea passage to Asia.

By about 1450 the old feudal system of western Europe was in decline. At about the same time a number of monarchs in Western Europe began to assert central control of taxation, law, trade, and military affairs. As monarchs consolidated power, their subjects identified them more closely with the state itself, spurring a rise in nationalist spirit. Late fifteenth century kings such as England's Henry VII controlled their countries more directly than the kings of the feudal age.

Another such leader was Prince Henry of Portugal. Although Portugal was a relatively poor nation, it had freed itself from control by the Moors, Muslims from Northwest Africa, who had occupied the Iberian Peninsula since the tenth century. Anxious to conquer the Muslim world, Henry, who became known as "the Navigator," organized expeditions into the unknown Atlantic Ocean. Aided by advances in navigation, mapmaking and shipbuilding, Portuguese seamen soon discovered one island group after another—the Madieras, the Canaries, the Azores—off the coast of Portugal and Africa. In 1487, Bernal Diaz and crew became the first Europeans to sail all the way down the west coast of Africa to the Cape of Good Hope. A decade later, another Portuguese, Vasco da Gama, reached even further. After rounding the Cape of Good Hope, da Gama and his men continued on up Africa's east coast and across the Indian Ocean, charting the path for Portuguese trading colonies in Goa, India and the Spice Islands (the present-day East Indies).

## European Mercantilism

The success of Portugal's overseas exploration signaled a major shift in Europe's economy, away from agriculture-based feudalism and toward a new system based on trade. Whereas feudalism operated on decentralized control by numerous powerful lords, mercantilism depended on strong central government, provided by newly powerful monarchs, to manage trade policies.

At the heart of mercantilist economics was a desire to balance the value of goods a country exported with the value of goods imported. Mercantilist economies increased exports by seeking overseas colonies that could generate raw materials or precious metals such as gold or silver; they worked to limit imports from other nations by imposing strict tariffs on foreign goods; and they encouraged the accumulation of wealth so that nations and individuals could create capital to expand production of finished goods.

Once Portugal initiated the age of European exploration, its neighbors—particularly Spain, France and England— saw that following in that nation's wake in founding overseas colonies as an economic necessity.

**BIRTH OF NATIONS** In the late fifteenth century, powerful monarchs began to centralize power over their kingdoms, initiating the rise of European nation states.

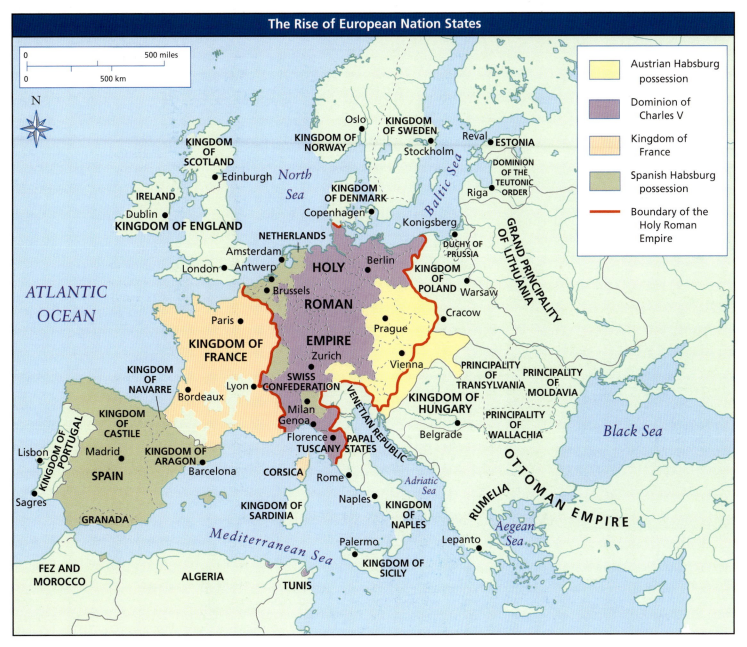

### The Rise of European Nation States

| | |
|---|---|
| | Austrian Habsburg possession |
| | Dominion of Charles V |
| | Kingdom of France |
| | Spanish Habsburg possession |
| | Boundary of the Holy Roman Empire |

# The Reformation

*"Blood alone moves the wheels of history."*

—Martin Luther

Along with the rise of nation states, the flowering of a new intellectual climate during the Renaissance, and the shift from agricultural feudalism toward mercantalist trade, conflicts in religion also influenced Western Europe's sixteenth and seventeenth century race for new lands. Twinned with the desire for material wealth, the opportunity to spread the Catholic faith to "heathen" lands spurred Portugal and then Spain. At the same time, the revolts against the Catholic church that swept Europe during the era would play out in the New World as well.

In April 1521, a 37 year-old friar named Martin Luther stood in front of the Imperial Diet of the Holy Roman Empire, in Worms, Germany. Presiding over the assembly was Emperor Charles V.

Luther had been summoned to Worms to face charges of heresy against the Catholic Church. A devout Catholic, Charles V ruled over a vast empire that stretched across much of Europe. Among the holdings of the Holy Roman Empire was the Kingdom of Spain, in which Charles held the title King Charles I. One of the goals of the Spanish exploration of the Americas that began a few decades earlier was to extend the reach of the Catholic faith. To Charles V, Martin Luther ideas threatened that faith in the heart of his empire.

Beginning in 1517, Luther had published a series of works that accused the church hierarchy, including the pope himself, of straying far from the teachings of Jesus Christ. To the German people Luther was a national hero, but to the Church he was a dangerous radical. Asked at his trial if he would take back his accusations against the church, Luther refused. As news of Luther's trial spread through Europe, revolt against the Church exploded across Europe.

Calls for reform in the Catholic Church predated Luther's stand at Worms. In the late fourteenth and early fifteenth centuries, John Wycliffe, an Englishman, and Jan Huss, a Bohemian, had condemned popes for placing their authority above that of scripture and for living lives of secular affluence. The Renaissance popes who ruled from Rome from 1447 to 1534 were patrons of the arts and collectors of ancient manuscripts, and were protected by private armies. Despite vows of chastity, many popes and bishops had sired numerous children.

Martin Luther went further than merely condemning church corruption. True, one of his strongest criticisms had to do with the Church practice of selling "indulgences" as atonement for sin. Yet his critique went directly to the heart of Catholic theology. He condemned the Catholic belief that salvation could be won through doing good works, arguing that only personal faith in God guaranteed eternal life.

Luther also directly attacked the authority of the pope by stating that the Bible itself, rather than the pope or any priest, was the sole authority on Christian life. Thus, every believer was capable of interpreting the Bible without a priest's guidance. In God's eyes all believers, regardless of circumstance, were equal.

Luther's theological argument was a direct assault on Rome's political authority as well. He called on German princes to assert control over religion in their states rather than submit to Rome's domination. Coming at a time when monarchs were strengthening the concept of the nation-state, Luther's anti-Roman political arguments appealed to growing nationalist sentiment. His protests against the Catholic Church would give the movement he began its name, Protestantism.

## The Anglican Church

In this climate England's monarch, Henry VIII, challenged the pope's authority over the church in his kingdom. Henry was no religious reformer—a devout Catholic, he detested Luther, once describing him as "a great limb of the Devil." Yet in 1527, Pope Clement VII refused to set aside Henry's marriage to Catherine of Aragon, the aunt of Holy Roman Emperor Charles V. At the time, Charles V's army had seized Rome and taken Pope Clement prisoner. Charles V refused to allow the pope to end his aunt's marriage to the English king. In response Henry called upon Parliament to strip away the pope's power over England. At Henry's direction Parliament then founded the Church of England, or Anglican Church, with England's king as its authority.

Parliament then granted Henry permission to leave Catherine. Upon doing so, Henry VIII married a dark-eyed 20 year old named Anne Boleyn, whom he hoped would bear him a son.

Henry VIII's three children, Edward VI, Mary I, and Elizabeth I, would each

**MARTIN LUTHER** In 1517, a monk and theology professor Martin Luther posted 95 theses condemning the Catholic hierarchy on the door of a church in Wittenberg, setting the Protestant Reformation in motion.

reign after his death. Both Edward and Elizabeth were staunch Protestants, but Mary, a Catholic, returned England to the authority of the pope.

## Huguenots, Presbyterians, and Puritans

Henry VIII's conflict with the Catholic Church was personal rather than theological. The doctrines of the Church of England remained quite similar to those of Catholicism. Yet Martin Luther's theological arguments with Rome were a major influence on other religious thinkers. In 1519, Swiss priest Ulrich Zwingli began preaching ideas, leading Zurich to become the first state in Europe to formally renounce the authority of the pope. In 1533, French reformer John Calvin expanded on the doctrines of Luther and Zwingli. Calvin believed that men and women are by nature sinful. Yet a select few were chosen by God to be saved from sin. Calvin called these few people "the elect," and declared that the identities of the elect had been predetermined by God. This doctrine is known as "predestination."

Calvin also advocated for a presbyterian form of church government, with laymen sharing control of church government with ministers.

Calvin believed that the elect had a duty to rule over society in order to bring glory to God. In his view, the ideal government was a theocracy in which church leaders controlled the lives of the community's citizens. Calvin personally acted on these principles when the people of Geneva, Switzerland asked him to lead their government. Under his rule, all citizens of Geneva were required to attend religion classes. Wearing bright clothing or playing card games were banned.

Calvin's ideas spread through France, Scotland, and England, where his followers eventually became known, respectively, as Huguenots, Presbyterians, and Puritans. The Huguenots and Puritans would be among the first to come to the Americas as pilgrims seeking to establish cities of God on earth.

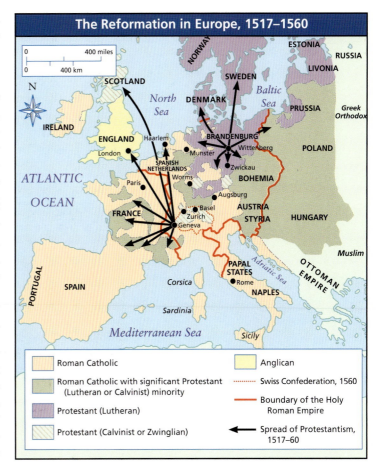

**The Reformation in Europe, 1517–1560**

Roman Catholic

Roman Catholic with significant Protestant (Lutheran or Calvinist) minority

Protestant (Lutheran)

Protestant (Calvinist or Zwinglian)

Anglican

Swiss Confederation, 1560

Boundary of the Holy Roman Empire

Spread of Protestantism, 1517–60

**THE MOVEMENT OF REFORM** During the early 16th century, Protestantism spread throughout much of Europe, ignited by the Lutheran and Calvinist movements in Germany and Switzerland, respectively. Other important Reformation movements included the Zwinglians, Anabaptists and Anglicans.

*"You must submit to supreme suffering in order to discover the completion of joy."*

—John Calvin

**JOHN CALVIN** The Swiss theologian John Calvin, who promoted the idea that God had chosen a select few to be saved from sin. To Calvin, these "elect" were called upon to lead the affairs of both church and state.

# Chapter 3: The African Heritage

During the early centuries of the past millennium, there arose in West Africa a series of kingdoms and empires. Based on trade, they mixed elements of the indigenous cultures of the region with the Islamic civilization of North Africa and the Middle East, a culture to be discussed at greater length in the next section of this chapter.

The wealth of these kingdoms—and most especially of Mali—is revealed in the spending of their rulers. In the 13th century A.D., one ruler named Kankan Mansa Musa led a caravan of 25,000 camels to Mecca, as part of the pilgrimage all good Muslims are expected to take at least once in their lifetime. Indeed, Mansa Musa ordered the construction of a new mosque—or Islamic temple—every Friday, to honor the weekly Muslim sabbath. Moreover, the caravan contained so much gold that it brought down the price of the precious metal wherever it went.

As with much of African history, the origins of Mali lie in a complex interplay of indigenous developments and outside influences. Around 1000 b.c., the Mande-speaking people of what is now western Sudan and Chad shifted their economy from hunting and gathering to agriculture, domesticating native plants like sorghum and millet. Farming, of course, can support far greater numbers of people than hunting. Among the Mande it produced a population explosion that led them to settle across a vast territory stretching to the Atlantic Ocean by 400 CE. As population densities increased, federations of villages under a single king spread across the Sahel, the semi-dry grassland region south of the Sahara. But what turned these small federations into great empires—of which Mali was just one—was only partly the doing of the Mande. In fact, the foundations of Mali and the other great Sahelian empires rested on the back of the camel.

**A WORLD WONDER** The Great Mosque, in Djenné, Mali, is the world's largest mud brick structure. It was originally built in the 13th century by Koy Konboro, Djenné's first Muslim ruler. The mosque towered over the town for six centuries, and stories of its splendor reached as far as Europe.

**ISLAM IN AFRICA**
The Muslim faith spread quickly across northern and western Africa following the death of the prophet Mohammed. Immediately after his death, his followers declared holy war on non-Muslim territories.

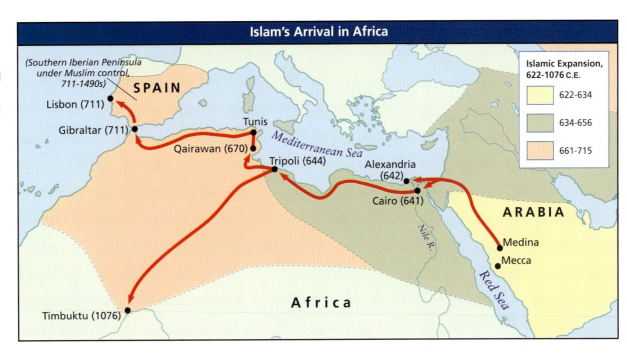

**Islam's Arrival in Africa**

(Southern Iberian Peninsula under Muslim control, 711-1490s)

SPAIN

Lisbon (711)
Gibraltar (711)
Tunis
Qairawan (670)
Tripoli (644)
*Mediterranean Sea*
Alexandria (642)
Cairo (641)
*Nile R.*

ARABIA
Medina
Mecca
*Red Sea*

Timbuktu (1076)

Africa

**Islamic Expansion, 622-1076 C.E.**
- 622-634
- 634-656
- 661-715

## The Spread of Islam

While camels are difficult to handle, they are ideally suited for desert travel and desert commerce—able to carry 500 pounds 25 miles a day and do so without a sip of water for a week at a time. Not surprisingly the camel—originally from Asia—spread rapidly through North Africa after its introduction around 200 A.D. It opened up an immensely lucrative trans-Saharan trade network between the Mediterranean and sub-Saharan Africa, a network that put the Mande in the middle. Great cities arose at the southern edge of the Sahara, where the main caravan routes emerged from the desert: Walata (in present-day Mauritania); Tekedda and Agades (Niger); and, most famously, Gao and Timbuktu (Mali). There Arab, Berber, and Mande merchants—all Muslim peoples from North and West Africa—exchanged silk cloth, cotton cloth, mirrors, dates, and salt (essential to the diets of people in tropical climates) for ivory, gum, kola nut (a stimulant), and gold. By the 11th century the mines of West Africa had become the Western world's greatest source of gold, turning out nine tons of the precious metal annually.

Also making its way across the Sahara—not on the backs of camels but in the minds of the merchants who drove them—was a new faith. Islam was born in the Arabian cities of Mecca and Medina in the early 7th century. A crusading religion that preached the power of Allah and the equality of all men, Islam—under the Prophet Muhammad and his successors—

quickly spread throughout the Middle East and North Africa. By 1100 CE, the Maghreb—Arabic for "land of the setting sun," that is modern-day Morocco, Algeria, and Tunisia—boasted major Berber and Arabic Islamic empires. South of the Sahara, a major kingdom—built on the wealth of the trans-Saharan trade—was emerging in what is now Mauritania and Mali. While its subjects—a Mande-speaking people known as the Soninke—called it Aoukar, outsiders referred to it as Ghana, after the title taken by its warrior-kings, and the name stuck.

The Kingdom of Ghana was a remarkable place, so well-administered that scholars throughout the Western world praised it as a model for other kingdoms. To assure the royal lineage, for example, the kingdom was inherited not by the king's son—in an age before genetic testing, paternity could never be determined with one hundred percent accuracy—but by his nephew, that is, his sister's son. And while the king and his people retained their ancestral religion—commissioning exquisite altars and statues to worship ancestors and guardian saint-like spirits—much of the merchant class and the government bureaucracy were Arabic-speaking Muslims. It was a potent combination of ideas, wealth, and military strength. By the end of the first millennium, Ghana had conquered almost all of the trading cities of the western Sahel, covering a territory roughly the size of Texas, where it exacted tribute, or taxes, from trans-Saharan merchants, subordinate kings, and local chiefs.

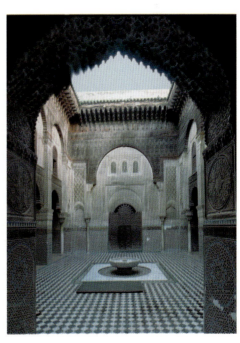

**RELIGIOUS TEACHINGS** Madrasas, or religious schools like this one in Fez, Morocco, helped spread Islam to believers in Africa.

# Kingdoms of Africa

**ENSLAVED** A 19th-century illustration of slaves in Zanzibar from *The Life and Exploration of Dr. Livingston, LLD* by David Livingstone.

Despite its good governance, Ghana collapsed around 1100 and divided into small kingdoms, which warred on each other for more than a century until a new dynasty of warrior-kings, founded by the great Sundiata, united the region from their capital at Niani (present-day Mali). More extensive than Ghana, the kingdom of Mali and its successor—the Songhai Empire—dominated much of West Africa from the 13th to 16th centuries. Even more than Ghana, these were thoroughly Islamic empires, where many of the rulers, such as Mansa Musa, were driven as much by faith as power. And as medieval Islam valued literacy and learning above all other earthly pursuits, the kingdoms of Mali and the Songhai were renowned for their scholarship. By the late 15th century, Timbuktu was home to the largest university in Africa outside of Egypt, funded by the wealth derived from trans-Saharan trade.

But while that wealth went to build mosques, universities, and great cities, it came at an immense cost. Along with the gold, salt, and cloth transported by trans-Saharan caravans, there was human cargo—slaves.

## Slavery in Africa

While never reaching the scale of the transatlantic slave trade of the 16th through 19th centuries, the trans-Saharan trade was still immense. It is estimated that up to 10,000 slaves were annually carried northward across the Sahara (along with a small trickle southward) at the height of the trade in the 10th and 11th centuries. In all, historians estimate over 4 million men, women, and children were transported from West Africa to the Islamic realms of the Mediterranean and Middle East between the years 650 and 1500. As in the Americas, the black slaves of the Arab world were largely put to work as

**MANSA MUSA** In this illuminated manuscript page from 1375, Mansa Musa, King of Mali, is seated on his throne, wearing a crown and holding an orb and sceptre, is portrayed at the center of a map of his realm.

## Major Kingdoms of Africa

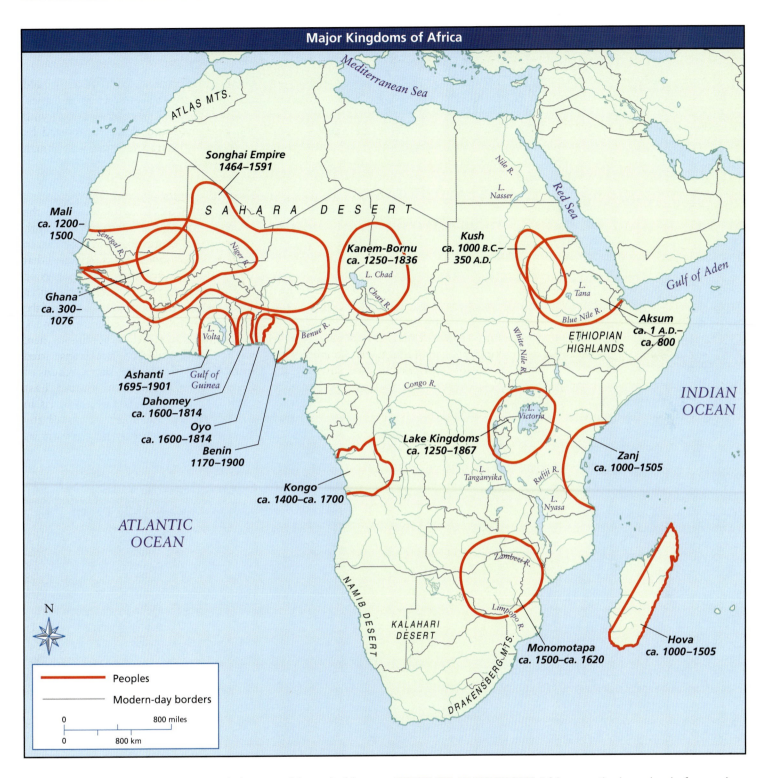

Songhai Empire
1464–1591

Mediterranean Sea

ATLAS MTS.

Nile R.

L. Nasser

Red Sea

S A H A R A   D E S E R T

Mali
ca. 1200–1500

Senegal R.

Niger R.

Kanem-Bornu
ca. 1250–1836

L. Chad

Chari R.

Kush
ca. 1000 B.C.–350 A.D.

L. Tana

Blue Nile R.

Gulf of Aden

Ghana
ca. 300–1076

L. Volta

Benue R.

Aksum
ca. 1 A.D.–ca. 800

ETHIOPIAN HIGHLANDS

White Nile R.

Ashanti
1695–1901

Gulf of Guinea

Congo R.

INDIAN OCEAN

Dahomey
ca. 1600–1814

L. Victoria

Oyo
ca. 1600–1814

Lake Kingdoms
ca. 1250–1867

Zanj
ca. 1000–1505

Benin
1170–1900

L. Tanganyika

Rufiji R.

Kongo
ca. 1400–ca. 1700

ATLANTIC OCEAN

L. Nyasa

N

Zambezi R.

NAMIB DESERT

Limpopo R.

KALAHARI DESERT

Monomotapa
ca. 1500–ca. 1620

Hova
ca. 1000–1505

DRAKENSBERG MTS.

Peoples

Modern-day borders

0          800 miles

0          800 km

---

laborers—in mines, plantations, workshops, and households.

Still, there were significant differences between Islamic and transatlantic slavery. For one thing, many of the Islamic slaves became soldiers, where they could often earn their freedom through military valor. And because race and color had little to do with status—the Arab world also imported slaves from Europe and western Asia—there was far more social intermingling of free people and slaves, including extensive intermarriage. Indeed, it was in this multi-cultural Mediterranean setting that African slaves first came to the attention of European Christians, including the Spanish and Portuguese. And when these Europeans looked for people to work the plantations of their transatlantic empires after 1500, they increasingly turned to Africa.

**SPECTACULAR KINGDOMS** Africa was the homeland of several great civilizations. On the west coast alone were the great kingdoms of Ghana, Mali, and Songhai.

*"Kill neither man, woman nor child. Are they not the children of Chembe (God), and have they not the right to live?...."*

—Shamba Bolongongo, King of Kongo (1600–1620)

# The Rise of the African Slave Trade

"Sir," began the letter that the king of Kongo, Nzinga Mbemba, wrote in 1526 to King João III of Portugal. "Your Highness should know how our Kingdom is being lost in so many ways . . . by the excessive freedom given by your agents and officials to the men and merchants who are allowed to come to this Kingdom to set up shops with goods and many things which have been prohibited by us, and which they spread throughout our Kingdoms and Domains in such abundance that many of our vassals [subjects], whom we had in obedience, do not comply because they have the things in greater abundance than we ourselves; and it was with these things that we had them content and subjected under our vassalage and jurisdiction. . . . "

Mbemba, the son of the first central African king to encounter Europeans, was probably not the first African ruler, and certainly not the last, to learn that the trade goods that Europeans brought with them in their ships came with a steep price tag. In 1506, Mbemba had invited Portuguese merchants, administrators, and government officials to live in his kingdom and introduce European ideas, faith, and commodities to his subjects. But as the 1526 letter between Mbemba and King João III makes clear, the European presence proved to be destructive. Portugal's representatives freely sold Mbemba's subjects alcohol, firearms, and other goods, thereby undermining the Kongo government. And, of course, the goods were only part of the trade. In exchange, the Portuguese demanded the kingdom's most valuable asset. "We cannot reckon on how great the damage is," Mbemba's letter goes on to say, "since the mentioned merchants are taking every day our natives . . . and get them to be sold; and so great, Sir, is the corruption of licentiousness [sin] that our country is being completely depopulated."

The king of Portugal's response to the African leader was less than encouraging; Kongo had nothing else of value to Europeans. If Mbemba wanted to receive the European goods his kingdom now depended on, he would have to let Portuguese slave traders conduct their business without interference. Although Mbemba's successors would attempt to prevent Portugal from dominating the kingdom's affairs by fostering trade with the Dutch as well, by the late 17th century

Kongo had splintered apart. Two centuries later French and Belgian colonies, known as French Congo and Congo Free State (later renamed Belgian Congo) would complete Kongo's transformation from independence to subjegation.

## Slavery in Pre-Colonial Africa

As in many regions in ancient times, slavery was part of everyday life in Africa. As the biblical book of Exodus recounts, the Egyptians enslaved thousands of Hebrews—and Nubians—putting them to work constructing some of the greatest monuments of the ancient world. The Phoenician trading empire of Carthage—in modern-day Tunisia—exported African slaves throughout the Mediterranean world several centuries before Christ. The Romans took the trade to another level, enslaving tens of thousands of Africans (including a small number of black Africans) to work the plantations and crew the sea-going galleys of the empire. The barbarian successors to Rome in North Africa maintained slavery, and the coming of the Arab armies in the 7th and 8th

**CARTHAGINIAN SLAVE** An enslaved African carries a serving platter in this Carthaginian mosaic dating from between 180 and 90 CE. Carthage used slaves throughout its Mediterranean empire.

centuries expanded the trade, even as their religion established some of the first moral codes on the treatment of slaves.

Humans were among the most common and valuable commodities of the trans-Saharan trade, with Arab merchants working with local officials and traders to secure the cargo. While evidence of slavery in all great medieval kingdoms of Africa is relatively scarce, a pattern seems to emerge: the more trade-oriented the kingdom, the more common was slavery. Thus, in the great West Africa trading empires of Mali and Songhai, slaves did much of the backbreaking labor in salt mines and on plantations, as well as served as a lucrative export.

Evidence of a slave trade also exists for the early kingdoms of Oyo and Benin from the 15th century onward and in the kingdom of Great Zimbabwe in southern Africa from 1200 to 1500. The trade was an essential component of the economies of the Islamic city-states established by Arab merchants along the Indian coast of Africa.

Amongst the villages and tribal confederations of sub-Saharan Africa, slavery was a more intimate affair. In terms of numbers, it was much smaller in scale and slaves lived with, worked among, and often married into the families who owned them. Before the arrival of European slavers and outside the orbit of the great Islamic and African empires, slaves were not simply commodities in a vast trading system. While slaves in such societies were not always treated benignly—wherever one person holds power over another there is the potential for abuse—they were still treated as human beings. A person became a slave because of misfortune—losing a war and becoming a prisoner or losing a crop and being a debtor—or because of individual misdeeds, as in the case of criminals. Thus, slavery was rarely an inherited status and slaves were not necessarily viewed as an inferior form of humanity.

## The Transatlantic Slave Trade

While slavery in Africa predates the European Transatlantic trade, it is important to understand that Europeans expanded the slave trade beyond any scale ever dreamt of by the most ambitious trans-Saharan merchant. The development of New World plantation agriculture and the

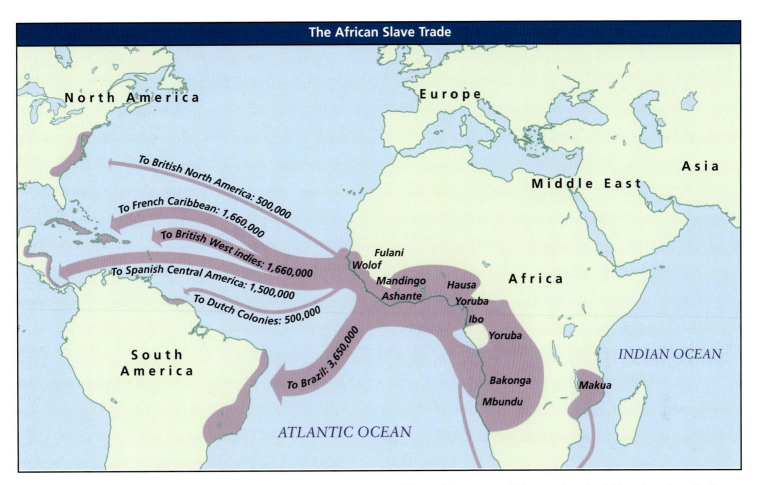

## The African Slave Trade

To British North America: 500,000
To French Caribbean: 1,660,000
To British West Indies: 1,660,000
To Spanish Central America: 1,500,000
To Dutch Colonies: 500,000
To Brazil: 3,650,000

North America

Europe

Asia

Middle East

Africa

Fulani
Wolof
Mandingo
Ashante
Hausa
Yoruba
Ibo
Yoruba
Bakonga
Mbundu
Makua

South America

INDIAN OCEAN

ATLANTIC OCEAN

**THE AFRICAN SLAVE TRADE** Between roughly 1500 and 1870, over 9 million Africans were kidnapped and sold into bondage in the Americas. Most came from West Africa. The largest enslaved African population was in Brazil, which finally banned slavery in 1870.

decimation of Native American populations by disease and war after 1500 led to an insatiable demand for labor, and the African slave trade was expanded exponentially to meet that demand. Over the course of the 16th century, the trade gained momentum slowly, with the Portuguese dominating. By 1600, the transatlantic trade drew, even with the trans-Saharan network, about 5,000 slaves being transported every year along each of these routes. With the arrival of the more efficient Dutch, British, and French traders in the 17th and 18th centuries, the transatlantic trade easily outdistanced the trans-Saharan trade. By 1800, nearly 80,000 Africans were being forcibly transported to the New World. During the course of the 19th century, the numbers leveled off and then declined, as first Great Britain, then the United States, and finally other European countries banned first the trade in slaves and then the practice of slavery itself.

All of these numbers are estimates. But one fact should always be kept in mind: the numbers of slaves actually taken to the New World represents only a fraction—probably less than half—of the total numbers of Africans enslaved. Historian Patrick Manning estimates that about 9 million persons were brought to the Caribbean, Brazil, and the United States as slaves between 1700 and 1850. But, he adds, some 12 million died within a year of their capture and another 7 million were enslaved for use within Africa. Altogether, it is estimated that as many as 18 million persons were forcibly taken from tropical Africa: 11 million from West Africa across the Atlantic; 5 million more from the Sahel across the Sahara and Red Sea; and yet another 2 million from central and southern Africa to the

Middle East and the sugar islands of the Indian Ocean. The demographic effect of this trade was even greater than these numbers indicate. Scholars estimate the population of sub-Saharan Africa at about 50 million in 1850; absent the slave trade, however, it would have been closer to 100 million.

## Europeans in Africa

If, by some magic, all European settlers had disappeared from sub-Saharan Africa in 1800, they would have left behind scant evidence of their presence: some British, and French slave forts along the coasts of western and southwestern Africa, a few Portuguese trading posts along the southern and east African coast and, most notably, a scattering of Dutch towns and farms at the Cape of Good Hope (modern South Africa), where the Mediterranean climate was more conducive to European settlement. Until the 19th century, European settlers and colonists kept their distance from Africa, and for good reasons. First, the tropical parts of the continent were full of diseases deadly to outsiders, with malaria in particular felling most of those who tried to settle there. Even the freed slaves from North America who settled in Liberia—all distant descendants of the African motherland—often succumbed to disease. Not for nothing had tropical Africa earned the terrifying name "white man's grave."

Topography also played a role in keeping the Europeans at bay. Much of interior Africa is made up of high plateaus, which drop

**THE PORTUGUESE** Portugal was the first European nation to explore and, in time, colonize coastal Africa. In 1472, Bartolomeu Dias founded the settlement at Elmina. Eventually, the Portuguese would reach the west coast of India.

off steeply near the coast. Turbulent rapids and falls mark the lower reaches of most of the great African rivers, making them all but impassable to navigation. Finally, there was the human factor. For European governments and merchants of the 17th and 18th centuries, there was no need and little chance to penetrate more than a few miles from the coast. Africa's most valuable and coveted export—slaves—was largely controlled by powerful, militaristic African states. Until the advent of more sophisticated and deadly weaponry in the late 19th century—such as the Maxim gun—no European force could effectively challenge the African middlemen of the slave trade, armed as they were by those same Europeans.

### European Settlements

As with exploration and the slave trade, the Portuguese were the first to settle in sub-Saharan Africa. For much of the 15th century, the Portuguese monarchs—most notably Prince Henry the Navigator—sent ships southward, looking for an all-sea route to the Indies. Two years after Christopher Columbus's 1492 "discovery" of America, Pope Alexander VI helped arrange the Treaty of Tordesillas, dividing the non-European world into Spanish and Portuguese spheres: most of the Americas and the Pacific for Spain; Asia, Brazil, and Africa for Portugal. In 1497, Portuguese explorer Vasco da Gama finally rounded the Cape of Good Hope at the southern tip of Africa, sailed on to India, and returned to Portugal. Although his expedition was less than successful financially—his European trinkets were of little interest to local African merchants—it did prove three things: the voyage was possible; the Portuguese had bigger guns than the locals (and could force them to sell); and the spice price differential between India and Europe (the source of profits) was enormous.

Over the next several decades, the Portuguese would establish trading posts and factories at Elmina (modern-day Ghana) and Luanda (Angola), while forcibly taking the Arab trading cities of Sofala, Moçambique, Pemba, Zanzibar, and Mombasa on the Indian Ocean coast. In 1652, the Dutch East India Company established a colony of farmers and traders in the region around the modern-day city of Capetown, to serve as a provisioning station for ships bound to and from the East Indies. At the same time, and on through the 18th century, British, Dutch, French, Spanish, and even Danish merchants built slave factories, or fortified trans-shipment centers, along the West African coast from Senegal to Nigeria, many of which thrived well into the 19th century.

## Portuguese Exploration of Africa

← Bartolomeu Dias, 1487–88
← Vasco da Gama, 1497–98
▨ Area under Portuguese control, ca. 1550
● Major town

Mediterranean Sea

CANARY IS.

Nile R.
Red Sea

Sierra Leone 1460
GUINEA
IBERIA
Elmina 1472
SLAVE COAST
ETHIOPIA

Santa Maria 1462
Principe Is. 1472
Cape St. Catherine 1474
KINGDOM OF KONGO
Malindi
Mombasa
Kilwa 1488–89
INDIAN OCEAN
COMORO IS.
to India

ATLANTIC OCEAN
KINGDOM OF NDONGO
Benguela 1484
Mozambique 1489–90

Walvis Bay 1486
Sofala 1488–89
Madagascar

Lüderitz Bay 1487
Cross erected by Bartolomeu Dias 1488
São Bras (Mossel Bay) 1497
Capetown

**HUMAN CHATTEL** The Slave Market, Zanzibar

## European Slave Forts in West Africa

**European Trading Forts or Castles**

- 🟥 Danish
- 🟨 English
- 🟪 French

Contemporary boundaries and place names are provided for reference.

**European Trading Forts or Castles in the Gold Coast Region**

| | | |
|---|---|---|
| 12 English | 3 Brandenburger (Germany) | |
| 10 Dutch | 3 Portuguese | |
| 4 Danish | 1 French | |

**SLAVING FORTS** At the height of the African slave trade in the late 1700s, England, Holland, Portugal, Spain, and France were among the European nations operating slave forts in Africa.

But while the early years of the 19th century saw the peaking of the transatlantic slave trade, subsequent decades would see its decline, outlawing, and disappearance. In 1807, the British—then the most powerful maritime power in the world—banned the trade in slaves, followed by the Americans a year later. Naval patrols scoured the Atlantic in an effort to prevent the illegal trade. But the struggle was a long and frustrating one. As the quantity of slaves diminished, prices went up, encouraging even more ruthless and greedy traffickers in human flesh. Eventually, as first the British (1833), then the French (1848), the Americans (1865), and the Spanish and Portuguese (1880s) outlawed slavery in territories under their control, the transatlantic slave trade died out. (The trans-Saharan trade continued well into the 20th century; while internal African slavery survives in pockets—such as Sudan—today.)

**GOREE ISLAND** Goree Island, one of the most notorious slave forts in Africa, is located in what is now the nation of Senegal.

# Chapter 4: The Arrival of the Europeans

**COLUMBUS** An artist's depiction of Christofo Columbo, or Christopher Columbus. Columbus' actual likeness is unknown.

**CHARTING THE CARIBBEAN** Columbus led a total of four voyages to the Caribbean. He went to his death still believing he had reached Asia.

In an age when explorers were trying to discover new sea routes to the riches of the Far East, Genoan mariner Christopher Columbus proposed to get there by sailing west. Most educated people agreed that the Earth was spherical, but many believed that the ocean separating East Asia and western Europe was too vast to cross. Based on geographical analysis and many wishful assumptions, Columbus argued that the distance from the Canary Islands to Japan was only 2,400 nautical miles; in fact, it is more than 10,000. If he had been right, then Japan would have been only as far from Europe as Haiti. In any case, he proposed sailing west from the Canary Islands, propelled by the easterly trade wind.

After much discussion, Ferdinand and Isabella of Spain agreed to fund the expedition. On August 3, 1492, Columbus set sail from Palos, Spain, with a modest expedition consisting of 90 men, most of them Spanish, and three ships: the *Santa Maria*, probably less than 100 feet long; and the caravels *Pinta* and *Niña*, each probably less than 70 feet long. Columbus commanded the *Santa Maria*, while two Spanish brothers commanded the other ships: Martín Alonzo Pinzón on the *Pinta* and Vicente Yáñez Pinzón on the *Niña*. After stopping for provisions at the Canary Islands, on September 6 they sailed due west for regions unknown.

By late September, progress was dramatically slowed by doldrums and weak winds, causing crew members to threaten mutiny. A month after setting sail, the expedition had covered 2,700 miles, surpassing Columbus's estimate of 2,400 miles for the entire journey. Rather than disclose his miscalculation to his rebellious crew, he began keeping two logbooks: one with fake calculations, and a second accurate but secret account. At 2:00 a.m. on October 12, Rodrigo de Triana, the Spanish lookout on the *Pinta*, spotted land. After sunrise the explorers anchored their ships and stepped ashore on an island in the Bahamas that the Native peoples called Guanahaní. Columbus, a deeply religious Catholic, knelt and thanked God; then, claiming the island for Spain, he christened it San Salvador, or "Holy Savior."

The people of San Salvador, the Arawak, soon came out to meet the newcomers. The Arawak bore gifts of parrots, cotton, and wooden spears, which they readily exchanged for the trinkets the Spanish offered, such as glass beads and

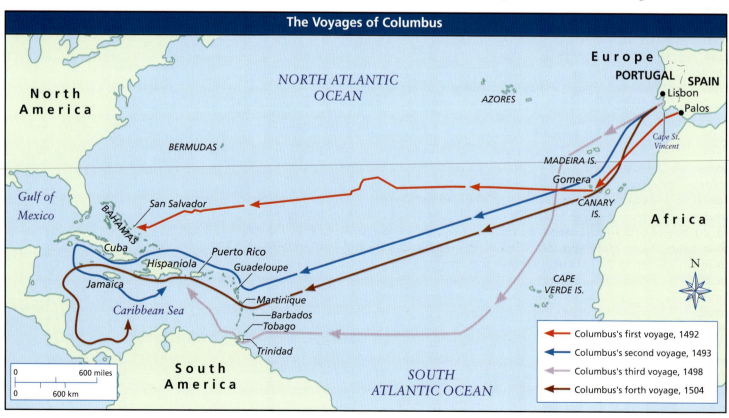

**The Voyages of Columbus**

Columbus's first voyage, 1492
Columbus's second voyage, 1493
Columbus's third voyage, 1498
Columbus's forth voyage, 1504

hawks' bells. A handsome people who went naked or nearly naked, they impressed Columbus with their hospitality and guilelessness. "Of anything they have," wrote Columbus, "if you ask them for it, they never say no; rather they invite the person to share it, and show as much love as if they were giving their hearts." Columbus wrote at first that he had high hopes of converting them to Christianity, using not force but love. Despite these good intentions, they were soon to be exterminated, with Columbus's help.

Columbus called them Indians, since he believed he had reached the Indies, or East Asia. He was convinced that the advanced civilizations of Japan and China lay nearby, and with them the gold he was seeking. Some of the Arawak wore gold ornaments in their noses, a sign to Columbus that vast gold reserves were close at hand. Following hints from the Arawak, he sailed from island to island, landing on Cuba and Hispaniola (from española, "Spanish lady"), the latter now divided into the Dominican Republic and Haiti. But gold fields did not materialize, nor any signs of advanced civilization. Worse, on Christmas Day 1492, the *Santa Maria* broke up on a coral reef off Hispaniola. But Columbus, ever the optimist, took it as a sign that God wanted him to found a settlement on the island. Using timbers from the ship's wreckage, his crew constructed a fort called Navidad, or "Christmas." Columbus left fewer than 40 men there with orders to keep looking for gold and to treat the Native peoples well. On January 4, 1493, he set sail with the *Niña* and *Pinta* for Spain, which he reached on March 15.

## Columbus' Later Voyages

Ferdinand and Isabella then sent him on a second voyage, intended to establish a colony. The expedition consisted of 17 vessels and about 1,200 men, including priests to do the converting and soldiers to do the conquering. Lasting nearly three years, from September 25, 1493, to June 11, 1496, the expedition stopped in Puerto Rico, Jamaica, Dominica, Guadeloupe, and Antigua. Columbus also returned to Navidad on Hispaniola, where he found the fort destroyed and the settlers killed. Columbus learned that the garrison had demanded gold, food, and labor from the Arawak. As a contemporary Spanish diarist euphemistically wrote, "Bad feelings arose. To eliminate this outrage . . . [the

## The Columbian Exchange

It has been said that 1492 did not mark the meeting of an Old World and New but rather that of two Old Worlds. Upon their meeting, the two world's began what is called the Columbian Exchange, exchanging plants, animals, microorganisms, and people. The impact of this exchange is still felt worldwide today. Some examples of the exchange are listed below.

### To the Americas from Europe

By 1580, herds of wild horses, descended from horses brought to the Americas by Spain, stretched from Argentina to the Great Plains of North America.

The most dangerous items brought from Europe with the Spanish were germs. Native Americans had no immunity to smallpox, for example, which first spread through Hispaniola in 1518, killing half of the region's Indians before spreading throughout the rest of the Americas, killing millions in its path.

### To the Americas from Africa

Over 9 million slaves may have come to the Americas, bringing aspects of African culture that influenced religion, cooking, music, language, and many other facets of daily life.

### From America to Europe, Asia, and Africa

Corn, or maize, was first grown in Mexico, and potatoes in the Andes. Today, they are two of the world's most important staple crops.

Although historians debate the origins of syphilis, evidence exists that it came from the Americas. A major epidemic of the disease swept Europe in 1500, shortly after the first voyages to the New World. No signs of the disease exist in Europe prior to that year.

### From Asia to the Americas

Bananas, originally from Indonesia, became a major crop in Latin America only after arriving there with Spanish settlers. Today, they are one of the region's most important export crops.

Arawak] attacked the Christians in great force."

Columbus established the colonies of Isabella and Santo Domingo on Hispaniola. Santo Domingo, capital of the Dominican Republic is the oldest surviving European city in the Americas. Columbus' next voyage took place from May 1498 to October 1500. During this journey, Columbus came ashore on what is now Venezuela. By then, however, a number of colonists had complained to the Spanish crown about Columbus's tyrannical style, leading Ferdinand and Isabella to ask for his resignation as governor. When he refused, he was arrested and returned to Spain in shackles. While the sovereigns later released him and approved plans for a fourth voyage, they did not restore him to the governorship of Hispaniola.

On the final voyage, which began in May 1502 and ended in November 1504, Columbus concentrated on trying to find a westward passage to the mainland of Asia, which he still felt must lie near Hispaniola and the other islands that he had explored. Cruising the coast of Central America, he

landed in what are now Honduras, Nicaragua, Costa Rica, Panama, and Colombia, and even briefly established a settlement in Panama. By the time he died, he did acknowledge that what he had found did not correspond to any previously known lands: it was, he said, an *otro mundo*, or "other world." Even so he died convinced that this New World was very close to Asia, and that with a little more sailing, he might have reached his original goal.

*"I promise, that with a little assistance afforded me by our most invincible sovereigns, I will procure them as much gold as they need . . . ."*

—CHRISTOPHER COLUMBUS, IN A LETTER DATED MARCH, 1493, REPORTING TO ONE OF HIS PATRONS WHAT HE HAD FOUND IN THE CARIBBEAN

# Early Portuguese and Spanish Settlement

*"[The] Spaniards still do nothing save tear the natives to shreds, murder them and inflict upon them untold misery, suffering and distress, tormenting, harrying and persecuting them mercilessly."*

—BARTOLOME DE LAS CASAS,
SPANISH MISSIONARY

**SOUTH AMERICA** Amerigo Vespucci explored the coast of South America in 1499. Missions by the Spanish, Portuguese and English would soon follow in his wake.

Even while Columbus was still exploring, Spain acted quickly to solidify its claims in the New World. As Catholic sovereigns, Ferdinand and Isabella believed the pope had the responsibility to authorize monarchs to evangelize the pagan peoples in newly discovered territories and, for this purpose, to grant temporal sovereignty to monarchs over those territories. They appealed to Pope Alexander VI, who was Spanish himself, to grant them this sovereignty in the New World, and this he did in a series of bulls in 1493 that established what has become known as the Papal Line of Demarcation. The precise terms of the arrangement dissatisfied Portugal, which managed to get them modified in the Treaty of Tordesillas of 1494. Under the revised arrangement, Portugal was given title to all lands east of a line of demarcation 370 leagues west of the Cape Verde Islands, while Spain won title to all lands west of the line.

The agreement was meant to protect Spain's interest in the New World and Portugal's interest in Africa, but it had an unintended consequence. When eastern Brazil, which lay east of the line of demarcation, was reached by Portuguese explorer Pedro Álvares Cabral (ca. 1468–1520) in April 1500, it gave Portugal a claim to vast territory that would become Brazil. This claim was upheld despite the fact that he had been beaten to Brazil in January 1500 by the Spanish explorer Vicente Yáñez Pinzón (ca. 1460–ca. 1523). Hence Brazil became a Portuguese colony, with Salvador founded in 1549, São Paulo in 1554, and Rio de Janeiro in 1567. It remains to this day a Portuguese-speaking nation.

Despite competition with Portugal and to a lesser extent France and England in the early sixteenth century, early exploration of the New World was almost entirely a Spanish affair. Spain moved so rapidly to capitalize on Columbus's discoveries that vast regions of the American interior were already shipping wealth to Spain while European rivals were still skirting the coasts. Spain's first holdings were in the place Columbus had first colonized: Hispaniola.

## The Spanish, the Native Americans and Hispaniola

Shortly after the Spanish conquest of Hispaniola, the new colonial government set up a system they called *repartimento*. Under the system, a conquistador was made, in effect, the lord of a given area, and the Indians living there were required to work for him without pay—in the gold-fields, for example. The system soon developed into another, called *encomienda*, which granted the Spanish overlord not only the right to free labor, but also the right to demand tribute from the Indians in such forms as woven fabric, gold dust, and harvested crops.

The result of the encomienda system in Hispaniola was genocide. This phenomenon was repeated elsewhere, including Cuba and Puerto Rico. Estimates for the number of Native Americans living in the Caribbean before Columbus are uncertain; there may have been hundreds of thousands, perhaps millions.

**European Exploration of the South Atlantic**

Vera Cruz · Gulf of Mexico · North Atlantic Ocean · Treaty of Tordesillas (1494) · N

Santiago de Cuba · Caracas · VENEZUELA · Spanish · Portuguese

Pacific Ocean · Negro R. · Amazon R. · LOWER PERU · Madeira R. · BRAZIL

Lima · Cuzco · Paraguay R.

UPPER PERU · Paraná R. · São Paulo

Santiago · Plate R. · Buenos Aires · South Atlantic Ocean

Strait of Magellan

Legend:
- Amerigo Vespucci, 1499–1500
- Pedro Álvares Cabral, 1500
- Hernán Cortés, 1519–21
- Ferdinand Magellan, 1519–21
- Sebastian Cabot, 1526
- Francisco Pizarro, 1531–35
- Francis Drake, 1578
- Inca Empire
- Aztec Empire

0 — 1000 miles
0 — 1000 km

**CARVING THE GLOBE** In 1493, the pope divided the globe between lands open to Spanish settlement and lands open to Portugal. A year later, Spain and Portugal agreed to adjust the boundary.

The Treaty of Tordesillas

In attempting to explain this genocide, some historians have pointed to Spanish history. The centuries-long effort to wrest land away from the Moors on the Iberian Peninsula had made the Spanish warriors battle-hardened and contemptuous of non-Spanish people. They were prepared to conquer and rule ruthlessly. Spanish nobility considered treasure won in warfare to be honorable, while manual labor was beneath the dignity of a gentleman.

Atrocities against the Native Americans of Hispaniola, many of them well documented by Spanish missionary Bartolomé de Las Casas, were legion. Soldiers murdered and tortured, took slaves, stole provisions, and raped women at will. For sport, Arawak babies were dashed against rocks or fed to dogs. At one point all adult Arawak were ordered to deliver a certain amount of gold every three months, at which time they would receive a token to wear around their necks as proof of delivery. Anyone found without his token would have his hands cut off.

When the Arawak resisted, the massacres grew worse. For every European killed, 100 Indians would be executed. In return, the Native Americans tried to hide in the hills or flee to neighboring islands, but the Spanish presence soon pervaded the whole of the Caribbean, and there was nowhere to hide. As the Native Americans abandoned their crops in order to flee, many died of starvation. Countless others died of diseases brought in by the Spanish to which the Native Americans had no natural immunity.

Other islands suffered similar fates. The Spanish launched successful campaigns to conquer Puerto Rico in 1508, Jamaica in 1509, and Cuba in 1511—the three large islands that, with Hispaniola, compose the Greater Antilles. The Native American populations of all these islands were soon wiped out. In 1542, describing the Spanish Caribbean in his blistering *A Short Account of the Destruction of the Indies*, Las Casas wrote: "All those islands . . . are now abandoned and desolate."

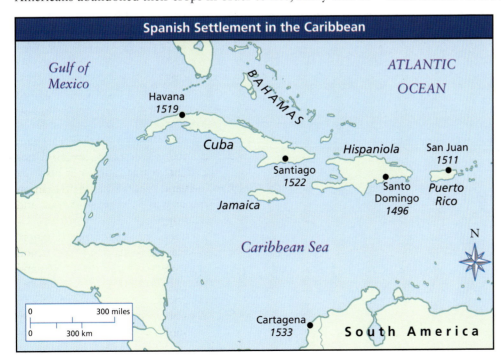

Spanish Settlement in the Caribbean

*"In [Hispaniola], there are mountains of great size and beauty, vast plains, groves, and very fruitful fields, admirably adapted for tillage, pasture and habitation. . . ."*

—CHRISTOPHER COLUMBUS, MARCH, 1493

**THE SPANISH CARIBBEAN** Early sixteenth century settlements in today's Cuba, Puerto Rico, and Hispaniola (shared in the present-day by the Dominican Republic and Haiti) helped Spain establish a major presence in the Caribbean that continues to this day.

# Early English, French and Dutch Exploration

*"Westward the course of empire takes its way...."*

—ENGLISH PHILOSOPHER GEORGE BERKELEY

For Europeans, the Americas were a New World. As early as 1502, Florentine navigator Amerigo Vespucci, who explored the South American coast for both the Spanish and Portuguese, wrote that the Americas were a separate continent rather than a part of Asia as Columbus believed. In 1519, Spanish explorer Ferdinand Magellan led an expedition around South America and across the Pacific to Asia. Although Magellan was killed in the Philippines, his crew's surviving members completed the first circumnavigation of the globe, returning to Spain in 1522.

Amerigo Vespucci claimed that he had been the first European to see the American mainland, and it is based on this false claim that German cartographer named the New

World "America." However, that honor belonged to another Italian. Sailing under an English flag, Italian-born navigator Giovanni Caboto, or John Cabot (ca. 1450–1499), explored the coasts of Labrador, Newfoundland, and New England in two voyages in 1497 and 1498. Like Columbus, he was searching for a short route to Asia and was convinced that Japan and China lay right around the bend. Cabot may have reached America again in 1498, but he disappeared during that journey. His son Sebastian claimed to have reached Hudson Bay in 1509.

Cabot's journey was the first European expedition to the Americas undertaken under a flag other than that of Spain or Portugal. Although Spain would dominate

**SEARCHING FOR A NORTHWEST PASSAGE**

The first European explorers of North America sought passage through North America to Asia. Europeans would not settle on the continent until Spain founded St. Augustine in Florida in 1566.

**Early French, English, and Dutch Exploration of North America**

Legend:
- John Cabot, 1497
- Giovanni da Verrazano, 1524
- Jacques Cartier
- Martin Frobisher, 1576
- Henry Hudson, 1609
- Hudson, 1610–11
- Sir Thomas Button, 1612
- William Baffin, 1616

the Americas, England and France would send voyages of exploration to the Americas during the early sixteenth century. Like Spain and Portugal, these new nation states were eager for natural resources to support their domestic industries. The establishment of colonies allowed these nations to procure valuable trade goods, such as timber, fur, and other valuable items from North America. These goods would spur the development of the mercantile system that would come to dominate Europe's economy from the sixteenth to eighteenth centuries.

### From Verrazano to Baffin

Despite its desire to compete with Spain, Portugal, and then England, France entered the race for New World resources relatively later. From 1494 to 1559, France was embroiled in a series internal struggles as well as external wars with Italy. As a result the French government was too burdened with military and political struggles at home to sponsor expeditions on the same scale as the Spanish. The first French expedition was undertaken by Italian explorer Giovanni da Verrazano (ca. 1480–1527), who explored the Carolina coast for France in 1534 and then proceeded north to New York Harbor, Narragansett Bay and Nova Scotia. Jacques Cartier (1491–1557) found and explored the Gulf of St. Lawrence in 1534, and the following year, led a journey up the St. Lawrence River to present-day Montreal. Yet Cartier's failure to discover either a northwest passage or New World treasures such as spices, gold or other natural resources discouraged the French monarchy from further exploration of the Americas for over 50 years. Yet Cartier's exploration of the St. Lawrence river laid the basis for later French claims to the territory that became Canada.

Despite the failures of earlier expeditions to find a Northwest passage during the late sixteenth century and early seventeenth century, the hunt continued in the second half of the century. In 1576, Martin Frobisher reached what is now called Frobisher Bay on Baffin Island, believing that it opened up to a passage. In 1609, another Englishmen, Henry Hudson sailed up the river that would later carry his name. This first Hudson expedition was commissioned by Holland, which by the seventeenth century had become one of Europe's fastest rising commercial powers. The following year, Hudson, this time sailing under an English flag, claimed what became Hudson's Bay in Canada during another failed hunt for a shortcut to Asia. However, when Hudson's crew mutinied, the explorer was cast adrift and died.

Despite Hudson's demise, his northern voyage was followed by two more English expeditions—in 1612, by Sir Thomas Button, who made undertook further exploration of Hudson's Bay, and then, in 1616, by William Baffin, who investigated the area north of the island that would later be known as Baffin Island. Baffin ultimately concluded correctly that there was no passage between the polar ice sheet and the mainland of North America. Although the French, English and Dutch failed to find a passage to Asia, each would establish their first permanent settlements in North America during this period, which will be covered in greater detail in Chapter 6. By the time they had, however, Spain had established not only settlements in the New World, but a vast empire.

**HUDSON'S LANDING** English explorer Henry Hudson, sailing his ship *The Half Moon* under a Dutch flag, comes ashore along the river that will bear his name.

# Chapter 5: The Conquistadors

**THE CONQUEROR** Hernán Cortés destroyed his crew's ships after landing in Mexico to prevent the timid from returning to Cuba.

*"Broken spears lie in the roads; we have torn our hair with grief. The houses are roofless now, and their walls are red with blood."*

—FROM AN AZTEC ACCOUNT OF THE FALL OF TENOCHTITLÁN

**W**ithin a mere 30 years of Columbus' first landing, Spain had successfully conquered and subjugated or slaughtered much of the population of the Caribbean basin. Yet despite the efficiency of their conquest, Spanish settlement in 1518 was still limited to Hispaniola, Puerto Rico and Cuba. Over the next thirty years, the Spanish would extend their dominion in the New World from the central Plains of the present-day United States to the southern tip of South America. In doing so they established the authority of Spanish military and governmental rule over this vast territory, as well as the religious authority of Catholicism. In the process, the Spanish would topple the two most powerful civilizations in the Americas: the Aztec of central Mexico, and the Inca of Peru. They would then use Mexico as a base of operations for extending their reach northward into the Americas.

## Cortés and Montezuma

Hernán Cortés, an ambitious young man of noble lineage but little money, had come to the New World in 1504. He had aided in the conquest of Cuba, became alcalde, or mayor, of Santiago de Cuba, and successfully angled to be named captain of an expedition to what is now Mexico. In February 1519 Cortés set sail from Cuba with 11 ships; about 500 soldiers; 12 arquebuses, or muskets; 14 cannon; and an assortment of horses, war dogs and Native American and African servants.

Before moving inland with his army, Cortés captured the coastal town of Tabasco and founded the settlement of La Villa Rica de la Vera Cruz, "The Rich City of the True Cross" (present-day Veracruz, Mexico). Then, in a dramatic

gesture, he destroyed his expedition's ships—thus preventing the timid or rebellious among his crew from sailing home. With no way back to Cuba, his men had nowhere to go but forward under his command.

From Vera Cruz, Cortés' expedition set out for Tenochtitlán, the capital city of the powerful Aztec empire. A daring general and cunning politician, Cortés used every advantage in his single-minded drive to conquer the Aztecs. He needed every advantage he could get, for his position was almost laughable: an army of 500 against an empire of tens of millions, with an extensive, battle-hardened warrior class and a practice of sacrificing and eating defeated enemies.

But Cortés had advantages. The Aztec had never encountered muskets and cannon and were appropriately terrified by their fire, noise, and destructive power. With their steel armor and strange white skin, the conquistadors looked like gods or demons rather than men. They won their early battles easily and were magnanimous at first to their defeated enemies, giving them a reputation for both invincibility and graciousness.

Another Spanish advantage was the vacillation of the Aztec emperor Montezuma II (ca. 1466–1520), who distrusted Cortés but failed to destroy him when he had the chance. While Cortés was still at Vera Cruz, Montezuma sent emissaries laden with gold and silver, requesting that the Spanish not venture inland to Tenochtitlán. The gifts only whetted the conquistador's appetite and made him more determined than ever to take control of this rich land.

By 1521, just two years after Cortés and his 500 men had left Vera Cruz, the Aztec empire had fallen. Cortés razed Tenochtitlán, and on its ruins built Mexico City, capital of the new colony of New Spain. Colonists flowed in from Spain to make it the greatest city in the Spanish American empire, with churches, palaces, a printing press built in 1535 (the New World's first), and a university in 1551.

The locals were made to swear allegiance to their new Spanish overlords, just as they had once done to their Aztec overlords. Native Americans who had worked for the Aztec now worked for the Spanish,

**CONQUISTADORS**
Hernán Cortes' army, seen at left, faces off against Aztec warriors. While the Aztec succeeded in destroying most of the Spanish force, Cortés raised a new army and burned Tenochtitlán to the ground.

**PIZZARO** Forces under Francisco Pizarro toppled the once-mighty Inca empire in 1533.

who introduced the same encomienda system that had reduced the Caribbean peoples to virtual slavery.

With the conquest of Mexico, there seemed to be endless possibilities for empire in the New World. In the years that followed, Spanish conquistadors acted exactly as if there were no limits. In Peru, Francisco Pizarro conquered yet another empire, that of the Inca. The Caribbean became a Spanish sea, Central America a Spanish land-bridge, and colonies sprouted from California to Chile. By the early eighteenth century, Spanish America was a thriving entity: centrally controlled but full of potential for disunion; ripe with extremes of rich and poor; and blending Spanish, Native American, and African peoples and traditions.

### Pizarro and the Inca

Like Cortés, Francisco Pizarro (ca. 1476–1541) was a daring and unscrupulous man of little money but gentle birth (illegitimate, in Pizarro's case) who came to the New World to seek his fortune. Eager to follow Cortés's example of conquering an empire, he was thrilled to learn in his travels of the existence of the Inca Empire, a vast and wealthy state based in Cuzco, Peru, that governed millions of people throughout the Andes. With royal backing from Charles I and fewer than 200 men, Pizarro sailed from Panama in 1531 and landed in Peru in 1532. Taking advantage of internal divisions among the Inca, Pizarro captured Cuzco, their capital city, within a year.

### New Spain and Global Trade

By 1550, Spain had seized control of the entire Caribbean, Mexico, Central America, and the west coast of South America. From these vast territories, Spanish overlords extracted sugar, wood, gold, and especially silver, and shipped these east across the Atlantic back to the Spanish crown. From the outset of the Spanish colonial era, the Spanish throne worked to assure itself that no European rival would share in its newfound wealth. Every ship leaving from Spain for the Americas left with instructions to collect whatever resources it could in the name of the crown. Individuals were permitted to oversee work at gold and silver mines, but the Spanish monarch claimed one-third or even half of whatever riches were found.

The Spanish government also controlled the flota, or fleet of ships that provided the means of transport to the Americas. Twice a year, a convoy of 40 to 70 Spanish galleons carried the resources to Europe, and returned from home carrying finished trade goods, slaves from Africa, and colonizers from the home country. No merchants from any nation but Spain was permitted to trade with Hispanic America. Spain's European competitors would have to content themselves with commissioning privateers such as Sir Francis Drake to plunder Spanish ships, taking some treasure for themselves and some for their governments. Tentative settlements by French Huguenots in Florida and English entrepreneurs in the late sixteenth century failed. The challenge to Spanish supremacy in the Americas would have wait until the next century.

**New Spain, 1600**

Santa Fe
NEW SPAIN
Gulf of Mexico
Florida
ATLANTIC OCEAN
Mexico City
Acapulco
Cuba
Jamaica
Hispaniola
Puerto Rico
Santo Domingo
San Juan
Caribbean Sea
Cartagena
NEW SPAIN
Panamá
Bogotá
PACIFIC OCEAN
BRAZIL
Lima
PERU
Santiago
Buenos Aires
N

Spanish claims
Portuguese claims
Viceroyalty borders

0   600 miles
0   600 km

**GLOBAL EMPIRE** The Viceroyalty of New Spain was the richest colony in the world in 1600. Spain also controlled the Vice Royalty of Peru, which stretched from Panama to Argentina.

# Spanish Exploration in North America

Besides colonizing much of what is now called Latin America, the Spanish were the first European colonizers of what is now the United States. Forty-two years before 1607 when the English would found Jamestown, Virginia, England's first permanent settlement in the Americas, the Spanish founded one in St. Augustine, Florida.

### The Spanish Southeast

Florida's European discoverer was Juan Ponce de León (1460–1521), who traveled with Columbus on his second voyage (1493–1496) and who conquered Puerto Rico beginning in 1508. According to a dubious legend, he came to Florida searching for a mythical "Fountain of Youth." What is certain is that he landed on the northeast coast near present-day St. Augustine on April 2, 1513, and claimed the land for Spain, calling it Florida because he discovered it in the season of Easter, known in Spanish as Pascua Florida, "Floral Passover." He returned in 1521 and attempted to found a settlement on the peninsula's west coast, facing the Gulf of Mexico, but a Native American attack drove him off, leaving him with an arrow wound that killed him once he reached Cuba.

Spanish exploration of Florida and adjacent areas continued in the coming decades. In 1526, Lucas Vásquez de Ayllón (ca. 1475–1526) founded a colony in what is now North or South Carolina but died of fever that year; the colony foundered soon after. Two years later, in 1528, an expedition headed by Pánfilo de Narváez landed on the Gulf Coast at Tampa Bay and marched inland almost to the present-day border with Georgia. But through Narváez's mismanagement, the explorers lost contact with their ships and were forced to build barges to try to sail across the Gulf of Mexico to New Spain. The barges were wrecked near present-day Galveston, Texas, and all but four men were lost. They managed to stay alive and return to tell their astonishing tale. Led by Álvar Núñez Cabeza de Vaca (ca. 1490–ca. 1557), they walked for years across Texas and what is now the American Southwest, becoming the first Europeans to see American bison and making their living as healers among the Native Americans before arriving back in Mexico in 1536.

After this dismal start, Spain had little reason to continue exploring Florida. The terrain was difficult, there was no gold or silver, and the Native Americans were skilled fighters. Even so, Hernando de Soto (ca. 1500–1542) came to Florida in 1539, searching for gold. His expedition (1539–1543) slogged across parts of what are now Florida, South Carolina, North Carolina, Alabama, Mississippi, Tennessee, Arkansas, Oklahoma, and Texas. Although he discovered the Mississippi River in 1541 (where he was buried after dying of fever), his expedition's reports did not make Florida or the American Southeast sound any more attractive to Spanish ears. The Spanish claim to the territory languished for two more decades.

What brought Spain back to Florida was not desire for wealth but a strategic interest in keeping foreign rivals from grabbing the peninsula, particularly since Florida threatened the sea lanes through which Spanish ships carried New World treasure home to Spain. In 1564 a group of Huguenots, or French Protestants, founded a colony at Fort Caroline in northeast Florida. The very

**DE SOTO** Governor Hernando de Soto and his men were the first Europeans to come across the Mississippi River. Despite De Soto's extensive exploration of Florida, the Southeast, and the Mississippi valley, his death made other Spanish explorers wary.

next year, Spain sent Pedro Menendez de Avilés (1519–1574) to the region, where he founded the Spanish colony of St. Augustine and destroyed Fort Caroline, massacring its inhabitants. St. Augustine endured attacks by both French and English (including a 1586 raid by English privateer Sir Francis Drake in which the settlement was burned to the ground and had to be rebuilt), earning its present-day status as the oldest permanent European settlement in what is now the United States. Its Castillo de San Marcos, begun in 1672, is the oldest masonry fort in the continental United States.

Spain's sense of what constituted La Florida was vague at first: roughly the Florida peninsula and anything north and west of it, even as far north as Newfoundland. Spain's more extravagant claims to distant northern lands were challenged in the early seventeenth century as European rivals at last established their own enduring colonies, including France's Quebec in 1608, England's Plymouth in 1620, and Holland's New Amsterdam (later captured by the English and renamed New York) in 1624. But closer to the southern heartland of Spanish America, Spain did what it could to press its claims.

## The Spanish Borderlands

Soon after the Spanish settled in Florida, they also settled in another part of what is now the United States: the Southwest. To them it was the far north of New Spain. By the end of the Spanish colonial era, far northern territories claimed by Spain included all or part of what are now California, Arizona, New Mexico, Texas, Nevada, Utah, Colorado, Kansas, Wyoming, and Oklahoma. Despite these grandiose claims, these territories were thinly populated by the Spanish, and in many areas Native Americans continued their ancient ways unmolested by Spain. Other European powers contested Spanish claims and encroached on their colonies, particularly in Texas. The area was a frontier, a region at the edge of an expanding state—or, as many historians now prefer to call it, a borderlands area, a region where boundaries are contested or ill-defined and different cultures are cohabiting. Within these borderlands were some thriving Spanish colonial communities, particularly Santa Fe, New Mexico; San Antonio, Texas; and San Diego, California.

The first Spanish explorer to enter what is now the state of New Mexico was Álvar Núñez Cabeza de Vaca, the shipwrecked survivor of Narváez's ill-fated Florida expedition (1528–1536) who walked across Texas and New Mexico before returning to New Spain. After him, in search of the legendary riches of the Seven Cities of Cíbola, came Francisco Coronado, whose overland expedition from Mexico (1540–1542) reached present-day Arizona, New Mexico, Texas, Oklahoma, and Kansas. The Coronado expedition encountered such wonders as the Grand Canyon of the Colorado River but no wealthy empires. The fabled Cíbola turned out to be only the pueblos, or adobe villages, of the Zuni people.

*"[H]e ordered that all the other men enter in groups of twenty, and he took leave of all of them with much sadness on his part and many tears on theirs. He charged them with the conversion of those natives and with the increase of the Crown of Spain, saying that death had stopped him in the achievement of these desires. . . ."*

—Garcilaso Vega, on the last wishes of Hernando de Soto before his death from fever in 1541

**Spanish Entradas in North America**

0 — 300 miles
0 — 300 km

Mississippi R.
Arkansas R.
Red R.
Rio Grande
Gulf of California
Culiacán
Compostela
Colima
Mexico City
Zacatula
Acapulco
Veracruz
Gulf of Mexico
Havana
Cuba
Santiago
Jamaica
Utatlan
Guatemala
Trujillo
Panama City
Florida
St. Augustine
ATLANTIC OCEAN
BAHAMAS
Hispaniola
Santo Domingo
Caribbean Sea
PACIFIC OCEAN

Legend:
- Vincente Yañez Pinzón and Juan Díaz de Solis (1508–1509)
- Luis Ponce de León (1513)
- Hernán Cortés (1519–1521)
- Hernán Cortés (1524–1526)
- Pánfilo de Narváez and Álvar Núñez Cabeza de Vaca (1528)
- Cabeza de Vaca (1528–1536) (solo continuation of earlier journey)
- Hernán Cortés (1532–1536)
- Hernando de Soto (1539–1542)
- Francisco Vásquez de Coronado (1540–1542)

**THE NORTHERN FRONTIER** Spain's vast holdings in North America were claimed by a series of explorers. Yet outside of St. Augustine Florida, Spain would not found any permanent settlements until the late 17th century.

# Chapter 6: Colonists in the Americas

In 1542, seven years after Jacques Cartier's second expedition to the coasts of Newfoundland, Labrador and Prince Edward Island and the St. Lawrence River to present-day Montreal, the French crown made its first attempt to colonize Canada. The sieur de Roberval's attempt failed, and the monarchy abandoned its efforts, to focus instead on religious strife at home and wars abroad in Europe.

The year before Roberval had received his grant, French theologian Jean Calvin, living in the independent city-state of Geneva on France's border, established a system of government based upon his Protestant beliefs. Calvin's Geneva had become a strict theocracy, and Calvin had absolute authority over government policy and the personal conduct of Geneva's citizens. Most distressing to Europe's Catholic hierarchy, Calvinist missionaries had begun traveling all over Europe from Geneva in order to spread their faith. While France itself maintained its strongly Catholic majority, Calvin attracted rapidly growing number of followers. By 1545, the first community of Calvinists in France, known as Huguenots, was founded. Soon thereafter, their rapidly growing numbers allowed the Huguenots to become a political force in France. Beginning in 1562, conflicts with the French Catholic majority led a series of Wars of Religion that would not end for three decades. In the meantime, the Huguenots suffered severe persecution for their faith and in the mid-16th century, many Huguenots were imprisoned.

### The Huguenots in Florida

By 1564, the struggle between Catholicism and Protestantism found its way for the first time to American shores, where it would mesh with the geopolitical race for control of the New World. This struggle began with the arrival of French Huguenots in Florida in 1564. Seeking a place in which to live and worship freely, the Huguenots made several attempts in the 1560s to settle in Florida where the Spanish had already established settlements.

On June 22, 1564, the Huguenots landed on the northern Florida coast. The new settlers were greeted warmly by the local Indians, who offered French commander René de Laudonniere garments made of skins including "a large skin decorated with pictures of wild animals." The French then explored several rivers along the Atlantic coast of modern-day Florida before deciding to settle along the St. Johns River. However, lack of food and other supplies ultimately drove the first Huguenot colonizing effort back to France later that year.

A second attempt in 1565 failed because of mutiny and fighting with local Indians. That same year, the French settlement, Fort Caroline, was destroyed by the Spanish. Near the site of the devastated French fort, the Spanish founded St. Augustine, which remains the oldest continuously inhabited city in the United States.

### New France

It was not until the 1590s, when the French king Henry IV began to grant fur-trading monopolies that colonization efforts began anew, led primarily by missionaries and traders. From 1604 to 1607, Samuel de Champlain accompanied an expedition of French settlers to the New World. During the summers, he explored the northern Atlantic coast and the inland rivers. During the harsh winters when waterways were frozen, Champlain and his crewmates did little more than try to survive.

In 1608, Champlain, now leading the expedition, founded the colony of Quebec. The colony was to become the capital of New France and the foundation of France's empire in Canada. On one of the earlier expeditions, the French had allied themselves with the Huron, who now controlled much of the territory that had been held in the sixteenth century by the Iroquois. In 1609 and 1610, Champlain and the French helped the Huron defeat the Iroquois in several battles, strengthening the ties between the two peoples. As a result, the French were able to establish a trading network that stretched all the way to Huron settlements along the Great Lakes. In the 25 years under Champlain's leadership, France won control of both the St. Lawrence seaway and the fur trade that depended so heavily on this river.

**French Exploration on the Great Lakes and Mississippi**

Route of Jacques Marquette and Louis Joliet, 1673

Route of Robert Cavelier de La Salle, 1682

**FRENCH EXPLORATION** Explorers René Robert Cavelier, sieur de La Salle, as well as Louis Joliet and Jacques Marquette, gave France a foothold deep within the North America interior with their travels throughout the Mississippi River valley.

In the 1660s, France moved to expand its American holdings beyond the St. Lawrence. Its goal was, in part, to expand the fur trade. Yet equally important as an incentive was religion. In the 1670s and 1680s, French adventurers began moving westward from Quebec, the capital of France, into the Great Lakes region.

Fur trader Louis Joliet explored the Great Lakes and the surrounding territory from 1669 to 1672. Commissioned by the governor of New France to find a route to the Pacific in 1674, Joliet and Jesuit priest Jacques Marquette explored the Mississippi River Basin. They canoed as far south as the Arkansas River and discovered from the friendly Quapaw Indians that the Mississippi flowed into the Gulf of Mexico rather than the Pacific.

Another Frenchman, René Robert Cavelier, sieur de La Salle, explored the territory around the Great Lakes during the 1670s, often accompanied by Father Louis Hennepin, a Franciscan friar who became La Salle's chaplain in 1678. With the support of both King Louis XIV of France and Comte de Frontenac, the governor of New France, La Salle pushed southward down the Mississippi from the Great Lakes territories.

By claiming the Mississippi, the French hoped to confine English colonies to the east coast of North America. Yet New France never managed to attract many settlers. Efforts to build plantations were largely unsuccessful; saving Indian souls and collecting beaver fur remained the twin linchpins in the social and economic life of New France. The colony's meager population became rooted in a network of trade and military alliances with Native Americans. This inherent weakness left New France vulnerable to attacks from both the English in the east and from the Spanish to the south. By the end of the Seven Years War in 1763, the only geographical remnants of the once vast colony of New France were the small St. Lawrence river islands of St. Pierre and Miquelon. Nonetheless, the French imprint on Canada would endure as many of the colony's 50,000 citizens would remain, maintaining their unique identity, even under English rule.

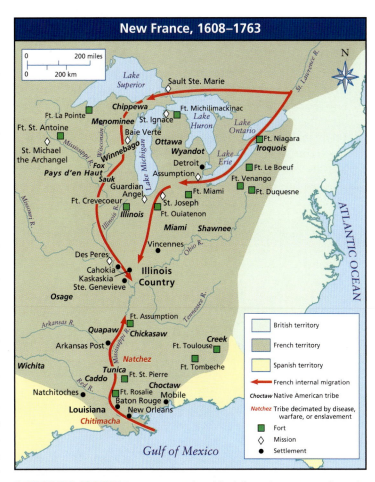

**A TRADING EMPIRE** France's vast land holdings in eastern Canada and the Mississippi Valley were centered around the immensely profitable fur trade. Yet unlike the English colonies along the eastern seaboard, New France was sparsely populated.

# The Spanish Far North

For several decades after the Coronado expedition of the 1530s, Spain lost interest in its Far North territory. But as New Spain grew, and its northern frontier expanded as far as Santa Bárbara, Mexico, soldiers and missionaries again became curious about what lay beyond the Rio Grande. Spain's strategic interest increased when England's first successful circumnavigation of the globe was completed (1577–1580) by the privateer Sir Francis Drake, who explored the California coast as far north as present-day San Francisco and claimed the region for England. Whatever the lands north of Mexico contained, Spain did not want England to possess them.

Beginning in the 1580s, several small expeditions reconnoitered the region they called Nueva México, "New Mexico." Beginning in 1598, Juan de Oñate (ca. 1550–ca. 1630) set forth from Mexico with a royal contract to settle the region and renew the search for precious metals. He founded San Juan de los Caballeros, near present-day Santa Fe, in 1598. His successor, Pedro de Peralta, founded the new provincial capital of Santa Fe in 1610.

Nearly 2,000 miles from Mexico City, this far northern outpost of New Spain had little to attract settlers, and it grew slowly as a farming and ranching community, with missions to indoctrinate the local Pueblo people in the Catholic faith. As usual, the Native Americans were pressed into servitude by various mechanisms and whipped or murdered on the slightest pretext. In 1680, Spanish abuse prompted a Native American rebellion known as the Pueblo Revolt, led by a Tewa shaman of the San Juan Pueblo named Popé and supported by the Hopi, the Zuni, and the people of Acoma. Wanting to restore their traditional religion and drive out the Spanish, the Pueblo destroyed the missions, killed 400 Spanish, and forced out the rest. For more than a decade, they occupied Santa Fe. But the Spanish returned in 1692, recapturing Santa Fe that year and reconquering the whole region by 1696.

After their return, the Spanish were marginally more respectful of the Pueblo, permitting them to hold ancient religious ceremonies. The Spanish and Pueblo also became allies against the Apache—nomadic, buffalo-hunting people who raided them both. While his people had occupied Santa Fe, Popé had traded horses acquired from the Spanish to the Apache, who began using the horse not only in hunting but also in raids on both the Spanish and on Pueblo Indians.

Despite the hardships of New Mexico, colonization increased there during the eighteenth century. In 1692 the Jesuit missionary Eusebio Kino came to what is now Arizona and was then part of New Mexico. There he began founding missions among the Yaqui, Yuma, and Akimil O'odham (Pima). In 1752 the Spanish built a presidio, or fort, at Tubac, the first permanent European settlement in

## Wild Horses on the Great Plains

Before the arrival of the Spanish to North America, Native Americans in the Great Plains and Southwest did not use horses. The horses that spread northward into the Great Plains from Mexico City starting in the 16th century were descended from Spanish Barb horses brought to North America by Spanish Conquistadors in the sixteenth century. While many of these horses may have escaped into the wild and migrated north on their own, historians also believe that Plains Indians traded for these horses with Indians of the Southwest, who had, in turn, obtained them from Spanish settlers in New Mexico. In either case, by the end of the century, horses roamed the Plains, transforming the way of life of the peoples who lived there.

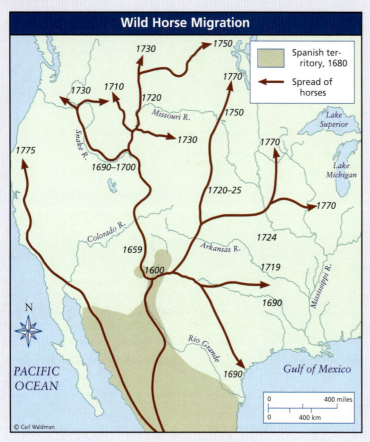

Wild Horse Migration

Arizona. By then the Spanish had learned the value both of sending missionaries to the frontier as vanguards of colonization and of establishing a paid, standing garrison in a presidio to guard the missionaries. The presidio guarding the mission church became a central feature of Spanish colonies from California to Florida.

By 1800 the Hispanic population of New Mexico was about 20,000. Many of these inhabitants were not Spanish but poor, Spanish-speaking mestizos (a mix of Spanish and Indian) from New Spain, induced to move north by offers of land—a technique used in colonizing Texas and California as well. Trade grew throughout New Mexico in the eighteenth century, with Native Americans exchanging skins and buffalo meat for Spanish manufactured goods at annual trade fairs

such as those at Taos and Pecos. These fairs were an extension of a complex system of trade in New Spain that included El Camino Real, "The Royal Road," the name for the overland trade routes in New Mexico, Florida, California, and Texas connecting the north with Mexico City. Other land routes connected Mexico City to Mexico's east coast port of Veracruz, center for transatlantic trade with Europe; and to the west coast port of Acapulco, center for transpacific trade with the Philippines.

Illicit trade with the French also took place, as the French, pressing their territorial claims to Louisiana, established a presence in what are now the states of Kansas, Oklahoma, and Texas. The international jockeying between Spain and France did not end until 1763, when France transferred to Spain its claim to the Louisiana Territory from the Mississippi River to the Rocky Mountains. Even then the conflict was not over: this territory was ceded back to France in 1800 and then ceded to the United States as the Louisiana Purchase in 1803, prompting American explorers to venture west across the plains.

### Texas

Although Cabeza de Vaca, Coronado, and Oñate all visited what is now Texas, Spain showed no major interest in the region until the 1680s, when France began laying claim to it as part of its Louisiana Territory. The Spanish sent expeditions to drive out the French and to found missions and presidios in eastern Texas, but Native American resistance forced the Spanish to abandon these in 1694. Then, in 1714, the French founded a settlement on the Rio Grande in southwestern Texas near what is now Eagle Pass. This was getting perilously close to New Spain. The Spanish reclaimed Texas with a vengeance, in time founding more than 30 missions in Texas by the end of the eighteenth century. The most important of these was San Antonio in south-central Texas, founded in 1718. The same year, France founded New Orleans near the Gulf Coast, just east of Texas.

### Alta California

Baja (Low) California, the peninsula that today is part of Mexico, was first seen by Cortés in the 1530s. The European discovery of Alta (High) California, the region we call simply California, soon followed. In 1540–1543, Portuguese explorer Juan Rodríguez Cabrillo traveled north along the Pacific coast beyond Baja California and

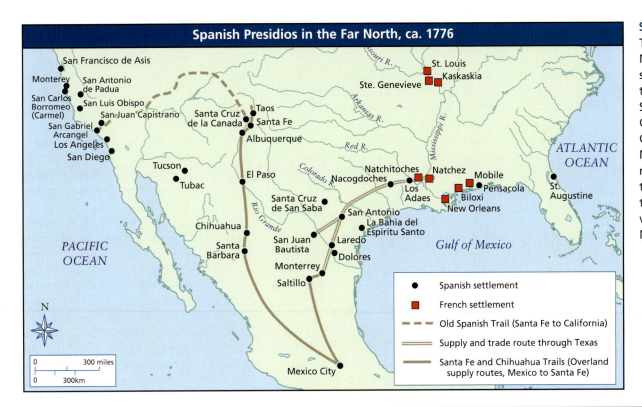

**Spanish Presidios in the Far North, ca. 1776**

Legend:
- ● Spanish settlement
- ■ French settlement
- – – Old Spanish Trail (Santa Fe to California)
- ═══ Supply and trade route through Texas
- ═══ Santa Fe and Chihuahua Trails (Overland supply routes, Mexico to Santa Fe)

**SPANISH FORTS**
The Spanish Far North was sparsely settled for much of the time it lay in Spanish hands. Colonists in California, New Mexico and Texas relied on overland trade routes to keep them in contact with the capital in Mexico City.

encountered San Diego Bay. He sailed farther north than present-day San Francisco, then turned back and sailed to San Miguel Island near present-day Los Angeles, where he died of illness, leaving others to finish the expedition.

No apparent gold or silver beckoned in California, so the Spanish left it alone. Drake explored and claimed northern California for England in 1579, but the English also left it alone. Finally, in the mid-eighteenth century, Russian ships began to trade for seal fur along the Pacific coast north of California, spurring the Spanish to defend their claim to California.

As they had been in New Mexico and Texas, Catholic missions were the advance guard of colonization. The Franciscan priest Junípero Serra (1713–1784) founded a mission and presidio at San Diego. By the 1820s the Franciscans had built more than twenty missions near the California coast, from San Diego to north of San Francisco Bay. Local Native Americans were taught the Catholic faith, forcibly resettled near the missions and compelled to work as manual laborers under the direction of the missionaries. Poor Hispanic settlers from New Spain were induced to settle in the pueblos, or towns, that grew up around missions. Cattle ranching became a primary occupation, with hides and tallow among colonial California's chief exports. California cities that originated as missions founded by Father Serra include Carmel (1776), San Francisco (1776), Santa Clara (1777), and Los Angeles (1781). The Spanish presence is still felt in California, not only in Spanish place-names but in the many examples of Spanish colonial architecture that survive, including San Francisco's presidio.

Despite the burst of colonizing energy represented by the vast California mission system, Spain's heyday as a colonial empire in the Americas by that time had long since past By the 1830s, nothing would remain of Spain's American empire but Cuba and Puerto Rico, and those fragments would be gone by the end of the century.

**Spain's California Missions**

Legend:
- Presidio
- † Mission
- ■ Pueblo
- *1787* Date founded

*Note:* Map shown with modern boundaries for reference.

**THE MISSION TRAIL** Spanish priests founded 20 missions in California—the last two years after Mexico won its independence.

# Early English Settlement on the Eastern Seaboard

Although John Cabot had sailed under an English flag to America in 1497, England was in no position during the sixteenth century to compete with Spain for American colonies. Yet England would become the dominant force in the Americas during the two centuries that followed. How did this happen?

For historian Charles Beard, one answer lies in geography. As an island nation, England was protected from wars that ravaged its continental competitors. Rather than drain its treasury on expensive land wars, the English built a navy, initially for defense. In 1588, that navy, led by privateer Sir Francis Drake, destroyed the powerful Spanish Armada (or navy), cleared the Dutch from the English channel, and bottled up the French navy.

By the late sixteenth century, England was ready to compete. Unlike France and Spain, which directly controlled exploration and colonization, England placed these enterprises in the hands of merchants. English merchants believed America would provide markets for woolens, and become a source for products such as naval supplies, wine, and oil that the English had to buy from other nations. The English also had a religious incentive for colonization, as Eng-land's Protestant monarchs were unwilling to cede the Americas to Catholic Spain and France.

Sir Walter Raleigh organized the first English attempts to colonize, at Roanoke Island, off the coast of present-day North Carolina in the 1580s. The first colonists settled the island in 1585. According to one colonist, local Indians received them "with all love and kindness, and with as much bounty, after their manner, as they could possibly devise." Yet the colony failed in 1586, when the colonists, short on supplies and wary of Indian hostilities, abandoned Roanake and returned to England.

A second attempt to colonize Roanoke, in 1587, became known as the "Lost Colony." Governor John White's supply ships, delayed by the Spanish Armada, failed to return to Roanake until August 1590. By then, the colonists had disappeared, leaving no clue to their fate except the word 'CROATAN'—the name of a nearby Indian tribe—carved into a tree.

Others soon took up the challenge. In 1602, Bartholemew Gosnold navigated from Maine to Narragansett Bay, collecting a cargo rich in furs, lumber, and sassafras, prized in England as a medicinal herb.

## Jamestown Colony

When James I granted the private Virginia Company of London a colonization charter in 1606, Gosnold was named vice admiral of the fleet sent to establish the colony.

That expedition, led by Gosnold, Christopher Newport, and John Smith, established Jamestown Colony the following year. Jamestown became the first permanent English colony in America.

Life at Jamestown was harsh. The settlers endured food shortages and disease, made worse by tense relations with the Powhatan Confederacy, the dominant Indian nation in the region. The colonists frequently bickered among themselves. In September 1608, John Smith became president of the colony and managed to secure corn from the Powhatan to feed the colony during the winter of 1608–1609.

Smith returned to England in 1609, and the colony fell into chaos. The winter of 1609–1610 was so brutal that colonists called it the "Starving Time." The survivors were preparing to abandon the settlement when a relief expedition arrived, led by Lord De la Warr, a director of the Virginia Company. De la Warr found the settlement a "very noisome and unwholesome place" and restored order through his firm rule.

The true savior of the Jamestown colony was not De la Warr, but tobacco. In 1613, colonist John Rolfe crossed native seeds with seeds imported from the West Indies to produce a smooth smoke that captured European tastes. The colony was

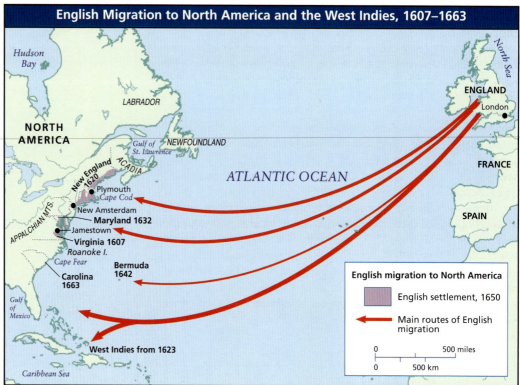

**THE ENGLISH MIGRATION** During the 17th century, colonists from England crossed the Atlantic for colonies in the West Indies, Bermuda, and the Atlantic seaboard. Reasons for the crossings varied, but by the end of the century, the English had surpassed both Spain and France to become the strongest European power in the Americas.

**English Migration to North America and the West Indies, 1607–1663**

Hudson Bay
North Sea
LABRADOR
ENGLAND
London
NORTH AMERICA
Gulf of St. Lawrence
NEWFOUNDLAND
ACADIA
FRANCE
New England 1620
ATLANTIC OCEAN
Plymouth
Cape Cod
New Amsterdam
Maryland 1632
SPAIN
APPALACHIAN MTS.
Jamestown
Virginia 1607
Roanoke I.
Cape Fear
Bermuda 1642
Carolina 1663
Gulf of Mexico

**English migration to North America**
- English settlement, 1650
- ← Main routes of English migration

0 — 500 miles
0 — 500 km

West Indies from 1623
Caribbean Sea

transformed, and tobacco could soon be found planted not only in outlying fields, but along the main streets of Jamestown itself. Between 1616 and 1628, tobacco exports from Virginia would climb from 2,500 to more that one million pounds.

To accomplish this rapid growth, Virginians needed land and labor. As tobacco rapidly depletes soil, planters needed more and more land to keep up with demand. By 1630, tobacco plantations stretched thirty miles up the James River from Jamestown. As the number of plantations expanded, so too did the labor required to work them. Much of that work would be done by enslaved Africans, who the Virginia colony first began to import in 1619.

## Maryland is Founded

Despite the growth of Virginia, the Virginia Company itself failed in 1624, forcing the English crown to assume control of the colony. In 1632, Charles I approved a second land grant in the region to Sir George Calvert, a former investor in the Virginia Company. Yet Calvert was less interested in profit than in religious faith. Calvert was Catholic, and he decided to use the land to establish a haven for those of his faith. He named the colony Maryland, in honor of Charles' wife, Queen Henrietta Marie, and planned to divide it into small kingdoms that would be populated and farmed by peasant labor. Calvert's son, Cecil, realized that few people would emigrate to work as what would amount to being permanent feudal serfs on other people's land. Instead, the younger Calvert offered land to all those who would settle Maryland, regardless of title or religion.

## Pilgrims and Puritans

The same year that James I granted a charter to the Virginia Company to settle the southern coast on the Atlantic seaboard, he granted another to the Plymouth Company to colonize in the north. After one settlement on the mouth of the Kennebec River in present-day Maine failed, the company sent John Smith to scout the northeast coast. Smith reported back with an enthusiastic report, *Description of New England*.

Yet it was religion that finally brought the first permanent English settlement to New England. Thirteen years after Jamestown was founded, the Pilgrims—or Separatists for their desire to separate from the Church of England—became the first permanent European settlers in what would become New England. The Pilgrims first left England for Holland to escape persecution. Seeking greater freedom, thirty-five Pilgrims, joined by almost seventy hired hands, came to the New World aboard the *Mayflower* in 1620. The ship left Plymouth, England, on September 16, 1620, heading for territory its passengers had been granted in Virginia. Bad weather altered the ship's course and the ship came ashore far to the north.

Because the Pilgrims would land outside the territory granted to them, their leaders realized that some form of self-government would be necessary to organize their settlement. The result was the Mayflower Compact. The forty-one men who signed the agreement while still onboard the *Mayflower* bound themselves into a civil body and promised to abide by the laws that they would later make. After stopping briefly at Cape Cod in November, the Pilgrims founded New Plymouth Colony in December 1620.

A decade after the Pilgrims landed, the Puritans followed. The Puritans and Pilgrims held the same basic beliefs, but the Puritans aimed to "purify" the Church of England from within rather than

separating completely. During the 1630s, about 20,000 Puritans founded Boston, Salem, and the Massachusetts Bay Colony, governed as "Puritan Commonwealth," in which only church members could vote. The Commonwealth was led with a firm hand by John Winthrop.

Puritan rigidity led to the departure of some settlers. In 1636, Roger Williams, banished from Massachusetts for his "dangerous" views on freedom of religion, founded Providence and the colony of Rhode Island. A year earlier, Thomas Hooker had left the colony, leading a group of followers seeking religious liberty. Hooker objected to the tight-fisted control exercised over both religious and civil matters by Reverend John Cotton, head of the First Church of Boston. After Hooker established a settlement at Hartford, Connecticut, his congregation joined him there in 1636. Two years later, another wave of Puritans founded New Haven colony on the Connecticut coast.

Throughout this era, the Puritans gained greater power in the English Parliament. In 1649, the Puritan army, led by Oliver Cromwell, defeated the forces of Charles I, and executed the king. While Cromwell ruled England with an iron fist, he allowed the American colonies to govern themselves with little interference. Two years after Cromwell's death in 1658, his son Richard was overthrown and a constitutional monarchy was under Charles II was installed.

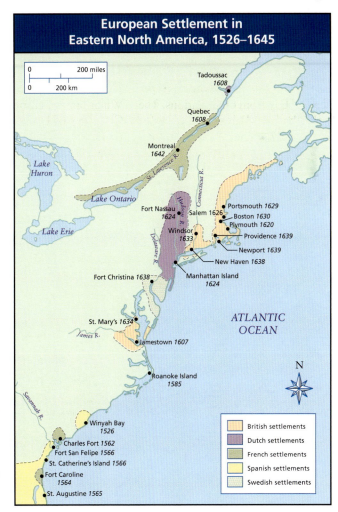

**European Settlement in Eastern North America, 1526–1645**

0 — 200 miles
0 — 200 km

Tadoussac 1608
Quebec 1608
Montreal 1642
Lake Huron
Lake Ontario
Fort Nassau 1624
Salem 1626
Portsmouth 1629
Boston 1630
Plymouth 1620
Lake Erie
Windsor 1633
Providence 1639
Newport 1639
New Haven 1638
Fort Christina 1638
Manhattan Island 1624
St. Mary's 1634
James R.
Jamestown 1607
ATLANTIC OCEAN
N
Roanoke Island 1585
Savannah R.
Winyah Bay 1526
Charles Fort 1562
Fort San Felipe 1566
St. Catherine's Island 1566
Fort Caroline 1564
St. Augustine 1565

British settlements
Dutch settlements
French settlements
Spanish settlements
Swedish settlements

**THE RACE FOR AMERICAN EMPIRE** By the mid-1600s, European nations had colonized much of the eastern seaboard.

# New Amsterdam and the Later English Colonies

In 1609, the Dutch East India Company sent English navigator Henry Hudson across the Atlantic, where he claimed all the territory along the Hudson River for the Dutch. The United Provinces, as the Netherlands were then known, thus established New Netherland, which stretched from the Hudson and Connecticut rivers in the north to the mouth of the Delaware River in the south, to include parts of present-day New York, New Jersey, Connecticut, Delaware and Pennsylvania. A new company, the Dutch West India Company, received responsibility for colonizing New Netherland, and in 1624, thirty Dutch families founded New Amsterdam on the southern tip of Manhattan.

The initial impetus behind New Netherland was the fur trade, not large-scale settlement. Two years later, in the interest of fostering good relations with local Indians, a party of colonists led by Peter Minuit "purchased" the island of Manhattan from the Canarsee Indians for the equivalent—according to legend—of $24. The Indians had no idea that they were bargaining away their land rights. They believed they were merely allowing the Dutch to use small tracts of land as trade outposts. Yet in 1629, Kiliaen Van Rensselaer, a stockholder in the Dutch West Indies Company, convinced the firm to shift focus from trading to settlement. As a result, the company provided for the creation of patroonships to spur the development of the colony. Any investor who brought at least fifty colonists to New Netherland could purchase a large tract of land from the Dutch West India Company. Management of the deeded land was essentially feudal. The landholder, or patroon, provided farmland, tools, and building materials to the farmer in exchange for receiving one-third of all crops as rent.

As the Dutch focus moved from trade to larger settlements, colonists were less attentive to Indian rights—often resorting to force to clear the way for new patroonships. Although the Dutch preserved good relations with the powerful Iroquois Confederacy to the north, relations with the Lenape and Wappinger Indians in the lower Hudson River valley worsened. Between 1640 and 1664, a series of bloody Dutch–Indian wars were fought. The Dutch fur trade also pitted the Mohawk of the Iroquois Confederacy against the Mahican nation. With the help of Dutch muskets, the Mohawk forced the Mahican from their lands east of Albany and into the Housatonic Valley of Massachusetts and Connecticut.

In 1638, Dutch investors helped finance a Swedish effort to establish a foothold in the Americas. Peter Minuit, who had been instrumental in the founding of New Amsterdam, purchased land from the Lenape Indians near present-day Wilmington, Delaware. There he founded Fort Christina. The Dutch were initially unable to move against the settlement, since New Netherland was occupied with Indian wars to the north. In 1655, however, forces under governor-general Peter Stuyvesant captured Fort Christina and allowed the 300 Swedish and Finnish colonists to stay on under Dutch rule.

Stuyvesant's acceptance of Scandanavians had more to do with necessity than tolerance. In 1660, he banned immigration to New Netherland by Quakers—and fined colonists who provided them shelter; this act led the people of present-day Flushing, New York to issue the Flushing Remonstrance, the first petition against a government in the Americas for greater religious freedom. But unlike the rapidly growing English colonies, New Netherland's population remained modest. The Netherlands did not have a large population, and the Dutch, on average, were comparatively well-off and less inclined to leave home. Thus, to attract a larger population, the Dutch welcomed not only Swedes and Finns, but also French, Germans, Italians, and the first Jewish community in North America.

Still, New Amsterdam's population numbered just 2,000 in 1664. The colony, already weakened from Indian wars on the frontier, war with England at home, and Stuyvesant's growing unpopularity, quickly surrendered when an English fleet sailed into New Amsterdam harbor and captured the city.

## New York and New Jersey

Upon the capture of New Amsterdam, Charles II of England granted the land to his brother, James, the Duke of York. In his honor, the victors renamed the city and the surrounding region New York.

Although the Duke of York had absolute political authority over the territory, he appointed a royal governor to oversee the territory and allowed Dutch patroons to maintain their large estates, while granting equally large estates to English supporters. James granted the southern portion of the territory to two friends, Sir George Carteret and Lord John Berkeley. Because the

**New Netherland and New Sweden**

IROQUOIS CONFEDERACY

Mohawk R.
Schenectady
Fort Orange
Mahican
Hudson R.
Susquehanna R.
Catskill Cr.
CATSKILL MTS.
Roeloff Janso Kill
Esopus Cr.
Esopus
Fort Good Hope
Connecticut R.

NEW NETHERLAND
HUDSON HIGHLANDS
Wappinger
Long Island Sound
Delaware R.
Lehigh R.
Pavonia
Haarlem
New Amsterdam
Breukelen

ATLANTIC OCEAN

Schuylkill R.
Delaware R.
Delaware

NEW SWEDEN Fort Nassau
Fort Christina
Fort Casimir

Delaware Bay

0 — 50 miles
0 — 50 km
N

Areas of Dutch and Swedish settlement

Land claimed by New Netherland

■ Dutch fort
■ Swedish fort
*Delaware* Native American tribe
→ Native American migration

**THE DUTCH AND THE SWEDES** The short-lived colony of New Sweden was financed and later captured by the Dutch.

governor of New York had granted the same territory to a group of Puritans before learning of the Duke's bequest, the territory was divided in 1676 into two—East Jersey and West Jersey. In 1702, the colony united as New Jersey.

## The Quakers Arrive in the Colonies

The Society of Friends, or Quakers, were a religious group that first formed in England in about 1650. Among the most radical of all Protestant groups, they went even further than the Puritans in their rejection of the Church of England. They had no organized ministry and no churches; instead, they held meetings in which each person spoke "as moved by the Spirit." They also opposed war and slavery. Quakers were persecuted in England, and in the seventeenth century, Quaker groups began arriving in New England and New Netherland in search of religious freedom. Yet they fared no better. The Puritans believed the Quakers to be a dangerous sect and drove them from New England. Peter Stuyvesant, governor of New Netherland, fined colonists who sheltered Quakers. The Quakers found Rhode Island friendlier.

Then, in 1682, Quakers settled in Pennsylvania in larger numbers, drawn by William Penn's promise of religious tolerance. Penn had been expelled from Oxford University for associating with religious "radicals." His father, Admiral Sir William Penn, was deeply disappointed in his son and sent him to Ireland in an effort to separate him from the group. In Ireland, however, Penn met and joined the Quakers. In 1681, Penn used a large grant of land in the colonies, left to him by the king in payment for a debt to his father, to establish his "holy experiment"—Pennsylvania, a colony dedicated to religious tolerance. Penn also designed his colony to offer economic opportunity and political freedom to all who lived there. Penn lived in Pennsylvania from 1682 to 1684 and again from 1699 to 1701. He died in England in 1718.

As Penn intended, Pennsylvania flourished as a haven for religious minorities from Europe and from other American colonies. The Quakers remained the most influential, although not necessarily the most numerous group. Most Quakers settled in and around the colony's capital, Philadelphia, which means "City of Brotherly Love" in Greek. Scotch-Irish settlers also arrived in great numbers, and tended to settle on the frontier country in the southwest part of the colony.

## The Carolinas

The year before the English captured New Netherland, Charles II made another grant —this time to a group of eight nobles including Sir William Berkeley, governor of Virginia. The colony extended from the southern border of Virginia to the northern border of Spanish Florida. The grant set the eastern border as the Atlantic Ocean, and the western border as the Pacific Ocean—over three thousand miles away. Berkeley and the other proprietors of the colony created huge estates for themselves and, assuming the role of feudal lords, parceled out the remainder of the land to tenants. The proprietors proposed the Fundamental Constitutions of Carolina, written by philosopher John Locke. Locke's draft set up Carolina society along rigid class lines, ruled by a hereditary nobility. Problems arose immediately when settlers rejected all but a few provisions of the proposed constitution and immigration came to a virtual standstill.

Eventually, a more democratic Carolina constitution was written, and in 1712, the colony divided into North and South Carolina. Most of North Carolina's original settlers came from

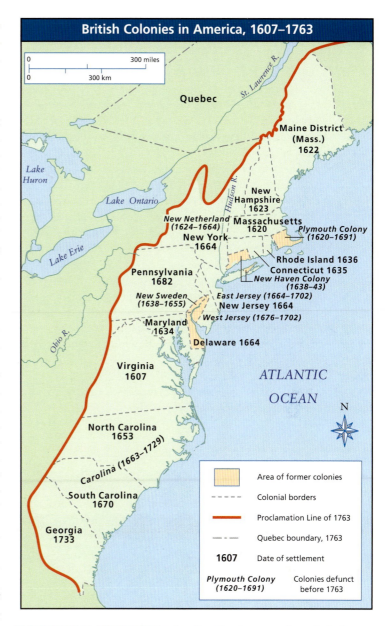

**British Colonies in America, 1607–1763**

**THE ORIGINAL COLONIES** England's colonies were founded along the Atlantic seaboard from 1607 to 1733.

other colonies, whereas most of South Carolina's came from either English colonies in the West Indies or directly from England.

## The Founding of Georgia

The final English colony to be founded was Georgia. In 1732, James Oglethorpe, a member of the British Parliament, decided to establish a territory south of the Carolinas in order to create a buffer between South Carolina and Spanish Florida. Rather than create the colony as either a money-making venture or as a religious refuge, Oglethorpe wanted the colony to provide a place where imprisoned English debtors could receive a new start.

Despite Oglethorpe's noble intent, few debtors actually migrated to Georgia. Even so, it did attract a number of poor English and Scottish shopkeepers, as well as Protestant refugees from Switzerland, Germany, and elsewhere. However, Catholics were banned from the colony, on the fear that they would side with Catholic Spain in the event of a war.

# The Struggle for Empire

In 1672, eight years after the English navy captured New Amsterdam from the Dutch and renamed it New York, the Dutch navy sailed into New York harbor and took the colony back. This time, the Dutch had no great interest in keeping the colony. Instead, they used it as a bargaining chip in a larger geopolitical game.

The war, known as the Third Anglo-Dutch War, was actually a much larger conflict involving trading rights around the world. In 1674, the Dutch returned New York to England, exchanging it for the colony of Madras, India. This episode would be little more than a historical footnote if it did not underlie a larger point—the competition for empire in the Americas, pitting at various times over more than two centuries English against Dutch, French against English, Spanish against French, and English against Spanish—took place as part of a larger global drama, in which these nations and others battled each other in Europe and abroad. The shifting forces behind this struggle were also multi-dimensional, often fusing economic, nationalist, and religious rivalries.

## King William's War

Even in the midst of its competition with the Dutch United Provinces over territory in North America, England had far greater rivals to worry about. Chief among them was France, Europe's most powerful empire. Although England agreed to ally itself with France against the United Provinces from 1672 to 1678, by 1686, England joined with the United Provinces and others to form the League of Augsburg to defend against France's territorial expansion. In 1688,

William of Orange, a Dutch prince, became King William III of England. William then launched what was known in Europe as the War of the League of Augsburg against France.

Meanwhile in North America, the governor of New France, Louis de Baude, Comte de Frontenac, was desperate to stop Iroquois attacks on his settlements. One raid destroyed the village of Lachine, across the river from Montreal, massacring 200 men, women, and children and capturing another 120. Other Indian nations were doubting French power.

Frontenac considered the English and Iroquois to be allies, in competition with New France for the fur trade. He used the war in Europe as an excuse to strike at British frontier settlements. On February 8, 1690, 300 French-Canadian woodsmen and their Indian allies surprised unguarded Schenectady, New York, and wiped it out. Other raids destroyed remote settlements in New England and along the coast.

In retaliation, New Englanders allied with New Yorkers to attack French-Canadian coastal towns and raid close to Montreal.

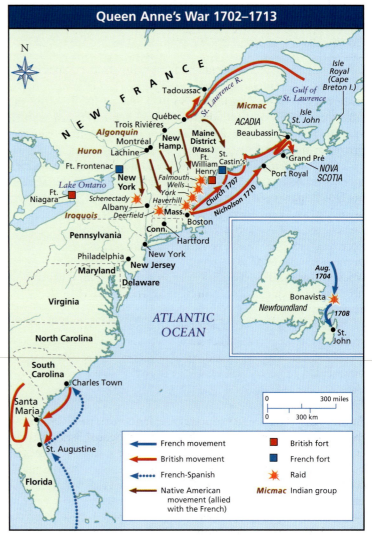

**King William's War 1690–1697**

**Queen Anne's War 1702–1713**

**WARS FOR KIND AND QUEEN** King William's War was a seven-year-long series of skirmishes between France and Britain. During the war, a British fleet tried and failed to capture Quebec City. A few years later, during Queen Anne's War, the British failed to capture Quebec again when a powerful storm devastated the British fleet. Nonetheless, Britain captured Nova Scotia from France and St. Augustine from Spain.

That fall, a British fleet of 35 vessels and 1,300 colonial militia sailed into the St. Lawrence River to besiege Quebec City. Frontenac mounted an effective defense, although there was little actual fighting. The onset of cold weather and a smallpox epidemic among the troops forced the invaders to withdraw.

Known in America as King William's War, the conflict dragged on for seven years in a series of skirmishes and raids that set the stage for future struggles between the British and French in North America.

### Queen Anne's War

English and French colonies in America entered the eighteenth century under a cloud of hostility. The legacies of King William's War—raids and counter raids, massacres and destruction—had generated enduring hatred between New France and English America.

New France was vastly outnumbered, however. By mid-century, there were fewer than 80,000 French colonists, while the population in the English colonies approached a million and was steadily growing. That population would soon turn westward, toward territory claimed by France.

But the next clash between Europeans in the Americas would once again start in Europe. Beginning in 1701, the War of the Spanish Succession pitted the English and their allies against France and Spain in a struggle to decide the next king of Spain. The fighting in colonial America was called Queen Anne's War, after the English queen.

In 1702, Carolina militia and Indian allies sacked Spanish St. Augustine. In reprisal, the Spanish and French mounted a seaborne attack on Charleston, South Carolina in 1706, but the expedition failed and withdrew. A year later, the British moved against the Spanish at Pensacola, but French reinforcements drove them off.

The winter of 1703-04 saw surprise raids by the French-allied Indians, who destroyed remote New England communities, including Deerfield, Massachusetts. New England and New York militias, along with Iroquois warriors, conducted their own raids against the French towns. A combined British and colonial expedition captured Port Royal on the island of Acadia (Nova Scotia) in 1710. This opened the way for an invasion up the Saint Lawrence River in 1711, when a 64-vessel fleet with 5,000 troops sailed toward Quebec. The fleet was devastated by a storm that drowned more than 900 men, aborting the invasion.

The war's peace terms left Nova Scotia in British possession, so New France was somewhat smaller. Hostility between French and British colonies had deepened, and another war was only a matter of time.

### The War of Jenkins' Ear

At the same time, a series of naval and land skirmishes known by the curious name the War of Jenkins' Ear highlighted Britain's rivalry with Spain in the Americas. Although Spain was no longer the pre-eminent New World power it had been a century before, it still controlled Florida, much of the Caribbean, as well as vast territories in the North American southwest and Latin America. In 1731, a British merchant named Robert Jenkins attempted to encroach on the Spanish trading monopoly in the Caribbean. His ship was boarded by Spanish, who seized his cargo and cut off his ear. In 1738, Jenkins appeared before Parliament with his severed ear. Using the seven-year old Jenkins incident as justification for renewing hostilities with Spain, in 1739 England began a series of raids on Spanish ships and settlements. Engagements in the

**British, French, and Spanish Possessions in North America, 1713**

British
French
Spanish

**DIVIDED CONTINENT** While Spain and France controlled more land, by 1713 Britain held economic supremacy in North America.

Caribbean spilled over to the southern colonies. In 1742, British forces repelled a Spanish attack on Georgia's St. Simon's Island in the Battle of the Bloody Swamp. The next year, southern colonial forces failed in an attack on St. Augustine.

### King George's War

The next war between French and British America sprang from the War of the Austrian Succession (1740–48). In North America, this struggle was named after British king George II.

In 1744, the French failed to recapture Nova Scotia, but built massive Fort Louisbourg on Cape Breton. Louisbourg dominated fishing grounds and merchant traffic in the North Atlantic. British colonists asked Parliament to capture Fort Louisbourg but the government refused, claiming it would be too difficult. Undaunted, in 1745 New England and New York militias launched their own expedition, supported by a British naval squadron that blockaded Louisbourg. The colonials astounded Parliament by capturing the fort that June.

This triumph made colonists proud, but to their dismay, the 1748 peace treaty handed Louisbourg back to the French. Many colonials never forgave this undoing of their great victory. Their bitterness fostered anti-Parliament hostility that helped bring on the American Revolution in 1775.

# Chapter 7: Politics, Religion, and Economics

Although all thirteen English colonies were largely self-governing by the middle of the eighteenth century, their governments had been shaped by very different histories. Many were originally chartered colonies; of these, some were corporate colonies created by stock-company ventures, while others became proprietary colonies, held essentially as private estates by individuals or groups of individuals. Chartered at different times for different reasons, many saw transformations in their colonial governments over the years, often starting out as private ventures but ending up as Crown, or royal, colonies. Due largely to their isolation from England, almost all enjoyed relative freedom from direct Parliamentary supervision.

### Chartered Colonies

Issued by the king, royal charters allowed the grantees, whether individual proprietors or corporations, the right to colonize specified tracts of land and to administer themselves as long as they did not pass legislation contrary to the laws of England.

Proprietary colonies were issued to individuals or groups of people who essentially held the land as a private estate. Proprietors could earn income from the land by selling, leasing, or renting parts of it to settlers.

Colonies that began as proprietary ventures included Maryland, Carolina (later North and South Carolina), New York, New Jersey, Pennsylvania, Delaware, and Georgia. By 1776, only Maryland, Pennsylvania, and Delaware remained as proprietary colonies.

Charters for corporate colonies, on the other hand, were obtained by corporations called joint-stock companies. These companies owned and managed their colonies in the name of its investors, who often were among the colony's original settlers. A corporate colony might also be formed when a proprietor sold or leased land to another organization. Colonies that began as corporate colonies included Virginia, Massachusetts, Connecticut, New Hampshire, and Rhode Island. By 1776, Connecticut and Rhode Island were the only two remaining corporate colonies.

### Crown Colonies

Crown, or royal, colonies were under direct protection and supervision of the British monarch. Many colonies became royal colonies after their corporate or proprietary ventures failed. Although royal colonies set up legislative assemblies for self-governance, their acts were technically subject to the approval of Parliament. Royal colonies included Virginia (as of 1624); New Hampshire (as of 1679, when it separated from

**COLONIAL CHARTERS** The early English exploration and colonization of the Atlantic coast was done by the Virginia Company of London and the Virginia Company of Plymouth, both private enterprises. While their respective territories were distinct in 1606 (see map at left), the boundaries began to overlap as the colonies grew (see map at right).

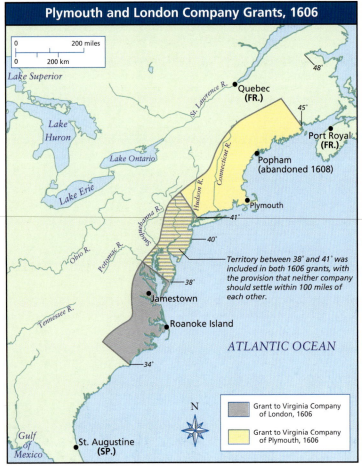

**Plymouth and London Company Grants, 1606**

0   200 miles
0   200 km

Lake Superior
Lake Huron
Lake Ontario
Lake Erie
St. Lawrence R.
Quebec (FR.)
48°
45°
Port Royal (FR.)
Connecticut R.
Hudson R.
Popham (abandoned 1608)
Plymouth
41°
Susquehanna R.
40°
Ohio R.
Potomac R.
Territory between 38° and 41° was included in both 1606 grants, with the provision that neither company should settle within 100 miles of each other.
38°
Jamestown
Tennessee R.
Roanoke Island
34°
ATLANTIC OCEAN
Gulf of Mexico
St. Augustine (SP.)
N

☐ Grant to Virginia Company of London, 1606
☐ Grant to Virginia Company of Plymouth, 1606

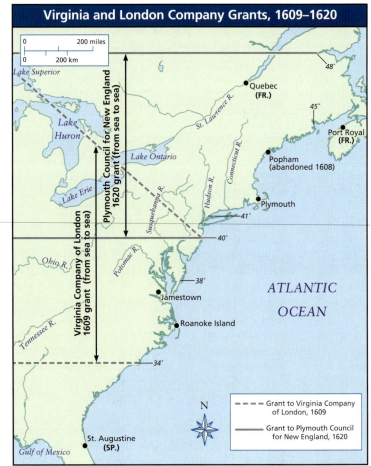

**Virginia and London Company Grants, 1609–1620**

0   200 miles
0   200 km

Lake Superior
Lake Huron
Lake Ontario
Lake Erie
St. Lawrence R.
Quebec (FR.)
48°
45°
Port Royal (FR.)
Plymouth Council for New England 1620 grant (from sea to sea)
Connecticut R.
Hudson R.
Popham (abandoned 1608)
Plymouth
41°
Virginia Company of London 1609 grant (from sea to sea)
Susquehanna R.
40°
Ohio R.
Potomac R.
38°
Jamestown
Tennessee R.
Roanoke Island
ATLANTIC OCEAN
34°
Gulf of Mexico
St. Augustine (SP.)
N

– – – Grant to Virginia Company of London, 1609
——— Grant to Plymouth Council for New England, 1620

## Early Colonial Land Grants, 1621–1639

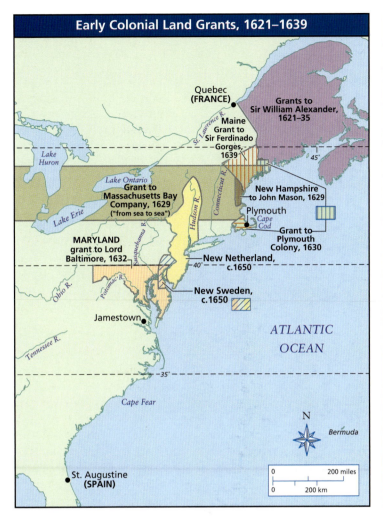

## Early Colonial Grants, 1662–1732

**NEW GRANTS, NEW COLONIES** During the 1620s and 1630s the English crown awarded further land grants that would eventually become parts of Maryland, New Hampshire, and Maine. At the same time, the Netherlands and Sweden would also found territories and the claims of Massachusetts Bay would stretch far to the west.

**FURTHER GRANTS** Colonies in Connecticut, New Jersey, Pennsylvania, Delaware, the Carolinas, and Georgia would all emerge by 1732. New Netherlands would become New York.

Massachusetts); New York (as of 1685); Massachusetts (as of 1691); New Jersey (as of 1702); Maryland (from 1692–1715, when it reverted to proprietary status); and Georgia (as of 1752).

### The Roots of Representative Government

Differences among the colonies were most apparent at the local government level. Colonial governments were generally based on the English system of a head of state (the governor) and a bicameral legislature, made up of two houses. (Pennsylvania and Georgia had only one legislative house.)

Except in Rhode Island and Connecticut, governors were appointed by the crown or by its proprietors. Governors had the power to convene and dissolve a colony's legislature as well as veto its laws. They had command over the colonial militia and the authority to appoint public officials and to administer justice.

Common to most colonies was a council appointed by the crown. Although the number varied, this usually consisted of twelve men who served as the upper house of the legislature, as a board of advisors to the governor, and often, as the highest court in the colony.

Legislative assemblies were made up of representatives elected by colonists. The House of Burgesses, the first elected representative government, appeared in Virginia in 1619. A Massachusetts assembly followed in 1634, after which other colonies followed suit. Although the assembly was the chief legislative arm of the colonial government, its acts could be vetoed by the governor or overridden by the Crown. However, the legislature did hold the right to approve of any taxation of the colony.

In the North, local government took the form of small towns run by selectmen elected at annual town meetings. In the South, where settlers were more scattered, the county was the basic administrative unit rather than the town. The Middle Colonies adopted a mixture of township and county government, depending on population and local necessity.

*"...[W]ee must Consider that wee shall be as a Citty upon a Hill, the eies of all people are uppon us; soe that if wee shall deale falsely with our god...wee shall be made a story and a byword through the world..."*

—JOHN WINTHROP, 1630

### Different Types of Colonial Government

Hudson's Bay Company

St. Lawrence R.

Nova Scotia

Province of Quebec

Lake Huron

Lake Ontario

Lake Erie

Maine District (Mass.) 1622

New Hampshire 1623

Hudson R.

New York 1664

Massachusetts 1620

Rhode Island 1636
Connecticut 1635

Pennsylvania 1682

New Jersey 1664

Maryland 1634

Delaware 1664

Ohio R.

Virginia 1607

Indian Reserve

ATLANTIC OCEAN

N

North Carolina 1653

Carolina 1663–1729

South Carolina 1670

Georgia 1733

West Florida

East Florida

Corporate or self-governing colonies

Proprietary colonies

Royal colonies

Other British territory

Proclamation Line of 1763

**PROPRIETARY AND CROWN COLONIES** Although Virginia had originally been operated as a privately chartered colony, by the 1620s, the English government ruled it in its own name, as it did all other colonies in the South. Northern colonies were generally private.

**JOHN COTTON** Cotton was the powerful pastor of the First Church of Boston.

*"The placing of a people in this or that land is from the appointment of the Lord . . ."*

—JOHN COTTON, FROM HIS SERMON "GOD'S PROMISE TO HIS PLANTATION", 1630

# The Religious Foundations of the English Colonies

In 1625, a lawyer, trader and poet named Thomas Morton arrived in New England with a Captain Wollaston and thirty indentured young men. Once there, Morton and his associates settled at Mount Wollaston (present-day Quincy, Massachusetts), where they formed a new colony known as Mary Mount. They began trading with local Native Americans, and Morton soon came to admire the ways of the Native peoples. When the profit-minded Wollaston began selling the new colony's indentured servants to Virginia tobacco planters, Morton convinced the remaining servants to abandon Wollaston and and join with the free members of Mary Mount as they live in peace with the local tribes.

Mary Mount prospered, and soon began attracting runaway servants from nearby Plymouth Plantation to the south. Alarmed by Morton's activities—and his free-thinking ways—the Pilgrim leaders at Plymouth condemned Morton as a heathen drunk. In 1626, when Morton erected a giant maypole at Mary Mount and hosted local tribes at a May Day celebration for the purpose of wooing Indian wives for his colony's bachelors, the Plymouth leaders could take no more. A force led by Miles Standish invaded Mary Mount, arrested Morton, and scattered the rest of the colony's residents.

### New England's Christian Utopia

The Mary Mount episode is perhaps an extreme example of the unyielding devotion of early Puritan separatists to protecting their vision of Plymouth Colony as a New

World utopia. With the establishment of Massachusetts Bay Colony in the 1630's the Puritan grip on the reins of the daily political, religious and social lives of the colony's residents only tightened. Diversity of religious opinion was not tolerated. Only church members could vote at town meetings, and until 1630, one could become a church member only by the minister's endorsement.

While most colonists were not church members, and most came to America for social, political, and economic reasons, Puritanism dominated the lives of all New Englanders. Biblical law was common law. Puritans believed they were on a holy mission to order the church and society as a living utopia in the wilderness. In 1633, John Cotton, England's leading Puritan minister, joined Massachusetts Bay Colony and became the powerful pastor of the First Church of Boston. His "True Constitution of a Particular Visible Church," laid the foundation for the Congregationalist denomination that grew out of the Puritan movement.

As discussed in Chapter 6, rigid insistence by Cotton and other Puritan leaders led dissenters like Thomas Hooker and Roger Williams to leave or be banished from Massachusetts Bay Colony to found more religiously tolerant colonies, in Connecticut and Rhode Island.

## Religious Tolerance and the Middle Colonies

New England was not alone in the role that religion played in the initial settlement of the English colonies. Religion played a central role in the formation of Pennsylvania and Maryland as well. Unlike Massachusetts, the Quaker founders of Pennsylvania and the Catholic founders of Maryland, were open to new settlement by

### Religious Membership in the Colonies in 1775

| Denomination | Number |
| --- | --- |
| Congregationalist | 575,000 |
| Anglican | 500,000 |
| Presbyterian | 310,000 |
| German Churches* | 200,000 |
| Dutch Reformed | 75,000 |
| Quaker | 40,000 |
| Baptist | 25,000 |
| Roman Catholic | 25,000 |
| Methodist | 5,000 |
| Jewish | 2,000 |

*includes German Reformed, Lutheran, Mennonite, and Moravian
Source: Encyclopedia of American History

a wide spectrum of believers. The Dutch colony of New Netherland (which under English rule became New York and much of New Jersey) was founded for trade rather than religion. While it would be a stronghold of the Anglican Church, the colony would remain tolerant of most religious minorities, including Catholics and Jews.

This tradition of greater religious tolerance in the middle colonies is reflected in the second wave of migration to the colonies in the late seventeenth and early eighteenth centuries. During the 1700s, about 90,000 Germans would arrive in the English colonies. Many belonged to Protestant denominations, such as the Lutheran, Mennonite or Moravian sects.

Many of the Scots-Irish immigrants who arrived in the Americas at this time belonged to the Presbyterian Church. Some settled in the same frontier territories as the Germans, while others pushed the boundaries of the western frontier over the Appalachian mountains, deep into Indian territory. A small number of Scots-Irish settled in New England, although they faced resistance from the Puritan leadership.

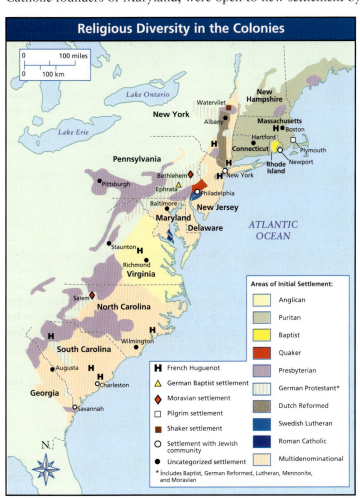

### Religious Diversity in the Colonies

Areas of Initial Settlement:
- Anglican
- Puritan
- Baptist
- Quaker
- Presbyterian
- German Protestant*
- Dutch Reformed
- Swedish Lutheran
- Roman Catholic
- Multidenominational

- H French Huguenot
- △ German Baptist settlement
- ◆ Moravian settlement
- ☐ Pilgrim settlement
- ■ Shaker settlement
- ○ Settlement with Jewish community
- ● Uncategorized settlement

*includes Baptist, German Reformed, Lutheran, Mennonite, and Moravian

*"[N]oe person or persons whatsoever within this Province . . . professing to believe in Jesus Christ, shall . . . [be] troubled, Molested or discountenanced for or in respect of his or her religion."*

—From the Maryland Toleration Act, 1649

**RELIGION IN AMERICA** While the earliest settlers to Virginia and Massachusetts were Anglicans and Puritans, respectively, later colonization brought greater religious diversity.

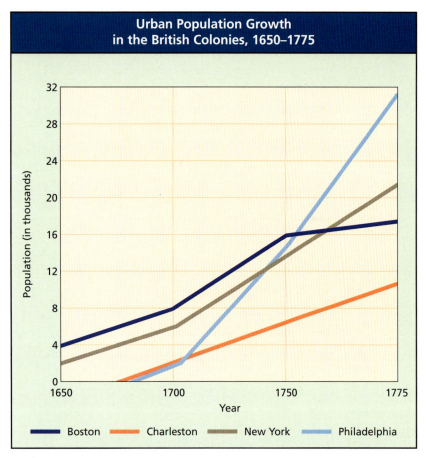

### Urban Population Growth in the British Colonies, 1650–1775

Population (in thousands)

Year

Boston — Charleston — New York — Philadelphia

**GROWING COLONIES** Rapidly expanding coastal cities (top) helped the population of the thirteen English colonies far exceed those of other European colonies in North America (bottom).

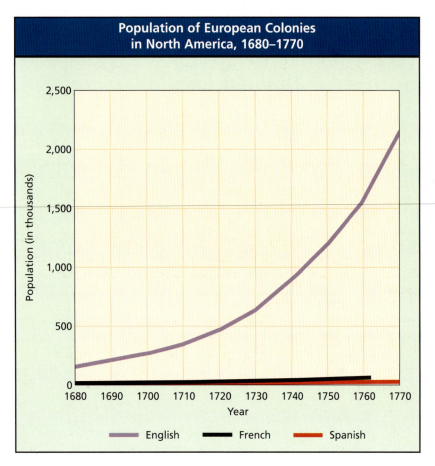

### Population of European Colonies in North America, 1680–1770

Population (in thousands)

Year

English — French — Spanish

## The Anglican Church and the Southern Colonies

In Virginia, the Carolinas, and Georgia, the Church of England, or Anglican Church, was the official religion. Much as the Congregationalist Church stood at the center of New England society, and only church members had the right to vote in Massachusetts Bay Colony, the Anglican Church in the South also occupied a special status. Anglican ministers were paid from public taxes and—unlike Massachusetts where most residents were not members of the Church—all residents of Virginia, the Carolinas and Georgia were required to be members of the Church of England.

The chief difference between Congregational churches in New England and Anglican churches in the South had to do with the reasons the colonies were founded in the first place. Where Plymouth and Massachusetts Bay colonies had been founded to serve God, Virginia and the Carolinas were founded to make money. Thus, in New England, political, social, and economic life was a reflection of the role played by the Congregational church. On the contrary, in the South, the Anglican church's role was a reflection of political, social, and economic life.

The power behind the Anglican Church was a reflection of class. Leading planters controlled most congregations and their finances and appointed all ministers. For this reason, Anglican ministers paid special attention to the wealthiest families, who represented a very small percentage of the population, and to yeoman farmers. These ministers paid little attention to the spiritual needs of white tenant farmers, white servants, and enslaved African Americans, who made up the majority of the population in South Carolina and nearly half of it in the Chesapeake region. By the late 1600s, the social, economic and political tensions that underlay this class system would deepen as new immigrants—generally poorer, often non-Anglican—would arrive in the colonies.

# The Expanding British Colonies

During the period stretching from 1680 and 1770, the thirteen British colonies underwent explosive growth. While the number of major colonial cities during the 1600s had been limited to the ports of Boston, New York, Philadelphia, and Charleston, in the 1700s newer cities, such as Norfolk, Virginia and Baltimore, Maryland, Providence, Rhode Island, and Salem, Massachusetts were founded.

In 1670, the population of England's colonies in North America was around 85,000. By 1713, it had reached 386,000, and by 1754 stood at 1.5 million. In the same period, the land area settled by Europeans tripled.

### A New Wave of Immigration

Several forces accounted for the dramatic population increase in the colonies. First of all, unlike the largely male colonists of New Spain and New France, the English colonies had a significant female population, high rates of marriage, and large families. Second, the population of enslaved Africans in the colonies also grew rapidly. As late as 1674, there were roughly 10,700 indentured white servants working in Virginia, and only about 2,700 enslaved Africans. Yet in the years that followed, the number of white servants in the colony leveled off, particularly after a series of armed rebellions by white servants and small farmers. At the same time, the number of Africans enslaved in the colony rose dramatically. Just after the turn of the eighteenth century, the colony's enslaved African population surpassed the white servant population.

Even as the number of slave ships arriving from Africa and the Caribbean increased, the number of slaves born in the colonies increased even more quickly. By 1720, most enslaved Africans in the thirteen colonies were born there.

Another significant cause of the population boom in the colonies was immigration. The initial European wave of migration to New England and the Chesapeake region in the early 1600s had ended by 1640—halted in large part by the English Civil War. But by the 1680s, a new wave had begun. This time, most of the new European immigrants were not English. Instead, they were German, Scots Irish, Scottish, Irish, French, and even Welsh. Also included in this wave were several hundred Sephardic Jews.

Of all these groups, the Germans and Scots Irish came in the greatest numbers. Scotch Protestants from Northern Ireland began arriving in large numbers after Queen Anne's War (1702–1713) between England and France came to an end and Atlantic sea lanes that had been closed reopened. Many of them settled on the Appalachian frontiers of the Carolinas and Georgia, while others settled further north, particularly in the western frontier of Pennsylvania.

The inland regions of Pennsylvania also became home to exiled Protestants from Germany, including Lutheran, Mennonite and Moravian communities. Like the Scots, most of these were small farmers. German communities also sprung up in colonies from New York to South Carolina. Place names such as Herkimer, New York and Mecklenberg, North Carolina bear their imprint.

While the original charters granted ownership of the colonies to commercial interests or sole proprietors, by the eighteenth century, the crown had taken direct control of most of them. What's more, the British also claimed ownership of an indefinite expanse of land stretching to the west.

At the start of the eighteenth century, much of this land lay unexplored by Europeans. Yet colonial officials were quick to realize its value. In Virginia, Governor Alexander Spotswood personally set out in 1716 with an expedition into the western wilderness of Virginia. Spotswood and his men traveled roughly 200 miles inland to the mountain range they named the Blue Ridge mountains. They then crossed into the Shenendoah River valley between the Blue Ridge and the Appalachians. By 1730, Virginia settlers had established villages, farms and towns throughout the

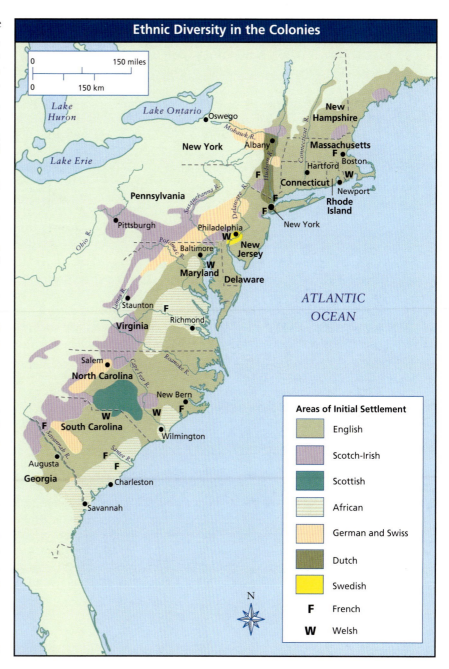

**Ethnic Diversity in the Colonies**

*Areas of Initial Settlement*
- English
- Scotch-Irish
- Scottish
- African
- German and Swiss
- Dutch
- Swedish
- F  French
- W  Welsh

**ETHNIC TAPESTRY** Enslaved Africans and others soon joined English settlers in America.

valley. By 1740, a few Virginians had moved beyond the Appalachians into Ohio country.

As settlers from the English colonies poured into these western lands, they came in greater and greater conflict with the Native Americans and French who also claimed the land as their own.

## Bustling Coastal Cities

Even as part of America's growing population pressed westward, once small settlements on the eastern seaboard, especially those founded on rivers that emptied into the Atlantic, were transformed into thriving cities. Norfolk, Virginia, chartered in 1682, became an outlet for North Carolina's lumber. Baltimore, Maryland, founded in 1730, flourished by exporting grain from Maryland and Pennsylvania.

As port cities began to compete with each other, they tried to improve their connection with the frontier settlements. In 1733, for example, Philadelphia spurred by Baltimore's success, built the "Great Road" to the mouth of the Conestoga River. To help bring farm products to the city, settlers developed the Conestoga wagon. By 1764, Philadelphia had become the most modern city in the colonies. Its population, which reached 18,766 in 1760, enjoyed paved streets, with sidewalks lit by whale-oil lamps and patrolled by sheriffs and constables. The city had large public buildings like the Statehouse (later known as Independence Hall, where the Declaration of Independence would be signed), libraries, three newspapers (including one in German), the only hospital in North America, a botanical garden (on the estate of naturalist John Bartram), a post office run by Benjamin Franklin, and several prosperous markets.

Philadelphia was not alone in its success. Growing wealth throughout the colonies brought schools, colleges, newspapers, and printing presses to many communities. Merchants in Boston, New York, Philadelphia, and Charleston were becoming rich on trade. A new elite class of merchants enjoyed imports from Europe. Those who could afford to wore the latest European fashions, kept up with European literature, decorated their homes with imported European furniture, and rode about town in European-made carriages.

The growth of cities, immigration to North America by less wealthy, more ethnically diverse settlers, and the expansion of the frontier into regions either previously uncharted by Europeans—or already claimed by France—sowed the seeds for a complex web of coming social, religious, racial and economic conflicts.

## The Great Awakening

In 1636, the Puritan leaders of Massachusetts Bay Colony, concerned about the potential for a shortage of trained ministers in the colony, established the first college in North America in the town of Cambridge, Massachusetts. In its earliest days, Harvard College (named for one of its chief benefactors) accepted livestock as payment for tuition. While the regular course of study at the school lasted four years, those training to be ministers were enrolled for an additional three years.

Funded by Royal Charter in 1693, the College of William and Mary in Williamsburg, Virginia became the second college established in the colonies. Founded to educate sons of the planter gentry and to prepare young men for ordination in the Anglican Church, the colonial college included a preparatory school, an Indian school, a collegiate curriculum and a seminary.

Although Harvard and William and Mary were founded by very different denominations in very different settings, they both reflected the stature that the Congregational and Anglican churches held in their respective colonies. They were schools for the elite members of New England and Virginia society only. In 1701, Congregationalists founded Yale College in New Haven, Connecticut. Like Harvard and William and Mary, Yale was also governed by the church. Thus, almost a century after the first English settlers founded the Jamestown colony, there were still only three institutions of higher learning in all of the North American English colonies. What's more, no new colonial colleges would be founded for almost another half century.

One explanation for the dearth of colleges in the colonies has to do with changes in the relationship between citizens of the colonies and their respective churches. As both colonial populations and economies expanded, making societies in the Middle and Southern colonies at once both more diverse and more prosperous, many people began straying from the church. Some members of the new merchant class were distracted by the promise of wealth and property. Others, particularly members of the second wave of European immigrants from Germany, Scotland, Ireland and elsewhere, brought with them brands of Protestantism that were new to the colonies.

### A Religious Revival

These forces, among others, led some to feel a greater need for inspirational meetings and sermons. This desire led to a widespread and wide-ranging religious movement known as the Great Awakening. Occurring at different times in different places, by the mid-1700s, the Great Awakening had not only reshaped the doctrines of some of the long-established denominations in the Americas, but also become an outlet for democratic impulses that had not existed in the early colonial experience.

The first stirrings of the Great Awakening took place in New Jersey in the 1720s, led by an evangelical Dutch Reformed preacher named Theodorus Frelinghuysen. The movement gained

**JONATHAN EDWARDS**

momentum among Scotch Presbyterians trained under William Tennent. His son Gilbert Tennent became the leading Great Awakening figure in the Middle colonies.

In New England, the leading figure was the Congregationalist minister Jonathan Edwards. Edwards admonished his parishioners in Northampton as "sinners in hands of an angry God," and urged them to repent. Provoked into fear of the torments that Edwards said awaited them in Hell if they did not change their ways, the citizens of Northampton began preparing for religious conversion, to be "born again" with a personal experience with God.

In 1739, the Great Awakening gained full steam as a national movement when George Whitefield, England's leading Methodist preacher, began a two-year tour of the colonies, attracting thousands to open air revivals. Whitefield dispensed with written sermons and preached spontaneously—urging audiences to take personal responsibility for their salvation and "fly to Christ."

In this way, Whitefield and other Great Awakening preachers challenged the authority of establishment, college-educated clergy. Parishioners—male, female, rich, poor, slave or free—were even urged to participate in "lay exhorting," or giving testimony of their own personal religious experiences. The Great Awakening directly challenged the class and social boundaries that had shaped the early history of both the

Puritan and Anglican traditions in the Americas.

## Old Lights and New Lights

One outgrowth of the Great Awakening in New England was a schism within Puritanism between the rationalist "Old Lights" represented by the Boston establishment, and the "New Lights" of western New England that stressed the deep emotionalism of the religious experience. Old Lights favored sober adherence to the letter of Puritan teachings; New Lights sought a personal sense of spiritual conversion.

As the eighteenth century progressed, the Old Lights were increasingly influenced by the intellectual climate of the Enlightenment. Charles Chauncy, a leader of the Old Lights, condemned the irrationality of the open air revivalists and proposed that just as basic physical laws could be determined by rational thought, a basic set of religious principles could likewise be proven through reason. If Newton's universe was a well-ordered machine, Chauncy believed, than specific moral principles could be arrived at to ensure a well-ordered and harmonious society. In this view, which in time evolved into what became known as Deism, an individual's personal experience of religious fervor was not only secondary to adherence to doctrine, but it was also a recipe for chaos. In time, the Old Light faction of the Congregational church would evolve into the Unitarian denomination, and be embraced by such founding fathers as John Adams and—informally, at least—by Thomas Jefferson.

## The Great Awakening in the South

As it had in New England, the Great Awakening also caused a religious schism in the South. Anglican ministers had paid little attention to the spiritual needs of small farmers on the far-flung frontier, yet the revival inspired a New Light Presbyterianism. Beginning in the mid-1740s, itinerant preachers like Samuel Davies traveled the Virginia countryside, taking the message of personal salvation directly to the people.

By the 1760s, the Baptist denomination arose in western Virginia and the Carolinas, often led by uneducated, poor farmers who heard the call to preaching. Condemning the wealthy Anglican elites for their worldly ways, Baptist preachers stressed the equality of humankind in the eyes of God. To unschooled backwoods country folk—and to the thousands of African-Americans enslaved in Virginia and the Carolinas, these were powerful words indeed. To Anglican gentry, they were alarming in the extreme.

## The Impact of the Great Awakening

The Great Awakening was one of the transformative events in American history. First off, it had a democratizing effect. No denomination, even Puritan or Anglican, could claim a monopoly on religious truth. All believers were equal in God's eyes. The arrival and growth of new denominations in the colonies proved that there was room in American spiritual life for denominational diversity, and that despite some tensions, these denominations could live together. This helped foster the separation of church and state in daily life, for no single faith could claim special status.

The Great Awakening also led to the establishment of a number new colonial colleges. While the College of New Jersey (later Princeton), King's College (later Columbia), the College of Rhode Island (later Brown), and Dartmouth were affiliated with the Presbyterian, Anglican, Baptist and Dutch Reformed, and Congregational churches, respectively, all were governed by bodies made up of men from a diversity of faiths.

**George Whitefield** To Whitefield, no Christian denomination had a special status over any other. As he said in a sermon, "Father Abraham, whom have you in heaven? Any Episcopalians? No! Any Presbyterians? No! Any Independents or Methodists? No, No, No! Whom have you there? We don't know those names here. All who are here are Christians . . . God help us to forget your party names and to become Christians in deed and truth."

**Founding of Colonial Colleges, 1636–1769**

0 / 150 miles
0 / 150 km

Quebec
Maine District (Mass.)
New Hampshire
Lake Ontario
Dartmouth College, Hanover, (1769)
Hudson R.
New York
Massachusetts
Harvard College, Cambridge, (1636)
Lake Erie
Yale college, New Haven 1701
College of Rhode Island (Brown), Providence, 1764
Pennsylvania
Rhode Island
Connecticut
Queen's College (Rutgers) New Brunswick, 1766
King's college (Columbia), New York, 1754
College of Philadelphia (Univ. of Pennsylvania), Philadelphia, 1754
College of New Jersey (Princeton), Princeton, 1746
New Jersey
Maryland
Delaware
ATLANTIC OCEAN
N
Virginia
College of William and Mary, Williamsburg, 1693

☐ Colonial college
---- Colonial borders
—— Quebec boundary, 1763

**COLLEGES OF CHURCH AND STATE** While all of the earliest colleges in the British colonies were affiliated with religious bodies, by the 1700s many of them were run by men of diverse faiths.

# Chapter 8: Slavery and the Colonial Economy

Within fifty years of Columbus's arrival in 1492, the Taino and Carib population on the island of Hispaniola (modern Dominican Republic and Haiti) had been nearly annihilated. Some were killed by Spanish swords, muskets, and dogs; most, however, were felled by diseases such as smallpox and measles. On the mainland, the numbers were even more appalling, with millions dying. Again, most succumbed to disease, though a significant minority were worked to death in mines or starved when their lands were taken from them to raise Spanish cattle. Horrified by the carnage he was witnessing, Spanish priest Bartolomé de Las Casas pleaded for mercy for his Indian charges. "For God's sake and man's faith in Him, is this the way to impose the yoke of Christ on Christian men?" he asked King Charles I. "They are our brothers."

Ultimately, the king agreed with Las Casas. But if not American Indians, then colonizers would need others to work the mines that fed the Spanish treasury and the ranches and farms that fed the miners. Las Casas suggested Africans, though he would later regret the idea and condemn African slavery as well.

## Slavery in New Spain

By 1600, Spanish America had imported about 75,000 African slaves. In the seventeenth century the number rose to 292,000; from 1701 to 1810, the total was 578,600. All told, roughly 1.5 million Africans would be imported into New Spain over roughly two and a half centuries.

Despite these numbers, African slavery took root on the periphery of New Spain. Because Spanish settlement in North America did not begin until the very end of the sixteenth century—and remained sparse even into the early eighteenth century—the scope of the threat from Spanish settlement was not as great for Native Americans in North America as it was for their counterparts in other parts of New Spain. And while formal Indian slavery was banned after 1542, other forms of coerced labor—such as the *encomienda* system—assured a steady supply of Indian muscle for Spanish mines and ranches during the sixteenth and seventeenth centuries.

Equally important, the Spanish—more interested in plundering gold and silver than settling—were slow to invest in plantation agriculture. Instead, the Spaniards reaped gold, silver and copper from Peru, and silver from Mexico, sending riches home to Spain or across the Pacific to their colony in the Philippine Islands. Following the exhaustion of the gold supply in the Caribbean, the Spanish did make some effort to harvest sugar into profit. The first African slaves were shipped to Hispaniola in 1502, the first sugar mill was built there in 1516, and by 1565, as many as 30,000 enslaved Africans may have arrived in the colony.

Yet agricultural production in the Caribbean was of less initial importance to the Spanish crown than precious metals from elsewhere in New Spain. It would take the more enterprising and emigration-oriented countries of northern Europe to realize that wealth and economic development could be gained through new products, new markets, and new sources of labor. During the 1500s and 1600s, the Dutch, English, and French would come to supplant the Spanish in much of the Caribbean and the southern part of the North American mainland, turning these tropical islands and subtropical lands into vast plantations worked largely by African slaves growing crops for a mass European market. The western third of Hispaniola became the French colony of Saint-Domingue in 1697, and over the next century developed into the richest colonial economy in the world. The colony's wealth was derived primarily from its large sugar and coffee plantations and the hundreds of thousands of African slaves that labored in them.

## Slavery in French North America

Slavery was also part of France's North American empire. Colonists in New Fance seeking inexpensive, readily available labor were able to capitalize on the Native American practice of enslaving captives of other tribes. Soon the French were purchasing captives from their Indian allies. Many were Pawnee captured farther west, and *panis* became the generic French term for Indian slave. Ownership of Indian slaves was formally legalized in a 1709 colonial ordinance. On the eve of New France's demise in the early 1760s, there were some 3,000 "panis" in the St. Lawrence region. Indian slavery was more limited in the sparsely settled Great Lakes region. In Louisiana the importation of African slaves by the 1720s had largely supplanted the use of Indian slave labor. Both the English and Spanish officially prohibited Indian slavery on taking possession of their respective parts of New France in 1763.

There was little demand for African slaves in Canadian New France. The climate did not support large-scale agriculture. Most slaves in the St. Lawrence region were household servants. But Louisiana, with its warmer climate, saw the widespread introduction of black slavery. Shipments of African slaves began arriving in the colony in 1717. A Code Noir (black code), written in 1724, codified the slavery system in Louisiana. About 28,000 African slaves in all were imported into French Louisiana. Most were employed on indigo and tobacco plantations along the Mississippi River. Small numbers of slaves were taken to scattered French settlements further north. Despite high death rates, a strong African-American community developed in the region with a distinctive Creole, or mixed black and white, culture.

## The Middle Passage and the Triangle Trade

The transatlantic triangle slave trade began with the Portuguese and Spanish in the 1400s, and was greatly expanded by Dutch, English, and French slavers in the 1600s and 1700s. North American—and, after 1776, U.S.—slavers were also active, particularly toward the end of the eighteenth century.

Most scholars estimate that roughly 9 to 12 million Africans were taken from Africa to the Americas, with about 50,000 coming in the fifteenth century, 300,000 in the sixteenth, 1.5 million in the seventeenth, 5.8 million in the eighteenth, and 2.4 million in the nineteenth, many of the latter being smuggled despite international sanctions against the slave trade.

## European Colonies and Exports from the Americas

ICELAND

Hudson's Bay Company

*Hudson Bay*

Labrador

**Pelts**

PRINCE RUPERT'S LAND

Newfoundland

QUEBEC

Cape Breton

*Missouri R.*

Nova Scotia

Boston

*St. Lawrence R.*

**Area disputed by Russia and Spain**

*Mississippi R.*

Whale meat, fish

Louisiana

Philadelphia · New York

UNITED STATES

Jamestown

VICEROYALTY OF NEW SPAIN

· Santa Fe

*Rio Grande*

**Tobacco, grain**

*ATLANTIC OCEAN*

New Orleans

Bahamas (Br.)

Mexico

*Gulf of Mexico*

Cuba

*West Indies*

**Tobacco, sugar, coffee**

Mexico City (Tenochtitlan) ·

Santo Domingo

*Caribbean Sea*

**Silver**

**Tobacco, cacao, hides, skins**

*PACIFIC OCEAN*

· Bogota

Guiana

Belem (Nossa Senhora de Belem) ·

VICEROYALTY OF NEW GRANADA

*Amazon R.*

**Tobacco, sugar, cotton, coffee**

**Gold**

VICEROYALTY OF PERU

VICEROYALTY OF BRAZIL

Bahia (São Salvador) ·

Lima · · Cuzco

**Silver**

**Gold, diamonds**

Rio de Janeiro ·

**Copper, grain**

VICEROYALTY OF LA PLATA

**Meat**

Rio Grande ·

**Silver, skins and hides**

Valparaiso · · Santiago

Buenos Aires

*PATAGONIA*

N

→ Important exports

**European possessions in the Americas, 1775–1800**

British

Dutch

French

Portuguese

Russian

Spanish

0          1000 miles

0          1000 km

**AMERICAN COLONIES** By the eighteenth century, Britain, France, and Spain had enjoyed the fruits of colonial trade for over 150 years. The resource-rich Americas had supplied Western Europe with precious metals, valuable furs, and a huge variety of foodstuffs. Yet, by 1775, the colonial competition was entering its final phase.

Africans were settled across the length and breadth of North, Central and South America and the Caribbean. Overall, about 40 percent (or 4 million) of all enslaved Africans were sent to the Portuguese colony of Brazil. The next most common destination were the British holdings in the Caribbean, with about 20 percent of all slaves (or 2 million). Spanish American colonies on the mainland and in the Caribbean took about 17.5 percent (or 1,750,000), French holdings in the Caribbean (mostly, Saint-Domingue, modern Haiti) took in 13.5 percent (or 1,350,000), and the tiny Dutch and Danish Caribbean islands received about 2.5 percent (or 250,000). Finally, British North America and, after independence the United States, took in 650,000 slaves, or 6.5 percent of the total.

## The Middle Passage

The slave trade was enormously profitable. In the context of the transatlantic trading system, the shipment of slaves from Africa to the Americas represented what was known as the Middle Passage, one leg of a triangular trade that saw European manufactures transported to Africa, where they were exchanged for slaves, and American plantation crops carried to Europe. (In reality, the system was far more complex, with ships traveling to and from many different ports in many different lands and with all kinds of goods.) At the height of the trade in the 1700s, an adult male slave could be purchased at a slave-trading post on the African coast such as Goree Island off French Senegal; Bonny, off British Nigeria; or Benguela, off Portuguese Angola, where hundreds or even thousands of captured Africans were kept in holding pens called barracoons.

While a slave ship merchant might pay about twelve ounces in gold for a slave in Africa, Africans sold for several times that amount in an American port. Therefore, with ships carrying anywhere from a few dozen to more than 200 slaves, the human cargo on a larger ship could equal more than a million dollars in today's money.

Conditions aboard ranged from the awful to the horrendous, depending on the attitude of the captain, the company he worked for, the quality of the ship, and the length of the voyage. Some slavers believed in tight-packing, cramming as many slaves into the hot and unsanitary holds as possible, while others were loose packers. The former, of course, meant more cargo, but also more loss of lives and potential profits. Death rates for slaves in the Middle Passage therefore ranged greatly between voyages, but they averaged about fifteen to twenty percent in the first couple of centuries of the trade, dropping off to about five to ten percent in the latter years. (Nor was the crew much better off, suffering similar mortality rates on the voyage from diseases picked up on shore or from the slaves themselves.)

But while these numbers explain the deadliness of the business, it requires the words of participants to convey the true horrors of the middle passage. "I was soon put down under the decks, and there I received such a salutation in my nostrils as I had never experienced in my life: so that with the loathsomeness of the stench and crying together, I became so sick and low that I was not able to eat," wrote Olaudah Equiano, an African enslaved near the Bight of Benin in the 1750s. He continued, "I now wished for death to relieve me." Not surprisingly, during this loading period—as during the transatlantic trip itself—the crew

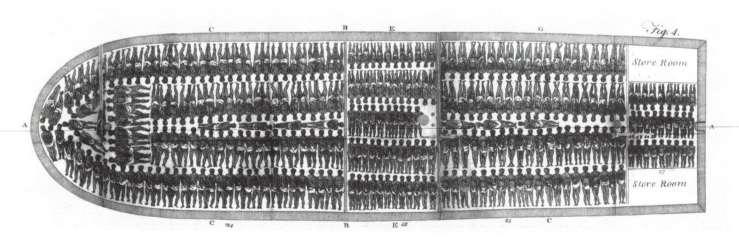

**CRUEL PASSAGE** Captured Africans are shown "tight-packed" in the hold of a slave ship. Conditions on board such ships were abysmal, and as many as one in five typically died from rapidly spreading illness, suicide, and starvation before even reaching American shores.

had to remain ever vigilant. Escapes, rebellions, and suicides were common occurrences throughout the process, but particularly so in the first few weeks. Indeed, crews let the slaves out of the holds for only a few brief moments while the ship was still in sight of land, and sometimes confined them to the hold for the entire voyage.

To keep their human cargo alive on the voyage, the crews sometimes forced food on them. The provisions—usually little more than a mealy porridge and perhaps some fish heads for protein—was unfamiliar to the Africans. Moreover, in the tropical climate, it often became rotten and bug-infested, leading to stomach illness, diarrhea, and vomiting, which further polluted the crowded holds in which they were kept.

After a voyage that could take weeks or months, the vessel arrived in an American port, usually in the Caribbean or in Brazil. Slaves were then prepared for sale by being given plentiful fresh water and local produce and meats, so as to make them appear healthier and hence more valuable. Depending on the facilities available, the slaves would either be herded ashore or local slave traders would come on board to examine the merchandise. The first to go were the youngest and strongest, with the sick and the old being sold to the poorest colonists. It was, recounts Equiano, yet another terrifying episode in a saga of fear and suffering. "Without scruple," he later wrote, "are relations and friends separated, most of them never to see each other again."

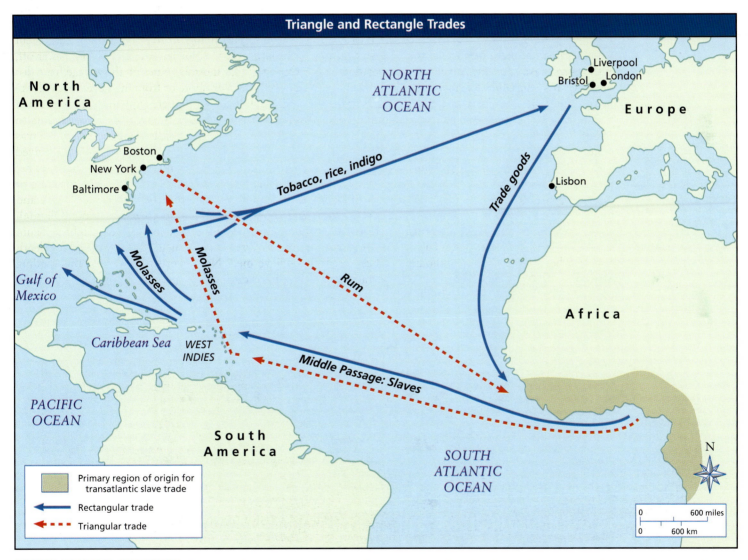

**Triangle and Rectangle Trades**

ROUTES OF THE SLAVE TRADE The term triangle trade has often been used to describe the trade routes used during the years of the transatlantic slave trade. For example, African slaves would be traded in the Caribbean for molasses, which would then be sent to North America, where it would be used to produce rum, which in turn would then be traded in Africa for more slaves. In recent years, historians have also begun referring to the rectangle trade, in which North American agricultural products such as tobacco, rice and indigo were sent to Great Britain, which in turn would send trade goods to Africa in exchange for slaves, thus adding another leg to the trade cycle.

# Economic Life in the British Colonies

Immediately preceding the American Revolution, the economic life in the thirteen British colonies in North America was flourishing. Cultivated crops and harvested natural resources were in abundance: tobacco, rice and indigo from the southern colonies; grains and livestock from the central colonies, known as the "bread colonies"; and salted fish and lumber from the New England colonies. The colonists, who had little cash to spend, exchanged their products for British goods such as furniture, wine, and material for clothing. Many enterprising colonists had also begun their own manufacturing industries, creating everything from finely crafted wood furniture, pewter tableware, and silver home ornaments to everyday necessities such as nails, glass, and paper goods.

## Mercantilism and America

The eighteenth-century trade system between the thirteen colonies and Great Britain operated according to mercantilism, the dominant economic theory in Europe during the era. According to mercantilist principles, a nation's wealth was based on the accumulation of precious metals through a surplus of exports over imports. Colonies were therefore regarded as means toward mercantilist ends with their trade strictly controlled. Beginning in 1650, England instituted a series of laws known as the Navigation Acts, aimed at controlling the trade of the English colonies. For example, these laws required that only English ships be used for trade; that manufactured goods competing with England's well-developed businesses, such as woolens and hats, not be exported; that non-English ships be forbidden from trading with the English colonies; that certain products, such as sugar, tobacco, cotton, indigo, rice, beaver skins, iron, and lumber, could only be shipped to English ports.

The economic relationship between the mother country and colonies was not completely one-sided. Colonial commodities often received a monopoly of the English market and preferential tariff treatment. For example, Americans benefited when tobacco cultivation was made illegal in England, just as British West Indian planters were aided by the Molasses Act of 1733, which imposed high duties on French sugar.

Nonetheless, resentment against royal trade restriction grew. The same Molasses Act that aided planters in the British West Indies hurt American rum distillers who had grown accustomed to lower-priced French molasses. Molasses was particularly important as a key product in the triangle trade. Rum from New England was exported to Africa, where it was traded for African slaves; the slaves were brought to British sugar plantations in the West Indies, where they were traded for molasses; and the molasses was then traded to New England where it was then used to produce more rum. Even after the act's passage, colonial

**SHIPWRIGHT AND BLACKSMITH (both pictures to right)** Colonial artisans, such as the shipwright and blacksmith shown here, possessed valuable and specialized skills. After first working in their chosen trades as apprentices, artisans would rise to become journeymen or master craftsmen.

merchants regularly circumvented the Navigation Acts by trading with the French and other non-British colonies in the West Indies. By the time of the American Revolution, the smuggling of products from foreign sources was considered perfectly respectable. It was also extremely profitable.

## Colonial Merchants

Not all merchants in the colonies, of course, were directly involved in smuggling, nor did all merchants own fleets of trade ships. Instead, colonial merchants reflected the diversity of the colonial economy. While international shipping merchants held the greatest prestige and owned the greatest wealth, most colonial merchants were shop owners, who sold or traded goods within the colonies, or between colonies. Large or small however, merchants negotiated with colonial planters and craftsmen, and ordered goods and materials for the colonies from England. Those that were engaged in the international shipping trade coordinated the sea voyages required to export products like furs, fish, grain, indigo, lumber, rice and livestock, and import products like glassware, copperware, ironware, silk goods, iron nails, printed cotton, linen and beaver hats.

## Farmers and Planters

Like merchants, those involved in agriculture ran the spectrum from wealthy plantation owners to modest small farmers. Planters were wealthy educated men who oversaw the operations on their plantations. They dealt more with logistics than with hard labor. They could be found supervising slaves and staff and inspecting crops. Whether cultivating tobacco in Virginia or Maryland or rice and indigo in the Carolinas, planters profited by selling crops to merchants for export or for distribution in the colonies.

A far greater number of colonists throughout the colonies were small farmers. While a minority of these farmers may have owned a handful of slaves, the vast majority, whether in the North or South, did not. They did their own labor — clearing land, digging ditches, building fences and farm buildings, plowing fields, and caring for livestock if they owned it. Like large planters, small farmers also grew some crops to sell, but much of it was grown to feed their own families.

## Colonial Artisans

Another common and very important occupation in Colonial America was that of the artisan. Artisans were involved in a wide range of crafts. Some were blacksmiths who supplied other craftsmen and townspeople with iron tools or supplies like axes or horseshoes. Others were coopers, who made barrels to store grain, cornmeal, beer, molasses, syrup, salted fish, and meat. Coopers also made kegs for gunpowder and rum, as well as tubs and pails for everyday use. Other artisans were tinsmiths who worked with tin to make lanterns, pans, and other items.

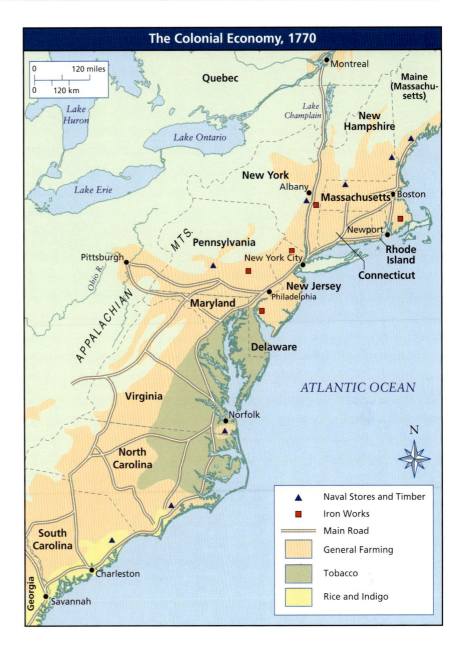

**The Colonial Economy, 1770**

Legend:
- ▲ Naval Stores and Timber
- ■ Iron Works
- ═ Main Road
- General Farming
- Tobacco
- Rice and Indigo

Then there were the printers, who published everything from newspapers and books to legal forms and advertising handbills.

Artisans were highly valued for their special expertise. To gain expertise, artisans began as apprentices, and moved up with experience to become journeymen. The most experienced artisans—and most highly esteemed—were called masters. In the South slaves would sometimes be trained as artisans. Although their skills were valued, their legal status as human possessions did not change.

## Laborers

Most slaves belonged to the large class of laborers. Most performed the hardest work on southern plantations, including clearing and plowing land, and planting, picking and processing crops.

Slaves were far from the only laborers in the colonies. There were also indentured servants—men and women who agreed to work for a certain period of time in exchange for passage to the colonies. After the service period ended, indentured servants were free, and

**DIVERSE ECONOMIES** Economic life in the colonial era varied with geography, from the slave-based plantation agriculture of the South to the small farms and manufacturers of the North. Important seaports such as Boston, New York and Charleston were centers of overseas and inter-colonial trade, as the rudimentary roads made for slow long-distance travel.

**CARIBBEAN SLAVES** The European colonies in the Caribbean were usually the first stop for enslaved Africans that eventually came to North America. Jamaica and Saint-Domingue in particular had large slave population. Slaves would often be "seasoned" in the Caribbean sugarfields before being resold to North American planters.

*"If any man shall out of wantonness . . . or cruel intention, wilfully kill a negro, or other slave, of his own, he shall pay into the public treasury fifteen pounds sterling."* —FROM BARBADOS SLAVE CODE, CA. 1780

received clothing, tools, and sometimes land from their former masters with which to start their new lives. Many then became small farmers, working their own land. Others remained laborers, although free. Freedom was not possible for slaves, however, who were bought and sold as property.

# The Caribbean Plantation System

Africans came to be the labor of choice for the grueling work on the sugar plantations of the Caribbean, particularly after the Dutch, English, and French secured Hispaniola (Saint-Domingue, later Haiti), Jamaica, and most of the Lesser Antilles in the 1600s. (The Spanish-speaking islands of Cuba and Puerto Rico—which remained in Spanish hands until the Spanish-American War of 1898—would not see large-scale plantation agriculture and importation of slaves until the nineteenth century. The Dominican Republic on the eastern two-thirds of Hispaniola was politically and economically linked to Saint-Domingue or Haiti almost continuously through 1844.)

Barbados, the first Caribbean island settled by the British, offered a model for African life and labor in the English-speaking Caribbean. The Spanish had been the first Europeans on Barbados, and had killed or driven away the entire native population of Carib in the sixteenth century. The first English ship landed in 1627, carrying eighty British colonists and ten African slaves. Laboring on small tobacco and cotton farms, much of the population consisted of white indentured servants until the 1640s, when sugar cultivation was introduced from Brazil by Dutch traders. Involving grueling work and large-scale capital investment for refining equipment, sugar cultivation soon displaced cotton and tobacco, even as plantations took over farms and African slave labor replaced independent white farmers and servants. In 1645, Barbados counted just under 6,000 slaves; by 1685, there were ten times that number; and by the end of the century, some 135,000. In the process, the vast majority of whites—some 30,000—fled to other Caribbean islands, England, or the British colonies in North America, particularly South Carolina. Thus, like much of the Caribbean but unlike most mainland North American colonies, Barbados became predominantly black. More than 90 percent of its population was of African descent by the end of the 1700s.

## Social Conditions in the Caribbean

Another factor differentiated Barbados and other Caribbean islands from the mainland of North America—a constant influx of new African slaves, until the out-lawing of the slave trade in the early 1800s. While it might seem pointless to discuss the relative merits of slavery in one place or another—slavery was brutal business wherever it took hold—it was less fatal on the North American mainland than it was in the Caribbean, mostly due to two inter-related reasons. First, North American slaves ate better. For example, while mainland slaves enjoyed diets with ample vitamins and minerals, it is estimated that Caribbean slaves received only 90 percent of their vitamin A needs, less than 50 percent of their calcium needs, and only a third of the vitamin C they required. Second, the more poorly fed Caribbean slaves were more likely to succumb to disease. A look at mortality statistics bears this out. Nearly 40 percent of Jamaican slaves were listed as dying from fevers, compared to just 11 percent of Virginia slaves. At the same time, twice as many slaves in Virginia—albeit a still minuscule 7.3 percent—died of old age.

This difference was due more to economic calculation than the relative kindness of the master class. On Caribbean islands, most land was devoted to sugar, forcing planters to import costly foodstuffs, which they rationed out parsimoniously. Plentiful land in North America allowed planters and farmers to raise both commercial and food crops. Moreover, mainland planters soon came to the realization that healthy slaves worked harder, had more babies, and did not need to be

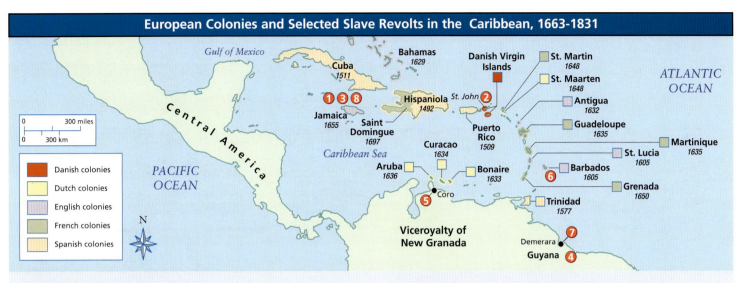

**European Colonies and Selected Slave Revolts in the Caribbean, 1663-1831**

1. 1663 The first serious slave revolt in Jamaica takes place. It involves 400 slaves.
2. 1733 At least 150 slaves are implicated in a slave revolt on St. John in the Danish West Indies.
3. 1760 On Jamaica, an uprising known as Tacky's rebellion involves about 1,000 slaves.
4. ca. 1763 Two thousand slaves revolt in Berbice, Guyana, and kill 200 of the settlement's 350 whites.
5. 1795 Three hundred slaves rise up at Coro.

6. 1816 On Easter Sunday, slaves on approximately 60 plantations rise up on Barbados.
7. 1823 Between 10,000 and 20,000 slaves on 50 plantations revolt in Demerara, Guyana.
8. 1831 The Christmas Uprising of 1831, a revolt by 20,000 slaves, takes place in Jamaica. The revolt leads to the end of slavery in the British Caribbean.

**FIGHTING FOR FREEDOM** Unlike plantations in North America, Caribbean and South American plantations often had huge slave populations. This fact led to a greater frequency of large-scale rebellions.

replaced. Thus, by the early 1700s, the North American slave population had reached a point where it could sustain growth without further imports while the English-speaking Caribbean islands required slave imports right up until abolition in 1833 to sustain their populations. (It should be noted that sugar cultivation in a tropical climate is far more grueling than tobacco or cotton farming in a temperate climate.)

Quality of life issues go beyond nutrition, disease, and work. Because of the high proportion of Africans in the population and the constant influx of new Africans, Caribbean blacks were able to retain more of their culture, especially in terms of language, religion, and social customs. Even today, Caribbean blacks are more likely than their North American counterparts to practice a faith that blends Christianity with traditional African religions, and their English is laced with more Africanisms. Moreover, their demographic dominance also gave birth to a fuller history of rebellion and resistance, especially on the largest of the English-speaking Caribbean islands, Jamaica.

Encountered by Columbus on his second voyage to the Americas in 1494, Jamaica saw virtually its entire indigenous population of Taino wiped out by infection, overwork, and murder within a few decades. First settled in 1506, Jamaica developed slowly under the Spanish, with only about 1,000 white and black inhabitants in 1655 when it was conquered by the British, who quickly took advantage of its tropical climate and, for the Caribbean, abundant land. Soon, more than 100,000 African slaves—along with 10,000 European masters, overseers, and skilled workers—were working in gangs producing the largest sugar crop in the English Caribbean.

## The Maroons

From the late 1600s onward, Jamaican runaway slaves established numerous independent settlements in the mountainous interior, where they effectively fought off British soldiers and Mosquito Indian troops, recruited by the English from Central America. Known as maroons (from the Spanish cimarrones, or runaway cattle), they numbered nearly 40,000 by the time slavery was prohibited in 1833.

The first maroons emerged in 1655 when their Spanish masters freed them as the English captured the island. The British tried to recapture them but the maroons' familiarity with the nearly impenetrable interior frustrated their efforts. In the 1680s, war broke out between the maroons and the British. Led by such legendary fighters as Accompong, Quao, and Nanny, the maroons held out for some 50 years.

In 1739, maroon leaders signed a controversial treaty with the British. While granted their freedom, the maroons agreed to stop raiding plantations, stop protecting runaways, and assist the British in quelling slave insurrections. The treaty preserved the maroon communities, but at the cost of dividing them from the much larger slave population. Still, after the 1833 declaration of emancipation in the British Empire, many former slaves migrated to the maroon communities, rather than work as wage laborers on the European-owned sugar plantations of the lowlands.

# Slavery in the Thirteen Colonies

In 1676, a group of yeoman farmers from the backcountry of Virginia asked Governor William Berkeley to protect their frontier settlements from Indian raids. Berkeley, who was involved in profitable trade with the Indians, refused. In response, the farmers, led by Berkeley's own nephew, Nathaniel Bacon, began raiding Indian settlements themselves. Berkeley charged Bacon with treason, although he later dropped the charges.

The farmers had other complaints as well—high taxes and a lack of representation in Virginia's planter-dominated House of Burgesses—and a rebellion took place. The farmers marched to Jamestown in September 1676, seized control of the House of Burgesses, and passed reform laws. At the height of the rebellion, Bacon died of malaria. With his death—and the arrival of an English warship—the governor's troops regained control of Jamestown. In the aftermath of the rebellion, 23 rebels were executed without trial.

Among the last to surrender was a mixed group of white and black yeomen. Victorious, the planters and burgesses were also wiser for the near-death experience. Indentured servants became yeomen and yeomen insisted on their rights as Englishmen, even if some were African. Slaves could make no such claims. But—for both cultural and legal reasons—it was not possible to enslave Englishmen. The planters instead began importing slaves from the Caribbean who had already been "seasoned" to plantation agriculture. By 1700, the population of Africans in Virginia had multiplied tenfold to 20,000. Over the next 50 years, no less than 100,000 slaves would be imported into the region.

**SLAVERY'S STATISTICAL RISE** The legal codification of slavery in the English colonies was a gradual process, reflected by social customs that saw black Africans as inferior to white Europeans as well as by labor and class struggles between different segments of the white population.

## Slavery Emerges as a Legal System

Although the first Africans arrived in Jamestown in 1619, there has long been debate about their status as slaves. Legally, at least, no Virginia laws specifically identified African servants as enslaved for life until 1641, when four white indentured servants and an African named John Punch was convicted of running away from their service. The whites were punished with an extra year of service. Punch on the other hand was sentenced to lifetime servitude. By the second half of the century, and particularly after Bacon's Rebellion, the House of Burgesses began writing laws that more specifically defined the difference in status between white and black laborers. Most crucial were a series of laws passed between 1667 and 1671 that said baptism and Christianity did not qualify African servants for eventual freedom. In 1692, marriage and sexual relations between whites and blacks were outlawed. Finally, in 1705, the burgesses ended all half measures by passing a law that read: "All servants imported or brought into this country by sea or land who were not Christians in their native country shall be accounted and be slaves." With this law, race rather than class became the prime dividing line in Virginia society. Even the poorest whites now had a stake. Their white skin alone conferred to them a commonality of purpose with the wealthy planter class, even as their economic interests differed.

## Slavery in Georgia and the Carolinas

Aside from the Chesapeake region of both Virginia and Maryland, slavery's deepest roots were in the Carolinas. Among that region's early settlers were the sons of wealthy West Indian planters—short on land, but rich in slaves. They settled the

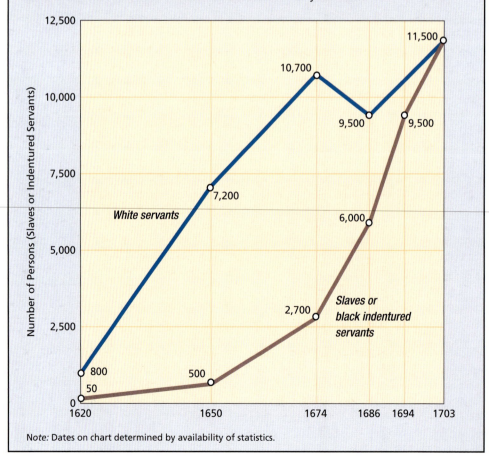

## The Rise of Slavery in Virginia

The number of African slaves in the Virginia colony during the 17th century rose rapidly, while the number of indentured servants declined before rising again at a slower rate, particularly after armed white servants and small farmers began a series of revolts, which culminated in Bacon's Rebellion in 1676. After that date, the number of slaves imported into the colony skyrocketed. While 3,015 enslaved Africans were imported into Virginia in the 82 years between 1619 and 1701, three times that number would arrive in the next 18 years alone.

Note: Dates on chart determined by availability of statistics.

Carolina lowcountry, taking control of millions of the best acres. Yet malaria was a constant threat in the lowlands, and one planters strove to avoid. Most therefore lived in Charleston, away from their actual plantations, while plantation overseers supervised the day-to-day business of agricultural production. This produced a very different pattern of slave-master relations in Carolina, with slaves living and working separately from their owners and enjoying an unusual degree of cultural autonomy. This would become even more the case once Carolina discovered a lucrative commercial crop.

The main Carolina crop also set the master-slave relationship in the region apart from its characteristics elsewhere. Carolina's lowcountry is ideal rice growing land. But rice is hard to grow, even in the best conditions, and English planters knew little about rice farming. But Africans did and brought their knowledge to the Carolina coast, which led to enormous wealth for the planter class. Beginning in the 1680s, rice exports rose from almost none to 17 million pounds in 1730 and 75 million pounds by the American Revolution, not including millions more that were consumed locally.

The slave population of the colony grew from a few thousand at the beginning of the eighteenth century to nearly 82,000 seventy years later. By 1770, there were two blacks for every white in South Carolina, Since most of those blacks lived away from their masters, they were able to preserve many aspects of their African culture. Even today remnants of a community known as the Gullah still inhabits the coastal islands of South Carolina. The distinctive Gulluh language, a hybrid of English and various African dialects, exists nowhere else. Yet despite the relative autonomy enjoyed by the lowcountry slave community, its worklife was brutal. Malaria and other diseases were a constant threat. What's more, slaves saw little of the wealth that their labor generated and enjoyed even fewer material comforts than their counterparts in the Chesapeake.

Moreover, the fact that South Carolina remained a majority black and slave colony (and later, state) made whites particularly edgy. And for good reason. Situated near the edge of British North America, they represented the first line of defense against hostile Spanish Florida. The Spanish offered freedom and land to any black who fled the colony. In 1738, sixty-nine slaves made their way to St. Augustine. When war broke out between England and Spain in 1739, seventy-five South Carolina slaves killed several whites, seized weapons, and headed for Florida "with Colours displayed and two Drums beating." Most of the Stono rebels—named after the river where they plotted their uprising—were quickly hunted down and killed before they could make it to Florida or spark a general uprising. Still, the rebellion put enough fear into the hearts of southern planters that imports of African slaves declined for a time, for fear that the slave to citizen ratio was becoming dangerously high.

### African Americans in the North

Not all eighteenth-century African Americans were slaves and not all lived in the southern colonies. Small communities of free blacks survived, in southern ports like Charleston, in older rural regions like the Chesapeake, and in northern cities. Slavery was also both legal and practiced in all of the British North American colonies, including New England. Particularly in the middle colonies—and especially New York—slavery thrived, though in a very different form than the South. According to the first national census in 1790, 7.6 percent, or 25,875 persons, of the population of New York State was African American; in Pennsylvania, the figure was 2.4 percent, or 10,238 persons, and in Massachusetts just 1.4 percent, or 5,369.

In rural areas of the North, African Americans were rare. Colder weather and a shorter growing season made it impossible to farm labor-intensive crops like tobacco, sugar, and rice, which required nearly year-round maintenance. Those commercial crops that did thrive in the North—largely grains—had highly seasonal labor demands. Lots of hands were only needed at planting and harvest time. Thus, it made little economic sense to buy and maintain slaves who only worked part of the year. It was better to hire labor as it was needed. But African Americans were were common in the colonial cities. Approximately ten percent of Boston and twenty percent of New York—both with total populations under 20,000—were black. Whether slave, indentured, or free, African Americans were often among the most impoverished urban residents, and held the poorest-paying professions like day laborers, cartmen, or merchant seamen.

Harsh conditions bred discontent and, on some occasions, rebellion. Not surprisingly, given the multicultural nature of the city, African Americans often found allies among other the members of oppressed groups. In 1712, about twenty-five Indian and black slaves set fire to an outhouse, then lay in ambush, killing nine men and wounding seven others who came to put the fire out. The punishment meted out was even more horrific than the crime. More than twenty slaves—including a pregnant woman—were hanged; another three were burned to death; one was broken on the wheel. Moreover, slave codes were toughened—slaves found meeting in groups larger than three were subject to a punishment of forty lashes—and arson was made punishable by death for anyone in the colony.

Harsh codes, however, did little to assuage the fear of wealthy white New Yorkers living in a city increasingly dominated by the poor and nonwhite. A series of suspicious fires in 1741—just two years after the Stono Rebellion in South Carolina—led to rumors of a slave and indentured servant insurrection. Although no conclusive evidence of a conspiracy could be found, authorities rounded up poor African Americans and whites. Some of them were tortured; others were offered a reward for turning in other slaves and servants. In all thirty blacks and four whites were executed for their supposed roles in the alleged conspiracy. This episode illustrates that although not as dependent on slaves for their wealth as southern planters, northern merchants nevertheless feared those whom they had enslaved—the black people who served them daily and helped keep the city running.

*"Whereas the plantations and estates of this province cannnot be well and sufficiently managed and brought into use without the labor and service of negroes and other slaves; and foreasmuch as the said negroes . . . are of wild, savages natures . . . it is therefore enacted that all negroes, mulattoes, mestizos, or Indians are hereby made and declared slaves . . . ."*

— SOUTH CAROLINA SLAVE CODE, 1712

# Chapter 9: The American Revolution

Less that seven years after the end of King George's War, Virginia colonel George Washington led a small force toward Fort Duquesne, the French stronghold defending the Ohio River. The Virginians, who had come to claim the region, built a stockade they called Fort Necessity in July 1754. The French and their native allies soon surrounded Washington, who had no choice but to surrender and retreat to Virginia. This minor episode sparked the French and Indian War, part of a worldwide struggle for dominance known as the Seven Years' War. By 1763, Britain had taken control of vast French holdings in North America that stretched from the mouth of the St. Lawrence River in the north, through the Great Lakes and Ohio Valley and south along the Mississippi River. Yet the war's end would open a new set of conflicts—between American colonists and a British government that sought to recoup some of its wartime expenses by raising colonial taxes, and between American colonists who moved to settle these new lands and the Indians who lived in them.

## The French and Indian War

The French and Indian War took place in four main theaters: the Ohio Valley, northern New York, Canada, and the Caribbean. In 1755, the French and their Indian allies won a spectacular victory, ambushing General Edward Braddock's 2,000-strong expedition as it marched on Fort Duquesne in western Pennsylvania. Half the men were killed, including Braddock. Refusing to heed most colonial advice, including Washington, Braddock insisted on fighting in the American wilderness in the same way that battles were fought on the open fields of Europe. Although Washington won fame by conducting a fighting retreat that saved many troops, 1755 was a disaster for the British. Only a colonial force under New York's William Johnson was victorious, defeating French and Indians at the Battle of Lake George.

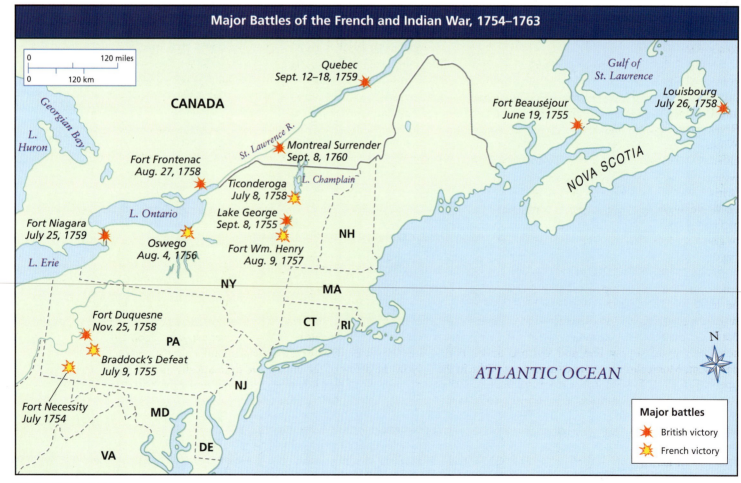

**Major Battles of the French and Indian War, 1754–1763**

**SEVEN YEARS' WAR** The French and Indian War, also known as the Seven Years' War, began with series of French victories. Yet by 1768, the tide had turned in Great Britain's favor. For Britain, however, the war had been costly, both financially and politically as it unleashed a series of events that spelled independence for its 13 North American colonies.

Indian raids drove thousands of settlers from the frontier, filling colonial cities with refugees. In 1757–1758, Fort Oswego on Lake Ontario and Fort William Henry on Lake George fell to the French. The Marquis de Montcalm won a key victory in taking Fort William Henry, but his triumph was soiled by massacre. Indian warriors fell on the unarmed British captives at the fort and killed hundreds of soldiers and civilians before the French could intervene.

Montcalm made his base at Fort Carillon (later named Ticonderoga by the British), defending the water route up Lake Champlain toward Quebec. In 1758, he and 3,200 troops were besieged by an army of 15,000 under General James Abercrombie. Abercrombie had one of the finest armies ever assembled in North America, but instead of surrounding Montcalm, he launched frontal attacks that left hundreds of his men dead. Abercrombie soon withdrew in defeat.

### The End of New France

Yet the tide was turning. In July 1757, the British captured Fort Louisbourg, the massive French garrison at the mouth of the St. Lawrence that had been at the center of King George's War. They also took Fort Duquesne and Fort Frontenac, endangering Montreal and Quebec. By mid-1759, British and colonial forces captured Fort Oswego and Fort Niagara to seize control of Lake Ontario. In July the last French defenders abandoned and blew up Fort Carillon rather than allow the British to seize it.

Soon, 9,000 British troops under James Wolfe surrounded Quebec, where Montcalm commanded a mixed garrison of 14,000 French Regulars, Canadians, and Indians. The city stood above the Saint Lawrence River, protected by high cliffs. Near the end of July, Wolfe launched an ill-fated attack to take the top of the cliffs, but he was repulsed with more than 440 killed and wounded. Montcalm could afford to wait out the British, who would have to depart before cold weather. Wolfe, however, had to bring on an open battle. His artillery pounded the city as he desperately sought a way to get to the level land known as the Plains of Abraham, beyond the cliffs.

By mid-September, Wolfe's men had found an undefended pathway to the top. On the night of September 13, he led his troops to the crest, unchallenged. Sunrise revealed thousands of redcoated British troops arrayed for battle on the Plains of Abraham. With the British now across his main supply line and Quebec under bombardment, Montcalm was compelled to meet Wolfe in the open field. Each force numbered approximately 4,000 Regulars, but superior British firepower and tactics won the day. Quebec surrendered, but both Wolfe and Montcalm died from their wounds.

### The Fall of Montreal

British commander Sir Jeffrey Amherst was slow to move against Montreal, the last French stronghold. He planned for three armies to advance on the city in the coming year. One force would come from the west, another from the south over Lake Champlain, and a third from Quebec. In the early spring of 1760, the French managed to rally an army and attack Quebec, briefly laying their own siege to the city. The arrival of a British fleet ended the siege, however, and the campaign against Montreal soon began.

By September 1760, overwhelming force compelled Montreal's surrender to Amherst, ending the fighting in North America. Final peace terms were approved in 1763, as the French ceded Canada and a vast territory along the Ohio River and east of the Mississippi. After 70 years of war, French power in North America was broken, and the British ruled supreme. Britain was master of the seas, and her American colonies grew richer with every passing year. Soon, they were too powerful to remain colonies subordinate to Britain, and they demanded equal rights, respect, and eventually independence.

# Taxation Without Representation

"I have been told . . . that the English colonies in North America, in the space of thirty or fifty years, would be able to form a state by themselves, entirely independent of Old England." wrote Peter Kalm, a Swedish botanist who visited America from 1747 to 1751. "But as the whole country which lies along the seashore is unguarded," he continued, "and on the land side is harassed by the French in times of war, these dangerous neighbors are sufficient to prevent the connection of the colonies with their mother country from being quite broken off. The English government has therefore sufficient reason to consider the French in North America as the best means of keeping the colonies in their due submission."

What Kalm did not foresee was that the French threat to the British colonies would come to an end by 1763, with France's defeat in the Seven Years' War. Yet Kalm was prescient in his assessment of how France's defeat would impact British-American relations.

With the removal of the French from most of North America, Britain became one of the world's greatest powers and colonizers. Its North American colonies were among the most economically vibrant in the world. The colonies not only supplied the mother country with abundant resources, but also served as an ever-expanding commercial market for Britain's own manufactured goods. Now the defeat of the French had dramatically increased the amount of North American territory under the British flag. To British authorities, maintaining this expanded territory demanded tighter control.

Tighter financial control topped the agenda. The war with France had nearly doubled the British national debt. Large sums had been spent defending the colonies against French and Indian hostilities, and even more would be needed to protect against further Indian attacks. To the British, it seemed only reasonable that the colonies pay more for the services provided.

## Pontiac's Rebellion and the Proclamation of 1763

The continuing danger of Indian attacks was highlighted in 1763 by bloody fighting in the Ohio Valley known as Pontiac's Rebellion. In the aftermath of France's defeat, tensions between France's former Indian allies and British authorities grew, sparked in part by Britain's refusal to supply Indians with gunpowder as French traders had done. Despite promises to the contrary, the British had also failed to prevent colonists from migrating into Indian territory.

In protest, Pontiac, war chief of the Ottawa nation, convinced other nations to join him in an alliance against the British. In May 1763, Pontiac and a force of 300 laid siege to Fort Detroit. Other bands captured 9 of the 11 other British forts on the frontier. Soon after, the tide turned. By October, 1763, the Indian offensive had weakened. Pontiac, realizing that many bands of Indians had begun to make peace, lifted the siege on Fort Detroit.

The same month, Britain issued the Proclamation of 1763. The edict outlined the organization of the lands acquired from France. New settlement would be permitted in territory that had been previously "civilized" by European settlement, such as Canada, East Florida, and West Florida. "Uncivilized" lands, such as the Ohio Valley and other lands west of the Appalachians, were to be reserved for Indians. Whites were banned from settling in the region and only licensed traders could deal with the Indians who lived there.

Although welcomed by Native Americans, the Proclamation angered colonists who had expected that the end of the French and Indian War would allow them to move westward. Most important, American colonists saw the Proclamation of 1763 as another restraint on freedom. Despite the law, many Americans would move west anyway.

## The Stamp Act

Over the next several years, Parliament passed a series of measures to raise revenue. Of all the new acts, the Stamp Act of 1765 was the most far-reaching. A tax on such everyday items as newspapers, licenses, almanacs, and playing cards, it applied to all citizens.

Many colonists felt that because they did not have their own representatives in Parliament, they were being taxed without their consent. "No taxation without representation" became their rallying cry. To protest the act, many colonists agreed not to buy any goods imported from Great Britain. In Virginia, Patrick Henry, a member of the House of Burgesses, drafted resolutions known as the Virginia Resolves, stating that Parliament had no right to tax the citizens of Virginia. Although Henry delivered the Resolves to shouts of "Treason!" from more cautious members of the Burgesses, the Virginians voted in their favor.

News of the vote spread through the colonies. By midsummer, the General Court of Massachusetts asked for a meeting of delegates from all colonies to devise a united response to the Stamp Act. Although only nine of the colonies agreed to participate in the Stamp Act Congress, delegates from Massachusetts to South Carolina meeting in New York in October agreed that Englishmen in the colonies were entitled to the same rights as Englishmen in England. Therefore, they argued, only colonial legislatures had the right to impose taxes on the colonies.

By the time that the Stamp Act Congress convened, however, many colonists had already expressed their dissatisfaction through direct, and sometimes violent action. In Boston, New York, Philadelphia, Charleston and elsewhere, secret organizations that would become known as "Sons of Liberty" organized protests against the act. The first major outbreak of violence took

**The Proclamation of 1763 and Anti-Tax Rebellions**

Legend:
- Proclamation Line of 1763
- British territory
- Thirteen British colonies
- Indian Country
- Anti-tax riot, 1764–74

**THE COLONIES REBEL** In the years following their victory over France in the Seven Years' War, Great Britain declared the western frontier off limits to western settlement and began to impose taxes on the 13 colonies in order to recoup the cost of the war. Both of these actions infuriated colonists, who ignored the Proclamation of 1763's settlement ban, and rioted repeatedly against the imposition of taxes.

## The Boston Massacre

In 1770, a crisis arose when Lord Hillsborough, a British foreign minister, ordered the governor of Massachusetts to disband the colonial assembly. To enforce his demand, he sent two British regiments into Boston, a provocative move that all but guaranteed tension between the citizens of Boston and the soldiers. On March 5, a fist fight broke out between a soldier and Bostonian laborer. When a crowd of colonists gathered and began throwing stones, coal and other objects at guards outside of the Old State House, a scene deteriorated into a riot. In response, British soldiers fired into the angry crowd, killing five, including an African-American sailor named Crispus Attucks. The colonial press dubbed the event the "Boston Massacre" and fear and anger spread through the streets of Boston. To avoid a full scale uprising, Parliament recalled troops from Boston.

REBELS A Boston mob protests the Stamp Act.

place in Boston on August 14, 1765 when Andrew Oliver, a British tax agent was hanged in effigy, and the building containing his tax office was destroyed. Oliver resigned his post. Less than two weeks later, a second Boston mob ransacked the home of Lieutenant Governor Thomas Hutchinson, mistakenly believing he had helped win the act's approval. The following day, Sons of Liberty in Newport, Rhode Island burned pro-British figures in effigy and over the next several days engaged in riots that destroyed the homes of two Stamp Act supporters. On November 1, a mob in New York City destroyed the royal coach of Acting Governor Cadwallder Colden. By the time the act was set to go into effect, no stamp tax collector in the colonies was willing to stay on the job. By March 1766, Parliament was forced to repeal the act.

### The Stamp Act's Legacy
The Stamp Act protests marked an important signpost on the road to revolution. First, they united the colonies. Second, support for resistance cut across class lines. The Sons of Liberty were generally supported by wealthy American merchants, and most of the group's founders came from the middle class. Some were intellectuals like the firebrand Samuel Adams, who hoped to make Massachusetts into a conservative Christian community. Others were artisans like silversmith Paul Revere.

Though British officials considered the Sons of Liberty radicals, the group's middle-class leaders did not think themselves that way. The Sons of Liberty in New York explained its aims this way: "[We] are not attempting . . . any change of Government—only a preservation of the Constitution." Independence was not a serious consideration, and many of the various Sons of Liberty groups reaffirmed their loyalty to George III.

Yet much of the violence and destruction done in the group's name during the Stamp Act protests came not from the wealthy or middle class, but from ordinary artisans and mariners. Thus, to wealthier colonists, the mob fury unleashed by the Stamp Act protests were a double edged sword. As long as the poor's anger was directed at British tax collectors, many middle– and upper–class colonists were supportive. At the same time, many members of the merchant class also recognized that if anti-British sentiment among the working class became fused with a general class resentment, then the dangers would be serious indeed.

# The March Toward Revolution

The very same day that Parliament repealed the Stamp Act, it passed a new measure that enraged the colonies. The Declaratory Act stated that Parliament could pass any law it wished "to bind the colonies and people of America." Determined to maintain its power, Parliament imposed new taxes in June 1767, in the form of the Townshend Acts. These acts taxed glass, lead, paints, paper and tea imported into the colonies. As with the Stamp Act, protesters, who had begun to refer to themselves as Patriots, responded with a fresh round of boycotts against British goods. The boycotts lasted for three years, until 1770, when Parliament repealed all of the Townshend Act taxes—other than the one covering tea.

## The Burning of the *Gaspee*

To get around the tax on British tea, colonial merchants followed their long-standing practice—they smuggled less expensive tea and other products from other nations. To halt the practice, Britain used customs ships to patrol the Atlantic coast. One of them, the *Gaspee*, was particularly forceful, confiscating goods from even the smallest of vessels. In 1771 the *Gaspee* ran aground near Providence, Rhode Island. A colonist named John Smith led a band of men aboard the ship. Once on board, Smith and his men shot and killed the ship's captain, sent the crew ashore, and then set the ship on fire.

Although all of the culprits in the *Gaspee* affair were caught, no witnesses would come forward to give evidence against them. The incident convinced many in Britain that the colonists in North America could not be brought to justice by customary rules.

## The Boston Tea Party

In 1773, another incident solidified this view. To avoid taxes on tea, colonists began smuggling less expensive tea from Holland. As a result, the British East India Company, which had a monopoly on the sale of British tea, was losing money. In the Spring of 1773, Parliament passed the Tea Act to protect the East India Company from further losses. The Tea Act allowed the East India Company to sell its tea in the colonies at far lower prices. In this way, other tea merchants, unable to match these prices, were driven out of the colonial tea market. While some colonists were tempted to buy the East India Company's high-quality tea at very low prices, others resented the manner in which Parliament was using the Act to interfere in the American marketplace. Protesting this latest outrage became a matter of patriotic honor. Tea ships were turned away from American ports. Many Americans refused to drink tea altogether. Huge cargoes of unsold tea rotted in warehouses.

Tensions surrounding the Tea Act increased dramatically after the merchant ship *Dartmouth* arrived in Boston on November 27, 1773. Angry members of the local Sons of Liberty, led by Samuel Adams, were determined to stop the ship from landing its cargo of tea. Governor Thomas Hutchinson was equally determined to collect the tax and enforce the law. On the night of December 16, a band of colonists disguised themselves as Indians and boarded the ship. While a crowd cheered them from the wharf, they dumped all the chests of tea into Boston Harbor.

Parliament responded to the Boston Tea Party the following Spring by passing the Coercive Acts, which became known in the

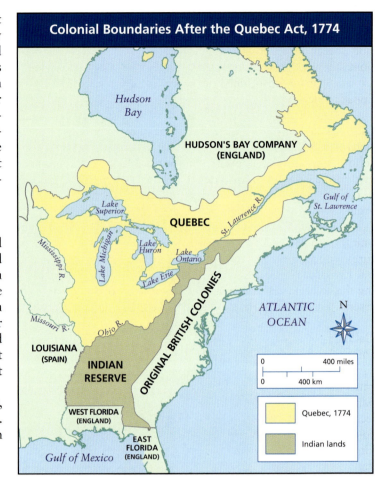

**Colonial Boundaries After the Quebec Act, 1774**

**QUEBEC IN THE OHIO VALLEY** The Quebec Act of 1774 extended Quebec's southern border to the Ohio River.

colonies as the "Intolerable Acts." The first of these harsh new laws, the Boston Port Act, closed the Port of Boston to all ships until its citizens paid for the destroyed tea. The Massachusetts Government Act changed the governing charter of Massachusetts by granting more power to the royal governor and weakening the authority of local meetings.

The Intolerable Acts, which punished the entire population of Massachusetts for the acts of a few, angered the citizenry—not only in Massachusetts, but throughout the other colonies as well. The Virginia House of Burgesses declared a day of fasting to show solidarity with the citizens of Boston, who were now facing food shortages due to the closing of their port. South Carolina sent rice and money to the city, while New York offered sheep.

In June, Parliament passed an act that had a more direct impact on all of the colonies than the Intolerable Acts. The Quebec Act extended the Quebec border down to the Ohio River—in effect annexing the Ohio Territory to Canada. The act also extended religious liberties to French Catholics in the area. Many Americans viewed the act as yet another repressive measure to enforce British authority. They also believed it was a malicious attempt to permanently ban settlers from expanding into the Ohio Territory (even though that right had previously been restricted by the Proclamation of 1763).

## The First Continental Congress

In the aftermath of the Intolerable Acts and the Quebec Act, many in the colonies realized that the best way to approach Britain with complaints was through a unified governmental body. Many Patriots feared that dependence on mob action such as protests and riots would only encourage Parliament to impose harsher restrictions and higher taxes. On September 5, 1774, the first Continental Congress, made up of delegates from 12 of the colonies met in Philadelphia.

For moderate delegates such as Joseph Galloway and John Dickinson of Pennsylvania, the goal of the Congress was to ease tensions with Britain. For radicals such as Samuel Adams and his cousin John Adams of Massachusetts, and Patrick Henry of Virginia, the goal of the Congress was to devise a way to force Britain to give in completely to the colonies' demands. Failing that, the radicals argued, the colonies should declare their independence.

Initially the moderates held sway. Galloway proposed a union of the colonies under British authority. Colonial legislatures would retain the powers that they had had prior to 1763, but Parliament would still be entitled to pass regulations affecting the colonies. However, a "grand council" of American representatives would be empowered to veto Parliament's laws.

Largely due to the work of Samuel Adams, many questioned Galloway's assumption that Parliament had the right to regulate colonial trade. Instead, they accepted the view of a young Virginian named Thomas Jefferson, who had written a pamphlet called *Summary View of the Rights of British America*. In his pamphlet, Jefferson argued that Parliament could neither tax nor legislate for the colonies. In fact, the only connection between the colonies and Britain, wrote Jefferson, was mutual loyalty to the king. For Jefferson, the British empire was not a united whole, but a loose affiliation of independent states, each governed by its own representatives, and not by Parliament.

While delegates to the Continental Congress dared not go so far as declaring independence, they did take several key steps toward it. They first drafted a statement to King George III that declared the rights of the colonies and listed their grievances. Second, they formed the Continental Association to organize a formal boycott of British goods. This move differed from previous boycotts because it also proposed to ban American exports to Britain. The colonists hoped this plan would bring pressure on Parliament to relax its trade restrictions. Third, they recommended that each colony arm its citizenry and form its own militia. Finally, the delegates also agreed to meet again in Philadelphia on May 10, 1775.

# Declaring Independence

"Government is dissolved and we are in a state of nature," argued the fiery Virginian Patrick Henry during the First Continental Congress in 1774. "The distinctions between Virginians, New Yorkers, and New Englanders are no more. I am not a Virginian, but an American."

Despite Henry's rhetoric, very real differences still existed between the delegates as the Congress broke up. Only a handful joined Henry in favor of independence as a desired outcome. Yet by agreeing to prepare for a boycott on British trade should the Intolerable Acts not be repealed, the twelve colonies in attendance moved closer to a permanent break with London.

### Concord and Lexington

But as the delegates also recommended that each colony organize armed militias, a match was struck to the colonial tinderbox. Just weeks before a Second Continental Congress was to meet, the confrontation between King and colonies turned to armed conflict. On April 19, 1775, British general Thomas Gage sent seven hundred soldiers toward Concord, Massachusetts to confiscate a cache of weapons and arms and to capture Samuel Adams and Boston merchant John Hancock. Three Bostonians, Paul Revere, William Dawes, and Samuel Prescott, learned of the maneuver and rode through the area to warn of the British advance. Patriots across the Massachusetts countryside rushed to Lexington, just east of Concord. The volunteers were known as Minutemen because they had pledged to be ready for battle at a minute's notice.

**BATTLE ROAD** British Regulars retreating from Concord were attacked by local militiamen from behind stone walls and from inside houses along the road. In counterattacking, the Regulars frequently bayoneted those they caught.

When the British reached Lexington at dawn, seventy Minutemen were waiting on the village green. After rebels refused an order to lay down their arms, the first shot was fired—though which side fired first is unknown. In the skirmish that followed, eight Patriots were killed and nine wounded.

Marching on to Concord, the British destroyed part of the Patriot weapons cache and began heading back to Boston. However, at the Old North Bridge, a group of Minutemen fired on the British, killing three. Soon farmers and townspeople throughout the area joined the fray, firing at the retreating redcoats from behind roadside stone walls and trees. After a deadly sixteen mile march, the British reached Boston. In the day's fighting, they had lost seventy-three men and another 174 had been wounded. The Patriots, on the other hand, had lost forty-nine men, while forty-one had been wounded. By then, Patriots had seized Fort Ticonderoga in northern New York without firing a shot and had surrounded Boston to begin a siege of the city. While British troops would drive Patriots from their positions at Breed's Hill and Bunker Hill north of Boston in June, the siege of Boston would continue for almost a year. War had begun.

## The Second Continental Congress

The Continental Congress met for the second time on May 10, 1775, in Philadelphia. Most delegates had attended the first Congress, which had met the previous year, but joining the delegates this time were Benjamin Franklin, a well-known inventor and printer from Philadelphia and Thomas Jefferson, the author of the influential pamphlet, *Summary View of the Rights of British America*. In addition, Georgia, which had not sent a delegation to the first convention, did send one this time, marking the first time all thirteen colonies met at once. The Continental Congress that convened that day would serve as the central government of the colonies for the next six years.

Now that military action had begun, the first order of business for the new government was to organize a Continental army and appoint its commander. Local militias serving the interests of a single colony were not well-suited to a long-term war involving thirteen colonies. Thus, Congress established the Continental Army, and placed Virginia's George Washington, one of the heroes of the French and Indian War, at its helm.

**Loyalist Strongholds and Rebel Support**

Legend:
- Loyalist stronghold
- Strongly contested areas
- Patriot stronghold

**DIVIDED OPINION** While virtually all of New England and Virginia were Patriot strongholds during the Revolutionary War, some major cities, such as Philadelphia, New York City, and Charleston, South Carolina were strongly loyal to the crown.

## The Olive Branch Petition

Even after war broke out in the spring of 1775, many delegates to the Continental Congress still hoped that the conflict with Britain could still be settled peacefully. On July 5, Congress drafted the Olive Branch Petition—a final plea to Britain for peaceful reconciliation. While the petition respectfully identified the colonies as subjects of the "Mother Country," it also asked the British government to answer colonial grievances. On receiving the petition, King George III refused to even read it.

The next day, the more radical delegates, led by Thomas Jefferson, submitted a document called "A Declaration of the Causes and Necessity of Taking Up Arms." In it, the authors expressed their willingness to fight for their freedom.

## A Continental War

In the fall of 1775, American forces invaded Canada, hoping to divert British troops from New England. The first expedition, led by General Richard Montgomery, captured Montreal in November. By December,

Montgomery had joined with a second Patriot force, led by Colonel Benedict Arnold, and attacked Quebec. Outnumbered and exhausted by the difficult journey through the wilderness, the Americans failed to take the city. Montgomery died in the fighting, the British took many prisoners and the remainder were forced to retreat back to New England by the spring of 1776.

Despite these setbacks, the Americans did achieve several victories during the winter and spring of 1775–1776. On March 17, after General Henry Knox arrived in Boston with cannons captured at Fort Ticonderoga in New York, the British withdrew from the city. Then on June 28, the Patriots fought off a British naval attack on Charleston, South Carolina.

# The Fight for Independence

After the Olive Branch petition failed to secure peace, many Americans began to accept that a permanent break with Britain was unavoidable. On June 7, 1776, Richard Henry Lee of Virginia proposed to the Continental Congress a resolution stating that the colonies were "free and independent states." The members of Congress appointed Thomas Jefferson, Benjamin Franklin, John Adams and Connecticut's Roger Sherman to draft a declaration based on Lee's resolution. Jefferson wrote the initial draft, thanks to what Adams termed his "peculiar felicity of expression."

On July 1, the committee presented its draft to the full Congress. For three days, fifty-six delegates held a heated debate over the document. Jefferson's draft contained an attack on slavery—though Jefferson owned slaves. Southern delegates insisted that this section be removed. In addition, some of Jefferson's harsh attacks on King George III were softened in the final document. At last, on July 4, all delegates added their signatures. As he signed, Franklin remarked, "We must all hang together or assuredly we will all hang separately."

There were two parts to the declaration. The first, the Preamble, stated that "all men are created equal" and possess certain God-given rights such as "Life, Liberty and the pursuit of Happiness." The second listed British injustices against the colonies.

**Major Battles of the Revolutionary War, 1775–1778**

★ American victory
★ British victory

0   200 miles
0   200 km

Despite passage of the Declaration, the colonies remained divided on the issue of independence. John Adams's own estimate placed one third of the population as Patriots, another third as Loyalist, and the final third as neutral. Patriots generally supported the war, but not all of them believed in independence. They fought as militiamen when the war came to their

**WAR IN THE NORTH** For the first three years of the war, most major engagements were in the North, particularly in New York, New Jersey, and Pennsylvania, as George Washington played a three year game of cat and mouse with the British army, the world's greatest military force. In doing so, Washington's rag-tag army was transformed into an effective fighting force.

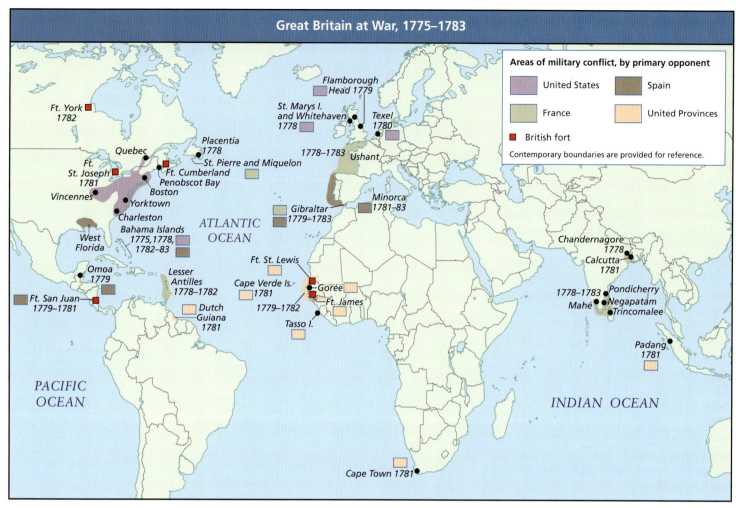

**Great Britain at War, 1775–1783**

Areas of military conflict, by primary opponent
- United States
- Spain
- France
- United Provinces
- British fort

Contemporary boundaries are provided for reference.

Ft. York 1782
Placentia 1778
Quebec
Ft. St. Joseph 1781
St. Pierre and Miquelon
Ft. Cumberland Penobscot Bay
Vincennes
Boston
Yorktown
Charleston
Bahama Islands 1775, 1778, 1782–83
West Florida
Omoa 1779
Lesser Antilles 1778–1782
Cape Verde Is. 1781
Ft. San Juan 1779–1781
Dutch Guiana 1781
Flamborough Head 1779
St. Marys I. and Whitehaven 1778
Texel 1780
Ushant 1778–1783
Gibraltar 1779–1783
Minorca 1781–83
Ft. St. Lewis
Gorée
Ft. James 1779–1782
Tasso I.
ATLANTIC OCEAN
PACIFIC OCEAN
Chandernagore 1778
Calcutta 1781
1778–1783
Mahé
Pondicherry
Negapatam
Trincomalee
Padang 1781
INDIAN OCEAN
Cape Town 1781

**A WORLD WAR** When France, Holland (United Provinces), and Spain entered the war on the Patriot side, Britain's military resources were stretched thin. The empire had to be defended, not only in North America, but also in the Caribbean, India, and Africa.

colonies, but were often hesitant to join the Continental army in support of other regions.

Loyalists, or Tories, remained loyal to the crown. While many were critical of British policy, many thought it foolhardy to challenge the greatest military power on Earth. Loyalists were often harassed, beaten and on rare occasions killed by Patriot mobs. Before the war's end, as many as 60,000 Loyalists would leave for England, while others would sail for Canada or the British West Indies.

# The Revolutionary War

On July 2, 1776, as the Continental Congress was debating the Declaration of Independence in Philadelphia, 10,000 British troops under the command of General William Howe landed on Staten Island in New York. Within a month, the force had grown to 32,000. Howe's brother, Admiral Richard Howe, commanded a huge fleet of warships and transports. In response, General George Washington sent 19,000 heavily outnumbered men to defend the western end of Long Island. When British forces stormed Washington's position on August 27, American resistance collapsed. The Patriots lost over 1,000 men, while Howe lost but 400. Washington avoided what might have been a total disaster only by crossing the East River into Manhattan, and then retreating north into Westchester County.

## The British Take New York

In September, the British took New York City. New York had been a Loyalist stronghold, and the city's Tory community cheered the arrival of the King's army. Then on September 21, a fire broke out, raging through the streets and destroying 500 buildings. British forces and Tories were certain that Patriots had started the fire, though no proof existed. Suspects were rounded up and some were hanged without trial. Others were tossed back into the still-burning flames to their deaths.

Although it's not known if the Patriots had set the fire, Washington himself had considered ordering the city burned rather than turn it over to the enemy. In the end, he decided against the plan. Still, the fire benefited the Patriot cause. Charred and gutted by fire, New York was of little use to Howe and his men. One Loyalist wrote that New York was "a most dirty, desolate, and wretched place." For his part, Washington remarked about the fire, "Providence, or some such good honest fellow, has done more for us than we were disposed to do for ourselves."

On October 28, the British defeated Washington once more, at the Battle of White Plains. However, in another fortunate turn, General Howe opted not to pursue Washington's main force into New Jersey. Instead, he turned over that duty to Lord Charles Cornwallis and headed back to northern Manhattan, where his troops captured Fort Washington, still under the command of Patriot General Nathanael Greene. The British would hold New

York for the next seven years, earning the city the nickname "Tory capital of America" for the remainder of the war.

## Crossing the Delaware

Following the British victory at White Plains, Cornwallis pursued Washington into New Jersey. Once again the Patriots narrowly escaped, this time by crossing the Delaware River into Pennsylvania. However, as the British approached Philadelphia, the Continental Congress was forced to flee Philadelphia for Baltimore.

Desperate for a victory, Washington decided to launch a surprise attack. On Christmas night, 1776, with about 2,400 troops, Washington crossed back across the Delaware River and marched on Trenton, New Jersey. At dawn Patriot forces surprised British troops and Hessian mercenaries, who were still recovering from their Christmas celebration. About 920 Hessians were captured, 25 killed and 90 wounded. The triumph immediately boosted morale and secured Washington's reputation as a military strategist. On January 3, 1777, his force attacked a British force at Princeton, New Jersey and captured the town.

## The Tide Turns

The defeats in the fall and winter of 1776 were a tremendous blow to the Continental Army. Still, the impact would have been far worse had Washington not been secretly receiving military supplies from France, Holland and Spain that allowed his army to stay in the field. Yet France's aid was secret. Although the French government had been closely following the war in the hope of striking a blow at Great Britain, the French were not prepared to openly support the Patriots. Doing so would surely have brought on a new war.

In the autumn of 1777, events shifted in favor of the Americans. That summer, British general John Burgoyne led 7,700 troops from Canada into northern New York. Allied with Burgoyne was a Iroquois Indian war party. Burgoyne planned to move on Albany, and after uniting with Howe, seize control of the Hudson Valley. If successful, the British would divide New England from the rest of the colonies.

They may have, had General Howe kept to his end of the plan. Instead, he moved south from New York to attack Washington's army in Pennsylvania. Although Howe managed to capture Philadelphia, the elusive General

**Major Battles of the Revolutionary War, 1779–1783**

Washington eluded the British once again. Without aid from Howe, Burgoyne lost the series of battles that took place near Saratoga, New York in September and October. On October 17, 1777, he was forced to surrender about 5,000 men to American general Horatio Gates.

Back in Pennsylvania, Washington's men wintered at Valley Forge. Suffering through blizzards, mud, and epidemics of

**WAR IN THE SOUTH** In 1779, the war shifted to the South, and the British won victories in Georgia and South Carolina. Nathanael Greene's campaign won back the South, and when Washington was victorious at Yorktown, the Americans began negotiations to gain their independence.

typhus and other diseases with only limited supplies, many of Washington's soldiers deserted. Yet after a former Prussian military officer named Baron Wilhelm von Steuben arrived to drill the remaining ragtag troops, the Continental Army left Valley Forge well-trained and better prepared.

After the American victory at Saratoga, France openly allied with the Patriots. By the end of the 1770s, France was sending a steady supply of soldiers, ships, and money across the Atlantic.

### The War in the South

Even after France entered the war, hostilities were far from over. As the 1770s came to an end, British forces won control over much of the southern colonies. Still, a spirited guerrilla campaign managed to keep pressure

on the British, and in combination with a better-trained Continental Army, these guerrillas gradually drove the British into a smaller and smaller area. A second front was opened against the British when Spanish troops under Bernardo de Gálvez captured British settlements on the lower Mississippi and along the Gulf Coast. The Spaniards swept far to the north to capture a British post in what is now Michigan. Critical to these offensives was a supply of beef cattle that Gálvez had ordered driven from the Spanish settlement of San Antonio in present-day Texas. Finally, in October, 1781, General Cornwallis' army found itself trapped by American forces on land and French forces at sea. Cornwallis surrendered, and the hope of British victory came to an end.

In 1782, the United States and Great Britain signed a temporary peace treaty, ending most of the hostilities. However, the agreement angered France, which had expected as an ally of the rebellious colonies to be included in the negotiations. France only accepted the treaty with the understanding that it would not go into effect until France had concluded its own peace treaty with the British.

One year later, a formal peace treaty was signed in Paris. The goal of American independence had been achieved. The world had witnessed the birth of a new nation—the United States of America.

# War Opens the Frontier

In the summer of 1777, reports spread that an Iroquois war party traveling with General Burgoyne's British troops near Fort Edward, New York, had killed a young woman named Jane McCrea. Miss McCrae, had been on her way to join her fiancé, a lieutenant in a Loyalist militia accompanying Burgoyne. Although the Iroquois warrior that took her scalp claimed that Miss McCrae had actually been killed by a bullet from a Patriot militia, her death enraged Patriot settlers, and many joined the American forces that were preparing to attack Burgoyne that fall near Saratoga.

### Indians and the War

Most tribes that lived in British North America wished to stay neutral during the war. "We are unwilling to join on either side of such a contest," argued one Oneida chief diplomatically when the war began, "for we love you both—old England and new."

Many became involved nonetheless. Although both the British and Americans believed the Indians should not be involved, the British had longstanding ties with the Iroquois and other tribes long before the war broke out. For example, Thayendanekea, also known as Joseph Brant, was an Iroquois chief of the Mohawk nation. He had been educated at the Indian School in New Hampshire (later renamed Dartmouth College). The British made Brant "Colonel of Indians" and beginning in the late 1770s, he led the Iroquois on a series of devastating raids on the New York frontier.

**Siege of Yorktown, September 28–October 18, 1781**

York River

Choisy

Gloucester

Chesapeake Bay

Swamp

**Cornwallis**

Yorktown

Yorktown Creek

**De Grasse**

Deux-Ponts

Hamilton

**Rochambeau**

Moore's house

Surrender field

Mill Pond

French artillery park

Lincoln

**Washington**

Steuben

American artillery park

Lafayette

N

| | | | |
|---|---|---|---|
| American advance | | American trenches | |
| American artillery | | British infantry | |
| American camp | | British redoubt | |
| American infantry | | British ships | |
| American redoubt | | French ships | |

0    .5 miles
0    .5 km

**YORKTOWN** By surrounding the British at Yorktown, American troops under George Washington and French forces under Comte de Rochambeau forced British commander Charles Cornwallis to surrender in the last major engagement of the Revolutionary War.

**TRAIL OF DESTRUCTION** In 1779, American forces under John Sullivan and James Clinton ransacked the Iroquois homeland in New York, burning villages, killing women and children, and ending Iroquois military resistance for good.

## The War in the West

In 1779 Washington sent a force led by John Sullivan and James Clinton to weaken the Iroquois. Although only scattered fighting occurred, the Americans left a trail of destruction—burning native villages and fields and killing men, women and children in their wake. The purpose of the expedition was simple: with their food and homes destroyed, the Iroquois were in no position to help the British.

Meanwhile, General George Rogers Clark brought the war to British outposts in the Northwest Territory, which stretched from the original colonial frontier, beyond the Great Lakes, to the Mississippi River. From June 1778 to February 1779, Clark led 200 frontiersmen through flooded swampland to capture British posts on the Mississippi and Wabash Rivers.

Clark's greatest triumph was taking Fort Sackville at Vincennes in February 1779. His victories, almost bloodless, helped establish American claims to the Northwest Territory when final peace terms were negotiated between Great Britain and the United States. Yet American claims—and settlement—on the western frontier dated back to well before the start of the

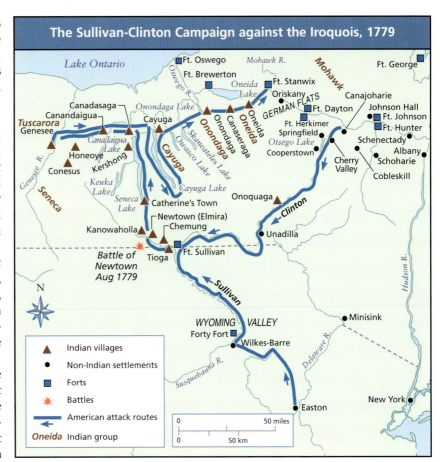

**The Sullivan-Clinton Campaign against the Iroquois, 1779**

▲ Indian villages
● Non-Indian settlements
■ Forts
✴ Battles
→ American attack routes
*Oneida* Indian group

0     50 miles
0     50 km

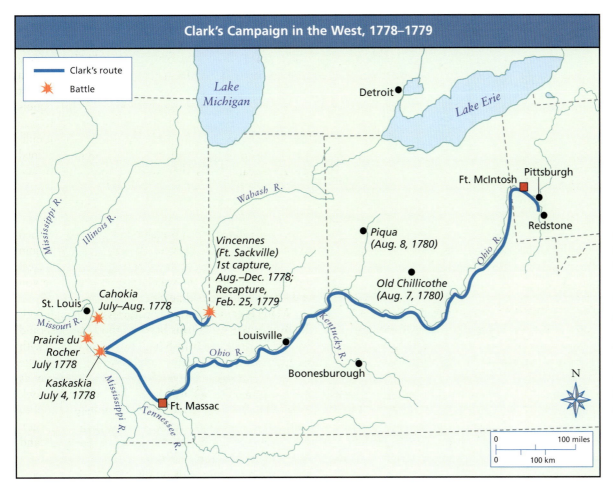

**Clark's Campaign in the West, 1778–1779**

— Clark's route
✴ Battle

0     100 miles
0     100 km

**A GRUELING CAMPAIGN**

In the winter of 1778–1779, George Rogers Clark journeyed to the Falls of Ohio, near present-day Louisville, Kentucky. There he gathered backwoods fighters for a campaign against British forts at Kaskaskia and Vincennes, which he captured.

Revolution. The Proclamation of 1763, in which Britain banned American settlement west of the Appalachian Mountains, slowed but did not halt American settlers. In 1773, legendary frontiersman Daniel Boone had attempted to lead a party of family and friends over the mountains, from North Carolina, but was turned back by an Indian attack that killed his son. The following year, he led a Virginia militia in defeating 300 Shawnee and Delaware warriors at Point Pleasant on the Ohio River. In 1775 Boone led a party that cut the Wilderness Road across the Cumberland Gap into Kentucky, where he founded the settlement of Boonesborough. Boone's adventures— one year rescuing his daughter and two others from Shawnee kidnappers, escaping from captivity himself and then holding off Shawnee warriors during a siege of Boonsborough, to name a few—turned the frontiersman into a genuine folk hero in his own time.

### The Treaty of Paris and the Western Territories

Following Yorktown, one of the most important questions to be settled became how much territory the United States

## The Smallpox Epidemic of 1775–1782

Between 1775 and 1782, as war raged along the eastern seaboard, the people of North America were also struck by another devastating and deadly threat called smallpox. Smallpox, caused by a contagious virus known as Variola major, began with an infection of the respiratory tract. After about twelve days, early flu-like symptoms appeared— including headache, backache, fever, vomiting, and general weakness. After another few days, painful lesions appeared in the mouth, throat, and nasal passages. In some patients, the infection caused internal haemorrhaging beneath the skin, which then led to bleeding from the eyes, nose, gums and elsewhere.

Patients that did not experience haemorrhaging had a better chance of survival. In them, the pus-filled lesions, or pustules, pushed to the surface of the skin, where they blistered, and if the patient survived, scabbed over.

During the war years there were numerous major outbreaks of smallpox. Three major occurances took place between 1775 and 1776 alone. The first occurred in 1775, during the siege of Boston the second, the next year, during the siege of Quebec, and the third, also in 1776, in Virginia among a group of black loyalists fighting under Lord Dunmore, the Royal governor.

While vaccination against smallpox would not be discovered for another twenty years, health practitioners of the Revolutionary era did take steps to prevent the disease. The controversial practice of inoculation—by which people were intentionally exposed to the disease, after which they would come down with a far less severe case of it, and then be immune from more

Spread of Smallpox through North America, 1775–1783

serious outbreaks—was used during the Boston outbreak, and then, on George Washington's orders, on much of the Continental Army.

Between 1777 and 1778, the virus appeared to be relatively contained. Yet, in 1779, it rose again. As fighting moved to the southern colonies, so too did the pox. A combined force of British and Pennsylvania loyalist troops, for instance, carried the disease with them from Jamaica to Pensacola, Florida. The disease also swept through the ranks of formerly enslaved African Americans who had escaped captivity for freedom on the British side. In many instances, British abandoned their end of the bargain and forced ill Africans to return to captivity at the point of a gun.

The same year, a major outbreak hit Mexico City, afflicting over 44,000 and killing about 18,000. The virus also moved south into South America, and north in the the Spanish Far North Frontier of Texas and New Mexico. At the same time, it swept across the Great Plains, possibly carried by warriors of the Comanche Nation, as far as Montana, and from there into the Pacific Northwest and Canada, leaving a trail of decimation in its wake.

would gain. Benjamin Franklin, one of the American negotiators suggested that Britain turn over to the United States all of Canada to prevent "future difficulties." The British refused, but hoping to reduce French influence over the United States, decided to offer the rest of its territory in North America, from the Ohio Valley in the north to Florida (which Spain had regained) in the south, and west all the way to the Mississippi River. The exact location of the Spanish border remained in dispute until 1819 when Spain ceded all of Florida, including the disputed land, to the United States.

The vast new territory won in the war would grip the imagination of the new nation. The men who would shape the government of the United States would face innumerable new conflicts. Each individual state would scramble to stake competing claims to these lands. The question of how to manage the territory for the good of the nation rather than for the interests of individual states would be one of the first questions to arise.

## Black Loyalists and Migration to Nova Scotia

As revolution began in the thirteen American colonies in the late 1770s, the British were badly outnumbered. When in desperation they promised freedom to any slave of a rebel who fought the Americans on their behalf, the response was greater than they could have imagined; as many as 30,000 slaves escaped to British lines. Working as soldiers, laborers, pilots, cooks, and musicians, they were a major part of the war effort. As defeat became inevitable, these free blacks were evacuated to Nova Scotia with the other Loyalists. But many faced discrimination, and most were reduced to a position not so different from slavery, where they were dependent on the meager wages they could earn from manual labor. Then in 1787, the British government established a settlement for free blacks called Freetown, which today is the capital of Sierra Leone. Before long, most black loyalists left Nova Scotia for the new settlement. Today, their descendants number more than 60,000.

### North America, 1783

*(map)*

ARCTIC OCEAN

ALASKA

Baffin Bay

Baffin Land

NEWFOUND-LAND

Hudson Bay

LABRADOR

RUPERT'S LAND

Area disputed by Spain, England, and Russia

Area disputed by England and U.S.

PACIFIC OCEAN

Columbia R.

Snake R.

ST. PIERRE and MIQUELON (FRANCE)

QUEBEC

NOVA SCOTIA

UNITED STATES

Mississippi R.

Area disputed by Spain and U.S.

ATLANTIC OCEAN

N E W S P A

Rio Grande

FLORIDA

British West Indies (ENGLAND)

Gulf of Mexico

CUBA

JAMAICA

ST. DOMINGUE

Caribbean Sea

BRITISH HONDURAS

MOSQUITO COAST PANAMA

0    500 miles
0    500 km

**Legend:**
- French possessions
- Russian claims
- Spanish possessions and claims
- Disputed areas
- United States
- Area unexplored by non-Indians
- British possessions

### Black Loyalist Settlements in Nova Scotia, 1783

- ○ Black Loyalist communities
- ◻ Black Loyalist landing places

N

St. John River area

Ft. Cumberland

Sydney area

Parrsboro

Cornwallis/Horton area

Tracadie/Guysborough area

Annapolis area

Windsor area

Digby area

Preston area

Halifax

Weymouth area

ATLANTIC OCEAN

Port Mouton
Shelburne

0    100 miles
0    100 km

**A NEW NATION** The Treaty of Paris in 1783 ended the Revolutionary War and brought independence for the thirteen United States. Spanish-held territory hemmed in the new nation to the south and west, while Great Britain continued to hold Canada.

# Chapter 10: Thirteen Independent States

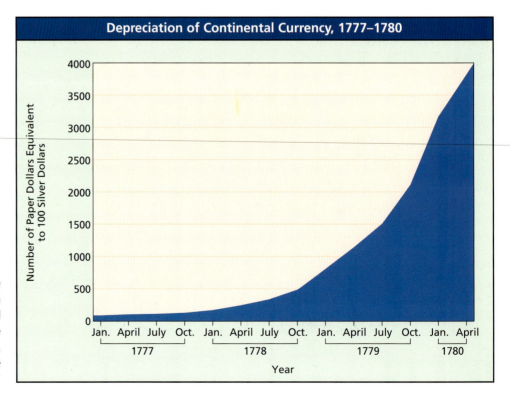

ARTICLES OF CONFEDERATION The Articles of Confederation were in effect from 1781 to 1789.

On July 12, 1776, eight days after the passage of the Declaration of Independence, a congressional committee presented for discussion a document called the Articles of Confederation. Intended as a constitution for the colonies after independence, the Articles reflected the Patriots' distrust of central authority. For example, the Articles granted Congress no authority to levy taxes or even to raise troops.

The Articles were sent out to the colonies—which by then were beginning to be called states—for approval in November 1777. After amendments, the Articles of Confederation were adopted on March 1, 1781. Their adoption would help establish the idea of rule under a written document.

Yet even before the states ratified the Articles, their shortcomings as a governing document for a nation at war were clear. The "united" states were only very loosely united. Under the Articles, the states were practically separate countries. Congress was powerless to make trade treaties with foreign nations in the name of the United States as a whole. Instead, only individual states could make trade agreements. Rivalries developed between major seaports like Baltimore and Charleston.

New York antagonized its neighbors with taxes on goods passing through its ports.

## Economic Crisis

To Patriots in 1776, independence from Great Britain meant that Americans would face no more taxes levied from across the Atlantic. No longer would they be restricted in what products they could trade, or with whom. Yet during and after the war, the thirteen new states faced serious economic problems, and the lack of a single, unified economic policy would hamper Congress's ability to address them.

For well over a century, economic life in the colonies had been strictly intertwined with Britain's worldwide imperial economy. Colonial merchants sent raw materials such as wheat, rice, tobacco, and indigo to Britain and received, in return, manufactured goods such as furniture, clothing, tea, and innumerable other items. As members of the British empire, the American colonies also had access to other key British colonies. Most important were the West Indies, from which the colonies received sugar and other crops as well as labor in the form of enslaved Africans.

Pre-war merchants had chafed in the face of Parliamentary restrictions that out-

RAPID INFLATION During the war, the Continental Congress issued so much paper currency that its value decreased rapidly—its decline sped by an effective British blockage of American ports. Worthless objects were said to be "not worth a Continental."

**BUSY PORT OF TRADE** Although Salem, Massachusetts (seen here in about 1790) and other American ports would thrive once more in the last years of the 18th century, during the Revolutionary War, overseas trade virtually collapsed.

lawed trade with nations such as France and Holland. Yet the British mercantile system offered stable markets for American exports and a wealth of manufactured imports that found a ready supply of colonial consumers. Despite growing anger over taxes, free Americans in all colonies had benefited from the arrangement—from fisherman, shipbuilders, and sea captains in New England to small farmers in Pennsylvania and large slave-owning planters in South Carolina. By the early 1770s, the economies of the thirteen British colonies were among the healthiest in the world.

With the onset of war, the American economy fell into fiscal chaos. Transatlantic trade and trade between colonies along the Atlantic coast and with the West Indies had come to a grinding halt as British warships controlled and blockaded the coastline. The loss of trade also meant a loss of jobs—for merchant seamen and for all those involved in building and supplying American merchant ships.

American soldiers, whether they were members of local militia or enlisted in the Continental Army rarely had sufficient supplies. While states did have enough food and clothing to feed and clothe the army, many states were hesitant to ship provisions elsewhere. Besides, transportation was slow by land and next to impossible by sea since the British controlled the Atlantic coastal shipping lanes. Neither state governments nor the Congress had

political power or capability to efficiently manage a continental war. As the war dragged on, the cost of waging it increased.

To pay these costs, Congress and the states printed and issued millions of dollars worth of paper money. Yet because the money's value was not supported by gold or any other commodity, its value was essentially based only on Americans willingness to use it. By the last years of the war, the federal currency was worth little, and state-issued currency even less. In this climate, inflation spiraled skyward. A bushel of corn in Massachusetts that cost less than a dollar in 1777 was selling for nearly $80 two years later.

Despite the chaos, states strongly resisted any attempt to centralize fiscal policy. For example, Superintendent of Finance Robert Morris's called for the wartime government to assume the entire national debt, issue new interest-bearing debt certificates, and impose tariffs and internal taxes to pay the interest costs. Yet the Morris plan greatly exceeded the limits of federal power set by the Articles of Confederation. Rhode Island, for example, objected to the idea of a national tariff (an import duty of 5 percent on foreign goods), leading to its defeat in Congress. In many ways, the Morris plan was a precursor to the fiscal ideas of Alexander Hamilton, but with a war for independence raging, the former British subjects had little desire to trade one central authority for another.

# Revolutionary State Governments

During the Revolutionary era, the colonies had to create frameworks for self-government as they nullified their colonial charters with England. Though the United States proper was created with the ratification of the national Constitution in 1788, many states drafted their own constitutions after—or even before—the signing of the Declaration of Independence on July 4, 1776. All state constitutions expressed the same basic philosophical tenets, framing government around the idea of representation, checks and balances, and individual liberties. The details of state constitutions varied widely, expressing the diversity of social, economic and political interests as well as the characteristics of each state's history. Variations among states often played out in the dichotomies of rural vs. urban interests, North vs. South, small state vs. large state, and conservative vs. radical. Though nationalism surged around the signing of the Declaration, between 1776 and 1787, most Americans' primary allegiance rested not with the developing nation but with their home state.

## State Constitutions

The similarities and differences between the various states can be seen by examining some of the main features behind the new constitutions of Virginia, Delaware, Pennsylvania, New York, and Massachusetts.

In June 1776, even before the Continental Congress signed the Declaration of Independence, Virginia's new three-part constitution took effect. One part consisted of a declaration of independence, a second a detailed Frame of Government, and the third a bill of rights based on ideas of equality and inalienable rights that became a national model. The Virginia constitution also created a bicameral legislature, based on the colonial House of Burgesses. It stipulated that the governor be elected by legislative ballot. In another departure from its colonial charter, the state ended its official sanction of the Anglican Church.

The first state to pass a constitution written by elected delegates was Delaware. The state's constitution, which took effect in September 1776, called for a Privy Council. The Council's members were chosen by the General Assembly, which was divided into an upper and lower house. Laws passed by the assembly did not need approval from the state president. Delaware's constitution also stipulated that only white male landowners had voting privileges.

The same month, Pennsylvania's new constitution also went into effect. Its constitution created a ruling executive council rather than a governor. However, the council did not have the power to veto laws passed by the legislature. Unlike most other state governments, Pennsylvania only had a one-house legislature. Its power was held in check by a Council of Censors, elected once every seven years. Voting rights extended to free white male taxpayers.

In keeping with its liberal tradition of representative democracy, religious tolerance, cultural diversity and anti-slavery sentiment, Pennsylvania became the first state to outlaw slavery when the legislature passed the Gradual Abolition Act in 1780.

In New York, the new constitution took effect in April 1777, creating the first state in which the governor was elected by the popular vote, even if voting rights were limited to white male landowners. The governor's appointments were subject to approval from a Council of Appointment. The New York Constitution also stipulated that voters could change the constitution every twenty years.

**New State Constitutions**

- United States in 1783
- U.S. territory, 1783
- Territory in dispute
- **1776** Date of state constitution
- **1776** Altered original charter to exclude allegiance to the crown

**STATE CONSTITUTIONS** In 1776, twelve former British colonies approved new or altered original constitutions. The documents expressed many of the ideas that later appeared in the U.S. Constitution. The most important was that government power was derived from the people and that the people should be governed by elected officials. But some states were more conservative than others. For instance, Massachusetts, which did not ratify its constitution until 1780, made substantial property ownership a qualification for voting and holding office. Pennsylvania, on the other hand, gave voting rights to all adult males who paid taxes and had lived in the state a year.

### Western Land Claims, 1783

**Disputed Western Claims**
- Massachusetts and New York
- Massachusetts and Virginia
- Connecticut and Virginia
- States having no Western claims

### The Northwest Ordinance of 1787

- United States
- U.S. territory
- British territory
- Spanish territory
- Disputed territory
- Fort

**ORGANIZING THE WEST** The Northwest Ordinance of 1787 put an end to the competing land claims of Virginia, Massachusetts, New York, and Connecticut. Prior to the Ordinance's passage, Virginia had claimed land the entirety of what are now the states of Kentucky, West Virginia, Ohio, Indiana, Illinois, Wisconsin, Michigan and parts of Minnesota.

Power in New York was divided between the governor, legislature and courts. The legislature was split into two houses. New York's constitution, which was largely written by John Jay, codified the state's long tradition of religious freedom by guaranteeing it in writing. Yet the political interests of New York City often clashed with upstate, rural interests. This antagonistic urban vs. rural relationship would remain a hallmark of politics in New York.

### Territorial Conflict

With the Peace Treaty of 1783, the United States gained the large land area known as the Old Northwest. Citing territorial charters signed before the war's end, the larger states of Virginia, Connecticut, New York and Massachusetts immediately laid claim to the vast majority of the land. Other states argued that the earlier land divisions had been created haphazardly and that the nation as a whole should own the entire area, which measured some 265,878 square miles. In 1780, New York agreed to cede its claim to western land to the federal government.

Thomas Jefferson, a consistent advocate for a coast-to-coast democracy, played a key role in the eventual reorganization of the area. Jefferson drafted the Ordinance of 1784, which divided the Northwest Territory into various smaller territories and created a plan for the temporary government of the area. Though Jefferson's plan was never enacted, it did become the basis for a future settlement of the issue.

The next year, the Ordinance of 1785 created the township system for surveying land in the Northwest Territory. The Ordinance put in place a rectangular grid system to divide the land for sale at public auction, with proceeds going to the federal government. In 1785 and 1786, both Massachusetts and Connecticut ceded their western land claims to the federal government. The following year, on July 13, 1787, Congress passed a revised Ordinance of 1787, also known as the Northwest Ordinance. The land in question was located north of the Ohio River and stretched between the Mississippi River and the Great Lakes.

The much-needed revenue that would be generated by land speculation hastened the Northwest Ordinance's passage. In October, 1787, the sale of the land began as Manasseh Cutler and Winthrop Sargent, director and secretary of a new company called the Ohio Company of Associates, purchased 1.78 million acres of Ohio land. In the Spring of 1788, settlement of the new territory began.

A bill of rights for the Northwest Territory established trial by jury, freedom of religion, and an emphasis on public education, with lands being set aside for the construction of public schools. The Ordinance also banned the entrance of slaves into the territory.

According to the Ordinance, any territory carved from the Old Northwest was to be governed by a congressionally appointed governor, secretary and group of three judges. Once the population of a new territory reached 5,000 free adult males, a legislature could be elected, and a non-voting representative could be sent to Congress. Once the population of a territory reached 60,000, the territory could apply for statehood. Eventually, five states (Ohio in 1803, Michigan in 1805, Illinois in 1809, Indiana in 1816 and Wisconsin in 1836) were created entirely from former Northwest Territory lands. In 1858, part of Minnesota would also be created from the territory. The Northwest Ordinance created the nation's first organized system of rules governing territorial land, encouraged settlers to move west, and established clear procedures for the admission of new states to the Union. At the same time, the admission of new states from the Northwest Territory differed in one major respect from future state admissions. In the future, the slavery issue would be far more contentious

# Into the Backcountry

The United States in 1783 still hugged the Atlantic seaboard. Americans saw the continent stretching to their west as a vast wilderness awaiting their taming and development. The frontier was the western edge of settlement, "the meeting point," in the words of historian Frederick Jackson Turner, "between savagery and civilization." To Thomas Jefferson, the frontier was the place that his vision of a nation of yeoman farmers would become real. His proposed Ordinance of 1784, and the Ordinances of 1785 and 1787 that followed it, created the practical framework through which, he believed, that vision might be fulfilled.

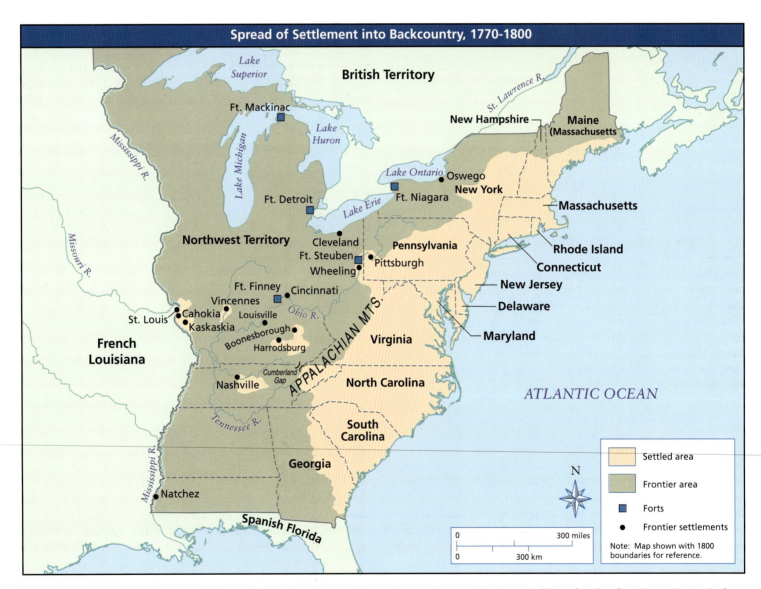

**Spread of Settlement into Backcountry, 1770-1800**

**WESTERN SETTLEMENT** Between 1770 and 1790, American settlement moved across the Appalachians for the first time. Control of the Ohio Valley became the prize in the fierce warfare that broke out between settlers and Native Americans of the region.

## Pinckney's Treaty, 1795

Area claimed by Spain after 1793

Line of Pinckney's Treaty, 1795

**PINCKNEY'S TREATY** Unclear borders between the United States and Spanish territory in North America led to tension between the two countries. In particular, the Spanish and Americans differed over the border of West Florida, which had been ceded to Spain by Great Britain after the war. In addition, Spain also claimed former British territory as far north as the Ohio and Tennessee rivers. American settlers ignored these claims. In 1795, Pinckney's Treaty settled the issue temporarily.

### British, Indians and the Old Frontier

Despite the legal framework for settlement, many Americans had severe doubts that the federal government could effectively promote territorial growth and settlement. In 1787, four years after the end of the Revolutionary War, Great Britain still occupied forts on the western frontier. What's more, that frontier was still occupied by American Indian nations that viewed the United States with hostility.

To Americans in the post-Revolutionary era, the Indians were a conquered people, who as allies of Great Britain during the war, had lost all claim to it by virtue of Britain's defeat. Indian tribes were not sovereign nations, but subjects of the American government. To enforce this view, the federal government demanded that American Indians living west of the Appalachians cede their lands to the United States.

In 1784, the United States reached an agreement with a number of Iroquois who claimed to be representatives of their people. According to the terms of the Treaty of Fort Stanwix, the Iroquois ceded all lands in western Pennsylvania and Ohio. Members of the once powerful Iroquois Confederacy were now forced to live on an assortment of isolated reservations, as destitute wards of the state.

Immediately, Iroquois opponents of the treaty argued that the agreement was illegitimate, that it had been signed at gunpoint, and that those who signed the treaty had not been authorized to do so. Warfare continued in the area for almost another 20 years.

Other treaties, involving the Indians of the Northwest Territory, followed Fort Stanwix—at Forts McIntosh (1785) and Finney (1786). In 1789, the Wyandot, Delaware, Potawatomi, Ottawa and Sauk nations met with federal officials at Fort Harmer in present-day Marietta, Ohio to confirm the cessions made at these treaties.

### Jay's Treaty and the Northwest Territory

In addition to hostile Indians, the United States also still had to contend with British forts that remained active on the frontier, despite provisions in the Treaty of Paris in 1783 that they would be dismantled. In 1794, the Washington administration sent Chief Justice John Jay to Great Britain to negotiate for their removal, as well as for British acknowledgement of neutrality and commercial rights at sea. In signing the controversial Jay's Treaty, Britain agreed to remove the forts by 1796, to pay $10 million in reparations for American ships seized at sea, and to open the British West Indies to American trade on a very limited basis. Although critics harshly condemned Jay's Treaty as far too accommodating of the British, it did bring about peace with Great Britain for the next decade, and ended British occupation of forts on the frontier.

### Pinckney's Treaty

As American settlers moved into the Old Northwest, territorial disputes between the United States and Spain over land in the Old Southeast territory that stretched from the Atlantic Ocean to the Mississippi River came to a head.

Florida had been a flashpoint between the countries since the end of the Revolution. Borders were disputed. Immigrants to Florida from the United States pressed for Florida's annexation. The Treaty of Paris, which ended the war, failed to establish a border between the United States and West Florida, which the Spanish had won from Britain. Because of their military victories against the British in the Mississippi River valley, Spain viewed as its own the land between the Yazoo River and the east side of the Mississippi River up to the Ohio and Tennessee rivers. The American government—and particularly American settlers—ignored these claims, recognizing that the Spanish had little recourse. On October, 27, 1795, the United States and Spain signed Pinckney's Treaty, or as it was officially known, the Treaty of San Lorenzo.

According to the terms of the treaty, Spain recognized the Mississippi River to be the border to the west and the 31st parallel to be the border to the south, Most important to the United States, Spain also agreed to grant the United States the right to deposit goods at the port of New Orleans. The treaty helped the United States gain control over its vast western lands.

# Chapter 11: The U.S. Constitution

During the Summer of 1786, a dispute arose between Virginia and Maryland over navigation rights on the Potomac River. To resolve the issue, a meeting was held at Mount Vernon, the home of George Washington. Encouraged by the meeting's success, representatives from Maryland proposed a larger meeting to address reforming trade policy between the states. Under the Articles of Confederation, trade policy had been left up to individual states. Only five states sent delegates to the resulting September 1786 Annapolis Convention, but Alexander Hamilton, New York's representative, took the opportunity to arrange a meeting the following year which would be devoted exclusively to revising the Articles of Confederation. Delegates at Annapolis agreed to ask all states to send representatives to Philadelphia, where the meeting would be held.

## Shays's Rebellion

As the Annapolis Convention was taking place in Maryland, a crisis in western Massachusetts broke out that for many leaders of the Confederation underscored that need for revision of the Articles. The economic depression that followed the Revolutionary War had hit the farmers of New England especially hard. Many were heavily in debt. Crop prices were falling, and creditors often refused to accept almost worthless paper money as payment. In western Massachusetts, a former Continental army officer named Daniel Shays led a revolt in 1786.

Shays and his followers demanded an end to imprisonment for debt and called for the issuance of more paper money. On September 26, 800 "Shaysites" confronted state militiamen at Springfield. Tempers cooled temporarily, but in February 1787, fighting broke out again and the militia finally broke up the rebel band. Shays himself fled to Vermont where he remained in hiding. He was sentenced to death in absentia but later pardoned.

### SUPPORT FOR THE FEDERAL SYSTEM

Support for ratification of the U.S. Constitution varied by state and by region within states.

## The Constitutional Convention

Shays's Rebellion, while relatively bloodless, convinced many Americans that a strong central government was needed to solve the states' growing economic troubles. To many delegates, the rebellion was a dark omen. To them, only a stronger national government could provide order and uphold property rights against the threat of mob rule.

In May 1787, delegates from all states other than Rhode Island (whose leaders believed the convention was a conspiracy to overthrow the established government) arrived in Philadelphia to revise the Articles. Delegates included many wealthy,

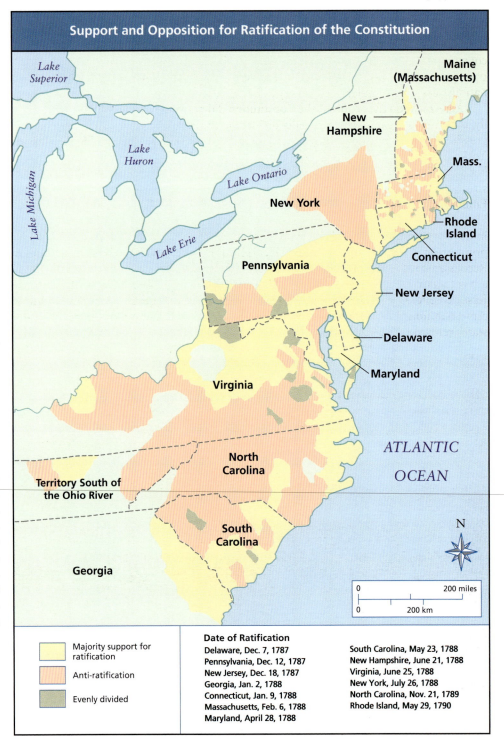

**Support and Opposition for Ratification of the Constitution**

Lake Superior
Lake Huron
Lake Michigan
Lake Ontario
Lake Erie

Maine (Massachusetts)
New Hampshire
Mass.
Rhode Island
Connecticut
New Jersey
New York
Pennsylvania
Delaware
Maryland
Virginia
ATLANTIC OCEAN
North Carolina
Territory South of the Ohio River
South Carolina
Georgia

N

| | 0 | 200 miles |
| | 0 | 200 km |

Majority support for ratification

Anti-ratification

Evenly divided

**Date of Ratification**
Delaware, Dec. 7, 1787
Pennsylvania, Dec. 12, 1787
New Jersey, Dec. 18, 1787
Georgia, Jan. 2, 1788
Connecticut, Jan. 9, 1788
Massachusetts, Feb. 6, 1788
Maryland, April 28, 1788

South Carolina, May 23, 1788
New Hampshire, June 21, 1788
Virginia, June 25, 1788
New York, July 26, 1788
North Carolina, Nov. 21, 1789
Rhode Island, May 29, 1790

influential figures, such as George Washington and James Madison of Virginia, Benjamin Franklin of Pennsylvania, and Gouverneur Morris of New York.

After some debate, the delegates agreed that the Articles were too weak and that a stronger central government and a document to support it were needed. The new constitution created a federal government divided into three branches (executive, legislative, and judicial), each with different roles and the ability to act as controls on the others—a system known as checks and balances. This system corrected a weakness in the Articles of Confederation, which had placed almost complete power in the hands of legislators alone. The concept of checks and balances had first been suggested by English theorist James Harrington and later expanded upon by John Locke, William Blackstone, and Montesquieu, but it was the framers of the Constitution who perfected it. By ensuring that governmental responsibilities would be shared among three branches, they created an administrative system that necessitated cooperation and protected the rights of states. This model was later passed down not only to state and local governments but to other nations seeking to emulate democracy and stability.

Agreement on the details of the Constitution did not come easily, however. Delegates were especially divided on the issue of congressional representation. Larger states, like Virginia and New York, argued for proportional representation, by which the number of representatives from each state would be determined by the size of that state's population. Representing this view was Edmund Randolph of Virginia. Randolph proposed his Virginia Plan, which included a bicameral (two house) legislature, wherein the lower house is elected according to the size of each states' population and the upper house is elected by the lower. Recognizing that strict proportional representation was to the disadvantage of smaller states like his, William Paterson of New Jersey countered with the New Jersey Plan, which called for equal representation by all states in both houses. Small and large states refused to agree to either plan.

## The Question of Slavery

Although Thomas Jefferson's first draft of the Declaration had condemned slavery, his attack on the institution had been deleted from the final draft. At the Constitutional Convention, the idea of abolishing slavery was not one that was seriously considered. Instead the issue arose mainly in arguments on how slaves were to be counted. Southern states wanted each slave to be counted as a person. This would give the South a greater number of seats in the House of Representatives, even though southern governments had no intention of allowing African American slaves to vote. Eventually, delegates agreed that each slave would be counted as three-fifths of a person for the purposes of representation and taxation. Any other system, argued James Madison, would lead to fraud in the way states counted their populations.

Finally, Oliver Ellsworth and Roger Sherman submitted the Connecticut (or Great) Compromise. Their plan called for proportional representation in the lower house, or House of Representatives, and equal representation of the states in the upper house, or Senate. The convention also gave Congress the power to implement taxes, among other responsibilities. In July 1787, delegates approved the Great Compromise. The following month, despite continuing opposition from leading signers of the Declaration of Independence like Samuel Adams and John Hancock of Massachusetts, and Patrick Henry and Richard Henry Lee of Virginia, a majority of delegates accepted a first draft of the new Constitution. On September 28th the Constitutional Convention passed it on to the states for ratification.

**CONSTITUTIONAL CONVENTION** Delegates from all states other than Rhode Island gathered in Philadelphia in May, 1787 to negotiate the details of the new federal Constitution. George Washington can be seen presiding over the gathering.

# Ratification and the Bill of Rights

According to the terms of the Constitution, nine states needed to ratify the Constitution before it could become the country's governing document. All but Rhode Island elected delegates to state conventions to consider ratification. Consequently, letters, articles, essays, and pamphlets were published to influence the vote for or against ratification. On one side were the Federalists, who

**JAMES MADISON** Together with Alexander Hamilton and John Jay, Virginian James Madison drafted the Federalist Papers, a series of articles arguing in favor of the Constitution. Madison, who later parted ways with Hamilton over the rights of individuals, was also the author of the Bill of Rights.

had largely written the Constitution and supported it unreservedly. Leading the campaign in favor of ratification were Alexander Hamilton and John Jay of New York and James Madison of Virginia. The three published a series of articles in New York newspapers that were later collected under the name The Federalist Papers. When they first appeared, the articles were signed "Publius," and the identity of the authors was kept a secret for several years afterwards. Although the articles only reached a small number of readers when they were first published, their winning defense of Constitutional government has since been recognized as one of the greatest achievements of American political thought.

Opposing the Federalists, was a loose coalition called the Antifederalists. Antifederalists believed the Constitution as written belied the republican principles upon which the nation had been founded. Many of the foremost leaders of the

## The Bill of Rights

**Amendment I:** Prohibits Congress from establishing a national religion or preventing the free exercise of religion; forbids Congress to abridge freedom of speech or of the press; acknowledges the people's right to assemble peaceably and to petition the government.

**Amendment II:** Noting the importance of a "well regulated militia," guarantees the right of the people "to keep and bear arms."

**Amendment III:** Prohibits the lodging of soldiers in any home without the consent of its owner.

**Amendment IV:** Protects against "unreasonable searches and seizures"; requires probable cause and an oath or affirmation to issue warrants in necessary searches and seizures.

**Amendment V:** Requires the indictment of a grand jury to prosecute capital crimes, except for military personnel during a time of war or national threat; forbids trying a person twice for the same offense; forbids compelling someone to be a witness against himself or depriving him of his rights without "due process of law"; forbids

the taking of private property for public use "without just compensation."

**Amendment VI:** Guarantees the right to "a speedy and public trial, by an impartial jury" in the district where the crime has occurred; allows an accused person to know the nature of the charges against him, to face his accusers, and to obtain both counsel and witnesses for his defense.

**Amendment VII:** Ensures a trial by jury in cases of common law involving amounts over $20.

**Amendment VIII:** Prohibits the imposition of excessive bail and fines as well as "cruel and unusual punishments."

**Amendment IX:** Ensures that rights not specifically covered in the Constitution are "retained by the people."

**Amendment X:** Powers that are constitutionally neither assigned to the federal government nor denied to the states are assumed to be the province of the states or of the people themselves.

**CARTOON CONVENTION** The Connecticut debate over ratification of the US Constitution is illustrated in this cartoon by Amos Doolittle. The state is represented by a wagon stuck in a muddy ditch while two factions pull it in opposite directions. On the left are the Federalists (supporters of the Constitution) and on the right, the anti-Federalists, while in the center foreground, various characters make obscene gestures to show their diverse opinions.

Revolution, including Samuel Adams and John Hancock of Massachusetts, and Patrick Henry, Richard Henry Lee, George Mason and James Monroe of Virginia were strongly opposed to the Constitution. Henry and Mason, together with Elbridge Gerry of New York, also wrote a series of articles—the *Antifederalist Papers*—in response to Hamilton, Jay and Madison. To the Antifederalists, the Constitution did not do enough to limit the power of the federal government. Its terms, they argued, allowed the federal government to infringe not only on the rights of the states but on individuals as well. As Mason put it, the Constitution had "no declaration of rights." The Federalists saw no need for such a declaration. They believed that the new government, with its specified powers and systems of checks and balances, would automatically protect civil liberties. They also believed that lists of inherent rights belonged in state constitutions, not in the national document.

Eventually, the debate centered around the Constitution's one omission: a bill of rights, which the Antifederalists were for and the Federalists were against. By late 1788, all states except North Carolina and

Rhode Island had ratified the Constitution, but the support of many of those states was contingent on the addition of a bill of rights.

To satisfy Antifederalist demands, James Madison worked out a series of amendments between March and June 1789. Drawing on over 200 recommendations as well as the Virginia Declaration of Rights that Mason had authored in 1776, Madison submitted 17 proposed amendments to the House of Representatives. After the House approved the amendments, they were sent to the Senate. There, several of the proposed rights, including a clause allowing conscientious objectors to be exempted from military service, were rejected. The remaining twelve amendments were approved by the Senate, and then sent back to the states for final ratification. Two more amendments—one concerning the number of representatives and the other covering compensation for senators and representatives—were rejected, leaving a final list of 10 amendments that were ratified by 10 states. With the addition of these amendments to the Constitution, national support for the document was assured, and the new Bill of Rights became the nation's bedrock of civil liberties.

# The Presidency and the Origin of the Two-Party System

On April 30, 1789, according to terms set out in the new Constitution, George Washington was inaugurated as the first president of the United States. Washington, who had led the Continental Army to victory during the Revolutionary War, and then presided over the Constitutional Convention in Philadelphia, had been reluctant to take the post, preferring to enjoy the "domestic felicity" of private life at his estate in Mount Vernon, Virginia. Yet Washington, universally respected in both northern and southern states alike, had been the only man that electors had seriously considered for the post. Closely tied to neither Federalist nor Antifederalist factions of the government, Washington was perhaps the only man in the nation with the stature to assume the presidency. John Adams of Massachusetts, who had helped negotiate the Treaty of Paris with the British, was elected Vice President.

While the Constitution gave the Congress responsibility for authorizing all spending of federal money, the president had the power to veto congressional bills. In addition, he could check the power of the judiciary by nominating judges to the Supreme Court and lower federal courts.

In addition to president and vice-president, the Executive Branch also came to include a cabinet of federal department heads. Although the Constitution made no specific mention of a presidential cabinet, it was assumed that department heads would advise the president and Congress on policy. In fact, department heads originally reported to Congress rather than the president, but gradually they came under the president's authority. It was Washington's idea to call together the heads of all departments for regular meetings.

Although the Constitution set basic parameters for the scope of the presidency, Washington's personal achievements in the post should not be understated. He was well aware upon taking office that every act, large and small, would be measured by history as a precedent for other, less-talented men to follow. As he put it, "Many things which appear of little importance in themselves and at the beginning, may have great and durable consequences from their having

**MR. PRESIDENT** Although John Adams proposed nicknaming him, "His Highness," George Washington rejected that grandiose title in favor of the simpler "Mr. President."

**WASHINGTON'S CABINET** Members of the first presidential cabinet included (left to right) Secretary of War Henry Knox, Secretary of State Thomas Jefferson, Attorney General Edmund Randolph and Secretary of the Treasury Alexander Hamilton.

been established at the commencement of a new general government."

Therefore, Washington proceeded slowly, using his executive power cautiously at first. He was prepared to consult with Congress, but he decided that the president should not attend Congressional debates. He also recognized the symbolic power of the office of the presidency, and it was important to him that the public see his office as one of dignity. In keeping with that view, for a time he even accepted the title "His Highness, the President of the United States and Protector of the Same." Vice President Adams suggested the shorter, but no less exalted, "His Most Benign Highness." Congress was equally aware of the precedent-setting importance of Washington's first term, and the thought that after defeating the armies of George III the new nation would call its new leader "His Highness" sent Antifederalist members of Congress into a fury. Ultimately, the less imperial title "Mr. President" was adopted.

## The Rise of the Two-Party System

Washington's most important cabinet members were Secretary of the Treasury Alexander Hamilton and Secretary of State Thomas Jefferson. Although the framers of the Constitution had attempted to avoid factionalism and corruption by making no mention of political parties, Hamilton and Jefferson headed two opposing factions. Hamilton, as leader of the Federalists, advocated strong executive and judiciary branches,

and pushed for heavy government involvement in the national economy. Hamilton and his allies believed that the proper role of government was to promote economic growth. With their base of strength in the Northeast, the Federalists supported commercial and industrial interests over agriculture. Hamilton in particular favored strong diplomatic and economic ties with Great Britain. While Hamilton had supported the war for independence—and had in fact served as one of Washington's top aides—he also admired the stability provided by the British monarchy and class system. To Hamilton, the wealthiest elites were best suited for governing. On the other hand, he had a deep distrust of the ability of ordinary citizens to govern, as they "are turbulent and changing; they seldom judge or determine right." Not surprisingly, he and his Federalist allies deeply opposed what they saw as the dangerous excesses of the French Revolution that began in 1789.

The Antifederalists, who would by 1794 emerge in Congress as the Democratic-Republican party, had Jefferson as their prime spokesman. The party preferred limited federal government, especially in the economy. Jefferson and his allies favored agricultural, rural interests over urban, commercial interests. The party promoted the ideal of Jeffersonian Democracy, which stressed a strict interpretation of the Constitution, as well as simplicity and frugality in government. In foreign affairs, the Jeffersonians supported the democratic ideals of the French Revolution, and opposed close ties with Great Britain. Farmers, artisans and southerners were the party's strongest supporters.

While Washington and Jefferson shared similar backgrounds as Virginians and gentlemen farmers, Hamilton used his long-standing relationship with Washington—as well as enormous talents as a political operator—to sway the president to his viewpoint time and time again during Washington's first term in office. In July 1793, Jefferson resigned from the administration in frustration over Hamilton's influence.

It was a controversy that took place after Jefferson's departure that led most directly to the formal birth of the two opposing political parties. In 1794, Washington sent Supreme Court Justice John Jay to London to negotiate agreements on a number of conflicts. Among these was Great Britain's continued occupation of forts in the Northwest Territory in violation of the Treaty of 1783. Another was interference with neutral American shipping and the impressment of American seamen. Still another was an American demand for compensation for African American slaves freed by British forces during the Revolution.

When Jay returned from his mission, he carried with him a treaty that had held only meager concessions from the British. Britain agreed to leave the western forts—

but not for another two years. It refused to compensate American slave owners for their losses. It also refused to recognize American neutrality or to stop the impressment of American sailors.

Although the administration argued that the treaty was the best that could be negotiated and that it prevented greater hostilities with Great Britain, the agreement angered Americans across the geographic spectrum. Southern planters were furious about the denial of slave compensation, northern merchants and sailors objected to the treaty's failure to halt impressment, and westerners were angry that the British would remain in their forts for another two years. So great was the anger over the treaty that a New York mob attacked Hamilton with stones when he tried to defend the treaty. By the time Washington's second term ended in 1796, political division lines had hardened. Even Washington himself came under attack. Thomas Paine, the Revolutionary-era propagandist, wrote an open letter to Washington in the Philadelphia *Aurora*, stating, "As to you, sir . . . treacherous in private friendship . . . and a hypocrite in public life, the world will be puzzled to decide . . . whether you have abandoned good principles or whether you ever had any." Marked by vicious and personal attacks such as this, the deeply divided American political climate would virtually paralyze the administration of John Adams, Washington's successor. The two-party system had been born.

**JOHN MARSHALL** Appointed by John Adams in 1801, Chief Justice John Marshall was instrumental in solidifying the constitutional powers of the Supreme Court.

# John Marshall and the Making of the U.S. Supreme Court

The third branch of the federal government, as set out by the U.S. Constitution, is the judiciary. The judiciary is composed of the Supreme Court and two lower levels, both created by the Judiciary Act of 1789: the federal circuit courts and district courts. The judiciary's role is to check the legislative branch, and occasionally state legislatures by declaring laws unconstitutional, and to check the power of the executive by declaring the president's actions or those of his subordinates to be unauthorized or unconstitutional.

While the judiciary's theoretical function was outlined in the Constitution, it took putting constitutional theory into practice for the federal courts to become

truly defined. John Marshall, the fourth Chief Justice of the U.S. Supreme Court, gave the court that definition. Marshall achieved greatness by shaping the court's role in the American legal system and securing its place in the U.S. government. A Federalist with flexible views, Marshall was intellectual, principled, and frequently at odds with his fellow Virginian Thomas Jefferson. After President John Adams appointed him chief justice in 1801, Marshall worked to strengthen the Supreme Court's status and responsibilities. He worked to make the court a cohesive unit, in part by initiating the now-traditional black robes worn by all Supreme Court justices. He also altered living and working

arrangements while the Court was in session, requiring justices to work together. Marshall also changed the method by which decisions were issued. Prior to his arrival on the court, decisions were announced as individual opinions rather than as the opinion of the Court as a whole.

Under his leadership, the Court became an equal partner with the executive and legislative branches by asserting its authority to judge the constitutionality of those branches' acts and decisions. His ruling in the case of *Marbury v. Madison* (1803) was a turning point in American law. From this point forward, the Supreme Court would always judge cases according to its interpretations of the Constitution, setting the precedent for the practice known as judicial review. Through the use of judicial review, Marshall established the Constitution as the law of the land and the Supreme Court as its final interpreter.

In 1807, during Thomas Jefferson's second term as president, Marshall faced one of his greatest challenges. After Jefferson learned that his former vice-president, Aaron Burr, had been secretly plotting to seize Spanish lands in the West and make himself emperor of a new state, Jefferson attempted to use his presidential powers to remove the privilege of habeus

corpus and condemn Burr on the basis of "constructive treason." Marshall determined that the Court, not the president, presided over the trial, dealing a blow to Jefferson after Burr was acquitted.

In landmark decisions such as *Fletcher v. Peck* (1810), *McCulloch v. Maryland* (1819), *Cohens v. Virginia* (1821) and *Gibbons v. Ogden* (1824), he also established the Court's jurisdiction over state courts in federal matters and authored landmark decisions that still resonate in American legal venues. Marshall served as chief justice for 34 years.

*"The government of the Union, then, is emphatically and truly a government of the people. In form and in substance it emanates from them. Its powers are granted by them, and are to be exercised directly on them and for their benefit."*

—JOHN MARSHALL, IN McCULLOCH V. MARYLAND

**COMPETING VISIONS** Marshall, seen administering the oath of office to Andrew Jackson in 1829, served for 34 years as chief justice, longer than almost any other justice in history. During the Jackson Administration, the two men would repeatedly clash over the constitutional powers of the executive and judicial branches.

# Chapter 12: Westward Expansion and Manifest Destiny

The nation that declared its independence from Great Britain in 1776 existed primarily around the busy seaports of the East Coast. Yet by 1867, the United States stretched all the way across the North American continent. The story of the years between tells of the pioneers who crossed the vast expanse of land, the technology that made it possible, and of the impact this migration had on the native peoples who had lived on these lands for thousands of years beforehand.

After the Revolution, the first wave of pioneers crossed the Appalachian Mountains, and slowly settled the Ohio Valley, the Great Lakes region, and the Old Southeast. These pioneers depended on water travel to reach their homes and to keep connected to the communities they had left behind. The Great Lakes, along with the Ohio, Missouri, and Mississippi rivers, were the nation's inland waterways.

The Louisiana Purchase of 1803 eventually inspired another great wave of migration into the West. By the 1840s, settlers were traveling from the Missouri River across the western mountains and deserts, all the way to California and Oregon. The acquisition of Texas in 1846, and the capture of the lands that are now California, Utah, New Mexico, Nevada, and Arizona in 1848, filled in the patchwork map of the country.

## The Roads West

While colonial Americans relied mainly on waterways for transportation, roads became increasingly important as the nation grew westward. In 1775, Daniel Boone blazed a trail from North Carolina into what is now Kentucky and Tennessee and this was probably the single most important road for pioneers moving across the Appalachian mountains. The road, which became known as the Wilderness Road, allowed for the settlement south of the Ohio River, and by the 1790s, the admission of Kentucky (1792) and Tennessee (1796) as the fifteenth and sixteenth states in the Union. Pennsylvania's Lancaster Turnpike, built between 1791 and 1797 from Philadelphia to Lancaster, was important for its method of construction: it was the first "macadam" road, a road paved with crushed stone, and therefore passable year-round.

The National (or Cumberland) Road was the first to receive funding from the federal government. The idea of a federal east-west road was first approved by Congress in 1802. In 1806, the idea was expanded to extend from the Atlantic Ocean to the Mississippi River. Construction began in 1808, and in 1819, the National Road reached the Ohio River, 130 miles from its start. The project ended in 1852 when it reached Vandalia, Illinois, short of the Mississippi.

## River and Lake Transportation

Despite the construction of new roads in the early nineteenth century, travel along them was still quite slow. For many settlers, the best and most reliable means of westward travel was by water. Until the railroads arrived, the Ohio River, together with the Great Lakes, served as the nation's highway west. Once across the Appalachians, a pioneer could travel the Ohio River all the way to the Mississippi River, the nation's western

**WEST TO THE MISSISSIPPI** As the 19th century opened, the young United States, once limited to the Atlantic coast, had stretched west to the Mississippi.

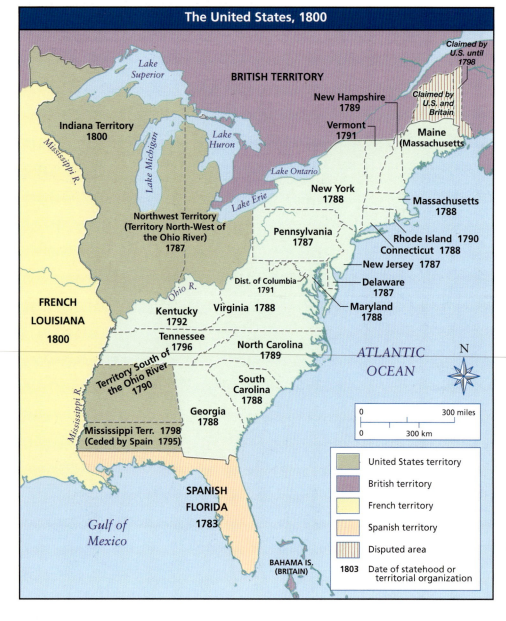

### The United States, 1800

Lake Superior

**BRITISH TERRITORY**

*Claimed by U.S. until 1798*

Lake Huron

**Indiana Territory 1800**

Lake Michigan

Mississippi R.

New Hampshire 1789

*Claimed by U.S. and Britain*

Vermont 1791

Maine (Massachusetts)

Lake Ontario

**Northwest Territory (Territory North-West of the Ohio River) 1787**

Lake Erie

New York 1788

Massachusetts 1788

Pennsylvania 1787

Rhode Island 1790
Connecticut 1788

New Jersey 1787

Ohio R.

Dist. of Columbia 1791

Delaware 1787

**FRENCH LOUISIANA 1800**

Kentucky 1792

Virginia 1788

Maryland 1788

Tennessee 1796

North Carolina 1789

**Territory South of the Ohio River 1790**

South Carolina 1788

Georgia 1788

Mississippi R.

**Mississippi Terr. 1798 (Ceded by Spain 1795)**

*ATLANTIC OCEAN*

N

**SPANISH FLORIDA 1783**

*Gulf of Mexico*

BAHAMA IS. (BRITAIN)

| 0 | 300 miles |
| 0 | 300 km |

- United States territory
- British territory
- French territory
- Spanish territory
- Disputed area
- **1803** Date of statehood or territorial organization

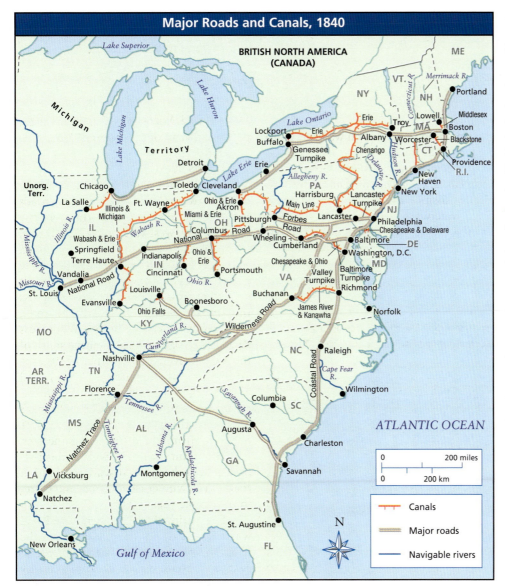

**Major Roads and Canals, 1840**

Legend:
- Canals
- Major roads
- Navigable rivers

0 — 200 miles
0 — 200 km

N

**ROADS AND CANALS** Although early roadways like the National Pike and the Natchez Trace eased transportation somewhat, travel by road in the early 1800s was slow. By 1840, over 3,000 miles of canals had been built in the United States. The most famous and successful was the Erie Canal from Buffalo to Albany, New York.

boundary until 1803. Towns at the westernmost points of the Missouri—Independence, Westport, and St. Joseph, Missouri—would become the jumping-off points for wagons traveling further west. Keelboats, flatboats, and barges that carried passengers and freight along America's waterways floated easily downstream with the river's current. To journey upstream was more arduous and slow-moving—and was accomplished by sail, or by paddling or pushing with poles.

### The Erie Canal

The major limitation of the waterways as highways to the west was that few of them were connected. To get from New York City to Pittsburgh, where the Ohio River began, required a long trip by land. To get to Chicago or Detroit, people could travel up the Hudson River to Albany, but then faced a long journey by land to Buffalo, where water transport was again available on the Great Lakes. A solution to this problem was the building of canals.

The first major canal in America was the Erie Canal. Between 1817 and 1825, the state of New York dug a 363-mile channel from Troy, just north of Albany, to Buffalo on Lake Erie. When it opened, travelers and goods could reach the Midwest from the Atlantic coast entirely by water.

The Erie Canal was a tremendous success, and other states rushed to imitate New York. Pennsylvania completed a canal from Philadelphia to Pittsburgh in 1834, aided by an early railroad system that dragged barges over difficult terrain. Ohio, Illinois, Michigan, Indiana, and Wisconsin also built important canals. By linking the major waterways of the Northeast and midwest,

## Movement of White and Black Population into Trans-Appalachia, 1800 to 1830

| Free Whites | 1800 | 1820 | 1830 | Free Blacks (continued) | 1800 | 1820 | 1830 |
|---|---|---|---|---|---|---|---|
| Illinois | — | 53,788 | 155,061 | Missouri | — | 347 | 569 |
| Indiana | — | 145,758 | 339,399 | Ohio | — | 4,723 | 9,568 |
| Kentucky | 179,871 | 434,644 | 517,787 | Tennessee | 309 | 2,727 | 4,555 |
| Michigan | — | — | 31,346 | | | | |
| Missouri | — | 55,988 | 114,795 | **Slaves** | 1800 | 1820 | 1830 |
| Ohio | — | 528,572 | 928,329 | Illinois | — | 917 | 747 |
| Tennessee | 91,709 | 339,727 | 535,746 | Indiana | — | 190 | 3 |
| | | | | Kentucky | 40,343 | 126,732 | 165,213 |
| **Free Blacks** | 1800 | 1820 | 1830 | Michigan | — | — | 32 |
| Illinois | — | 457 | 1,637 | Missouri | — | 347 | 10,222 |
| Indiana | — | 1,230 | 3,629 | Ohio | — | 0 | 6 |
| Kentucky | 741 | 2,759 | 4,917 | Tennessee | 13,584 | 80,107 | 141,603 |
| Michigan | — | — | 261 | | | | |

*"I've got a mule and her name is Sal,
Fifteen miles on the Erie Canal."*

—FROM "LOW BRIDGE, EVERYBODY DOWN"

# The Lewis and Clark Expedition

canals created a transportation network that was crucial to the nation's economic development. The canals also rapidly boosted westward migration and settlement: Four hundred thousand white men and women moved to Ohio during the 1820s alone. Illinois' white population more than tripled in size during the same decade.

Although virtually all the major canals were built in the Northeast and Midwest during the 1820s and 1830s, the new roads that were completed in both the North and South also allowed for a rapid increase in migration from southern coastal regions to trans-Appalachian settlement in the inland South. These new roads, along with the invention of the cotton gin, helped encourage the western spread of the slave system. The slave population of Tennessee, for example, grew from about 13,000 in 1800 to more than 140,000 two decades later. While the expanded transportation infrastructure in the North helped boost new industry, new means of reaching the inland South helped perpetuate that region's slave-based agricultural economy.

In 1784, as a delegate to the Confederation Congress, Thomas Jefferson called for the division of territory in the Old Northwest. His "Report of Government for the Western Territory" created a framework for what would become the Ordinance of 1787, which set the guidelines by which Western territories were created and later admitted into the Union as states.

Jefferson's interest in these western lands was motivated by more than practical considerations. Other founding figures, like Alexander Hamilton, saw America's strength in its potential for harnessing financial capital in the name of commerce and industry. Jefferson, the gentlemen farmer, saw it in land—vast stretches of land, rolling westward over thousands of miles—that offered the possibility of making his vision of a democratic nation of yeoman farmers a reality. In 1803, during Jefferson's first term as president, the United States paid $15 million to France for 820,000 square miles of land stretching from the Mississippi River to the Rocky Mountains, an agreement known as the Louisiana Purchase.

A TERRITORIAL BARGAIN The United States paid France $15 million for the vast Louisiana Territory.

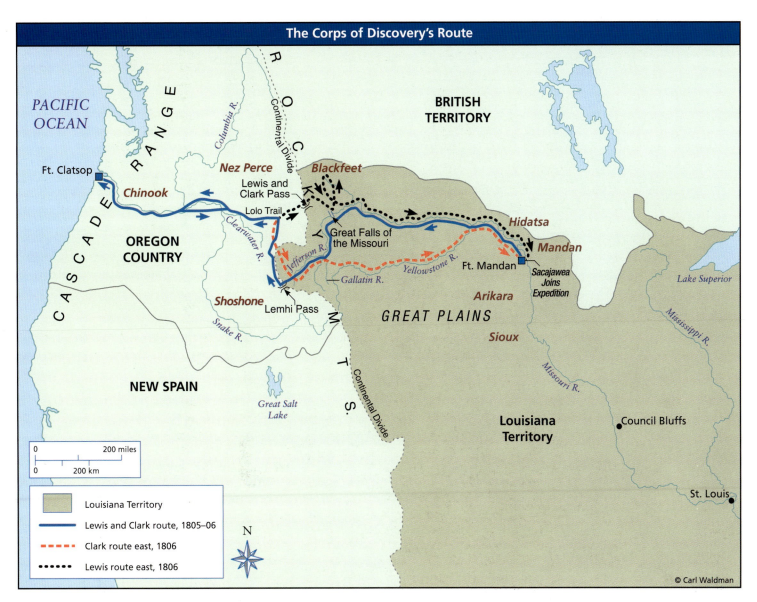

**The Corps of Discovery's Route**

**TO THE PACIFIC** In April 1805, the Corps of Discovery proceeded from Fort Mandan in present-day Montana up the Missouri River, then traversed the Rocky Mountains and three rivers before reaching the Pacific.

Even before the Louisiana Purchase, Jefferson had been eager to explore this territory and beyond, believing that the newly acquired lands would yield important information about its natural wealth and political significance. This information could be used to generate public support for acquisition and settlement of western territories. Explorers of the Pacific Northwest could also report on the fur trading activities of British fur trading enterprises in the region and locate an overland route to the Pacific that American traders could use.

In 1803, Congress agreed to finance a small expedition. Once the Louisiana Purchase was made, the expedition took on national importance. Jefferson commissioned his secretary, Army captain Meriwether Lewis to conduct a scientific exploration of lands west of the Mississippi to the Pacific Coast. Although Lewis had little formal education, he had spent his youth exploring the wilderness and was an experienced frontier soldier.

Jefferson's interest in western exploration went beyond the economic and political. As an avid student of the natural sciences, he was curious about the climate, soil, flora and fauna of the West.

To fulfill the scientific goals of the expedition, Lewis studied astronomy, medicine, and the natural sciences for months before assembling a party he would lead west.

### The Westward Journey
In time, Lewis mapped out a route and, with former Army officer William Clark, assembled an expedition of twenty-nine men called the Corps of Discovery. Clark, the brother of Revolutionary war frontier hero George Rogers Clark, had served with Lewis in the army, and Lewis admired Clark's skills as a frontiersman. Clark was also accompanied by his African slave, York, who spoke several American Indian dialects. York would prove a valuable addition to the group. Part of the party were an assemblage of blacksmiths, carpenters, and other craftsmen whose skills would be required during the mission.

The Corps started from St. Louis in May 1804, traveling up the Missouri River in cumbersome supply-laden boats. From the start, they were plagued by mosquitoes, bad weather, and the Missouri's difficult currents.

**INTERPRETER** Sacagawea, at right, conveys Lewis and Clark's peaceful intentions to the Chinook Indians as the Corps of Discovery nears the Pacific Ocean. William Clark stands at her right.

At last, the group arrived at a site near present-day Bismarck, North Dakota, where they set up winter camp. Here they built Fort Mandan, made peaceful contact with the Minnetaree Indians, and gathered plant, animal and mineral specimens. The Corps also hired French-Canadian fur-trapper Toussaint Charbonneau as its interpreter. Charbonneau informed the group that they would need horses for the journey ahead. Charbonneau's wife Sacagawea, a Shoshone who had been captured by the Minnetaree, could help purchase horses from her tribe further west. Charbonneau and Sacagewea joined the expedition, with Sacagawea also acting as an interpreter and sometime guide.

In April 1805, the expedition proceeded from Fort Mandan up the Missouri. Portaging their canoes over treacherous bluffs at Great Falls in present-day Montana, they continued forward, catching site of their first grizzly bears and bighorn sheep. Nearing the lands of the Shoshone, they floated down raging rivers, and, on foot, crossed the Continental Divide on August 12, 1805. Nearby they met Sacagawea's tribe, and with her help, purchased horses before moving on through the Bitteroot Mountains and toward the Clearwater River. In October 1805, they arrived at the Columbia River, and followed it into the Cascade Mountains. By November, they could see the Pacific Ocean. There they set up a new winter camp.

### The Journey Home

In March 1806, the Corps of Discovery headed east along the Columbia River. They returned to the Clearwater River to retrieve the horses they had left behind and moved through to the Bitteroot Mountains along the same Indian trail they had used the previous year. Lewis and nine men then crossed the Continental Divide by way of a pass, now known as Lewis and Clark Pass, in present-day Montana.

Clark and his party, meanwhile, headed south, exploring the Yellowstone River until it reached the Missouri River, where they rejoined Lewis and his men in August 1806. After parting ways with Sacagawea and her husband, the rest of the Corps moved down the Missouri toward St. Louis. Reaching their destination on September 23, 1806, the Corps of Discovery were received as returning heroes.

The Lewis and Clark expedition covered 7,500 miles, often through unmapped territory. It proved that it was possible to reach the Pacific Ocean by land. Their notes and specimens of plant and animal life would aid scientists for years to come. Perhaps most important were the detailed maps created by the expedition. It was these maps that would guide traders and trappers who traveled west throughout the 19th century.

### Further Expeditions

The next expeditions to explore the American West, however, would not have the benefit of the Corps of Discovery's maps. Even before Lewis and Clark had returned from the Pacific Northwest in 1806, President Jefferson had sent more explorers west. In 1804, scientists William Dunbar and George Hunter were sent to investigate the Red River. Thomas Freeman, an astronomer and surveyor was sent in 1806 to survey the Red River again, but he was turned back by Spanish soldiers.

In 1805, Zebulon Pike led a party to locate the source of the Mississippi River. After mistakenly identifying the source as Leech Lake in present-day Minnesota, he returned to St. Louis. The next year, he set out again, this time to explore the region between the Arkansas and Red rivers. Pike followed the Arkansas to the Colorado Rockies, where he sighted and named—but did not climb—the peak that today bears his name.

On his return journey, Pike led his men into Spanish territory, where they were arrested. Spanish officials eventually released them in Mexico, but without the notes and maps they made. Pike reconstructed most of the confiscated data, and supplemented it with additional information he secretly gathered as he was escorted from Mexico. With this information, he was able to publish a report that brought him wide acclaim.

By the time of Pike's return, however, Congress had begun to focus on the foreign policy conflicts that would eventually lead to the War of 1812. Although American fur trappers continued to traverse the West during the 1810s, government-sponsored exploratory missions were temporarily suspended.

### Trappers and Mountain Men

Hearing reports from the Lewis and Clark expedition of territory rich in beaver and game and relatively free of hostile Indians, fur trappers and traders flooded west. Among the first was John Colter, a frontiersman and member of the Corps of Discovery who left the expedition before it returned to Missouri. Over several years, Colter traveled throughout what are now Wyoming and Montana, and to become the first white man to see the the thermal springs at Yellowstone that are known now as Colter's Hell. George Drouillard, who had also been with Lewis and Clark, returned to the West to trap and explore what is now Montana, including the Tongue and Bighorn river basins.

Manuel Lisa, a St. Louis merchant of Spanish descent, roamed the northern Rockies during the winter of 1807–1808, and in 1811, Ezekial Williams explored the North Platte River valley, despite clashes with Indians who were alarmed by the invasion of their lands.

### The Mountain Men

In the latter part of the fur trading era, the "Mountain Man" emerged in popular lore. These men—including legendary names such as Jim Bridger, James Beckwourth, Kit Carson, and Joseph Walker—were solitary trappers who spent long months in the mountains searching for beaver pelts. These men roamed countless miles, learning intimately a geography that was alien to most Americans. Many went on to lead settlers west or to scout for the army. Jedediah Smith, who established numerous trails from 1822 to 1831, was first to discover an overland route to California through South Pass and first to travel across the Great Basin. He was followed followed in the 1840s by John C. Frémont, who surveyed areas along many important routes into Oregon and California. The Santa Fe Trail, established in 1821, ran approximately 780 miles from Independence, Missouri, to Santa Fe, New Mexico, by way of the Arkansas River, Raton Pass, and Great Plains. The Oregon Trail started along the

**THE PIKE EXPEDITION** In the winter of 1807, American explorers Zebulon Pike and his men built a fort squarely within Spanish territory. Whether this act was purposeful or not, Pike (above, center) was arrested by Spanish authorities. The arrest proved fortunate, as it enabled Pike to travel through the Spanish Southwest, normally closed to foreigners.

same route, then branched northwest, along the Platte and Sweetwater rivers, across South Pass, and up into Oregon. Both trails become essential to American trade and western settlement. An observer, writing in 1847, said, "All this vast country . . .would even now be terra incognita to geographers . . . but there is not an acre that has not been passed and repassed by the trappers in their perilous excursions."

Yet as more trappers went west, competition for pelts increased. Trappers penetrated remote areas to find pelts, heedless of the need to preserve the resource that provided their livelihood. By 1835, it was apparent that beaver was becoming scarce, and by 1840, the West was nearly "trapped out."

# The War of 1812

Thomas Jefferson's foresight in negotiating the Louisiana Purchase stands today as the crowning achievement of his presidency. Yet as the nation looked west toward the untapped western wilderness of the North American continent, trouble was brewing from the east—in the Atlantic Ocean and in the capitals of Europe. During his second term, Jefferson faced growing conflict with Great Britain, France, and Spain. War was raging in Europe, and the United States struggled to remain neutral. To reinforce U.S. neutrality, Jefferson proposed and Congress passed the Embargo Act of 1807. The law, which forbade American ships from trading with foreign nations was a disaster, and it caused an immediate economic slump in New England. As his popularity dwindled, Jefferson chose not to seek at third term, instead supporting James Madison, his good friend, close ally and Secretary of State as his successor. In 1808, Madison easily defeated Federalist party nominee Charles C. Pinckney to become the fourth president.

Madison's two terms in office would be dominated by the dangerous international situation. France, led by Emperor Napoleon Bonaparte, remained at war with Great Britain. The British navy, as it had for years, continued to seize American ships and sailors. In his inaugural address, Madison criticized both Britain and France, but continued to back Jefferson's policy of trade restriction to bring about a peaceful settlement.

To many Americans, however, it looked as if Madison was unable or unwilling to fight for American rights. When a British ship attacked the American warship *Chesapeake*, killing or wounding twenty-one Americans, the nation seethed with anger. In Congress, a group of young legislators, led by Henry Clay of Kentucky and John Calhoun of South Carolina condemned Madison for his caution.

In 1812, after negotiations and economic embargoes failed to change British policies, Madison reluctantly declared war on Great Britain. To 'War Hawks" like Clay and Calhoun, the war was "the Second War of Independence." Yet from the start, the war was a dis-

aster. Although simultaneously at war with the French, the British generally had the upper hand throughout the conflict. They easily repulsed U.S. efforts to invade Canada in 1812, seizing Detroit and winning the battle of Queenston Heights on the Canadian side of the Niagara River. They successfully defended Canada again in 1813, despite American victories at the battles of York (which the Americans burned to the ground), Lake Erie, and the Thames. Although Madison had been reluctant to start the war, Federalist opponents of the war took to derisively calling it "Mr. Madison's War."

The most humiliating moment for the United States came in 1814, when the British, assisted by escaped Maryland slaves, attacked Washington D.C., setting fire to the Capitol and the White House in retaliation for the destruction of York. In the midst of the American army's headlong retreat from Washington, Madison himself was seen unsuccessfully trying to rally the troops into battle.

Two days later, Madison returned to work, never having even considered surrender. A month after the burning of Washington, the British laid siege to Baltimore. This time, they were driven off by stiff American resistance. Suddenly, American military fortunes took a turn for the better. In September 1814, an American naval victory on Lake Champlain caused the British to cancel plans for an invasion from Canada.

Despite this major victory, opposition to the war, particularly from from New England Federalists, continued. In December 1814, Federalists gathered in Hartford, Connecticut where they demanded Madison's resignation and threatened to secede from the Union. Madison refused to give in. Since the previous August, American and British diplomats had been meeting in Ghent, Belgium to negotiate an end to the fighting. On December 24, a peace treaty was signed. One last battle would take place, on January 8, 1815. Unaware that a treaty had been signed, 7,500 veteran British troops attacked a combined force of 4,500 American frontiersmen and Choctaw Indians under the command of Major General Andrew Jackson at New Orleans. Firing from behind cotton bales, Jackson's crack troops shot the neat redcoat lines to pieces. The British lost 2,000 men, including their commander, before retreating. The Americans lost just seventy-one.

The Battle of New Orleans made Andrew Jackson a national hero. The battle also helped transform President Madison's reputation as president. That the United States had battled the greatest military power in the world once more and if not won had at least held its own led to celebrations throughout the country. At the same time, the Federalist Party, having just attempted to force Madison's resignation upon threat of New England's secession lay in disgrace. Although the Federalists would run a token opposition candidate in the 1816, he would be overwhelmingly defeated by James Monroe, a close ally of Madison and Jefferson. Following that defeat, the Federalist party would collapse altogether.

## Major Battles of the War of 1812

Lower Canada

Lake Superior

Quebec

Upper Canada

*Lake Huron*

District of Maine

Ft. Mackinac
July 17, 1812

Chateaugay
April 26, 1813

Chrysler's Farm
Nov. 11, 1813

Lake Champlain
Sept. 11, 1814

Michigan Territory

York (burned)
April 27, 1813

Plattsburg
Sept. 11, 1814

Vermont

*Lake Michigan*

*Lake Ontario*

New Hamp.

Illinois Territory

Ft. Detroit
Aug. 16, 1812

Thames
Oct. 5, 1813

Sackett's Harbor
May 28–29, 1813

Mass.

Boston

*Mississippi R.*

River Raisin
Jan. 22, 1813

*Lake Erie*  Presque Isle

New York

Conn.

Ft. Dearborn
Aug. 15, 1812

Lake Erie
Sept. 10, 1813

Pennsylvania

Rhode Island

Ft. Meigs
May 1–9 and
July 24, 1813

Ft. Stephenson
Aug. 2, 1813

Ft. McHenry
Sept. 14, 1814

*Hudson R.*

New Jersey

Ohio

Indiana Territory

Cincinnati

Bladensburg
Aug. 24, 1814

Baltimore

Delaware

*Ohio R.*

Virginia

Maryland

Kentucky

Washington, D.C.
(burned)
Aug. 24, 1814

Unorganized Territory

Tennessee

North Carolina

Tallasahatchee
Nov. 3, 1813

South Carolina

Talladega
Nov. 9, 1813

Georgia

ATLANTIC OCEAN

Mississippi Territory

Horseshoe Bend
March 27, 1814

Louisiana

Fort Mims
Aug. 30, 1813

Pensacola

New Orleans

New Orleans
Jan. 8, 1815

Florida (Spanish)

Gulf of Mexico

N

**Major battles**

★ British/Indian victory

★ U.S. victory

0        200 miles

0        200 km

**WAR OF 1812** Although many battles in the North were inconclusive, victories against Indians in the South helped clear the frontier.

# The United States, Florida, and the Spanish Southeast

By the mid-1700s, the Spanish Empire was in decline, challenged by the rise of British and French colonial forces. Although France had ceded the Louisiana Territory to Spain following the French and Indian War, and Britain had returned Florida to Spanish control after the American Revolution, the once-powerful Spanish empire was in no position to defend itself against encroachment by American settlers. By 1788, Spain had responded to the demands of American settlers by offering free land in the Mississippi valley, hoping to cultivate loyal Spanish followers. In 1795, Spain ceded northern Florida to the United States, accepting the 31st parallel as its northern border and allowing the United States free use of the Mississippi River.

### The French Revolution and Spanish America

Spain's major concern during this period was not American settlers. Like all of Europe, it's main concern was the cataclysmic upheaval brought on by the French Revolution (1789–1799). The Revolution, which temporarily abolished the French monarchy and led to decades of war, was partially inspired by the American Revolution, which Spain had helped bring to fruition. Like other European nations, Spain was terrified to see republicanism take root closer to home and joined in fighting republican France in the Wars of the French Revolution (1792–1795).

Some of that fighting took place on the island of Hispaniola, which was divided in two—with the French colony of Saint Domingue in the west and the Spanish colony of Santo Domingo in the east. In 1791, African slaves in the north of Saint Domingue revolted, launching a campaign for control of the island. (Although France defeated Spain so soundly that the latter nation surrendered Santo Domingo to France, by 1804, the former slaves of Saint Domingue had won control of the entire island, which they would rename Haiti. By the 1840s, the two parts of Hispaniola would at last become independent of each other, with the culturally-French Haiti in the west and the culturally-Spanish Dominican Republic in the east.)

In 1796 Spain changed direction and formed an alliance with France against Britain. As a result, Spain became a puppet of the powerful French leader Napoleon Bonaparte (1769–1821), who became first consul, or dictator, of France in 1799 and emperor of an expanding empire in 1804. In 1800, Napoleon forced Spain to cede Louisiana back, thus taking away a large section of its North American empire, and an important buffer between northern New Spain and the aggressive frontiersmen of the young United States. The buffer was lost for good in 1803, with Thomas Jefferson's purchase of the territory.

Meanwhile in Europe, the British navy was largely able to cut Spain off from its valuable American colonies, and it won a devastating victory over the allied Spanish and French navies at Trafalgar, on the southwest coast of Spain (1805). The final Napoleonic insult for Spain came in 1808, when Napoleon occupied Madrid, deposed Spain's King Ferdinand VII, and placed his brother, Joseph Bonaparte, on the Spanish throne.

For the next six years, Spain would fight for its independence. The Spanish people rose in revolt, as did the Portuguese, whose country had been occupied by Napoleon in 1807. In what was known as the Peninsular War (1808–1814), Britain came to the aid of Spanish and Portuguese rebels, working with Spanish guerrillas to liberate the entire Iberian Peninsula by the time of Napoleon's first abdication in 1814. Though sent into exile that year by his victorious enemies in the Napoleonic Wars (1799–1815), Napoleon escaped, returned, and was not finally defeated until the battle of Waterloo (in present-day Belgium) in 1815.

The Peninsular War, which Napoleon called his "Spanish ulcer," contributed to his defeat by tying down troops and devouring resources. But it also drastically weakened Spain's control of its empire. Not only did it prompt revolutions throughout many parts of Spanish America, but it left its far northern territories—Florida, Texas, New Mexico, and California—in peril of takeover from a foreign power: the United States.

### The Adams-Onís Treaty

Florida had been a flash point for contention with the United States since the end of the American Revolution. Borders were disputed and immigrants to Florida from the United States pressed for American annexation. The Treaty of Paris in 1783, which ended the war, failed to establish a clear border between the new United States and West Florida, which had been won by Spain from Great Britain. What is more, because of their military victories against the British in the Mississippi River valley during the war, Spain viewed as its own the land running along the east side of the river up to the Ohio and Tennessee rivers. The American government—and particularly American settlers—ignored these claims, recognizing that the Spanish had little recourse. Finally in 1810 American settlers in West Florida rebelled and established an independent republic, which the United States annexed over Spanish protests. During the War of 1812, which in many ways was an offshoot of the Napoleonic Wars, Spain allowed Britain to establish a naval base in Pensacola, and American troops under General Andrew Jackson drove the British out. Later, in the First Seminole War, Jackson invaded Florida again to retaliate for border raids by the Seminole.

By this time, Napoleon's 1808 conquest of Spain had ignited independence movements across Spanish America. As Mexican patriot Carlos María Bustamante put it, "Napoleon Bonaparte . . . to you Spanish America owes the liberty and independence it now enjoys. Your sword struck the first blow at the chain

**The Acquisition of Florida**

Louisiana

Mississippi

*Mississippi R.*

*Pearl R.*

Alabama

*Alabama R.*

*Perdido R.*

West Florida

Georgia

*Apalachicola R.*

ATLANTIC OCEAN

East Florida

*Gulf of Mexico*

N

0        80 miles
0        80 km

Seized from Spain in 1810

Seized from Spain in 1813

Acquired by Adams–Onís Treaty, 1819

---

which bound two worlds." From Mexico in the north to Argentina in the south, eleven Latin American countries would gain their independence from Spain.

In the midst of these rebellions, the last thing Spain needed was a war with the United States over Florida. So, in the Adams-Onís Treaty of 1819, Spain agreed to cede East Florida to the United States in return for American agreement to assume payment of up to $5 million in claims by American citizens in Florida against Spain. In addition, the United States received recognition of its control of West Florida; Spain gave up its claims to the Oregon Territory; and the border between the Louisiana Territory and New Spain was settled, with American acknowledgement that Texas was not part of Louisiana. In 1821 the United States took formal possession of Florida, cutting away yet another piece of Spanish America.

# Slavery and Territorial Expansion

From the earliest days of the American republic, the question of slavery and the limits, if any, to its westward expansion were a central problem in American political life. Proponents of slavery had been angered by its exclusion from the Old Northwest by the Ordinance of 1787. Yet as America's network of rivers, lakes, roads,

and canals expanded to bring more people across the Appalachians, slavery moved west as well.

Yet some historians have argued that by the early 1790s, slavery appeared to be on the road to gradual extinction. Revolutionary ideals about "all men [being] created equal" prompted some planters to manumit, or legally free, their slaves. More important, grain farming was on the rise in the North and the upper South. Grains—like wheat and corn—required heavy labor at sowing and harvest times only. It made more economic sense to hire labor when it was needed than to make a heavy investment in slaves who would only be used part of the year. Thus, in 1790, the institution of slavery thrived largely along a narrow, coastal corridor of tobacco, rice, and long-staple cotton plantations from Virginia to Georgia. While hugely profitable, the agricultural economy of this region was not replicable in the territories of the West for climatic reasons.

Eli Whitney's simple invention of the cotton gin changed all that. By making short-staple cotton—which could be grown across much of the lower South—profitable, the gin revived slavery as an institution. And by creating an insatiable demand for the commodity, the Industrial Revolution—which began in England and soon spread to New England—made short-staple cotton farming hugely profitable.

As new territories in the West were carved into states and admitted into the union, the economic demand for more and more cotton fused with the political issues surrounded slavery and the U.S. Constitution.

**ACQUISITION OF FLORIDA**

Facing independence struggles in Latin America and fearful of American settlement in northern Mexico, Spain ceded both East and West Florida to the United States in 1819.

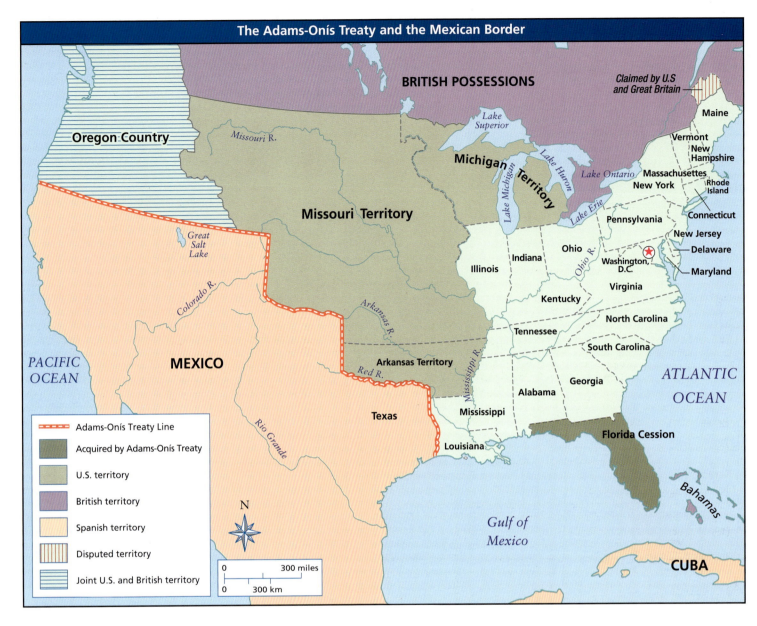

## The Adams-Onís Treaty and the Mexican Border

**BRITISH POSSESSIONS**

Claimed by U.S and Great Britain

Oregon Country

*Missouri R.*

Lake Superior

**Michigan Territory**

Lake Huron

Lake Ontario

Lake Michigan

Lake Erie

Maine

Vermont

New Hampshire

Massachusettes

New York

Rhode Island

**Missouri Territory**

*Great Salt Lake*

Pennsylvania

Connecticut

New Jersey

Delaware

Ohio

Indiana

*Ohio R.*

Washington, D.C.

Maryland

Illinois

Virginia

*Colorado R.*

Kentucky

*Arkansas R.*

North Carolina

Tennessee

South Carolina

**MEXICO**

PACIFIC OCEAN

**Arkansas Territory**

*Red R.*

*Mississippi R.*

ATLANTIC OCEAN

Georgia

Alabama

**Texas**

Mississippi

Florida Cession

*Rio Grande*

Louisiana

Bahamas

N

Gulf of Mexico

CUBA

**Legend:**
- Adams-Onís Treaty Line
- Acquired by Adams-Onís Treaty
- U.S. territory
- British territory
- Spanish territory
- Disputed territory
- Joint U.S. and British territory

0   300 miles
0   300 km

**THE MEXICAN BORDER** In addition to ceding East and West Florida to the United States, the Adams-Onís Treaty also established a border between the United States and Spain's colony of Mexico.

In creating a document that would appeal to southerners, northern statesmen—who wanted a constitution that created a strong, pro-trade central government—had agreed to a compromise whereby slaves would count as three-fifths persons for the purposes of apportioning representation. As the South was then the largest region of country, it was expected that it would have the largest population and the most representatives. In short, northerners got the kind of government they wanted but at the price of allowing southerners to run it. This compromise rested, however, on a premise that ultimately proved to be false. Because of the presence of a slave labor force, few immigrant laborers moved to the South and the North soon surpassed it in population.

### Missouri Compromise

In 1819, a challenge to the three-fifths compromise emerged. After accepting the admission of several slave states in the 1810s, northern politicians finally put their foot down when Missouri asked to join the Union as yet another. For two years, Congress divided bitterly over the issue, until a compromise was hammered together by House Speaker Henry Clay of Kentucky. Under the Missouri Compromise, that state would join the Union alongside the free state of Maine. Thus was inaugurated a new sectional balancing act, whereby states would enter in pairs—one free state for every slave state. And so while the House of Representatives—which was based on population—came to be dominated by northerners, the Senate—which guaranteed each state two members—would maintain a balance of power between the two regions. Moreover, to satisfy lingering northern suspicions of slavery dominating the West, a line was drawn from Missouri's southern border—at 36° 30' latitude—to the Pacific Ocean, even though most of this territory belonged to the newly independent country of Mexico. To many Americans—including an aging Thomas Jefferson—the Missouri Compromise portended dangerous divisions within the republic. "This momentous question, like a firebell in the night," wrote the retired president, "awakened and filled me with terror."

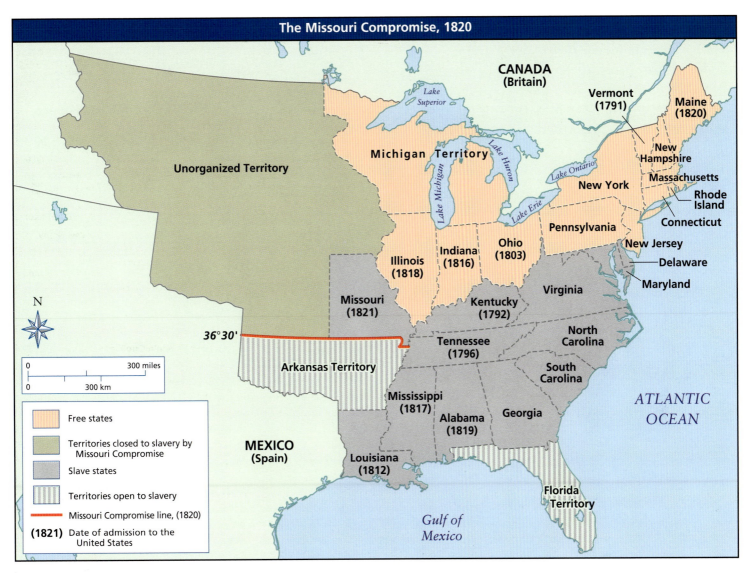

The Missouri Compromise, 1820

CANADA (Britain)

*Lake Superior*

Michigan Territory

Unorganized Territory

Vermont (1791)

Maine (1820)

New Hampshire

*Lake Huron*

*Lake Michigan*

*Lake Ontario*

New York

Massachusetts

Rhode Island

*Lake Erie*

Pennsylvania

Connecticut

Illinois (1818)

Indiana (1816)

Ohio (1803)

New Jersey

Delaware

Maryland

Missouri (1821)

Virginia

Kentucky (1792)

North Carolina

N

36°30'

Tennessee (1796)

South Carolina

Arkansas Territory

ATLANTIC OCEAN

0        300 miles
0        300 km

Mississippi (1817)

Alabama (1819)

Georgia

MEXICO (Spain)

Louisiana (1812)

Florida Territory

Free states

Territories closed to slavery by Missouri Compromise

Slave states

Territories open to slavery

Missouri Compromise line, (1820)

(1821) Date of admission to the United States

*Gulf of Mexico*

# Indian Removal from the Old Southwest

As American settlers moved west, carrying with them the institution of African enslavement, conflict with American Indians of the Old Northwest and Old Southeast increased. The initial conflicts after the Revolution took place in the Northwest.

### Little Turtle and the Battle of Fallen Timbers

Although the British had ceded the Northwest Territory to the United States with the Treaty of Paris, Indians in the region asserted that that since they had never given their lands over to the British, the British had no authority to bargain them away. Yet having been supplied for decades with guns and ammunition by British-held garrisons at Detroit and elsewhere, Indians of the Old Northwest held out hope that the British would join them to prevent American invasions. By 1786, Algonquian-speaking peoples of the region were organizing into a powerful alliance that included the Shawnee, Miami, Ottawa, Wyandot, Chippewa, Delaware, Sac, Potawatomi, Mingo, and Fox. Their war chief was Little Turtle—Mishikinakwa to his own people, the Miami.

In 1790 and 1791, Little Turtle, who had participated in many attacks on white settlements in the Ohio and Kentucky frontiers, led his coalition of warriors to victory against American forces, first against General Joseph Harmer and then against General Arthur St. Clair.

Following St. Clair's defeat, he was replaced by General Anthony Wayne as governor of the Northwest Territory. By 1793, Wayne had ordered the construction of a series of forts throughout Indiana Territory and advanced deep into Indian country, laying waste to the countryside. Although Little Turtle advised his people to make peace with the far larger American force rather than fight, the tribes refused to hear of it. On August 20, 1794, at the Battle of Fallen Timbers, Little Turtle and his coalition of Indian nations were crushed. The following year, he was forced to sign the Treaty of Greenville, one of several treaties that forced the Indians of the southern Ohio to cede their lands and move westward.

### Tecumseh and the War of 1812

From 1795 until the War of 1812, Indian resistance to American settlement in the region was limited. An uneasy tension remained, however. President Jefferson

**MISSOURI COMPROMISE**

The Missouri Compromise set the border between slave states and free states at the 36° 30' latitude, with Missouri being the one state above that line in which slavery would be allowed. Though the Compromise was an uneasy and temporary settlement of the territorial expansion of slavery question, its guidelines helped keep the peace for thirty years.

*"When your time comes to die, be not like those whose hearts are filled with fear of death, so that when their time comes they weep and pray for a little more time to live their lives over again in a different way."*

— TECUMSEH

**TECUMSEH**

**TENSKWATAWA**

encouraged William Henry Harrison, the governor of Indiana Territory, to seek "legal" title to as much territory as possible. Between 1802 and 1811, Harrison concluded treaties that added millions of acres of land to the United States—usually without making sure he was dealing with legitimate representatives of the tribes.

As a result, dissension grew among the tribes throughout the region. Tecumseh, an Ohio-born chief of the Shawnee, maintained that land could not be sold or purchased from individual tribes because the land belonged to all Indians. To halt further white encroachment, by 1806 he had created a powerful confederation of tribes. Threatening war against the United States in order to buy time, he traveled throughout the Ohio country, west to the lands of the Sioux, and south to the lands of the Creek, Chickasaw and Choctaw, trying to convince them to refuse the white man's gifts and to join together against the Americans.

Tecumseh's mission was only partly successful. In 1809, Harrison concluded the Treaty of Fort Wayne with the Delaware, Potawatomi, and Miami leaders, granting about three million acres in tribal lands to the United States in exchange for $7000 in goods and an annuity of $1,750. Even worse, while Tecumseh was away, Harrison attempted to destroy the heart of Tecumseh's confederacy. Harrison took a militia of a thousand men and marched on the confederated Indian settlement of Prophetstown. On November 7, 1811, Tenskwatawa, Tecumseh's brother, made a crucial mistake. In an effort to pre-empt the American attack, Tenskwatawa led a raid on Harrison's camp on the Tippecanoe River. The Indians were soundly defeated, Prophetstown was destroyed, and Tenskwatawa was disgraced. When Tecumseh returned to the region, he too rebuked his brother for his rash attack. The confederacy in tatters, Tenskwatawa left Ohio country and settled for a time in Canada where he lived on a British pension.

For his part, Tecumseh opted to continue the fight against the United States. Rather than swear off all contact with the white man, he joined the British against the United States. To the British, the Indians of the Ohio valley served as a buffer between the United States and Upper Canada against American encroachments.

During the War of 1812, Tecumseh participated in most of the major British campaigns in the West. In January 1813, U.S. forces occupied a vulnerable position on the River Raisin and were attacked by a combined force of British and Indians. Losses on the American side, mostly captured, were as high as 800, but thirty-three of the wounded prisoners were killed by Indians. Rumors quickly exaggerated the numbers killed, and a new battle cry for U.S. troops became "Remember the Raisin!" At the Battle of the Thames, Harrison led an army of 5,000 and defeated the remaining British and Indian forces in western Ontario. Tecumseh was killed. His death dissolved any substantial resistance to settlement between the Ohio and Mississippi Rivers for the next twenty years.

## The Black Hawk War

The final conflict between the United States and Indians of the northern states east of the Mississippi began in 1831. The Sauk and Fox of northern Illinois had accepted a treaty in 1804 that ceded their lands to the United States. They were allowed to remain until the late 1820s, when settlers begin to appear, and the government arranged with leading chief Keokuk to move the Sauk and Foxes into Iowa. A group led by the elderly Chief Black Hawk refused to go.

In the summer of 1831, Illinois militia mustered against Black Hawk, who fled with 1,000 people across the Mississippi. After a hungry winter, Black Hawk's folk returned to their homeland to reap corn they had planted before leaving. Now, more than 1,600 troops marched against these "hostiles," but Black Hawk again led his people to safety. American troops pursued them, bringing on small engagements that cost a few lives and created the false impression that Black Hawk had large numbers of hostile warriors on the loose. In fact, some of his men did join with other renegades to attack settlers, killing more than 200.

Army Regulars struck the Sauk and Foxes at the Battle of Wisconsin Heights, which cost seventy Indian lives, only one American. As Black Hawk's people again fled, they offered several times to surrender. The whites refused to accept, however, and attacked in the Battle of Bad Axe River, as the Indians were trying to cross the Mississippi. With an armed steamboat firing grape shot, 300 Sauk and Foxes were slaughtered, half of them women and children. The Americans suffered only twenty-seven dead and wounded. Black Hawk got away, but later was captured and imprisoned. This was the last Indian war fought east of the Mississippi.

**DEATH OF TECUMSEH** Shawnee chief Tecumseh meets his end at the hands of Colonel Richard Mentor Johnson during the Battle of the Thames, Ontario.

## Indian Removal in the South

While the battles for the Old Northwest between the United States and Indians came to an end, a separate series of conflicts over territory were occurring to the south. The initial conflicts were played out in the context of the War of 1812, and took place among the Creek nation in Alabama and Georgia. The Creek nation was divided into the Upper Creeks and Lower Creeks. The Lower Creek, or White Sticks, were mainly farmers, living like whites, with whom they intermarried. The Upper Creek largely rejected white culture and opposed American incursions into their country. Civil strife developed among the Creek, with a warlike anti-American faction taking the name Red Sticks. Early in 1813, conservative Creek executed several Red Sticks found guilty of killing white settlers. The executions caused a deep rift in the nation, with Red Sticks attacking their own council headquarters.

That spring, the Red Sticks struck at white settlements in Alabama and Georgia. Led by William Weatherford, a mixed-blood also known as Red Eagle, they captured Fort Mims on the Alabama River in August, killing almost all 550 whites there.

Tennessee militia general Andrew Jackson campaigned against the Red Sticks, leading militia and Creek and Cherokee allies. Jackson's force sometimes numbered 5,000 men. Other military expeditions, from Mississippi and Georgia, burned Red Sticks villages. Jackson defeated 700 Red Sticks at Talladega, killing 300. Weatherford then withdrew to the Talapoosa River, where he fortified a peninsula at Horseshoe Bend, Alabama. Jackson followed, but in January 1814 was defeated in several engagements. Reinforced, he attacked the Red Stick stronghold on March 27, 1814, in the Battle of Horseshoe Bend. More than 500 Creek men and many women and children died, while seventy of Jackson's men were killed and more than 200 wounded. Weatherford escaped, but later surrendered. The resulting Treaty of Fort Jackson cost both hostile and peaceful Creek 23 million acres, ceded to the states.

### Slavery and the First Seminole War

With the end of the Creek War, clashes between the United States and Indians in the region were limited to Florida. With the pacification of Creek in Georgia and Alabama, white farmers and planters began to move onto land formerly in Creek territory. With the aid of Eli Whitney's cotton gin, hundreds of square miles of ideal short-staple cotton-growing land was now available. Loans from Britain and the financial and industrial centers of the northern states now poured into the South, and new cotton plantations sprouted throughout the former Creek lands and elsewhere.

Providing labor on these new plantations were African-American slaves. While Congress had banned U.S. participation in the international slave trade in 1807, a booming domestic slave trade flourished in the period between the War of 1812 and the Civil War. While the spread of cotton lands had increased the demand for slaves, the ban in international trade had slowed the supply, causing the price of slaves to rise dramatically.

The record of African-American resistance to slavery is a long and proud one that will be discussed in greater detail elsewhere in this book. Whether resistance from Africans took a subtle form, such as stealing a master's food or property or sabotaging equipment, or a more direct one such as escape or even armed rebellion, slave resistance and subversion was a constant economic threat to the Southern planter class.

The chances of a slave successfully escaping all the way from the Deep South to the North or Canada were small. However, in the years immediately following the War of 1812, the swamps of Florida provided another option. Prior to 1819, Florida was still Spanish territory. Yet Spanish settlements were relatively few, and largely on the coastlines. Most of the territory was sparsely settled marsh, subtropical forest and scrubland. Ensconced in these wilds were the Seminole. For decades before 1816, relations had been uneasy between southern whites and the Seminole of southern Georgia and Spanish-owned Florida. The Seminole—named for a Creek version of the Spanish word for "runaway"— were one of the "Five Civilized Tribes" of the Southeast. Unlike the other tribes of the region—the Cherokee, Chickasaw, Choctaw and Creek—the Seminole lived in territory that was not within the U.S. borders. Even after Florida became a state, many Seminole were able to resist capture and removal to the West for decades.

The Seminole welcomed escaped slaves, and African Americans and Seminoles often intermarried. Southern slave owners demanded the federal government send a military expedition against the Seminoles. In early 1816, General Andrew Jackson, hero of the Battle of New Orleans and the Creek War, led an expedition against the Seminole at Negro Fort, a stronghold which had been built by runaway slaves on Apalachicola Bay. Surrounded by cannon fire from land

**WEATHERFORD SURRENDERS**
Creek chief William Weatherford, also called Red Eagle, survived the destruction of the Red Sticks at Horseshoe Bend, but with his followers defeated, he eventually surrendered to General Andrew Jackson. Weatherford was allowed to return to his people.

**The First and Second Seminole Wars**

Conecuh R.
1817  Fowltown
Ft. Scott
1818
Apalachicola R.
Tallahasee
Negro Fort  1818
1816  St. Marks
Pensacola
Ft. Gadsden
Apalachee Bay
Suwanee R.
St. Johns
St. Augustine
Ft. Peyton
1818  Suwanee
Old Town  Osceola's Capture 1837
Ft. Micanopy
Ft. Drane  1835
Gaines's Battle 1836  Ft. King
Withlacoochee R.
Clinch's Battle 1835  Ft. Mellon
Wahoo Swamp 1836  1837
Ft. Armstrong
Ft. Dade  Dade's Battle 1835
Ft. Brooke  Taylor's Battle 1837  Jesup's Battle 1838
(Tampa)
Gulf of Mexico  Tampa Bay  Big Cypress Swamp 1855–58  Lake Okeechobee  Ft. Jupiter
Colee Hammock 1842  Ft. Lauderdale
Ft. Dallas
THE EVERGLADES

N

0      200 miles
0      200 km

⚶ Indian villages
● Non-Indian settlements
■ Forts
✳ Battles

© Carl Waldman

**SEMINOLE WARS**
Despite fighting a series of three wars against them, the United States failed to militarily defeat the Seminole people of Florida. Although most Seminole did relocate west, some only did so after receiving payment.

and sea, 300 Seminole and African American men, women and children held out until a well-placed shot from a warship struck the fort's ammunition dump, killing most of the fort's inhabitants.

Hundreds of other Seminole living in the Pensacola region continued to resist. By 1818, the year before Florida was purchased from the Spanish and incorporated as a U.S. territory, most Seminole had been pushed farther south. With this U.S. victory, the First Seminole War had ended, although scattered skirmishes continued over the next several years.

### The Trail of Tears and the Second Seminole War

In 1830, Andrew Jackson and the state government of Georgia decided that any Indians remaining east of the Mississippi would be forcibly removed to territory in the West. The Indian Removal Act of 1830 allowed the government to offer Indians land further west in exchange for their eastern lands. Although the land specifically required the Indian's consent for such trades, this provision was never enforced. Instead, over the next decade, tens of thousands of Indians were forced from their land. The Cherokee, Chickasaw, Choctaw and Creek were driven to a new "Indian Territory" in what is now Oklahoma. They were forced to travel under terrible conditions, and thousands died en route from hunger, cold, and disease. The Cherokee, who bitterly resisted their

removal and marched under army guard, called the journey the Trail of Tears, a phrase that has come to symbolize the barbarity of the U.S. removal policy.

The U.S. government also pressured the Seminole to join the other "Civilized Tribes" in emigrating west. In 1835, some of the Seminole chiefs were tricked into signing a misleading treaty that appeared to promise them the right to remain in Florida but actually called for their removal. When the truth about the treaty was revealed, an army of black and Native American Seminole launched new attacks on white plantations and U.S. Army outposts, sparking the Second Seminole War.

For several years, the U.S. Army and the Seminole fought skirmishes and battles throughout northern and central Florida. Under the leadership of chiefs Osceola, King Philip, and Wild Cat, Seminole warriors hit the U.S. Army when they least expected it, and then disappeared into the swamps.

However, using trickery and overwhelming force, General Thomas Jesup and the U.S. Army were eventually able to capture Osceola and wear down much of the Seminole's resistance. By 1842, most of the Seminole had surrendered, with hundreds sent west to Arkansas and Oklahoma and many blacks forced back into slavery. A reporter for *Harper's Weekly* noted in that year, "The negro slaves are, in fact, the masters of their own red owners. . . . The negroes were the master spirits, as well

103

**Relocation of Eastern Indians**

**INDIAN REMOVAL** During the 1830s, the United States forcibly removed the major Indian peoples of the Southeast—the Cherokee, Chickasaw, Choctaw, Creek, and Seminole.

as the immediate occasion, of the Florida wars. They openly refused to follow their masters if they removed to Arkansas; it was not until they capitulated that the Seminoles ever thought of emigrating."

Still, a small band of African Americans and Seminole continued to hold out in the Everglade swamps of southern Florida. A series of sporadic skirmishes, sometimes called the Third Seminole War, continued until 1858. These last survivors won a major concession from the federal government, which allowed them to stay on in southern Florida, where they live to this day. Today's mixed-race Florida Seminole are proud to say that they fought the longest war in American history against the U.S. government and that they never signed a treaty ending the war.

# The Texas Independence Movement

Two years after Spain ceded Florida to the United States in 1819, Mexico, the heart of Spain's once mighty New World empire gained its independence. The independence movement had been rooted in clashes among European colonial powers. When French emperor Napoleon forced his brother Joseph onto the throne of Spain, the Creole (American-born) elite had been mostly willing to submit to Spain's legitimate King Ferdinand VIII, but they refused to submit to the Bonapartes. In city after city, they formed juntas to rule themselves rather than by Spain's governing viceroys.

## Indian Cessions Through 1850

CANADA

Columbia R.
Blackfoot
Flathead
Crow
Nez Perce
Bannock
Sioux
Mandan
Shoshoni
Snake R.
Great Salt Lake
Arapaho
Ute
Pawnee
Cheyenne
San Francisco
Monterey
Paiute
Cheyenne
Santa Barbara
Navajo
Osage
Kiowa
Albuquerque
Santa Fe
Creek
Cherokee
San Diego
Apache
Pueblo
Seminole
Comanche
Chickasaw
Choctaw
Tucson
El Paso
Natchitoches
Nacogdoches
San Antonio
Rio Grande

Lake Superior
Mississippi R.
Missouri R.
Lake Michigan
Lake Huron
L. Ontario
Lake Erie
St. Lawrence R.
Fort Detroit
Cincinnati
St. Louis
Fort Orleans
Ohio R.
Louisville
Fort Prudhomme
Arkansas Post
Natchez
New Orleans
Pensacola

Portland
Boston
New York
Philadelphia
Pittsburgh
Baltimore
Washington, D.C.
Richmond
Raleigh
Charlotte
Augusta
Charleston
Savannah
St. Augustine

ATLANTIC OCEAN

PACIFIC OCEAN

MEXICO

Gulf of Mexico

N

Indian lands ceded before 1784
Indian lands ceded, 1784–1810
Indian lands ceded, 1810–50

0     250 miles
0     250 km

For many, the juntas were not a call for independence but a effort to restore the Spanish monarchy.

### Independence for Mexico

On September 16, 1810, independence from Spain was declared by Miguel Hidalgo y Costilla, a Catholic priest in the small town of Dolores, causing a long war that ultimately led to Mexican independence from Spain in 1821. Agustín de Iturbide, a conservative who had spent ten years fighting against the rebels before joining the cause of independence, was named Agustín I of the First Mexican Empire.

Almost immediately, the Mexican government was in chaos. After General Antonio López de Santa Anna proclaimed Mexico to be a republic, Agustin I was forced to resign. A year later he attempted to regain power, but was arrested and executed.

Iturbide's death did not end the chaos in Mexico. In 1824, Mexico became a republic with a president and a two-house Congress heading the national government, and governors and legislatures heading the states. Although General Santa Anna initially supported the republic, Mexico's power struggles continued, with nine

different men leading the country over the next nine years. In 1828, Santa Anna supported the rule of Vincente Guerrero, backed his overthrow in 1832, and then overthrew Guerrero's successor himself the next year, seizing control of the country and ruling as dictator on and off until 1847.

### Mexico's Northern Frontier

From the moment Mexico first gained its independence in 1821, the United States—and particularly American settlers—kept a close watch on events there. Mexican independence also meant Mexican control of all lands formerly in Spanish hands north of the Río Grande and west of the Mississippi River. This vast territory encompassed what is today New Mexico, Arizona, California, Nevada, Utah, New Mexico, Texas, and parts of Wyoming, Colorado, Kansas and Oklahoma. Over the next several decades, however, Mexico would lose all of this territory to the ever expanding settlement from the United States. Among the first Americans to take interest in the changing government in Mexico were merchants and traders. Under Spanish rule, Santa Fe, the largest Spanish settlement north of the Río Grande, was

VANISHING HOMELAND By the 1840s, the vast majority of American Indian peoples living east of the Mississippi River had ceded their lands to the United States.

prohibited from contact with the rest of North America. Since the 1770s, however, American fur trappers and traders had regularly snuck into Mexico from the east along an old Indian trail to hunt and sell goods. The trail, which eventually stretched from Independence, Missouri to Santa Fe, became known as the Santa Fe Trail.

### Americans in Texas

While few Americans lived in Santa Fe during the early 1800s, a larger number lived just to the east in the Mexican territory of Texas. The first Americans had arrived in 1803, and in 1820, an American named Moses Austin was given permission to found a colony of American settlers along the Gulf Coast between the Colorado and Brazos rivers. When Mexico won its independence from Spain the next year, the American colonists backed the Mexican government.

Still, the Mexican government questioned the loyalty of the American settlers and in 1829 decided to ban slavery in Mexican territory as a way of discouraging further American immigration. The policy was a disaster. With Mexico's government in chaos, Anglo-Americans in Texas found it easy to ignore the ban. Under protest from Anglo slaveowners, application of the law to Texas was suspended. With the suspension of antislavery laws, the production of cotton began to increase. In just six years, between 1827 and 1833, the number of cotton bales produced in Texas doubled.

In 1830 Mexico enacted even more direct legislation to control the Anglo menace. The new law closed the border to further Anglo-American immigration into Texas, prohibited the slave trade, encouraged Mexicans and Europeans to settle in Texas, and imposed customs duties on imports from the United States. Troops were sent and new forts built to reinforce Mexican authority. Anglo-Americans in Texas responded with outrage, some launching military attacks on customs houses and army posts. Many Texans resorted to smuggling to avoid duties. The influx of Anglo immigrants, though illegal, continued to be at least as heavy as before.

In 1833 a convention of Texans sent Moses Austin's son Stephen to Mexico City to argue for rescinding the laws and making Texas a Mexican state with its own U.S.-style constitution. Austin could not get an answer from the chaos-ridden Mexican government, so after 11 weeks he sent a letter to the city council of San Antonio, back in Texas, advising that Texas form its own state government without the central government's support.

Austin's letter had an unintended effect, for most San Antonio city council members were Mexican Texans, or Tejanos. Alarmed, they forwarded it to Santa Anna, who had seized control of the government by this time and suspended the federal constitution of 1824. Santa Anna judged the letter treasonable and had Austin locked up until 1835. In response, Texan delegates, some Tejano but most Anglo, covened at San Felipe de Austin, and, on November 7, 1835, provisionally declared their independence from Mexico until such time as the Constitution of 1824 was restored.

### Independence for Texas

On October 2, 1835, a month before formally declaring independence, the first battle in the Texan Revolution, or Texan War of Independence took place

**THE ALAMO** Once a Spanish mission called Missión San Antonio de Valero, the fortified Alamo shielded 200 Texans for two weeks aganst Santa Anna's attackers.

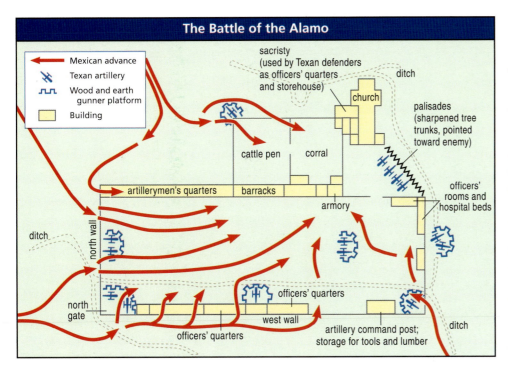

**The Battle of the Alamo**

- ← Mexican advance
- Texan artillery
- Wood and earth gunner platform
- Building

sacristy (used by Texan defenders as officers' quarters and storehouse)

ditch

church

palisades (sharpened tree trunks, pointed toward enemy)

cattle pen    corral

artillerymen's quarters    barracks

armory

officers' rooms and hospital beds

ditch

north wall

north gate

officers' quarters

west wall

officers' quarters

artillery command post; storage for tools and lumber

ditch

**ASSAULT ON THE ALAMO** As Mexican forces scaled the fort's walls during the final assault on the Alamo, most of the Texan defenders, who were stationed throughout all areas of the fort, died where they fought.

at Gonzales when Texan rebels refused to hand over an old cannon they had been given for protection against Native Americans. The rebels captured the presidio at Goliad a week later, then captured San Antonio on December 11 after five days of fierce house-to-house fighting. Santa Anna, eager to avenge the defeat, amassed an army of perhaps 5,000 and marched into San Antonio on February 23, 1836. He found the town only thinly defended by a force of about 150 men, all holed up in the fortified mission called the Alamo. It would become the symbol of Texan independence.

Led by William Travis, a South Carolina lawyer who came to Texas in about 1832, the tiny force in the Alamo also included pioneer James Bowie and Tennessee frontiersman and politician Davy Crockett, who had come to aid the rebels in the Texan War of Independence. During the siege, thirty-two other men joined the defenders, bringing the total force to about 182. Some Tejanos were in the Alamo, including San Antonio colonel Juan Seguín.

Upon arriving, Santa Anna surrounded the Alamo and raised the red flag, the sign of "no quarter," indicating that the Texans must surrender immediately or die upon being captured. The Texans replied with cannon fire. Santa Anna besieged and bombarded the Alamo for thirteen days, then attacked. On March 6, his forces captured

the Alamo. All 182 Texan soldiers were killed, either in battle or after capture. Only women, children, and slaves in the mission were spared.

Santa Anna had won the battle but lost the war. Word of the Anglo stand at the Alamo reinforced Texan zeal and earned Santa Anna the reputation of butcher, as did his massacre of Texan prisoners outside Goliad on March 27. In the Battle of San Jacinto on April 21, Sam Houston led a force of fewer than 800 men in a surprise attack on Santa Anna's sleeping army of about 1,500. In the 18-minute rout, Houston's soldiers killed Mexicans with vengeful abandon, disregarding many surrender attempts, shouting "Remember the Alamo!" and "Remember Goliad!" Stephen Austin's nephew, Moses Austin Bryan, described it as "the most awful slaughter I ever saw." By Houston's account, 630 Mexicans were killed and 730 taken prisoner, while fewer than 10 Texans died. Among the prisoners he took was Santa Anna, who, in exchange for his freedom, signed treaties recognizing Texan independence and agreeing to withdraw Mexican forces beyond the Rio Grande.

Disgraced by his defeat, Santa Anna was forced out of office. The new Mexican government refused to recognize Texan independence, but was in no position to pursue its claim.

# The Mexican-American War

The independent Republic of Texas, founded in 1836, chose Sam Houston as its first elected president. Texas became known as the Lone Star Republic for its flag with a single star, but for many Texans, including Houston, the goal was not independence but to join the United States as a new state. Some voices in the United States called for annexation, but others resisted. Opponents of slavery recognized that Texas would enter the Union as a slave state, upsetting the balance of free and slave states in Congress. Further, annexation of Texas would probably lead to war with Mexico, since Mexico still claimed Texas as its own.

The years 1836 to 1846 were tense ones in the disputed borderlands. Texas was plagued by debt and wars with Native Americans. Mexico did not recognize Texan independence, invading twice in 1842 but failing to capture territory. The two nations also disagreed about boundaries. Texas claimed that the Río Grande from mouth to source was the republic's southern and western border, an assertion that would have allotted Texas parts of what are now New Mexico and Colorado. Mexico argued that the southern border of Texas was the Nueces River, about 150 miles north of the Rio Grande.

Some Texans had even grander notions of their republic's extent, asserting dominion as far as the California coast. In 1841 Texan president Mirabeau Bonaparte Lamar sent an expedition of 300 merchants and soldiers to Santa Fe to try to incite a revolt against Mexico. The expedition was a disaster, as the participants became lost in the wilderness, were attacked by Comanche and Kiowa Indians, and then captured by New Mexico's government and imprisoned in Mexico City, from which they were released only after American and British protests.

Tensions also rose between Mexico and the United States. In October 1842 American Commodore Thomas Catesby Jones, acting on a rumor that war had broken out, sailed to Monterey, California, and forced the Mexican garrison there to surrender. The embarrassed officer was forced to give Monterey back the next day on learning that he had been mistaken.

The affair gave Mexico good reason to be suspicious about U.S. intentions, for California was becoming ever more attrac-

## The Texan Revolution

0 — 75 miles
0 — 75 km

N

Bastrop

Washington-on-the-Brazos

Groce's Ferry

*San Jacinto* (April 21)

The Alamo (March 6)

Harrisburg

Anahuac

San Antonio de Bexar

Gonzales

San Felipe de Austin

Coleto (March 19–20)

Fort Bend Brazoria

Galveston

Presidio de Rio Grande

**Coahuila Texas**

Guadalupe Victoria

Velasco

Rio Grande

Matagorda

**Chihuahua**

Goliad (March 24)

*Refugio* (March 13–14)

Laredo

San Patricio (February 27)

*Gulf of Mexico*

**Tamaulipas**

Agua Dulce

• Monclova

Mier

**Nuevo León**

← ···· Route of Martín Perfecto de Cos
← --- Route of Antonio Gaona
← Route of Sam Houston
← Route of Antonio López de Santa Anna
← --- Route of José Francisco Urrea
← ···· Route of Juan Morales and Cayentano Montoya

Matamoros

• Monterrey

Saltillo •

**TEXAS WAR FOR INDEPENDENCE**
Early in 1836, General Santa Anna moved against an Anglo uprising in Texas. Following the Mexican capture of the Alamo after a two-week seige, Santa Anna divided his army to pursue the Texans, only to be defeated at San Jacinto in April.

tive to the United States. New England shipowners were getting rich on the maritime trade with the California ports of Monterey and San Francisco. New England whalers docked in those ports on their hunting expeditions. In 1844 a treaty opened five Chinese ports to American commerce, increasing the importance of having Pacific harbors available on the American mainland. American merchants had much to trade, because American manufacturing was on the rise, as the country rebounded from a depression that had lasted from 1837 to 1841. Through immigration and natural increase, the population of the United States was burgeoning, nearly doubling from 12.9 million in 1830 to 23.2 million in 1850—and many of those people wanted nothing more than cheap land, no matter how far west it lay. In addition to these factors, the United States had a foreign policy stake in preventing other nations from acquiring California, particularly Britain, which was then contesting the United States for possession of the Oregon Territory, just north of California. For all these reasons, the United States had a strong interest in acquiring Mexico's Far North, especially California. For its part, Mexico—as New Spain had done when settling California and Texas a century before—viewed the northern frontier as a defensive buffer against its expansionist neighbor. Therefore, even though its northern frontier was still relatively sparse in population, Mexico had a strong interest in not letting the United States have it.

As early as the 1820s, the United States had offered to buy Texas, an offer rejected as an insult by

Mexico. In 1835 United States president Andrew Jackson offered to buy San Francisco Bay. In 1845 President John Tyler offered to buy New Mexico and California. Such offers only fueled Mexico's distrust and resentment of the United States.

At the same time, the Anglo-American population in the remainder of Mexico's Far North kept growing. Just as in Texas before the Texan Revolution, Anglo-American immigrants poured into California, attracted by such reports as that of former New Mexican Louis Robidoux, who called northern California "the promised land where the arroyos run with virgin honey and milk. Another Texas." Among those who came was Baden-born John Augustus Sutter, who settled in the Sacramento Valley with a grant of 49,000 acres, to which he attracted many American settlers. After the U.S.-Mexican War (in which Sutter sided with the United States), Sutter became even more famous for the gold found on his lands.

The Mexican authorities tried the same strategies for control that had failed in Texas: clamping down with tougher anti-immigration laws, sending more troops, and trying to encourage immigration from outside the United States. The strategies failed in California too—in part because Californios, who welcomed the local development the immigrants brought and lacked the military strength to expel them, tended not to enforce the restrictions. One young Californio, Pablo de la Guerra, said the foreigners "are about to overrun us, of which I am very glad, for the country needs immigration in order to make progress."

In New Mexico, Governor Manuel Armijo had better luck restricting immigration, but Anglo-Americans could turn up anywhere. Even during the U.S.-Mexican War, one determined group of Anglo-Americans took up residence in a Far Northern region as yet unsettled by Hispanics: the Mormons, who, fleeing persecution in the United States, established their first colony in what is now Utah in 1847.

The threat of war between the United States and Mexico grew in November 1844, when Democrat James K. Polk was elected president. Polk was an expansionist committed to territorial growth, beginning with annexation of Texas and ideally extending to California. The notion of annexing Texas was becoming increasingly popular, as southern states pressed for addition of a new slave state to aid their cause in Congress, and as British and French influence grew in Texas, making it possible that the United States would permanently lose its chance to acquire the Lone Star Republic.

On February 28, 1845, before Polk had been inaugurated, the U.S. Congress approved a joint resolution inviting Texas into the Union. Mexico protested and broke off diplomatic relations with the United States, but the tide of U.S. expansionist sentiment grew. In the summer of 1845, John L. O'Sullivan, editor of the *United States Magazine and Democratic Review*, coined the phrase Manifest Destiny, saying it was the United States' "manifest destiny to overspread the continent allotted by Providence for the free development of our yearly multiplying millions." O'Sullivan had not originated this idea; many Americans, including Polk, felt that their country should and would expand from coast to coast, bringing with it the blessings of democracy and free enterprise. Some saw no limits to this destiny—up into Canada, down into Mexico, even into South America or Europe. One American soldier wrote prior to the U.S.-Mexican War that with a "gigantic effort" the United States "could sweep the continent from Panama to the Pole and from ocean to ocean in a year." Others, like Polk, were more restrained; they wanted only North America, from sea to shining sea.

Polk made one major effort to acquire the Far North peacefully. In November 1845 he sent diplomat John Slidell to Mexico to try to gain recognition of the Río Grande border for Texas and buy New Mexico and California. As a bargaining tool, Slidell was to use claims of damages to American property during Mexico's civil wars, claims that the United States was willing to drop in return for Mexican cooperation. The Mexicans refused to negotiate.

While Slidell was in Mexico, Texas entered the Union, becoming the 28th state on December 29, 1845. At about the same time, another revolt broke out in Mexico, with General Mariano Paredes coming to power on January 2, 1846. As Polk saw it, he had tried peaceful means to acquire Mexico's Far North, and those had failed. His next move was war.

## War with Mexico

On January 13, 1846, Polk ordered General Zachary Taylor to advance from his position on the Nueces River to the Rio Grande. The president did so knowing that Mexico rejected the American claim to the territory between the rivers and would therefore regard this move as an invasion. On March 28 Taylor arrived at the Rio Grande, across from the Mexican city of Matamoros, and began constructing forts. Shortly thereafter, General Pedro de Ampudia, commander of Mexico's Division of the North, ordered Taylor to withdraw or face hostilities. Taylor refused.

On April 25 a large Mexican cavalry force crossed the Rio Grande. They surrounded a small squadron of American dragoons, killing or wounding sixteen and taking the rest prisoner. Taylor sent word to Polk, who informed Congress heatedly, "Mexico has passed the boundary of the United States, has invaded our territory and shed American blood upon the American soil." Some congressmen objected, questioning whether the east bank of the Rio Grande could really be considered American soil, but they were in the minority. Congress declared war on Mexico on May 13, 1846. A subordinate of Taylor's, Colonel Ethan Allen Hitchcock, commented: "It looks as if the government sent a small force on purpose to bring on a war, so as to have a pretext for taking California and as much of this country as it chooses."

The American strategy for winning the war centered on Taylor, who had won two victories on the northern side of the Rio Grande even before the declaration of war: at Palo Alto on May 8 and Resaca de la Palma on May 9. On May 18 Taylor advanced into Matamoros, which the enemy had abandoned, and raised the American flag there. The plan was for Taylor to keep pushing into northern Mexico, while a separate force, the Army of the West, conquered New Mexico and California, and the navy attacked California and blockaded both Mexican coasts. President Polk hoped these strategies alone would convince Mexico to make peace, ending the war swiftly. He had not counted on the stiffness of Mexican resistance, which would keep Mexico in arms for more than two years, not making peace until their capital was taken.

## New Mexico and California

In June 1846, while Zachary Taylor battled in northern Mexico, the campaign to capture New Mexico and California began. On June 27, Brigadier General Stephen Watts Kearny, commander of the Army of the West, left Fort Leavenworth in what is now Kansas with about 1,500 troops. After marching more than 1,000 miles along the Santa Fe Trail, Kearney's forces captured Santa Fe, New Mexico, without a fight on August 16. The Neuvomexicanos varied in their responses to the takeover. They had no great love for the Mexican government but were wary of Americans. The attitude of New Mexican official Juan Bautista Vigil seemed a typical one: "No mat-

### The Bear Flag Revolt

Captain John C. Frémont, 1845

Captain John C. Frémont, 1846

Commodore John D. Sloat

*Note:* Contemporary borders and state names are provided for reference.

Oregon

Klamath Lake

*Sacramento R.*

Nevada

Lake Tahoe

**Bear Flag Revolt**
*Sonoma*
June 14, 1846

Sutter's Fort

*San Joaquin R.*

San Francisco

Santa Cruz

San Juan Bautista

**Monterey—**
July 7, 1846

California

PACIFIC OCEAN

Los Angeles

N

0    100 miles
0    100 km

*from Mexico*

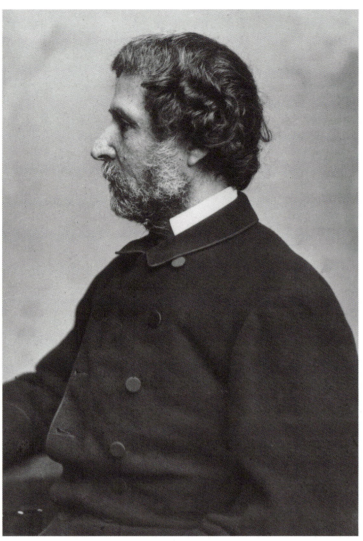

**THE BEAR FLAG REVOLT** The Bear Flag Revolt began on June 14, 1846, when Anglo settlers in Sonoma placed Mexican general Mariano Vallejo under arrest, declaring California an independent republic they called the Bear Flag Republic.

**THE PATHFINDER** Western explorer John C. Frémont is credited with launching the Bear Flag Revolt when he gave his support to a revolt against Mexican rule by a group of Anglo settlers in Sonoma, near San Francisco.

ter what her condition, [Mexico] was our mother. What child will not shed abundant tears at the tomb of his parents?"

By the time New Mexico was captured, California had fallen to the United States as well. Captain John C. Frémont, who had been in the region on an exploratory expedition since the previous year, gave his support to a settlers' revolt at Sonoma, north of San Francisco. At dawn on June 14, the rebels rousted General Mariano Vallejo from his bed, placed him under arrest, and forced him to surrender. Since they were not yet certain that the United States was at war with Mexico, the rebels could not claim the territory in the name of the United States. Instead, they proclaimed California's independence, raising a flag decorated with a grizzly bear. The event was called the Bear Flag Revolt, even though the Bear Flag Republic's flag was taken down and replaced with an American flag once confirmation of the state of war came.

Soon after the Bear Flag Revolt, Commodore John D. Sloat closed in from the sea, capturing Monterey on July 7 and San Francisco three days later. In August, Commodore Robert F. Stockton, who had replaced the ailing Sloat, captured Los

Angeles, Southern California's strongest garrison, without opposition. Stockton proclaimed himself governor of the territory, but the Californios only appeared to submit to him. In September Californios, led by Captain José María Flores, rebelled and took back Los Angeles. In the following months, the Californios took possession of most of the towns in the interior. The tide of battle turned when Kearny, who had been advancing west from Santa Fe, arrived in December and fought through enemy lines until he could join Stockton's forces. With Kearny's help, Stockton recaptured Los Angeles on January 10, 1847. At about the same time, the people of New Mexico also revolted, but they were crushed at Taos early in 1847.

### Invading Mexico

While the struggle for California went on, General Taylor moved deeper into Mexico. His victories were aided by the superiority of American weapons over outdated Mexican ones and by the generally poor leadership and training of Mexican soldiers—despite the fact that they often fought more tenaciously and courageously than Americans had expected. On September 24, 1846, Taylor captured Monterrey, which guarded an important mountain pass leading into Mexico's interior. On February 22–23, 1847, at Buena Vista, Taylor faced an old fighter against Americans: General Santa Anna of Alamo fame. In exile in Cuba at the start of the war during one of his periods out of power, Santa Anna had convinced President Polk to allow him to pass through the naval blockade so he could regain control of Mexico and negotiate peace. As soon as the general got back home, however, he reneged on the deal and gathered an army of 20,000 to face Taylor's 5,000 at Buena Vista. Both sides suffered heavy losses, but Taylor held fast, and Santa Anna was forced to withdraw, leaving northern Mexico in U.S. control.

In March 1847 Alexander Doniphan, a lieutenant of Kearny's who had led an expedition from Santa Fe, captured Chihuahua in northern Mexico. But by then the focus of battle had turned to central Mexico. Polk realized that Mexico would not surrender unless its capital was captured, so he determined to seize it. The plan was to land troops at Veracruz, then follow the ancient invasion route to Mexico City that Hernán Cortés had used in overthrowing the Aztec Empire. The man appointed to head the campaign was General Winfield Scott.

On March 9, 1847, near Veracruz, Scott launched the largest amphibious assault yet undertaken by American troops, with 10,000 soldiers wading onto the beach under the cover of naval artillery. After a siege and bombardment, the walled city of Veracruz fell on March 29. Scott marched west to Mexico City as Cortés had, capturing town after town and defeating the Mexicans at Cerro Gordo (April 18), Contreras (August 19), and Churubusco (August 20). Scott was hampered by high rates of disease and desertion, which had also plagued Taylor's army. However, he was aided by the effective soldiering of his West Point–trained junior officers, who would go on to fight each other in the American Civil War. They included Ulysses S. Grant, Robert E. Lee, George McClellan, P. G. T. Beauregard, and Thomas (later called "Stonewall") Jackson.

Notwithstanding the superior training of the U.S. officers, Mexican forces fought vigorously to defend their country against the American invasion, and some battles were hard-won, such as Churubusco, in which the Americans suffered about 1,000 casualties and the Mexicans 4,000. Particularly fierce were the battles of Molino del Rey (September 8) and Chapultepec (September 13), both fought over fortified positions guarding the entrance to the capital. During the Battle of Chapultepec, in which Americans stormed the castle and military school of the same name, the young Mexican cadets showed great

**BATTLE OF BUENA VISTA** Five thousand men under American general and future president Zachary Taylor held off 20,000 Mexicans at the Battle of Buena Vista.

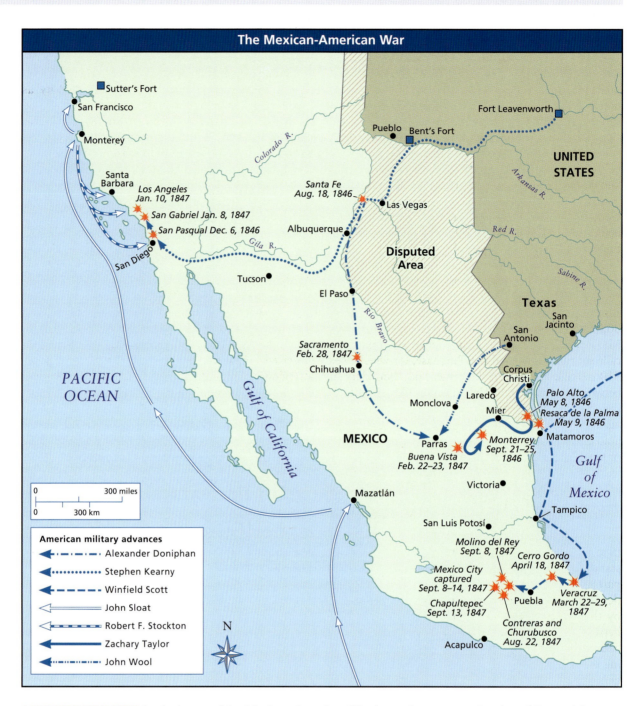

## The Mexican-American War

Sutter's Fort
San Francisco
Monterey
Santa Barbara
Los Angeles Jan. 10, 1847
San Gabriel Jan. 8, 1847
San Pasqual Dec. 6, 1846
San Diego
Tucson

Fort Leavenworth
Pueblo  Bent's Fort
UNITED STATES
Santa Fe Aug. 18, 1846
Las Vegas
Albuquerque
Disputed Area

*Colorado R.*
*Gila R.*
*Arkansas R.*
*Red R.*
*Sabine R.*

El Paso
*Rio Bravo*

Texas
San Jacinto
San Antonio
Corpus Christi

PACIFIC OCEAN

*Gulf of California*

Sacramento Feb. 28, 1847
Chihuahua
Monclova
Laredo
Mier
Parras
Buena Vista Feb. 22–23, 1847
Monterrey Sept. 21–25, 1846
Matamoros

Palo Alto May 8, 1846
Resaca de la Palma May 9, 1846

MEXICO

*Gulf of Mexico*

Victoria
Mazatlán
San Luis Potosí
Tampico

Molino del Rey Sept. 8, 1847
Mexico City captured Sept. 8–14, 1847
Chapultepec Sept. 13, 1847
Cerro Gordo April 18, 1847
Puebla
Veracruz March 22–29, 1847
Contreras and Churubusco Aug. 22, 1847
Acapulco

0    300 miles
0    300 km

**American military advances**
— · — · —  Alexander Doniphan
· · · · · · ·  Stephen Kearny
— — — —  Winfield Scott
—▷—▷—  John Sloat
—◁·—◁·—  Robert F. Stockton
————  Zachary Taylor
—··—··—  John Wool

N

**AMERICAN INVASION** At the heart of the Mexican-American War lay a dispute over the size of Texas. After annexing the Lone Star Republic—as independent Texas was called—the United States claimed that the Texas border followed the Rio Grande all the way from the Gulf of Mexico to territory north of Santa Fe in New Mexico, including land in present-day Colorado and Wyoming.

courage, many of them fighting to the death rather than surrendering. Mexicans still commemorate them as Los Niños Héroes, "The Boy Heroes."

With Chapultepec fallen, the road to Mexico City lay wide open. Santa Anna evacuated his troops, and on September 14, 1847, Scott occupied the Mexican capital. Santa Anna tried a last attack on Scott at Puebla, but it failed, and he fled into exile once again. The citizens of Mexico City gave some resistance in the form of riots and sniping, but Scott suppressed it within a matter of days. For the first time, the American flag waved over a foreign capital.

### The Treaty of Guadalupe Hidalgo

Peace came with the Treaty of Guadalupe Hidalgo, signed in a Mexico City suburb by that name on February 2, 1848. The treaty gave the United States everything for which it had fought. Mexico surrendered its claim to Texas and accepted the Rio Grande boundary. In what was called the Mexican Cession, Mexico ceded the remainder of its Far North, including California, New Mexico, and all or part of what are now Arizona, Nevada, Utah, Wyoming, Colorado, Kansas, and Oklahoma. In return the United States paid Mexico $15 million and took on $3 million in unpaid claims of American citizens against Mexico.

Mexican citizens who chose to remain in the acquired territories would be granted "all the rights of citizens of the United States," including full property and civil rights and religious liberty—paper promises that would soon suffer many violations. The two nations ratified the treaty in March, and on June 12 American forces left Mexico City.

About 13,000 Americans had died in the war—1,733 on the battlefield, most of the rest from disease. Thousands more Mexicans died in battle than did Americans, though the precise number is not known. The *Whig Intelligencer* commented that the $15 million payment to Mexico showed "we take nothing by conquest. . . . Thank God." But since Mexico had refused to sell its Far North at any price before the war, and was persuaded to do so only under threat of continued occupation, many people then and since have regarded the Mexican–American War as a war of conquest.

The transfer of land from Mexico to the United States was not yet over. In 1853, in what became known as the Gadsden Purchase, American foreign minister James Gadsden convinced Mexico to sell 30,000 square miles in what is now southern Arizona and New Mexico, a region coveted for its mineral wealth and potential as a railroad route. The Gadsden Purchase, for which Mexico received $10 million, established the present-day boundary in that region between Mexico and the United States. The Mexican president who negotiated the transaction was none other than Santa Anna, back again from exile and in need of cash. The purchase once again disgraced Santa Anna and contributed to his being yet again forced out of power, this time for good.

# Border Disputes with Britain

In its first seventy years, the United States' boundaries were constantly changing, and disputes with other countries also claiming parts of the continent were predictable. In the Northeast, the border between New Brunswick and Maine had been left indistinct by the Treaty of Paris (1783), creating ongoing disagreements between the United States and Great Britain. Subsequent treaties and arbitration failed to clarify the border question. In 1839, fighting broke out along the Aroostook River between Canadian loggers and the Maine militia. The skirmishes, known as the Aroostook War, were quickly halted by a truce. The matter was settled for good when Secretary of State Daniel Webster negotiated the Webster–Ashburton Treaty of 1842 that set the boundaries between Maine and New Brunswick as well as between Wisconsin Territory and Canada.

Meanwhile, Oregon had been under joint British and American occupation since 1824, but the situation became increasingly unacceptable to westward-migrating Americans who believed it was their manifest destiny to extend their country and culture across the continent. By 1844, presidential candidate James K. Polk was leading the call for "Fifty-four Forty or Fight"—claiming all Oregon territory up to the latitude 54°40' (the Alaska boundary). However, with the Mexican–American War looming, the need for peaceful compromise became paramount. Consequently, as president he entered into negotiations with Great Britain that culminated in an 1846 treaty setting the northern border of U.S.-owned Oregon at the 49th parallel. With its northern boundaries established on both coasts, the young nation truly stretched "from sea to shining sea."

**OREGON TERRITORY** Despite James K. Polk's popular calls for American possession of the entire Oregon Territory up to latitude 54°40' (the Alaska boundary), the Oregon Treaty of 1846 set the border at the 49th parallel.

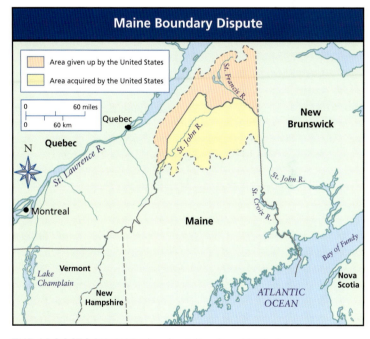

**THE AROOSTOOK WAR** The short-lived and little-known Aroostook War of 1839 was a series of border skirmishes between the Maine militia and Canadian loggers. The Webster-Ashburton Treaty of 1842 set permanent boundaries between Maine and New Brunswick, as well as between New Hampshire and Canada and between Wisconsin Territory and Canada.

*"That an end is put to the wholesale murder in Mexico is truly just cause for rejoicing . . . but we are not the people to rejoice; we ought rather blush and hang our heads in shame."*

—FREDERICK DOUGLASS

# Chapter 13: A Changing Nation

In 1789, when Samuel Slater, a cotton spinner's apprentice with ambition and a good memory, slipped out of England and came to the United States, he set in motion a profound shift in American economic life. When he arrived in the United States, economic life in the still young republic was centered around agriculture, as it had been for generations. Most Americans worked the land, as small farmers, plantation owners, servants or slaves. Others worked as artisans, producing specific items by hand.

Because it was a crime to carry plans for English manufacturing equipment out of the country, Slater had memorized the designs of England's most modern and carefully guarded textile machinery rather than write them down. After arriving in New York, Slater moved to Pawtucket, Rhode Island, where he worked with two machinists and a wheelwright to make an intricate Arkwright spinning frame. In 1790, the equipment went into operation at Slater's mill—turning out spindles of cotton yarn. By the early years of the nineteenth century, the technology had spread like wildfire—one Pittsburgh factory was selling carding machines, drawing frames, spinning mules with up to 200 spindles, and twisting frames for yarn stockings. Cotton mills sprouted up everywhere in southern New England. In 1807, there were fifteen or twenty mills with 8,000 spindles. In 1810, the number had climbed to 90 mills and 80,000 spindles. By 1820, more than 190,000 spindles were in use. America's industrial revolution had begun.

## America's Industrial Revolution

Slater's arrival coincided with the first year of George Washington's presidency. During Washington's first term, the views of his two most important advisors, Thomas Jefferson and Alexander Hamilton clashed frequently. For Jefferson, a national economy based around self-sufficient small farmers would be an economy free of European domination. America's vast western lands—which Jefferson would greatly expand during his own presidency—would serve, he believed, as a great democratizing agent, as small farmers would find plentiful lands for all as the nation expanded.

To Hamilton, however, the United States may have gained its political independence, but it was economically dependent on Europe. Hamilton saw America's future not on the farms of the South and West but in the finance and commerce of the Northeast.

During his first term, Washington more frequently sided with Hamilton. Yet the direction of the economy was not decided in the halls of government. Instead, it was decided at Samuel Slater's Rhode Island cotton mill. The technology that Slater carried in his head to the United States would reshape the lives of small farmers and all others. While farmers at the close of the eighteenth century might have lived out their days on the land, their children and grandchildren would grow up in an industrialized nation.

**SAMUEL SLATER'S MILL** Samuel Slater's Pawtucket, Rhode Island mill featured an intricate spinning frame that would be used to produce cotton yarn. Slater memorized plans for this technology and brought it to the United States, where it set America's industrial revolution in motion.

### Advances In Technology

Slater's mill was followed in 1793 by Eli Whitney's cotton gin (see Chapter 12), which revolutionized cotton production. By 1798, Whitney had created a new machine, which he used for milling interchangeable weapon parts. By making a metal mold, or a "jig" for most parts of a gun, Whitney could use less skilled metalworkers rather than experienced gunsmiths to hand tool the mechanisms. In this way, each part of the each gun would be a duplicate of the same part in another gun. Although Whitney did not originate the idea of interchangeable parts, his work advanced the new field of factory production. When his mill in New Haven, Connecticut was completed, it was deemed a model of efficiency and was widely copied. By 1810, 140 American factories were pouring out 40,000 firearms a year.

Commerce and industrial development took another leap forward due to the efforts of Robert Fulton. The son of poor Irish

*R. Fulton*

*From the original painting by Chappel in the possession of the publishers*

*Johnson Fry & Co. Publishers, New York*

**FULTON AND HIS FOLLY** By building a steamship capable of traveling the Hudson River from New York City to Albany at a speed of 5 miles per hour Robert Fulton's steamship helped to revolutionize transportation in America.

United States. Hamilton was correct that the fate of the United States was still to a large degree dependent on the capitals of Europe. In 1807, as Fulton was steaming his way into the history books, the Jefferson administration was pushing for a total ban on American shipping trade with Britain and France as a misguided means of remaining neutral in the ongoing Napoleonic Wars between Britain and France. The Embargo Act of 1807 proved to be a disaster, particularly for New England merchants, shipbuilders and mariners. Although James Madison, Jefferson's successor, attempted to chart a similar course of neutrality, both Britain and France continued to interfere with American merchant ships. By 1812, the War of 1812, often known as the Second War of American Independence, was all but inevitable.

Following the war with Great Britain, the United States faced a considerable economic challenge. Although the war helped the United States break from its economic dependence on Europe, Great Britain's process of industrialization remained far ahead of that of the United States. With trade restrictions between the United States and Britain lifted with peace, inexpensive British goods flooded into the United States. Hundreds of nascent American industries found it impossible to compete with low British prices and were forced into collapse.

Meanwhile, the Democratic-Republican Congress had allowed the charter for the First Bank of the United States, founded in the 1790s, to expire in 1811. At the same time, hundreds of new commercial banks, particularly in new western states like Ohio, Tennessee and Kentucky, had been founded. Many of these wildcat banks lacked sufficient specie (gold- or silver-backed currency) to support increasingly risky and speculative loan policies. To address the problem, Madison and the Democratic-Republicans reversed course in 1816 and supported the creation of the Second Bank of the United States. In 1819, directors of the Second Bank ordered that state banks redeem their notes from commercial banks in specie. A wave of foreclosures, commercial bank failures, and unemployment, coupled with slumps in agriculture and manufacturing, swept the country.

Proposals to address the crisis were varied and contradictory. Northern manufacturers favored an increase in tariffs to restrain the sale of cheap foreign-made goods; Southern planters favored a reduction in tariffs since they believed that free trade would stimulate the economy and increase demand. Some proposed suspending specie payment, while others favored even tighter enforcement of it. Some sought relief for debtors while others wanted stricter enforcement of anti-debt laws. Finally, a growing number of westerners favored the abolition of the Second Bank. By 1824, the crisis had ended, and gradual growth returned to the U.S. economy. The transformation of the American economy from agricultural to industrial, though a sometimes painful transition, was now permanent.

### The First Railroads

Among the most important innovations brought about by steam power was the steam locomotive. In 1830, New York industrialist Peter Cooper built a steam-powered locomotive, called the *Tom Thumb*, as an experiment for the Baltimore and Ohio Railroad,

immigrants, Fulton had little education, but possessed a sharp gift for mechanics and engineering. Among his early inventions were machines for spinning flax, sawing marble, and making rope. He also invented a power shovel for digging canals and an inclined plane for raising and lowering canal boats. In 1802, Fulton was commissioned by Robert Livingston, the U.S. Minister to France, to build a commercially practical steamship. In 1807, his boat *Clermont* steamed up the Hudson River from New York to Albany and back at a top speed of 5 miles per hour. By demonstrating the efficiency of steam power for navigation, Fulton helped usher in a new era of transportation.

### The Panic of 1819

Jefferson and Hamilton had both been right about certain aspects of the American economy. Jefferson was correct that the American interior would provide an impetus for tremendous growth for the

## Early American Railroads, 1850–1860

**AMERICAN RAILS** The introduction and expansion of a network of railroads ended the era in which canals were the main system of transportation in the United States.

which was founded that year and carried passengers in horse-drawn cars. In a race against a horse-drawn car, the Tom Thumb lost, but only because of mechanical trouble. Even so, it proved that steam-powered transportation was possible both on water and on land. Later that year, the South Carolina Canal and Railroad Company opened the first genuine railroad; its steam locomotive *Best Friend* pulled a train of cars that could carry passengers a full six miles.

By the mid-1830s, small railroads had been established all over the East Coast. By the end of the decade, there were railroads in almost every state in the Union—almost 3,000 miles of track. But these early railroads were short in length and served mainly to carry passengers and freight between neighboring cities or to waterways. During the next decade, as mileage was added, and more and more cities were linked, the rail-

roads developed into a major industry.

Almost 10,000 miles of track existed at the beginning of the 1850s, when the development of a reliable, standard locomotive made travel easier. During the next several years, railroads began to build longer "trunk" lines, connecting distant cities with each other and with important waterways. By the end of the decade, it was possible to get all the way from the East Coast to the major western waterways of the west by rail; railroads connected New York City to the Great Lakes and the cities of Pittsburgh, Pennsylvania and Wheeling, West Virginia, to the Ohio River.

### Growing Urban Centers

Most Americans, whether in the North, South or West, lived in rural communities during the early nineteenth century. At the same time, the industrialization of the

American economy during this time led to the growth of old colonial financial centers and port cities of the eastern seaboard, like Boston, New York and Philadelphia. The completion of the Erie Canal made New York City the nation's largest center of commerce and population. With its direct water-route connection to the West, New York held the largest share of the nation's import-export business as it still does today.

Industrialization also led to the development of smaller cities centered around abundant sources of water power, such as waterfalls and river rapids. These all-important water sources powered textile and other manufacturing mills in cities like Wilmington, Delaware, Trenton, New Jersey and Lowell, Massachusetts. Mill owners in these cities worked to attract farm girls as a labor source by promoting their factory towns as something akin to a finishing school. Instruction in social manners and foreign languages were offered to workers after hours, and parents were promised that their daughters would be strictly supervised—both while at work in the factory and at local boarding houses where the young women often lived. Thousands of young women accepted jobs in mills in order to learn a trade and be self-supporting.

Once a young woman accepted a position in a factory, she quickly learned that she had little control over her life. Employers assumed almost complete control over employees. Those young women whose work days were limited to 10 hours were among the lucky few.

Finally a number of cities in the West also developed in the decades after the Erie and other canals went into operation. Cities like Chicago, St. Louis, Pittsburgh and Detroit had long been major transportation hubs. During the early nineteenth century, Chicago became the most important of these cities, developing into the region's leading commercial center.

### Irish and German Immigration

In the first 50 years after the Constitution went into effect in 1789, the population of the United States ballooned at a greater rate than it has ever since. During that period, the population grew more than fourfold, from 3,929,214 in 1790, the year of the first census, to 17,069,453 in 1840. (By comparison, the population grew less than twofold from 1890 to 1940.)

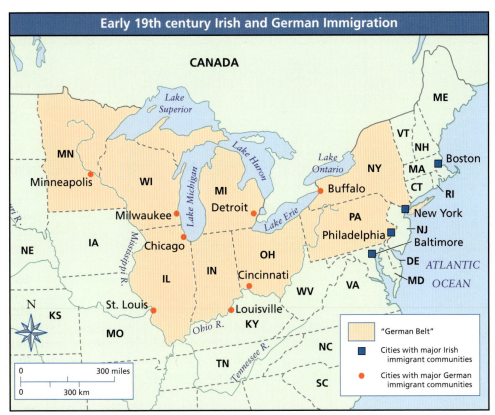

**Early 19th century Irish and German Immigration**

CANADA

Legend:
- "German Belt"
- ■ Cities with major Irish immigrant communities
- ● Cities with major German immigrant communities

**IRISH AND GERMAN IMMIGRANTS**
The 2.2 million Irish and Germans that came between 1845 and 1854 were equal to 10 percent of the U.S. population in 1850.

*"I am now in a fair way bettering myself, but I will tell you . . . that I have suffered more than I thought I could endure, in a strange Country far from a friend . . . [The experience] may serve me for the remainder of my life."*

—IRISH IMMIGRANT, 1852

This growth occurred despite relatively low immigration from 1790 to 1820, when Great Britain sharply restricted emigration and European wars hampered transatlantic shipping. After 1820 immigration began to grow, particularly from Ireland, which was wracked with overpopulation and poverty; and, in the 1830s, from Germany, where the Industrial Revolution was displacing farmworkers.

Natural increase made up the rest of the population growth: a large percentage of Americans were young people starting families, and those families were big. The average woman in 1800 gave birth to about seven children, and since mortality rates were declining, many of those children lived to have children of their own. With the nation's gross area doubling from 891,000 square miles in 1790 to 1.8 million square miles in 1840, most Americans believed there was plenty of land for all.

Despite the seemingly endless supply of land, most immigrants did not have enough money to purchase land. Poorer Irish and German immigrants had little choice but to remain in eastern cities and search for work. By 1860, as many as one third of all Americans living in the Northeast were immigrants. The Irish, who had fled famine and poverty at home, made up the largest single immigrant group in the Northeast. They also made up significant populations in cities in other regions, such as New Orleans.

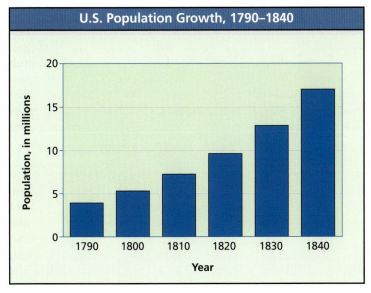

**U.S. Population Growth, 1790–1840**

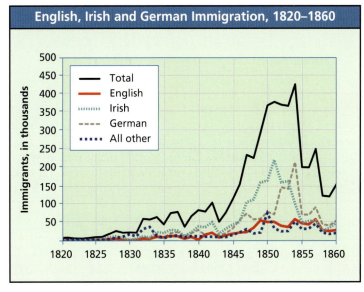

**English, Irish and German Immigration, 1820–1860**

Legend:
- Total
- English
- Irish
- German
- All other

**IMPACT OF IMMIGRATION** Although the total U.S. population climbed steadily between 1790 and 1840, German, Irish, and to a lesser extent, English immigration to the United States during the 1840s and 1850s was responsible for an even more rapid increase.

## Five Most Populous States, 1790–1840

**1790**
1. Virginia
2. Pennsylvania
3. North Carolina
4. Massachusetts
5. New York

**1800**
1. Virginia
2. Pennsylvania
3. New York
4. North Carolina
5. Massachusetts

**1810**
1. New York
2. Virginia
3. Pennsylvania
4. North Carolina
5. Massachusetts

**1820**
1. New York
2. Pennsylvania
3. Virginia
4. North Carolina
5. Ohio

**1830**
1. New York
2. Pennsylvania
3. Virginia
4. Ohio
5. North Carolina

**1840**
1. New York
2. Pennsylvania
3. Ohio
4. Virginia
5. Tennessee

**A SHIFTING POPULATION** Whereas the most populous states in 1790 were all among the original thirteen colonies hugging the Atlantic seaboard, by 1840, Ohio and Tennessee had surpassed North Carolina and Massachusetts in population. The nation's most populous cities underwent a similar shift, as newer western cities like St. Louis, Chicago, and Buffalo topped established eastern ones like Salem, Providence, and Richmond.

## Ten Most Populous Cities, 1810–1860

**1810**
1. New York
2. Philadelphia
3. Baltimore
4. Boston
5. Charleston
6. New Orleans
7. Salem
8. Providence
9. Richmond
10. Albany

**1860**
1. New York
2. Philadelphia
3. Baltimore
4. Boston
5. Charleston
6. New Orleans
7. St. Louis
8. Chicago
9. Buffalo
10. Newark

### Strains to the Public Health

As the populations of American cities grew, so too did strains to the public health system. During the early nineteenth century, public sanitation was primitive at best. Only the wealthy could afford running water, which meant many poorer residents had no toilets. Diseases such as cholera, malaria, and yellow fever were common, particularly in slum areas where poorer immigrants lived. In New Orleans, for example, Irish immigrants lived along the waterfront, and worked in construction, digging canals in steaming hot weather, standing in stagnant water. And because much of New Orleans is actually below sea level, such work usually was performed amid swarms of mosquitoes. As the *London Illustrated News* wrote in the summer of 1853 about an epidemic of yellow fever in the city, "New Orleans has been built upon a site that only madness or commercial lust could have tempted men to occupy."

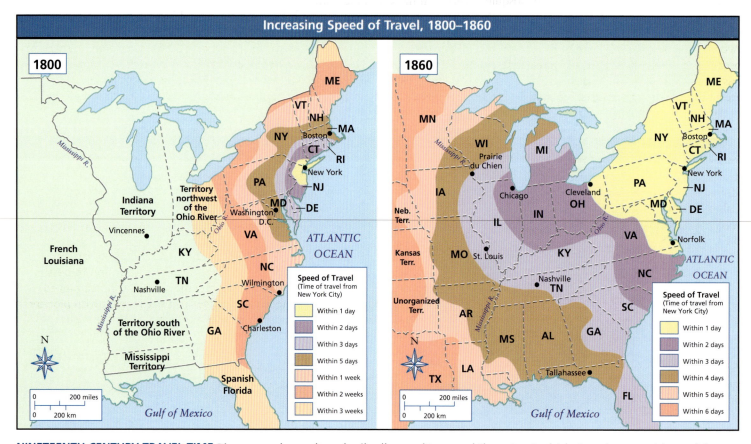

**Increasing Speed of Travel, 1800–1860**

**NINETEENTH CENTURY TRAVEL TIME** Rivers, canals, roads and rails all served to speed the rate at which Americans could travel from one section of the country to another.

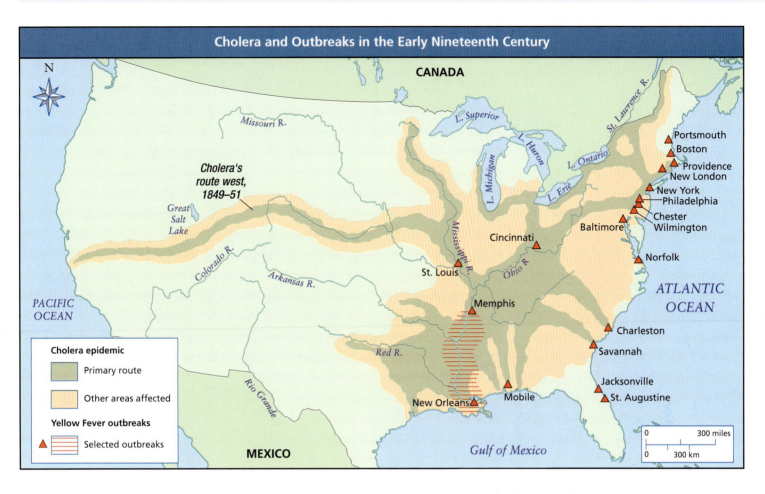

## Cholera and Outbreaks in the Early Nineteenth Century

**Cholera epidemic**
- Primary route
- Other areas affected

**Yellow Fever outbreaks**
- ▲ Selected outbreaks

Because their work and their waterfront neighborhoods exposed them more frequently to mosquitoes carrying the yellow fever virus, the New Orleans' immigrants were blamed for spreading the disease. According to the *Orleanian*, the Irish were falling ill only because they were "poor—reckless and indifferent . . . less cautious and careful of themselves than those that are habituated to our summers." Some lifelong residents of the city argued that New Orleans would have no diseases if outsiders had just stayed away.

Cities like New Orleans, Philadelphia, St. Louis, and Pittsburgh, served as transportation hubs, and diseases that broke out in those cities often spread elsewhere rapidly along river routes and other byways. During the California Gold Rush, for example, a major outbreak of cholera spread along the wagon trail route west across the Great Plains and Rocky Mountains.

# The Growth of the Slave System

Eli Whitney's invention of the cotton gin revolutionized the cotton industry and sent the demand throughout the South for slave labor skyrocketing. From the South Atlantic coast to the fields of East Texas and beyond, cotton became king.

Between 1800 and 1860, cotton production doubled every ten years. By the latter year, the American

South was producing two-thirds of the world's supply. At the same time, cotton exports were worth double the amount of all other goods and crops exported by the United States. Although of paramount importance, cotton was not the only commercial crop grown in the slave South. Rivaling the spectacular growth of cotton—although on a much smaller geographic scale—was sugar. Primarily grown in Louisiana, sugar production multiplied fivefold between 1800 and 1860. Meanwhile tobacco remained important, with exports doubling between 1790 and 1860, even though its percentage within the total exports of the country fell from fifteen to six percent. In short, slavery—and the agricultural commodities it produced—was a very big business in antebellum America.

Production of the commercial crops—sugar, tobacco, rice, and above all cotton—of the South required three critical ingredients: land, capital, and labor. Land, of course, was the foundation. In 1790, the farms and plantations of the South—from Maryland in the north to Georgia in the south—were largely confined to a strip of land between the Atlantic coast and the Appalachian Mountains, although pioneers had begun to settle the future states of Tennessee and Kentucky. Divided into low-lying tidewater and upland piedmont areas (areas by the base of the mountain), the settled territories of the eastern seaboard ranged between fifty and 200 miles in width.

As discussed in Chapter 12, between 1790 and 1840, the federal government and state militias largely cleared the vast territory between the Appalachian

**THE SPREAD OF DISEASE** Poor sanitation in rapidly growing cities helped bring on frequent outbreaks of deadly diseases like cholera and yellow fever. Yellow fever, which is spread by mosquitoes, was a constant threat in port cities along the Atlantic Coast and Mississippi. Cholera, which can be spread by person-to person contact, moved west with pioneers. Cholera was especially deadly to American Indians that came in contact with the settlers, as their bodies had no natural resistance to the disease.

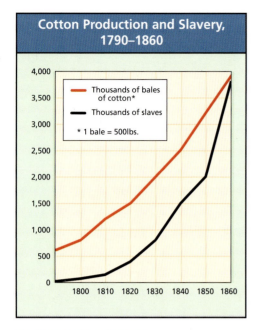

## Cotton Production and Slavery, 1790–1860

Legend:
- Thousands of bales of cotton*
- Thousands of slaves

\* 1 bale = 500lbs.

**COTTON AND SLAVERY** Cotton production was tied closely to slave labor, and as the demand for cotton rose, so too did the demand for slave labor.

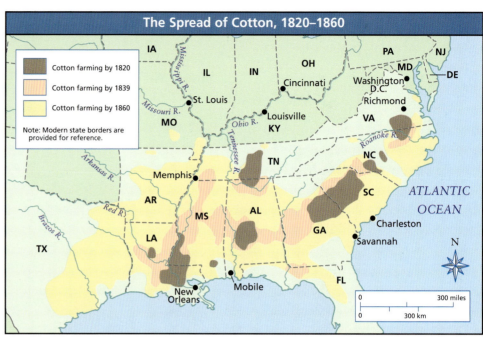

## The Spread of Cotton, 1820–1860

Legend:
- Cotton farming by 1820
- Cotton farming by 1839
- Cotton farming by 1860

Note: Modern state borders are provided for reference.

**A GROWING HARVEST** Although cotton growing had once been limited, the invention of the cotton gin allowed it to spread rapidly across the South by 1860.

*"Trade cannot stagnate here. Industrious and ingenious mechanics must see that the inhabitants of such a country will want houses, furniture, farming utensils, leather, saddles, boots, shoes, etc., and will be able to pay good prices for them. The upper country on the Tennessee and Holston rivers and their branches will afford, at very trifling expense for water carriage down the river, abundant supplies of provisions, iron, lumber, and other raw materials."*

—FROM A FEBRUARY 1818 ADVERTISEMENT FOR LAND IN ALABAMA, PLACED IN A LOCAL SHELBYVILLE, TENNESSEE NEWSPAPER

mountains in the east and the Mississippi and Missouri Rivers in the west of Indian tribes through a series of illegitimate treaties, bloody wars and forced migrations. At the same time, the settlement of former Indian lands in the Old Southwest (Alabama, Arkansas, Mississippi, Louisiana, Tennessee, and the western parts of Georgia and North Carolina) was accelerated by developments in transportation technology. Steam linked the South and West into an integrated economic region based on the Mississippi River and its tributaries, until the development of the railroad network re-oriented trade along an east-west pattern in the 1840s and 1850s. This early economic integration had important political repercussions, creating a South-West alliance in Congress dedicated to the protection of slavery, at least in the South and Old Southwest. (The Old Northwest Territory was declared free under the Northwest Ordinance of 1787, with most new states there banning slavery).

## Financing the Slave System

Meanwhile, former tribal lands in the Old South began to fill up with white farmers and planters determined to expand the cotton empire. And to the hundreds of thousands of square miles of ideal short-staple cotton-

growing land now available, the planters and farmers of the antebellum South now added the two other crucial ingredients previously mentioned—capital and labor. The former came largely from Britain and the northern states. Like all commercial farmers, the cotton growers of the Old South were perpetually in debt, borrowing to meet this year's living and operation expenses against next year's crop. To meet this economic contingency, there arose a financing system stretching as far as New York City and London and linking northern and British money and textile interests with southern farmers and planters. Much of the business was handled by commission merchants or "factors"—some independent and some working directly for northern and English financial interests—who lived in the South and offered a variety of services to planters, including loans, warehousing, and shipping. In addition, these factors helped finance western settlement, providing large loans to cover the first four or five costly years of plantation development. But these services came at a high price. Factors typically skimmed off a fifth to a quarter of the crop in payment. By the 1850s, more than $100 million in cotton profits was annually siphoned off to northern banks, giving major financial centers in the North a direct stake in preserving the slave-based cotton system of the South.

This outside financing was also heavily responsible for supplying the final ingredient in the spread of slavery to the

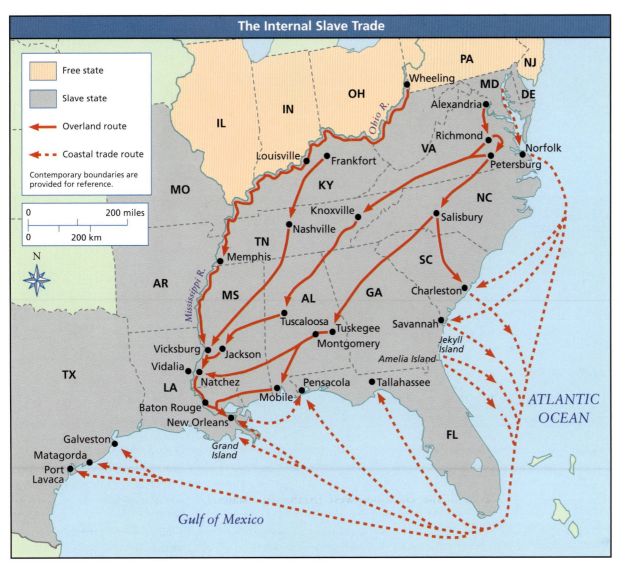

### The Internal Slave Trade

Free state

Slave state

Overland route

Coastal trade route

Contemporary boundaries are provided for reference.

0         200 miles

0         200 km

N

PA
NJ
OH
Wheeling
MD
DE
IN
Alexandria
IL
Richmond
VA
Norfolk
Louisville
Frankfort
Petersburg
MO
KY
NC
Knoxville
Salisbury
Nashville
TN
SC
Memphis
Charleston
AR
MS
AL
GA
Tuscaloosa
Tuskegee
Savannah
Vicksburg
Jackson
Montgomery
Jekyll Island
Vidalia
Amelia Island
TX
LA
Natchez
Pensacola
Tallahassee
Mobile
Baton Rouge
New Orleans
Galveston
Grand Island
FL
Matagorda
Port Lavaca
Gulf of Mexico
ATLANTIC OCEAN
Ohio R.
Mississippi R.

## A BOOMING TRADE

After 1807 when legal U.S. participation in the slave trade was banned, the majority of slaves bought and sold in the American South were born in the United States, and sold—like other possessions— through a vast network of coastal and overland trade routes.

territories of the Old Southwest: labor. New plantations needed new labor forces, and factors helped finance the huge growth in the domestic slave trade between 1820 and 1860. Like many aspects of slavery, the domestic trade and price of slaves was a market-driven phenomenon. With the growth of slavery increasing demand and the abolition of the international slave trade in 1807–1808 reducing supply, the price of slaves began to climb. Indeed, areas of early slave population concentrations along the eastern seaboard began to see rising profits from the sale of slaves, even as their depleted land (both cotton and tobacco drain nutriments from the earth) resulted in decreased productivity. By the 1850s, slave-owners were shipping more than 25,000 slaves from east to west, in the process breaking up African-American families and communities. (Westward expansion was not the only cause for the breakup of slave families and communities, as planters often divided their estates—including their labor force—among various heirs.)

Slave sales represented some of the

**SLAVE AUCTION** Slave auctions were among the cruelest aspects of the American slavery system. Family members, including children, were frequently sold to distant plantations, usually never to be seen again.

121

## The Mormon Trek

CANADA

Lake Superior

Lake Michigan

Lake Huron

Lake Ontario

Lake Erie

**New York**

Fayette

Kirtland

ATLANTIC OCEAN

**Wyoming**

*Great Salt Lake*

**Nebraska**

**Iowa**

Nauvoo
*1839*

**Indiana**

Salt Lake City
*1847*

Liberty
*1831*

Ohio

**Illinois**

N

**Utah**

**Missouri**

PACIFIC OCEAN

MEXICO

| | Proposed State of Deseret |
| --- | --- |
| | Mormon Trail |
| | Migration route |
| *1839* | Date of arrival |

Contemporary boundaries are provided for reference.

0 — 300 miles
0 — 300 km

**MORMON MIGRATION** In 1830, Joseph Smith founded the Mormon Church in upstate New York. After Mormon settlements in Ohio and Missouri were driven out by local opposition, the group moved to Nauvoo, Illinois. After Smith was killed by a mob in 1844, his followers headed west, finally settling near Great Salt Lake. In 1849, Smith's successor, Brigham Young proposed a new state called Deseret, which would have included much of the American Southwest. Congress refused and created the Utah Territory in 1850 instead.

most cruel and frightening moments in an African American's life. Often purchased by slave traders—notorious even among whites for their vicious barbarity—slaves would be shackled and forcibly marched up to hundreds of miles to auction houses, where they were kept in barracks and pens for days, weeks, and months on end. Paraded in front of potential buyers—who poked and prodded them like cattle, often peering into their mouths to check their teeth—slaves were auctioned off to the highest bidder, often with little regard to family and marriage ties. (Some planters—both as buyers and sellers—made a point of keeping families together for fear that breaking them up would produce an unhappy and, hence, unproductive or recalcitrant slave force.)

## Settling the West

By the 1840s, reports from explorers and traders had sparked a massive wave of migration to the American West. Oregon was a favorite destination for many—especially farmers—and the best means for getting there became the Oregon Trail. The Trail did not follow a single route but was spread out over miles of rugged open country, developing many branches and way-stations over the years. For most emigrants, the Oregon Trail began in Independence, Missouri. After following the Santa Fe Trail for the first 40 miles, it took a northwesterly direction along the Platte River, past Fort Laramie (Wyoming) to the Sweetwater River, and west through the Rocky Mountains' South Pass to the Colorado River basin. Travelers then went either southwest to Fort Bridger or west through Sublette's Cutoff to the Bear River, then northwest again to Fort Hall, Idaho, following the Snake River up to Fort Boise. After crossing the Blue Mountains, different routes could be taken to final destinations. For many of the earliest settlers, this was Oregon's Willamette Valley.

The Oregon Trail saw its heaviest use during the 1840s and 1850s. The 2,000-mile trip generally took six months, and approximately one in ten emigrants died along the way. By the 1870s, railroads had displaced wagon trains, and the trail fell into disuse. Portions of it are preserved today by the Oregon National Historic-Trail. Even now one can see its testament in wagon-wheel ruts, the remains of abandoned wagons, and skeletons of horses and cattle.

### The Mormon Trek

In 1830 Joseph Smith Jr. founded the Church of Christ (later the Church of Jesus Christ of the Latter-Day Saints), whose adherents are commonly known as Mormons. Claiming to have received divine instructions, Smith sought to restore the "true church" according to the teachings of Jesus Christ. He quickly attracted followers, and within a few years Mormons were spreading his gospel throughout the United States and overseas. After Smith's assassination in 1844, Brigham Young, who headed the Quorum of the Twelve Apostles, became the church's prophet, or leader. Persecuted for their beliefs and their practices of polygamy and collective ownership, the Mormons were frequently forced to move. In February 1846, under Young's leadership, they left Nauvoo, Illinois, and began a trek through Iowa, Nebraska, Wyoming, and Utah that took them over old Native American trails and parts of the Ox-Bow, Oregon, and California trails. By the time the first band of Mormons arrived in Utah's Salt Lake Valley in July 1847, they had covered 1,297 miles. Over the next twenty-two years, nearly 70,000 Mormons would migrate to Salt Lake City, following the trail blazed by Young and maintained by Mormons. Here the church flourished, and approximately 350 settlements were established in Utah, Idaho, Wyoming, Nevada, Arizona, and California. By the late twentieth century, the church boasted more than 9.7 million members worldwide.

## The California Gold Rush

Although gold had been found in southeastern California as early as 1775, it was the discovery at Sutter's Mill in northern California that set off the most famous stampede of fortune hunters in history. On January 24, 1848, James Marshall—then supervising the construction of a sawmill for his employer, John Sutter—spotted what he quickly realized was gold. Word of the discovery soon leaked out, and before long, local gold seekers were swarming over the area. Nine days after Marshall's discovery, the treaty ending the Mexican–American War was signed, and Mexico ceded over 500,000 square miles of territory to the United States—including California. With the United States in a financial depression, the prospect of making a fortune seemed irresistible. After news of the gold find reached the eastern United States in 1849, the rush intensified. Hopeful treasure hunters migrated to California from all over the country, earning them the name "Forty-Niners." As many as 90,000 Forty-Niners went to the gold fields during a 17-year period. They arrived by land and by sea: traveling by wagon train across the Great Plains; sailing to the Isthmus of Panama and then traversing the jungle to other ships in the Pacific; or sailing around Cape Horn and up the coasts of South and North America.

Many treasure hunters created clubs that allowed them to pool their savings and send representatives into the fields. Similar lotteries were held in other countries. Forty-niners came from as close as Canada and Mexico and from as far away as Chile, England, France, Germany, Norway, Turkey, China, and Australia. Within two years of the discovery of gold

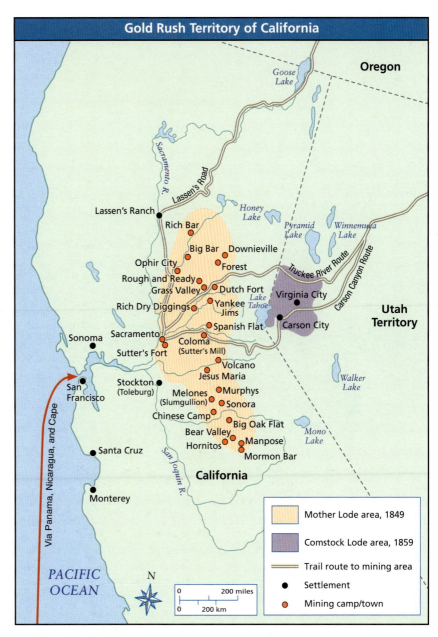

**Gold Rush Territory of California**

Legend:
- Mother Lode area, 1849
- Comstock Lode area, 1859
- Trail route to mining area
- ● Settlement
- ○ Mining camp/town

**SILVER AND GOLD** The discovery of gold near Sutter's Mill in 1848 and silver at the Comstock Lode in present-day Nevada in 1857 led a legion of fortune hunters to the Far West. While most of the old mining camps are long gone, some, such as Sacramento, grew into major cities.

at Sutter's Mill, 58,000 fortune seekers had descended on California from around the globe. By 1854, as many as 24,000 Chinese were working in and around the goldfields. The Chinese sent home stories of the riches to be had in what they called *Gam San*, or "Gold Mountain."

Few of these fortune hunters, however, became rich from their efforts; most suffered tremendous hardships, digging for months and gaining little or nothing. Nevertheless, the gold rush stimulated western migration to such an extent that California's Anglo-American population rose dramatically—while its Mexican and Native American peoples were persecuted, driven out, or put to work in the gold fields.

# Chapter 14: Democracy and Discontent

Andrew Jackson, the nation's seventh president, was the first self-made citizen to be elected president. Born in 1767 in the backwoods settlement of the Waxhaws, South Carolina, Jackson was also the first president not closely associated with the Revolutionary-era founders. (Jackson's predecessor, John Quincy Adams, was the son of the president, and had already spent a lifetime in government service before reaching the presidency.) Prior to becoming president, Jackson had served relatively quiet terms as a Representative and then Senator from Tennessee, among other government posts. But he was best known as the hero of the Battle of New Orleans, and more temperamentally suited for military command than political compromise. When his name first began circulating as early as 1816 as a possible future president, Jackson was quick to disavow the attention. "I know what I am fit for," he said. "I can command a body of men in a rough way; but I am not fit to be president."

By 1824, he had reconsidered. In the first popular presidential election—in which all white men, regardless of their status as property-owners, were allowed to vote—Jackson won more popular votes and electoral votes than John Quincy Adams, or the two other candidates, Senators Henry Clay and William Crawford. But he did not win an electoral majority as required by the Constitution. Thus, the election was thrown into the House of Representatives, where Clay threw his support to Adams, guaranteeing Adams the presidency and the enduring anger of the western frontiersmen who made up the core of Jackson's support.

To the eastern establishment, who feared the hero of New Orleans could become an American Napoleon, Jackson's near victory was alarming. But his supporters formed the Democratic Party for the express purpose of seeing Jackson run again—and win the 1828 election. When the rematch between Jackson and the unpopular Adams came, Jackson won convincingly. His popularity was such that, at the reception following his inauguration, the White House was nearly wrecked by his supporters' robust celebrations. Jackson himself was forced to flee the White House to avoid the danger.

While fears that he would seek the power of a Napoleon were unfounded, the dynamic, plain-spoken, and temperamental Jackson exercised more executive power than all previous presidents combined. Using the veto with great frequency, he put the presidency on an equal footing with Congress—a balance that had been lost during the John Quincy Adams administration. Although Jackson frequently argued that his vetoes were made on constitutional grounds, he largely governed by instinct: if he disagreed with a congressional action, he moved to block it.

At the same time, Jackson was a fierce defender of the Union. In one of the most dramatic incidents of his presidency, he nearly sent troops into South Carolina after states rights advocates, led by John C. Calhoun, Jackson's own vice-president, argued that states had the right to ignore or nullify federal laws that contradicted the laws of a state. He was also an avid expansionist, ordering thousands of Indians from their tribal homelands in the Southeast to clear the land for white settlers.

## Jacksonian Democracy

Andrew Jackson's rise could not have happened without an expansion of voting rights during the 1820s. Prior to 1824, the ideal that every individual should have an equal voice in government was not reflected in practice. When the Constitution was drafted in 1787, all of the original thirteen states excluded poorest citizens from voting: ten states required a certain amount of property; three required payment of a tax.

The Constitution left the question of who should have suffrage, or the right to vote, to the states. But within those states, clamor grew in the late eighteenth and early nineteenth centuries for expansion of suffrage to all adult white males, regardless of economic status. The demand was loudest on the frontier, where egalitarian spirit was especially strong. No states admitted to the Union after the original thirteen required property for voting, and only a few required a tax. This example put pressure on the older states, which abolished all property qualifications by 1860, with five retaining tax requirements. (While states were enacting white male suffrage, they tightened other requirements, setting residency and age qualifications and excluding criminals, the mentally ill, African Americans, and women.)

### "The Common Man"

Jackson's brand of politics, with its appeal to ordinary white men, became known as Jacksonian Democracy. Behind his forcefulness —and the public's support for him—lay a growing antipathy for the moneyed class. Jackson's destruction of the Second Bank of the United States was based less on economic considerations than on his perception that the bank was a tool of the eastern moneyed establishment.

Jackson's attitude was in keeping with the egalitarian fervor that swept the nation during the 1820s and 1830s. Many Americans came to believe that the United States had a special destiny, where men would govern themselves, live in harmony with the laws of nature and

**ANDREW JACKSON**

War hero, Indian fighter, and symbol of the emerging "Common Man" in American political life, Andrew Jackson dominated his age, and reshaped the powers of the presidency.

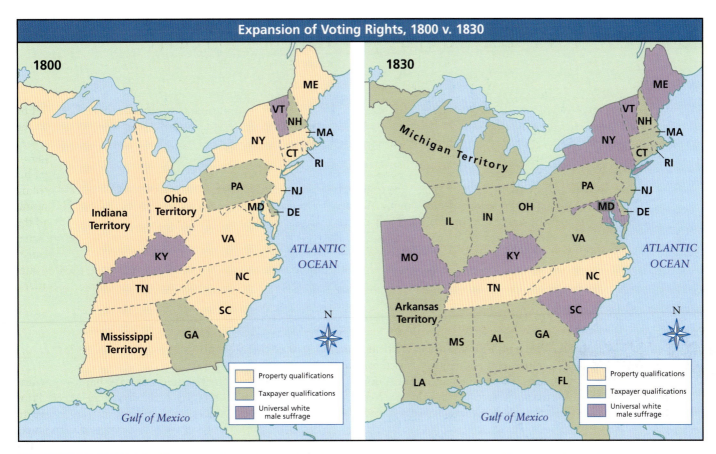

## Expansion of Voting Rights, 1800 v. 1830

**1800**

ME
VT
NH
MA
NY
CT
RI
PA
NJ
Ohio
Territory
MD
DE
Indiana
Territory
VA
KY
ATLANTIC
OCEAN
NC
TN
SC
Mississippi
Territory
GA

Property qualifications
Taxpayer qualifications
Universal white
male suffrage

*Gulf of Mexico*

N

**1830**

Michigan Territory
ME
VT
NH
MA
NY
CT
RI
IL
IN
OH
PA
NJ
MD
DE
MO
KY
VA
ATLANTIC
OCEAN
Arkansas
Territory
TN
NC
SC
MS
AL
GA
LA
FL

Property qualifications
Taxpayer qualifications
Universal white
male suffrage

*Gulf of Mexico*

N

**EXTENDING THE FRANCHISE** During the 1820s and 1830s, a growing number of states ended restrictions of white male voting rights. At the same time, women and minorities would continue to wait.

## Jackson and the Second Bank of the United States

THE DOWNFALL OF MOTHER BANK.

**"THE DOWNFALL OF MOTHER BANK"** In this cartoon, Andrew Jackson refuses to renew the charter of the Bank of the United States, choosing to remove all government funds from the bank and to deposit them in state banks around the country.

The Bank of the United States was a controversial institution from its inception in 1791, with Thomas Jefferson and others maintaining that the Constitution did not grant Congress the authority to create a central bank. This argument and anti-bank interests prevailed when its twenty-year charter failed to be renewed in 1811. However, following the financial chaos created by the War of 1812, a new bank was chartered in 1816. Under Nicholas Biddle's management the bank prospered—and became too powerful, according to state banks and frontiersmen who, like Andrew Jackson, felt it operated solely in the interests of wealthy eastern businessmen. Encouraged by Senator Henry Clay, Biddle applied to renew the bank's charter in 1832, but President Jackson vetoed the bill, thus pitting himself against Biddle and Clay. Interpreting his re-election that same year as a mandate, he set out to bring the bank down—and succeeded.

| GROWTH OF NEWSPAPERS, 1783–1880 | |
|---|---|
| **YEAR** | **NEWSPAPERS IN CIRCULATION** |
| 1783 | 43 |
| 1814 | 346 |
| 1850 | 2,526 |
| 1880 | 11,314 |

eradicate social injustice or inequality. Unlike the monarchies of Europe, the United States, in this hopeful view, was a nation based on the good judgement of the "Common Man" rather than the dictates of the elite.

During the early nineteenth century, any and all social or political institutions that smacked of elitism came under fire. Elite professions such as the law and medicine found themselves on the defensive. By the 1830s, most states made local judges stand for election by the people, rather than be appointed by a politician. To widen the number of lawyers and doctors, many states even did away with rules requiring special training, allowing men with no prior understanding of the legal system to offer legal services for hire and allowing alternative medical practitioners—many of them women—to prescribe concoctions of herbs, roots or alcohol on an equal footing with more orthodox treatments.

# Religion and Reform

The impulse for social change in the early nineteenth century was infused with religious overtones, and those who led the fight for reform in many areas of American life were almost always deeply religious. During this era, two major and vastly different trends in Protestantism helped stimulate the desire for reform. The first was religious liberalism and the second evangelical revivalism.

### Deism and the Decline of Orthodox Calvinism
During the Great Awakening of the mid-1700s, the Congregationalist Church in New England split into two factions, known as the "New Lights" and "Old Lights." The leading figure among the New Lights was Northampton's charismatic minister Jonathan Edwards. Edwards preached a strict brand of Calvinism to his rural western Massachusetts flock, emphasizing the power of personal salvation in saving the sinner from damnation. To Edwards, God was an omnipotent presence in the daily lives of impotent humans. Those who were saved felt an emotional and sometimes physical connection to the spirit of God.

The Old Light Congregationalists, on the other hand, disavowed such emotionalism. As Charles Chauncy, the leading Old Light figure in Boston, scoffed about the New Lights, "Nay, [hasn't it] been common in some Parts of the Land, and among some Sorts of People, to express their religious Joy by singing through the Streets, and in Ferry Boats?" To Old Lights, such emotional displays were to

be discouraged in favor of more "rational" behavior. In keeping with the age of the Enlightenment, Old Lights reassessed Calvinist theology and disavowed many of its core principles. For example, Old Lights rejected the doctrine of predestination, in which the vast majority of humanity was condemned to Hell while a small number of predetermined souls were saved for Heaven. Instead, they argued that human action determined one's eternal fate, and that humankind was essentially good, not sinful. Some eighteenth-century New England preachers also embraced Arianism, which rejected the divinity of Jesus Christ, and Socinianism, which rejected both predestination and the Holy Trinity.

To many of the founding fathers of the American Revolution, such as Jefferson, Franklin, and Thomas Paine, this new theological thinking—more rational and more humanistic—proved attractive. All three men withdrew from more traditional churches and embraced Deism, which held that God had created the universe according to a specific set of natural laws, and that having done so, had withdrawn to let it run its course. If the universe ran according to natural laws, so the Deist belief ran, then human behavior could be modeled on natural laws as well. Thus, the American and French revolutions, which emphasized respect for the natural rights of the individual and the capacity for human beings to improve themselves and their world, were rooted in the liberal theology of Deism. As Paine himself wrote, "I believe in the equality of man, and I believe that religious duties consist in doing justice–loving mercy, and endeavoring to make our fellow creatures happy."

### Unitarians and Trancendentalists
While Deists generally abandoned organized Christianity altogether, by the early nineteenth century other religious liberals influenced a shift in theology from within established congregations. William Ellery Channing, minister of Boston's First Federal Church, became involved in a controversy that split New England Congregationalism. In 1819, Channing delivered a sermon in Baltimore entitled "Unitarian Christianity," where he laid out the intellectual foundations of American Unitarianism. Channing stressed the importance of the individual human conscience in guiding one's actions. Linking liberal religion with humanitarian reform, Unitarians stressed the importance of working for the betterment of humanity in this life over preparing the way for life in the next.

In theology, Unitarians emphasized humankind's God-given rational powers. Endowed with free will, man was charged with drawing his own conclusions about the material and spiritual world. According to Channing:

> If reason be so dreadfully darkened by the fall that its decisive judgements on religion are unworthy of trust, then Christianity, and even natural theology, must be abandoned: for the existence and veracity of God, and the divine original of Christianity, are conclusions of reason and must stand or fall with it.

**WILLIAM ELLERY CHANNING**

**RALPH WALDO EMERSON**

**HENRY DAVID THOREAU**

In applying the test of reason to Calvinist theology, Unitarians rejected such bedrock principles as the Holy Trinity, the divinity of Jesus Christ, original sin, and predestination, in favor of a single unifying God, a human Jesus whose life individuals should emulate, and a world populated with human beings who are born essentially good and are able to bring progress to the world through the application of free will.

As benign as Unitarian theology appeared, it was not without critics. Like Old Light Congregationalism and Deism with which it shared its roots, Unitarianism was sometimes seen as a religion of Boston's urban, intellectual elite. Critics argued that the Unitarian emphasis on reason over all other senses lent it a cold and passionless formality.

Among those critics was the essayist Ralph Waldo Emerson, a Unitarian minister who had resigned his pulpit in 1832 because he believed that Unitarianism had forsaken the life of the spirit in its concern for people's material well-being. The foremost American intellectual of his era, Emerson urged people to look beyond reason and experience to the emotion and intuition inside the self for spiritual truth. While he shared with the Unitarian establishment the belief that individuals should strive to improve the material conditions of their fellow human beings, the impulse for reform must be found in the spirit rather than in the mind. "To acquaint a man with himself," he argued, was to instill "reverence" for self and others, which would in turn inspire the desire for social change. He wrote,

What is man born for but to be a Reformer, a Re-maker of what man has made; a renouncer of lies; a restorer of truth and good, imitating that great Nature which embosoms us all, and which sleeps no moment on an old past, but every hour repairs herself, yielding to us every morning a new day, and with every pulsation a new life.

If the seeds of rationalist Unitarianism lay in eighteenth-century Enlightenment thought, Emerson was also influenced by the Romantic movement of the early nineteenth century. Even as Emerson argued that Americans should cast off the European intellectual tradition, he shared much with leading European Romantics such as Kant, Hegel, Carlyle, and Wordsworth. For these writers, experience and reason could only reveal a portion of the truth. The instinctual, emotional man—the "Common Man"—was favored over the rational elite.

At the same time, Emerson fostered a uniquely American brand of literature and thought. In 1836, he moved to Concord, Massachusetts, where his home became the gathering place for a small circle of like-minded intellectuals, including Theodore Parker, Henry David Thoreau, Amos Bronson Alcott, George Ripley and Margaret Fuller. Because the group shared the belief that individuals could transcend experience to find truth in intuition, Emerson's Concord neighbors were dubbed the Transcendentalist Club. The great American novelists Nathaniel Hawthorne and Herman Melville were also regular visitors to Emerson's home.

In 1841, George Ripley founded a cooperative community called Brook Farm to put transcendentalist philosophy into daily practice. The community's 200 residents, which for a time included Hawthorne, supported themselves through farming, teaching and making clothing. The experiment lasted until 1847, when a fire destroyed the community's main building.

At the same time that the Brook Farm experiment in communal living was taking place, another trancendentalist undertook an experiment in solitary living. From 1845 to 1847, Henry David Thoreau lived in a small hut at Walden Pond, on the outskirts of Concord. Convinced that "the mass of men live lives of quiet desperation," Thoreau wanted to see if it was possible to live truly free, as close to nature as possible. "I went into the woods, because I wanted to live deliberately, to confront only the essential facts of life, and to see if I could learn what it had to teach, and not, when I came to die, discover that I had not lived." In 1846, while at Walden, Thoreau refused to pay a one dollar poll tax in order to protest the Polk administration's war against Mexico. Thoreau was jailed—though for just one night—since to his great disappointment a relative paid his tax. Nonetheless, the arrest inspired him to write his landmark essay "Civil Disobedience." In it, he argued that the moral individual was duty-bound to protest government laws that came in conflict with moral laws.

### The Second Great Awakening

As influential as the Unitarian and transcendentalist movements came to be, the number of followers committed to each remained relatively small. Most Americans still believed in original sin, in the Holy Trinity, and in the active hand of both God and the Devil in day-to-day life. While an educated, relatively well-off man like Thoreau could make the conscious decision to go live in the woods, he did so knowing that a hot meal could be had should he just head into town to his friend Emerson's household. To Americans living on the frontier, or in one of the nation's overcrowded and unsanitary slums, suffering was a daily fact of life. Epidemics like cholera could kill off one's children swiftly and virtually without warning. To make sense of this suffering, and the ever-present nearness of death, many Americans actively sought comfort and salvation from a God who offered a better life in the next world.

Nonetheless, by the early nineteenth century, some of the sharp edges of the old Calvinist theology had softened. In the optimistic early 1800s, God came to be seen increasingly as a benevolent father who granted the opportunity for conversion to all believers rather than just the elect. Thus, a number of Protestant denominations went through a period of enormous growth. In particular, Presbyterians, Baptists and Methodists won converts by the thousands.

One of the main factors behind this growth was the revival meeting. In 1801, some 25,000 men, women and children poured into the tiny settlement of Cane Ridge, Kentucky for a religious camp meeting that lasted a full week. Baptist, Methodist and other ministers traded turns at the pulpit. Similar revivals popped up elsewhere in Kentucky and the Ohio Valley, each with itinerant preachers exhorting the masses to abandon their drinking, gambling, or otherwise sinful ways.

In 1830, a Presbyterian minister with no formal training named Charles G. Finney sparked what came to be called the Second Great Awakening. Between September 1830 and March 1831 alone, Finney traveled the countryside, preaching a total of ninety-eight sermons, sometimes as many as three a day. Some of his revivals lasted from 6 A.M. to late into the night. So many people once packed into a church where Finney was preaching that the building nearly collapsed under the weight.

One of Finney's most effective methods of spreading the word was a technique called "the anxious seat." Keeping benches at the front of the church empty at the start of his preaching, he asked believers to come forward and "offer themselves up to God, while we make them subjects of prayer." Those in the anxious seats would eventually publicly declare their faith in God, as the rest of the community looked on. Finney's methods were soon adopted at other revivals. In 1832, Frances Trollope,

mother of the English author Anthony Trollope, wrote with alarm about observing the frenzied passion at a woodland revival in Indiana:

> Above a hundred persons, nearly all females, came forward, uttering howlings and groans so terrible that I shall never cease to shudder when I recall them. They appeared to drag each other forward, and on the word being given, "Let us pray," they all fell on their knees; but the posture was soon changed for others that permitted greater scope for the convulsive movement of their limbs; and they were soon all lying on the ground in an indescribable confusion of heads and legs. They threw their limbs about with such incessant violent motion that I was every instant expecting some violent accident to occur.

Although religious doctrines behind the Great Awakening differed greatly from that of Unitarianism and the transcendentalist movement, in many respects they shared a common democratic impulse. Finney's philosophy was in many ways grounded in transcendentalist thought. Although his conception of God may have differed from that of Emerson, Finney also believed that humankind was perfectible, and that all individuals, regardless of race or creed were worthy of receiving God's salvation by tapping the spirit within. Finney lent his support to a wide variety of religious and secular reform movements. In 1835, he joined the faculty of Oberlin College, the first non-segregated, coeducational institution of higher learning in the country. In 1851, he became Oberlin's second president.

## The Temperance Movement

At the height of the Second Great Awakening, religious fervor reached well beyond the church or camp meeting. Schools organized midday prayer sessions, businesses closed early so that employees could go home to pray with their families, and a new concern about the dangers of alcohol gave birth to one of the longest-lived reform efforts in American history: the temperance movement.

One of the earliest and most influential leaders of the temperance movement was the Presbyterian minister Lyman Beecher. At his "continuous revivals," Beecher railed against what he called "ruff-scruff" clergy who tolerated the sins of ostentatious dress, dueling, dancing, stage theatrics and waxworks shows. (He also attacked Roman

Catholicism, and religious tolerance in general, which would indirectly inspire Bostonians to plunder that city's Ursuline Convent in 1831.) Beecher had some of his most profound influence as a moral reformer in the fight against alcohol, helping to shepherd passage of Connecticut blue laws.

Another advocate of temperance was a Finney disciple named Theodore Dwight Weld. Weld was such a powerful speaker that following a lecture in Rochester, New York, Albert and Elijah Smith, the most successful whiskey dealers in Rochester publicly smashed their supply in the streets, vowing never to provide it again.

By today's standards, Americans of the early nineteenth century were, inarguably, heavy drinkers. While the average American adult today consumes under three gallons of pure alcohol a year, in 1820 Americans took in more than seven gallons. Because corn could be easily and cheaply converted to whiskey, small farmers produced a steady flow. At the same time that physicians began to warn of alcohol's physical harm, preachers warned of its spiritual and moral dangers. Women began to speak out about physical abuse and deteriorating finances caused by male intoxication.

In 1826, the American Temperance Society was born. The organization promoted complete abstinence from alcohol. By 1829 222 temperance groups had followed in its wake. By 1835 these groups claimed a total of 1.5 million members. The movement did not end drinking, but it did temper it. By 1840, the per capita consumption of alcohol had fallen to 3 gallons. At the same time, the movement also began to emphasize a new strategy: rather than simply use moral pressure to convince drinkers to abstain, temperance advocates began calling for legal restrictions, and sometimes outright bans on the sale or consumption of alcohol. In 1851, Maine became the first state to pass a prohibition law.

## The Criminal and the Insane

Some of the most far-reaching reform efforts born of the early 19th century involved those on the fringes of society—criminals and the mentally ill. If society was perfectible through moral and social reform, then the institutions dedicated to the mentally ill or criminal members of that society needed reform as well. After the turn of the nineteenth century, a number of states built asylums, reform schools and jails in which to house society's outcasts. Yet the insane and sane, debtors and murderers were often thrown together without thought. In 1841, a Unitarian teacher named Dorothea Dix traveled to the East Cambridge House of Corrections to teach a Bible class. What she found shocked her: imprisoned mental patients, chained, naked and beaten, sometimes in total darkness. Two years later—after visiting every jail and poorhouse in Massachusetts and recording the abysmal conditions at each—Dix presented her findings to the Massachusetts State Legislature and recommended that special hospitals or asylums, staffed by trained professionals, be founded.

Behind Dix's idea was not simply the notion that the mentally ill be treated more humanely. Rather, she and other reformers believed that all human beings, including the poor, the mentally ill and even the criminal, had an inherent dignity, and that by reforming society's institutions, even the most hardened criminal could be rehabilitated.

Although the penitentiary movement reflected this belief, its results were not always satisfying. Much thought went into designing the proper prison design. One prison in Auburn, New York, featuring tiny rectangular cells and common work rooms served as a popular model. Others followed the design of the Pennsylvania prison system, in which buildings were star-shaped, and each inmate was in solitary confinement. Regardless of the shape of the prison, the isolated inmates were supplied with Bibles so that they could reflect on their sins. Despite the good intentions of prison reformers, however, prisons and mental asylums developed into large, understaffed, warehouses for marginalized members of society.

# The Lives of Women

At the start of the nineteenth century, women were forbidden from voting or being elected to office; they could not own property, nor could they receive a college education. Married women had no legal status separate from their husbands—meaning they could not control their own wages or even contest the custody of their children in case of a divorce.

As a variety of reform movements, including antislavery, temperance, and education took shape, a number of women began to argue that their gender had a duty to exert their role in restoring morality to American society.

Among those women was Catharine Beecher, the eldest daughter of Lyman Beecher. Beecher, whose younger sister Harriet Beecher Stowe would gain worldwide fame as author of the novel *Uncle Tom's Cabin*, became one of the nation's leading advocates of female education. In 1824, she founded Hartford Female Seminary to train women not for a profession outside the home, but for the moral education of children inside the home. For Beecher, the lives of women and the lives of men existed in two separate spheres, with men providing for the family through a profession outside of the home and women providing for the family through her moral guidance inside of it. When the question of women's suffrage arose, Beecher strongly disapproved of women winning the right to vote.

At the same time, the gap between male and female power widened greatly during the first half of the 1800s—particularly after suffrage was extended to all white men, including recent immigrants. In this context,

**A COMICAL COMMENTARY**

A cartoon satirizes the campaign for women's suffrage by showing women protesting for their rights while leaving the care of children in the hands of a befuddled husband.

129

interest in granting legal and political rights to women eventually gained ground.

Although popular opinion ran against woman suffrage, some women voiced dissatisfaction at being unable to vote or own property, despite holding jobs or being educated. To address these issues, Quaker reformers Elizabeth Cady Stanton, Lucretia Mott, and others organized a convention in July 1848 to discuss "the social, civil, and religious conditions and rights of women." At the convention, the assembled women and men, including former slave Frederick Douglass, unanimously approved and signed a Declaration of Sentiments, based on the Declaration of Independence. Two weeks later, a larger meeting was held, which led in turn to a similar meeting in Rochester, New York and to annual meetings thereafter. Soon other women's right meetings were occurring across the nation. At the National Women's Rights Convention in 1850, the ex-slave and abolitionist Sojourner Truth made explicit the link between women's rights and the abolition of slavery. That same year, Elizabeth Cady Stanton met Susan B. Anthony, who had attended Stanton's 1848 Seneca Falls Convention. Anthony did not actually commit herself to the cause of women's suffrage until she was denied the chance to speak at a temperance meeting. After their 1850 meeting Stanton and Anthony formed a close working partnership and friendship. In 1860, they secured passage of the New York State Married Woman's Property Act. In 1869, they cofounded the National Women's Suffrage Association, which became the most important suffrage organization prior to the twentieth century.

# The Anti-Slavery Movement

Between 1803 and and 1853, the United States underwent an enormous territorial expansion. The sectional divisions that had first divided Federalists from Democratic-Republicans and then Democrats from Whigs, widened each time new territory came into the nation. At the core of this split was the issue of slavery and the federal government's right to restrain its expansion, if not ban it outright. As discussed in Chapter 12, the Missouri Compromise of 1820 divided the nation along a line extending along Missouri's southern border at the 36° 30' latitude to the Pacific Ocean—even though much of the western portion of that territory was still Spanish in 1820. Although Missouri sat north of the line, it was opened to slavery, while Maine was admitted as a new free state.

Although the Compromise seemed to permanently divide the nation into two—one part slave, one part free, the precarious political compromise held for thirty years. Even so, as the nation expanded to the west, slavery spread and so did the controversy surrounding it. Northern politicians feared that the addition of new slave states would upset the balance of power between North and South. Southern politicians and planters suspected that the opponents of slavery hoped not merely to limit slavery's spread but ban it outright. Such a ban, they knew would devastate the South's labor intensive, agricultural economy and threaten what they said were the rights of individual states to set their own policies. By the 1830s, pro-slavery forces felt under siege, and for several reasons. There was the ever-present physical danger of rebellion from enslaved blacks themselves. There was also an economic cost each time a slave escaped. And finally, there were the increasingly loud calls from northern abolitionists calling for an end to the slave system.

## Slave Rebellions

Throughout the history of slavery in the Americas, enslaved Africans plotted to gain their freedom, either through escape or rebellion. When the slave population of Saint Domingue overthrew French colonial power to become the first majority black government in the Americas, slaveowners feared the news would inspire rebellion within the United States. To be sure, several major rebellions did take place in the early years of the republic. In 1800, a self-educated blacksmith in the Richmond area named Gabriel organized a rebellion that may have involved up to 600 slaves. Angry that his master kept most of his earnings as an itinerant craftsman—and believing that the nation was facing an imminent political crisis during an election year that saw Democratic Republicans take over the government from Federalists—Gabriel selected the night of August 30 for the uprising. But a major thunderstorm forced him to postpone the rebellion for 24 hours, during which time several slaves betrayed the plot to whites. Though hundreds of African Americans were arrested, Gabriel escaped on a schooner to Norfolk. Unfortunately for him, another slave—enticed by a $300 reward—revealed his whereabouts. Sixty-five slaves were tried, and of that number Gabriel and 26 others were hanged. Of the remainder, some were sold into other states, some were found innocent, and a few were pardoned. In response, Virginia strengthened its laws against slave assemblies and literacy, as well as bolstering its militia.

Betrayal also doomed the new republic's second major rebellion, this one in Charleston, South Carolina, in 1822. Fear of slave uprisings was particularly acute in the state as the population of blacks had outnumbered that of whites for nearly a century. Moreover, Charleston was one of the few cities of the Deep South with a significant number of free blacks. Among these was Denmark Vesey, a former slave who had purchased his freedom after winning a state lottery in 1799. A successful carpenter, Vesey had amassed $8,000 in savings by 1822, a fortune for a free black man of the South in those years. Yet, despite his personal prosperity, Vesey dedicated his life to destroying slavery, by speaking at gatherings in black churches and workshops. By 1822, he had gathered a small

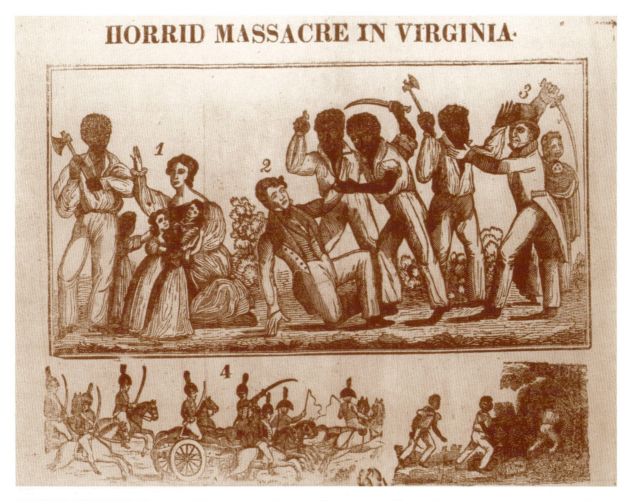

# HORRID MASSACRE IN VIRGINIA·

**TURNER'S REBELLION** The broadside above depicts Nat Turner's Rebellion as follows: 1. A woman pleads for the lives of her children; 2. Mr. Travis is murdered by his own slaves; 3. Mr. Barrow defends himself so that his wife and children escape; 4. Mounted dragoons in pursuit of rebel slaves.

cadre of like-minded blacks—both enslaved and free—willing to launch an uprising against the white population. Planned for late July, the conspiracy was betrayed by several slaves in May. On July 2, Vesey was arrested. Refusing to confess, he and 34 other African Americans were executed.

Despite such measures, rebellions large and small continued across the South, reaching a culmination in the bloodiest slave uprising in American history: the Nat Turner revolt of 1831. Turner was born a slave in Virginia's Southampton County on October 2, 1800, just five days before the execution of Gabriel. His father had run away when Turner was a boy, where it is believed he lived out his life as a runaway slave in the Great Dismal Swamp along the North Carolina border. Turner's mother was just seven years removed from Africa when she gave birth to Nat and constantly told her son that he was destined for great things. Deeply spiritual and a self-educated biblical scholar, Turner claimed to receive visions all of his life. In 1821 his master, Benjamin Turner, hired a particularly violent overseer and Nat escaped for a month, during which time he claimed God told him to lead a slave rebellion. Over the next decade, Turner became an itinerant preacher, traveling from plantation to plantation giving sermons on the necessity of violent liberation.

An eclipse of the sun in February 1831 was, in Turner's mind, a signal that the time for revolt was ripe. He soon began recruiting a small cadre of followers with the symbolic date of July 4 as their day to launch the rebellion. When Turner got sick, the date was pushed back six weeks.

On August 22, Turner and his band of followers began their attack, striking first on the plantation of Joseph Travis, where Turner then lived. The strategy was simple and brutal; they would move from plantation to plantation slaughtering masters and their families until they had intimidated the local white community and raised an army of rebel slaves. At that point, the killing would cease and the slave army would head for Jerusalem, Virginia, Southampton's county seat and the site of a major arsenal. Armed, they would make their way to the Great Dismal Swamp where they would establish an armed free black community impervious to white counterattack. Over the next couple of days, the rebels—now some 60 or 70 in all—murdered 57 whites, though it is believed that Turner himself killed no one. But as the element of surprise faded, local white militias counterattacked, killing some 100 blacks, in the process and ending the uprising. While many of those killed had nothing to do with Turner's activities, Turner himself escaped and was not apprehended until October 30.

Following a brief trial he was executed on November 11, 1831, after offering a detailed confession and biography to a court-appointed attorney.

Like the Gabriel and Vesey rebellions before it, the Nat Turner uprising led to harsh new disciplinary edicts and practices. Beyond that, the Turner rebellion marked a pivotal moment in the history of American slavery and in the development of the anti-slavery movement. The uprising ended any lingering thoughts that slavery might fade away peacefully in the South while, at the same time, dispelling the belief that slaves were largely contented with their lot. Coming in the same year that William Lloyd Garrison launched his fiercely abolitionist news-paper—*The Liberator*—Turner's rebellion sharpened the conflict between antislavery and proslavery forces in the North and South.

## The Underground Railroad

While most slave escapes were only temporary, thou-sands of African Americans did manage to break free of slavery altogether and escape the South, usually by fleeing to the North and Canada. A few in the Deep South made it to the swamps of Florida, where they joined the Seminole Nation or stowed away on boats bound for the Caribbean.

But the odds against escape were long. White patrols, supplemented with bloodhounds, constantly patroled the roads. Any black person off the plantation was presumed to be a runaway—and if stopped by a white, who was usually armed—would be forced to pro-duce a pass. Thus, the odds were best for those who lived near the free states. Still, it is estimated that approximately 1,000 slaves annually made it to freedom

**FREEDOM TRAIL**
The Underground Railroad was a complex network of escape routes from South to North, or into Mexico and the Caribbean.

The Underground Railroad

by the 1840s and 1850s. Many, if not most, were aided in their escape by a network of black and white abolitionists that came to be called the Underground Railroad.

Because of the intense secrecy that shrouded its operations, much about the Underground Railroad has been lost to history. As slaves were property, freeing them was a form of theft under state and federal law. Penalties for those who participated were severe, especially for blacks. While whites risked arrest, prison, and fines, black "conductors" and "station masters"—as guides and owners of safe houses (places where runaway slaves could hide) were respectively called—risked being sent back into slavery. Even free blacks in the North could be enslaved if caught aiding runaways. For instance, abolitionist Frederick Douglass, born a slave on the Eastern Shore of Maryland, made his way north by borrowing the papers of a free black sailor. Had Douglass been caught, it is highly likely that the sailor would have been punished by enslavement.

While some slaves, like Douglass, made their way north by boat, most traveled by land routes. In general, a slave's best chance of escape came if he or she was escorted northward by a "conductor," a free black or former slave living in the North who traveled south to serve as a guide. The most famous of these was Harriet Tubman. Like Douglass, Tubman was born a slave on Maryland's Eastern Shore, not far from the free state of Pennsylvania. As a teen, she was severely injured when her owner threw a two-pound weight at a runaway slave Tubman was shielding. The weight hit Tubman in the head, leaving a deep scar and a propensity for headaches and dizzy spells the rest of her life. After marrying a free black man in 1844, Tubman searched for ways to escape bondage. She first tried the law and, when that failed, she escaped to the North in 1849. (Her husband refused to go along so she went alone.)

Working as a maid and cook in Philadelphia, Tubman saved her earnings and plotted a trip to Baltimore to free her sister and her sister's two children in 1850. Between that year and the outbreak of the Civil War, Tubman—despite a bounty on her head, dead or alive—made more than 15 trips into the South, liberating some 200 slaves, including her entire family. Unlike in the early years of the Railroad—when most runaways were settled in the free black communities of the North—Tubman was forced to deal with the 1850 Fugitive Slave Act, which required northern authorities return all runaways or face federal criminal prosecution. To cope, she connected up with a network of safe houses and guides who could lead escaped slaves to Canada.

## The African Colonization Movement

The Turner Rebellion strengthened the idea—particularly in the upper South, where slavery was increasingly seen as no longer economically viable—that the only way to deal with the presence of blacks in America was to eliminate it, by banishing blacks to Africa. The idea of sending African Americans back to their African homeland was not a new one in the 1830s. Indeed, many of the founding fathers, including Thomas Jefferson, believed that the African and Caucasian races—given the history of black subjugation and the supposedly different abilities of the two races—could not live in peace in the same land. As a Virginia legislator, Jefferson had advocated sending freed blacks to "a far away place selected as the circumstances of the time should render most proper." As hopes that the American Revolution might lead to a more equal society for African Americans faded in the late eighteenth century and early nineteenth century, the idea of "colonization"—as the return to Africa proposal was called—caught on among leading whites and a few free blacks.

Among the free blacks who supported re-Africanization was Paul Cuffe, a wealthy black shipowner from New Bedford, Massachusetts. Cuffe believed he had a duty to help his fellow Africans, both in America and Africa. Sending blacks back to Africa offered a way to do both. For African Americans, it would mean an opportunity to escape white racism and build a community of their own, proving to the world that blacks were capable of self-government. At the same time, these settlers would bring civilization and Christianity to their long-lost brothers in Africa. In 1811, Cuffe visited Sierra Leone, a British colony established as a haven for former slaves from Britain, North America and the Caribbean. Four years later, he sent the first shipload of settlers to Sierra Leone at his own expense. But his death two years later ended the project.

Meanwhile, a group of influential whites—including Kentucky senator Henry Clay, future president Andrew Jackson, "Star Spangled Banner" author Francis

**HARRIET TUBMAN**

**FREDERICK DOUGLASS**

Scott Key, and Bushrod Washington, nephew of George—established the American Colonization Society (ACS) in Washington in 1816. The goals of the society were decidedly mixed. "Can there be a nobler cause," Clay, a wealthy planter and slaveowner, asked his fellow colonizationists, "than that which, while it proposes to rid our own country of a useless and pernicious, if not dangerous, portion of the population, contemplates the spreading of the arts of civilized life, and the possible redemption from ignorance of a benighted portion of the globe?" Indeed, from the beginning, colonization was tainted by its association with slaveholders and denounced by free blacks and, later, abolitionists as a way to force free African Americans—many of whom traced their ancestry in America back for generations—out of the country, while preserving slave status for the vast majority of blacks. "We have no wish to separate from our present homes for any purpose whatsoever," declared a statement issued by 3,000 African Americans meeting at Philadelphia's Bethel Church in 1817, adding "we only want the use of those opportunities . . . which the Constitution and the laws allow to us all."

Still, the ACS achieved some success. In 1820, it sponsored its first shipment of eighty-six blacks to the British colony of Sierra Leone. After a sojourn ridden with disease, colonists moved southward to found the colony of Liberia. Over the next four decades, more than 10,000 African Americans settled in Liberia. In 1847, the colonists—a mix of free blacks from the North, freed slaves from the South, and Africans recaptured from slavers on the high seas—declared their independence from the ACS, making Liberia Africa's first republic. Indeed, aside from Ethiopia, it would remain the only part of Africa to escape European colonialism in the 19th and 20th centuries. For roughly 150 years, Liberia was ruled by the descendants of African Americans—the so-called Americo-Liberians—until their regime was overthrown in a 1980 coup.

### The Abolitionists

Largely a failure, the colonization idea was displaced in the 1830s by a militant abolitionism. While colonizationists spoke of a gradual end to slavery through emigration—an impossible proposal given the millions of blacks already living in America—abolitionists called for the institution's immediate demise. They dismissed the colonizationists as co-conspirators of planters, seeking to rid the country of its unwanted free black population.

Meanwhile, throughout the North, free black communities in the 1820s were endorsing ever more radical measures to end slavery, even if they involved violence. In 1829 came the most incendiary statement yet. The pamphlet *An Appeal . . . to the Colored Citizens of the World* declared to whites: "We must and shall be free . . . in spite of you. . . . And woe, woe, will be it to you if we have to obtain our freedom by fighting." Written by David Walker, a used clothing salesman and pamphleteer living in Boston, and commonly

known as *Walker's Appeal*, the tract also violently refuted white claims to racial superiority. "I do declare that one good black man can put to death six white men," wrote Walker, who soon gained an enthusiastic black audience. The pamphlet went through three printings and even showed up among free black communities in the South.

Meanwhile, sentiment was shifting among white opponents of slavery as well. The wave of evangelical Christianity that swept much of the upper Midwest, upstate New York, and New England in the 1820s inspired a new condemnation of slavery. The religious message of the Great Awakening—as the movement was called—emphasized the individual moral agency of all human beings. Being a good Christian meant choosing to follow God's plan. By keeping African Americans in bondage, slave owners were keeping them in darkness, unable to make the moral choice God had given all human beings. The implications of this argument were clear: slavery was a sin and slaveholders were contravening God's will. To many evangelicals, there could be no compromise with slavery, no gradualist approach to its extinction. Nat Turner's 1831 uprising seemed like a sign to many that God's patience with America and its compromise with the forces of evil—that is, with slavery—was running thin.

That same year, William Lloyd Garrison, a Boston-based printer and evangelical Christian, launched a weekly abolitionist newspaper, *The Liberator*. In its first issue, the editor made his intentions clear: "I will be harsh as truth and as uncompromising as justice. . . . I am in earnest—I will not equivocate—I will not excuse—I will not retreat a single inch—AND I WILL BE HEARD." In later issues, Garrison would go on to denounce the American Constitution—with its unwritten acceptance of slavery—as "a covenant with death, an agreement with Hell." Garrison's fiery language and uncompromising convictions attracted other like-minded opponents of slavery. In 1833, Garrison joined with Theodore Weld—an upstate New York preacher—and Arthur and Lewis Tappan—wealthy merchant brothers from New York City—to form the American Anti-Slavery Society.

The society's members took two approaches to their crusade. The first was aimed at the public. Borrowing techniques from the revivalist churches, they held public meetings where eloquent and passionate speakers offered the equivalent of sermons on the theme of abolitionism. Many evangelical women became caught up in the crusade, going so far as to speak to mixed sex audiences on the subject, unprecedented events that shocked the gender sensibilities of the day. (Indeed, the antislavery movement proved to be one of the seedbeds of the women's movement, which grew to fruition in the same abolitionist strongholds and culminated in the 1848 women's rights convention Seneca Falls, New York.)

And, of course, the abolitionist movement drew on black speakers as well. In 1841, a white abolitionist in

**THE LIBERATOR** The fiery abolitionist William Lloyd Garrison began publishing his newspaper in 1831.

New Bedford, Massachusetts invited a young, escaped slave named Frederick Douglass to speak at a meeting on Nantucket Island. The power and conviction of Douglass's testimony won him a role as abolitionism's most famous and effective spokesperson. In addition, abolitionists published hundreds of thousands of pamphlets, flooding the North and the South with antislavery propaganda. The purpose of this approach, known as "moral suasion," was to create a moral climate in which slave owners would recognize the error of their ways and move to end slavery. While the campaign did little to change the moral stance of most slave owners, it did increase the public pressure on them. In response, southern officials began routinely raiding post offices to seize and destroy the literature.

The abolitionists also published—and sometimes ghost-authored—slave narratives. Usually written in the melodramatic style of 19th century literature, these narratives told of the unspeakable barbarities of the slave regime—beatings, torture, rape, and the anguished cries of mothers torn from their children at slave auctions. To modern readers, the most powerful narratives were those written in the clear and unadorned prose of the former slaves themselves. Among the most famous of these tracts are Frederick Douglass's *Narrative of the Life of Frederick Douglass, an American Slave*, Solomon Northrup's *Twelve Years a Slave*, and Harriet Jacobs's *Incidents in the Life of a Slave Girl*.

A second strategy of the abolitionists was aimed at politicians. In order to convince Congress of the depth of antislavery sentiment in the North, the Anti-Slavery Society encouraged local chapters to inundate Congress with petitions calling for

laws that were in its purview to pass, including the abolition of slavery in Washington, D.C.; a ban on the interstate slave trade; the removal of the "three-fifths compromise" in the Constitution, which enhanced southern legislative representation; and a ban on the admission of new slave states. (As slaves were considered legal property, slavery was protected by the Constitution; banning slavery required a constitutional amendment.) So many petitions flooded Washington that, in 1836, southern Congressmen and their northern sympathizers pushed through the "gag rule," whereby all petitions against slavery were automatically tabled so that they could not become the subject of debate. The law—a clear denial of the First Amendment—would remain in effect for eight years.

Eventually, the efforts of the political wing of the abolitionist movement led to the establishment of the Liberty Party in 1840, the first political party in American history expressly devoted to ending slavery. Although winning less than 3 percent of the northern vote in the 1844 presidential elections, the Liberty Party eventually gave way to the Free Soil Party in the late 1840s, a much larger party with a more popular—although less radical—mandate of preventing the spread of slavery to the West. The Free Soil Party—with ex-president Martin Van Buren as its nominee—won more than 10 percent of the vote in 1848 and paved the way for the antislavery Republican Party of the 1850s.

Despite this success, the political strategy helped split the abolitionist movement. Radical white abolitionists—led by Garrison—believed that working with politicians compromised the idea of abolitionism as a moral crusade against evil. At the same time, more moderate white abolitionists and the majority of black abolitionists—

**WILLIAM LLOYD GARRISON** In addition to publishing his abolitionist newspaper, Garrison also co-founded the American Anti-Slavery Society. By 1838, the organization had about 100,000 members.

135

coalescing around Douglass—took a more pragmatic approach, hoping that political and legislative action would gradually put slavery on the road to extinction. Ultimately—with proslavery power increasing in the 1850s—Douglass and anti-Garrisonian radicals like John Brown would come to the conclusion that neither the political nor the moral suasion route offered a solution to the slavery problem. Instead, direct action was necessary, though when Brown and a number of radical white abolitionists suggested an invasion of the South in 1859, Douglass dismissed the idea as folly.

The abolitionists' place in history—and their role in ending slavery—is a complicated one. On the one hand, most of their efforts—either radical or pragmatic—failed. Few slave owners were ever convinced of the errors of their ways and Congress failed to pass any of the legislation desired by the abolitionists, at least until the Civil War. Indeed, the rhetoric and action of the abolitionists stirred up a hornet's nest of protest in the North, where many whites feared a flood of unwanted black migrants should slavery be ended in the South. Abolitionist speakers like Douglass and Garrison were often attacked verbally and even physically by anti-abolitionists. In 1837, the movement got its first martyr in Elijah Lovejoy, an abolitionist editor murdered by a white mob in Alton, Illinois.

And yet through this very controversy, abolitionists achieved success of a kind. Until the crisis decade of the 1850s, most Americans accepted slavery as a fact of national life. For southerners, it was a way of life; for northerners, it was a distant and abstract issue. For almost all Americans, it didn't seem worth fighting over. And politicians did their best to keep things that way. Slavery was a no-win issue; support it too strongly and one offended northerners; oppose it, and one alienated the South. It was best to just ignore it. But abolitionists, with their speeches, pamphlets, and petitions, made it increasingly hard to ignore slavery as a political and moral issue. Moreover, as proslavery politicians and white mobs attacked abolitionists, they turned them into martyrs, not so much to the cause of black freedom but to the causes of freedom of speech, assembly, and press. Most northerners were both racist and against slavery. They wanted to keep blacks—enslaved or free—out of the North and West. As southern politicians and their northern allies passed proslavery legislation, northerners felt that their political will was being ignored or actively subverted. Abolitionists, then, were critical in raising the national political temperature to a degree high enough to spark the Civil War, which ultimately destroyed slavery.

### The Compromise of 1850

As discussed in Chapter 12, Texas won its independence from Mexico in the mid-1830s—partly to escape the latter's edicts against slavery—and sought to enter

the American Union as a slave state, a move blocked by antislavery forces in the North. Angry southerners then began pressuring the national government to acquire western lands open to slavery below the Missouri Compromise line, a plan that was bound to lead to hostilities with Mexico. In 1845, southerners won the admission of Texas into the Union as a slave state. A year later, President James Polk, a slave owner from Tennessee and a determined expansionist, provoked a war with Mexico by sending American troops into disputed territory along the Rio Grande. When Mexican soldiers fired on the Americans, Polk and southerners in Congress declared war. David Wilmot, a Free Soil congressman from Pennsylvania, tried to undermine the southerners' plans by introducing a proviso making all territories acquired from Mexico free, but his efforts were brushed aside by proslavery forces in Congress.

From the beginning, the war was an unequal one. Mexico proved to be no match for the United States and, after two years of hostilities, was forced to cede the northern third of its territory to the United States for a nominal payment of $15 million. Suddenly, southerners had what they wanted—vast new American territories for the expansion of slavery. Although somewhat mollified by the acquisition of the Oregon territory from Britain in 1846, northerners cried foul, arguing that the war was part of a south-

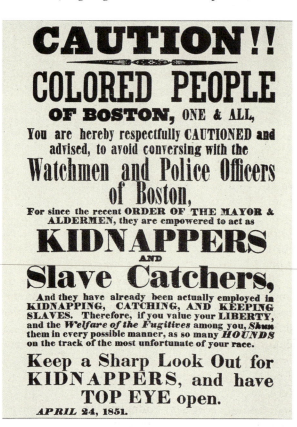

**FUGITIVE SLAVE ACT** The Fugitive Slave Act of 1850 made it illegal for whites to assist runaway slaves. Nonetheless, many whites continued to help runaways avoid capture.

## The Compromise of 1850

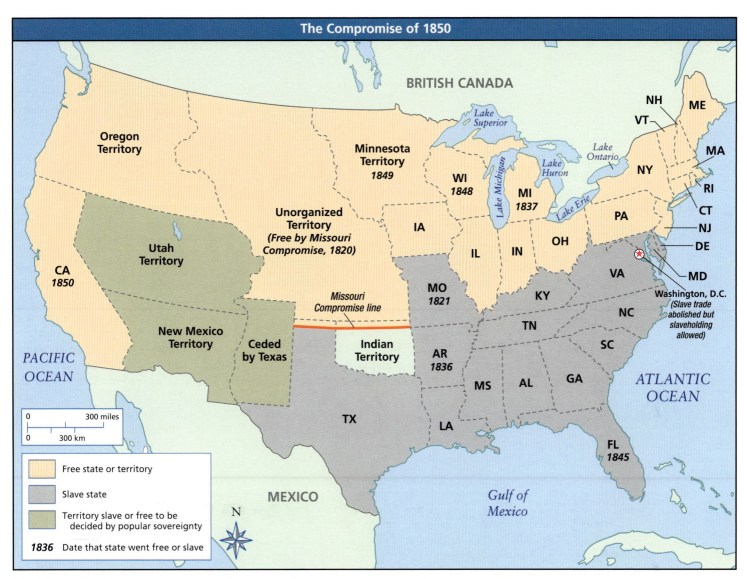

**BRITISH CANADA**

Oregon Territory

Minnesota Territory *1849*

Unorganized Territory (Free by Missouri Compromise, 1820)

Utah Territory

CA *1850*

New Mexico Territory

Ceded by Texas

Missouri Compromise line

Indian Territory

WI *1848*

MI *1837*

IA

IL

IN

OH

MO *1821*

AR *1836*

TX

LA

MS

AL

GA

KY

TN

NC

SC

VA

FL *1845*

NH

VT

ME

MA

NY

PA

RI

CT

NJ

DE

MD

Washington, D.C. (Slave trade abolished but slaveholding allowed)

*Lake Superior*

*Lake Michigan*

*Lake Huron*

*Lake Ontario*

*Lake Erie*

**PACIFIC OCEAN**

**ATLANTIC OCEAN**

**MEXICO**

*Gulf of Mexico*

N

0          300 miles
0          300 km

☐ Free state or territory

☐ Slave state

☐ Territory slave or free to be decided by popular sovereignty

*1836* Date that state went free or slave

**COMPROMISE OF 1850** By recognizing the concept of popular sovereignty, the Compromise of 1850 opened vast western territories to slavery.

ern conspiracy to spread slavery and dominate the Union. The sense of crisis was stoked by the discovery of gold in newly acquired California in 1848. With hundreds of thousands of settlers—largely from the North—pouring in, the Pacific Coast territory asked to join the Union as a free state in 1850.

But with no equivalent slave territory ready to enter the Union, California's request provoked the most serious sectional crisis since Missouri. Over the course of the year—and after some of the bitterest debate in congressional history—an elaborate new compromise was reached. Although involving a series of delicately balanced elements, the Compromise of 1850 boiled down to two controversial provisions. First, California would be admitted into the Union as a free state, giving the North a sixteen to fifteen state advantage in the Senate. Second, as a concession to southerners, Congress passed the infamous Fugitive Slave Act. For the first time, the federal government became a seriously active participant in enforcing the law against runaway slaves. Under the act, fugitive

slaves and even free blacks anywhere in the Union were subject to potential enslavement or re-enslavement. Moreover, the Fugitive Slave Act made it a crime for any northerner to interfere in the apprehension of an alleged escapee. Northerners were outraged, and not just because law-abiding blacks were subject to arrest. Suddenly, it seemed to them as if the entire federal government had been hijacked by what was coming to be called the "slave power conspiracy."

*"The South asks for justice, simple justice, and less she ought not to take . . . She has already surrendered so much that she has little left to surrender."*

—Senator John C. Calhoun, in a speech opposing further compromise on the slavery question, March 4, 1850

# Chapter 15: The Road to War

**THE KANSAS–NEBRASKA ACT** The Kansas–Nebraska Act opened both Kansas and Nebraska to slavery, invalidating the Compromise of 1820.

With pioneers beginning to settle the lands to the immediate west and northwest of Missouri, a proposal was floated by the powerful Illinois senator Stephen Douglas in 1854 to establish two organized territories—Kansas and Nebraska. To gain southern support for the measure, Douglas insisted that the settlers decide their status as slave or free. Because the territories lay north of the Missouri Compromise line, antislavery northerners cried foul, arguing that the lands were supposed to be free. Despite their protestations, the "popular sover-eignty" elements of the Kansas-Nebraska bill passed, providing yet more evidence to suspicious northerners that the "slave power conspiracy" was determined to enforce its will on the entire country.

In the aftermath of the act's passage, the memberships of the nations two principal political parties—the Whigs and the Democrats—became severely divided. Out of various factions a new party, the Republican party, was formed. The Republicans, while not necessarily aboli-tionists, were opposed to the further spread of slavery. In the 1856 presidential election, the Republicans nominated John C.

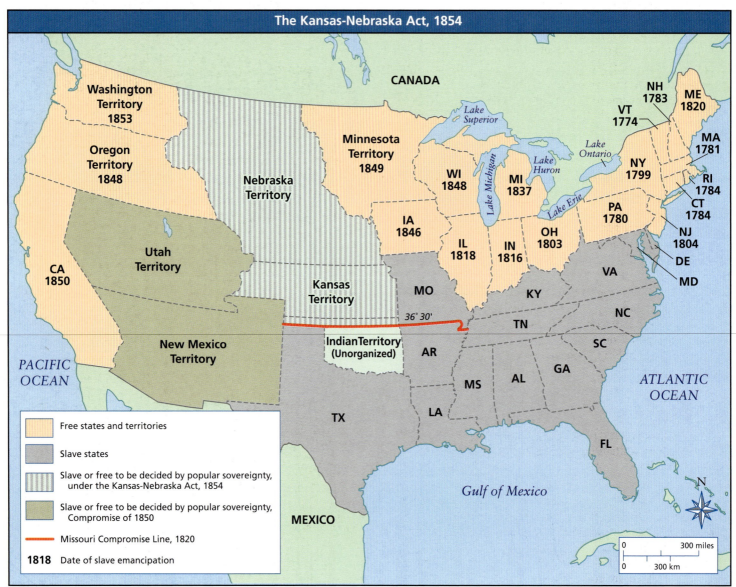

**The Kansas-Nebraska Act, 1854**

Legend:
- Free states and territories
- Slave states
- Slave or free to be decided by popular sovereignty, under the Kansas-Nebraska Act, 1854
- Slave or free to be decided by popular sovereignty, Compromise of 1850
- Missouri Compromise Line, 1820
- **1818** Date of slave emancipation

Frémont, the famous explorer, hero of the Bear Flag Rebellion in California, and an ardent abolitionist. The Democrats nominated former Secretary of State and career diplomat James Buchanan. Buchanan, who had been posted in Britain during the Kansas-Nebraska debate, had thus avoided taking a stand on the issue.

# John Brown and Dred Scott

In the midst of the campaign, violence erupted in Kansas as pro- and antislavery forces clashed, leading to murders, skirmishes, and massacres. In the summer of 1856, more than 700 proslavery men attacked the free town of Lawrence, burning it to the ground. In response, abolitionist John Brown and a small gang of followers descended on a settlement at Pottawatomie Creek, where they murdered five proslavery settlers in their homes. The violence over the slavery issue even penetrated Capitol Hill. Following a fiery speech on the floor of Congress—in which he denounced South Carolina senator Andrew Butler for taking up with "the harlot slavery"—Massachusetts senator Charles Sumner was beaten unconscious by Butler's nephew, Representative Preston Brooks.

### The Dred Scott Case

In November, Buchanan won the election, but Frémont's relatively good showing, despite a total lack of support in the South, highlighted the growing national division. With Kansas in flames and Congress bitterly divided, the Supreme Court moved into the breach, seeking to resolve the issue through a broad judicial ruling. The case that came to them involved a slave named Dred Scott who, with the help of abolitionist lawyers, was suing for his freedom. Scott's master, an army surgeon, had taken his slave with him when assigned to serve in the free state of Illinois and the free territory of Wisconsin. When his master died, Scott—citing his habitation on free soil—claimed his freedom. His late master's heirs insisted he belonged to them. In March 1857, in a highly controversial decision delivered just days after Buchanan naively stated in his inaugural address that he hoped the controversy over slavery was "approaching its end," the Supreme Court ruled against Scott. Writing for the majority, Chief Justice Roger Taney stated that Scott was a slave no matter where he lived. Taney's reasoning was as follows: as an African American, Scott had no rights. As a slave he was merely property, whether or not he had set foot on free soil. To northerners, the implications were dire. Legally, a slaveowner could now bring his slaves with impunity to any northern state, rendering the entire Union slave territory. Once again, it seemed to many in the North that the "slave power conspiracy" was winning the day. The Court's contention that slaves had the same legal status as livestock or a piece of land, was for some abolitionists, proof that the spread of slavery could not be checked by anything less than violent action. War fever heightened, and increasingly contentious politics fired the national disposition for a bloodletting.

### John Brown's Raid

Southerners, meanwhile, had their own fears. Outnumbered and outpaced by a rapidly growing and industrializing North, they felt hemmed in on all sides. Britain had outlawed slavery in its empire in 1833, followed by France in 1848. The bestselling novel of the day—popularized in countless theatrical productions across

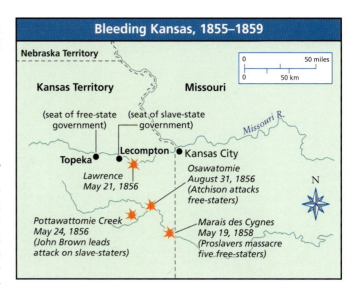

**Bleeding Kansas, 1855–1859**

**OPEN WARFARE** Civil war raged in Kansas Territory after the passage of the Kansas-Nebraska Act left residents to decide on slavery's status. Pro- and antislavery parties established territorial capitals, and abolitionist John Brown took part in several murders.

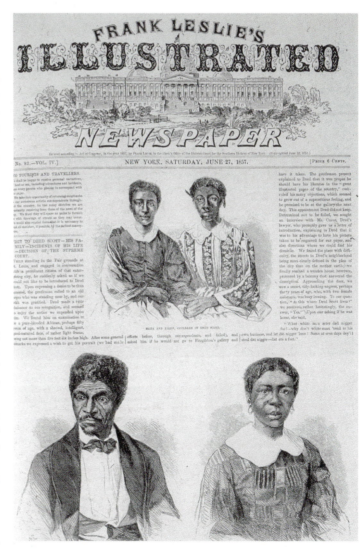

**DRED SCOTT AND FAMILY** Dred Scott, at bottom left, is shown with his wife Harriet to his right, and their daughters, above. The Supreme Court ruled that he and his family remained slaves, regardless of where their owner lived.

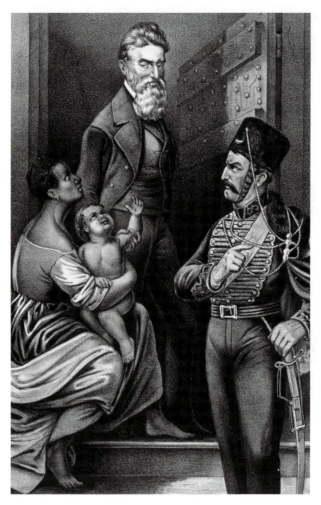

**JOHN BROWN UNDER ARREST** John Brown's violent methods divided even ardent abolitionists. To some, he was a heroic martyr. To others, a dangerous fanatic.

**THE DIVIDED UNION** Eleven slave states seceded from the Union, while four would remain. In 1863, anti-slavery West Virginia would break from Virginia.

the North—was Harriet Beecher Stowe's *Uncle Tom's Cabin*, a powerful melodrama on the evils of slavery. A new and popular antislavery party—the Republicans—was fast becoming the majority in the northern states. Then, in 1859, came the final blow. In October, John Brown—the abolitionist fighter from Kansas—led an armed gang on a raid of the federal armory at Harper's Ferry, Virginia (now West Virginia), hoping to launch and arm a general slave insurrection in the process. Brown's plan was as crazy as it was audacious. There were few African Americans in the mountainous region around Harper's Ferry and Brown's small force was quickly killed or dispersed by a Virginia militia company headed by Robert E. Lee, future commander of Confederate forces in the Civil War. Brown himself was captured alive.

At first, northerners and southerners were largely in agreement on Brown; he was seen as a dangerous and misguided fanatic who threatened the peace and welfare of the country. But during his trial, Brown spoke with such great eloquence on the evils of the slavery system and on the necessity of destroying it that he won over the majority of public opinion in the North. Following his conviction and subsequent death by hanging, Brown's body was shipped northward to a burial site in New York's Adirondack Mountains, where he had lived much of his life. In Philadelphia, his body was taken from its original coffin—which had been built by slaves—and placed in one made by free blacks. Along the train's route, large crowds came out to pay their respects to the man

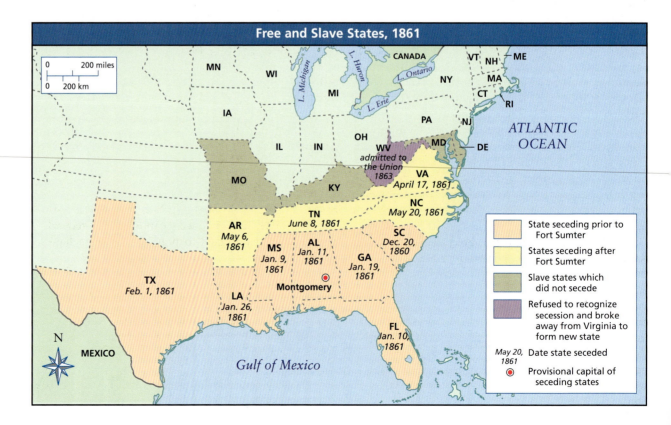

Free and Slave States, 1861

Legend:
- State seceding prior to Fort Sumter
- States seceding after Fort Sumter
- Slave states which did not secede
- Refused to recognize secession and broke away from Virginia to form new state
- *May 20, 1861* Date state seceded
- Provisional capital of seceding states

they now viewed as a national hero. To proslavery southerners, this was further proof that all northerners were secret abolitionists. This was a mistaken assumption, of course. Most northerners did not want to ban slavery in the South, but instead just prevent it from spreading to the West. But, in politics, opinion often counts for more than fact, a rule that would be proven—with disastrous results—in the presidential election year of 1860.

## The Union Sundered

By the end of the 1850s, many of the institutions that had previously bound the nation together had divided into mutually hostile northern and southern wings. Fraternal organizations, churches, and the Whig Party had all broken over the question of slavery. During the election campaign of 1860, the only remaining national party—the Democrats—would come apart as well. At their national convention in Charleston, South Carolina, southern and northern delegates debated the question of popular sovereignty and the expansion of slavery in the western territories. When the northerners—who only weakly supported both—won out, the southerners walked out on the convention. Ultimately, the Democratic Party ran two candidates for president—Stephen Douglas and Kentucky senator John Breckinridge. Along with a third party candidate, former Tennessee senator John Bell, who ran under the banner of the Constitutional Union Party, the Democrats split the southern and border states of Delaware, Kentucky, Maryland, and Missouri between them.

The Republicans ran Abraham Lincoln of Illinois. Lincoln's opposition to extending slavery to the territories put him squarely at odds with proslavery southerners. United behind Lincoln, the Republicans swept the northern states and took the election with a plurality of just forty percent of the national popular vote.

As far as southerners were concerned, the election results were the final straw. In their opinion, Lincoln was a closet abolitionist, despite his protestations that he did not intend to ban slavery where it already existed. Lincoln had also made clear his belief that the Union would "become all one thing, or all the other."

In December, Senator John J. Crittenden of Kentucky, backed by the National Unity Party, made one last-ditch effort to solve the slavery question. Crittenden introduced a proposal to Congress that would have confirmed the free-and-slave state boundary set by the Missouri Compromise, allowed slave trading in the District of Columbia to continue, prohibited the importation of slaves from Africa, and slightly modified the Fugitive Slave Law. The proposed compromise was supported by border states and acceptable to the South, but Lincoln and the Republican party opposed

**THE LITTLE GIANT**
Senator Stephen A. Douglas of Illinois promoted the idea of popular sovereignty to settle the slavery issue. Although his pro-compromise views helped him defeat Abraham Lincoln in their famed Senate race of 1858, he lost to Lincoln in the presidential election of 1860.

it. The Crittenden Compromise was defeated in both the House and Senate, making war inevitable.

That same month, staunchly proslavery South Carolina became the first state to adopt an ordinance of secession. Within hours of Lincoln's election, the South Carolina legislature called for a state convention, and the convention's delegates voted unanimously to break with the Union. The decision sparked a state-wide celebration. Soon the state demanded that federal troops be withdrawn from Fort Sumter in Charleston harbor, an ultimatum which would lead to the bombardment of the fort and the first shots of the Civil War. South Carolina's secession was followed in January by those of Mississippi, Florida, Alabama, Georgia, and Louisiana. Texas seceded in February.

As 1860 ended and 1861 began, secessionists began to seize federal forts and arsenals in the Southern states. Two forts guarding the valuable harbor of Mobile, Alabama, were captured. The federal government, determined to prevent that from happening at Fort Sumter in Charleston Harbor, South Carolina, sent 250 troops to Charleston aboard the merchant ship *The Star of the West* to reinforce the beleaguered fort's garrison. As *The Star of the West* approached Charleston on January 9, 1861, by Confederate-held shore batteries fired upon it. In an effort to avoid confrontation, President Buchanan ordered that *The Star of the West* return to New York with the reinforcements still aboard. The incident heightened tensions already near the breaking point.

**GUNS OF SECESSION** Confederate forces fire on Fort Sumter in Charleston harbor on April 2, 1861, beginning the Civil War.

On February 4, 1861, delegates from these states met in Montgomery, Alabama to create a new nation, the Confederate States of America. Within five days, they had adopted a provisional constitution and elected a provisional president, former U.S. Senator, and Pierce administration Secretary of War Jefferson Davis. As one of his first acts, President Davis demanded that Federal troops evacuate all their posts in the Confederacy, including Fort Sumter in Charleston harbor. Without hesitation, President Lincoln refused. The stage was set for war.

### The Divided Nation: North, South and West

Even before the formal secessions took place, the United States was, as it had been through history, sharply divided—not just over slavery—but culturally and economically as well. In particular, the years before the war had been a time of dramatic change in the North. Quiet farming communities now bustled with activity as mills and factories sprang up. The cities of the Northeast teemed with immigrants from Ireland, Germany and Scandinavia. Railroads and canals crisscrossed the land, transporting the products of the North to the rest of the nation. New techniques in manufacturing made northern industry the wonder of the world.

At the same time, the growth of industry had led to the rise of a new class of people: factory workers, many of them immigrants, living and working in terrible conditions, "wage slaves" whose lives were often just as difficult as those of agricultural slaves in the South. Immigrants were often confronted with prejudice and suspicion.

But the people of the Northeast were at least free, and with luck and determination could move west to homestead on the frontier. By the mid-nineteenth century, manifest destiny, the idea that it was America's destiny to occupy the entire North American continent, from the East Coast to the West, was largely a reality. The western lands were rapidly being settled by hardy and adventurous men and women. Some of these pioneers sought religious freedom, like the Mormons in Utah; others had been motivated by the desire for quick riches, such as the forty-niners who arrived in California during the Gold Rush. Most, however, were seeking their own land to homestead and a better life than could

## TWO PRESIDENTS: LINCOLN AND DAVIS

The 16th president of the United States, Abraham Lincoln (1809-65) and Confederate president Jefferson Davis (1808-89) were both born in southern Kentucky, less than a year apart.

Davis attended college, then entered West Point, eventually serving as an officer in the 1832 Black Hawk War and on the Northwest frontier. In 1845, he was

**Jefferson Davis**

elected as a Democratic congressman for Mississippi, resigning to serve in the Mexican–American War, which began that year. When he left the military in 1847, Davis was appointed as a senator from Mississippi. In 1853, he became secretary of war in the Franklin Pierce administration. Returning to the Senate in 1857, he was a staunch advocate of states' rights, and by 1860 favored secession and the establishment of the Confederacy.

Lincoln's youth was spent mainly in frontier Indiana, with

little formal education. As a young man he moved to Illinois, where he briefly volunteered as a militiaman in the Black Hawk War. Lincoln worked in a grocery while he studied law, soon becoming a successful lawyer. He served several terms as a Whig member of the Illinois state legislature and was a congressman for one term, 1847-1849. His outspoken opposition to the Mexican-American

**Abraham Lincoln**

War cost him reelection to Congress. In 1858, Lincoln won a national reputation for debating Stephen A. Douglas, promoter of the 1854 Kansas-Nebraska Act, which allowed the residents of those territories to decide whether they would become slave or free states.

As the Republican candidate, Lincoln won the November 1860 presidential election. The Confederate Congress appointed Davis its provisional president in February 1861.

---

be found in the Northeast, the South or in Europe. Alone, in small groups, or in wagon trains of hundreds of families, thousands of people moved west to farm, raise livestock, mine, and build towns and cities on the prairie.

As discussed, as the western territories were settled and applied for admission to the Union, the question of whether the new territories would be slave or free arose. To proslavery advocates, the assumption was that western life would revolve around agriculture, and specifically cotton, just as it did in the South. South of the Mason-Dixon line, tobacco, sugar, and other crops were cultivated, but by the 1850s, cotton was the undisputed "king" of the South. By the 1860s, southern cotton made up over half of all U.S. exports. The South's economy depended almost totally on cotton to sustain it; having no other industry, the South needed cotton profits to purchase manufactured goods from the North or from Europe. Most southern whites, however, were not slave-owners but poor farmers who barely grew enough to feed themselves and their families. But even poor whites supported the institution of slavery, partly out of fear of competition if blacks were freed, and partly because they were aware of how vital slave labor was to the South's overall economy. Conditions for slaves varied widely, with some treated decently and many others suffering greatly under abusive masters. But no matter how they were treated, they were slaves, without basic rights as human beings.

### The First Shots Are Fired

"The government will not assail you," Lincoln told secessionists in his inaugural address on March 4, 1861. "You can have no conflict without being yourselves the aggressors." Upon his inauguration, President Lincoln was facing the worst crisis in the history of the Republic. His inaugural speech offered familiar concessions to the South—no punishment for secession and assurance that slavery would remain undisturbed there—and tough measures if the seceding states did not return to the Union. It was a difficult balancing

act, threatening the Deep South with punishment while easing fears in the critical states of the upper South, most especially Virginia.

Fort Sumter presented Lincoln with his first immediate decision. To abandon it would be to destroy the Union's credibility. To break the blockade by armed force risked making the North the aggressor and thereby causing the states of the upper South to join their Deep South sisters in secession. Ultimately, Lincoln chose the middle ground. Occupying an artificial island, Sumter was commanded by Major Robert Anderson of Kentucky, whose eighty-four officers and men were low on ammunition, food and water. The Confederacy's President Davis intended to force Sumter's surrender before Lincoln could resupply and reinforce the fort.

Lincoln dispatched a relief expedition. With the new supplies, southern leaders realized, Fort Sumter could hold out for months. A federal fort situated in the symbolic capital of the South was intolerable to Confederate leaders. On April 12, Confederate batteries under the command of General P.G.T. Beauregard opened fire on Sumter. Thousands of Charlestonians gathered to watch the bombardment, which continued through the night, lasting thirty-four hours. When fires broke out in the fort, Anderson had to give up. Ironically, given the enormous bloodshed of the Civil War that began there, the only death occurred on April 14, when a Union soldier was killed by the explosion of a Federal cannon that had been firing in salute as the flag was lowered. And, though lost to the South, the fort represented a symbolic victory for Lincoln: he had forced the other side to fire first. Within days, his call for 75,000 new federal soldiers had been easily met, though the call to arms was enough to push Arkansas, North Carolina, Tennessee, and Virginia to secede. Davis called for for 82,000 volunteers to serve in the Army of the Confederate States of America, and Lincoln called for 75,000 three-month volunteers for the United States. Hundreds of militia companies that had been drilling in the North and South rallied to their cause. The Civil War had begun in earnest.

# Chapter 16: The American Civil War

*"I am loathe to close. We are not enemies but friends. We must not be enemies. Though passion may have strained, it must not break the bonds of affection.*

*The mystic chords of memory, stretching from every battlefield and patriot grave to every living heart and hearthstone all over this broad land, will yet swell with the chorus of the Union, when again touched, as surely they will be, by the better angels of our nature."*

—ABRAHAM LINCOLN, FIRST INAUGURAL ADDRESS, 1861

When the first shots were fired on Fort Sumter in Charleston harbor in April, 1861, few could imagine the violence of the storm being called down upon the nation.

The Civil War cost the lives of more than 620,000 Americans, who died in battle or from disease. Slavery, too, died in the war. The years 1861 to 1865 would be the most important watershed in United States history, helping to define the nature of the nation—both in terms of the relationship between the states and the federal government and in terms of the relationship between individuals — regardless of race — that made up the nation's population.

## The Confederacy

One week after the Confederate attack on Fort Sumter, President Lincoln took the advice of his general-in-chief, Winfield Scott, and ordered a blockade of all southern ports. Because the Confederacy had to import most of its military supplies—as well as manufactured goods for civilian use, Lincoln and Scott hoped to destroy the southern economy and thus the Confederacy's ability to fight. Eventually, the blockade stretched 3,500 miles across the Southern coastline and involved hundreds of ships. Since few of the Union navy's 90 warships were suitable for this sort of guard duty, many civilian vessels, ranging from fishing boats to ferries, were hastily armed and pressed into service.

Meanwhile southerners worked to evade the blockade by slipping "blockade runners" past Union vessels in order to deliver cargo to its destination. Many of the owners of blockade running ships were not so much motivated by Southern patriotism as the profit motive. As the blockade began to strangle the Southern economy, luxuries as well as everyday items began to command fantastically high prices. It was not unusual for owners of a blockade runner to gar-

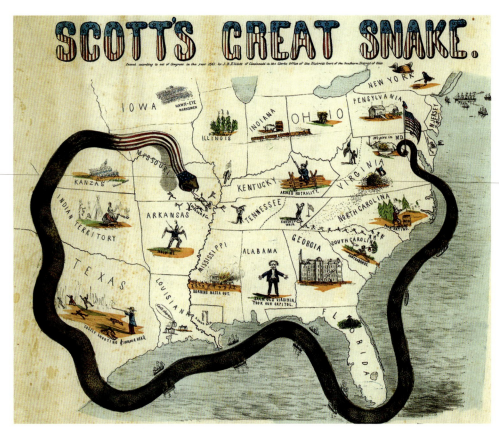

**THE ANACONDA PLAN** This 1861 cartoon depicts General Winfield Scott's plan to crush the Confederacy as a great snake. Scott, however, saw control of the Mississippi as the key to the strategy.

**CONFEDERATE CABINET** Jefferson Davis, president of the Confederate States of America (seated, fourth from left), and his Cabinet were frequently at odds with each other. Many Cabinet officers were chosen for regional balance rather than competence.

ner $150,000 for a single load of cargo. Goods destined for the Confederacy were shipped from European ports to the Caribbean or Bermuda and placed aboard the blockade running ships, which would then make a dash for the coast, usually under cover of darkness, hoping to sneak into a Confederate port or to land their vessel in a quiet cove. Many blockade runners got through but many more were captured and destroyed. By war's end, the blockade managed to reduce the flow of supplies to the Confederacy to a trickle.

## Challenges for the Confederacy

For its part, the blockade caused the Confederacy an enormous and immediate challenge. The initial challenge was to equip and arm the vast number of volunteers who answered the rebel call to arms. So many young southerners signed up that initially thousands had to be turned away for lack of supplies.

In time, enlistment fell as stories detailing the harsh reality of war trickled back to training camps. Rumors of enormous blood-shed certainly focused the minds of even the most gung-ho soldiers, but so too did the rigors of day-to-day soldiering. Union and Confederate troops alike were housed in tents that gave scant protection from wind and weather. They were clothed in uniforms that were flimsy in cold weather and stifling in heat, and they were fed a diet that consisted mostly of salted meat and hardtack— a sometimes mealy hard bread. Disease due to poor sanitation, boredom, and the difficulty of being far from home took their toll. By the spring of 1862, the one-year enlistment period for many Confederate soldiers would run out, forcing the Confederacy to authorize conscription.

At first only men between the ages of eighteen and thirty-five were affected, but as the war dragged on the age limits were widened to seventeen and fifty. Many southerners protested, pointing out that conscription violated the very principles of states rights and individualism for which the South was fighting. Others criticized the class-biased exceptions for those owning twenty or more slaves and those who could afford to hire a substitute. (The latter practice was outlawed in 1863.) Even slaves were drafted throughout the war to aid construction and other labor tasks, but were not authorized for active military service until 1865, too late to make a difference.

Another problem for the Confederacy was the quality of their political leadership. Jefferson Davis, Secretary of War during the Pierce Administration, had begun serving as provisional president in February, 1861, and then ran unopposed when squabbling delegates could not agree on another candidate.

As president, one of Davis' first decisions was to united the diverse opinions of the southern population by making sure each state in the Confederacy was represented in his Cabinet. Unfortunately, that meant that geography sometimes took priority over competence. The original Secretary of War, for example, was not even able to keep up with his mail. Davis's action also brought some of his harshest rivals into the government: his archrival Robert Toombs served as secretary of state, and Vice President

145

Alexander Stephens came to openly despise Davis. Only two original Cabinet officers served in the Cabinet through the collapse of the Confederacy in 1865. During the Confederate Cabinet's brief existence, there would be three secretaries of state, four attorneys general, five secretaries of war, and two secretaries of the treasury.

The Confederate Congress was even worse. Notorious for infighting and inefficiency, it often met in secret, undermining public confidence. Robert E. Lee, the South's leading general once said that all the Congress seemed to do was "chew tobacco and eat peanuts" while his ill-equipped soldiers starved.

Jefferson Davis had a virtually impossible job—to win a war while creating a nation out of eleven states that had little interest in federal government. Davis was routinely accused of violating states's rights, the very thing he was fighting to protect. His stern manner also made it difficult for him to inspire loyalty in a wary public.

### The Southern Economy

Charles Memminger, the first Confederate treasury secretary, had an especially daunting task. In the initial months of the war, life in the South seemed unchanged as small towns carried on sleepily, and planters maintained their genteel standards of living. Slaves too carried on in their expected roles. But the South would pay a bitter price for its attempt at independence. Even before the war, the South had never developed a self-sufficient economy. Cotton and tobacco were the chief crops; food and manufactured goods needed to be imported. While the North had a skilled class of industrial workers, many factories, access to vast resources and an excellent rail system to transport goods from factories, the South had none of these. The minimal industry of the Confederacy was hard-pressed to supply the rifles, cannons, bullets and bayonets, ships and shells that its forces required. The South began the war with some arms captured from federal arsenals and many weapons were purchased overseas and smuggled into the Confederacy by blockade runners, but as the Union blockade tightened, the Confederacy was forced to rely on its own industry to keep its forces functioning. Under the circumstances, the South did a remarkable job producing arms and sustaining its war effort, largely through the cooperation of civilians, who donated every last church bell to be melted and recast as cannon. Despite this resourcefulness, the war would be fought almost entirely on southern soil, meaning that wartime conditions, coupled with the impact of the Union blockade, would soon lead to desperate conditions.

With hardly more than a million dollars in specie in its possession at the start of the war, the rebel Treasury was hardly in a position to finance a lengthy war. Domestic loans brought in money, and $400,000 in gold bullion was seized from the federal mint in New Orleans, but for the most part, the Confederates relied on "printing press money." Never declared legal tender, one billion dollars worth of local and national currency was nevertheless printed in the South. As the war dragged on, the Confederate bills fell in value. During the war, prices rose dramatically in many parts of the South, people resorted to bartering as a means of exchange.

By April 2, 1863, food shortages in Richmond had become so bad that a mob, mostly consisting of women, ransacked shops and bakeries demanding food. President Davis himself addressed the crowd, demanding they disperse or be fired on by a company of militia. The looters broke up, but the riot was a reminder of the desperate shape into which the Confederate economy had come. By 1864, a Confederate dollar was worth only five cents in gold.

### The Confederacy and the World

The South's economic troubles were compounded by poor economic and foreign policy decisions in regard to the major powers in Europe. Because Great Britain generally favored the Confederacy's aristocratic culture, the South worked mightily to win its formal recognition and aid. Their cause was helped in November 1861, when two Confederates were taken prisoner by Union forces while traveling aboard a British ship. The enraged British government secured the prisoners' release, but U.S.–Anglo relations were badly strained. That same year, the British began secretly producing ironclad rams and commerce raiders—including the infamous *Alabama*—for Confederate use, delivered through third parties. In late Summer 1862, British Prime Minister Lord Palmerston considered offering a mediation proposal which would have favored the rebel cause. But as the South's military position weakened, English interest waned and the proposal was dropped.

The Confederacy's frustration with European unwillingness to offer open support led to its greatest diplomatic error. Knowing that textile mills in England and France drew eighty percent of their raw cotton supply from the South, the Confederacy imposed a ban on cotton exports in the hope that economic hardship would force Britain and France to recognize the Confederacy, and perhaps even intervene militarily. The ban placed Britain and France in difficult political positions. Britain was forced to choose between Southern cotton, which it needed for its extensive textile industry, and Southern slavery, which many British vigorously opposed.

As for France, Napoleon III, the nation's emperor, sympathized with the Confederates but could not endorse rebellion for fear that it would be "catching," nor could he support a cause that preserved slavery. Despite the appeals of Confederate diplomats for recognition and arms, both France and Britain proclaimed their neutrality. In response to the Confederate cotton ban, Europe fell back on alternate supplies of cotton, from India, Egypt and elsewhere. Meanwhile, the South found itself without much needed money to buy weapons.

While Lincoln was willing to accept European neutrality, when Napoleon III tried to effect a six-month armistice with the support of Britain and Russia, Lincoln and his administration interpreted the proposal as an unfriendly act. When both the British and Russians also hedged on the plan, France opted against pursuing the idea by itself.

Unlike Britain and France, Russia openly supported the Union cause. In the fall of 1863, two Russian fleets sailed into American harbors—one in San Francisco and the other in New York, to spend the winter. Northerners believed that the Russians had arrived to discourage the French and British from intervening on the side of the Confederacy or to strengthen the Union blockade of the South. In fact, the Russian navy's arrival had nothing to do with the American war. Russia was involved in a squabble with Britain and did not want its fleet frozen in Russian ports during the winter. Nonetheless, the presence of the Russian ships was seen as a goodwill gesture in the North, and Russian sailors spent the winter being lavishly feted by the people of New York and San Francisco.

# The Union

From the moment he took office in 1861, Abraham Lincoln was guided by a central vision that the Union had to be preserved at all costs. But not everyone in the North agreed on how to proceed when the war began. Lincoln had to please a wide range of voters and politicians who had often loud and opposing views of what the North should fight for—or if it should fight at all. When the secession crisis first began, some argued it would be better to let the South go its own way. Horace Greeley, editor of the influential New York Tribune, wrote, "If the Cotton States [are] satisfied . . . they can do better out of the Union, we insist on letting them go." Lincoln, however, believed that if secession prevailed, the Union was finished.

## A Political Balancing Act

Lincoln also faced divisions within his administration. Four of his cabinet members, including Secretary of State William Seward, had been Lincoln's rivals for the Republican presidential nomination. Others, like the incompetent Secretary of War Simon Cameron (who would be replaced by Edwin Stanton in 1862), were appointed for political reasons.

In addition to trying to keep peace within his cabinet, Lincoln had to walk a fine line with Congress: some congressmen believed the war should only be fought to preserve the union, while others demanded that the end of slavery be one of the war's primary aims. Then there were the "Copperheads," mostly northern Democrats who favored reunion with the South through negotiation rather than armed conflict. Their opposition to the war was largely racial in that

**WOMEN AT WAR** Nurses and officers of the U.S. Sanitary Commission at Fredericksburg, Virginia in 1864.

## Southern Women and the War

With most able-bodied men enlisted or conscripted into the Confederate army, the maintenance of the civilian war effort turned largely to women. First and foremost, women tended the legions of wounded rebel soldiers, defying traditional southern custom that thought of nursing as too indelicate for ladies. In one instance, after the Battle of Seven Pines, when nearly 5,000 casualties were brought to Richmond, one woman reported, "Almost every house in the city was a private hospital . . . and almost every woman a nurse." Once military hospitals were established, women still had to contend with the loud disapproval of male surgeons, and some doctors regarded the women nurses as evidence of a new "petticoat government." Some women sidestepped any discrimination: Sally Tompkins of Richmond started her own infirmary, eventually earning a captains commission from Jefferson Davis. During the war, "Cap'n Sally" treated over 1,300 men.

Women also became important fundraisers for the Confederate cause: one statewide women's drive in South Carolina garnered $30,000. Other women worked in mills weaving fabric or as seamstresses fashioning uniforms and linens for the soldiers. Sewing circles turned out everything from caps to sandbags, at times supplying entire regiments with uniforms, flags and blankets. While most states initially furnished cloth for these projects, volunteer organizations had to find their own material after the first two years of the war.

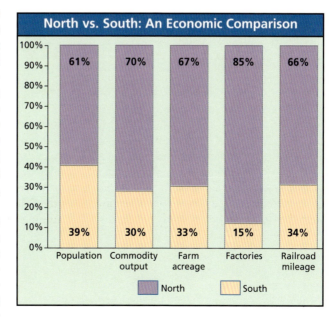

**North vs. South: An Economic Comparison**

| | Population | Commodity output | Farm acreage | Factories | Railroad mileage |
|---|---|---|---|---|---|
| North | 61% | 70% | 67% | 85% | 66% |
| South | 39% | 30% | 33% | 15% | 34% |

**NORTHERN ADVANTAGE** The Union's larger population and industrial infrastructure gave it a heavy advantage during the Civil War.

they opposed the emancipation of enslaved African Americans. Some "War Democrats" also opposed emancipation, but felt the Union could only be preserved through military victory.

Also known as "Peace Democrats," the Copperheads used the issue of emancipation to stand up to Lincoln and the Republican party. Arguing that they were standing against tyranny, they raised troubling questions about individual liberty in times of war. The most celebrated civil liberties case involved Clement Vallandigham of Ohio. As a candidate for Ohio governor, Vallandigham aroused fears among the working class that the end of slavery would lead to lower wages and a loss of jobs. In April 1863, General Ambrose Burnside, then the commander of the Department of the Ohio, declared that any person who committed "implied treason" would be arrested. At a campaign rally in May 1863, Vallandigham denounced the war as "wicked, cruel, and unnecessary." He was arrested, convicted of treason by a military court and sentenced to death. Although Lincoln altered his sentence to banishment to the Confederacy, Vallandingham had succeeded in raising important questions regarding civil liberties including whether or not a speech could be treason, and whether it was legal for a military court to try a civilian.

### The Northern Economy

When the Confederate states seceded, they took with them $300 million in unpaid debts to Northern businesses. The federal government, however, would eventually spend more that $2 million a day to finance the war.

To raise money Congress authorized sweeping tax measures, including the Internal Revenue Act of 1862, which authorized the first income tax in the nation's history. The government also issued "greenbacks"—paper money that Congress declared legal tender but was not backed by gold. Yet one crucial difference existed between greenbacks and the Confederate paper currency that plummeted in value during the war: gold and silver continued to flow into the Union's treasury from mines in California, Nevada, and Colorado. Eventually, the gold backed the paper, helping to stabilize its value.

The North's already vigorous industrial economy expanded to meet the needs of the Union army and navy, while its efficient farms were able to feed the nation and export wheat to Europe. In 1860, cotton exports had made up half of the value of all American exports, and many predicted that the loss of the South's cotton would ruin foreign trade. By 1865, however, the Union's own crop exports had more than made up for the loss.

Many northerners prospered as factories scrambled to produce all the things needed to wage war, from locomotives and rifles to blankets and shoes. Yet wartime inflation kept most ordinary workers from reaping the benefits of this booming economy.

### Northern Women and the War

Many of those ordinary workers were women. During the war, women worked in civil service, manufacturing, and agriculture. On April 29, 1861, physician Elizabeth Blackwell organized a meeting of 3,000 women in New York City, which resulted in the Women's Central Association for Relief (WCAR). The United States Sanitary Commission, founded out of the WCAR, was composed of 7,000 local chapters devoted to tending the wounded and reducing the spread of disease in army camps. The commission was the most important institution developed by women in the course of the war.

In recognition of the contributions women were making to the war effort, the government appointed Dorothea Dix superintendent of nurses for the Union army. Dix established a minimum age of thirty for her corps of nurses, and specified that women must be "plain in appearance." While most worked in hospitals, some took their skills to the front. Mary Ann "Mother" Bickerdyke, for example, tended the sick and injured at nineteen different battle sites.

### American Indians and the Civil War

While the North and South waged war in the East, American settlers continued to move into the Great Plains, Rocky Mountains and Far West. In 1862, Congress passed two far-reaching laws that encouraged further white migration into the West. The first, the Homestead Act, gave away millions of acres of the frontier to those willing to settle on it. The second authorized construction of a transcontinental railroad to the West Coast.

The increase in migration to the Plains and elsewhere during the war meant that women and children settlers became more vulnerable to Indian attacks and uprisings, at a time when many men were away from home serving in the army, and military garrisons that had previously been protecting frontier settlers were reassigned to the East to fight the Confederacy. For six weeks in the late summer of 1862, the Santee Sioux in Minnesota rose up in violent protest against the unlivable conditions on their reservations. Union forces put down the revolt, but not before nearly 300 white settlers were killed. Two thousand Indians were captured, and 303 were sentenced to hang. Lincoln ultimately commuted the sentences of all but thirty-eight of the Indians, and they were hanged on December 26, 1862 in the largest mass execution in American history.

Confrontations between settlers and Indians continued across the Western frontier, in territories as diverse as Missouri, Nebraska, and Colorado, through the war's end. The Lincoln administration made some effort to continue the practice of treating American Indian tribes as nations and conducting relations with tribal governments through treaty negotiations. Tribal delegations were welcomed to Washington and shown great courtesy—which generally masked the poor terms of the treaties that they signed while visiting.

There were some Indians that worked closely with the Union as well. Ely Parker, a Seneca Indian, served as a general in the Union army, and served as Ulysses S. Grant's military secretary.

Generally speaking, because the Confederacy did not have the great frontier that the Union did, fewer direct conflicts emerged between white Southerners and Indians. In fact, representatives from the Five Civilized Tribes of the Indian Territory that is now Oklahoma (Cherokee, Choctaw, Creek, Chickasaw, and Seminole) were among the non-voting members of the Confederate Congress. The best-known Indian fighter for the Confederates was Stand Waitie, a Cherokee who had gained notoriety among his people for signing away tribal lands in Georgia.

# The Early Battles

Once the war began, one of Lincoln's greatest immediate challenges was bringing his army up to readiness. In early 1861, the regular army of the United States stood at about 16,000 men, most of whom were scattered along the frontier. Shortly before the war began, one third of the nation's most experienced officers resigned their commissions to fight for the Confederacy. After Fort Sumter, Winfield Scott warned Lincoln that it would take at least 300,000 men and as long as three years to defeat the Confederacy. Although many scoffed at the aged Scott's assessment, Lincoln was quick to call for 75,000 volunteers. As a result, the Army of the Potomac was formed.

## Blue versus Gray

For military strategists in the Union and Confederacy, the Civil War was actually fought as three wars. The first took place east of the Appalachian Mountains, mainly in Virginia. Here, the Union objective was to capture the rebel capital, Richmond. But the North's hope for a quick victory was dashed in July, 1851, when the Confederates defeated a Union advance on Richmond at Bull Run, the first major battle of the war.

Chastened by the humiliating defeat, Lincoln moved to strengthen the Army of the Potomac by placing a young general named George McClellan at its command. In July, McClellan lead an army of Indiana and Ohio volunteers in a campaign to drive Confederate forces from western Virginia. McClellan's personal aide, William S. Rosecrans, who had been made a general based on his ability to turn raw recruits into professional soldiers, executed a difficult flanking maneuver through the mountainous terrain to secure a victory that would help keep western Virginia under Union control.

The second war took place in the region between the Appalachians and the Mississippi River. Here the Union was more successful. In the spring of 1862, a brigadier general named Ulysses S. Grant led Union troops in the capture of Forts Henry and Donelson in Tennessee. These victories in the West began to split the Confederacy in two. But success proved costly; the heavy Union casualties under Grant at the Battle of Shiloh, fought on April 6–7, 1862, shocked the North.

The third war was the war at sea. In this conflict, the North won important victories in 1861 and 1862 as the Union navy seized bases on the southern coast to tighten its blockade and cut the Confederacy off from overseas help.

Just as the land war saw the introduction of new weapons technology by both sides, so too did the war at sea. On April 21, 1861, just as the Civil War was getting under way, Union forces hastily abandoned the critical Norfolk Navy Yard—after destroying most of the yard's facilities and twelve ships to prevent them from falling into rebel hands. One of the warships scuttled at its dock was the five-year-old steam frigate *Merrimack*. Captured by the Confederates, the *Merrimack* was refitted and renamed the *C.S.S. Virginia*. On March 8, 1862, the remodeled *Virginia* attacked the Union frigate, *Cumberland*. While cannonballs shot from the *Cumberland* in defense clanged harmlessly off the side of the metal *Virginia*, fire from the *Virginia* destroyed the *Cumberland*. Hearing the news of this new iron vessel, the Union soon pressed its own ironclad, known as the *Monitor*, into action. The *Monitor*, with its flat deck

and revolving gun turret, was nicknamed the "cheesebox on a raft." In the first ever battle between ironclads, the *Monitor* met the *Virginia* off the Virginia coast and traded shots for several hours. The battle ended with neither vessel destroyed, but with the *Virginia* withdrawing to safer waters. Returning to Norfolk, the *Virginia* saw no more action because the Union Army soon invaded, and the ship was scuttled rather than allowed to be captured. The *Monitor* sank in a gale off Cape Hatteras on December 31, with some loss of life.

Both the Union and Confederacy quickly set about building more ironclads, which caught the eye of navies around the world, and warship design was changed forever.

**GEORGE McCLELLAN**

## New Orleans Falls to Farragut

In April 1862, Union admiral David Farragut's fleet steamed toward New Orleans, the key port of the Mississippi Delta and one of the Confederacy's leading cities. New Orleans was guarded by two major forts—Fort Jackson and Fort St. Philip. Farragut attacked the forts using yet another new weapon of war: mortar schooners—converted sailing ships that lobbed huge explosives into the forts. Despite intense bombing, the forts held out against Farragut's fleet. The aggressive Farragut decided to bypass the forts by risking a dash up river. Early on the morning of April 24, the fleet steamed for two miles through a storm of shot from the forts' 100 guns. But Farragut's gamble paid off: he lost only one ship, and by dawn, the Union fleet had reached New Orleans. On the morning of April 25, residents of New Orleans found Union guns pointed at the heart of what was probably the most important Confederate city other than the capital of Richmond. Fearing a ruinous bombardment, New Orleans authorities could do nothing but await the inevitable military occupation of their city. On April 29, a Union force under General Benjamin Butler arrived and received the city's surrender. Meanwhile, Farragut and his ships advanced up the Mississippi, capturing Baton Rouge and Natchez without resistance. The fleet's progress was halted only at Vicksburg, Mississippi.

**ULYSSES S. GRANT**

**THOMAS "STONEWALL" JACKSON**

## The End of the Beginning

The spring of 1862 was a hopeful time for the North. Victories in the West and at sea took some of the sting out of the defeat at Bull Run. George McClellan began plotting to capture Richmond by way of an advance up the Virginia peninsula. But in April, a hard-hitting Confederate offensive led by General Robert E. Lee drove them back. Meanwhile Stonewall Jackson conducted a brilliant campaign in Virginia's Shenandoah Valley. Lee's chief fighting force, the Army of Northern Virginia further humiliated the North by defeating Union forces once again near the old Bull Run battlefield in August.

**ROBERT E. LEE**

## Weapons of War

The American Civil War was the first war to see the use of ironclad warships. Although the French and British had developed earlier ironclads, it was the Union and Confederate navies that first built and fought whole fleets of ironclad ships and riverboats. One of the most effective naval innovations was the rotating gun turret used on "Monitor" class warships.

Most ironclads belonged to the North, whose overwhelming industrial superiority would give them the heavy advantage. This was the first "railroad war," with both sides using trains to shift troops and supplies from place to place. The South's awkward mixture of unconnected rail lines, various track gauges and engines caused transport difficulties, while the North built thousands of miles of new track to support military operations. Rapid troop movements were facilitated by the widespread use of the electric telegraph.

In 1862 the rapid-fire Gatling Gun was patented, but it was little used during the war. The Civil War saw rifled cannon made of high-quality cast iron developed. One such, the Parrott Gun, was an accurate artillery piece favored by both sides for field and naval guns. A few imported breech-loading cannon saw service with the Confederacy.

The seven-shot Spencer repeating rifle using metallic cartridges was introduced in 1863 and found immediate favor, especially in the federal cavalry. Late in the war some Union infantry were armed with these weapons. Their firepower astonished the enemy, who believed they faced a whole division rather than just one regiment.

Although the North had superior numbers, the South had the superior military leadership in Lee and Jackson. Encouraged by victory on the Peninsula and at Bull Run, Lee invaded Maryland in September. Lee's men met with Union troops under McClellan at Antietam Creek near Sharpsburg, Maryland. Neither side was able to win the upper hand in the fighting, but Lee lost over a quarter of his men to Union artillery and rifle fire in what was savage, no-holds-barred and often hand-to-hand fighting. Meanwhile Union general Ambrose Burnside sent many of his troops to their unneccesary deaths by asking them to storm a shallow stream in pursuit of Lee by crossing an easily defended narrow stone bridge—even though the shallow stream could have been forded easily in several spots. Not until the afternoon were Burnside and his men able to cross the bridge and continue their pursuit of Lee. September 17, 1862 would become the bloodiest single day of the war. McClellan lost more than 12,000, Lee almost 14,000.

When McClellan refused to follow Lincoln's advice the next day and renew the battle, Lincoln replaced McClellan—with the incompetent Burnside.

As 1862 ended, the Union met with little success in the East. In December, Burnside launched a fruitless and costly attack at Fredericksburg, Virginia. The only bright spot for the North was in the West, where the Union grip on the Mississippi River continued to grow tighter.

# 1863: The Crucial Year

At the start of 1863, the North's military fortunes were at a low point. The Army of the Cumberland was in the midst of a brutal three-day battle at Murfreesboro, Tennessee on New Year's Day. Farther west, Grant's campaign against Vicksburg, the Mississippi River stronghold, had stalled. In the East, the Army of the Potomac, still recovering from a bitter defeat at Fredericksburg, prepared for yet another ill-fated advance on Richmond.

For the Confederacy, the first half of 1863 would mark a high point. Jefferson Davis, unlike Lincoln, had found a general in Robert E. Lee who could bring him victories. When the Army of the Potomac again moved through Virginia that spring, Lee was ready. He and his army scored a brilliant victory at the Battle of Chancellorsville—a triumph made tragic by the death of Stonewall Jackson.

After Chancellorsville, Lee's Army of Northern Virginia seemed invincible to many people in both the North and the South. As summer approached, Lee and Davis planned the South's boldest move—an invasion of the North. In June, Lee's army left Virginia with the Army of the Potomac in pursuit. As July 1863 began, the two great armies met, at a small Pennsylvania town called Gettysburg.

### Gettysburg

The battle of Gettysburg began in earnest on July 1, when Confederate general A.P. Hill sent a division to discover why an expected Confederate force had not reached the area. Hill's men ran into Union artillery fire and cavalry. More Confederates joined the battle and the two forces fought fiercely between the ridges east of the town. Outnumbered Federal troops withdrew to Cemetery Ridge, on a hill just south of Gettysburg. Lee and his men arrived in the afternoon to press the attack. Despite the capture of many Union troops, Lee and his generals, uncertain of the strength of possible Union reinforcements, hesitated. A chance for a quick rebel victory was lost when at day's end, Union reinforcements did arrive.

Fighting did not resume until late the next day. Union general George Meade's men positioned themselves along Cemetery Ridge and two hills at its southern end: Big Round Top and Little Round Top. Little Round Top was vital to the battle's outcome—it commanded a three-sided field of fire, and Confederate general James Longstreet was determined to take it. At 4 p.m., he and his men charged the hill through a rock strewn field called Devil's Den where they met a Union force under General Dan Sickles.

While that fight raged, Union general Gouverneur Warren discovered that Little Round Top had been abandoned and was open to rebel conquest. Warren found reinforcements however, who arrived just in time. The troops help their positions in the face of the intense assault, as the battle raged into the night.

As the fight for Little Round Top raged, General Lee laid plans for a full-scale assault the next day. As July 3 dawned, Meade's Union force prepared itself for the attack they knew would come. Then, just after 1 p.m. rebel artillery fired on the Union positions. The Union forces held their fire, hoping to mislead the Confederates. Later, some Union units were withdrawn, leaving a football field sized gap in the Union line. Lee, sensing a chance to overrun Union positions, ordered Longstreet and his men to attack. Longstreet's subordinate, General George Pickett, was sent with a corp to charge the Union line, in a fight that would be remembered, somewhat unjustly, as neither Longstreet nor Pickett agreed with the idea of a full frontal assault—as "Pickett's Charge." The efforts of Pickett and his men were valiant but in vain. They charged almost directly into the barrels of Union cannon, but were forced back by withering fire, taking terrible casualties.

The doomed charge marked the turning point in the battle that was itself the turning point of the war. By the next day—Independence Day—Lee's army was in full retreat. Despite Lincoln's urgings, Union forces followed the retreat at a distance rather than attacking the fleeing army, and thus possibly missing a chance to destroy Lee's army. On July 12 and 13, Lee—lighting fires to deceive Meade's forces into thinking the Confederates had stopped to make camp—led his men back across the Potomac River to the relative safety of Virginia.

Yet the setback at Gettysburg, coupled with the capture of Vicksburg on the very same day, crippled the Confederate military. Lee had failed in his gamble for a conquest in the North. From that point on, the Confederacy was forced to fight a defensive war for survival. Confederate victories would follow Gettysburg, and the war would drag on for two more years, but the offensive had passed to Lincoln and his generals. Still, the cost of stopping Lee's advance had been appalling: nearly 28,000 Confederates and more than 23,000 Union soldiers dead or wounded. These casualty rates amounted to an astounding one quarter of the entire Union army and one third of the Confederate army.

## The South Under Seige

One of the main goals of Lee's failed northern offensive had been to draw Union forces away from the Mississippi River city of Vicksburg, which had been under siege since the end of the previous year. Grant had spent the early months of 1863 attempting to devise a strategy to capture the vital stronghold. With the city situated in a nearly impregnable maze of high bluffs and waterways, land assaults proved too costly, and attempts at a waterborne advance—including an effort to cut a canal which would allow Union vessels to bypass Confederate outposts on the Mississippi—repeatedly failed. By Spring, Grant had a new plan: troops were sent out on diversionary maneuvers on the river bend and inland, and with the Confederates distracted, Grant marched an army of 33,000 men past Vicksburg to attack the town from its vulnerable east side. Despite fierce resistance, within days Grant

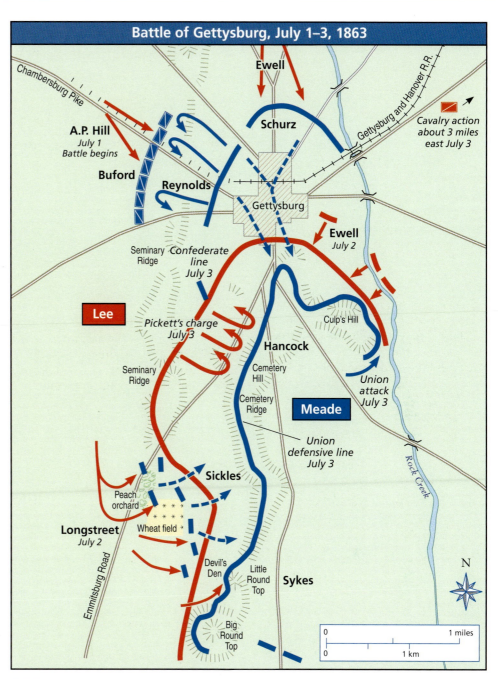

**Battle of Gettysburg, July 1–3, 1863**

**THREE DAYS OF BATTLE** Union cavalry and infantry bought time for reinforcements to arrive at Gettysburg on July 1. Lee attacked the Union forces on July 2 but was beaten back, convincing him the enemy center was most vulnerable. He underestimated the number of Union troops opposing him.

had trapped a rebel army of more than 30,000 inside Vicksburg's fortifications.

As the spring proceeded, Grant's lines around the city grew tighter. Shells from Union gunboats and artillery crashed into the town, and its citizens had to build underground shelters to escape the bombardment. With the city cut off by land and water from outside commerce, ordinary articles were in short supply—by late spring, the town's newspaper was printed on wallpaper. When food became scarce, the population was forced to eat mule meat. Somehow despite the shelling

only ten civilians lost their lives during the siege.

Beginning in May, Grant joined forces with naval commander David Porter to devise a wide-ranging plan of attack on Vicksburg's fortifications and the seven-mile row of rebel trenches which guarded the port from north to south. Eventually, the combined firepower of Grant's artillery and Porter's gunboats paved the way for the Union capture of Vicksburg.

By July, it had become clear to Joseph Johnston, the Confederate commander in charge of the troops at Vicksburg, that

**UNION DEAD** Soldiers from the 24th Michigan Infantry lay dead after the first day of battle at Gettysburg.

there was no way for his men to fight their way past Grant and Porter. On July 4, Johnston surrendered, effectively cutting the Confederacy in half at the Mississippi.

Together the Union's twin victories at Gettysburg and Vicksburg marked the turning point of the Civil War. The Confederacy would still win battlefield victories, but from now on the South would be fighting not just for its independence but for its survival.

As the second half of the year began, the focus of the Union effort shifted to Tennessee. Union forces had suffered a bloody defeat at Chickamauga and retreated into Chattanooga, where Confederates held them under seige. Then Grant arrived on the scene. In November, he swept the Confederates away from Chattanooga at Lookout Mountain and Missionary Ridge.

Thus, the year had seen the South's hopes raised and then dashed. Jefferson Davis, addressing a downcast Confederate Congress, admitted, "we now know that the only reliable hope for peace is the vigor of our resistance." Meanwhile in Washington, Lincoln had begun to feel confident enough to begin outlining plans for the South's "reconstruction" after the war.

# African–Americans and the War

Within days of the capture of Vicksburg, Confederate forces at Port Hudson surrendered as well, opening the Mississippi River to Union navigation from New Orleans. The surrender, which ended a long siege at Port Hudson, is also remembered for the service on the Union side of two particular regiments—the 2nd and 3rd Louisiana Native Guards. The Louisiana Native Guards, among the first African American regiments brought into the Union army, were engaged in some of the heaviest assaults at Port Hudson, and they performed with great valor, helping to settle the debate that had raged throughout the early years of the war about the worthiness of African-Americans as soldiers.

For African-Americans in both the North and the South, 1863 would stand as a turning point. Issues involving the goals of the war, the role of blacks as Americans with obligations to their nation, and the future of slavery all came into sharp relief during the year, beginning, on January 1, with Lincoln's emancipation of all enslaved African-Americans in the Confederacy.

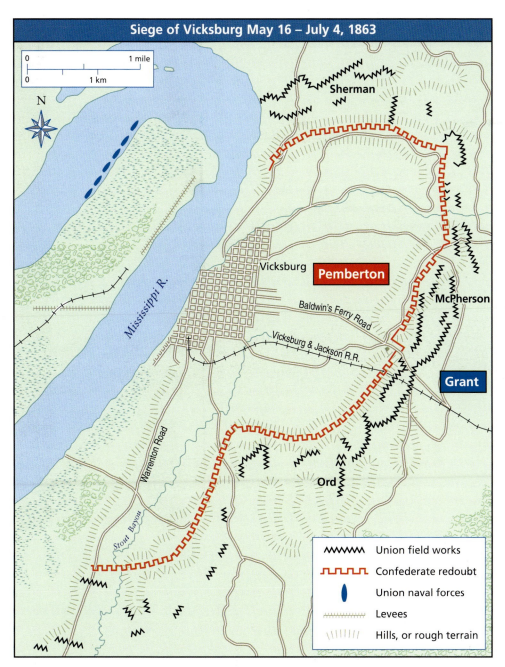

## Siege of Vicksburg May 16 – July 4, 1863

Union field works
Confederate redoubt
Union naval forces
Levees
Hills, or rough terrain

**VICKSBURG** Ulysses S. Grant risked his career by disregarding orders to march on Port Hudson, and instead brilliantly defeated rebel forces in the field and drove on to Vicksburg.

## The Emancipation Proclamation

From the beginning, both northerners and the Republican Party were divided over the war's meaning. To Democrats, moderate Republicans, and Lincoln himself, the main aim of the conflict was to preserve the Union. But to abolitionists, free blacks, and the so-called Radical Republicans, the war was about saving the Union and destroying slavery. At first, the former group—with its talk of gradually abolishing slavery over many years—predominated. But as casualties mounted in the first year of fighting, public and congressional opinion began to shift toward more immediate abolition, if only to

punish secessionist planters who most northerners felt had started the war.

Meanwhile, as Union armies pushed into the South, a new problem arose: runaway slaves. When three showed up at a Union army encampment on the Virginia coast in 1861, commanding officer General Benjamin Butler refused to return them to their masters, declaring them "contraband" of war. It was, in short, a legal cover for emancipation. With white southerners off at war, those three Virginia slaves were soon joined by thousands of African Americans.

In Washington, changing opinion and the problem of runaway slaves was forging

an ever more radical antislavery coalition between Lincoln and congressional Republicans. In April 1862, slavery was outlawed in the District of Columbia; in June, it was outlawed in the territories. Neither act freed many slaves, but it showed a growing commitment to immediate abolition, a commitment bolstered by the Second Confiscation Act passed in July. Under this bill, all "contraband" was declared "forever free." The way was being paved for the most radical measure of all. On September 22, 1862, Lincoln issued the historic Emancipation Proclamation, declaring all slaves in rebel-held territories free as of January 1, 1863. Technically speaking, the proclamation did not free a single slave. Slaves in Union-held territory would remain in bondage (to maintain the support of border state leaders); and slaves held in rebel territory were out of reach of the act. But the proclamation changed the meaning of the war. From then on it was about abolishing slavery and, with every mile of territory captured by Union armies, African Americans would be emancipated by an act of the federal government.

### African-American Soldiers

Moreover, just as African Americans had helped force emancipation by their decision to leave the plantations, so black leaders helped push into effect the recruitment of black soldiers into the Union army. At the beginning of the war, few people outside the abolitionist and free black communities believed in recruiting blacks. In the thinking of the day, blacks were considered too cowardly and undisciplined for soldiering. And the notion of giving guns to blacks in order to kill whites—even if those whites were traitors to the Union—was anathema to the vast majority of northerners. But as the war ground on—and casualties mounted—the unthinkable became possible then desirable.

On the other hand, from the moment southern guns opened up on Fort Sumter, African Americans clamored to serve the Union. Blacks understood from the beginning that the war would decide the fate of slavery. This, they believed, was their struggle. And, as Frederick Douglass understood, "once let the black man get upon his person the brass letters, 'U.S.,' let him get an eagle on his buttons and a musket on his shoulder and bullets in his pockets, and there is no power on earth which can deny that he has earned the right to citizenship in the United States." Indeed, in nineteenth-

### African-American Participation in the Civil War

**FIGHTING FOR FREEDOM** African-American soldiers participated in large and small battles in all theaters of the war.

century America, citizenship was often defined by one's willingness to serve in the military. Still, politicians hesitated, fearing public opinion and racial conflict in the ranks of soldiers.

But public opinion in the North was changing fast. As the idea that the war was about abolition—as opposed to simply preserving the Union—began to sink in, more whites came to accept the idea that if blacks were going to benefit by the war, they ought to share in the fighting. Northern commanders were also realizing that the only way to win the war was to grind down both southern armies and the South's ability to make war. Such a strategy required the North to sacrifice enormous numbers of soldiers and material, knowing that the region's greater population and resources would outlast those of the South.

Once African American soldiers took to the battlefield, their performance also changed public opinion. In January 1863, Thomas Higginson, an abolitionist-

turned-commander, wrote a well-read newspaper account, praising the African-American First South Carolina Volunteers. "No [white] officer in this regiment," Higginson noted, "now doubts that the key to the successful prosecution of the war lies in the unlimited employment of black troops." Shortly thereafter, the War Department authorized the enlistment of free northern blacks and runaway southern slaves.

Meanwhile, Boston abolitionists organized the Fifty-fourth Massachusetts Regiment, an all-black regiment commanded by white abolitionist Robert Gould Shaw. At first, the Fifty-fourth was either kept in camp or ordered to perform routine noncombat duties. They were not even issued guns or ammunition. But protests by Shaw and his men—as well as drops in white recruitment—pushed higher-ups in the military to authorize combat duty for the regiment.

The authorization coincided with Union efforts to take Charleston, South Carolina, which had been

**COLONEL SHAW FALLS** Colonel Robert Gould Shaw, from a prominent Boston family of white abolitionists, was killed leading the charge of the all-black Fifty-fourth Massachusetts Regiment at Fort Wagner, South Carolina.

under siege for a year. On July 18, 1863, Colonel Shaw and the 54th Massachusetts led the assault on Fort Wagner, an important coastal battery. Making a reckless charge along a narrow front, the Union regiments were cut to pieces before the Confederate ramparts. During the battle, Shaw was killed. Charleston would not be retaken until 1865. Yet the assault had finally proved to whites that they were able to fight and were willing to die in the cause of freedom. Nor could the pride and satisfaction in their new duties be disguised. One black soldier, seeing his former master among the prisoners he was guarding, greeted him with: "hello massa, bottom rail on top dis time."

Still, even as military commanders recognized the valor and discipline of black troops, racism prevailed. Blacks were kept in segregated camps and usually assigned to menial labor or guard duty. And, until mass protests by black troops in June 1864, they received little more than half the pay of white soldiers: $7 versus $13 a month. Even as black troops experienced discrimination within the Union army, they faced a threat on the battlefield that whites did not. That is to say, as the number of black troops rose, the Confederate government issued a dire warning: any blacks captured

in war would either be executed or returned to slavery. When word came back that black prisoners of war were being routinely executed by southern military authorities, Lincoln cut off all prisoner exchanges, although he did not carry through on his own threat to begin executing southern POWs in retaliation.

Despite discrimination on the northern side and the executions on the southern side, blacks flocked to the military. By the end of the war, approximately 200,000 African Americans were serving in the Union army and navy. Their critical role in the war effort was recognized by Lincoln when he said that without black soldiers, "we would be compelled to abandon the war in three weeks."

### Northern Unrest

Despite black willingness to serve the Union cause, prejudice in the North remained high. Many parts of the Midwest, largely inhabited by migrants from the South, were bastions of pro-southern sympathizers. These so-called copperheads—named after a particularly venomous snake of the region—turned increasingly against the Union war effort as it became associated with abolitionism.

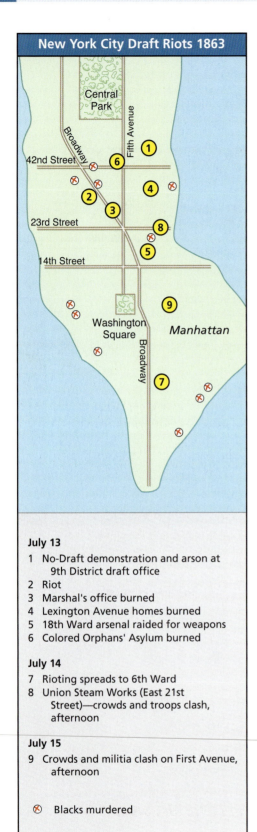

### New York City Draft Riots 1863

**July 13**

1 No-Draft demonstration and arson at 9th District draft office
2 Riot
3 Marshal's office burned
4 Lexington Avenue homes burned
5 18th Ward arsenal raided for weapons
6 Colored Orphans' Asylum burned

**July 14**

7 Rioting spreads to 6th Ward
8 Union Steam Works (East 21st Street)—crowds and troops clash, afternoon

**July 15**

9 Crowds and militia clash on First Avenue, afternoon

⊗ Blacks murdered

**CHAOS IN THE STREETS** The New York Draft Riots were the largest riots in New York City history.

Ironically, however, the most violent demonstrations against the war effort, abolitionism, and blacks was in a place far from the South—both geographically and demographically: New York City. When the war began, New Yorkers—like the majority of northerners—supported the Union cause enthusiastically. The largely working-class and immigrant communities of the city had little sympathy for white planters, even if the city's economy was closely bound up with that of the South. Moreover, most New Yorkers—like most northerners—believed the war would be short, glorious, and relatively bloodless. When that proved to be far from the case, sentiment began to change and, by 1863, recruitments began to dry up. To maintain effective troop numbers, Lincoln and his War Department authorized two measures: one was the recruitment of black soldiers; the other was the Enrollment Act of 1863, the nation's first military draft. Among the provisions of the act was a commutation fee. Any draftee who could come up with $300—more than half a year's income for the average worker—could buy his way out of the war.

By the summer of 1863, when the draft was set to commence, tensions in working-class neighborhoods of the city were high. There was resentment. The largely Democratic population was not particularly fond of Lincoln and the Republicans, whom they saw as agents of the city's business leaders. There was also anger over high prices and war profiteering by the same merchants and factory owners who could pay the commutation fee. And there was fear. Immigrant and working-class New Yorkers believed that abolition would lead to a flood of southern black workers into the city who would drive wages down as they competed for the same unskilled positions.

Thus, when draftee names were announced in early July, the city exploded, particularly its Irish neighborhoods. The draft office was the first to receive the rioters' torch, then the mobs attacked buildings associated with the Republican Party and business elites. While the undermanned metropolitan police force was able to keep the rioters out of the wealthier residential neighborhoods, they lost control over most of the city. Ultimately, the mobs turned their wrath against the city's free black community, lynching dozens of African Americans and burning the Colored Orphans Asylum to the ground, forcing hundreds of terrified children to flee the city in the middle of the night. It took several days for Lincoln and the federal government to react, but when they did, they came down hard. Federal troops were rushed back from the battlefield to put down the rioting. Dozens of rioters were shot and thousands were arrested. In the end, more than 100 people died in the New York City draft riots of 1863, making them the worst civil disturbance in American history.

# The Road to Appomattox

In April 1861, what was expected by both sides to be a short and glorious war was ushered in with cheering crowds, waving flags, and patriotic songs. By the start of 1864, after thirty-two months of total war that had left hundreds of thousands of casualties, the glory was gone but the war remained. The Civil War had become not just between armies but between populations.

Victories at Vicksburg, Gettysburg, and Chattanooga had given the North the upper hand early in 1864. On battlefield after battlefield, however, the South proved that its superior leadership and the raw courage of its soldiers could overcome greater Northern strength in men and munitions.

But the superiority of the southern troops soon ended with Lincoln's appointment of Ulysses S. Grant as the new supreme Union commander. Under Grant, the Northern military effort gained two things it had lacked—a coordinated strategy between its eastern and western armies, and a willingness to fight Lee's army to the death.

In the spring of 1864, Grant confronted Lee in a series of bloody running battles outside of Richmond. Grant's strategy as commander in chief was to fight a war of attrition, destroying Confederate armies in order to weaken the South's ability to fight. Neither side had seen fighting like this before: alone the Army of the Potomac's losses for the week of May 5 were greater than the combined losses Union forces had suffered in any previous week of the war. By summer, Grant was stalled at Petersburg, Virginia. Undaunted, he settled down for a siege, while unleashing a campaign of devastation against Confederate resources in Virginia's Shenandoah Valley—a strategy that

William Tecumseh Sherman would repeat in Georgia.

By the fall of 1864, the number of Confederate troops was dwindling from desertion and casualties. But war weariness was growing in the North as well. Grant's spring offensive in Virginia had led only to drawn out trench warfare at Petersburg. In the West, Sherman's army held Atlanta under seige, but still failed to take the city, even after months of campaigning.

Many people in the North, including Lincoln himself, believed that the Republicans faced defeat in the upcoming presidential election. Because the Democratic party favored a negotiated peace with the Confederacy, the hope of a Democratic victory fueled rebel resistance at Atlanta and Petersburg.

In this same time, Admiral David Farragut and the Union Navy defeated the harbor batteries and warships of Mobile, Alabama, one of the last ports open to blockade runners. Farragut's victory in the Battle of Mobile Bay on August 5 helped seal the fate of the Confederacy, now virtually unable to import armaments or manufactured goods. Then, on September 1, after a four-week siege, Confederate forces evacuated Atlanta for Sherman to occupy the next day.

## The Election of 1864

To mount his reelection campaign, Lincoln headed a coalition of Republicans and "War Democrats" calling themselves the National Union party. Although the Union party ultimately renominated Lincoln unanimously for the presidency, his nomination had not gone uncontested. Both Lincoln's Treasury Secretary, Salmon P. Chase, and former Republican nominee John C. Frémont made early, unsuccessful bids. Though Lincoln was opposed by some Radical Republicans, his moderate approach widened his politician base, as did the nomination of Democrat Andrew Johnson of Tennessee as his running mate. The Union party's platform rejected compromise with the South and proposed a constitutional amendment to abolish slavery.

In August, the Democratic Party held their convention and nominated General George McClellan, the former commander of the Army of the Potomac. Although fired by Lincoln, McClellan still enjoyed wide popularity. His running mate, George Pendelton, was the choice of Clement Vallandigham, the prominent copperhead. Vallandigham and his associates demanded "immediate efforts . . . for a cessation of hos-

GRAND, NATIONAL UNION BANNER FOR 1864.
LIBERTY, UNION AND VICTORY.

**NATIONAL UNION PARTY BANNER** In 1864, Lincoln chose Senator Andrew Johnson, a Democrat from Tennessee who had remained loyal to the Union as his running mate in the 1864 election campaign. The weak Johnson would become president upon Lincoln's assassination.

*"With malice toward none, with charity for all, with firmness in the right as God gives us the strength to see the right, let us strive on to finish the work we are in, to bind up the nation's wounds, to care for him who shall have borne the battle and for his widow and his orphan—to all which may cheive a just and lasting peace among ourselves and with all nations."*

—Abraham Lincoln, Second Inaugural Address, 1865

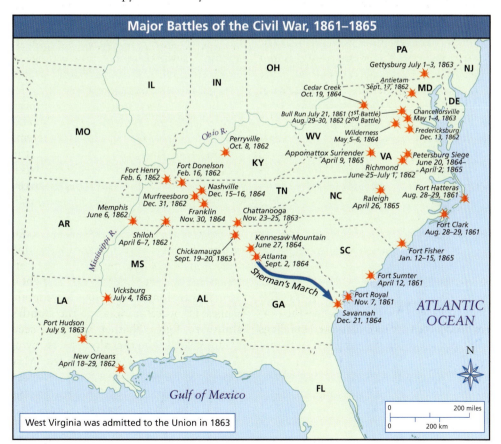

## Major Battles of the Civil War, 1861–1865

Gettysburg July 1–3, 1863
Antietam Sept. 17, 1862
Cedar Creek Oct. 19, 1864
Bull Run July 21, 1861 (1st Battle) Aug. 29–30, 1862 (2nd Battle)
Chancellorsville May 1–4, 1863
Wilderness May 5–6, 1864
Fredericksburg Dec. 13, 1862
Perryville Oct. 8, 1862
Appomattox Surrender April 9, 1865
Petersburg Siege June 20, 1864–April 2, 1865
Fort Henry Feb. 6, 1862
Fort Donelson Feb. 16, 1862
Richmond June 25–July 1, 1862
Nashville Dec. 15–16, 1864
Fort Hatteras Aug. 28–29, 1861
Murfreesboro Dec. 31, 1862
Raleigh April 26, 1865
Memphis June 6, 1862
Chattanooga Nov. 23–25, 1863
Franklin Nov. 30, 1864
Fort Clark Aug. 28–29, 1861
Shiloh April 6–7, 1862
Kennesaw Mountain June 27, 1864
Chickamauga Sept. 19–20, 1863
Fort Fisher Jan. 12–15, 1865
Atlanta Sept. 2, 1864
Fort Sumter April 12, 1861
Vicksburg July 4, 1863
Sherman's March
Port Royal Nov. 7, 1861
Port Hudson July 9, 1863
Savannah Dec. 21, 1864
New Orleans April 18–29, 1862

ATLANTIC OCEAN
Gulf of Mexico

West Virginia was admitted to the Union in 1863

0   200 miles
0   200 km

**PATHS OF WAR** The Civil War's heaviest fighting took place around Richmond and Washington, and crucial campaigns were fought for control of the Mississippi River and Tennessee.

A LITTLE GAME OF BAGATELLE, BETWEEN OLD ABE THE RAIL SPLITTER & LITTLE MAC THE GUNBOAT GENERAL.

**POLITICAL GAME** In this cartoon satirizing the election of 1864, Lincoln takes aim, as his opponent, George McClellan, holding the other cue, awaits his turn, as his running mate, Representative George Pendleton of Ohio (far left), Union general Ulysses S. Grant (to Lincoln's right), Senator Andrew Johnson of Tennessee, Lincoln's running mate, and Copperhead Clement Vallandigham comment on the match.

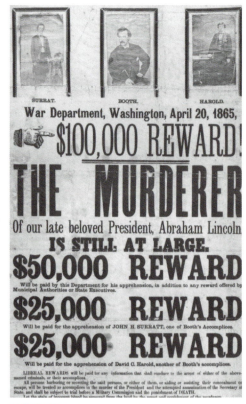

**WANTED** This poster calling for the capture of John Wilkes Booth and his associates was circulated after Lincoln's death.

tilities." Though McClellan had misgivings about such a "peace plank," Democrats hoped that a war-weary public would support him.

Thus, the stakes on November 8, 1864 could not have been higher: the vote was widely understood as a test of whether the northern public was willing to continue the conflict. As conscription fell, inflation rose, and casualties mounted, many expected Lincoln to lose. The victories at Mobile Bay and Atlanta helped to turn the tide in his favor. On election day, Lincoln received 55 percent of the popular vote and 90 percent of electoral vote. He carried every participating state except Delaware, Kentucky and New Jersey, while his fellow Republican candidates swept Congress and the state legislatures. Lincoln's most solid support came from soldiers in the field, allowed to vote for the first time, who expressed confidence in their commander-in-chief by an overwhelming margin of 78 percent.

With Lincoln's reelection, the war could only end with the Confederacy's defeat. Sherman further crippled the South's faltering economy. His "March to the Sea" devastated Georgia. Meeting little organized resistance, his 60,000-strong army destroyed railroads and plantations, confiscating or ruining any property that could be of mili-

tary value to the South. Sherman captured undefended Savannah on December 21.

Meanwhile, General Philip Sheridan conducted a successful Shenandoah Valley Campaign in late 1864, defeating General Jubal Early and helping to increase the hardship for the defenders of Richmond and Petersburg. Sheridan laid waste the fertile Shenandoah, killing or running off livestock, ruining farms—burning more than 2,000 barns—and destroying flour mills.

When the Spring of 1865 came, Lee launched one final, unsuccessful offensive at Petersburg. Then, on April 3, Richmond fell. Jefferson Davis escaped the capital and urged further resistance, but on April 9, Lee surrendered to Grant at Appomattox Court House. Although Lee's starving troops pleaded with him not to go, Lee, clad in his best uniform, mounted on his horse Traveller, rode out to surrender to Grant. Although Grant was dressed informally in a private's uniform and muddy boots, he magnanimously allowed Confederate cavalry to keep their mounts, and officers their side arms. Grant also refused to allow his men to celebrate, on the grounds that the defeated Confederate soldiers were now their countrymen again. Although some Union officers stole furniture from the Maclean house as souvenirs, many Union troops poured into Confederate positions, sharing their rations

with the nearly-starved Southerners, trading stories of the war, and talking of home.

## Lincoln is Assassinated

Seventeen days after Lee's surrender, General Joseph Johnston surrendered his army to Sherman in the Carolinas. Except for minor skirmishes in the West, peace had finally arrived. Yet Abraham Lincoln would not be present to welcome it. On April 14, he and his wife attended an English comedy called "Our American Cousin" at Ford's Theater in Washington. At about 10 p.m., John Wilkes Booth, a deranged actor with strong Southern sympathies, entered Lincoln's box, shooting him in the head and stabbing a companion, Major Henry Rathbone. Then Booth leapt down to the stage, breaking his leg in the process, and managed to escape through a side door to a waiting horse. Lincoln was taken to a house across the street, where he died early the next morning. As a doctor pronounced Lincoln dead, Secretary of War Edwin Stanton said, "Now he belongs to the ages"—a fitting eulogy for the remarkable leader who led his nation through its severest trial only to die almost at the moment of victory.

Lincoln was memorialized on April 19, at a White House service. His coffin lay in

state in the rotunda of the capital building before being placed on a special seven-car funeral train for the 1,700-mile journey to his final resting place in Springfield, Illinois. The train stopped several times en route for memorial services. In Cleveland, no building was big enough to hold the throngs of people who wanted to pay their respects, so a special viewing structure was built in a city park.

### The Legacy of the Civil War

Shortly before his death Abraham Lincoln gave a speech urging that Louisiana be readmitted into the Union. Although his plan was not well received, his speech served to present the American people with two difficult goals for the days ahead: readmitting the rebel states on terms of complete acceptance and reconciliation, and accepting blacks as full citizens enjoying every right and protection of the Constitution.

Lincoln's plan for Reconstruction was moderate, and that did not sit well with the radical Republicans who came to dominate Congress after the election of 1864. Lincoln's plan, which may well have proved more successful than the harsh Reconstruction urged by the radicals, was never implemented. With Lincoln's death the task of reuniting the nation fell to unpopular Andrew Johnson.

During Johnson's first year as president, the Union Army was demobilized and troops reduced drastically. Former soldiers and sailors were reabsorbed into northern society; the northern economy allowed for numerous job opportunities. Daily life resumed most of its normalcy; as most fighting had taken place in the South, the North did not experience the same extent of property loss, destruction and ruin. The North also had proportionally fewer casualties than the South. As a result, the Northern economy soon prospered. For blacks however, even in the North, discrimination and denial of political rights were still obstacles, and for many years, education for blacks were completely inferior to that of whites.

If Union forces returned home as victors to triumphant parades and acclaim, the homecoming for the Confederate soldier was far different. Thousands returned to find their homes and possessions looted or destroyed, crops laid to waste, and their families scattered as refugees. With slaves freed and many of the great plantations destroyed, wealthy Confederate officers found themselves in the same dire straits as the poor farmers that had so recently commanded. In short, the South lay utterly devastated. Almost a quarter of its white population had been killed in the war. Its industrial base—railroads, bridges, shops and factories—had been minimal before the war and now virtually all of it lay in ruins. Even agriculture, the basis for the economy, had declined terribly.

Beyond this material destruction was an even deeper problem. The morale of the Southern people had been shattered. Their old institutions and customs had been destroyed. Union troops now occupied formerly Confederate states, and northern Republicans held many of the statewide offices. Four million slaves were also now free, sparking even more tension in the volatile region. The physical and psychic scars of the American civil war would not heal quickly, and some would argue that they they have not healed to this day. For southern blacks, the end of legalized slavery did not begin the enforcement of civil rights. Nor would it settle the age old debate over federal power versus states rights. Although Northern business and political interests would dominate the national agenda during the Industrial Age that would follow, the pendulum would swing back and forth on that issue, and it continues to resonate today.

| Estimated Union and C.S.A Battle Casualties | | |
|---|---|---|
| **Battle** | **Union** | **Confederate** |
| **First Bull Run** (July 21, 1861) | | |
| Killed: | 418 | 387 |
| Missing: | 1,216 | 12 |
| Wounded: | 1,011 | 1582 |
| **Shiloh** (April 6, 1862) | | |
| Killed: | 1,754 | 1,723 |
| Missing: | 2,885 | 959 |
| Wounded: | 8,408 | 8,012 |
| **Antietam** (September 17, 1862) | | |
| Killed: | 2,108 | 2,700 |
| Missing: | 753 | 2,000 |
| Wounded: | 9,549 | 9,024 |
| **Chancellorsville** (May 2, 1863) | | |
| Total Casualties: | 17,278 | 17,821 |
| **Gettysburg** (July 1-4, 1863) | | |
| Killed: | 3,155 | 3,903 |
| Missing: | 5,365 | 5,425 |
| Wounded: | 14,529 | 18,735 |
| **Chickamauga** (September 19, 1863) | | |
| Killed: | 1,657 | 2,312 |
| Missing: | 4,757 | 1,468 |
| Wounded: | 9,756 | 14,674 |
| **Chattanooga** (November 25, 1863) | | |
| Killed: | 753 | 361 |
| Missing: | 349 | 4,146 |
| Wounded: | 4,722 | 2,160 |
| **Petersburg** (June 1864–May 1865) | | |
| Total Casualties: | 42,000 | 28,000 |

# Chapter 17: Reconstruction

Between 1865 and 1877, the United States of America embarked on one of the greatest experiments in social transformation ever attempted in history. The period—known as Reconstruction—has been called the "second American Revolution," for its far-reaching efforts to fulfill the political and social promise of the first. Beginning during the Civil War and reaching its culmination in the decade that followed, Reconstruction saw a near total—though temporary—transformation of southern politics, economy, and society. Reconstruction involved several elements: reintegration of southern states into the Union, the punishment of leading Confederates, a battle between Congress and the White House for political supremacy, and a struggle by African Americans and their allies for integration into the mainstream of American society.

## Wartime Reconstruction

In 1861, 4 million African Americans in the South lived in bondage, as property of their masters. Several hundred thousand other blacks—in both the South and North—lived as free men in name only, with, in the words of Chief Justice Roger Taney, "no rights which the white man was bound to respect." Less than a decade later, not only had 4 million slaves been removed from bondage, but all African-American males had achieved political and legal equality with whites, including the right to vote. While this era of equality was short-lived—largely dying with the end of Reconstruction in 1877—it established the constitutional basis for the civil rights movement of the mid-twentieth century.

Of all the cataclysmic changes wrought by the Civil War on southern society, none was more important than the emancipation of African Americans from centuries of slavery. Emancipation was not a single event, but millions of individual events involving millions of individuals. Nor was emancipation primarily set in motion by Lincoln's Emancipation Proclamation, although that event is often been cited as its spark. In most regions of the South, freedom was either seized by the slaves themselves or offered by advancing Union armies. Emancipation came whenever slaves sensed that the authority of the master no longer held sway. Emancipation, was not just a legal act, but a psychological event in the life of every African American emerging from bondage.

### A Rehearsal for Reconstruction

Among the first places to experience emancipation—more than a year before the Emancipation Proclamation went into effect—were the Sea Islands off the coast of South Carolina and Georgia. Occupied by the Union as part of the North's blockade strategy, the islands saw its white planters flee at the first sign of trouble. When planters tried to force their slaves to follow them to the mainland, most simply refused. As it had for centuries, the number of slaves in the Sea Islands in 1861 far outstripped the number of whites—as most members of the planter class spent more of their time at their coastal homes in Charleston or Beaufort, South Carolina or Savannah, Georgia than on their island plantations. Plus, with northern armies coming, slaves understood that the authority structure of the slave system was breaking down.

On the Sea Islands, one of the first things that freedpersons did was destroy the cotton gins and other property of their former masters. As emancipation advanced across the South, former slaves took advantage of their new freedom. Some shed their slave surnames and took on ones appropriate to the times, like Freeman. Others sought out local black preachers and Union army chaplains to legitimize the informal marriage arrangements of slavery times. Many took to the road—some to finding loved ones separated on the auction block; others to simply experience the freedom of movement.

The Sea Islands were not only where emancipation happened first; they were also where the first efforts at Reconstruction began. As one historian described them, wartime events in the Sea Islands represented a "rehearsal for Reconstruction." As would be the case in other parts of the South, the course of Reconstruction was determined by victorious white northerners as much as by liberated black southerners. Two groups of the former descended on the Sea Islands within months of their liberation. One included abolitionists who wanted to prove that black people were "reasonable beings" who had a "capacity for self-government." Alongside former slaves, the abolitionists established schools and churches, in order to prepare the freedpersons for eventual citizenship. Their dream—a goal shared by the former slaves—was to create a community of small land-owning farmers, harking back to the Jeffersonian ideal—still widely held in much of America and shared by Lincoln himself—wherein political freedom was achieved through economic self-sufficiency. Beginning in 1863, as the federal government began auctioning off lands that belonged to planters who had fled, several groups of blacks pooled resources to buy land together.

Not all northerners with an interest in the Sea Islands were abolitionists. Northern investors, believing that cotton was still critical to the South's future and to the American economy, wanted to put the plantations

**RECONSTRUCTION SCHOOLS** During the Civil War, northern abolitionists founded schools for freed slaves in the Georgia and Carolina Sea Islands.

back into production, using wage labor instead of slaves. Ultimately, the northern economic philosophy that was based on paid wages to industrial labor ran up against the southern Jeffersonian preference for a self-sufficient agrarian economy. Most freedmen vastly preferred independent subsistence farming to trading one master for another—even if paid.

## Wartime Reconstruction in Louisiana

A second experiment with wartime Reconstruction occurred in another area of the South occupied early by the Union army—Louisiana. As in the Sea Islands, northern abolitionist reformers helped the former slaves found schools and churches. By the end of the war, the black community had founded more than 120 schools, serving some 13,000 students.

As in the Sea Islands, Louisiana's black community made it clear that they wanted land of their own. In February 1863, however, military governor General Nathaniel Banks struck a deal with local planters: if the latter would abstain from physical punishment, provide decent food and clothing, and pay black workers—either in wages or a portion of the crop—the army would assure

that former slaves would "return[ed] to the plantations where they belong . . . to work diligently and faithfully for one year, to maintain respectful deportment to their employers and perfect subordination to their duties."

In other words, rather than allow freedmen to farm their own land, the U.S. government ordered all former slaves back to their old plantations to continue their service as employees rather than as slaves. This strategy reflected the northern industrial model based on wage labor, as well as racist assumptions that blacks were not capable of independent work and needed to be coerced. Thus, the desire of African-Americans for land of their own in order to work on their own was subverted not only by white racism but also by efforts to impose the northern industrial model on southern agrarian society, even before the war had ended.

## The Freedmen's Bureau

In the waning days of the war, Congress began to assert its role in shaping Reconstruction. Dominated by Republicans, but divided between "radicals" who wanted to punish the South and establish full civil rights for blacks and "moderates" who sought southern white

rehabilitation and limited black freedom, Congress established the Bureau of Refugees, Freedmen, and Abandoned Lands in March 1865. Popularly known as the Freedmen's Bureau, the agency took on the task of feeding and clothing black and white refugees, renting out confiscated planter land to "loyal" whites and freedpersons, and writing up and enforcing labor contracts between freedpersons and planters. In addition, the bureau worked with northern volunteer associations to establish schools and to send teachers throughout the South. By the end of the war, the Freedmen's Bureau had settled about 10,000 black and white families on lands seized from planters in Georgia and South Carolina. While it was not its intention, the bureau often encouraged blacks—who hoped to gain land of their own—to hold out against signing labor contracts with their former masters. As one freedperson told South Carolina planter Thomas Pinckney, "we ain't going nowhere. We are going to work right here on the land where we were born and what belongs to us."

Land and labor were not the only wartime Reconstruction issues on the table. There were also the matters of political power and civil rights, questions that first came to the fore in Louisiana. With their base in New Orleans, the largest free black community in the South—allied with many antiplanter, pro-Union whites among the city's working class population—began to demand civil rights, including the vote, even before the war ended. At first, Lincoln made it clear that he hoped that the state government would be turned over to moderate white planters. In December 1863, the president announced his "ten percent plan." Under the proposal, any Confederate state where ten percent of the voters took a loyalty oath to the Union would be readmitted to the Union. But as black protests continued, Lincoln shifted his opinion, requesting that the state's 1864 constitutional convention grant the voting rights to "intelligent blacks" and black soldiers. Still, he did not make black voting rights a requisite for readmission to the Union.

Whether Lincoln would have shifted further in favor of African-American civil rights is only speculation. One certainty became clear, however, upon his assassination just days after the war's end: if there was to be a push for greater black civil rights, it would not come from Lincoln's successor, Andrew Johnson of Tennessee.

**Black Colleges and Other Aid for Freedpeople, 1865–1871**

# Andrew Johnson and Radical Reconstruction

Andrew Johnson was plainspoken about his views on his black countrymen. In one address to Congress, Johnson insisted African Americans had less "capacity for government than any other race of people . . . [W]herever they have been left to their own devices they have shown a constant tendency to relapse into barbarism." Still, many Radical Republicans held out hope for a pro-civil rights, anti-planter policy in the early days of the Johnson administration, as the new president—a self-made man from the hill country of eastern Tennessee—was also known to be deeply suspicious of the southern planter class. But when faced with a decision to back freedperson versus planter aspirations, Johnson sided with his fellow whites.

Like Lincoln, Johnson believed that the former Confederate states had never legally left the Union and, therefore, their readmission did not require acts of Congress. Assuming executive branch control over the process, Johnson merely requested that southern states ratify the Thirteenth Amendment—banning slavery—and revoke their acts of secession. Once southerners took an oath of allegiance to the Union, they would get back all of their civil rights and all their property, minus the slaves. Exempted persons—including high-ranking Confederate officials and officers and persons with taxable property exceeding $20,000—could personally petition Johnson, who turned virtually no one away. Southerners immediately moved to take back property seized by the Union army during and immediately after the war. In October, Johnson ordered Freedmen's Bureau head General Oliver Howard to tell Sea Island blacks that they had no legal title to the land they were working. When Howard reluctantly agreed, he was met with a barrage of protests. "Why do you take away our lands?" a petition from a group of dispossessed farmers begged to know. "You take them from us who have always been true, always true to the Government. You give them to our all-time enemies!" When blacks resisted, Union soldiers forced them off or ordered them to work for their former masters.

Despite involvement from the federal government, the struggle over land and labor continued. Planters had lost their inexpensive slave labor force. Most had seen their savings wiped out, as Confederate currency became worthless after surrender. Still, if they could regain their land and their labor, they felt they could return to economic health and political power. But maintaining a labor force posed a challenge. Many former slaves left plantations for towns and cities where they could find better-paying jobs. Others became subsistence farmers, growing their own food on small plots of land.

## Black Codes

To counter these moves, the new postwar southern state governments—largely run by planters and their sympathizers—passed a series of strict new laws called black codes. The codes were essentially designed to return the South to a facsimile of antebellum times. The codes restricted the freedom of ex-slaves granted by the 13th Amendment and ensured a supply of labor to help repair economic losses incurred in the war. In essence, the codes maintained the freedman in paid bondage. The first, and perhaps most restrictive black codes, were passed in Mississippi in 1865. Among the Mississippi codes were "vagrancy laws" that stated that "all freedmen over the age of eighteen who did not have written proof of employment at the beginning of each year are vagrants" which made it virtually impossible for an African American in Mississippi to be legally self-employed as a small farmer, craftsmen, any other type of work other than a laborer in the employ of a white man. Other black codes in Mississippi made it illegal for blacks to carry firearms, drink liquor or even to "preach the Gospel without a license." Faced with fines that they could not pay, the "guilty" parties were then hired out to employers, often the former masters.

Harsh as the black codes were, they proved difficult to enforce. Supported by Freedmen's Bureau officials and Union army officers, many blacks refused to abide by them. Labor shortages often enticed desperate planters to entice another planter's workers to come work for him—even though it was illegal to do so. Still, the general tendency in the South was an attempted return—sanctioned by President Johnson—to the social, economic, and political order of a de facto slave economy.

In many ways, the black codes had a more dramatic impact on the North than on the South. Seeing former Confederates back in power in the South passing laws aimed at overturning the aims of the Civil War, many northerners—most of whom had had immediate family members killed or wounded in the fighting—were upset. In Washington, radical and many moderate Republicans were outraged, especially as there was little any of them could do. Until the passage of the Twentieth Amendment in 1933, Congress was largely in recess during its second year. In the year after the Civil War, that meant Congress was not in session until December 1865. As the months rolled by, and the South was reconstructed under pro-southern rules set by Johnson, frustration among congressmen grew and, with it, a consensus that Congress should take control of the Reconstruction process.

## Congressional Reconstruction

By December 1865, then, Republicans were itching for a showdown with Johnson over Reconstruction policy. And while the Republican delegation was divided between minority Radicals—led by Pennsylvania congressman Thaddeus Stevens and Massachusetts senator Charles Sumner—and majority moderates under senators William Fessenden of Maine and Lyman Trumbull of Illinois—it did agree on one thing: outrage at the arrival of former Confederate officials—including Confederate vice president Alexander Stephens as the new Senator from Georgia—in Congress. As the Constitution mandates, "each House [of Congress] shall be the Judge of the Election, Returns, and Qualifications of its own Members."

**ANDREW JOHNSON**

**THADDEUS STEVENS** Thaddeus Stevens, the fiery congressmen from Pennsylvania, was one of Congress's leading Radical Republicans.

Congressional Republicans exercised that right by refusing to recognize the representatives sent to Washington by the southern states.

Next, Congress acted on the issue of confiscated lands. While moderate Republicans voted down a measure by Thaddeus Stevens to turn over the "forfeited estates of the enemy" to freedpersons, they did reverse Johnson's orders to the Freedmen's Bureau evicting blacks from lands in the Sea Islands. In early 1866 Congress also passed the Southern Homestead Act, opening up 45 million acres in the region to anyone—black or white—who cultivated eighty-acre plots for five years. The law typified northern attitudes toward the freedpersons and Reconstruction. Where Radicals wanted active measures to guarantee black rights—including gifts of former planter estates—moderates believed in equality of opportunity, whereby both blacks and whites would be given a chance to earn their land. The Southern Homestead Act avoided what moderates feared would set a dangerous precedent: that if southern property could be confiscated and given to the poor, so might northern factories and businesses.

In February Congress's showdown with Johnson intensified when the president vetoed legislation extending the life of the Freedmen's Bureau. Unable to bring northern Democrats and conservative Republicans on board, the Radicals failed to override Johnson's veto. But then, adding fuel to the fire, an allegedly drunk Johnson celebrated with prosouthern sympathizers in Washington, denouncing Radical Republicans as traitors in an impromptu speech. The ill-advised speech pushed many moderates into the arms of the Radicals. In March, Congress passed the Civil Rights Act of 1866. For the first time, the federal government had passed legislation defining citizenship rights, including the right to own or rent property, the right to make contracts, and the right for access to the courts. The historic act also authorized federal officials to sue on behalf of persons whose rights had been violated and guaranteed that civil rights suits would be heard in federal court.

Although advised by his cabinet that many of his moderate and conservative Republican allies were turning against him, Johnson vetoed the bill. To many the justification he offered—that the bill offering immediate citizenship to former slaves violated the rights of white immigrants who had to wait five years—was far-fetched. This time moderate Republicans overrode the veto. Now convinced that Congress had to take control of Reconstruction away from an increasingly reactionary and irresponsible president, moderate Republicans passed a watered-down extension of the Freedmen's Bureau extension—requiring Sea Island blacks to buy, rather than be given, confiscated lands—and then over-rode a second Johnson veto in July.

### The Fourteenth Amendment

Meanwhile, the Joint Committee on Reconstruction — established by both houses of Congress to recommend further measures that would anchor black civil rights and federal guarantees of citizenship in the Constitution itself—submitted to the Congress the 14th Amendment. Although failing to guarantee black suffrage—a key demand of Radical Republicans—the Fourteenth Amendment was one of the most far-reaching extensions of federal powers in the U.S. history. Until its passage, the civil rights of all Americans were largely guaranteed by the states, not the federal government. Moreover, the amendment made it unconstitutional for any state to abridge "the privileges or immunities of citizens of the United States" or deprive "any person of life, liberty, or property, without due process of law." Finally, the 14th Amendment penalized states that denied suffrage to any male by decreasing that state's representation in Congress proportional to the numbers of adult males denied the vote. (Much to the chagrin of women's rights supporters, this was the first time that gender-specified rights entered the Constitution.)

Johnson was outraged by what he considered to be a barely disguised black civil rights amendment to the Constitution. Under his urging, border states and former Confederate states refused to go along, denying amendment supporters the three-quarter state majority required for ratification under the Constitution. Johnson also tried to create a political consensus

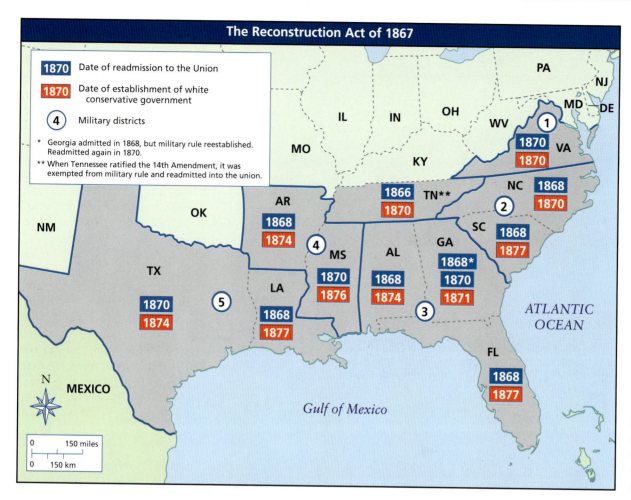

## The Reconstruction Act of 1867

**1870** Date of readmission to the Union

**1870** Date of establishment of white conservative government

**4** Military districts

\* Georgia admitted in 1868, but military rule reestablished. Readmitted again in 1870.

\*\* When Tennessee ratified the 14th Amendment, it was exempted from military rule and readmitted into the union.

**THE OCCUPIED SOUTH** The Reconstruction Act of 1867 divided the South into five military districts, each headed by a Union army general.

against congressional control of Reconstruction by forming a new national party of Democrats and conservative Republicans. With violence rising in the South—in New Orleans a white, largely Democratic mob attacked a black suffrage convention in July, leaving thirty-seven African Americans dead—Republicans refused to join Democrats, and Johnson's plan failed. Still, he remained determined. In late summer, he sought to win support through a railroad tour of the nation, even though personal campaigning by a sitting president was considered undignified at the time. Nor did Johnson help his case by drinking heavily and engaging in verbal shouting matches with hecklers.

Republicans responded with a strategy that would prove successful through much of the late 19th century. Known as "waving the bloody shirt," the strategy involved charging Democrats as the party of treason. It worked. In the congressional elections of 1866, Republicans won a three-to-one majority in both the House and the Senate, and gained control of governorships and legislatures in every northern and most border states.

### Johnson's Impeachment

With overwhelming control of Congress and state governments, the Republican majority gave its radical wing the lead in setting Reconstruction policy. First, in March 1867, came the Reconstruction Act, which divided the South into five military districts, each headed by Union army generals. Before a southern state could return to the

Union, it had to ratify a constitution acceptable to Congress and ratify the Fourteenth Amendment. Predictably, Johnson vetoed the bill and, just as predictably, Congress overrode the veto. To keep Johnson in line, Republicans then passed the Tenure of Office Act, requiring congressional approval for the dismissal of any executive department official whose position required congressional ratification.

Deemed by many judicial experts then and now to be unconstitutional, the act was passed to protect Secretary of War Edwin Stanton, a Lincoln cabinet holdover, and Radical Republican. When Johnson decided to fire Stanton in February 1868, the House voted to impeach him. As per the Constitution, the trial to remove Johnson from office then moved to the Senate. While Radicals were eager to do so, moderates feared establishing a precedent whereby a president could be removed from office for largely political differences with Congress. With presidential elections coming up—and Johnson virtually powerless already—the Radicals failed to win the two-thirds majority needed by just one vote. Johnson remained president for the remainder of his term, but largely as a figurehead.

In the election of 1868, the Republicans were again successful. Not only did the party retain more than a two-thirds, veto-proof majority in Congress, but Ulysses S. Grant, a national hero for his role as commander of the Union Army, was elected president. Grant who shared the belief that stern measures were needed to assure black civil rights and to humble for-

**THE FIFTEENTH AMENDMENT** A poster commemorating passage of the Fifteenth Amendment.

mer secessionists. Within months of the election, Republicans pushed through yet another amendment to the Constitution, this one forbidding states the right to deny citizens the vote on the basis of race, color, or "previous condition of servitude." However, as in the case of land confiscation measures, radicals failed to get everything they wanted in the Fifteenth Amendment, as the legislation failed to prohibit other voting restriction measures—such as literacy tests and poll taxes—that could effectively disenfranchise black (as well as poor white) voters without doing so by name.

Still, with the passage of the Fifteenth Amendment, congressional reconstruction had reached its high water mark. Between 1868 and 1871, both the Fourteenth and Fifteenth Amendments were ratified and all eleven states of the former Confederacy had met the requirements established by Congress—including the granting of full civil rights to black males—and rejoined the Union. And just as the radicals in Washington were reaching the zenith of their power in these years, so too were their political allies in the South. African Americans, freed from slavery just a few years earlier, were winning a degree of political power unprecedented in the nation's history.

## Social Reconstruction

On one level, the debates between Andrew Johnson and Congressional leaders that ultimately led to Johnson's impeachment and sweeping new legislation—and amendments to the Constitution—were the spark that ignited the Reconstruction of the former Confederacy. Even more than the debates in Washington, however, Reconstruction was a drama played out in the daily lives of southerners, both black and white, both rich and poor. It also featured northerners who came south either to assist in the region's social and political transformation or to profit from it.

During the mid-1860s, roughly four out of every thirteen Southerners was a former slave. Freedpersons included a majority of registered voters in five southern states: Alabama, Florida, Louisiana, Mississippi, and

South Carolina. The African-American community wanted land, economic independence from whites, a degree of political power equal to their numbers, and social equality, if not direct integration. Rallying behind the popular rallying cry "forty acres and a mule," the black community demanded that parcels of forty acres of farmland be awarded to each freedman.

Closely allied to former freedpersons, but often with an agenda of their own, came northerners. The immediate post–Civil War South was both conquered territory and a region of enormous economic opportunities, and both conditions drew northerners. First, there were administrators, both military and civilian. In greater numbers came the businessmen. From the cotton- and rice-growing Sea Islands of South Carolina and Georgia to the cattle-raising plains of Texas, northern business interests took advantage of land-poor southerners, people who owned land but had little money. With land cheap and cotton prices temporarily high due to war-induced shortages, many of these northern businessmen—as well as the politicians they helped elect—became quite rich. Southerners referred to them as "carpetbaggers," after the luggage they reputedly brought with them: the bags arrived empty and left full of money earned off southern land and labor.

Most white southerners in the mid-1860s were either poor or middle class. Most had little wealth and little land before the war, and they found themselves even more more desperate after it. Angry at wealthy planters for starting the war—and, often, refusing to fight in it—many were enticed into supporting Republicans, northerners, and even the freedpersons by offers of a better economic deal. The Radical Republican governments of the Reconstruction South created a host of programs—from public school building to progressive taxation—that poor whites could support. Still, many poor and middle-class whites could not overcome hostility to the North or their racism toward African Americans and therefore supported the planters and southern Democrats. In their eyes, white southerners who supported the Reconstruction governments were "scalawags," collaborators of a hated regime.

Finally, there were the planters. Once the unquestioned lords of southern politics and the southern economy, they had been crushed by the Civil War. Most had lost much of their wealth. Some had to sell their land and become overseers on plantations now owned by northerners. Planters also found themselves politically weakened. Still, they remained formidable opponents to Radical Reconstruction regimes. Using both violence and the ballot box, they eventually regained power and control in the region.

## Radical Republican Governments in the South

But that was still some years in the future. In the late 1860s, a new coalition of Republican forces—freedpersons, northerners, and progressive white southerners—had come to power in most of the South. Among these were a host of black politicians, such as senators Blanche Bruce and Hiram Revels of Mississippi, or Representative Robert Smalls of South Carolina. In addition, some twenty African Americans served in statewide offices, including governor, lieutenant governor, secretary of state, and superintendent of education. More than 600 African Americans won elections to serve in the various state legislatures.

Together with their white allies, these black politicians set forth an agenda that amounted to nothing less than the radical reconstruction of the South's social and economic order. Reconstruction governments rewrote state constitutions, extended the vote and made more offices elective. Debtor laws that had existed since colonial times were finally overturned and laws that turned over a married woman's property to her husband were done away with as well. Divorce—virtually illegal in most southern states—was made fairer and easier to obtain.

The Radical Reconstruction governments also attempted to rebuild, diversify, and expand the southern economy. Railroads were repaired and expanded and new manufacturing enterprises were promoted and subsidized. New roads were built into rural areas and city streets were paved. Institutions that had been established in the North during the early 19th century—including state hospitals, asylums for orphans and the insane, and more modern and humane prisons—were now founded in the South.

To pay for this vast expansion, Reconstruction governments passed a series of new taxes, in which those with more—which in the South meant planters—paid more. Not surprisingly, this created more opposition than almost anything else attempted by the Reconstruction governments. For years, the South had

**HIRAM REVELS OF ALABAMA**

**ROBERT SMALLS OF SOUTH CAROLINA**

lagged behind the North in taxation. With their governments run by planters, taxes on land and personal property were kept to a minimum. State governments offered almost no government services.

Intensifying the hostility of the planters were the methods used to assess and collect taxes. Because counties with large numbers of plantations usually had majority black populations, many of the new assessors and collectors were African Americans. Indeed, it was not unusual for a planter to find that

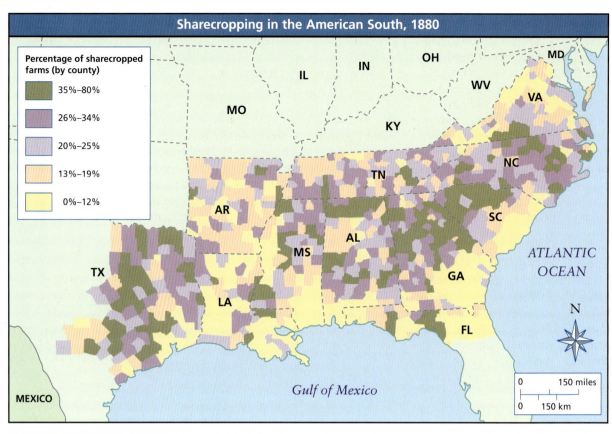

## Sharecropping in the American South, 1880

Percentage of sharecropped farms (by county)

- 35%–80%
- 26%–34%
- 20%–25%
- 13%–19%
- 0%–12%

OH
MD
IL
IN
WV
VA
MO
KY
NC
TN
AR
SC
AL
MS
ATLANTIC OCEAN
TX
GA
LA
N
FL
Gulf of Mexico
MEXICO

0     150 miles
0     150 km

**SHARECROPPING THE SOUTH** Although black land ownership rose from two percent of farm families owning farms in 1870 to twenty-one percent in 1890, the vast majority of black farmers were sharecroppers.

the person forcing him to pay taxes—with the power of the state government behind him—was one of his former slaves.

### The Sharecropping System

While some freedpersons were elected to local political offices, most remained in agriculture. Of those, the majority turned to sharecropping. As its name implies, sharecropping was a system of sharing, whereby planters provided the land, while "croppers" added the labor. When the crop was harvested, the two shared the proceeds—usually on a fifty-fifty basis. "Cropping," as it was popularly called, provided a reasonable solution to the many problems facing southern agriculture in the immediate post-war years. For cash-poor planters, it offered a guaranteed labor force without the need for wages. (In fact, it often increased the labor force as croppers, eager to maximize their own returns, reintroduced women into the fields at critical periods in the crop cycle.) For the former freedpersons, it meant relative independence. Croppers worked the land at their own pace and without direct white supervision, two benefits of supreme importance to people who had known the lash and the auction block all of their lives.

At first, "cropping" effectively served all parties. Cotton prices remained high during the first years after the Civil War and so returns to both planters and croppers were good. At the same time, as long as there were local black militias and officials, the cropper could be assured of a fair deal. Since the system inherently favored the planter—who controlled the weighing of the

crop and offered credit for seeds, tools, and food against next year's crop—it was critical that croppers could turn to the law to protect their interests. Under Republican Reconstruction regimes, black or procropper sheriffs, judges, and other local officials made sure that croppers could turn to the courts and find justice in the law if they felt their landlord planters were trying to cheat them. Planters—so recently used to having absolute command over their labor force—found the new arrangements noxious. Sharecropping, said one, "is the wrong policy. It makes the laborer too independent; he becomes a partner, and has a right to be consulted." Thus, from the very beginning of the post–Civil War era, the planter class of the South was determined to reassert its economic control over the region. But, as long as blacks, northerners, and their white progressive southern allies held the balance of political power, the planters were held in check. Not surprisingly, destroying that political power became the number one priority of the southern planter class during the Reconstruction era.

### The Birth of the Ku Klux Klan

Aside from the Civil War itself, the Reconstruction era was the most violent period in American history, as planters and their allies among the white population of the region employed systematic terror to destroy black political power and the Republican Party in the South. The backlash began just one year after war's end. In 1866, a group of planters and other whites met in Pulaski, Tennessee to form a secret organization dedicated to white power and white supremacy in the

South. Led by Nathan Bedford Forrest, a former Confederate army leader who had massacred northern black troops after they surrendered in the 1864 Battle of Fort Pillow, the group called itself the Ku Klux Klan. Allied closely with the Democratic Party in the South, the Klan—the name derived from a Greek word for "circle of men"—quickly spread across the region and, by decade's end, was operating in every southern state. It was particularly active in rural areas and in those parts of the South where the population of whites and blacks was relatively evenly balanced.

While most of the Klan's membership was drawn from the ranks of poor southern whites, its leadership was largely composed of planters, merchants, and other wealthy men of the region, including large numbers of Democratic Party officials.

At first the organization was largely a social fraternity, focusing on ritualistic ceremonies that celebrated white southern heritage. The rise of the Republican Party in the South, as well as black economic and political gains, turned the Klan into a vigilante organization that used violence and terror to achieve its ends, which included the return to power of the white planter class; the re-establishment of white social, economic, and political supremacy; and the resurrection of the

Democratic Party in the South. By early 1868, with chapters throughout the South, the Klan had turned to physical intimidation and violence. While white Republicans and other pro-black sympathizers were attacked by the Klan, the group's primary targets were African Americans themselves. Indeed, Klan violence was rarely random. Singled out were black Union army veterans—most of whom were armed and many of whom were leaders in their local communities—as well as freedpersons who appeared to be succeeding economically. Black women were also targeted for beatings, rape, and murder as a means of intimidating the black men, by showing them that they could not even defend their wives and daughters.

Not just individuals and families were targeted. A Republican rally in Eutaw, Alabama was assaulted in October 1870, leaving four African Americans dead and more than fifty wounded. While exact figures will never be known, it is estimated that as many as 10,000 southerners—largely black, but with a handful of pro-Reconstruction whites—were killed by the Klan between the late 1860s and the end of the Reconstruction era in 1877.

Not that there was no counteroffensive. For example, Klansmen employed hoods not just for the purposes

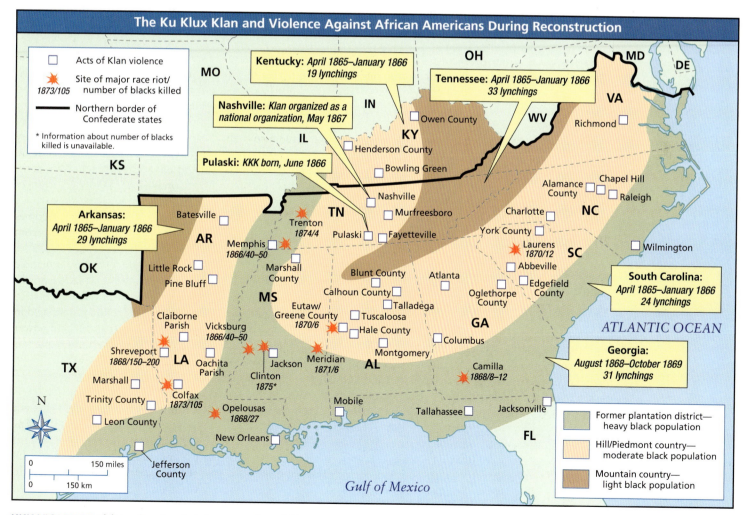

KKK VIOLENCE Although acts of violence against African Americans occurred throughout the South, much of the Klan's activity took place in the hill and piedmont regions.

of intimidation—they mistakenly believed that superstitious blacks might mistake the night riders for ghosts—but for anonymity as well. With federal troops still patrolling the South—and with local government often under the control of Republican officials—Klansmen faced prosecution, particularly after Congress passed the anti-Klan Force Acts in 1870 and 1871, which authorized federal prosecutions and the use of martial law to prevent vigilantism. Conviction under the Force Acts or the Ku Klux Klan Act of 1871—the first laws in U.S. history that made crimes by private individuals punishable by federal law—deprived convicted Klansmen of the rights to vote, hold elective office, or serve on juries.

For a time the federal government pursued the Klan vigorously. Agents infiltrated Klan chapters, gathering the evidence for more than 3,000 indictments. In South Carolina, a virtual state of martial law was declared and some 2,000 Klansmen were driven from the state. Still, the odds against destroying the organization were high. For one thing, the Klan enjoyed the support of much of the white South. It was relatively easy for Klansmen to blend into the general population. Aside from white Republicans and freedpersons—many of whom were effectively intimidated—it was difficult to find witnesses willing to testify or juries willing to convict. Ultimately, just 600 or so Klansmen were found guilty under the various federal acts aimed at the Klan, and only a fraction of those were punished with significant jail time.

### Northern Apathy

While Klansmen specifically targeted blacks and southern Republicans, they also effectively—if not entirely consciously—defeated another enemy: northern pro-Reconstruction Republicans. African American political power in the South rested on a shaky foundation: northern support. As long as Union troops remained in the South, the Radical Reconstruction regimes could remain politically viable in the face of relentless violence.

For a time, that northern political will was strong, particularly after the Republican sweep in the 1866 elections. But it did not last. Southern Democrats mounted a successful campaign to disenfranchise blacks, despite the existence of the Fourteenth and Fifteenth Amendments which prohibited racial discrimination. Through numerous election laws enacted by individual states and illegal schemes that made it difficult and dangerous for blacks to vote, the South effectively circumvented the federal statutes. Blacks were angered about their exclusion from the political arena. Southern Democrats ignored them.

By the late 1860s, northern Republicans did too, thanks to a growing weariness in the North with the "race question." Violence in the South left many northerners convinced that the region could never be changed. A commonly held sentiment was that it would be best to pull troops out of the region and let the locals fight it out amongst themselves.

At the same time, reports of corruption emerging from the South were turning northerners against the Republican regimes there. Indeed, there was enormous corruption in the South at this time. Planters and Democrats naturally blamed "carpetbagging" northern politicians and their "ignorant" black allies for the corruption. And with all of the new construction and new programs being initiated in the South, there was plenty of room for corruption. But the truth of the matter was that corruption tarnished every level of government and every region of the country in these years. It was endemic throughout the Union. Not for nothing have the decades following the Civil War come to be called the Gilded Age, an epithet coined at the time by Mark Twain and his writing partner Charles Dudley Warner to capture the excesses of wealth that characterized the period.

Northern frustration with the "race question" and corruption was compounded by tremendous labor and social strife in the northern states. In 1873, a series of business failures precipitated the worst depression in American history up to that time. Struggling to make ends meet on the farm—or battling factory bosses for a decent wage in industrial areas—made it hard for northerners to feel concern for the distant blacks. Meanwhile, the Republican Party establishment in Washington was coming to the realization that it no longer needed the southern vote to stay in power. A Republican coalition of Civil War veterans and middle-class northerners had come into being. The results could be seen in a collapse of Radical Republican leadership in Washington by the early 1870s.

Beginning in the upper South in the late 1860s and early 1870s—and then spreading to most of the Deep South by the middle part of the latter decade—Reconstruction governments fell as intimidated black and white Republicans were kept from the polls. By 1876, only three southern states—Florida, Louisiana, and South Carolina—remained under Republican governments, and their days were numbered.

# The End of Reconstruction

The Republican Party—in near complete control of the federal government since the election of Lincoln and the secession of the South in 1860–1861—was not looking forward to the elections of 1876 with much enthusiasm. The Grant administration had been rocked by corruption and scandal and the national economy was in the third year of economic depression. Businesses were failing, millions were unemployed and, in places, there was real starvation. To hold the presidency, the Republicans had nominated Rutherford B. Hayes, a whistle-clean governor from Ohio and a moderate on Reconstruction. Democrats put up the corruption-fighting governor of New York, Samuel J. Tilden.

On election night it appeared the Democrats had prevailed; Tilden had a slight majority of the popular vote and, more important, a 184 to 165 edge in the electoral college. Still, twenty electoral votes remained outstanding—nineteen in Florida, Louisiana, and South Carolina, and one from Oregon. Both Republicans and Democrats quickly claimed that they had won in the three southern states. As the Constitution offered no method for resolving such a circumstance, the nation was plunged into a period of rising tension. Congress voted to create a commission of fifteen to decide the outcome of the election, with seven Democrats, seven Republicans, and a presiding officer in Supreme Court Justice David Davis. At the last minute, however, the neutral Davis resigned from the court and was replaced by Joseph Bradley, a pro-Republican justice who voted along party lines, handing the election to Hayes.

Democrats were outraged by the results and determined to use every means within their power to block Hayes's inauguration. With the Senate in Republican hands and the House in Democratic hands, the balance of power lay with southern Democrats, and Hayes and other Republican leaders began to woo them in secret. Historians are not sure exactly who agreed to what—if

**SHARECROPPERS** Georgia sharecroppers picking cotton.

anything—during these talks. But the outcome—the so-called compromise of 1877—led to the final dismantling of the Reconstruction governments of the South. Not only were Florida, Louisiana, and South Carolina turned over to Democratic rule, but the new president agreed to confine all federal troops in the South to their barracks.

Reconstruction, which had been undergoing a slow death since the late 1860s, was not killed off by the "compromise" but it was hastened to its end. Southern blacks would continue to vote and elect their own to local, state, and federal office through the end of the century. Segregation and the full imposition of the misnamed "separate but equal" doctrine were still a decade or more in the future. Still, the "compromise of 1877" did mark the end of the federal government's commitment to one of the most remarkable efforts at social reconstruction in the nation's history. And nowhere was the loss of that commitment more sharply felt than on the plantations of the South and in the economic relations between sharecroppers and their landlords.

The presence of local politicians, judges, and law enforcement officials sympathetic to the freedperson was critical in assuring that fairness prevailed in sharecropping. It is not surprising, then, that the Klan specifically targeted African Americans, Republicans, and the candidates they voted for through intimidation, violence, and even murder. By destroying black political power, planters hoped to return blacks to subservience and assure profits generated from sharecropping would go to those who owned the land. This goal became critical to cash-strapped planters as the price of cotton began to decline from the highs that prevailed in the immediate post–Civil War shortage years.

In time, the economics of the sharecropping system came to be known as "debt peonage" or, as African Americans came to call it, "debt slavery." Croppers were forced to borrow from the

**The Emancipation of Slavery In Latin America, 1793–1888**

*1822* Date of emancipation

BAHAMAS *1834*
MEXICO *1829*
CUBA *1886*
PUERTO RICO *1873*
BELIZE *1834*
JAMAICA *1834*
HAITI *1793*
DOMINICAN REPUBLIC *1822*
GUATEMALA *1824*
EL SALVADOR *1824*
HONDURAS *1824*
NICARAGUA *1824*
COSTA RICA *1824*
PANAMA *1821–51*
VENEZUELA *1821–54*
GUYANA *1834*
SURINAME *1863*
FRENCH GUIANA *1848*
COLOMBIA *1821–51*
ECUADOR *1850*
PERU *1850*
BRAZIL *1871–88*
BOLIVIA *1831*
PARAGUAY *1840–70*
CHILE *1811–23*
ARGENTINA *1813–52*
URUGUAY *1842*
Lesser Antilles (see inset)
ATLANTIC OCEAN
PACIFIC OCEAN
ATLANTIC OCEAN
N

**LESSER ANTILLES**
BR. VIRGIN ISLANDS *1834*
ST.-MARTIN/ ST. MAARTEN *1848*
ST.-BARTHÉLEMY *1848*
ANTIGUA & BARBUDA *1834*
US. VIRGIN ISLANDS *1848*
GUADELOUPE *1848*
DOMINICA *1834*
MARTINIQUE *1848*
ST. LUCIA *1834*
ST. VINCENT *1834*
BARBADOS *1834*
GRENADA *1834*
TRINIDAD & TOBAGO *1834*
VENEZUELA

0        1000 miles
0        1000 km

**INTERNATIONAL SLAVERY COMES TO AN END** By the time that the Thirteenth Amendment to the U.S. Constitution abolished slavery in the United States in 1865, most nations and colonies in the Americas had done so decades earlier. Only Puerto Rico, Cuba, Brazil, and parts of Paraguay tolerated slavery longer than the United States.

planter to meet the farming and living expenses they accrued during the growing season. Sometimes this lending took the form of cash, but usually it was in goods such as seed, tools, and food. The interest and/or prices charged by the planter were often exorbitant. A sharecropper might find that at the end of the season, when the crop was weighed and the profits divided, he or she owed more to the planter than the cropper's half of the crop was worth. Moreover, operating the scales and keeping the books—many croppers remained illiterate—many planters cheated their tenants. If a tenant complained or threatened to find a better deal on another plantation, the planter could use law enforcement and the courts to keep the cropper in line. Laws were also passed at the state level to make it a crime to try to induce croppers away from a planter. Local industrialists and railroads were warned not to recruit black workers, except for the lowliest, poorest-paying positions. Gradually, croppers—both blacks and poor whites—found themselves so deeply in debt to their landlords that they could never leave. If they tried, they could be arrested and rented out by the state to work on their former master's land.

# Chapter 18: The Industrial Era

On May 10, 1876, President Ulysses S. Grant, accompanied by the Emperor Dom Pedro of Brazil, entered Machinery Hall at the Centennial Exposition in Philadelphia and started the largest steam engine in the world. "The Corliss engine does not lend itself to description,"wrote novelist and critic William Dean Howells after viewing the machine. "Its personal acquaintance must be sought by those who would understand its vast and almost silent grandeur. It rises loftily in the center of the huge structure, an athlete of steel and iron with not a superfluous ounce of metal on it; the mighty walking beams plunge their pistons downward, the enormous flywheel revolves with a hoarded power that makes all tremble, the hundred life-like details do their office with unerring intelligence."

To the throngs of visitors to the Exposition, the 56-foot-wide, 1400-horsepower, coal-burning steam engine represented the latest testament to American progress and innovation. Although the gathering at Philadelphia honored the one-hundredth anniversary of American independence, the gathering was not one of remembrance. Instead, the Exposition was a celebration of the American future.

The last three decades of the nineteenth century witnessed unparalleled and dramatic change in American society. The Reconstruction experiment came to an end, the western frontier was settled, and a massive new influx of immigrants from southern and eastern Europe arrived in the United States for the first time, swelling the populations of America's cities.

Meanwhile, heavy industry transformed the world of work as well as the class dynamics of American society. While antebellum America had also been divided into a rich, a middle class and a poor, the nature of wealth shifted after the war. Whereas many of the wealthiest Americans before the war had been born to wealth—and a wealth tied to land—after the war, many of the wealthiest Americans became rich through the control of industrial capital and resources—such as gold and silver mines, railroads, or steel mills.

The nature of the middle class was also transformed as technological improvements replaced the need for skilled craftsmen of the earlier part of the century. In the wake of this change, a new breed of middle class formed—often made up of manufacturing managers who supervised the work of laborers rather than directly produce goods themselves. Technology also

**THE CORLISS ENGINE**
The Corliss Bevel-Gear-Cutting Machine, seen in a wood engraving from 1876, was the premier exhibit of of Philadelphia Centennial Exhibition.

## Timeline of Technological Invention, 1870–1900

**1870** Richard Hoe invents a rotary press that can print on two sides of a page at once.

**1870** William Lyman patents the first can opener that uses a moving wheel to cut around the can's rim.

**1874** Joseph Farwell Glidden patents the first commercially successful barbed wire.

**1876** Alexander Graham Bell patents the telephone and transmits to his assistant Thomas Watson the first complete sentences to be sent via the device: "Mr. Watson, come here. I want you." The first commercial telephone operations will begin in 1877.

**1876** Thomas Alva Edison patents the first duplicating process that employs a wax stencil.

**1877** Edison invents the phonograph.

**1879** Edison patents the first commercially successful incandescent electric lightbulb.

**1881** Meat merchant Gustavus Swift invents the refrigerator car for transporting fresh meat.

**1883** The Brooklyn Bridge opens (built 1869–1883). Designed by John Augustus Roebling and completed after his death by his son Washington Augustus Roebling, it is the world's first steel-wire suspension bridge and the world's longest suspension bridge to that date.

**1884** Mechanic Ottmar Mergenthaler patents the Linotype typesetting machine.

**1885** Electrical engineer William Stanley invents the transformer.

**1885** The world's first skyscraper is erected in Chicago. Designed by architect William LeBaron Jenney for the Home Insurance Co., it is a 10-story steel-framed building.

**1888** Inventor George Eastman markets a camera suitable for amateurs, the Kodak, which costs $25 and contains a roll of film sufficient for 100 exposures.

**1888** The first successful electric trolley cars go into operation in Richmond, Virginia.

**1890** Engineer Herman Hollerith refines an electromechanical punch-card system for recording data. His company will develop into International Business Machines (IBM).

**1891** Edison invents the first motion picture system, the Kinetograph camera and the Kinetoscope, a peep-show–style viewer. Commercial operation will begin in 1894.

**1891** Inventor Edward Goodrich Acheson discovers silicon carbide, or carborundum.

**1895** Thomas Armat and Charles Francis Jenkins develop the Phantascope, one of several early devices for projecting movies on a screen. In 1896 Edison will acquire rights to it, rename it the Vitascope, and use it for commercial showings of movies.

**1900** Industrialist Harvey Samuel Firestone, who has patented a method for attaching tires to rims, founds the Firestone Tire & Rubber Co.

opened the floodgates for new service occupations, in transportation, in printing, publishing, and advertising, in finance, in telecommunications, and more.

Likewise, the nature of the lower classes changed. Certainly the greatest change was the end of slave labor in the South, replaced by paid field hands and debt-ridden sharecroppers. In the North more and more of the poor were immigrant laborers, working on the docks of port cities, as miners in the rural countryside, as laborers laying railroad tracks, as steelworkers forging the metal to make the rails, or as any of hundreds of other new occupations that were born out of America's industrial age.

In the South, whose plantation economy lay in tatters after the Civil War, economic rebirth came more slowly than in the North or Midwest, but when it came it came not because of a renewal of the pre-war agricultural economy, but because of the extension of railroads and other industrial infrastructure that allowed it to join the industrial boom.

### Inventors and Innovations

The industrial age saw one American technological innovation after another, each one helping to reshape industry and oftentimes the lives of ordinary Americans. Air brakes, barbed wire, bicycles, cash registers, electric stoves, fountain pens, gasoline engines, incandescent lamps, linotype, microphones, phonographs, railroad refrigerator and sleeping cars, steam turbines, steel alloy, telephones, typewriters, and much more all first appeared between 1865 and 1900. In fact, the pace of innovation was so rapid that by 1893, when the World's Columbian Exposition opened in Chicago, the Corliss Engine was already obsolete, the entire Exposition powered by electricity, rather than steam.

The harnessing of electrical power spurred the development of many of the most ground-breaking inventions of the period. Alexander Graham Bell's telephone, called a "toy" when displayed at the Philadelphia Exposition in 1876, became a necessity in short order; over 1 million and a half telephones were installed in family homes by 1900.

Even more important as an inventor than Bell was "The Wizard of Menlo Park," Thomas Alva Edison. At the 1876 founding of his Menlo Park, New Jersey laboratory, Edison promised to produce a "minor invention every ten days or so and a big thing every six months or so." He came close, developing the phonograph, lightbulb, an improved telephone, motion pictures, and hundreds of other inventions large and small. Edison received financial backing from New York banker J. P. Morgan, and launched the first electric company in 1882, in New York, and in 1888, followed with Edison General Electric Company to mass produce lightbulbs. Edison's only major error during his illustrious career was to choose direct electric

**THE TELEPHONE**
Alexander Graham Bell demonstrates his telephone at the Lyceum, in Salem, Massachusetts.

current, which limited electric transmission to a range of about 2 miles.

Edison's error proved costly when George Westinghouse purchased the patent rights for alternating current (AC) technology from a Croatian immigrant named Nikola Tesla. While Tesla worked for both Edison and Westinghouse at various times in his career, he preferred working independently. In doing so, Tesla invented an induction coil still used in radio technology today. He established an electric power station at Niagara Falls in 1893, and discovered stationary waves, proving that Earth is a conductor.

## Mining Natural Resources

Boosted by technology and the financial capital needed to develop them, the American industrial age of the late nineteenth century was powered by the nation's abundant natural resources. From the beginning of the European experience in the Americas, the search of gold and other riches had been a motivating force behind the exploration and settlement of North America. Until the California Gold Rush of the 1850s those riches remained a goal rather than a reality. Yet even the California gold fever only scratched the surface of the resources hidden in the North American landscape. For the most part the California "forty-niners" were solo operators, using inexpensive and inefficient placer mining techniques in which dirt was washed away to uncover ore. Likewise, the gold and silver strikes of decades that followed uncovered only the easiest ore to be found. Extracting underground gold and silver was much more expensive and required larger scale operations.

Until Andrew Carnegie began mass producing steel in the 1870s, most large-scale manufacturers in the United States were textile companies, rather than in heavy industry. As the mining industry developed, businesses began to focus not only on precious metals like gold and silver, but other minerals like iron, zinc, talc, copper, and oil. Although rich deposits of iron were discovered and mined in Minnesota and Michigan beginning in the 1850s, iron's lack of durability meant that it was only suitable for smaller-scale implements and equipment such as plows and hand tools. Although copper was first used primarily in household items, it proved much more adaptable than iron. By the 1880s it had become a key component in new industries like oil refining, telecommunications, and electrical power generation. By 1900 the value of copper produced by U.S. firms equalled that of gold and silver combined.

Likewise, coal production soared during the late 1800s, as coal-burning steam engines like the Corliss replaced water-wheel power. Where manufacturing had previously depended on proximity to a moving water source (often in remote rural areas), coal powered engines could be located anywhere, which meant that they were increasingly built in cities, which offered large labor pools and access to transportation hubs.

Even more dramatic was the harnessing of petroleum by industry. The presence of petroleum in western Pennsylvania was well-known. It was referred to as "rock oil" or "Seneca oil" after local Indians, whose chief Red Jacket had supposedly shared its healing secrets with the white man. While petroleum's healing properties were at best unsubstantiated, no other uses for it were known. In 1854, a lawyer named George Bissell decided to send a sample to a distinguished Yale professor named Benjamin Silliman, Jr., asking him to explore alternate uses for it for a fee of $526.08 (or the

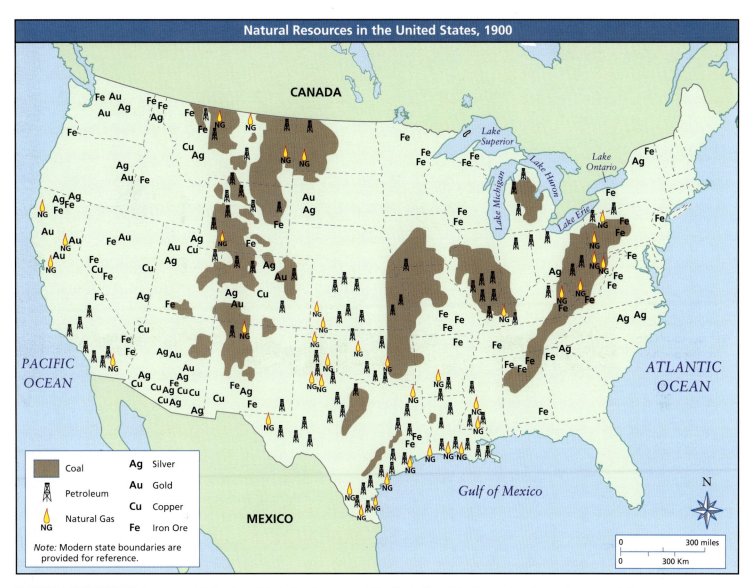

### Natural Resources in the United States, 1900

**Legend:**
- Coal
- Petroleum
- Natural Gas (NG)
- **Ag** Silver
- **Au** Gold
- **Cu** Copper
- **Fe** Iron Ore

*Note: Modern state boundaries are provided for reference.*

0 — 300 miles
0 — 300 Km

**NATURAL RESOURCES** Between 1859 when Edwin Drake tapped the first oil well in Pennsylvania, to the turn of the century, nationwide oil and natural gas discoveries along with mineral resources helped fuel the industrial age.

modern equivalent of about $5000.) When the professor reported that "rock oil" could be used as both a lighting source and industrial lubricant, Bissell began drilling. In 1859, Edwin Drake, a Bissell employee, tapped the first oil well in Titusville, Pennsylvania. While the well was initially mocked with the name "Drake's Folly," by the 1870s, an American oil industry was producing over 20 million barrels of oil a year.

### The Transcontintental Railroad

Before the completion of the first transcontinental railroad in 1869, mail, goods, and people moving between the eastern United States and the Pacific Coast faced a long, difficult overland journey, sea voyage or combination of the two. The limits to this system also greatly inhibited the geographic spread of industry out of the Northeast and Midwest. The effort to solve this prob-

lem began in 1861, when engineer Theodore Judah joined with four California businessmen to form the Central Pacific Railroad, which began laying track eastward from Sacramento in 1863. An 1862 act of Congress set up the westward-bound Union Pacific Railroad, but construction was held up until 1865 and the end of the Civil War. In that year, Union Pacific track began moving westward from Omaha, Nebraska.

For the next four years, the two lines moved toward each other, with Chinese laborers on the Central Pacific blasting and tunnelling through the snow covered high Sierra mountains, while Irish and other immigrant workers on the Union Pacific pushed across the desert and plains.

In May 1869, the two rail lines met at Promontory Summit in Utah Territory. When the famous "last spike" was driven in, uniting the east and west coasts by rail,

a newspaper joyfully announced "the annexation of the United States."

Six years later, as part of the 1876 centennial celebrations, a "Transcontinental Express" ceremoniously raced from New York to San Francisco in three days, 11 hours and 39 minutes. In 1881, a second transcontinental link was completed, when the Atchison, Topeka & Santa Fe Railroad met up with the Southern Pacific in Deming, New Mexico Territory, followed two years later by a third cross-country line, as the Northern Pacific linked the Great Lakes region to Seattle, Washington.

### Credit Mobilier

Financing construction of the transcontinental railroad—the biggest construction project of the nineteenth century—proved almost as difficult as laying the track. It was also rife with corruption. In 1872, a scandal

*"When I want to buy up any politicians I always find the anti-monopolist the most purchasable. They don't come so high."*

—William H. Vanderbilt, interview aboard his special train, approaching Chicago, October 8, 1882

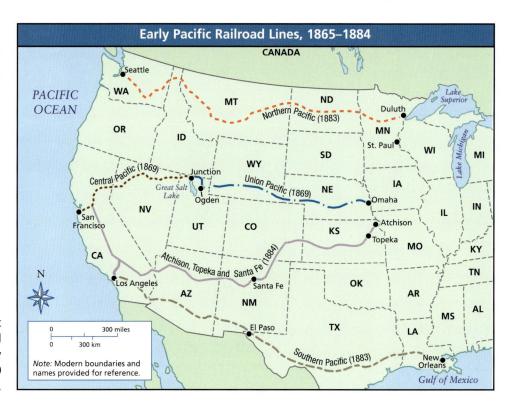

**Early Pacific Railroad Lines, 1865–1884**

Note: Modern boundaries and names provided for reference.

**THE AGE OF THE RAILROAD** The first transcontinental railroad was completed at Promontory Summit, Utah in 1869. By 1880, American railroads had laid 93,000 miles of track.

known as Credit Mobilier erupted in the press. During the railroad's construction it was learned Union Pacific Railroad directors formed a company called Credit Mobilier, and then used it to award themselves rich construction contracts. During the life of the company, millions of dollars in government money were siphoned off into the pockets of the directors and their friends. In order to forestall a congressional investigation, one of the directors distributed shares to congressmen (among those accused was future president James Garfield), Cabinet members, and even Vice President Schuyler Colfax.

While the press did uncover the Credit Mobilier scandal, it was far from an isolated incident. In New York City at this time, William Marcy "Boss" Tweed and his cronies plundered up to $200 million dollars from the city's treasury during the 1860s and early 1870s. During the same period, Louisiana's governor Henry Warmouth took in $100,000 a year despite an official salary of $8000. Contracts for the rebuilding and expansion of railroads in the South offered the unscrupulous opportunities for enrichment off the public till. On the federal level, civil service appointments were doled out to supporters based on favoritism rather than qualifications. Another future president, Chester A. Arthur, is said to have gained $40,000 by illegally using his influence as Collector of the Port of New York.

## The Birth of Corporate America

Between 1870 and 1900, industrialization vastly increased the wealth of the United States. Yet much of the wealth was held by a very small number of men. In 1900 the richest one percent of American households held 45 percent of the wealth. Some people considered these industrialists "captains of industry" because their business skills transformed the economy. Others called them "robber barons" because their wealth was not of their creation, was at the expense of workers, and was also bolstered by less-than-honest practices.

### Andrew Carnegie

One prime example was Andrew Carnegie. The son of a poor Scottish weaver, Carnegie immigrated with his family to Pittsburgh in 1848. His early career was spent with the Pennsylvania Railroad, which he left in 1865. In 1872–73, he founded a steel mill in Homestead, Pennsylvania, which eventually became the Carnegie Steel Company. Carnegie adopted the Bessemer and open-hearth manufacturing processes to successfully produce cheap and plentiful steel. He kept costs low in part through traditional means—by slashing worker wages while increasing the number of hours they worked. Carnegie also cut costs through

"vertical integration"—buying the land that contained the raw materials for steel and owning the ships and railroads that transported supplies. Many of Carnegie's purchases occurred during downturns in the national economy, allowing him to make his acquisitions on the cheap.

### John D. Rockefeller

Like Carnegie, John D. Rockefeller, a former hay, grain, and meat salesmen from Cleveland, also used new technologies and savvy management to build a fortune. Four years after "Drake's Folly" was drilled in Pennsylvania, Rockefeller sensed the expanding need for oil, and built his first refinery. In 1870 he created the Standard Oil Company, which bought out all of its local competitors by 1872, giving it enormous power when negotiating with railroads for good shipping rates on oil. In 1881 Standard's stock was placed under the control of a board of nine trustees, establishing the first major U.S. trust. Although Standard Oil would be found in 1910 to violate anti-trust legislation and be broken up into smaller firms, by the turn of the century, Rockefeller had become the richest man in the nation.

### Survival of the Fittest

In 1889, Andrew Carnegie published a volume called *The Gospel of Wealth and Other Timely Essays*. In it, he argued that the man of wealth had an obligation "to set an example of modest, unostentatious living,

## The Westward Movement of Iron and Steel Production to 1900

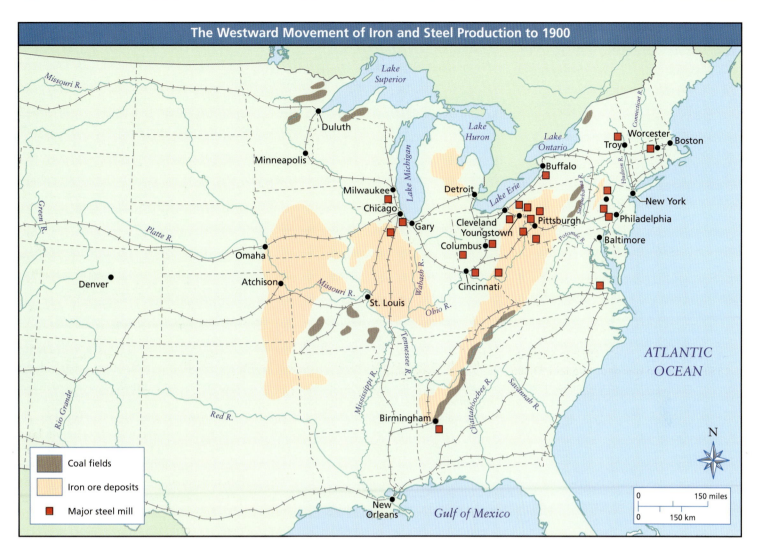

**Legend:**
- Coal fields
- Iron ore deposits
- Major steel mill

**INDUSTRY MOVES WEST** The nation's expanding railroad system allowed iron and steel production to spread throughout the eastern United States.

shunning display of extravagance; to provide moderately for the legitimate wants of those dependant upon him; and after doing so, to consider all surplus revenues which came to him as trust funds, which he is called upon to administer...in the manner which, in his judgement, is best calculated to produce the most beneficial results for the community..." In keeping with this belief, after Carnegie sold his company to J.P. Morgan in 1901 for $250 million, he turned his attention to philanthropy, giving money to fund music halls, education, the grant-giving Carnegie Corporation, and at least 3,000 public libraries.

At the same time, despite his pledge to modest living, Carnegie lived in a four-story, sixty-four room mansion on New York's Fifth Avenue. The enormous house was heated with the help of a miner's cart in the sub-basement that carried two tons of coal a day along a railroad track from a massive bin to three large boilers.

**ANDREW CARNEGIE**
Andrew Carnegie, seen here in 1900, created a steel industry monopoly by 1880. In 1901, when he sold his company, it had become the nation's first billion dollar corporation.

## Leisure Time

In late nineteenth-century, rural areas and small towns, family entertainment was central to maintaining the household. Mothers trained daughters in floral arranging and needlework. Everyone played card games like bridge and seven-up and board games such as Twenty Questions and checkers, and enjoyed music together on the player piano (pianola) in the parlor. Community cultural events consisted of lodge- or civic group-based picnics and annual county fairs, which offered amusements and displays of livestock and new products.

In cities, cramped living quarters necessitated entertainment that could be enjoyed by the masses. City parks, like New York City's Central Park, were designed to elevate the entire community. Parks also facilitated the rise of participatory sports, such as bicycling, tennis and swimming.

The era also witnessed the rise of professional sports. Baseball, which had developed out of various English ball games, became a professional sport in 1876 with the founding of the National League. By the 1890s, boxing fans were thrilling to the prowess of the bare-knuckled pugilist John L. Sullivan.

Beginning in the 1870s, vaudeville dominated popular urban entertainment, offering a variety of acts such as acrobats, contortionists, dancing, and ethnic comedy. Similarly, amusement parks like Coney Island's Steeplechase Park began to gain in popularity. Located away from the city, they provided urbanites an afternoon's vacation. The century's end also saw the beginnings of what would become the nation's most popular art: movies. Experiments with photographing moving objects had been taking place since the 1870s, and by the 1890s kinetoscope parlors let people pay to see everyday events played back on private viewers. More meaningful was the added attraction at the end of a vaudeville act at New York's Koster & Bial's Music Hall in 1896: a publicly projected moving picture.

To Carnegie, there was no contradiction between his written statement of modesty and the physical surroundings of his New York home. Most of the great industrialists of the era were firm believers in a philosophy known as Social Darwinism—a distorted application of Charles Darwin's biological theory of natural selection to social relations between the classes. Social Darwinist writers Herbert Spencer and William Graham Sumner argued that competition for survival applied to the marketplace as well. Just as survival of the fittest members of a species insured a species would survive longer and strengthen the species as a whole, competition in the business world would strengthen society by separating the weak from the strong. As Spencer argued, "If [individuals] are not sufficiently complete to live, they die and it is best that they die." Or as John D. Rockefeller told his Sunday School class, "The growth of large business is merely the survival of the fittest. This is not an evil tendency in business. It is merely the working out of a law of nature and a law of God." In other words, ruthless behavior by individuals in the business world was not only justified, but it was God's will.

### Corporate Personhood

If ruthless behavior in the business world was sanctified by God as some believed, by the 1880s it was also sanctioned by the courts. To understand how is to understand the changing nature of corporations—the institutions that took the dominant role in American society that they continue to enjoy today.

Corporations were not new in the industrial age, of course. The Virginia Company that settled at Jamestown in 1607 was a corporation, after all. But after the Civil War, the nature of corporations began to shift, as the courts began to affirm the concept of "limited liability." Prior to the war era, if a corporation went bankrupt, the individual owners of the corporation were liable and could have their personal property—homes, land, and other possessions—seized as well as merely the assets of their company. On the other hand, "limited liability" meant that the assets of a corporation could be seized, but not the personal property of that corporation's investors. This redefinition made investment in corporations a much safer and desirable venture. With more investors, a company could finance more technological innovations and advances.

In 1883, the nature of the corporation was altered even more dramatically. The headnote, or summary, of the Supreme Court's decision in *Santa Clara County v. The Southern Pacific Railroad* contained the following statement, written not by a Supreme Court justice, but by the court reporter, a lawyer who was closely affiliated with the railroad industry:

"The defendant Corporations are persons within the intent of the clause in section 1 of the Fourteenth Amendment . . . which forbids a State to deny to any person within its jurisdiction the equal protection of the laws."

In other words, the equal protection clause of the U.S. Constitution's Fourteenth Amendment, written to insure former slaves of their full rights as American citizens, was being used to shield corporations from government regulation. Technically speaking, because the headnote of a Supreme Court decision bears no direct legal weight, and is not meant to establish legal precedent in future cases, and because the actual *Santa Clara County v. Southern Pacific Railroad* decision did not establish "corporate personhood," debate continues to this day about this groundbreaking legal moment. Nonetheless, since 1883, corporations have been considered to be legal persons, entitled to "equal protection."

In point of fact, corporations in the last years of the nineteenth century received not equal protection but preferential treatment. Freed from personal responsibility for their actions, the flesh and blood individuals who ran the great corporations were rarely held responsible for actions undertaken in the name of their corporations. Advantages such as these inspired the saying that a corporation had neither a soul to be damned nor a body to be kicked. With this kind of competitive advantage, it is no wonder that the number of corporations rose dramatically in the last decades of the 1800s. By 1904, almost seventy percent of all workers in manufacturing—rich, middle class, and poor—were employed by corporations.

# Life in the Cities

As new industrial age technology allowed factories to be situated in cities, rather than in rural locations, the nation grew increasingly urbanized. By 1890 ninety percent of all manufacturing occurred in urban areas, and one-third of all Americans

**A BRIDGE TO BROOKLYN** The Brooklyn Bridge, which opened on May 24, 1883, connected New York City with the then-separate city of Brooklyn, New York. Prior to the bridge's opening, travel from Manhattan to Brooklyn depended on ferry service, which could be shut down in winter due to weather. After the bridge connected the two cities, New York City expanded rapidly, and in 1898 annexed Brooklyn entirely. This poster celebrates the bridge's completion.

lived in these cities. Eleven cities had populations of greater than 250,000, led by New York at 1.5 million, and Chicago and Philadelphia with more than 1 million. Yet while city dwellers of all classes in the late nineteenth century lived near one another, social and economic class affected where they lived, what they bought, and how they entertained themselves.

New immigrants, primarily those from eastern and southern Europe who swelled the nation's urban areas in the last two decades of the century, were largely less educated and poor. They generally worked at unskilled industrial jobs and lived in crowded, poorly designed apartments. A basic design was the multi-story tenement building with railroad flats of sequential rooms, often overpopulated with extended families and boarders.

Skilled wage laborers and middle-class salary workers lived in larger apartments with fewer inhabitants, and, once extensive public transportation systems were established, many left for the pastoral frontier of the suburbs.

If not living on inherited wealth, well-to-do families often made their living as industrial or business executives and tended to live in mansions on New York's Fifth Avenue or Chicago's Lake Shore Drive staffed by servants. The layout of a mansion was designed for maintaining staff, housing children, and entertaining. The top floor might contain a childrens's nursery, bedroom and baths, the second floor, separate bedrooms and baths for the husband and wife, and guest rooms. The main floor might boast a large foyer adjacent to a grand central staircase. The foyer would be used for greeting guests, who would then be entertained in a reception room or main parlor. The dining room would also be on the main floor, and would contain a dumbwaiter, or apparatus for conveying dishes downstairs to the kitchen in the basement, where servants worked.

These wealthy families, often leading members of the city, lived in social worlds defined by strict rules of etiquette and culture. The 400 families who comprised New York's elite society associated exclusively with one another at each other's homes, in private universities and clubs, and at socially exclusive cultural events, such as classical music performances and opera.

Unlike the rich, the middle- and lower-classes mixed more freely: They rode the same trolleys, buses, and new electric railways, and sometimes worked at the same workplaces. After 1876, when Philadelphia merchant John Wanamaker opened his "New Kind of Store," the store came to serve the entire population of his city. By 1900, Wanamakers and dozens of other department stores offered thousands of products and a variety of price levels—helping to define city living for shoppers of all means.

# Chapter 19: Immigration, Equality and Victorian America

*"[The Chinese] have never discovered the difference between right and wrong, never ceased the worship of their idol gods, or advanced a step beyond the tradition of their native hive."*

—California State Legislature Committee Report, "Address to the People of the United States upon the Evils of Chinese Immigration." (1878)

*As I write, news comes that in broad daylight in San Francisco, some boys have stoned an inoffensive Chinaman to death, and that although a large crowd witnessed the shameful deed, no one interfered.*

—Mark Twain, "Roughing It" (1872)

On May 10, 1869, when the last spike was driven to connect the Union Pacific and Central Pacific railroads, a crowd of dignitaries gathered at Promontory Summit for the celebratory ceremony. To reach this moment, a Union Pacific crew of 8,000 to 10,000 Irish, German, and Italian immigrants had met with crews of the eastbound Central Pacific, which included over 10,000 Chinese laborers. Earlier than morning, a small crew of Chinese began the final grading for the last two rails, and laid the last eastbound ties and rails in place. An Irish squad dropped the last Union Pacific rails into place.

The privilege of driving the ceremonial last spike was reserved for Leland Stanford of the Union Pacific and Thomas Durant of the Central Pacific. In actuality, the driving of the last spike was begun by a Chinese crewman. Stanford and Durant then gave light and ceremonial blows before turning the job over to railroad superintendants to finish the job.

The small crew of Chinese workers who worked to move the Promontory Summit ceremony along were actually the only members of the Chinese workforce invited to attend the ceremony. The rest of the 10,000-strong workforce, who had blasted through mountain tops and tunneled through deep winter snows to complete the Central Pacific rail, were not invited to the celebration.

## Chinese in the West

Although the first Chinese set foot in the United States in the 1790s, the California Gold Rush triggered the first significant mass arrival of Chinese to North America. Within two years of the discovery of gold at Sutter's Mill, at least 500 Chinese had arrived in California to seek their fortunes. These pioneers soon sent home stories of the riches to be had in what they called Gam Saan, or "Gold Mountain." A few made money supplying miners through retailing, restauranting, laundering, and truck farming. By 1854, as many as 25,000 Chinese were working in and around the goldfields. As their number increased, the resentment—and violence—against them from white miners rose. By the 1860s, when the Gold Rush was coming to an end, many of those not working on the Central Pacific set up shops in the growing

**IMMIGRANT FAMILY** This family of Chinese immigrants was relatively rare. Early Chinese-American communities were largely male.

**Chinese Population of the West, 1880**

Seattle
Columbia R.
CANADA
Washington Territory
3,186
Spokane
Great Falls
Missouri R.
Portland
Montana Territory
1,765
Billings
Dakota Territory
Oregon
9,510
Idaho Territory
3,379
Boise
Snake R.
Wyoming Territory
914
Nebraska
Sacramento R.
Reno
Nevada
5,416
Salt Lake City
Utah Territory
501
Colorado
612
Colorado Springs
Kansas
Oakland
San Jose
San Francisco
Fresno
Colorado R.
Arkansas R.
California
75,132
Las Vegas
Indian Terr.
N
Los Angeles
Arizona Territory
1,630
Albuquerque
New Mexico Territory
57
Amarillo
PACIFIC OCEAN
San Diego
Tucson
Texas
El Paso

Rio Grande

**Legend:**
- Chinese miners
- Chinese railroad workers
- Chinese miners and railroad workers
- ▲ Major Chinese immigrant community
- **1,765** Chinese immigrant population in 1880

0        300 miles
0        300 km

MEXICO

**PEOPLE OF GOLD MOUNTAIN** Two years before Congress passed the Chinese Exclusion Act most Chinese immigrants were centered in California, although smaller communities were spread out throughout the West. During the following decade new Chinese communities sprang up in eastern cities like New York as well.

Financial panics during the 1870s only increased hostility, resentment, and discriminatory legislation toward the Chinese. As the economy turned sour, unemployed white workers burned homes and stuffed Chinese workers onto railroad cars in a violent effort to literally force them off the land. From the San Joaquin valley to southern California's orange-growing counties, white mobs attacked and killed the Chinese, who record this time in their history as "the driving out." Denver experienced anti-Chinese violence in 1880, and five years later Rock Springs, Wyoming, saw twenty-eight Chinese murdered during a violent riot.

As anti-Chinese violence increased, many Chinese living in rural West Coast communities flooded into the segregated urban Chinatowns. Thus, the Chinese became even more physically separated from the larger white population, which in turn bred more fear and suspicion on both sides. The existence of the vice trade (drugs, organized crime groups known as tongs, gambling, and prostitution) in Chinatown further escalated anti-Chinese sentiment as it reinforced the notion of the Chinese as lustful and immoral non-Christian heathens.

Leadership at the federal level continued to discriminate against the Chinese, keeping the unfounded fear of a "Yellow Peril" takeover fresh in the minds of the public. Declared President Rutherford Hayes in 1879: "The present Chinese invasion . . . [is] pernicious and should be discouraged. Our experience in dealing with the weaker races—the Negroes and Indians . . . —is not encouraging."

Chinatown districts of San Francisco and other cities. Although many of these early Chinatowns rose and fell with the fortunes of the mines, some of the larger Chinatowns—around San Francisco's Portsmouth Square, and in Los Angeles, Denver, and Seattle, for example—grew to become vibrant and self-sufficient communities that still exist today. After the Gold Rush ended, some Chinese also trickled eastward, where new Chinatowns formed—the largest in New York City.

### The Anti-Chinese Movement

Although the thousands of Chinese arriving in America at the start of the gold rush had initially been welcomed by California officials, they soon faced growing hostility and racism. Some of the challenges came from the government in the form of discriminatory laws and court rulings. In 1854, for example, in the case of *People vs. Hall*, the California Supreme Court threw out the conviction of one George Hall, a white man who had been convicted of killing a Chinese. The Court ruled that Hall's conviction had been invalid as it was based on the testimony of three Chinese workers, who as non-whites were banned from testifying against whites in court.

The most virulent anti-Chinese racism came from white workers who saw the Chinese as a threat, and believed the newcomers were willing to work for lower wages and live in conditions that were unacceptable to white workers. But the anger of working people was also directed at those business and political leaders who they saw as encouraging Chinese immigration in order to depress white worker's wages. Anti-Chinese organizations such as the Anti-Chinese Union and Denis Kearney's Workingman's Party used a combination of political pressure and propagandizing on the government to deny Chinese immigrants their rights.

### The Chinese Exclusion Act of 1882

In 1882, the anti-Chinese movement reached its peak when, amid the hysteria and violence that raged across the West, Congress passed the Chinese Exclusion Act. This act barred the immigration of all Chinese laborers, "lunatics," and "idiots" into the United States for a 10-year period. Chinese merchants, students, and diplomats were exempt as long as they secured special papers, known as Section 6 certificates. The act was the first and only law in U.S. immigration history that banned a group of people of a specific nationality from U.S. shores.

The 1882 Exclusion Act was renewed in 1888 and again in 1892 with the passage of the Geary Act. This measure took anti-Chinese discrimination to an unprecedented level, requiring every Chinese person in America to register with the government. The Geary Act required that every Chinese immigrant carry a photo I.D. bearing a physical description. Congress deemed this necessary because so many Americans claimed to be unable to tell Chinese individuals apart since "they all looked and sounded alike."

The Geary Act also allowed for arrests without warrants, denied bail, and stipulated that white witnesses testify in any case involving Chinese immigrants.

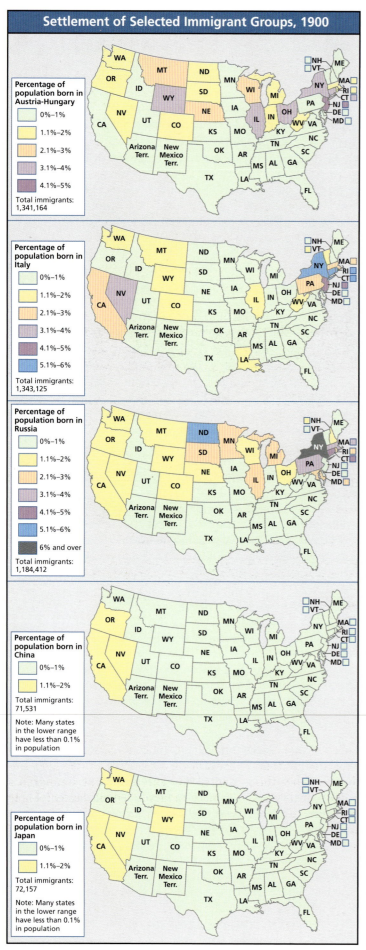

**Settlement of Selected Immigrant Groups, 1900**

Percentage of population born in Austria-Hungary
- 0%–1%
- 1.1%–2%
- 2.1%–3%
- 3.1%–4%
- 4.1%–5%

Total immigrants: 1,341,164

Percentage of population born in Italy
- 0%–1%
- 1.1%–2%
- 2.1%–3%
- 3.1%–4%
- 4.1%–5%
- 5.1%–6%

Total immigrants: 1,343,125

Percentage of population born in Russia
- 0%–1%
- 1.1%–2%
- 2.1%–3%
- 3.1%–4%
- 4.1%–5%
- 5.1%–6%
- 6% and over

Total immigrants: 1,184,412

Percentage of population born in China
- 0%–1%
- 1.1%–2%

Total immigrants: 71,531

Note: Many states in the lower range have less than 0.1% in population

Percentage of population born in Japan
- 0%–1%
- 1.1%–2%

Total immigrants: 72,157

Note: Many states in the lower range have less than 0.1% in population

**NATION OF IMMIGRANTS** While most Asian Americans settled in the West, other groups, including eastern and southern Europeans, were more concentrated in the East. New York City in particular welcomed millions of Italians, and Jewish immigrants from Russia and elsewhere in eastern Europe.

Renewal of the Exclusion Act came once more in 1902, this time with the date of expiration left blank. The Exclusion Act remained in effect until its repeal in 1943, when China and the United States allied together during World War II.

# Immigrants at the Golden Door

Compared with the enormous wave of immigration from Europe that began in about 1880, the number of Chinese in the United States at the time of the Chinese Exclusion Act was relatively small. In total, roughly 75,000 Chinese lived in California in 1880, while another 27,000 were spread out elsewhere. Yet the Chinese-American experience in the West highlights the manner in which the settlement of the West and the rise of the industrial era were shaped by America's ethnic minorities and immigrants, and by their treatment by the dominant white culture. The manner in which Asian Americans, African Americans, Hispanic Americans and the enormous late nineteenth-century wave of immigrants from southern and eastern Europe were treated called into question what it meant to be an American.

## Immigration from Eastern and Southern Europe

Between 1890 and 1920, nearly 18 million immigrants arrived in the United States. Whereas the "old immigrant" groups had mainly come from Ireland, England, Germany and other countries of northern Europe, most of the "new immigrants" came from southern and eastern Europe. About 4.5 million of these were Italian, another 4 million were Austrian, Czech or Hungarian, about 2.5 million were eastern European Jews, and another million were Poles.

Most of the new immigrants were uneducated peasants who settled in America's large cities, like New York, Chicago, Detroit, and Pittsburgh. There they filled employers' need for low-wage, unskilled labor. Most left conditions of poverty, famine, disease and/or political upheaval. Some, such as eastern European Jews, fled religious persecution as well. Once in America they found opportunities they could not have had at home, but they also met with hard labor, crowded and unsanitary living conditions, and prejudice.

In many instances immigrants from eastern and southern Europe, as well as from elsewhere, faced competition for jobs and resentment from the previous immigrant groups, such as Irish and German Americans. Increasingly, American-born nativists also viewed the newcomers as political subversives.

Religious differences played a role in this mistrust. With the exception of eastern European Jews, most European immigrants in the late nineteenth century, particularly Italians and Poles, were Catholics. Greeks and non-Jewish Russians generally belonged to the Greek and Russian Orthodox churches, respectively, while other Russians, as well as Slovaks and Hungarians, were Protestants. Chinese and Japanese, who mostly settled in California, were usually Buddhists. Because the rituals of many of these religions differed greatly from those of more widely-practiced

**A TENEMENT HOME** An immigrant family from Eastern Europe in their New York City tenement.

Protestant denominations, many native-born Americans condemned the religious beliefs of these immigrants as a threat to American culture.

## Urban Immigrant Communities

In order to protect their religious traditions and ethnic identities, immigrant groups often established ethnic mutual aid societies and parochial school systems for their children. Once established, these societies helped newcomers find housing in the community as well as work. In time this practice led certain ethnic groups to dominate specific professions. For example, two thirds of Slovak immigrants were coal miners in Pennsylvania, Italians became masons, bricklayers and builders in New York City, Jewish women worked in the garment trades of New York City, Poles in the Chicago, Omaha, and Kansas City meat-packing industry, and in mining and heavy industry in Pittsburgh, Buffalo, Milwaukee, Detroit and Cleveland. In each of these cities, members of an immigrant group often lived together in ethnically distinct neighborhoods. While this phenomenon was partly due to real-estate discrimination, it also provided a basis of community support and service.

Most immigrants resided in apartments, which frequently consisted of bedrooms and a kitchen. The kitchen, usually the only heat source, was the family center; bedrooms were sometimes rented to boarders to provide income. Public libraries and settlement-house centers provided instruction in English or civics.

Public schools, which might run from kindergarten through high school, aimed to protect children from urban vice and train them in citizenship. High school was a relatively new phenomenon, with the number of students rising nearly tenfold between 1890 and 1920, to 1,851,965 students. For entertainment immigrants attended vaudeville, ethnic theater (of note was Yiddish theater), and motion pictures. For excursions there were amusement centers, like New York's Coney Island or Memphis's Fairgrounds, reachable by trolley. In fact, the streetcar system was central to the early twentieth-century city, providing multiple spoke-like routes to and from the city center. Extensive and affordable, the trolley eased the immigrants' exit to the suburbs.

# African Americans and the Rise of Jim Crow

Just as the second wave of nineteenth-century immigration from Europe was getting under way, bringing millions of immigrants to the major cities of the Northeast and Midwest, Reconstruction, the nation's first great experiment in racial equality, was coming to an end. Still, many of the advances won by African Americans since the Civil War, such as the right of African Americans to vote and hold office, lingered on. In Mississippi and South Carolina, the two southern states with proportionally the largest black populations, voters sent African Americans to Congress through the end of the century.

Still, there were critical differences between Reconstruction and the period between 1880 and 1900. After 1880, blacks and their white Republican allies still held local and state offices, but not in nearly the same proportion as they had earlier. While blacks continued to vote in large numbers (when not deterred by violence), black voting rates hovered at about 90 percent, and their vote was tightly controlled.

**THE LOSS OF VOTING RIGHTS**
During the 1880s, 1890s and early 20th century, most governments in the South systematically stripped African-American males of their right to vote.

Segregation, or "Jim Crow" as it was called, once enforced by custom, became enshrined in law. All public places and conveyances were either strictly divided by race or restricted to whites only. At the same time, state after state in the South passed laws to effectively disenfranchise blacks. Among these were literacy tests (a difficult hurdle for those ex-slaves who could not read or write); poll taxes (almost all freedmen lacked money); all-white primary elections (particularly effective in single-party locations); and grandfather clauses, which barred grandsons of slaves from voting (all freedmen were grandsons of slaves). Coupled with disenfranchisement was legal discrimination through "Jim Crow" laws enforcing segregation and Black Codes outlawing conduct for freed slaves in such areas as vagrancy, work habits, and employment. Poverty, maintained through the sharecropping system which kept both black and white farmers in an endless debt cycle, also kept poor blacks in poor health, insufficiently educated, and tied to the land on which they worked. After federal troops left the South in 1877, lynchings and mob violence escalated, reaching all-time highs in the last decade of the century.

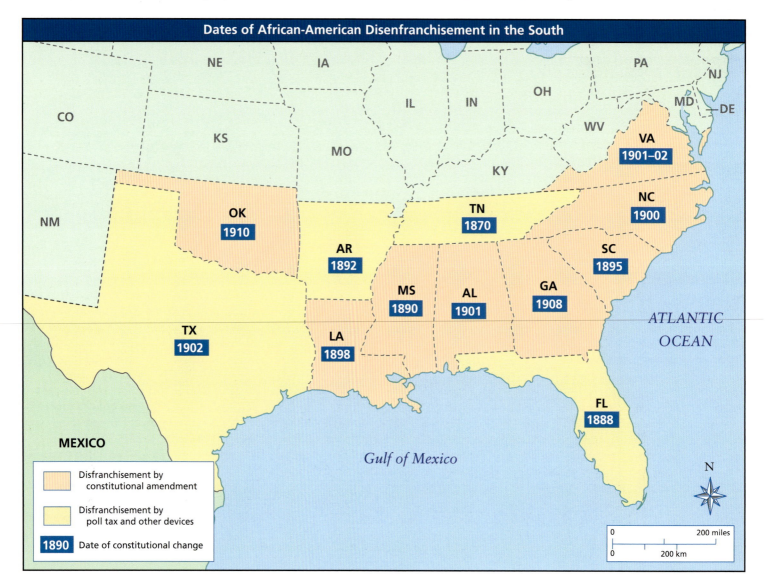

**Dates of African-American Disenfranchisement in the South**

Legend:
- Disfranchisement by constitutional amendment
- Disfranchisement by poll tax and other devices
- 1890 Date of constitutional change

State dates:
- VA 1901–02
- NC 1900
- TN 1870
- SC 1895
- OK 1910
- AR 1892
- MS 1890
- AL 1901
- GA 1908
- TX 1902
- LA 1898
- FL 1888

In addition the Democratic Party, which represented the wealthy white planter class, used fear-mongering tactics to prevent poorer whites from seeing the economic interests they shared with African Americans. With money, power, and influence on their side, white elites and Democratic Party politicians appealed to the lowest instincts of poor white southerners. Arguing that economic and political cooperation with blacks would lead to social equality—and even sexual intermixing—southern political leaders were able to browbeat many poor whites into voting Democratic. Indeed, Democratic rallies often featured bevies of white women appealing to their menfolk to protect them from the black man. When appeals to racial intolerance failed, white elites employed fraud, running up huge pro-Democratic tallies in the largely African-American counties that they controlled.

## "Separate but Equal"

As with the retreat from Reconstruction, the white South's efforts to reverse black gains were abetted by northern apathy. During the 1880s and 1890s, a series of Supreme Court decisions virtually undid all of the civil rights laws of the Reconstruction era. In an 1883 case, the court for all practical purposes eliminated the "equal protection" clause of the Fourteenth Amendment by exempting the actions of private citizens. That is to say, the court declared that the U.S. Constitution only applied in cases where the state itself discriminated. Thus, it was perfectly legal for a restaurant or a railroad to practice discrimination in its hiring or its offering of services to black citizens. The most infamous case reversing the gains of the Reconstruction era, however, was the 1896 *Plessy v. Ferguson* opinion. In it, the Supreme Court ruled that "separate but equal" facilities for blacks and whites were constitutional. In practice, however, facilities were far from equal. Black schools, for instance, were usually run down and underfunded. Following the *Plessy* decision, segregation became not merely custom but a legally sanctioned system through which African Americans would face daily reminders that they were considered inferior to whites. It would take nearly 60 years for the Supreme Court to reverse itself.

## Booker T. Washington

The institutionalization of African American inferiority also came into focus in the area of higher education. As early as 1862, Congress passed the Morrill Land Grant Act, under which the federal government offered large parcels of public land to individuals willing to establish agricultural colleges. Because African Americans were

**African-American Land Grant Colleges**

**HIGHER EDUCATION FOR BLACK AMERCANS** The Morrill Land Grant of 1862 offered large parcels of public land to those willing to establish agricultural colleges. Many of these "land grant" colleges offered African Americans an opportunity to learn practical vocational skills. The most famous of these schools was Booker T. Washington's Tuskegee Institute, later renamed Tuskegee University.

economically self-sufficient citizens. Many younger, educated, northern blacks saw Washington's caution as weakness. This conflict between Washington and more the younger generation of black leaders would grow in the decades to come.

# Women's Lives in the Industrial Era

Just as immigrants and ethnic minorities helped define the dramatic changes in American society in the last decades of the nineteenth century, so too did American women. After the Union victory in the war, the crusade for women's rights was reinvigorated. Women's rights leaders, who had lent their vocal support to the anti-slavery movement, refocused their efforts on fighting for their own rights.

In 1860, a number of new advocacy groups were formed, including Susan B. Anthony's female-only National Women's Suffrage Association (NWSA) and the rival American Women's Suffrage Association (AWSA), which accepted men as members. Women's rights periodicals included *Women's Journal* and Anthony's newspaper, *Revolution*. The idea of women's suffrage still had limited support during the 1870s, but women's

**BOOKER T. WASHINGTON**

seen as better-suited for the vocational education they would receive at agricultural schools rather than broad-based liberal arts educations, many all-black agricultural colleges were founded in the South after the war.

One such institution was the Hampton Institute, in Hampton, Virginia. In 1875, former slave Booker T. Washington graduated from the Institute. By 1881 he was heading another black agricultural school, the Tuskegee Institute, in Tuskegee, Alabama. Under Washington Tuskegee grew to become the premier industrial college for African Americans in the nation. Washington, who promoted economic self-help over political pressure on whites in the struggle for equality, was particularly popular with white leaders. To Washington it was far better for blacks to learn vocational skills so that they could support themselves than to press for rights. Acceptance of blacks as equals, thought Washington, would only come once African Americans had proven to be capable,

| Declining Birthrates in the 19th Century | |
|---|---|
| YEAR | NUMBER PER THOUSAND TOTAL WHITE POPULATION |
| 1860 | 41.4 |
| 1870 | 38.3 |
| 1880 | 35.2 |
| 1900 | 31.5 |

**SUSAN B. ANTHONY**

| Selected Private, Public and Catholic Women's Colleges, 1834–1897 | | | |
|---|---|---|---|
| NAME | LOCATION | TYPE | YEAR FOUNDED |
| Wheaton College | Norton, MA | Private | 1834 |
| Mount Holyoke College | South Hadley, MA | Private | 1837 |
| St. Mary's College | South Bend, IN | Catholic | 1844 |
| Rockford College | Rockford, IL | Private | 1844 |
| Marygrove College | Detroit, MI | Catholic | 1846 |
| Mills College | Oakland, CA | Private | 1852 |
| Elmira College | Elmira, NY | Private | 1855 |
| Vassar College | Poughkeepsie, NY | Private | 1861 |
| Barber-Scotia College | Concord, NC | Private | 1867 |
| Wellesley College | Wellesley MA | Private | 1870 |
| Bennett College | Greensboro, NC | Private | 1873 |
| Smith College | Northampton, MA | Private | 1875 |
| Spelman College | Atlanta, GA | Private | 1881 |
| Mississippi Industrial Institute (Mississippi State University for Women) | Columbus, MS | Public | 1884 |
| Bryn Mawr College | Bryn Mawr, PA | Private | 1885 |
| Goucher College (Woman's College of Baltimore) | Towson, MD | Private | 1885 |
| H. Sophie Newcomb Memorial College for Women | New Orleans, LA | Private | 1886 |
| Georgia State College for Women | Milledgville, GA | Public | 1889 |
| Agnes Scott College (Decatur Female Seminary) | Decatur, Georgia | Private | 1889 |
| Salem College | Winston-Salem, NC | Private | 1890 |
| Meredith College | Raleigh, NC | Private | 1891 |
| Goucher College (Woman's College of Baltimore) | Towson, MD | Private | 1885 |
| North Carolina College for Women (University of NC-Greensboro) | Greensboro, NC | Public | 1891 |
| Randolph-Macon Woman's College | Lynchburg, VA | Private | 1893 |
| Hood College | Frederick, MD | Private | 1893 |
| Trinity College | Washington, D.C. | Catholic | 1897 |

involvement in politics increased. For example, in 1872, the radical magazine editor Victoria Woodhull, who had made headlines for advocating free love, abortion and licensed prostitution, ran for President. By the end of the century, only two states—Utah and Wyoming—granted women voting rights, but women had increasingly gained stature through their efforts in social reform movements, such as temperance and women's higher education. Although Mary Lyons had founded Mount Holyoke College as early as 1837, after the Civil War a wave of women's colleges—some private, some public, some Catholic, and some for African-American women only—were founded. In 1890, the National American Women's Suffrage Association was founded, focusing its work on winning suffrage rights.

While they would not win voting rights nationally until 1920, women did make many advances during the late 1800s. Many stemmed from their growing importance in the labor force. In 1872, women working for the federal government were granted equal pay for equal work by Congress. More and more women worked outside the home, and new technology like the sewing machine and the typewriter only sped that process. The increase in the number of women in the workforce also had an impact on family life: as more women entered the working world, family sizes fell. In 1860, over forty-one babies were born for every 1000 white Americans (birthrates for non-whites were not tracked by the government). By the turn of the century, the number had fallen to just over thirty-one.

*"It would be ridiculous to talk of male and female atmospheres, male and female springs or rains, male and female sunshine.... how much more ridiculous is it in relation to mind, to soul, to thought, where there is as undeniably no such thing as sex, to talk of male and female education and of male and female schools."*

—SUSAN B. ANTHONY

# Chapter 20: The American Worker

**EDWARD BELLAMY**

*"Competition, which is the instinct of selfishness, is another word for dissipation of energy, while combination is the secret of efficient production."*

—EDWARD BELLAMY

In his 1888 novel, *Looking Backward, 2000–1887,* writer Edward Bellamy created a vision of America in the year 2000, in which all industry is nationalized, and wealth is distributed equally so that class divisions no longer exist. Bellamy traces the fictional evolution of American society from one rent by class struggle and inequality into a paradise featuring brotherhood, cooperation and an economy based on human need rather than unbridled profit.

*Looking Backward* met with enormous success, quickly becoming the best-selling and most influential American novel since *Uncle Tom's Cabin* more than three decades earlier. Selling more than a million copies, the book also inspired the formation of "Nationalist" clubs throughout the nation whose goal was to help bring about the society envisioned by the author.

Bellamy's rosy fictional future was certainly vastly different from the reality of the time in which he lived. The late nineteenth century economy, with its ever larger factories and automated assembly lines had revolutionized the manufacturing process—and turned factory workers into unskilled cogs in the machinery. Where once manufactured goods had been the product of skilled craftspeople who worked in their own homes or in small groups, laborers now often worked sixteen hour days, beginning work at dawn and returning home long after after dusk, six, and sometimes seven days a week. More than half of the workforce were women and children, who risked life and limb in poorly ventilated and dark buildings.

At the same time, farmers throughout the country found themselves growing deeper and deeper in debt, borrowing to meet mortgage payments, to buy new machinery or to pay hired hands until the next harvest. Caught in this perpetual cycle of debt, thousands of families lost their farms between 1870 and 1900.

## The Early Labor Movement

As the nature of manufacturing in America changed, as too did the nature of trade unions. Trade unions had existed as early as the 1790s, as skilled craftsmen such as shoemakers, printers, and carpenters joined together in local associations in cities like New York and Philadelphia. Still, union organizing was a challenging process in the early 1800s, especially as many courts held that unions amounted to illegal conspiracies. Even after 1842, when

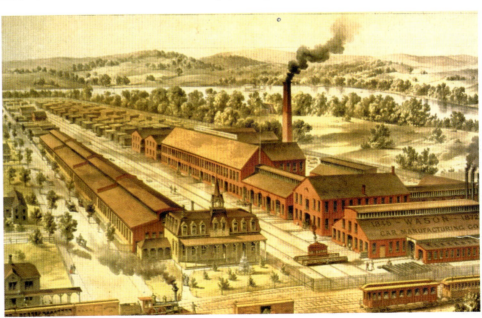

**FACTORY TOWNS** Watson Manufacturing of Springfield, Massachusetts, in about 1880.

the Massachusetts Supreme Court ruled in *Commonwealth* v. *Hunt* that both trade unions and strikes for closed shops were legal, large scale labor organizations were rare. By the time of the Civil War, only a handful of skilled trades, such as printers, stonecutters and cigarmakers had formed larger associations. By and large, however, labor associations remained local.

In about 1860, matters slowly began to change. That year, shoe-making workers of Lynn, Massachusetts formed the first successful worker's associations: the Daughters of St. Krispin and the Knights of St. Krispin struck successfully for higher wages. The strike soon spread throughout New England and involved 20,000 women and men. The workers won their major demands.

Yet as more and more industrial era businesses grew to become large corporations, the gap between workers and owners grew as well. Workers felt at the mercy of large corporations that could shut down a factory in one location and move to another region where wages were lower. Male workers also feared that women would replace them in the factory line as they received lower wages. In fact, in some factory occupations, such as

| Work Stoppages, 1883–1900 | |
|---|---|
| YEAR | NUMBER OF STOPPAGES |
| 1883 | 506 |
| 1884 | 485 |
| 1885 | 695 |
| 1886 | 1572 |
| 1887 | 1503 |
| 1888 | 946 |
| 1889 | 1111 |
| 1890 | 1897 |
| 1891 | 1789 |
| 1892 | 1359 |
| 1893 | 1375 |
| 1894 | 1404 |
| 1895 | 1255 |
| 1896 | 1066 |
| 1897 | 1110 |
| 1898 | 1098 |
| 1899 | 1838 |
| 1900 | 1839 |

**LABOR STRIFE** The late nineteenth century witnessed continual, strong and sometimes violent struggles between industrial labor and management.

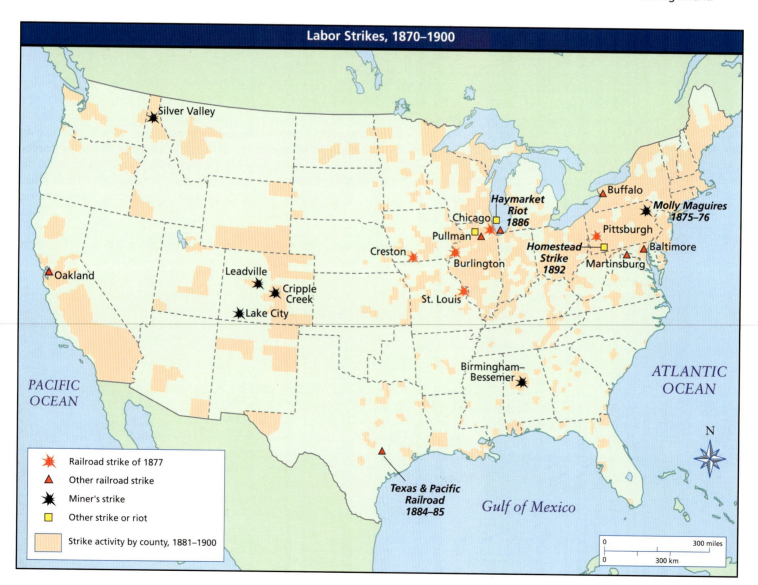

**Labor Strikes, 1870–1900**

Silver Valley

Buffalo

Haymarket Riot 1886

Chicago

Pullman

Creston

Burlington

Pittsburgh

Homestead Strike 1892

Martinsburg

Molly Maguires 1875–76

Baltimore

Oakland

Leadville

Cripple Creek

Lake City

St. Louis

Birmingham–Bessemer

PACIFIC OCEAN

ATLANTIC OCEAN

N

Texas & Pacific Railroad 1884–85

Gulf of Mexico

★ Railroad strike of 1877
▲ Other railroad strike
✴ Miner's strike
☐ Other strike or riot
▨ Strike activity by county, 1881–1900

0 — 300 miles
0 — 300 km

## Leading Occupations for Women (ca. 1880)

| JOB TITLE | NUMBER OF WORKERS |
| --- | --- |
| 1. Servants and waitresses | 1,216,639 |
| 2. Hired Farmhand | 447,104 |
| 3. Dressmakers | 292,668 |
| 4. Teachers, college professors | 246,066 |
| 5. Farm overseers | 226,427 |
| 6. Laundry workers | 216,631 |
| 7. Tailors | 64,509 |
| 8. Saleswomen | 58,451 |
| 9. Nurses, midwives | 41,396 |
| 10. Musicians, music teachers | 34,518 |

**WORKING GIRLS:** Young women at an Indianapolis cotton mill

textiles, women did dominate the labor force. In Atlanta thirty-five percent of the workforce in the 1880s was female. In Fall River, Massachusetts, the percentage was thirty-four percent, and in Philadelphia, twenty-six percent.

If a worker complained or went on strike, he or she could easily be replaced by a hired strikebreaker. As corporate power grew, the treatment of the labor force worsened.

Resentment of low pay, long hours, and unsafe conditions frequently led to battles between workers and their employers. In 1872, nearly 100,000 builders and mechanics in New York City went on strike, refusing to work more than eight hours in a day. Irish miners in Pennsylvania formed a secret labor society called the "Molly Maguires" that was blamed for numerous murders, beatings, knifings, armed robberies, and incidents of arson. In 1877, ten Molly Maguires were hanged, possibly on false evidence, for murder.

That same year a massive strike by railroad workers halted trains across the country, after the Baltimore and Ohio Railroad cut wages for the second time in a year. Many politicians urged President Rutherford B. Hayes to seize control of the railroads to break the strike. Hayes did send troops to several cities to keep the peace, and although he refused to take sides, on July 20 the Sixth Maryland militia opened fire on striking workers in Baltimore, killing twelve.

### The Knights of Labor
The first major national labor union was the Knights of Labor, founded in 1869 by garment cutters in Philadelphia. Initially the Knights were a secret society, but one that boasted a diverse membership that included blacks, women, farmers and merchants as well as both skilled and unskilled laborers. In its founding charter, "only lawyers, bankers, gamblers and stockholders" were excluded. In the West, most members of the Knights were farmers, in the East, most were trade unionists.

The Knights, under the leadership of the contradictory and charismatic Terrence V. Powderly, sought to reform the U.S. economy by uniting workers of all backgrounds and trades. The Knights grew in power and influence during the 1870s and 1880s. After a successful railroad strike against American millionaire Jay Gould by the Knights in 1885, membership in the Knights reached 700,000 and made the Knights the most influential labor organization of its time. The following year, however, the Knights would become wrongly associated with one of the worse labor disturbances in U.S. history—the Haymarket Riots—and membership in the Knights would fall off rapidly as a result.

The Haymarket Riots occurred on May 4, 1886, when Chicago police tried to break up a meeting of anarchists in Haymarket Square. During the chaos, a bomb exploded among the police who opened fire. Seven policemen were killed and seventy were wounded. Although the actual bomb thrower was never identified, seven of the radical agitators were sentenced to death or to prison sentences of one to fifteen years. As a result of petitions circulated by labor groups, only four were executed.

Although no evidence existed that the Knights of Labor were responsible for the violence at Haymarket Square, public perception of the group was severely damaged.

### Samuel Gompers and the AFL
The Knights of Labor was soon overshadowed by another union—the American Federation of Labor (AFL). Initially founded in 1881 as the Federation of Organized Trades and Labor Unions of the United States and Canada, the AFL was led by Samuel Gompers, a Dutch immigrant and official of the national Cigarmakers Union. The AFL consisted of separate autonomous member unions of skilled workers organized by trade or craft. Entrusting the AFL to the principle of federalism, Gompers allowed each union the internal freedom to organize and operate.

More conservative in its tactics than the Knights of Labor or other unions that were to come, the AFL worked to secure higher wages, shorter hours, and legislation against child labor rather than engaging in philosophical class struggles. Under the leadership of Gompers, the AFL would become the largest labor federation in the United States; it reached a membership of over 10 million at the time of its merger with another

**HAYMARKET RIOTS** When a bomb killed seven policemen at a Knights of Labor rally in Haymarket Square in Chicago (above, left), public condemnation virtually destroyed the Knights. Although no evidence proved union leaders were involved, authorities executed four. Because many members of the Knights were immigrants, the episode played into public fears of foreign radicalism. The handbill (right) announces the rally in German.

federation of unions, the Congress of Industrial Organizations (CIO) in 1955.

### The Strikes of the 1890s

The 1890s were an especially violent time for American labor, in large part because the nation underwent one of its most severe economic depressions in its history during the decade. As corporations slashed wages, armed conflict between strikers and police, militia, or even hired strikebreakers broke out on several occasions. Two of the best known incidents were the 1892 Carnegie Steel Company strike and the 1894 American Rail Union strike.

The Homestead strike took place at Carnegie's Steel Company, in Homestead, Pennsylvania, near Pittsburgh. After plant manager Henry Clay Frick hired 300 Pinkerton detectives as strikebreakers, some of the strikers fired upon them, killing seven, as they were being towed up the Mohongahela River. During the strike, a Russian-born anarchist named Alexander Berkman shot and stabbed Frick in an assault planned with his fellow anarchist Emma Goldman. The five-month-long strike finally ended with union leaders being fired and workers returning to 12-hour shifts.

The American Railway Union strike took place in the summer of 1894, after George Pullman, owner of the Pullman Palace Car Company cut his workers' wages by twenty-five percent. In response, Eugene V. Debs, head of the American Railway Union, called for a nationwide strike to support the Pullman workers. Soon, railways across the country were shut down as rail workers boycotted Pullman cars.

Because the strike stopped mail service, President Grover Cleveland decided to take direct action. Issuing an order to end the strike, he placed federal troops in Chicago to keep the peace. However, rather than bring a peaceful resolution to the crisis, the federal troops killed seven strikers in the process of quelling the strike.

Whether or not the federal government had the right to use injunctions and military force to end labor disputes was an open question at the time, and Cleveland's action was an unprecedented use of presidential power. Pro-business forces argued that anytime the "general welfare" of the public was threatened, the government had a responsibility to act. This view was upheld by the Supreme Court in the case of *In re Debs* (1895). The decision removed much of the protection that had been extended to labor by the 1842 *Commonwealth v. Hunt* case in Massachusetts.

# Populism and Political Reform

The period of labor turmoil between 1870 and 1900 was not limited to the eastern and midwestern industrial regions. In 1892, for example, martial law was declared at the Coeur d'Alene silver mines in Idaho after violence erupted between striking miners and strikebreakers. Yet much of the tension in the West—as well as in the rural South—was on the farm. During the Civil War, farmers

| Average Annual Wage, 1890–1900 | |
|---|---|
| YEAR | WAGES |
| 1890 | $475 |
| 1891 | $480 |
| 1892 | $482 |
| 1893 | $458 |
| 1894 | $420 |
| 1895 | $438 |
| 1896 | $439 |
| 1897 | $442 |
| 1898 | $440 |
| 1899 | $470 |
| 1900 | $483 |

throughout the nation had prospered as food was needed to feed the armies. With fewer farmers at home tending crops during wartime, the crops produced brought high prices. Yet after the war, prices stagnated, and then plummeted. A bushel of wheat that sold for $1.21 in 1873 brought just 49 cents by 1885. Cotton fell from 20 cents a pound in 1873 to just 5 cents twenty years later.

While droughts, grasshoppers and other naturally occurring challenges contributed to the problems, farmers looked to eastern bankers and the sheriffs that did their bidding when a bank foreclosed on a failing farm as the main source of their problems. To challenge these interests, farmers, like industrial workers elsewhere, began to organize.

### The Grange

Organized at almost the same time as the Knights of Labor, the Patrons of Husbandry became the first national farm organization with its founding in 1867. Founded by Oliver Kelley, a clerk at the federal Department of Agriculture, the Patrons began as an education and social society. By the late 1870s, there were twenty thousand local Patrons lodges—known as "Granges"—across the country.

**GIFT FOR THE GRANGERS** The Patrons of Husbandry, or the Grangers, became the nation's first farm organization when it was founded in 1867. The promotional poster seen here was distributed to Grange members after its publication in 1873.

While the Patrons of Husbandry was not formed for expressly political purposes, whenever farmers gathered at local Granges, they shared their common complaints, including the rise of absentee landowners and the fall of family-owned farms, higher and higher interest rates on bank loans, and ever-rising fees charged by railroad companies and operators of grain elevators. To address these problems, many farmers

### Coxey's Army Marches Against Hard Times

The Pullman strike of 1894 took place during a severe economic depression. Some historians have suggested that as many as one in five American workers was unemployed at the time. To protest the situation, Jacob Coxey of Masillon, Ohio proposed a plan of government work relief on public roads, to be financed by legal tender Treasury notes. By providing monetary inflation, internal improvements, and work for the unemployed, Coxey argued that his "Good Roads Bill" could end the depression. When Congress refused to pass the bill, a band of 500 jobless men, known as Coxey's Army, marched peacefully from Masillon to Washington, D.C. to protest. The protest ended in an anticlimax, as its leaders were arrested for marching on the Capitol lawn. "More money! Less Misery! Good Roads," went one of the chants used by Coxey's men on the move toward Washington.

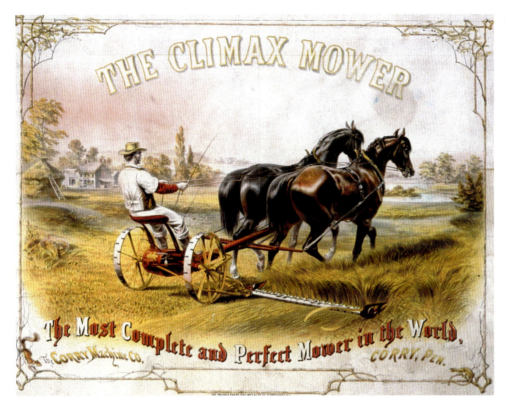

**NEW TECHNOLOGY COMES TO THE FARM**
The Climax Mower, introduced in 1869, featured blades that were attached to side wheels, which allowed for fewer movable parts and a less expensive product. The mower was an ideal tool for turning the western plains into farmland.

organized buying cooperatives in order to save on seed and fertilizer, as well as to purchase their own grain elevators. Some farmers' co-ops even set up their own factories to manufacture farm equipment for less.

### The Populist Party

While farmer cooperatives did address some of the problem of rising expenses on the farm, it did not resolve the problem of falling crop prices. What many farmers did not understand was that they could not grow their way out of the problem. When cheaper machinery, fertilizer and seed helped farmers cultivate an ever growing expanse of land, American farms found themselves with a surplus of food that outstripped the demand. As more food was produced, prices continued to fall.

To many farmers this situation defied common sense. If they were growing more food, they argued, they should be receiving more money. The cause of their problems could only be greedy banks, railroads and grain elevators. During the 1870s this anger began to translate into political action as new farmers' parties began to form in states throughout the Midwest and South. Many of these parties were radical—calling for state ownership of railroads and other private enterprises. They also called for "cheap money," or expanded access to credit. Attracting the votes of many Grangers, these political parties were able to push

through laws that regulated rail and grain elevator rates for the first time.

Railroads often ignored these new laws, arguing that states had no right to regulate interstate commerce. Yet in the 1876 case *Munn v. Illinois*, the Supreme Court upheld the right of states to fix maximum rates and to otherwise regulate businesses that served the public interest. The Court also held that state control of commerce did not interfere with federal control of interstate commerce. Ten years later, however, the court effectively reversed itself in *Wabash, St. Louis, & Pacific Railway Company v. Illinois*, which held that it was the exclusive right of Congress to regulate interstate commerce.

In 1887, Congress passed the Interstate Commerce Act, which created the Interstate Commerce Commission, the nation's first federal regulatory agency. The commission oversaw the conduct of the railroads, prohibiting pools and discrimination, and requiring the railroads to file their rates with the commission. It practiced the principles embodied in the Granger laws, that the government can regulate businesses that extend beyond state borders. The passage of the act was indicative of a changing economy that required changing methods of control.

During the late 1870s and early 1880s, prospects improved on American farms and the Granges attracted fewer members, but when the economy turned sour once more in the 1880s and 1890s, new organizations, called "Alliances," were born. In the West, Farmers' Alliances formed their own political parties while in the South, they became a wing of the Democratic Party,

| Percentage of Americans as Farmers, 1820–1900 | | | |
|---|---|---|---|
| YEAR | TOTAL LABOR FORCE (in thousands) | TOTAL FARM WORKERS (in thousands) | PERCENTAGE |
| 1820 | 3,135 | 2,470 | 78.8 |
| 1840 | 5,660 | 3,570 | 63.1 |
| 1860 | 11,110 | 5,880 | 37.5 |
| 1880 | 17,390 | 8,920 | 51.3 |
| 1890 | 29,070 | 11,680 | 40.2 |

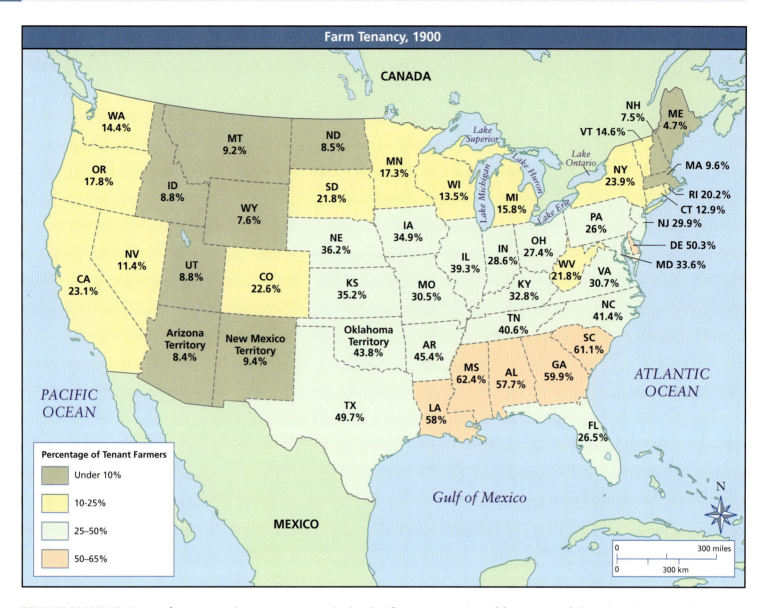

## Farm Tenancy, 1900

CANADA

WA 14.4%
OR 17.8%
ID 8.8%
MT 9.2%
ND 8.5%
MN 17.3%
NH 7.5%
ME 4.7%
VT 14.6%
NY 23.9%
MA 9.6%
RI 20.2%
CT 12.9%
NJ 29.9%
WI 13.5%
MI 15.8%
SD 21.8%
WY 7.6%
IA 34.9%
PA 26%
OH 27.4%
DE 50.3%
NV 11.4%
UT 8.8%
CO 22.6%
NE 36.2%
IL 39.3%
IN 28.6%
WV 21.8%
VA 30.7%
MD 33.6%
CA 23.1%
KS 35.2%
MO 30.5%
KY 32.8%
NC 41.4%
Arizona Territory 8.4%
New Mexico Territory 9.4%
Oklahoma Territory 43.8%
AR 45.4%
TN 40.6%
SC 61.1%
MS 62.4%
AL 57.7%
GA 59.9%
TX 49.7%
LA 58%
FL 26.5%

PACIFIC OCEAN

ATLANTIC OCEAN

Gulf of Mexico

MEXICO

**Percentage of Tenant Farmers**
- Under 10%
- 10–25%
- 25–50%
- 50–65%

N

0 — 300 miles
0 — 300 km

**TENANT FARMING** Tenant farmers, or sharecroppers, worked a significant proportion of farms east of the Mississippi River in 1900, particularly in the deep South. Farms farther west were more frequently worked by the settlers who owned the land.

**MARY ELIZABETH LEASE**

which, since the end of Reconstruction, was the only real party in the South. After success in local campaigns during the 1890 election season, western farmers decided to form a new national political party, known as the Peoples' Party, or the Populists.

The Populists called for widespread economic reform. To ease access to money, they called for the free coinage of silver and an increase in the money supply to $50 per American. They also called for a tax on incomes, public ownership of the railroads, and telegraph and telephone companies, a shorter day for factory laborers and the direct election of senators. (At the time, senators were still appointed by state legislatures.)

Leaders of the Populist movement were also intentionally provocative. As Mary Elizabeth Lease, a Kansas mother of four and Populist leader put it:

"What you farmers need is to raise a little less corn and a little more hell!.. Wall Street owns the country. It is no longer a government of the people, by the people, and for the people, but a government of Wall Street, for Wall Street, and by Wall Street. The great common people of this country are slaves, and monopoly is master."

### Populism in the South

Populist leaders hoped that southern farmers, regardless of race, would join the party as well. Even before the Populist Party formed, alliances between poor white and poor black farmers had begun to form. As the economic distress grew in the South, poor white farmers and sharecroppers had formed the Southern Alliance, a populist-style movement aimed at addressing low crop prices and

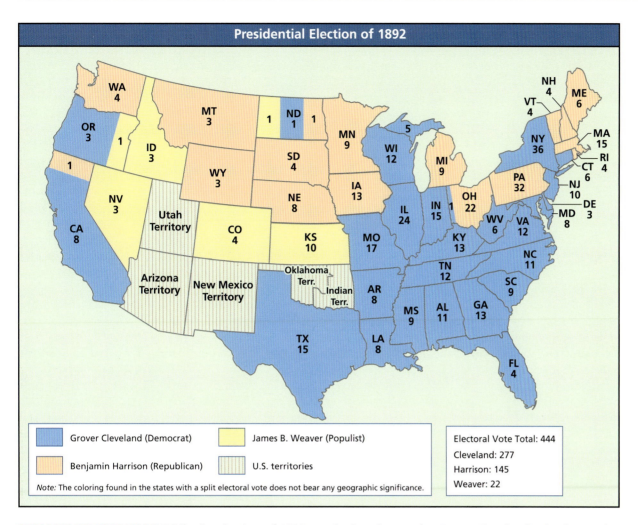

**Presidential Election of 1892**

| | |
|---|---|
| Grover Cleveland (Democrat) | James B. Weaver (Populist) |
| Benjamin Harrison (Republican) | U.S. territories |

Electoral Vote Total: 444
Cleveland: 277
Harrison: 145
Weaver: 22

*Note:* The coloring found in the states with a split electoral vote does not bear any geographic significance.

**POPULIST STRONGHOLDS** While the election of 1892 may be best known for Grover Cleveland's election to the only non-consecutive presidential term in history, it was also the high water mark for the Populist Party. Populist candidate James Weaver won four states and electoral votes from two others, all in the West.

burdensome debt. Blacks had followed suit with the Colored Farmers' Alliance. The organizations grew rapidly. By the late 1880s, the two organizations boasted a membership of 3 million between them.

The racial implications of these efforts were clear. Many members of the Southern Alliance understood that they had far more in common with black share-croppers and the Colored Farmers' Alliance than they did with the wealthy former Confederate planters that made up the elite of the Democratic Party. As Populist leader Tom Watson of Georgia remarked, "the accident of color can make no difference in the interest of farm-ers, croppers, and laborers. You are kept apart that you may be separately fleeced of your earnings." By 1890, both alliances were rallying behind the single largest challenge to the two-party system in the late nineteenth century. A movement designed to alleviate agricultur-al poverty through government action—including nationalization of the railroads, government purchase of crops, and inflationary monetary policy (inflation, by lowering the value of money and raising the price of crops, makes it easier for farmers to pay back their debts)—the Populists demonstrated enormous political appeal in both the South and Midwest.

Sadly, the Populist movement was broken in the South by the Democratic Party and its appeals to white supremacy. With money, power, and influence on their side, white elites and Democratic Party politicians appealed to the lowest instincts of poor white south-erners. As discussed earlier, the wealthy whites that made up the core of the Democratic Party in the South used racially-motivated scare tactics to dissuade poor whites from joining with blacks on economic and polit-ical issues. Southern Democrats charged that white-black political and economic alliances would lead blacks to seek social equality with whites. Such an out-come, they warned, would inevitably threaten the puri-ty of the white women and the future of the Caucasian race. In 1892, James Weaver, the Populist party can-didate for president said of such tactics:

"There is but one issue in the South. That is the com-petition to see who can most hate the Negro. The man that wins gets the nomination. The whole thing is a dead-drag on the Country . . . Slavery must be the greatest of crimes. Here we are, all these years after it as been abolished, and we're still paying the penalty for it."

When visceral appeals to racial intolerance failed, white elites employed fraud, running up huge pro-Democratic tallies in the largely African-American counties that they controlled. As Frank Burkitt, a Mississippi populist, complained, "a class of corrupt office-seekers ... hypocritically raised the howl of white supremacy while they debauched the ballot boxes ... disregarded the rights of the blacks ... and actually dominated the will of the white people through the instrumentality of the stolen negro vote."

### Greenbacks and "Free Silver"

During the 1892 election, James Weaver won over a million votes, and actually took Idaho, Nevada, Colorado, Kansas, part of the electoral vote from Oregon and North Dakota. The majority of the Populist Party then fused with Democrats, helping to elect many congressional members, three governors, and hundreds of local officials.

Even more important than its electoral success was the influence that Populists had on the major parties. In 1890, Congress found itself faced with growing demands that it do something to help farmers, as well as small businesses. Monopolies like John D. Rockefeller's Standard Oil of Ohio were able to charge virtually whatever they pleased for their products. In response, Congress passed the Sherman Antitrust Act, named for Civil War general William Tecumseh Sherman's brother John, a senator from Ohio. The Act gave federal courts the power to prevent restraint on interstate trade and foreign commerce. In practice, the act was not strongly enforced, and big business continued to act with little restriction.

Two years later, Senator Sherman's name was also attached to a bill dealing with the growing demand for "free silver." The debate over what sort of specie (or coin) that paper currency should be backed with was already an old one by the 1890s—its roots predating the days of Andrew Jackson's "pet banks." During the Civil War, "greenbacks" (paper currency unsecured by specie but on a par with backed notes) were used to pay the costs of the war. But greenbacks were unpopular, as many were suspicious of them and tended to spend them while saving gold. In this way, the amount of gold in circulation fell dramatically. In 1866 Congress had begun to retire them, but a demand for an inflated currency brought them back into circulation. In 1869 a compromise was reached in Congress, which left more than half of the remaining greenbacks in circulation. The next year the Supreme Court briefly declared the act establishing greenbacks unconstitutional, but then reversed itself the very same day when President Grant appointed two new justices to the Court.

During the Panic of 1873 supporters of greenbacks founded the Greenback Party, but two year later Congress passed the Greenback Resumption Act, setting January 1, 1879 as the date for redeeming all greenbacks in specie.

The Populist's call for currency backed with silver brought the currency issue to the fore once again. In 1890 Congress passed the Sherman Silver Act. The act required the U.S. government to purchase monthly an amount of silver equal to U.S. silver production. It paid in paper money, redeemable in either gold or silver. Farmers, who especially supported the act, hoped it would increase the amount of money in circulation, boost the economy, and raise the price of their goods. Instead the act decimated the nation's supply of gold and threatened the stability of the currency. Grover Cleveland, the fiscally conservative Democrat who won reelection in 1892 as president after being defeated in his first attempt for a second term in 1888, campaigned vociferously against the new law. It was repealed in 1893.

Next, Cleveland worked to stem the drain of gold from the treasury. He did so by turning to J.P. Morgan, the New York financier, and asking him to organize a sale of United States bonds in Europe. Morgan did so, restoring $65 million in gold to the treasury and reaping a tidy profit for himself in doing so.

While Morgan may have profited, his assistance was not enough to stem the tide of economic panic. Despite the disastrous experiment with the Sherman Silver Act, the idea that the nation's economic crisis could be solved simply by securing the dollar to silver rather than gold remained attractive, especially to farmers.

**WILLIAM JENNINGS BRYAN** Bryan, a tireless campaigner, was the first presidential candidate to hold a national campaign stumping tour. Despite his energy and eloquence, he lost the 1896 campaign to William McKinley, who largely limited himself to speaking to assembled press from his front porch in Ohio.

*"No one can earn a million dollars honestly."*

—WILLIAM JENNINGS BRYAN

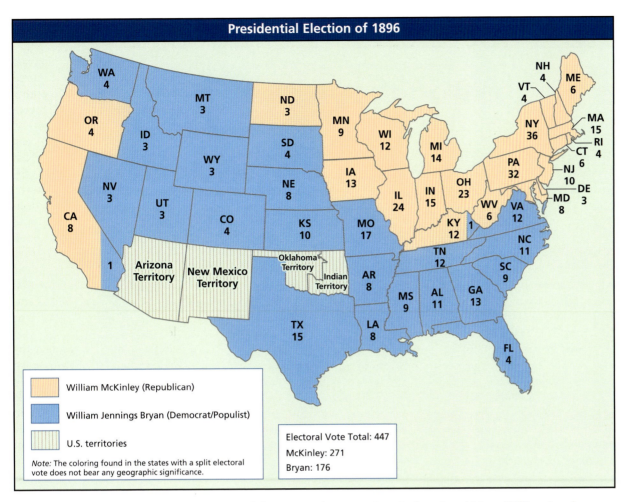

**Presidential Election of 1896**

William McKinley (Republican)

William Jennings Bryan (Democrat/Populist)

U.S. territories

*Note:* The coloring found in the states with a split electoral vote does not bear any geographic significance.

Electoral Vote Total: 447
McKinley: 271
Bryan: 176

**POPULISM'S DEFEAT** Despite running one of the most active campaigns in American history, William Jennings Bryan, candidate of both the Democrats and the Populists, failed to win a single state in the industrial Northeast or Midwest. Ohio's William McKinley, the candidate of the eastern business establishment, therefore won election by a safe margin.

## Bryan and the Cross of Gold

The concept of "free silver" would dominate the 1896 presidential campaign. Entering their presidential convention that year, the Democratic Party was divided into two camps: one, sympathetic to the more conservative fiscal policies of retiring President Cleveland, opposed free silver. In the other was a little-known but fiery 36-year old fundamentalist Christian congressman from Nebraska named William Jennings Bryan. At the convention, Bryan, whom some called "The Boy Orator from Platte" for his passionate speaking style, delivered a speech he had given time and time again to Nebraska farmers. It ended: "We will answer their demand for a Gold Standard by saying to them: You shall not press down upon the brow of labor this crown of thorns. You shall not crucify mankind upon a cross of gold." The thunderous applause for Bryan lasted a solid hour. Both the Democratic and Populist parties nominated Bryan as their candidate for president.

Meanwhile, the Republican candidate for president was William McKinley, a conservative, pro-business governor of Ohio. McKinley was also a close friend of millionaire Mark Hanna, who lent McKinley his support, strategic advice, and money for the campaign. While Bryan campaigned vigorously across the country, proclaiming himself to be the candidate of the "Common Man," Hanna had McKinley stay at home in Ohio. From there, Hanna made certain that McKinley received extensive press coverage, and saw to it that the McKinley campaign sent out as many as 5 million pieces of campaign literature a week. The Republican campaign fund was $7 million; Bryan and his supporters had just $300,000.

"A war of the East versus West," was how one historian described the election, "the farmers against the railroad tycoons and bankers; the workers against the industrialists; gold against silver . . ."

McKinley won the war with relative ease. Despite Populism's rapid growth in much of the country, the heavily populated Northeast and Midwest cast most of its votes for McKinley. Hanna spread word among northeastern workers that a Bryan victory would mean plant closings throughout the nation.

When the votes were counted, McKinley had won with about 600,000 more votes than Bryan and an electoral vote margin of 271 to 176 in the electoral college.

# Chapter 21: The Closing Frontier and Overseas Expansion

n 1828, the federal government set aside an "Indian Territory" on the Great Plains to be used as the permanent homeland for displaced "civilized tribes" of the southeastern United States. Over the next decade, the government forcibly removed the Cherokee, Creek, Choctaw, Chickasaw and Seminole to the seemingly barren territory west of the Mississippi that would eventually become Oklahoma Territory — a Choctaw word for "red people." Likewise, many of the last American Indians in the Northeast and Ohio River Valley were also forced west of the Mississippi River during this period. Even Black Hawk, a brilliant military leader of the Sauk and Fox Nation, had been unsuccessful in the guerrilla war he had waged against the Americans to stop the western advance of white settlement.

Yet even if U.S.–Indian wars east of the Mississippi were all but over by the mid-nineteenth century, as late as 1850 Indian nations west of the Mississippi still lived somewhat unhindered by what was still a relatively small population of whites in the West. Traditional ways of life, from Wichita Indian settlements in Kansas that contained as many as thousand grass lodges to the nomadic hunting and gathering ways of the Sioux in the Northern Plains and Cheyenne to the south, continued on as they had for centuries. Certainly a handful of American forts had begun

to appear on the Plains, in the Rockies, and on the Pacific coast in decades immediately following Lewis and Clark's trailblazing journey to the Pacific at the opening of the century, but those forts were largely for trading and not military purposes. In fact, the early Plains forts served as "neutral territory" where warring tribes could meet for trade.

By the 1850s, however, the trickle of whites in the West became a flood as goldseekers and other settlers headed for California and other points west via wagon train across the plains. In response the U.S. Army began building military forts to protect emigrants. The Indians, ill-equipped at first to combat the influx of people, were scattered from their territories in large numbers, leaving much of the Plains open for settlement.

## Iron Horses and Dead Bison

Shortly thereafter, the arrival of the railroads in the West proved far more devastating to the Indian way of life than the wagon train. In the 1800s bison roamed the Plains in great numbers of loosely-knit herds, containing thousands of smaller, single-family units. Herds were not permanent, and migration and grazing patterns were unpredictable. Indians hunted in small bands, fragmented the herd, and then used spears or bow and

**BUFFALO HUNT ON THE PLAINS**
Native Americans of the Great Plains relied on the bison for food, clothing, and many other necessities. Although the bow and arrow was the traditional weapon of choice, by the mid-nineteenth century, many Native American hunters had also mastered the hunting rifle.

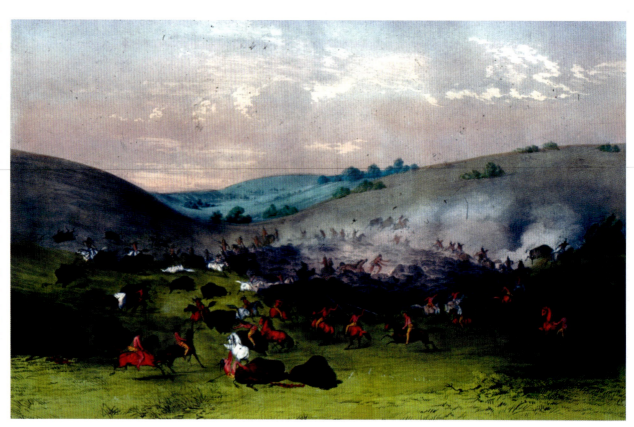

arrow to kill only as many as they needed. Little of the bison was wasted—the Indians would use the carcasses brought back to the tribe for food, fuel, clothing, shelter, and tools.

When the federal government began seizing Indian land for railroads, it set disaster in motion for the Plains Indian. First, the trains carried U.S. Army troops to quell Indian disturbances. The trains, which the Indians called "Iron horses," also brought farmers, ranchers, and other settlers who further infringed on Indian land. Even worse was the impact on bison populations. It was bad enough that railroad construction fed on bison, thereby competing with the main source of food for Plains Indians, but far worse were the whites who came west to "hunt" bison—often from moving trains—for their valuable skin, for their horns, or sometimes simply for "sport." Rather than using all parts of the animal as the Indians did, these hunters left the plains littered with bison carcasses, flesh rotting in the sun. Of the approximately 15 million bison on the Plains in 1865, only a few thousand still existed by the mid-1880s. Without the bison, the Plains Indians could barely survive.

## Indian Wars of the Late Nineteenth Century

As white settlers moved west, some Indian nations agreed to cede lands and allow the safe passage of settlers. In July 1851, for example, the Santee Souix ceded land to the federal government in exchange for $3 million, some allotted for agriculture and some for schools. The treaty was in keeping with federal policy, focused not merely on making peace with the Indians, but helping them to adjust to white society.

Several months later, Indian agent Thomas Fitzpatrick successfully gathered together 10,000 Indians with representatives of the U.S. government—the largest such assembly ever held—to negotiate the Fort Laramie Treaty. The treaty stated that in return for the land and safe passage of western trails, the Indians would be guaranteed specific "territories," or reservations. To compensate the Indians, the government agreed to pay them an annuity of $50,000 in provisions for fifty years.

**Settlement of the United States, 1890**

Settled areas

*Note:* Contemporary boundaries are provided for reference.

**THE CLOSING FRONTIER** By 1890 centuries of armed conflict between European and then American settlers and Native Americans came to an end. While parts of the Far West had been settled by whites beginning in the 1850s, much of the land between the Mississippi River and California was still sparsely settled. By 1890 most American Indians had been forced onto reservations.

While some Indian nations willingly entered treaty arrangements such as these, many believed that the government was unfairly coercing Indians into signing treaties that they did not truly understand. In 1855, for instance, the Walla Walla Council, held in what is now Walla Walla, Washington, members of the Cayuse, Umatilla, Yakima, Walla Walla and Nez Perce agreed to give up sixty thousand acres of land for an average price of three cents an acre.

In the face of these unbalanced treaties, many Indian nations continued to forcibly resist white settlement rather than accept life on reservations. The Brulé Sioux were particularly hostile to whites, and their attacks on white settlers led to war with the U.S. Army. In August 1855, the Army ambushed the tribe, killing 150, many of them women and children.

### The Sioux Uprising of 1862

In 1851, the Santee Sioux of Minnesota and Iowa had their lives uprooted when they ceded their land to the federal government. For 11 years they were entirely dependent of white merchants and U.S. government payments for their survival, while thousands of white settlers set up farms where once there had been open prairie. In August 1862, with most soldiers in the East fighting the Civil War, the Sioux attacked farms and towns and besieged an army post. Led by Little Crow, they killed more than 800 settlers.

The army put down the uprising quickly. Little Crow, who had at first opposed the attack, was murdered by white hunters in 1863. Meanwhile, most Santee Sioux were forced from their reservation in Mankato, Minnesota into camps in Dakota Territory. Without granting Indians any legal representation, Colonel Henry Hastings Sibley appointed a military court to try all Santee suspected of participating in the attacks. The court convicted 303 Sioux and ordered them hanged. However, President Abraham Lincoln refused to authorize so many executions and ordered a thorough review of trial records. In the end, thirty-eight Sioux were hanged en masse in December 1863.

### The Sand Creek Massacre

Like the Sioux of the Northern Plains, the Cheyenne of Southern Plains also warred with the U.S. Army. Yet in 1864, after several years of fighting, Cheyenne leaders opted to meet with Colonel John Chivington of the Colorado Militia at Camp Weld in Colorado Territory. Led by their elderly chief, Black Kettle, 200 Cheyenne warriors and 500 women and children assumed a peace treaty had been reached and settled forty miles away at Sand Creek, under the impression that they were under the protection of Fort Lyon. The group even flew an American flag and a white truce flag over their camp. Yet on the early morning of November 29, Chivington led a cavalry of 700 Colorado volunteers in a surprise attack on the settlement taking no prisoners, and killing and mutilating more than 300. Black Kettle escaped, and with the other survivors of Sand Creek moved south to a camp on the Washita River in Oklahoma.

### Red Cloud's War

With the 1864 massacre at Sand Creek, the Indian Wars on the Plains intensified. Chiefs willing to negotiate with the white man saw the massacre as the ultimate betrayal, and following the massacre, warriors from various band of the Sioux and Cheyenne began a prolonged and forceful retaliation.

One of the best known events in this period took place near Fort Phil Kearney in Wyoming. The fort had been built to protect the Bozeman Trail, an important route leading to goldfields in Montana. The trail was a major point of contention for the Sioux, as it led through their favorite hunting ground east of the Bighold Mountains. For two years, Red Cloud, Chief of the Oglala Sioux led a campaign to shut down the trail.

One of the most severe attacks on white settlers during Red Cloud's War began when Sioux attacked a supply train as it brought wood to the fort, and Captain William Fetterman and his men were called in to assist. When Fetterman spotted a small detachment of Sioux led by the warrior Crazy Horse, he disobeyed orders and followed them over a nearby ridge. Once Fetterman and his men came over the ridge, a party of 2,000 Sioux warriors ambushed them, wiping out the whole force.

### Cattle Trails on the Plains

Cheyenne and Sioux resistance continued the following spring as railroad construction advanced through the Central Plains and more and more wagon trains traveled to Colorado and the Southwest. Increasingly, Plains Indians also had to contend with a new kind of traffic from armed whites—namely cattle drives headed north from Texas directly through Indian Territory toward cattle railheads in Colorado, Kansas, and Nebraska. These new cattle trails were born out of the Civil War, as very few cattle east of the Mississippi had survived the war since Confederate Armies had generally relied on cattle for food. What's more, millions of easterners on both the northern and southern sides of the Mason-Dixon line had grown fond of beef during the war. Before the war, pork and chicken had been the main meat staples of the American diet, but the sudden demand for beef meant a steer might fetch as much as $50 in eastern markets.

At the same time, Texas was glutted with cattle. Because many herds had gone untended during the war, the populations had multiplied. Wild longhorn cattle were also plentiful, which meant that prices in western markets for cattle were as low as $3 per head. Thus, ranchers had an enormous profit incentive for moving their cattle herds to eastern markets. Beginning in 1866, a number of cattle trails, such as the famous Chisholm and Goodnight-Loving Trails, were born.

This new and lucrative cattle trade gave Indians a new target for raids. The logistics of moving large numbers of cattle over a long trails stretching across the lower Plains left cowboys vulnerable to raids. In turn, the U.S. Army had greater incentive to protect white passage through the Plains.

When General Winfield Scott Hancock tried to subdue a Sioux and Cheyenne village near Fort Larned, Kansas in 1867, he triggered a new round of war. Throughout the summer, Sioux and Cheyenne raided white settlements and ambushed travelers, constantly turning back attempts by General George Armstrong Custer's Seventh Cavalry to defeat them. Hancock, commander of the military district covering Texas and Oklahoma, responded in kind, torching Cheyenne villages. In September, a united force of 700 Cheyenne, Sioux, and Arapaho besieged 50 volunteers under Major George Forsyth at Beecher's Island in western Kansas. For seven days, armed with devastating repeating rifles, the volunteers held off assaults until saved by a charge from the Tenth Cavalry Regiment of African-American troops to end the assault.

Two months later, an 800-strong force of Seventh Cavalry led by Custer attacked Black Kettle's peaceful Cheyenne village on the Washita River. Among the dead was Black Kettle himself, who had survived the Sand Creek massacre a few years before and had continued to preach peace. More than 100 others, including many women and children, also perished in the attack.

Despite Custer's aggressive approach, the U.S. government had become eager to end Red Cloud's War. For his part, Red Cloud refused to meet with U.S. representatives until all U.S. troops along the Powder River section of the Bozeman Trail were withdrawn. In the summer of 1868, Fort Smith, Fort Phil Kearney and Fort Reno were all closed. In November, Red Cloud signed what became known as the Fort Laramie Treaty, securing the Powder River valley as a hunting ground for his people. Land in the Black Hills, sacred to the Sioux, was declared off-limits.

## Indian Policy Under Grant

Almost immediately after signing the Fort Laramie Treaty, Red Cloud noticed some discrepancies, particularly concerning the location of a Sioux trading post. The U.S. government had established the post 300 miles from Fort Laramie, which Red Cloud feared as an attempt to push the Sioux further south. Following the election of former Union Army commander Ulysses S. Grant as President in 1872, Red Cloud traveled to Washington to discuss the issue. Grant received Red Cloud as a vis-

**Cattle Trails and Cowtowns, 1866–1885**

- Shawnee Trail (dotted)
- Chisholm Trail
- Goodnight-Loving Trail
- Western Trail

Note: Modern boundaries and names provided for reference.

**CATTLE DRIVES** After the Civil War, western territories attracted cowboys who herded for later sale the approximately 5 million cattle that roamed there. Until federal laws ended open grazing in the mid-1880s, cowboys let their cattle feed freely along the famous several-hundred-mile Chisholm Trail from Texas to cattle towns like Abilene and Dodge City, Kansas. Other cattle drives used similar trails such as the Goodnight-Loving Trail. Provided cattle reached their destinations without being stolen by rustlers, they were purchased and moved by train to beef-hungry northern states.

iting dignitary, and Ely Parker, a Seneca Indian and former Grant military aide whom Grant appointed commissioner of the Bureau of Indian Affairs, helped Red Cloud interpret the treaty.

As commissioner of Indian Affairs, Parker worked to give Indians better advantage in negotiations. He opposed the treaty system as unfair. Thanks in part to his efforts, Congress abandoned the system in 1871, even though prior treaties remained in effect. After 1871, Indian

land continued to diminish, but as a result of negotiation and purchase rather than under the old treaty system.

Despite Grant's generally conciliatory approach, he could not stop Indian raids on settlements. Comanche and Kiowa raiders were using the safety of Indian Territory (later Oklahoma) and the Fort Sill Agency as bases from which to conduct these raids. In one particularly fierce attack, a combined Cheyenne and Kiowa force under Kiowa warriors Satanta and Satank and Cheyenne

**RED CLOUD**

**ELI PARKER**

chief Big Tree destroyed a supply wagon train at Salt Creek Prairie in 1871, torturing and killing several men and stealing 40 mules. Satanta then brought the mules back to the Fort Sill Agency and boasted openly about the raid. In response, the General-in-Chief of the Army, Civil War legend William Tecumseh Sherman, ordered Satanta arrested and tried. Satanta was sentenced to life in prison, where he committed suicide.

### The Long Walk and the Modoc War
Conflict between American Indians and the U.S. Army were not limited to the Plains. During the Civil War, tensions between the Navajo and the Army in the Southwest led to the Navajo War. In January 1864, a final standoff took place in Canyon de Chelly in Arizona Territory. A force led by the famous mountain man Kit Carson surrounded the Navajo, and began to systematically destroy their property. Carson then ordered the starving Navajo to walk through harsh winter conditions to the Bosque Redondo, a reservation on the Pecos River already occupied by Mescalero Apache. During their four-year exile from their homeland many Navajo died, victims of hunger and disease, as the government failed to provide sufficient support for the overcrowded reservation. In 1868 the Navajo were allowed to return to their homeland after promising never to war with the white man again.

Meanwhile in the California-Oregon border region, frequent clashes between whites and Modoc and Klamath Indians led to an 1864 treaty, by which the two tribes ceded their land in California and

moved north. But in 1870 the Modoc returned to California, and two years later the U.S. Army began a bloody campaign, known as the Modoc War, to try to dislodge the Indian nation. The Army effort failed and by 1873 a peace conference ended the war.

### Custer Enters Dakota's Black Hills
Though the Fort Laramie Treaty of 1868 had guaranteed the Sioux possession of the Black Hills of Dakota, army expeditions through the region in 1873 and 1874 led to a renewal of the Sioux Wars. After rumors spread that miners traveling with George Custer's 1874 expedition had found gold, legions of white fortune seekers flooded into the sacred Indian territory.

When the Sioux refused to sell their lands, the U.S. government opened the land to gold miners in 1875, breaking the Fort Laramie Treaty. In response many Sioux, allied with Cheyenne and Arapaho and led by Teton Sioux medicine man and diplomat Sitting Bull, left their reservations in order to resist.

In an attempt to pacify the Sioux before open war began, U.S. military leaders ordered Sioux chiefs to report to military authorities to discuss the situation. Crazy Horse, the Oglala Sioux who had formed a "Confederation of Sioux Warriors," refused. Three columns of U.S. soldiers were thus ordered to track down Sioux camps and force them back onto their reservations. In June 1876, on the Rosebud River in Montana, General George Crook attempted but failed to capture Crazy Horse. A brilliant military strategist, Crazy Horse defeated Crook, forcing him to retreat on June 17th.

### Battle of the Little Big Horn

Meanwhile, the other two U.S. military forces continued marching, unaware of Crook's defeat. Among these forces was the 650-man strong Seventh Cavalry under George Custer.

On June 25, Custer spotted a Sioux camp at the Little Big Horn River. Without any knowledge of how large the Sioux camp was, Custer divided his force in three. Expecting that each of the three smaller units would attack the Sioux camp from a different direction, Custer led 210 men on a reckless charge on the village. Custer was unaware that following Crazy Horse's victory at the Battle of Rosebud, Crazy's Horse's force had united with five other tribes, forming an army of almost 2,000 Oglala, Miniconjou, and Sans Arc Sioux, as well as Blackfoot and northern Cheyenne. In a bloody two hour battle the united Indian forces entirely wiped out Custer and the Seventh Cavalry.

Crazy Horse's victory at Little Big Horn was the highwater mark of Native American armed resistance to white advances. Following Custer's defeat the Sioux divided into smaller units, weaken-ing their power considerably. At the same time Custer's annihilation at Little Big Horn shocked the American public and inspired a thirst for revenge. George Crook, who had never previously defeat-ed a Sioux force, drove his men almost to the point of collapse in pursuit of the Sioux that had defeated Custer. In September his troops, now nicknamed "Custer's Avengers" defeated a Sioux force at the Battle of Slim Buttes in South Dakota. That same year, the Army built Fort Custer, an enormous fort just a few miles from Little Big Horn.

Meanwhile, at Cedar Creek in October 1876, General Nelson Miles defeated Sitting Bull, who fled to Canada. In November, Ranald Mackenzie defeated a Cheyenne encampment at the Powder River, Montana. Then, in January 1877, at Wolf Mountain, Montana, Miles defeated Crazy Horse. In May the legendary Indian warrior surren-dered. Just over three months later he was dead, killed while allegedly resisting his guards. In mid-1881 Sitting Bull also sur-rendered to save his homeless followers from famine.

**CUSTER'S LAST STAND** Expecting to find an unprotected Sioux village, the vain George Armstrong Custer (above) led 210 men in a reckless offensive only to find his force completely surrounded. His entire force was wiped out within two hours. Popular folklore, however, depicted Custer's ill-fated attack as a noble "last stand." In the fanciful illustration below, Custer is shown at center, with a pistol in each hand, standing tall against the enemy onslaught.

## RESERVATIONS

Despite strong resistance the U.S. Army successfully wrested control of western lands from the peoples who had lived on them for many centuries. By 1890 the main period of armed resistance to U.S. occupation of Indian lands had come to an end and most American Indians were forced to live on reservations.

*"Hear me, my chiefs! I am tired; my heart is sick and sad. From where the sun now stands I will fight no more forever."*

—CHIEF JOSEPH, NEZ PERCÉ

### Native American Territory Losses, 1850–1890

CANADA

Spokane
Washington
Yakima
Flathead
Blackfeet
Chief Joseph (Bear Paw Mountain), 1877
Sioux
Chippewa
Lake Superior

Umatilla
Warm Springs
Oregon
Idaho
Montana
Little Big Horn 1890
Powder River 1876
Slim Buttes 1876
Sioux
North Dakota
Minnesota
Wisconsin

Klamath
Crow
Rosebud 1876
Wolf Mountain 1877
Wounded Knee 1890
Sioux
South Dakota
Sioux War 1862

Modoc War 1873
Shoshone
Arapaho
Sioux
Sauk-Fox
Iowa

Paiute
Nevada
Wyoming
Nebraska
Omaha
GREAT PLAINS
Illinois

California
Utah Territory
Ute
Colorado
Ute
Sand Creek Massacre 1864
Kickapoo
Potawatomi
Kansas
Missouri

PACIFIC OCEAN
Tule River
Canyon de Chelly 1864
Hopi
Navajo
Apache
See detail area map
Washita 1868
Oklahoma
Arkansas

Walapai
Arizona Territory
Yuma
Zima
Apache
Pueblo
New Mexico Territory
Apache
Comanche
Mississippi

Pima
Gila R.
Rio Grande
Red R.
Texas
Louisiana
Arkansas R.
Mississippi R.

MEXICO
Rio Grande
Gulf of Mexico

#### (detail map)

Kansas
Cherokee Outlet
KAW
PONCA
TONKAWA
OTOE, MISSOURIA
PAWNEE
OSAGE
QUAPAW
OTTAWA
PAWNEE
WYANDOT
PEORIA
SENECA
MODOC
CHEROKEE
Oklahoma District
IOWAY
KICKAPOO
SAC, FOX
CREEK
CHEYENNE ARAPAHO
WICHITA
SEMINOLE
Greer County
KIOWA
COMANCHE
APACHE
POTAWATOMI, SHAWNEE
CHICKASAW
CHOCTAW
Arkansas
Texas

#### Legend

Land lost prior to 1850
Land lost 1870–90
Land lost 1850–70
American Indian reservations as of 1890
✹ Major battle
*Hopi* Indian group/tribe

*Note:* Contemporary boundaries are provided for reference.

---

CHIEF JOSEPH

### The Flight of Chief Joseph and the Capture of Geronimo

Following Crazy Horse's defeat, the Indian Wars of the West entered their final stage. By 1877 most conflict came from "reservation Indians" attempting to escape government control.

One of the best known episodes of this period involved Chief Joseph and the traditionally peaceful Nez Percé of the Pacific Northwest. In 1877, the U.S. government ordered Joseph and his people from their land. Joseph refused, though he did not want war. Soon U.S. Army troops clashed with Nez Percé braves. Despite early Nez Percé victories, the Army forced Joseph and about 750 men, women and children to flee for Canada. Several army detachments were sent to stop Joseph, who inflicted heavy casualties on the soldiers. Yet in October, after journeying 1,700 miles, Joseph and his exhausted people were trapped by Nelson Miles at Bear Paw Mountain, Montana, just 40 miles from the border. After Joseph's surrender, he and his followers were sent to Indian Territory and then to the Colville Reservation in Washington State, where he died in 1904.

The last major Indian leader to escape capture was the legendary Chiricahua Apache, Geronimo. Geronimo and his band of a few hundred followers continuously launched raids on white settlements along the Arizona-Mexico border. More than once Geronimo returned to the Apache reservation, but then fled, unwilling to live like a captive. In the early 1880s, George Crook's cavalry and Apache scouts joined with thousands of Mexican soldiers in campaigns against Geronimo. At last, in 1886, Nelson Miles persuaded Geronimo to surrender. Geronimo was taken from his homeland and confined to a reservation, never allowed to return.

### The Ghost Dance and Wounded Knee

By 1889 a religious inspiration known as the "Ghost Dance" had been sweeping

**MASSACRE AT WOUNDED KNEE** Immediately after the gunfire at Wounded Knee, a blizzard struck the region, delaying the burial of Indian dead. Finally, on January 1, 1891, U.S. soldiers collected the frozen bodies of the dead from the fields, and buried them in a mass grave. Authorities made little effort to identify the bodies and refused to allow the Indians to conduct any kind of burial ceremony.

through the reservations. Medicine men and shamans saw visions of an Indian savior who would destroy their enemies and restore freedom and happiness to the nations. The people joined in hypnotic dancing that caused trances and exaltation, worrying the Indian agents, who feared many Indians would be persuaded to take up arms again.

Since Sitting Bull was the greatest living symbol of Indian prowess, the army decided to place him in close custody. On December 15, 1890, the attempt resulted in a fight with Sitting Bull's followers, and he was killed by Indian police. Expecting to be arrested next, Chief Big Foot of the Miniconjou Sioux fled with several hundred followers toward Pine Ridge reservation. The army caught Big Foot and his band, and escorted them to a camp at Wounded Knee, South Dakota. On December 29 the captives were surrounded by 500 troops and four Hotchkiss guns, as soldiers began to search for weapons. When a shot rang out the troops indiscriminately opened fire, killing Big Foot and 150 men, women, and children. The Army's own gunfire was mainly responsible for killing 25 soldiers and wounding 39 more.

For the U.S. Army and white settlers, the slaughter at Wounded Knee marked the end of three hundred years of war between European and American settlers of North America and the American Indians who had inhabited the land. For Native Americans, Wounded Knee marked the tragic end of their hopes for autonomy.

# The Spanish-American War

With the end of the Indian wars of the late nineteenth century, the United States gained complete control of all U.S. territory from the Atlantic to the Pacific. The American frontier, which had once meant all lands west of the narrow strip of colonial outposts along the Atlantic coast, had been conquered.

That said, the idea of the American frontier as a key to America's cultural psyche was not one in the front of most people's minds as the nation moved forward toward the twentieth century. Thus, when an University of Wisconsin assistant professor of history delivered a speech entitled "The Significance of the Frontier in American History," at a meeting of the American Historical Association, as part of the 1893 World's Columbian Exhibition in Chicago, few people noticed. Yet Frederick Jackson Turner's thesis—that the territorial expansion from the Atlantic to the Pacific Ocean had shaped the character and institutions

## The United States and its Overseas Possessions, 1857–1917

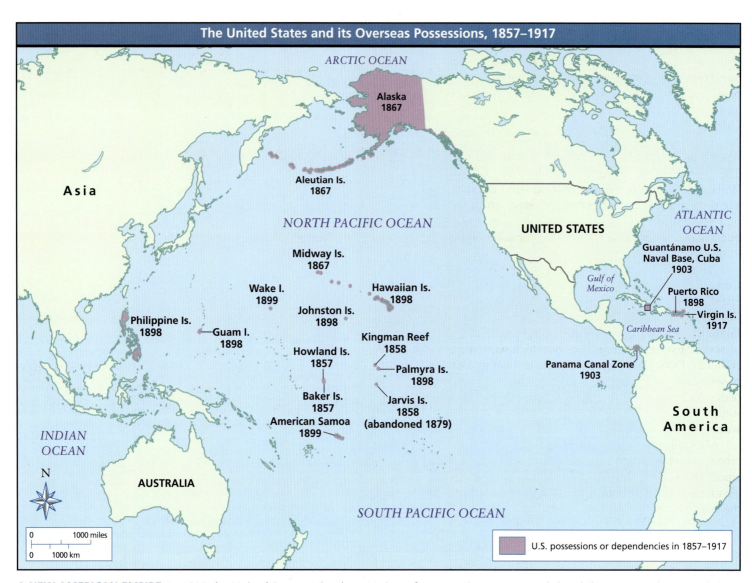

ARCTIC OCEAN

Alaska
1867

Asia

Aleutian Is.
1867

NORTH PACIFIC OCEAN

UNITED STATES

ATLANTIC
OCEAN

Midway Is.
1867

Guantánamo U.S.
Naval Base, Cuba
1903

Gulf of
Mexico

Wake I.
1899

Hawaiian Is.
1898

Puerto Rico
1898

Johnston Is.
1898

Virgin Is.
1917

Philippine Is.
1898

Guam I.
1898

Caribbean Sea

Kingman Reef
1858

Howland Is.
1857

Palmyra Is.
1898

Panama Canal Zone
1903

Baker Is.
1857

Jarvis Is.
1858
(abandoned 1879)

South
America

INDIAN
OCEAN

American Samoa
1899

N

AUSTRALIA

SOUTH PACIFIC OCEAN

0        1000 miles
0      1000 km

U.S. possessions or dependencies in 1857–1917

**A NEW AMERICAN EMPIRE**  In 1898 the United States gained possession of Puerto Rico, Guam, and the Philippines, and annexed the Hawaiian Islands. Yet as early as the 1850s the United States had gained a strong presence in the Pacific, thanks in part to a vibrant whaling trade.

of the United States, and that with the "closing" of the frontier, the nation would face a painful transition, from a land of endless boundaries to one with finite territorial limits. That transition, Turner argued, would call for Americans to recast their view of America as a land of infinite possibility.

In the midst of the unparalleled business growth and technological advancement that marked the Gilded Age, Americans had little patience for limits—even geographical ones. American sugar planters had gained virtual control of the Pacific island kingdom of Hawaii, and by 1898 it would become American territory. Closer to home, American business interests had eyed Spanish possessions in the Caribbean—Cuba and Puerto Rico—since before the Civil War. Rich in sugar, rice, and fruit, these colonies did a thriving

trade with the United States. By 1897, American politicians and businessmen were also considering building a ship canal across the Isthmus of Panama, territory that belonged to Colombia. To expansionist minds, control such a strategic canal required American dominance of the region. Civil strife in Cuba provided such an opportunity.

Since 1895 an insurrection had been raging in Cuba between the Spanish colonial government's forces and a determined Cuban independence movement. Despite facing 100,000 government troops and suffering from heavy-handed oppression, the 30,000 rebels kept up a guerrilla war that cost tens of thousands of lives. Taking the rebel side, the American press stirred up public opinion against Spain and called for Cuban independence.

### The Sinking of the *Maine*

In January 1898, the battleship USS *Maine* was sent to Havana to protect U.S. interests there, but on February 15 it exploded in Havana harbor killing 260. Although later investigations pointed to an internal explosion as the cause, American politicians and the sensationalist press—blaring "Remember the *Maine*!"—blamed Spanish sabotage for the sinking. Congress declared war on April 25, publicly stating it desired no more than Cuba's independence from Spain.

To wage the war President William McKinley called for 200,000 volunteers, and the public rallied behind the notion of waging a war against an oppressive European colonial power. In fact, the army was unprepared for the demands of training such a force.

The navy was ready, however, with a modern "steel fleet" of five battleships, two cruisers, another thirteen armored vessels, and six torpedo boats. Spain had a weak naval force, poorly maintained, and lacking convenient bases or coaling stations. While American troops mustered and trained in overcrowded camps at Tampa, New Orleans, and Mobile, the navy went into action.

### Attack on Manila Bay

The main American squadron, led by Rear Admiral William T. Sampson, steamed toward Cuba to blockade the Cuban ports of Havana and Santiago. A second squadron would would soon join Sampson in operations against Cuba and the other Spanish islands in the Caribbean.

Meanwhile, a third squadron, commanded by Commodore George Dewey, launched a blockade of Spain's colony in the Philippines. On April 30, six warships steamed into Manila Bay, risking the danger of floating mines. At 7 a.m. Dewey engaged a squadron of seven Spanish warships, one of which was wooden-hulled. Dewey's 100 guns were heavier than the thirty-seven carried by the Spaniards, and his gun crews better trained. By midday all the Spanish vessels were sunk or disabled. The Americans suffered only nine wounded, the Spanish 161 killed and 210 wounded.

Manila itself was already under siege by Filipino rebels, who had been waging a war of independence since 1896. The United States now arranged an alliance with the rebels and sent troops to help capture the city.

### A Splendid Little War

With Dewey's dramatic defeat of the Spanish Pacific squadron American strategy changed, and 20,000 troops were shipped to San Francisco for transport to Manila as other expeditions set off to invade Cuba. Meanwhile, a handful of Spanish warships, commanded by Admiral Pascual Cervera y Topete, entered Santiago de Cuba harbor. Cervera was soon blockaded by vastly more powerful ships under Sampson and Schley.

U.S. Marines cooperating with Cuban rebels took over Guantanamo Bay on June 10, and on June 22 and 24 General William R. Shafter landed 17,000 men at Daiquiri and Siboney, southeast of Santiago. Like Nelson Miles, the commanding general of the army, Shafter was a Civil War and Indian wars veteran. Miles was at the head of his own invasion force, which had not yet arrived.

### The Rough Riders

Though mainly regulars, Shafter's corps had several regiments of volunteers, one being the First United States Volunteer Cavalry, largely made up of Western cowboys and Eastern college boys. Calling itself the "Rocky Mountain Riders," the regiment later would be named the "Rough Riders." Logistical problems landed them in Cuba without their mounts, however, and only one officer found a horse. That officer was their second in

**Spanish American War: Caribbean Campaign, 1898**

| | |
|---|---|
| ← | Com. Winfield S. Schley |
| ← | Adm. William T. Sampson |
| ← | Gen. William Shafter |
| ← | Adm. Pascual Cervera |
| ← | Gen. Nelson Miles |

Norfolk

UNITED STATES

Tampa
Florida

*Gulf of Mexico*

Key West

U.S.S. Maine exploded Feb. 15, 1898

Havana

CUBA

*Naval Blockade*

U.S. captures Santiago July 17, 1898

Santiago

U.S. destroys Spanish fleet July 3, 1898

JAMAICA

*ATLANTIC OCEAN*

BAHAMAS

U.S. troops occupy Puerto Rico July 25–28, 1898

*Naval Blockade*

HAITI

DOMINICAN REPUBLIC

PUERTO RICO

*Caribbean Sea*

from Spain

N

0       300 miles
0    300 km

**NAVAL BLOCKADE AND BATTLE** The United States fleet blockaded Cuba, transported the main expeditionary force, and destroyed the Spanish squadron off Santiago; next it carried U.S. troops to take Puerto Rico.

command, Theodore Roosevelt, who had resigned as assistant secretary of the navy to serve in the war.

Other than minor skirmishing with American advance parties, the Spanish did not resist, but retreated toward Santiago. They numbered 12,000, many well-armed with modern Mauser rifles, but their artillery was deficient, and they lacked machine guns. On July 1 the Americans attacked Santiago's strongpoints at San Juan Hill and Kettle Hill and at El Caney to the north. The 6,600 American regulars attacking El Caney were held up by 520 dug-in Spanish defenders, who fought for more than eleven hours before retreating. Attacking San Juan Hill, Roosevelt's Rough Riders were joined by the Ninth and Tenth cavalry regiments, both African-American. Here 500 Spaniards were entrenched around reinforced blockhouses, and they put

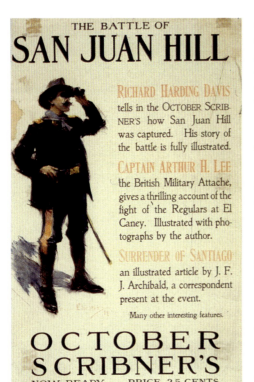

THE BATTLE OF
# SAN JUAN HILL

RICHARD HARDING DAVIS tells in the OCTOBER SCRIBNER'S how San Juan Hill was captured. His story of the battle is fully illustrated.

CAPTAIN ARTHUR H. LEE the British Military Attaché, gives a thrilling account of the fight of the Regulars at El Caney. Illustrated with photographs by the author.

SURRENDER OF SANTIAGO an illustrated article by J. F. J. Archibald, a correspondent present at the event.

Many other interesting features.

## OCTOBER SCRIBNER'S
NOW READY    PRICE, 25 CENTS

**THE SPLENDID LITTLE WAR** The popular press, which had helped push for the war at its outset, covered it in lavish detail once it began.

**A CARTOON CONQUERER** "I hardly know which to take first!" says Uncle Sam in the cartoon shown here, as he studies the menu listing Cuba, the Philippines, and the Sandwich Islands (a colonial-era name for Hawaii). President William McKinley, in a waiter's apron, looks on with approval.

up a fierce fight against the 8,000 American troops before them. San Juan Hill was taken after several hours, dooming Santiago, now under siege. The United States lost 205 killed and 1,180 wounded in the siege of Santiago, while the Spanish had 215 killed and 376 wounded.

## The Battle of Santiago de Cuba

Admiral Cervera was given direct orders by the colonial government to break out and escape. Cervera knew he could never succeed, but he gallantly obeyed, and on July 3, led his six ships on a dash out of the bay. The American blockading fleet, under tactical command of Commodore Schley, utterly destroyed the outgunned Spanish warships within four hours. More than 300 Spanish were killed, and 1,700 taken prisoner, including Cervera.

Santiago surrendered on July 17. Except for the capture of Puerto Rico at the end of July, and the fall of Manila to American troops and Filipino rebels in August, the fighting was over. The United States lost fewer than 400 men in combat, but another 2,000 would die from tropical disease. A general armistice took hold on August 12, with a final peace treaty signed in Paris on December 10, 1898. Secretary of State John M. Hay told Roosevelt this was a "splendid little war."

Spain was required to leave Cuba and cede Puerto Rico and the Pacific island of Guam to the United States, which paid $10 million for the Philippines. Filipino rebels, however, were unwilling to trade one foreign occupier for another. The Americans would have to fight harder than ever to control the Philippines.

## The Philippine-American War

Manila's surrender in August 1898 created a complicated situation, for a revolutionary army of 20,000 Filipinos had been besieging the city when the Americans arrived. In fact Dewey had transported Filipino leader Emilio Aguinaldo to the Philippines from Hong Kong, where he had been living in exile. Aguinaldo at first was supported by the Americans, but now his forces were not permitted to enter Manila, nor were they given any credit for the defeat of the Spanish colonial army.

The Americans occupied Manila, while Aguinaldo's powerful force was on its outskirts, each side entrenched and patrolling a no-man's land between them. By January 1899 a Philippine republic had been established, and Aguinaldo was named president. The United States, however, refused to recognize the government. The resentment of Filipino rebels and the imposition of American rule made for a volatile brew.

## A Short-Lived Peace

Taunts and insults were exchanged by the American Expeditionary Force and

WELL, I HARDLY KNOW WHICH TO TAKE FIRST!

Filipino rebel troops, and they often got into brawls. An uneasy few months exploded in February 1899 when an American patrol shot and killed Filipino sentries who challenged them. Full-scale combat erupted in and around the city, and 3,000 Filipinos died in just the first few days. The Philippine-American War, also known as the Philippine War for Independence, or the Philippine Insurgency, would rage for more than three years.

The major engagements took place on the island of Luzon, where Manila stood. General Ewell S. Otis led approximately 12,000 troops of the Eighth Corps, who were better-trained and armed than Aguinaldo's 40,000-strong army. American forces immediately pushed outward from Manila to split the Filipino forces and seize key towns and rivers. General Arthur MacArthur seized Caloocan in February and Malolos, the rebel capital, in March. Communications were cut between insurgent forces in north and south Luzon. American control was established over other important islands: Panay and Cebu in February, Negros in March, and Jolo in the Sulu Archipelago in May. In June, the American force numbered 47,500 men and would grow to 75,000 within a year.

## Atrocity and Starvation

By November 1899, the rebel field army was defeated, with heavy casualties, and its remnants began to wage a fierce guerrilla war. Otis was succeeded early in 1900 by MacArthur, who established martial law in certain military zones and filled concentration camps with civilians, separating them from the guerrillas. Both sides committed savage atrocities, and American troops often killed Filipinos without bothering to distinguish between combatant and civilian. Villages were wiped out or the population fled as their buildings were burned, livestock slaughtered, and crops ruined in order to starve out the insurgents.

In March 1901, General Frederick Funston and four American officers pretended to be prisoners of rebel troops—who actually were loyal Filipinos. They daringly entered the rebel camp, took Aguinaldo by surprise, and captured him. The war continued until July 1902, with more than 125,000 American troops eventually committed to finally winning the conflict.

Estimates put Filipino deaths at between 200,000-600,000—some say far higher. Most died of starvation and disease caused by economic disruption and by the concentration camps; about 18,000 died in combat. More than 4,500 Americans died, many of disease, with 2,800 wounded.

Warfare was not yet over in the Philippine islands, however, because the Moros—Muslims of the southern islands—had never been defeated by the Spanish and did not consider the Americans their overlords. Nonetheless, the United States would maintain political control over the Philippines for the next four decades. By 1946, when the U.S. Congress finally granted the islands their independence, the United States would have become the preeminent power in the world.

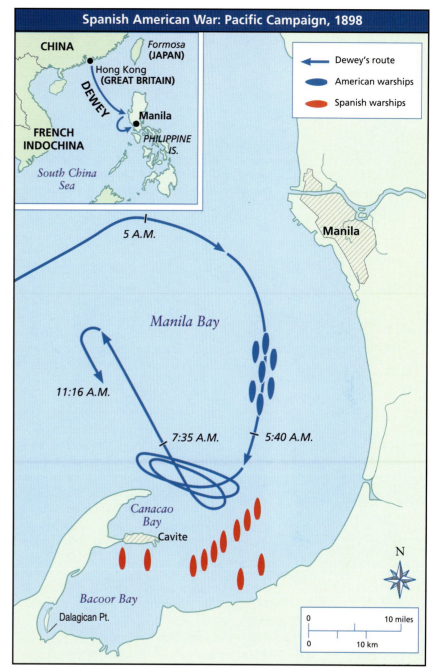

**BATTLE OF MANILA BAY** Spain's aging warships were outgunned by a modern U.S. squadron in the Philippines.

*"The Philippines are ours forever, territory belonging to the United States, as the Constitution calls them…We will not repudiate our duty in the archipelago. We will not renounce our part in the mission of our race, trustee, under God, of the civilization of the world."*

—Senator Albert J. Beveridge

# Chapter 22: The Progressive Movement

Theodore Roosevelt was not suited to be any man's Number Two. Yet as the presidential election of 1900 approached, Republican party bosses recognized Roosevelt, the popular governor of New York, as the strong vote-getter that he was. What's more, New York political boss Tom Platt figured that kicking Roosevelt up the ladder to the Vice-Presidency was worth the risk. From that post Roosevelt would actually have far less power than he had as governor.

Mark Hanna, President William McKinley's chief strategist, was unconvinced. Because his wing of the party represented the interests of the large business trusts, Hanna deeply distrusted New York's reform-minded governor. "Don't you realize," he argued, "there's only one life between that madman and the White House?"

Despite Hanna's fears, Roosevelt became the Republican nominee for Vice President. He then took the post when McKinley won a resounding victory in a rematch election contest over William Jennings Bryan. Yet on September 6, 1901, Hanna's worst nightmare came true. On that day, McKinley was shot by an anarchist named Leon Czolgosz while on a receiving line at the Pan-American Exposition in Buffalo, New York. A week later McKinley died, making the 42-year-old Roosevelt President of the United States.

Over the next dozen years, Roosevelt would tower over the nation's political scene as no president had since Andrew Jackson. As president Roosevelt used the "bully pulpit" of his office to reshape the presidency. He believed in using his full powers to ensure justice for all Americans, regardless of wealth or connections. He wielded the Sherman Antitrust Act to break up trusts he thought harmed the national interest. In one of his most far-reaching achievements he launched widespread conservation efforts that brought state and federal governments together to protect the nation's natural resources as never before.

## Origins of the Progressive Movement

Prior to Roosevelt's ascension to office, reforms efforts were limited by a number of factors. The poor economic climate that began in 1893 had discouraged states from developing new policy initiatives. The depression also encouraged further consolidation of corporations, which would make trusts a key issue during Roosevelt's term.

Finally, the Spanish American War distracted from domestic matters. Nonetheless, the reform impulse that flowered between 1901 and 1920 did not originate with Theodore Roosevelt. True, by sheer force of personality and the power of his position, Roosevelt came to personify his era. But the era's major achievements were not a direct result of Roosevelt but were instead as a wide-ranging response to the turmoil caused by rapid, unfettered industrialization.

In its broadest form the Progressive Movement crossed all political, social, and economic lines, and included nativists alarmed at skyrocketing immigration, populist followers of Bryan and other heartland crusaders, industrial labor union organizers, conservative prohibitionists and crusaders for moral purity, advocates for the rights of women and African-Americans, young and idealistic newspaper and magazine journalists, followers of a liberal religious movement known as the Social Gospel, or Christian Socialism, as well as many others.

The Social Gospel movement first flowered in the late nineteenth century among liberal clergymen who sought a means of helping the urban poor. One of the additional goals of the movement was to attract working class urban immigrants, many of whom were members of the Roman Catholic Church.

Perhaps the most prominent member of the movement was Walter Rauschenbush, a Baptist minister from the "Hell's Kitchen" section of New York City who called for a democratic society achieved through non-violence. Another was William Dwight Porter Bliss, who worked closely with the Knights of Labor and the Socialist Party.

Ultimately, the Social Gospel movement had limited success. While it liberalized some Protestant denominations and contributed to efforts by reformers like Roosevelt, Woodrow Wilson and Jane Addams, it failed to capture the hearts and minds of most poor laborers.

### Moral Reform Movements

Even if the Social Gospel Movement failed to cross class lines, the idea that human beings had a moral obligation to address the ills of society infused the progressive era reform movements. By 1913 thirteen states had banned the sale of cigarettes. Before long the difficulty of enforcing the ban led to a new strategy—the use of cigarette taxes to discourage their purchase.

More effective was the temperance movement, which dated back to the mid-nineteenth century, and took on a new fervor beginning in 1900. On June 1 of that year an anti-alcohol crusader named Carrie Nation gained nationwide attention when she took the law into her own hands.

## Recall, Referendum, and Initiative by State

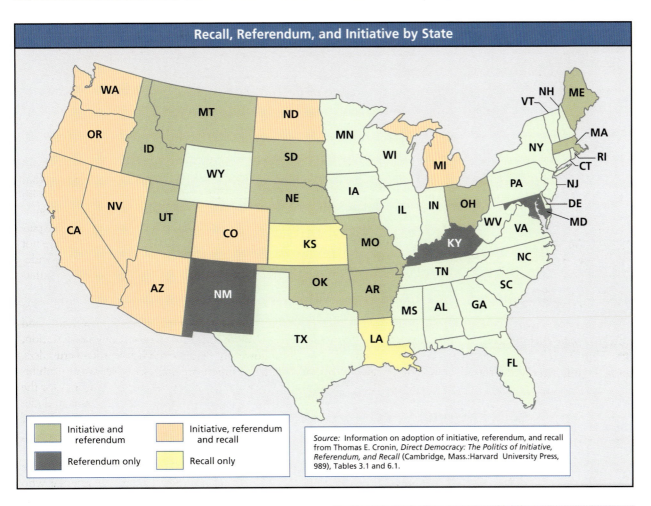

**Initiative and referendum**

**Referendum only**

**Initiative, referendum and recall**

**Recall only**

*Source:* Information on adoption of initiative, referendum, and recall from Thomas E. Cronin, *Direct Democracy: The Politics of Initiative, Referendum, and Recall* (Cambridge, Mass.:Harvard University Press, 989), Tables 3.1 and 6.1.

**ELECTORAL DEMOCRACY** Voter initiatives, referenda and recalls all aimed to make politicians more answerable to the average voter.

She attacked three illegal saloons in Kiowa, Kansas using stones, brickbats, full malt bottles, and one billiard ball as ammunition. Six months later, Nation added an axe to her arsenal, and it became her symbol. Over the next decade, Nation was arrested 30 times after leading her followers in attacks on one bar after another in states across the country, crying "Smash, ladies, smash!" as they went. The famous bare-knuckled prize-fighter John L. Sullivan was reported to have run and hid when the six-foot, 160-pound Nation burst into the New York City saloon that he owned.

While Carrie Nation garnered the most headlines in the early twentieth century fight against alcohol, her saloon-smashing antics were not as effective as the quiet action of the Women's Christian Temperance Union (WCTU), a group to which Nation belonged. The WCTU, founded in the 1870s, was one of the largest women's organizations in the nation. While the group's main focus was on temperance, the WTCU also worked to promote health and hygiene, prison reform, and world peace. Another important temperance group was the Anti-Saloon League, formed in the 1890s, which lobbied to convince states to ban alcohol within their borders. By 1915 more than a dozen states had banned alcohol, and temperance forces had begun to push for nationwide alcohol prohibition.

### THE MUCKRAKERS

Many progressive-era reforms came about on the state level, and to a lesser degree on the national level, thanks to the efforts of the press. Between 1900 and 1910 a new breed of journalist emerged, derisively called "muckrakers" for their tendency to stir up and expose the seamier side of American life. Lincoln Steffens, editor of

**UPTON SINCLAIR**

*McClure's Magazine*, published frequent articles exposing political and corporate corruption. Ida Tarbell, wrote *A History of Standard Oil* (1906), a book based on a series of articles on Standard Oil and its director, John D. Rockefeller. Her widely read articles would win support for Roosevelt's anti-monopoly efforts. But the work that had perhaps the greatest national impact was novelist Upton Sinclair's *The Jungle*. The book, focused on conditions in the Chicago meat stockyards, caused a sensation that led to the passage of the Pure Food and Drug Act of 1906.

## Selected Federal Child Labor and Child Welfare Laws

| LAW | YEAR PASSED | PROVISIONS |
| --- | --- | --- |
| The Children's Bureau Act | 1912 | Signed into law by President Taft, the bill created a new federal agency that had the stated purpose of investigating and reporting "upon all matters pertaining to the welfare of children and child life among all classes of our people." |
| The Keating-Owen Act | 1916 | Would have freed children from child labor only in industries that engaged in interstate commerce. Declared unconstitutional by U.S. Supreme Court as federal interference in local labor law. In 1941 the Court overruled its earlier decision against the act, outlawing the use of child labor in businesses that shipped goods out of state. |
| The Smith-Hughes Act | 1917 | Provided $1 million to each state that agreed to improve their public schools by providing vocational education programs. The National Child Labor Committee and other organizations believed that these programs would offer children an alternative to work. |
| Tax on Employment of Children | 1919 | Signed into law by President Wilson, this law placed a ten percent tax on net profits of businesses that employed children under age fourteen or made them work more than eight hours a day, six days a week. This law was also declared unconstitutional. |
| The Sheppard-Towner Maternity Act | 1921 | Authorized $1 million in federal funds for state aid, to be used for the promotion of the welfare of pregnant women and infants. |

When the United State entered World War I patriotic fervor helped swell support for prohibition further. With Americans dying in Europe many believed that the least they could do was forego alcohol. In January 1919 Congress passed the Eighteenth Amendment to the Constitution and a year later prohibition was the law of the land.

### Progressive Legislation in the States

While the Progressive Movement in its broadest sense crossed economic and social barriers, it differed from some of the other reform movements occurring at the time. Most of the leading figures in the Progressive Movement were upper- and middle-class white men—reformers not revolutionaries. While class, sex, and racial divisions led some of the more radical elements in the labor, women's rights and African-American civil rights struggles of the late nineteenth and early twentieth century to question the fundamental fairness of American society, the leading progressives believed in the American economic and social systems, and saw their work as an effort to broaden the core principles of democracy and freedom.

Progressives were united in their belief in clean government. Frequently referred to as "laboratories for democracy," the states and many efforts on the local and state level centered on anti-corruption campaigns. To make the electoral process more democratic a two thirds majority of the states ratified the seventeenth amendment in 1913, allowing for the direct election of U.S. senators by voters for the first time. All but three states also adopted direct primaries by 1916, which allowed voters to choose among several candidates for a party's nomination. To allow voters to express their dissatisfaction with elected officials Progressives proposed the recall, which allowed voters to remove them before the end of their term of office. To prevent employers or others from intimidating voters into voting a certain way, many states also began using secret ballots for the first time. Governments also took a more direct role in printing ballots, supervising elections and setting requirements for registration.

To give voters a greater voice in law making, Progressives also proposed the initiative and the referendum. The initiative allowed voters to propose a bill and legislation and the referendum permitted them to vote directly on an issue. Oregon, South Dakota, and Utah were the first states to adopt the initiative and referendum.

Among the most notable efforts at reform on the state level took place in Wisconsin, where Robert LaFollette was elected governor in 1901. As governor "Fighting Bob" promoted a series of labor, tax and comprehensive changes in his state's voting system that became known as "the Wisconsin idea." LaFollette quickly became recognized as one of the leading progressive politicians in the United States, a reputation he maintained as a U.S. Senator from 1906 to 1925.

Many states also designed labor and social welfare reforms to address the growing squalor of life in the urban slums. The model for some of these social programs came from Europe. Beginning in the 1880s Britain, France, Germany, and Scandinavian nations had adopted a series of social welfare programs—unemployment insurance, old age pensions, industrial accident and health insurance. During the Progressive era, many reformers borrowed these ideas and adapted them to meet American circumstances.

In part, these laws were a response to the work of investigative "muckraking" journalists. The laws were also a response to

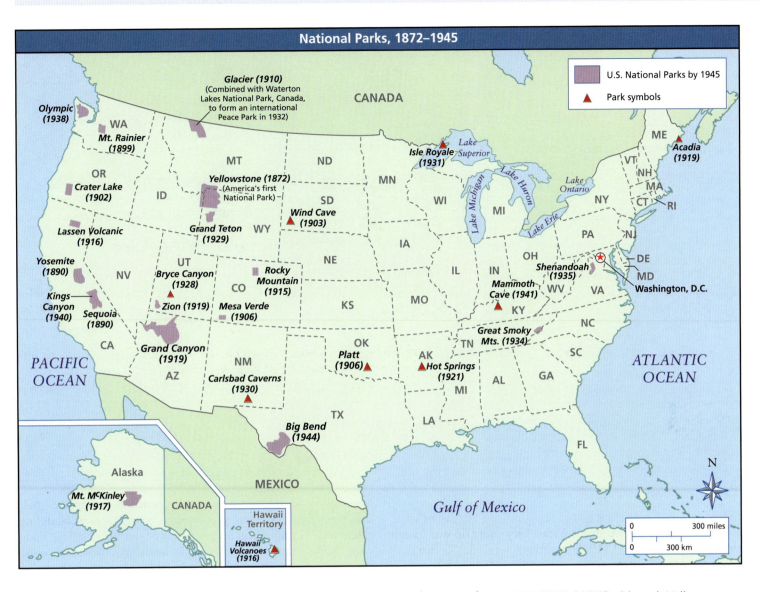

**National Parks, 1872–1945**

U.S. National Parks by 1945

Park symbols

CANADA

Olympic (1938)

WA

Mt. Rainier (1899)

Glacier (1910)
(Combined with Waterton Lakes National Park, Canada, to form an international Peace Park in 1932)

ME

Acadia (1919)

Isle Royale (1931)

Lake Superior

VT

NH

MA

MT

ND

MN

Lake Michigan

Lake Huron

Lake Ontario

OR

Crater Lake (1902)

ID

Yellowstone (1872)
(America's first National Park)

SD

WI

MI

NY

CT

RI

Wind Cave (1903)

Lassen Volcanic (1916)

Grand Teton (1929)

WY

IA

NE

PA

NJ

Lake Erie

Yosemite (1890)

UT

Bryce Canyon (1928)

Rocky Mountain (1915)

CO

IL

IN

OH

Shenandoah (1935)

DE

MD

Washington, D.C.

NV

Mammoth Cave (1941)

WV

VA

Kings Canyon (1940)

Sequoia (1890)

Zion (1919)

Mesa Verde (1906)

KS

MO

KY

NC

Grand Canyon (1919)

CA

NM

AZ

OK

Platt (1906)

AK

Great Smoky Mts. (1934)

TN

SC

PACIFIC OCEAN

Hot Springs (1921)

AL

GA

ATLANTIC OCEAN

Carlsbad Caverns (1930)

MI

TX

LA

FL

Big Bend (1944)

Alaska

MEXICO

CANADA

Gulf of Mexico

N

Mt. McKinley (1917)

Hawaii Territory

Hawaii Volcanoes (1916)

0    300 miles

0    300 km

events. In 1911, for instance, a small fire started in a rag bin at the Triangle Shirtwaist Company in New York City. The fire soon covered the clothing factory floor. Within an hour 146 workers, mostly women, choked to death from smoke inhalation. They could not escape because the owners kept all doors locked or blocked during the day. With no other way out, some jumped from windows, falling ten stories to their death.

After the fire New York and other states passed a wave of factory safety laws. Other state laws followed: by 1912 thirty states had abolished child labor, and by 1916 all states other than Mississippi had established compulsory school attendance laws. During the same period, laws limiting work hours for women and children passed in thirty-two states, and minimum wages for women workers were signed in eleven states; workmen's compensation programs, which provided compensation for workers injured on the job, became law in thirty-two states. Still other laws established an eight-

hour workday for state employees; authorized credit unions; created public utility commissions; established state employee pensions; and instituted a host of health and safety regulations.

Among the most dramatic American innovations were "widow's pensions." Adopted by most states, these programs provided widows with a monthly payment that allowed them to keep their children at home, and not have to put them in orphanages or out for adoption.

## Local Reforms

On the local level the drive for reform was equally apparent. In an effort to democratize local government Galveston, Texas established the first city commission in 1900. The change shifted power away from a mayor and alderman to five elected city commissioners, each responsible for a specific department.

Most city governments retained their traditional structure, but an increasing

**NATIONAL PARKS** Although Yellowstone National Park became the nation's first national park in 1872, the national park system did not expand rapidly until the administration of Theodore Roosevelt.

*How interesting everything is! Every rock, mountain, stream, plant, lake, lawn, forest, garden, bird, beast, insect seems to call and invite us to come and learn something of its history and relationship.*

—John Muir

## THE SUPREME COURT AND THE PROGRESSIVE ERA

In 1908 the Supreme Court again upheld a progressive era law when it ruled in the 1908 case *Muller v. Oregon* that a law limiting the number of hours worked by women was legal. The ruling denied that the law impaired the liberty of contract guaranteed by the Fourteenth Amendment. Attorney Louis D. Brandeis's brief on this case contained over 100 pages of data to prove that longer hours were dangerous to a woman's health, safety and morals, and that shorter hours result in better social and economic conditions. The case not only overturned the *Lochner v. New York* decision on 1905, which had ruled against the legality of states limiting working hours, but gave the Court power to render decisions in social and economic as well as legal cases.

**LOUIS D. BRANDEIS**

Just as often as it affirmed the legality of progressive legislation, however, the Supreme Court overturned it. In 1912 Congress established a bureau to deal with child labor concerns, and in 1916 the Keating-Owens Act became law. The act attempted to discourage child labor by banning its products from interstate trade. The Court declared the law unconstitutional two years later. In 1919 a similar attempt to limit child labor was made by taxing products made with child labor, but it too was declared unconstitutional by the Court in its 1922 *Baily v. Drexel Furniture* decision. Child labor would not be finally restricted until 1936, when Congress passed the Fair Labor Standards Act.

number of reform-minded mayors came to power. For example in New York Seth Low, a socialist, defeated the candidate of the local Tammany Hall machine, which had controlled city politics since the days of Aaron Burr, and in Detroit Mayor Hazen Pingree provided public baths, parks and work relief programs for the poor.

Perhaps the most aggressive reformer of all the nation's mayors was Toledo's eccentric Samuel "Golden Rule" Jones, who was elected four times between 1897 and 1904. Jones, a Welshman who had made a fortune in the oil industry, called for a ban on political parties, and public ownership of streetcars and utilities. Jones also established free kindergartens for Toledo youth, and granted a minimum wage, plus vacation pay to all municipal employees. He even called an end to the penitentiary system. When he sat in as a judge dealing with petty crimes, the born-again Christian mayor routinely dismissed all cases. In fact Jones could often be found, armed with a well-thumbed copy of Walt Whitman's *Leaves of Grass*, reading to inmates at the city jail. As he put it, "Anything which today separates me from the lowest soul in the penitentiary or tenderloin district is the very opposite of reli-

gion." Mark Hanna, Jones' fellow Ohioan, called Jones "a crank, but he is a moral crank..."

# The Progressive Movement and the Federal Government

The wealthy son of a New York merchant and director of many corporate boards, Theodore Roosevelt entered the presidency with a relatively modest reform agenda. Nonetheless, he still angered the "Big business" wing of his Republican party, which resisted even the smallest reforms. Several years after leaving the presidency, Roosevelt wrote this about those who had opposed reform:

I have always maintained that our worst revolutionaries today are those...who do not see and will not admit there is any need for change....If these [people] had lived at an earlier time in our history, they would have opposed free speech and free assembly, and voted against free schools; they are the men who today oppose min-

imum wage laws, insurance of workmen against the ills of industrial life and the reform of our legislators and our courts, which can alone render such measures possible.... It is these reactionaries...who, by 'standing pat' on industrial injustice, incite...industrial revolt, and it is only we who advocate political and industrial democracy who render possible the progress of our American industry...with a minimum of friction [and] with a maximum of justice.

### Roosevelt's First Term

During the first of Roosevelt's two terms, he showed right away that he was not afraid to use the power of his office. In 1902, the United Mine Workers of America called a strike in Pennsylvania's anthracite coal mines. When mine owners refused the union's offer of arbitration, Roosevelt stepped in and appointed a commission to mediate the strike. The commission succeeded in calling off the strike; it awarded workers a ten percent wage increase but refused to grant the union recognition. The anthracite coal strike marked the first major use of federal mediation in a labor dispute.

Most of Roosevelt's first term focused on two causes: trust-busting and conservation of natural resources. Since the 1890s Roosevelt had warned against the power of the trusts, which he believed led to social division and revolution. Roosevelt was not out to destroy all trusts, however—only to break up the most powerful.

In one of many efforts Roosevelt brought suit under the Sherman Antitrust Act to prevent the merger of several railroad companies into a holding company by the name of Northern Securities Company. In 1903 the government won its case against Northern Securities. The Supreme Court later upheld the victory.

Roosevelt's efforts as president to promote conservation began in 1902 when he established Crater Lake National Park in Oregon. The next year Roosevelt declared Pelican Island, Florida to be the nation's first federal bird reservation. Roosevelt's signature achievement in the area of conservation took place just before the end of his first term, when in February 1905 he established the U.S. Forestry Service.

### The Conservation Movement

Like other aspects of progressive era, the American conservation movement predates Roosevelt's presidency. As early as 1823

## SCHOOL ENROLLMENTS, 1900–1920

Between 1900 and 1920, the number of students in elementary and high schools grew rapidly.

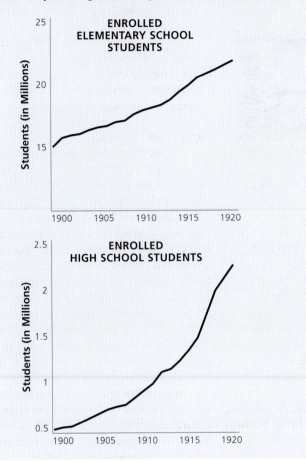

ENROLLED ELEMENTARY SCHOOL STUDENTS

ENROLLED HIGH SCHOOL STUDENTS

novelist James Fenimore Cooper had proposed that humans "govern the resources of nature by certain principles in order to conserve them. In 1832 Congress established Arkansas Hot Springs as a national reservation, and when an enormous sequoia nicknamed "Mother of the Forest" was cut down in 1852 simply to display its cross sections at carnivals, widespread outrage led to a series of federal laws and land grants that would eventually become the basis for a national park system.

Two of the conservation movement's leading champions were the naturalists John Burroughs and John Muir. Burroughs, who first began publishing in 1865, continued to release nature-themed works for the next four decades. In 1867 Muir traveled from Indiana to California, where he then centered his studies in the Yosemite Valley, and then Nevada and Alaska. Muir actively lobbied Congress to establish Yosemite National Park, which it did in 1890. Muir was later instrumental in pushing Congress to create Yellowstone National Park and many others.

### Taft v. the Bull Moose Party

In 1904, while running for election to a second term, Theodore Roosevelt promised that he would not run for a third term in 1908. When the time came he stepped aside to allow his friend and protegé, William Howard Taft, to win the election (sending William Jennings Bryan to a third defeat). But Roosevelt soon broke with Taft over his perception that Taft was abandoning his progressive path. In truth Taft actually achieved more in the fight against trusts than Roosevelt had. Yet when Roosevelt called for a "New Nationalism" that would increase conservation efforts, protect labor, begin a federal graduated income tax, and create new federal programs to aid women, children and the poor, the legalistic Taft questioned the constitutionality of such federal activism.

In the 1912 election Taft defeated Roosevelt to win the Republican Party's nomination. Yet Roosevelt then broke with the Republicans to become the candidate of the Progressive Party, which immediately became known as the "Bull Moose" when Roosevelt declared himself "fit as a bull moose." TR's continued popularity allowed him to win more votes than Taft—making Roosevelt the only third party candidate to outpoll a major party candidate in a presidential election. Nevertheless, Roosevelt also split Republican ranks, handing Democrat Woodrow Wilson the election.

### Civil Rights Policy Under Wilson

Woodrow Wilson had been governor of New Jersey and president of Princeton University before reaching the Presidency. Both an intellectual and an idealist, Wilson incorporated many progressive policies and ideals into his presidency—reforming currency, initiating an income tax, toughening antitrust and labor laws, and restricting child labor.

Unlike Roosevelt, Wilson promised that the United States would not seek to expand its territories—although he did send troops to Mexico, Nicaragua, the Dominican Republic and elsewhere in Latin America in the name of "stability." He initially sought to keep the United States out of the First World War, but by his second term reluctantly committed American forces to the "war to end all wars." His failed postwar campaign for American involvement in the League of Nations was a legacy of his vision of worldwide lasting peace.

Yet in the area of social equality Wilson was quite conservative. By the 1910s a new generation of African Americans—better educated, and mostly from the North—cast the struggle for African American civil rights in a more overtly political direction. Where Booker T. Washington, still the leading African Americans had preached conciliation and patience, intellectuals like W.E.B Du Bois demanded concrete political progress.

While campaigning for office in 1912 Wilson had promised justice to black Americans. "Should I become President of the United States," he wrote to one black leader, "they may count upon me for absolute fair dealing for everything by which I could assist in advancing their interests of the race." Yet immediately after the election he fired fifteen out of seventeen black supervisors who had been previously appointed to federal jobs, replacing them with whites. He also refused to follow the long-standing tradition of appointing African Americans as ambassadors to Haiti and the Dominican Republic, and allowed both the Postmaster General and Secretary of the Treasury to order that their departments be segregated. In 1913 William Monroe Trotter, founder of the National Equal Rights League, an African American civil rights group, called Wilson a liar to his face during a meeting in the White House, after Wilson denied that segregation existed in his administration. Not surprisingly Trotter was never invited back to the White House. Meanwhile the head of the Internal Revenue division in Georgia fired all black employees, stating, "There are no government positions for Negroes in the South. A Negro's place is in the corn field." The number of black civil servants in the Wilson government fell to just 74 by 1920—down from 400 in 1910 when Taft was president.

## Women's Suffrage Before the Nineteenth Amendment, 1920

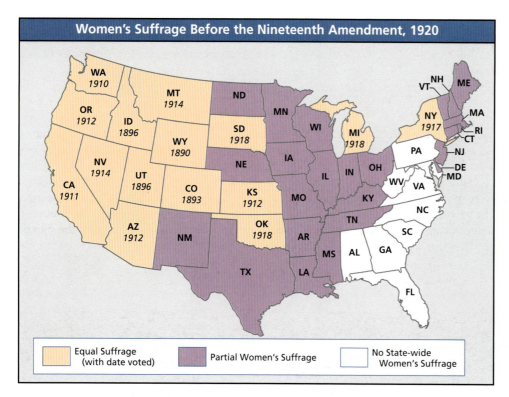

Legend:
- Equal Suffrage (with date voted)
- Partial Women's Suffrage
- No State-wide Women's Suffrage

Map labels: WA 1910, OR 1912, ID 1896, MT 1914, ND, MN, VT, NH, ME, MA, NY 1917, RI, CT, NJ, DE, MD, PA, SD 1918, WI, MI 1918, WY 1890, NE, IA, IL, IN, OH, WV, VA, NV 1914, UT 1896, CO 1893, KS 1912, MO, KY, NC, CA 1911, AZ 1912, NM, OK 1918, AR, TN, SC, GA, MS, AL, TX, LA, FL

**THE SPREAD OF WOMEN'S SUFFRAGE**
Prior to passage of the Nineteenth Amendment most states had already acted to grant women at least a limited form of voting rights.

# The Progessive Legacy

The suffrage movement's ultimate victory in winning the right to vote for women across the nation is one of the shining legacies of the progressive era. It was a change brought about not by progressive politicians but by citizens united to push their cause, and to sacrifice for it at great personal risk if necessary. The change had a long-lasting and dramatic impact on American politics as female voters became constituents rather than merely the spouses of male constituents.

Looking back on the optimistic first two decades of the twentieth century, this idea—that individual, ordinary citizens could effectively become agents of change—took hold. The progressive reforms towards more democratic elections remain with us in the form of direct election of senators, and in recall, initiative and referendum elections.

Government oversight of industry also reshaped the relationship between the federal government and American business. From the dismantling of Standard Oil to the passage of the eight-hour work day and worker safety laws, the progressive era softened some of the sharpest edges of industrial America.

At the same time many pieces of progressive-era legislation either failed to pass or were ineffective. Direct election of senators did not change the fact that U.S. senators came from the elite class of American society. The initiatives, recalls, and referenda were rare as organizing them cost considerable sums of money. And local governments, particularly in the cities, remained in the hands of machine politicians.

On the federal level, the trust-busting legacy launched by Roosevelt failed to ultimately increase competition or lower consumer prices. By the 1920s the federal government would revert to a hands off approach to business best symbolized by Calvin Coolidge's oft-repeated phrase that "the business of America is business."

## Women Win the Vote

Wilson was also resistant to calls for national women's suffrage. In 1890 the National Woman Suffrage Association (NWSA) had merged with its more conservative rival, the American Woman Suffrage Association (AWSA), to work together to form the National American Woman Suffrage Association (NAWSA) to work together in support of women's voting rights. From 1900 to 1904 and again from 1915 to 1920 the organization was led by Carrie Chapman Catt, a visionary leader who mobilized hundreds of thousands of citizens to support woman suffrage as a statement of justice and a road to world peace. Catt directed her campaign at both state and federal governments, and taught supporters how to use the system to lobby Congressmen and other officials. A longtime believer in the need for citizen involvement in politics, she later founded the League of Women Voters.

Yet despite Catt's leadership the suffrage movement split again during the progressive era—this time along generational lines. In 1913 28-year old Alice Paul, a member of NAWSA, tired of what she viewed as the quiet and slow legislative strategy of the organization. Paul had spent time in England where she had participated in the militant women's suffrage campaign there, led by Emmeline and Christabel Pankhurst. Radicalized by the experience, Paul left NAWSA in 1913 to form the Congressional Union for Woman Suffrage. The group later became known as the National Woman's Party (NWP).

Paul's provocative and highly visible tactics varied: She planned protest marches and hunger strikes as well as publicity campaigns. On the eve of Woodrow Wilson's inauguration in 1913 Paul led a peaceful march of 5,000 women to the White House. The march, featuring banners that asked "Mr. President — What will you do for woman suffrage?" sparked a riot. The picketing continued throughout Wilson's time in office, even as America readied for war.

Not all of Paul's tactics led to confrontation—one involved sending pro-vote valentines to all the members of Congress. But the NWP's more aggressive tactics often led to police violence and brutality. Wilson was personally offended by Paul's tactics, declaring her "unlady-like," and gave his tacit approval to her frequent arrests. During one incarceration Paul began a hunger strike, which ended with guards force-feeding her with a tube, locking her in solitary confinement and threatening to send her to an insane asylum. Nonetheless, Paul refused to back down. By the end of 1917 Wilson recognized the growing political support for women's rights and announced his support for a suffrage amendment to the Constitution. The Nineteenth Amendment giving women the right to vote passed in 1920.

On child labor and laws limiting the number of hours worked by women, the long-term record of progressive reform was also mixed, and often had unintended consequences. While the number of children between ten and fifteen in the labor force dropped from one in five in 1900 to one in twenty in 1930, the loss of income from the child, and from extra hours worked by women, created a new short-term strain on the already meager finances of the urban poor.

Laws such as the Pure Food and Drug Act and the Meat Inspection Act were certainly victories for consumers. But the unintended consequence of the new regulations was a contraction in the number of corporations able to profitably assume the financial costs of the new laws. Smaller businesses were more dramatically affected by the increased costs, and thus the new laws made the industry less competitive. Lobbying from the meatpacking industry also weakened the final form of the laws, as the federal government agreed to pay for the cost of inspections, and a requirement to date canned meats was stricken from the legislation.

In the fight for equality the Progressive Movement saw women win the vote, but that did not mean that most of the nation was prepared to accept women as the social equals of men. Minorities fared even worse—violence against blacks in particular increased during the era. The First World War, which the United States entered in 1917, also helped cool the fervor for progressive change. The Socialist and left-wing labor dream of peaceful, democratic redistribution of wealth in the United States receive a cold reception, particularly in the face of rising anti-foreigner sentiment during the war years.

Nonetheless, the progressive era had a significant impact on American society. It shone a bright light on some of the economic, social and racial abuses that had been allowed to fester during the industrial age. If the legislation that came out of the movement was not as far-reaching as intended, the progressive experience provided lessons for future generations who would attempt to address some of the same social ills.

**SUFFRAGE PARADE** After the suffrage movement revived during the Progressive era, pro-suffrage parades became common in many American communities. This one took place on Long Island, New York, in 1913.

# Chapter 23: World War I

President Wilson did not fully agree with the military goals of Britain, France, and Russia, the leading Entente Powers (or Allies), who wanted total victory over the Central Powers—Germany, Austro-Hungary, Turkey, and Bulgaria. Further, Wilson called for world disarmament after hostilities, and for addressing the claims of colonial peoples. The Allies did not support these and other such positions. Wilson declared the official status of the United States to be an "associate" of the Allies.

## Foreign Policy, 1867–1917

With the end of the Spanish American War and the annexation of the Kingdom of Hawaii at the end of the 19th century, the United States had gained an overseas empire and become a world power. The young empire soon flexed its diplomatic muscles on the international scene by proposing what became known as an Open Door Policy toward China. Starting in the 1840s, Great Britain and other European nations had taken advan-

tage of China's weak imperial government to demand special trading rights and commercial privileges. Soon several nations had carved out "spheres of influence" on the Chinese mainland. This arrangement put other nations, including the United States, at a disadvantage in the profitable China trade. In 1899 U.S. Secretary of State John Hay issued a "circular note" to the governments of nations with commercial interests in China. The note proposed, essentially, that China be treated as a "free trade zone" with equal trading access for all nations. Dubbed the "Open Door Policy," Hay's proposal was generally accepted by March 1900. Hay issued a second, more detailed note in July 1900 in the midst of a major crisis in China. This was the so-called Boxer Rebellion—an uprising by Chinese angered by what they saw as foreign domination of their country.

The Open Door Policy lasted nearly three decades. In 1917 the United States and other western nations agreed to recognize Japan's "special interests" in China, largely as a reward for Japan's joining the allies during World War I. In 1932, when Japan invaded the northern Chinese region of Manchuria, international protests from the West were not backed by the threat of force.

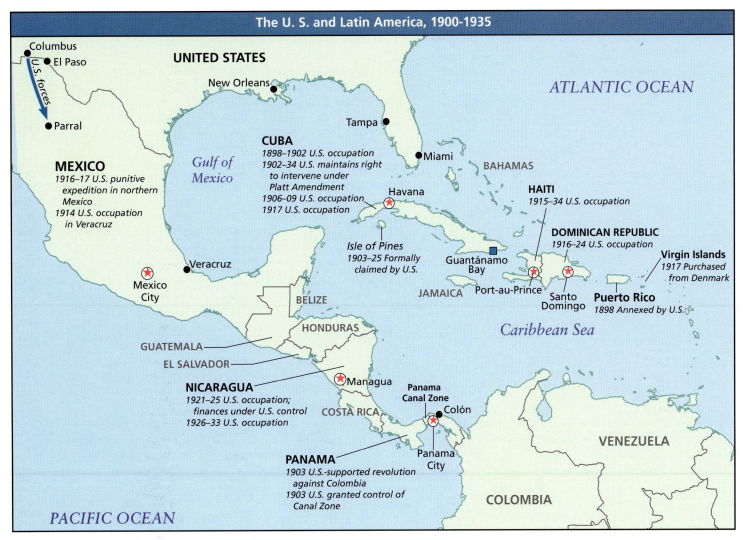

## The U. S. and Latin America, 1900-1935

**Columbus**
**El Paso**
*U.S. forces*
**Parral**

**UNITED STATES**

**New Orleans**

**Tampa**

**MEXICO**
1916–17 U.S. punitive
expedition in northern
Mexico
1914 U.S. occupation
in Veracruz

*Gulf of Mexico*

**CUBA**
1898–1902 U.S. occupation
1902–34 U.S. maintains right
to intervene under
Platt Amendment
1906–09 U.S. occupation
1917 U.S. occupation

**Miami**

**BAHAMAS**

**Havana**

**HAITI**
1915–34 U.S. occupation

**DOMINICAN REPUBLIC**
1916–24 U.S. occupation

**Veracruz**

**Mexico City**

Isle of Pines
1903–25 Formally
claimed by U.S.

**Guantánamo Bay**

**JAMAICA**

**Port-au-Prince**

**Santo Domingo**

**Virgin Islands**
1917 Purchased
from Denmark

**Puerto Rico**
1898 Annexed by U.S.

**BELIZE**

**HONDURAS**

*Caribbean Sea*

**GUATEMALA**

**EL SALVADOR**

**NICARAGUA**
1921–25 U.S. occupation;
finances under U.S. control
1926–33 U.S. occupation

**Managua**

**COSTA RICA**

**Panama Canal Zone**

**Colón**

**VENEZUELA**

**PANAMA**
1903 U.S.-supported revolution
against Colombia
1903 U.S. granted control of
Canal Zone

**Panama City**

**COLOMBIA**

**ATLANTIC OCEAN**

**PACIFIC OCEAN**

**A CENTURY OF INTERVENTIONS** The Caribbean and Central America saw considerable U.S. intervention in the twentieth century. American arms, influence, advice, and weapons toppled and raised governments, supported and quelled revolutions, and established American domination over the region's economy and politics.

When Japan extended its conquest of China in 1937, the Open Door era in China was dead.

### Roosevelt's Big Stick

Closer to home the United States in the early twentieth century had more success in shaping regional events to serve its interests. Ever since James Monroe had issued his Monroe Doctrine in 1923, the United States had warned that it would not tolerate European interference in the Western Hemisphere.

This principle first came into play in relation to former Spanish colonies in the Caribbean. In 1900 Congress passed the Foraker Act, which officially made Puerto Rico a U.S. territory. Although the act ended a two year period in which the island had been governed by the U.S. military, it angered most Puerto Ricans, who had dreamed of independence in the wake of Spain's departure. The act set up a new civilian government in Puerto Rico, headed by an American governor with veto power over all legislation. It also imposed high taxes on Puerto Rican sugar and tobacco exports to the United States. As legal residents of the United States, the Puerto Rican people would have neither full U.S. citizenship nor the citizenship of an independent nation, which meant Puerto Ricans would be deprived of their right to vote in national elections.

From 1898 to 1901 American troops were also stationed in Cuba, which some members of Congress were determined should likewise become an American territory. When troops did pull out in 1901 it was only after the United States obtained assurances from the Cuban government that American economic interests would be protected. Under U.S. pressure Cuba agreed to include in their new constitution a number of conditions that collectively became known as the Platt Amendment. Unlike Puerto Rico, Cuba would be a self-governing independent nation, but the Platt Amendment imposed so many conditions that Cuba's independence was in name only. For one, the amendment allowed the United States to establish a naval base at Cuba's Guantánamo Bay, on the eastern end of the island, and granted the United States the right to "intervene in order to maintain Cuban independence."

In short order the United States held a tight grip on the Cuban economy. American firms bought up many of Cuba's sugar mills, planted sugarcane (destroying jungle habitats in the process), and paid off corrupt officials in return for special treatment. American efforts increased sugar production in Cuba so rapidly that laborers from other Latin American and Caribbean countries had to be recruited to work the Cuban sugar plantations. Throughout the first two decades of the twentieth century world sugar prices rose with production. Yet, upon the end of World War I, an oversupply of

sugar caused prices to plummet. Although sugar production and prices rallied somewhat during the 1920s, they collapsed once more during the Great Depression.

U.S. intervention was not limited to territory lost by Spain in the Spanish American War. In 1904 Theodore Roosevelt formulated what became known as the Roosevelt Corollary to the Monroe Doctrine. To the general American public the Roosevelt Corollary became known as "big stick" policy after an adage that Roosevelt liked to quote: "Speak softly and carry a big stick; you will go far." The U.S. Navy, able to carry guns and troops anywhere in the world, was the "big stick."

In effect the Roosevelt Corollary gave the United States the right to interfere in the internal affairs of its Western Hemisphere neighbors whenever it detected "chronic wrongdoing" or political "impotence." Roosevelt's most notable assertion of this "international police power" in the Caribbean was in the Dominican Republic, where the United States began administering the customs department in 1905 to prevent the country's financial collapse.

## The Panama Canal

Prior to articulating the Roosevelt Corollary, Roosevelt had already acted in its spirit in Panama, which at the turn of the twentieth century was still part of the South American nation of Colombia. The United States and other countries had long been interested in digging a canal across Central America to provide a short sea route between the Atlantic and the Pacific. The addition of overseas possessions in both oceans made the building of such a canal even more urgent. In 1901 the Hay-Pauncefote Treaty between the United States and Britain gave the former nation free rein to build and regulate a canal across the Isthmus of Panama, provided that the zone remain neutral and open on equal terms to other nations' shipping. The government of Colombia agreed in subsequent negotiations to grant use of the necessary strip of

land, but the Colombian senate refused to ratify the agreement. Roosevelt's solution in 1903 was to encourage and support militarily a revolution in Panama against Colombia. The revolt was led by the canal's chief engineer.

That year the United States and the newly independent nation of Panama signed the Hay-Bunau-Varilla Treaty, which gave the United States rights in perpetuity over the canal and a Canal Zone on either side. It also gave the United States the right to intervene militarily in Panama to protect order, a right exercised often in the coming years. Panama received a guarantee of its independence and financial compensation: an initial payment of $10 million and an annuity of $250,000 that began in 1913 and was later raised.

A marvel of engineering that stretches fifty-one miles (eighty-two kilometers), the canal was completed in 1914. Completion required the virtual eradication of malaria and yellow fever in the canal area and the excavation of an estimated 175 million cubic yards (143 million cubic meters) of earth. The political marvel was almost as great: an entire country was created principally for the purpose of enhancing U.S. power and has been tied closely to the United States ever since.

Panamanians, like other Latin Americans with experience of the Roosevelt Corollary, resented U.S. domination of their country and long struggled to reduce that domination. A treaty ratified in 1939 removed the right of the United States to intervene in Panama's internal affairs, while giving the United States the right to intervene for the purpose of defending the canal. A 1977 treaty gave Panama possession of the canal beginning in 2000, but did not take away the right of the United States to defend the canal's neutrality. The most recent American military intervention in Panama took place in 1989, when the United States sent troops to capture dictator Manuel Noriega and force him to stand trial in the United States for drug trafficking.

The racism common among Anglo-Americans of the time against Hispanics laced much of Roosevelt's "big stick" foreign policy. Anglo-Americans regarded themselves as superior, upright, and mature, while considering Hispanics as inferior, corrupt, and childlike. Roosevelt justified his actions in Panama by calling Colombians "an inferior people" and remarking, "You could no more make an agreement with the Colombian rulers than you could nail currant jelly to the wall." He made light of potential Panamanian resistance to U.S. domination in a letter to his brother-in-law in 1905: "Sometime soon I shall have to spank some little brigand of a South American republic."

## Dollar Diplomacy

The Dominican Republic was another focal point for the American "big stick." In 1905, in response to the near collapse of the Caribbean nation's finances, Roosevelt arranged for the United States to administer its customs department. His aim was to ensure

829.
W.H Horne Co.

Gen. Fierro.

that customs money went to repay debts to creditors rather than to line the pockets of corrupt government officials. The arrangement, which lasted until 1941, was part of a policy that became known as "dollar diplomacy" during the administration of William Howard Taft (1857–1930; president 1909–1913). Dollar diplomacy was the use of the leverage provided by American economic might to extend American influence abroad. American bankers and industrialists were encouraged to invest overseas; the United States financed public debt in places as far-flung as Nicaragua, Haiti, and China. Wherever possible, notably in the Dominican Republic and Nicaragua, Americans were put in charge of collecting customs and administering finances.

Though the aim of dollar diplomacy was to achieve political stability by using "dollars instead of bullets," in practice these efforts were often enforced by bullets. In response to civil turmoil U.S. Marines occupied the Dominican Republic from 1916 to 1924.

For Latin Americans dollar diplomacy, the "big stick," and the Roosevelt Corollary were all different names for the same thing: American disrespect for their right to govern themselves. The same disrespect had been shown in the annexation of Puerto Rico and the legalized domination of Cuba.

### The U.S. and the Mexican Revolution

Of all the nations in Latin America during the early twentieth century, none was in crisis as consistently as Mexico. By 1910 the dictatorial president Porfirio Díaz had ruled Mexico for thirty-five years. While he had helped modernize Mexico's economy, he had done so by taking much of Mexico's *ejido*, or communal lands, from poor peasants and

**PANCHO AND PERSHING** Mexican revolutionary Pancho Villa (above, fourth from left) led raids into New Mexico during the Mexican Revolution. Although Villa was pursued by American troops under General John Pershing (below), he escaped capture.

selling them to large landowners, most of whom were investors from the United States. Ultimately, Díaz sold off about 75 percent of all of Mexico's natural resources to Americans and other foreigners. Americans owned a large proportion of Mexico's mines, oilfields, rubber plantations and even railroads. Meanwhile, most of Mexico's own population was desperately poor.

In 1910 Díaz attempted to steal the election by having opposition candidate Francisco Madero jailed until the election was over. In response Madero called for a revolution. Within a year Madero—supported by poor peasants throughout Mexico—had ousted Díaz to become the new president of Mexico. However, the moderate Madero soon found himself isolated—caught between the demands of revolutionary leaders such as Emiliano Zapata and Pancho Villa on the one hand and those of military leaders who had helped him overthrow Díaz on the other. In 1913, with support from the United States, General Victoriano Huerta overthrew Madero. When Huerta ordered Madero killed and then named himself president, he lost U.S. support. Woodrow Wilson, the new U.S. president, said of Huerta's government, "I will not recognize a government of butchers." Wilson's position signaled a change in U.S. policy, as he decided that his administration would only establish diplomatic relations with democratically elected governments.

To undermine the brutal Huerta Wilson allowed weapons to be shipped to Pancho Villa and Venustiano Carranza, another revolutionary leader. Then when several Americans sailors were arrested in Tampico, Mexico, Wilson used the incident to oust Huerta. He ordered that an American fleet set sail for Mexico. Wilson then learned that a German ship carrying weapons to Huerta was headed for the Mexican port of Vera Cruz. In response Wilson ordered U.S. forces to occupy the city. Huerta fell shortly thereafter, and Carranza took control of the government with Wilson's support.

Like Madero before him Carranza soon lost the support of Pancho Villa, who accused him of acting too slowly. Angered by Wilson's support of Carranza, Villa then launched a guerrilla attack on an American-owned mine. Killing 16 mineworkers, Villa and his men then crossed the border into the town of Columbus, New Mexico, where they killed another eighteen people. In response Wilson ordered General John J. Pershing to invade Mexico in search of Villa. After a fruitless eleven-month search Pershing gave up. Ultimately the two nations agreed to peaceful, if wary, co-existence.

In the end the Mexican Revolution cost about 1 million Mexican lives. Between 1910 and 1920, a torrent of Mexican refugees—poor farmers, soldiers, and wealthy immigrants alike—flooded into the United States to escape the violence. All told more than 200,000 Mexicans crossed the U.S. border during the Revolution. For Wilson calm on the southern border was critical. Far greater challenges lay ahead, as the United States prepared to enter a world war.

# The War to End All Wars

The global military conflict called World War I was triggered by an event that seemingly had only regional importance: the assassination of Austrian heir apparent Archduke Franz Ferdinand. The archduke was murdered in Sarejevo, Bosnia, then part of the Austro-Hungarian Empire, by Gavrilo Princip, a Bosnian Serb seeking to free his people from Austrian domination and unite them with Serbia. But because Europe was at the time a welter of imperial ambitions, with each great power trying to increase its colonies and influence around the world, and each linked to others in an intricate web of alliances, this small act of violence swiftly set off a slide toward war.

By August Austria had declared war on Serbia; Russia joined the war in support of Serbia; Germany had joined on the side of Austro-Hungary; and Britain and France had joined on the side of Russia. The Allies, or Entente Powers (chiefly Britain, France and Russia) were pitted against the Central Powers (chiefly Germany and Austro-Hungary, as well as the fading Ottoman Empire, or present-day Turkey).

## New Weapons of War

The Great War, as it was commonly called, brought with it a level of carnage never before seen in human history. During the war several new military technologies were introduced that killed with devastating efficiency. Some of these weapons, such as machine guns and artillery, predated the war but appeared in new and deadlier forms. Advancing armies were easily mown down by new machine guns firing 600 rounds a minute, artillery guns firing twenty shells a minute and infantry firearms that fired fifteen rounds a minute. One of the deadliest cannons was Germany's "Big Bertha," which could shoot its one-ton shells over a range of more than nine miles.

Against these weapons an advancing army could suffer 20,000 deaths in a single day, as the British did on the first day of the Battle of the Somme in 1916. For this reason the war was largely one of prolonged stalemate, in which opposing armies spent much of their time in trenches that insulated them from enemy fire, but were devastated whenever they left their trenches to try to gain ground.

A number of radically new weapons saw their first significant use in combat in World War I, including airplanes, tanks, submarines, and poison gas. Though none of these were decisive in this war, the first three would be indispensible to future armies and the last—as the predecessor of modern chemical weapons—would haunt arms negotiators to the present day.

**ARCHDUKE FRANZ FERDINAND**

## Europe at War, 1914–1918

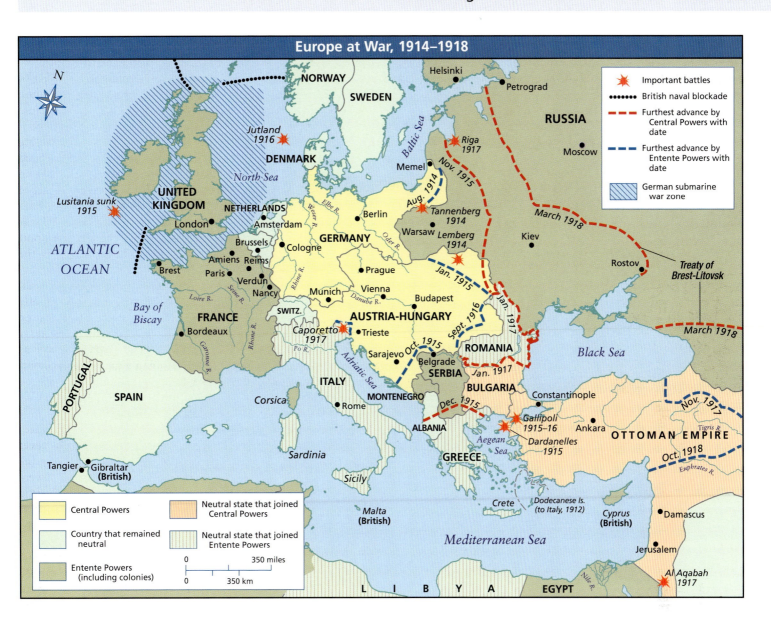

**Legend:**
- ✴ Important battles
- •••••• British naval blockade
- – – – Furthest advance by Central Powers with date
- – – – Furthest advance by Entente Powers with date
- ▨ German submarine war zone

- Central Powers
- Country that remained neutral
- Entente Powers (including colonies)
- Neutral state that joined Central Powers
- Neutral state that joined Entente Powers

0        350 miles
0        350 km

### "He Kept Us Out of War"

While the war in Europe raged for nearly three years, the United States worked to stay out of the conflict. After the war began in 1914 Woodrow Wilson urged the American people "to be neutral in fact as well as in deed." Many Americans, perhaps a majority at the time, were content with neutrality: this was Europe's war, and the United States had a long tradition of steering clear of European affairs. Furthermore, in a nation in which almost one in three Americans were of foreign birth or parentage, loyalties were divided. German-Americans were not disposed to rally against their mother country. Nor were Irish-Americans particularly sympathetic to Great Britain, since Ireland was in the midst of a rebellion against British rule at the time.

As the war dragged on, however, public opinion moved toward supporting the Allies. In 1914, 128 Americans had died on the British liner *Lusitania* when it was torpedoed by a German submarine off the Irish coast. Stories of German atrocities in France and Belgium—often exaggerated by Allied officials and journalists—horrified many Americans. Others, especially on the East Coast, felt a sense of kinship with Britain and

France. By 1916 the British government was also deeply in debt to U.S. banks, and profitable Allied orders for munitions poured into U.S. plants.

By 1915 a preparedness movement began to sweep the United States, as some Americans—most notably Theodore Roosevelt—urged that the nation prepare for war. The next year, even as he campaigned for re-election with the slogan, "He Kept Us Out of War," Wilson supported an expanded army and navy and warned Germany that the United States would not tolerate violations of its neutrality.

Despite Wilson's warnings, as 1917 opened German submarines targeted both Allied and neutral ships headed for Europe. Then in March American newspapers published the so-called Zimmermann Note—an intercepted German diplomatic communiqué that promised Mexico its support if it agreed to launch a war on the United States to reclaim territory lost in the Mexican-American War sixty years earlier.

### America Goes to War

On April 6, 1917, the United States declared war on Germany. In May General John Pershing, no longer

### ALLIANCES OF 1914

The Triple Entente (Allies) was led by Great Britain, France and Russia. They were joined by Belgium, Japan, Serbia, and Montenegro. Before the war, the Triple Alliance (Central Powers) was Germany, Austria-Hungary, and Italy, later joined by the Ottoman Empire and Bulgaria. In 1915, Italy entered the war on the side of the Allies.

**LIBERTY LOANS** Movie star Douglas Fairbanks takes to the megaphone to encourage people to purchase Liberty Bonds at a Wall Street rally.

chasing Pancho Villa on the Mexican border, was dispatched to Europe to ask the Allies what the United States could do for them. "Men, men, and more men," was the answer from French Marshall Joseph Joffre. That same month Congress passed the Selective Service Act establishing a military draft. By early June over nine million men between the ages of twenty-one and thirty were processed for the draft.

In addition to men the U.S. military also needed supplies. In July Wilson organized the War Industries Board, led by banker Bernard Baruch. Under Baruch's leadership the agency shifted factories from domestic to war production. It took over railroads and used them to ship arms and troops.

### The Home Front

To encourage public moral and financial support for the war a Committee on Public Information, led by journalist George Creel, recruited movie stars Mary Pickford, Charlie Chaplain and Douglas Fairbanks to sell Liberty Bonds that would pay for the war. George M. Cohan, John Philip Sousa, and Irving Berlin wrote patriotic songs, such as "Over There" and "The Caisson Song" to encourage patriotic fervor. Every day objects with German origins—such as dachshunds ("liberty hounds"), and hamburgers ("liberty sandwiches")—were renamed. In some public places German music and language were banned, and German-American and Austrian-American businesses were boycotted.

Meanwhile new taxes were imposed on businesses and unions agreed not to strike. With most draft age men headed off to war women went to work in munitions factories. Many southern blacks who were not in the military moved north to find better paying jobs in Chicago, Cleveland, Detroit, and other northern cities. The migration was not without incident, as attacks on African Americans broke out in St. Louis, Houston, and Philadelphia over jobs.

Although the war resulted in a 25 percent increase in overall domestic food production, the American public was being persuaded to eat less. To amass food to send to war-ravaged Europe the U.S. Food Administration, led by future president Herbert Hoover, asked Americans to decrease their consumption of meats, butter and sugar. It also asked the public to systematically abstain from certain staples throughout the week. In kitchens across the nation, for example, Mondays became "Wheatless Mondays" and Tuesdays, "Meatless Tuesday."

### Opposition to the War

Not all Americans favored the war effort. Although virtually all other labor unions supported the war effort, the radical International Workers of the World (IWW)

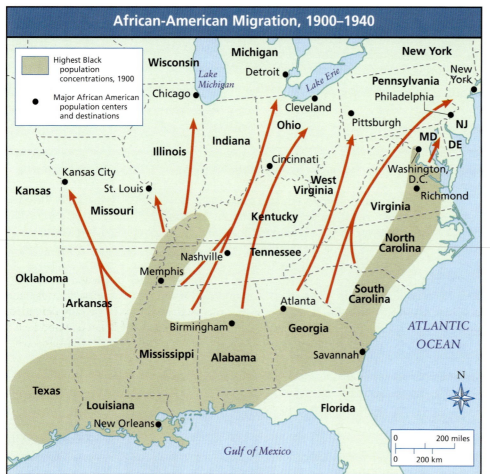

**African-American Migration, 1900–1940**

Highest Black population concentrations, 1900

Major African American population centers and destinations

**GREAT MIGRATION** During World War I, millions of African Americans moved north to take jobs in northern factories.

condemned it—and then never recovered from the backlash against them. The *New York Times* went so far as to call the IWW "German Agents."

A group of Oklahoma tenant farmers, calling themselves the Green Corn Rebellion, opposed the draft and hoped to join with other anti-war groups to march on Washington where they would overthrow President Wilson. Their plans fizzled quickly and the rebels dispersed when a citizen posse confronted the group.

One of the best known opponents of the war was labor leader Eugene Debs. Debs, a perennial candidate for President on the Socialist line, condemned the war as a grab for capitalist domination. In 1918, after an antiwar speech in Canton, Ohio, he was arrested and convicted in a Cleveland federal court under a war-time espionage law. Sentenced to 10 years in jail, he also had his U.S. citizenship—and thus his right to vote—revoked. Undeterred, Debs would run for president on the Socialist party ticket from his prison cell in 1920. He would win nearly a million votes. (On Christmas Day 1921, President Warren Harding pardoned Debs.)

## Americans at War

In November 1917, American units saw action for the first time in the Cambrai offensive launched by the Allies—notable for its use of massed tanks in the attack. By the end of 1917 five American divisions were in France, totaling more than 180,000 troops, a tiny force compared with the millions of Allied and German soldiers already in action. Fewer than 170 American had been killed in battle by then. The following autumn 1.4 million Americans would have seen action, and every available American soldier would be needed on the western front.

America's entry into the war came just in time for the Allies. On the eastern front Russia was collapsing. In March 1917, the Russian army had mutinied, leading to the downfall of Czar Nicholas II. Although the new democratic government, headed by Alexander Kerensky, promised to continue fighting, Russian peasants and workers had tired of the war and constant food shortages. Sensing an opportunity Germany ferried the exiled Communist leader V. I. Lenin back to St. Petersburg, where he and his Bolshevik party promised the people "peace, land, and bread." On November 6, two weeks before U.S. forces saw action at Cambrai, the Bolsheviks overthrew Kerensky and established the Soviet Union. Less than six weeks later, the new Soviet Union signed a cease-fire

**The Western Front in France and Belgium, 1914–1918**

Legend:
— Front line, August 22, 1914
– – – Front line, July–August, 1918
••••• German line at time of Armistice, November 11, 1918
✸ Major battle

**THE WESTERN FRONT** The 1914 German offensive nearly reached Paris before being forced back by the French and British. Until mid-1918 the Western Front remained relatively static, as even the largest offensives against fixed positions gained little ground.

agreement with Germany, and in March 1918 the two countries signed the Treaty of Brest-Litovsk, which handed a huge piece of the former Russian Empire to Germany. The fighting in the Soviet Union did not end however. A civil war broke out between Communist and anti-Communist forces. In June 1918, Britain, the United States and others sent troops to Russia to fight the Bolsheviks.

Meanwhile, peace with the Soviets allowed Germany to transfer its troops to the western front against France, Britain, and the United States. In the spring and summer of 1918, Germany launched several massive attacks in France.

## The Western Front

In early June 1918, the Germans pushed into the western Marne Valley in France to capture Belleau Wood, and threaten to cut the road between Metz and Paris. Believing that the Germans had left the forest only lightly defended, General Pershing, in command of U.S. forces, was determined to recapture it.

On June 6, the Americans went on the attack through these dense woods, and soon discovered it to be heavily defended. The bloody Battle of Belleau Wood lasted three weeks until the last Germans were forced by heavy artillery fire to withdraw. The Americans suffered almost 8,800 casualties in this, their first major engagement of the war.

In July Germany launched a new offensive. The turning point of the campaign took place at the Second Battle of the Marne. After two days of fighting, however, the Germans withdrew.

## THE INFLUENZA EPIDEMIC OF 1918

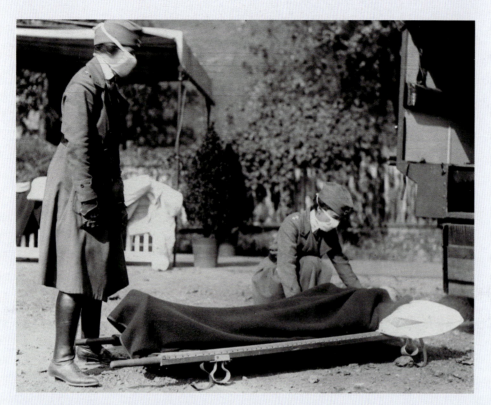

**PREPARING FOR THE WORST** A demonstration at the Red Cross Emergency Ambulance Station in Washington, D.C., during the influenza pandemic of 1918.

March 9, 1918 began like many others at the U.S. Army base at Camp Funston in Fort Riley, Kansas—with a dust storm. But it was not the wind that troubled company cook Albert Gitchell when he reported to the camp infirmary complaining of cold symptoms. Gitchell was soon joined by Corporal Lee Drake, who felt almost the same way. By lunch the infirmary had filled with 100 men, all suffering from the same illness—later identified as Spanish flu. A week later the number had climbed to five hundred. The first wave of the most deadly pandemic in human history had begun.

Two months later inmates at San Quentin prison in California came down with the same illness, as did people at other Army bases around the country. Nonetheless, with the United States now rapidly gearing up for the war in Europe, the nation had its attention elsewhere.

Just as influenza was hitting Camp Funston, two hundred thousand troops were preparing to ship out to Europe. Little did they know, but many carried with them a deadly strain of the influenza virus. Before their ship even reached Europe thirty-six members of the Fifteenth U.S. Cavalry fell ill; six of them died. Shortly thereafter the virus began taking its toll in Europe. In June 1918, thirty-one thousand cases were reported in Great Britain alone.

In July, the first concerted efforts to alert the public were made. Philadelphia health officials issued a bulletin regarding what they called "Spanish flu" due to inaccurate reports about the virus's place of origin.

By August far more serious cases were being reported—in Boston, Massachusetts; Sierra Leone, West Africa; and in the coastal port of Brest, in Brittany, France. While these three places were far from each other, doctors noted that they were all seaports actively involved in transporting men and arms to the battlefields of Europe.

The 1918–1919 influenza outbreak remains quite possibly the worst single pandemic in human history. All told, it killed an estimated 30 million people worldwide, including a staggering 20 million in India, and five hundred thousand in the United States. In New York City, where twenty thousand died in less than four months, there were reports of the virus killing at an amazing speed. Some reports claimed that passengers who had the first pangs of illness while boarding a subway on Long Island where dead by the time the train reached Columbus Circle in Manhattan. With so many sick and dead, social mechanisms virtually disintegrated.

As the death toll mounted, mass graves were dug and talk of divine or cosmic influence rose again. Others suggested that the Germans, unclean pajamas, nudity, or race mingling were responsible. Obviously, these claims were based in hysteria, not fact.

When the pandemic finally abated in the winter of 1919, more people had died of influenza than had died in four years of world war. Nonetheless, scientists were no closer to understanding why this was than they had been before the pandemic began. Medical investigation in the early 20th century was still severally handicapped. Every effort to identify the cause of the disease failed.

Finally, in 1932, an American doctor named Richard Shope proved that infected pigs could transmit the virus through nasal secretions by rubbing against the nostrils of other pigs. This discovery earned the virus the new name "swine flu." Shope later established that people who had lived through the 1918 outbreak were resistant to swine flu, signaling that they had developed antibodies to the virus. When he discovered that they did indeed possess such antibodies, it provided further evidence that swine flu was in fact the cause of the pandemic. No one has conclusively proven where the virus responsible for the pandemic came from. The initial outbreaks in humans in the spring of 1918 were followed only later by outbreaks among pigs. Then, later that year, the virus returned to humans in deadly form.

**WILSON IN PARIS** President Wilson (far right) traveled to Paris to join Georges Clemenceau of France, Vittorio Orlando of Italy and David Lloyd George of Great Britain in writing the Treaty of Versailles.

In September Americans captured the Saint Mihiel Salient, a German "bulge" in the Allied line, and pushed into the Argonne Forest, where fighting raged for forty-seven days before a U.S. victory. During the battle Sergeant Alvin York would become a national hero when he killed twenty-five Germans and captured 132. With the capture of the Argonne Forest, the Allies had pushed back the enemy from its strongest positions on the western front. The Germans were forced to surrender.

American forces had been crucial to the final Allied victory. The United States military had grown to almost 3.7 million men by mid-1918, with 1.39 million serving in France. American losses in the war were 50,475 killed and 205,600 wounded.

At 11:11 a.m., on the 11th day of the 11th month, the guns of World War I fell silent. The timing was no accident, as the number eleven symbolizes the last possible moment, or "the eleventh hour." Many believed that continued warfare would mean the end of civilization.

## Wilson and the League of Nations

Chief among those who believed that the Great War had to be the "war to end all wars" was Woodrow Wilson. In a January 8, 1918 address to Congress he laid out fourteen proposals for establishing a just and lasting peace. Known as the Fourteen Points the proposals rejected Allied territorial expansion and punishment of the Central Powers, opting instead for a high-minded commitment to justice, liberty, and security for all peoples. The first five articles called for open diplomacy, freedom of the seas, removal of trade barriers, disarmament, and settlement of colonial claims. The next eight dealt with territorial questions such as the restoration of conquered territory and self-determination for the peoples of the Austro-Hungarian and Ottoman empires. The final point called for the creation of a "general association of nations" dedicated to keeping the peace.

Coming as they did before the outcome of the war was certain, the Fourteen Points were aimed in part at convincing the Central Powers to make peace, and in that respect they may have shortened the war. But they were also intended as a guide to peace negotiations, and as such they were largely rejected at the Paris Peace Conference of 1919–1920 in favor of territorial rewards for the victors and punishment for the defeated. In particular the Treaty of Versailles forced Germany to cede considerable territory to the

**PALMER RAIDS** Attorney General A. Mitchell Palmer ordered the arrest and deportation of thousands of innocent immigrants on suspicion of being radicals.

Allies, pay reparations, limit its military, and accept blame for starting the war. Resentment in Germany over these clauses would help fuel the next, far more deadly, world war, which Wilson had hoped to prevent. The League of Nations was formed in accord with Wilson's fourteenth point, but even here he was disappointed.

Although the final Versailles Treaty rejected most of the Fourteen Points, the idealistic Wilson presented the treaty to the Senate, asking, "Dare we reject it and break the heart of the world?" To Wilson's chagrin isolationist opposition to foreign entanglements kept the U.S. Senate from ratifying the Versailles Treaty or the 26-article Covenant of the League of Nations that the treaty contained. Rather than compromise with the Republicans who controlled Congress, an exhausted Wilson toured the nation in a failed attempt to drum up popular support for the treaty's ratification. During the tour he suffered a stroke and nearly died.

The United States never joined the League of Nations, which seriously damaged its effectiveness. So too did its inability to compel its stronger members to submit their disputes to mediation. In 1923 the league was powerless to stop France from occupying the Ruhr Valley of Germany and Italy from occupying the island of Corfu. Though the League did resolve some minor disputes and begin the process of decolonization through its mandate system, it was powerless to prevent Germany, Japan, Italy and the Soviet Union

from aggressive expansion in the 1930s.

With the outbreak of World War II the League fell into limbo. In 1946 it voted itself out of existence. Much of its property, experience, and organizational structure would be absorbed into a new international organization—the United Nations.

### The Aftermath of War

The years immediately after World War I were troubled one's for the United States. Relations between black and white Americans reached a new low. Following incidents of racial violence that took place in some American cities as southern blacks moved north during the war to find work in armament factories, racial tensions only increased when armament factories closed after the war.

In 1919 over seventy-five blacks, including several in military uniform, were lynched by white mobs. Then in July, when a black teen named Eugene Williams decided to go for a swim at a Chicago beach reserved for whites, somebody hit him with a rock and he drowned. This death touched off five days of riots than left twenty-three blacks and fifteen whites dead.

### Labor Violence

During the war organized labor and business had had a generally cooperative relationship. Many unions had won recognition and workers in military munitions factories were granted an eight-hour workday. By 1919 the twelve-hour workday had been

abolished and half the country's workers now worked a forty-eight-hour week.

Yet trouble between business leaders and labor—muted during the war—exploded with the arrival of peace in Europe. During the war inflation had skyrocketed: the price of food, for example, had more than doubled between 1915 and 1920, while the cost of clothing more than tripled. In response labor continued to demand that more unions be recognized, that hours continue to be shortened where they still exceeded eight hours and that pay raises exceeding the rate of inflation be awarded to workers.

To back these demands one strike after another was launched across the country. In January a general strike began in Seattle. In Boston the police went on strike, leading to several days of rioting and crime, and inspiring Massachusetts governor Calvin Coolidge to declare, "There is no right to strike against the public safety by anyone, anytime, anywhere."

The most tumultuous strike of 1919 began in Chicago. A Chicago steel strike launched by the American Federation of Labor soon spread nationwide as 350,000 steelworkers in twenty-four separate craft unions demanded the right to organize.

To management the strikes of 1919 were about more that work hours or union recognition. From management's perspective the steel strike was a dangerous conspiracy by foreign radicals to undermine the American economic system.

### The Palmer Raids

Increasingly the general public agreed, and events seemed to confirm the worst of those fears. Overseas Italian laborers were seizing factories, while Communists were taking power in Hungary and staging revolts in Germany. Closer to home the news was even more alarming: In May, 1919, postal workers in New York discovered thirty-four letter bombs addressed to government officials and other well known figures, including J. P. Morgan, John D. Rockefeller and Supreme Court Justice Oliver Wendell Holmes. And in June a bomb detonated outside the home of A. Mitchell Palmer, the U.S. Attorney General. No one was hurt.

On November 6, the second anniversary of the Russian Revolution, the federal government struck back. In a series of raids called the "Palmer Raids," Attorney General Palmer arrested thousands of legal immigrants suspected of belonging to radical and Communist organizations. In

December, a ship nicknamed "the Soviet Ark" forcibly carried 294 legal aliens to Russia. Although the famous anarchist Emma Goldman was among them, most were innocent of any crime.

The methods used to make arrests verged on the criminal. In one case Gaspare Cannone was arrested in New York City. Cannone, who spoke limited English, was beaten and kicked when he refused to turn in others. After being held in secret for seventy-two hours, agents took Cannone to Ellis Island, where officials attempted to force him to admit that he was an anarchist. Although he refused, a forgery of his signature ended up on a written statement of guilt anyway.

On New Year's Eve, Palmer conducted an even larger sweep, arresting 6,000 people in one night. The arrests made Palmer a national hero.

A weary public now blamed all foreigners for the war itself and for the strife that followed it. Because many labor leaders and industrial workers were foreign born, the image of unions as tools of radical foreigners took hold in the public consciousness. In this climate winning concessions from business was next to impossible. The steel strike collapsed in total defeat.

Despite their popularity with the general public, the Palmer Raids did stir considerable controversy during their time. At the height of Palmer's sweeps, Assistant Secretary of Labor Louis F. Post, who feared Palmer was exercising extraordinary powers without any legal check, moved to cancel more than 1,500 of Palmer's deportations. When Palmer accused Post of "tender solicitude for social revolution," the House of Representatives initiating hearings to impeach Post. Testifying in his defense in front of Congress, Post defended his action by arguing that Justice Department lawyers had shown they knew nothing of immigration laws, the Fourth Amendment, or due process laws. Noting that most of the supposed radicals that had been picked up "couldn't tell you the difference between Bolshevism and rheumatism," Post also remarked that in thousands of searches of "radical" homes, Palmer's men had turned up a total of three .22 caliber pistols.

During the Spring of 1920, Palmer predicted one terrorist attack after another. On May 1, an international labor holiday, he ordered state militia and police nationwide to guard government buildings. When no threat materialized his power began to wane. That fall when a bomb did explode outside of J.P. Morgan's headquarters on Wall Street, most people viewed it as an isolated incident rather than a grand conspiracy.

Even as the Palmer Raids waned their impact continued to be felt. Among those who were arrested in the raids were two Italian immigrants from Massachusetts named Nicola Sacco and Bartolomeo Vanzetti. Despite flimsy evidence the two men were found guilty of robbery and murder. In 1927, despite a new trial, the men were sentenced to death in the electric chair.

Their case became a cause célèbre as many around the nation and the world believed the men had been found guilty based on their nationality and association with known radical groups, and not based on the crimes for which they were charged. For seven years, they sat on death row as lawyers appealed their case and protesters demanded a new trial. In August 1927, Sacco and Vanzetti were executed in the electric chair.

The years from 1920 and 1940 were marked by a mood of isolationism. Yet they would also be remembered for dramatic change—from fast-paced boom times to deep economic struggle.

## EXCERPTS FROM THE FINAL STATEMENTS OF SACCO AND VANZETTI, APRIL 9, 1927

Vanzetti (second from left) and Sacco (second from right)

**Nicola Sacco:**
I know the sentence will be between two classes, the oppressed class and the rich class, and there will be always collision between one and the other. We fraternize the people with the books, with the literature. You persecute the people, tyrannize them and kill them. We try the education of people always. You try to put a path between us and some other nationality that hates each other. That is why I am here today on this bench, for having been of the oppressed class. Well, you are the oppressor. . .

**Bartolomeo Vanzetti:**
Sacco is a worker from his boyhood, a skilled worker, lover of work, with a good job and pay, a bank account, a good and lovely wife, two beautiful children and a neat little home at the verge of a wood, near a brook. Sacco is a heart, a faith, a character, a man; a man—lover of nature and of mankind. A man who gave all, who sacrifice all to the cause of Liberty and to his love for mankind; money, rest, mundane ambitions, his own wife, his children, himself and his own life. Sacco has never dreamt to steal, never to assassinate. He and I have never brought a morsel of bread to our mouths, from our childhood to today—which has not been gained by the sweat of our brows. Never. His people also are in good position and of good reputation.

Oh, yes, I may be more witfull, as some have put it, I am a better babbler than he is, but many, many times in hearing his heartful voice ringing a faith sublime, in considering his supreme sacrifice, remembering his heroism I felt small, small at the presence of his greatness and found myself compelled to fight back from my eyes the tears, and quench my heart troubling to my throat to not weep before him—this man called thief and assassin and doomed. But Sacco's name will live in the hearts of the people and in their gratitude when Katzmann's and your bones will be dispersed by time, when your name, his name, your laws, institutions, and your false god are but a [dim] remembering of a cursed past in which man was wolf to the man.

# Chapter 24: The Roaring '20s

**PROHIBITION IN THE STATES**

By the time the Eighteenth Amendment banned the sale of alcohol, most states already had a ban in place.

"America's present need is not heroics but healing," declared Warren Harding before the Republican presidential convention of 1920, "not nostrums but normalcy; not revolution but restoration; . . . not surgery, but serenity."

After the upheaval of World War I Harding's words struck a chord. Most Americans wanted to resume the routine pattern of their lives and overwhelmingly elected the candidate who turned away from international affairs and promised a "return to normalcy."

Although Harding's Republican administration would be clouded by corruption, its pro-business approach resonated with striving middle-class voters. When Harding died in office in 1923, the outpouring of national grief was enormous. Yet the grief over Harding's death actually had less to do with the man himself than what he seemed to represent.

Harding was at worst oblivious to the scandals around him, not personally corrupt. (As he said himself about his abilities, "I am not fit for this office and never should have been here.") But his small town Ohio roots, and his call for a return to the normalcy of slower paced, simpler times were reassuring to the nation at a time when it was struggling to find its footing in a new and seemingly more complex world.

## The Roaring '20s

To many Americans, the whir of events seemed to be speeding up in the postwar years, not slowing down. Americans were on the move. Powered by mass produced Model T Ford automobiles and the expanding network of roads connecting city to countryside, many younger Americans from rural areas began leaving their rural lives in favor of resettling in the big cities. Flush with cash from a booming stock market, many younger Americans now also had the wealth to fully embrace a new, leisure-loving, urban way of life. Young women embraced the flapper look—bobbing their hair, raising their hemlines, and smoking cigarettes in public. Young men bought cars with rumble seats and talked of "free love." Together they went to nightclubs to hear "hot jazz," and dance to the Charleston or the tango.

The twenties were also a time in which a great many popular fads swept the nation. For younger people there

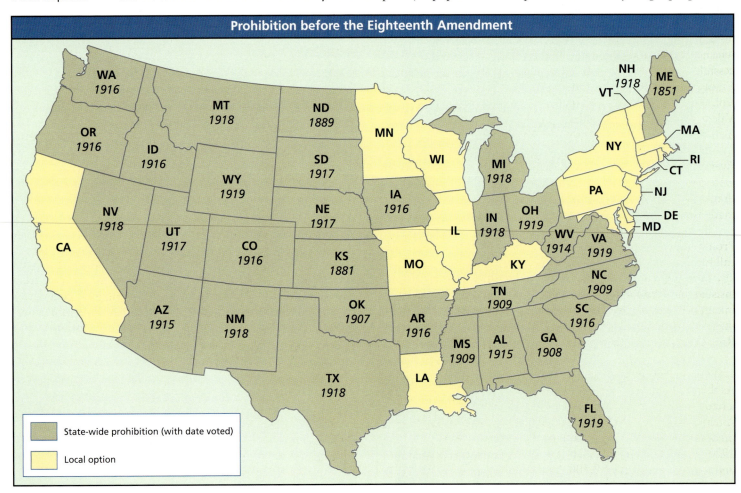

**Prohibition before the Eighteenth Amendment**

WA 1916 · MT 1918 · ND 1889 · MN · NH 1918 · ME 1851 · VT · OR 1916 · ID 1916 · WY 1919 · SD 1917 · WI · MI 1918 · NY · MA · NV 1918 · UT 1917 · CO 1916 · IA 1916 · IL · IN 1918 · OH 1919 · PA · RI · CT · NJ · CA · NE 1917 · KS 1881 · MO · KY · WV 1914 · VA 1919 · DE · MD · AZ 1915 · NM 1918 · OK 1907 · AR 1916 · TN 1909 · NC 1909 · SC 1916 · MS 1909 · AL 1915 · GA 1908 · TX 1918 · LA · FL 1919

Legend:
- State-wide prohibition (with date voted)
- Local option

were outlandish novelties like flagpole sitting and goldfish swallowing. For the more mature and sedate, there were new pastimes like crossword puzzles and mah jongg. But the most pervasive new form of entertainment was movies. By 1928, over 65 million Americans attended movies every week, allowing even the most timid to thrill vicariously to the adventures of vamp Clara Bow, sheik Rudolph Valentino, and other favorite stars.

# Social Attitudes of the 1920s

Hanging over the freewheeling frivolity of the 1920s was Prohibition. On January 16, 1920, the nationwide prohibition of alcohol, made legal with the passage of the Eighteenth Amendment to the Constitution the year before, went into effect. Prohibition was overwhelmingly supported by the public, particularly those in rural areas, who believed that the nation could finally end the scourge of alcohol.

Despite the long history of the temperance movement, Prohibition may actually owe its passage to World War I. During the war, grain that might have been used to make beer or whisky was needed to feed soldiers and refugees. What's more, many of the nation's biggest beer brewers, such as Anheuser-Busch, were of German ancestry and thus out of popular favor.

### The Impact of Prohibition

Soon after the passage of the Eighteenth Amendment the Volstead Act was passed to enforce it. Such enforcement was necessary because many Americans, particularly in the cities, had quickly found ways to obtain illegal liquor. Not only could liquor be obtained through doctors' prescriptions, it could also be brewed at home in bootlegging stills. More efficient was criminal bootlegging, which allowed for the transport of liquor nationwide. The most successful bootleggers, such as Al Capone and Dion O'Banion of Chicago, gained national notoriety for their fierce battles for turf control. The battle between Capone and O'Banion culminated on Valentine's Day in 1929, with the massacre of seven of O'Banion's men by members of Capone's gang.

Prohibition also changed social habits related to drinking. Average citizens went to speakeasies, which, unlike most saloons, were designed for both men and women. Privileged citizens still drank at home, however, including President Harding himself, who made the White House his private watering hole.

By 1925 there was already widespread opposition to Prohibition. The popular *Collier's* magazine became the first to call for its repeal. By the end of the decade, despite the widespread law-breaking that the law had inspired, President Herbert Hoover insisted that Prohibition was " a great social and economic experiment, noble in motive and far-reaching in purpose." The experiment continued until 1933, when Hoover's successor, Franklin D. Roosevelt, oversaw its repeal.

### 100 Percent Americanism

As the Prohibition experiment illustrates, the 1920s were far from a return to the supposedly simpler times represented by small town America. In fact, by 1920, the United States was no longer a nation predominately made up of small towns. According to the census of 1920, for the first time in U.S. history, more Americans lived in cities and towns of more than 2,500 people that lived in rural areas.

**FLAPPERS AGAINST PROHIBITION** A young woman shows her opposition to Prohibition on the back of her car.

One factor driving the growth of cities in the early 20th century was the arrival of millions of immigrants from southern and eastern Europe. Yet by 1920 many native-born Americans had come to fear the influence of "foreign" ideas. In 1921 Congress banned virtually all immigration from Europe and Asia with a "Quota Act" that limited immigration from any one nation to no more than 3 percent of the total number of people from that country living in the United States in 1910. The ban did not include immigrants from Mexico, however, and Mexican migration to the United States swelled throughout the decade.

### The Rebirth of the KKK

Anti-immigration sentiment also led to the rebirth of the Civil War-era white supremacist movement known as the Ku Klux Klan. Formally outlawed by a civil rights statute in 1871, the Klan was reconfigured in Georgia in 1915 as a patriotic benevolent association. While still grounded in hatred of African Americans, the modern Klan widened its assault to include Catholics and Jews, whose numbers had increased due to immigration. Some Klan groups also denounced drinking, birth control, union membership, women's suffrage, and the teaching of evolution. The view of the Klan as an all-American entity had been reinforced by its heroic depiction in the 1905 novel *The Clansmen* by Thomas Dixon Jr. and its 1915 film adaptation *The Birth of A Nation*, directed by D.W. Griffith. Woodrow Wilson had personally screened the film in the White House, declaring it "history written in lightning."

Adding to the Klan's popularity was the fear of alleged socialists, anarchists and communists in American society, as well as the large scale migration of African Americans to the North and Midwest during the war. Unlike the earlier Klan, which had been concentrated in the old Confederate South, the revived Klan had nationwide strength. During the early 1920s, the group boasted a membership of about 4 million Americans, with active members in cities from Los Angeles to New York City. Indiana was a particularly strong hotbed of Klan activity. Public demonstrations included a 1925 march in Washington DC, which included 40,000 hooded members, including women as well as men.

What the idealized portraits of the Klan did not show was the waves of violence perpetrated against its victims. The Klan, often with the direct support of local law officials, frequently used public lynching to spread its message of white supremacy. Accusing victims of some nonexistent crime, lynch mobs executed them without regard for legal rights or due process, often after torturing them first.

During the 1920s press coverage of Klan violence contributed to a decline in membership, but the group revived its strength once again in during the Civil Rights movement of the 1950s and 1960s.

## The Growth of Fundamentalism

Although most conservative Christians were not members of the Klan, the opposition of some Klan groups to the teaching of evolution highlights another important shift in American culture during the 1920s. During the nineteenth century, scientific advances had led some Christians to question beliefs that were based on a literal reading of the Bible. For example, geology suggested that the Earth had formed over millions of years, rather than in seven days, as held by the story of Genesis. Even more controversial was the theory, first stated by British naturalist Charles Darwin, that living creatures, including human beings, had evolved over millions of years from other creatures through natural selection.

**RACIAL UNREST** During the early twentieth century a new version of the Ku Klux Klan emerged. In addition to lynching African Americans, the new Klan, seen above right marching in Washington, also attacked immigrants and Catholics.

To some Christians, scientific theory and Christian theology were not mutually exclusive. Among the leaders of this "Liberal Theology" movement was Harry Emerson Fosdick, a professor of practical theology at Union Theological Seminary, and after 1926, pastor of New York's Park Avenue Baptist Church (later renamed Riverside Church). Fosdick argued that Christians did not have to believe in the literal truth of the Bible to have faith in Jesus Christ.

In rural parts of the nation, particularly in the Midwest and South, Fundamentalist Christianity, which preached the literal truth of the Bible, attracted legions of followers. Many of these followers were drawn to Fundamentalism by their rejection of the rapid social changes in society. Jazz music that emerged from African American culture, new roles for women, radical "foreign influences," rampant consumerism, liberal theology—all of these things seemed

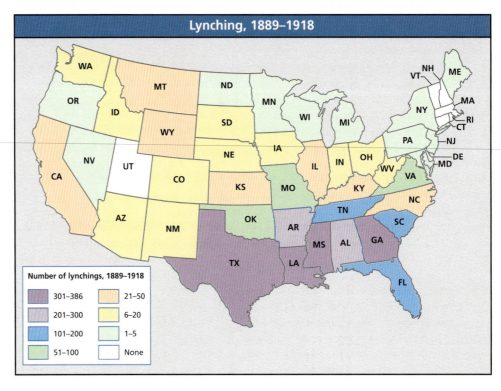

### Lynching, 1889–1918

Number of lynchings, 1889–1918

| | |
|---|---|
| 301–386 | 21–50 |
| 201–300 | 6–20 |
| 101–200 | 1–5 |
| 51–100 | None |

to be threatening the nation's traditional values.

## The Scopes Trial

Perhaps most threatening of all was the teaching of evolution in schools. In 1924, at the World's Fundamentalist Convention in Fort Worth, Texas, delegates passed a resolution calling on states "to force all teachers to sign . . . a statement of creed which affirms the steadfast faith in the Genesis account of creation. . ." The next year, State Representative John Washington Butler of Tennessee sponsored a law banning the teaching of evolution in all public schools in his state. The law passed, 71–5.

Almost immediately the American Civil Liberties Union (ACLU) challenged the ban by asking a young teacher in Dayton, Tennessee named John T. Scopes to discuss evolution in his classroom. Scopes agreed, was arrested, and a trial was set for July 1925. Roger Baldwin of the ACLU announced, " We shall take the Scopes case to the Supreme Court if necessary to establish that a teacher may tell the truth without being thrown in jail." Clarence Darrow, a brilliant and controversial lawyer defended Scopes. Arguing for the prosecution was an aging William Jennings Bryan, the three-time Democratic candidate for the presidency. Bryan, a Fundamentalist himself, had made a long career out of defending the interests of rural people and the poor against the wealthy and powerful elites. To Fundamentalists the elites were those who had turned away from religious faith in favor of science, while looking down upon believers for their unwillingness to abandon their faith.

When the trial began thousands of curious spectators swelled Dayton's streets, packing the courtroom. Vendors hawked souvenirs, bands entertained, and various groups paraded in support of their side in the courtroom drama. For five days lawyers and experts debated. Then Darrow called Bryan himself as his sole witness. For two hours he grilled Bryan on his beliefs, making Bryan appear weak, confused, and out of touch. As one reporter remarked, "Darrow never spared him. It was masterful, but it was pitiful."

Undeniably Scopes had broken the law, and thus he was found guilty. But the judge fined Scopes a token $100 dollars.

Five days later a broken William Jennings Bryan died in his sleep.

In the years since the Scopes trial some states had passed laws requiring that the Biblical story of creation be taught in schools. In 1988 the Supreme Court ruled that such laws violated the constitutional separation of church and state, but some communities have continued to challenge that ruling.

# Cultural Movements of the 1920s

As cultural debates over science and religion raged, the 1920s also witnessed a flowering of literature and the arts. In the early decades of the century, writers as diverse as Willa Cather and Sherwood Anderson were writing about the life on the frontier and in small town America. Frank Norris, Upton Sinclair, Theodore Dreiser and Edith Wharton wrote of the broad challenges and personal perils of the modern era.

Following World War I writers and artists addressed the war's desolation and the social excesses of 1920s society. Some American writers, such as Ernest Hemingway, F. Scott Fitzgerald, and Gertude Stein left the country altogether for Europe, becoming, in Stein's words the "lost generation."

## The Harlem Renaissance

Meanwhile, for African Americans leaving the rural South in search of better life in the North, New York City's Harlem became a cultural mecca. Newly arriving blacks, assisted by local chapters of the Urban League and other civic groups, spent most of their new income in the black community itself, fostering a black middle class and spirit of self-sufficiency. Harlem had long been home to African American intellectuals like W. E. B. DuBois and anti-lynching crusader Ida Wells-Barnett. And it was here that the creative movement known as the Harlem Renaissance flowered. Although the Renaissance was not an organized movement, it took its cue from DuBois, who had suggested that black Americans would only gain equality through greater awareness of their own cultural heritage. Leading writers associated with the Renaissance included lawyer, poet, songwriter and novelist James Weldon Johnson, editor Alain Locke, and poets Countee Cullen and Arna Bontemps, who also wrote novels and histories. The leading literary figure of the Harlem Renaissance, however, was the poet Langston Hughes, whose first collection, *The Weary Blues*, was published in 1926. Hughes's poetry protested the oppressiveness of a white society that excluded black America. Throughout his long career, which reached well into the Civil Rights era, Hughes continued to express and interpret the African-American experience, both in poetry and prose.

In addition to being a literary mecca Harlem was also an entertainment center. Home to the famous Cotton Club, which opened in 1922, Harlem became the nation's most important showcase for black musicians. The elegant interior, featuring primitivist decor, helped to inspire the "jungle sound" of conductor Duke Ellington who opened there in 1927. Other jazz greats who played there included Cab Calloway, Louis Armstrong and later, Lena Horne. Sadly during the 1920s, black audiences could not hear these artists since the club was for whites only.

The white audiences at the Cotton Club were—like audiences at other clubs, speakeasies and dance halls in urban areas across the country—generally wealthy, young, free spenders. The new fads and fashions, dance crazes, and music of the 1920s, were fueled by illegal drink and a booming stock market. They were also fueled by two more new factors: consumer advertising and easy credit.

Harlem also became home to the Jamaican nationalist leader Marcus Garvey, from which he spread his message of self-sufficiency, Pan-Africanism, and black separatism. Garvey, a Jamaican born civil rights activist, founded the United Negro Improvement Association in 1914, and moved it from Jamaica to Harlem in 1916. The organization's goals included better conditions for African-American communities as well as the economic development of Africa itself. A talented speaker, Garvey persuasively argued for a "Back to Africa" movement and an independent

## The Harlem Renaissance

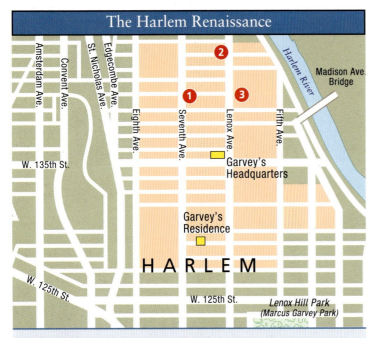

1. Founded in 1809 as the Free Baptist Church of New York city, the **Abyssian Baptist Church** became a center of civil rights activism when a young preacher named Adam Clayton Powell Sr. took over the pulpit a century later. The church building, dedicated in 1923, was a cavernous Gothic structure, featuring an Italian marble pulpit and imported stain glass windows. The congregation numbered over 7,000.

2. Opened in 1922, the **Cotton Club** became the premier showcase in America for black musicians. The elegant interior, featuring primitivist decor, helped to inspire the "jungle sound" of Duke Ellington, who opened there in 1927. Other jazz greats who played there included Cab Calloway, Louis Armstrong, and singer Lena Horne. Sadly, during the 1920s, black audiences could not listen to these musicians, since the club was for "whites only."

3. The **Harlem YMCA,** completed in 1919, offered some of the finest athletic facilities in New York City at the time. It also sponsored a host of conferences on subjects like women's suffrage, anti-lynching legislation, and civil rights activism. Among the figures who spoke there were Ida Wells, Mary McLeod Bethune and Booker T. Washington.

**AN ARTISTIC FLOWERING** Harlem in the 1920s was home to many prominent African-American artists, writers, political and cultural figures. Perhaps the best-known writer of the Harlem Renaissance was Langston Hughes, seen at right.

African state with its own high civilization. In 1925 Garvey was sentenced to five years in jail for mail fraud in a scandal involving his Black Star Shipping Company. Deported to Jamaica in 1927, he died in London in 1940.

# The Consumer Society

In the 1920s advertising became big business. As each new product was introduced, ad agencies moved to convince the public that this latest item was something that he or she could never live without. Advertisers hired psychologists to figure out how best to reach the psyches of potential customers. One surefire method was through the fear of being laughed at: the makers of Listerine, for instance, helped turn the term halitosis from a scientific term into a household name for bad breath.

Tied to the increased influence of advertising, the 1920s saw a shift in public attitudes about spending money. While previous generations had treasured thriftiness, self-reliance and self-sacrifice, many members of the general public had come to prefer free spending and accept rising personal debt.

While the average worker's income did rise during the 1920s, the number of purchases made by the average consumer skyrocketed. This became possible because of the installment plan. Before the war Americans had purchased all they needed, other than their homes, with cash. Now manufacturers and retailers urged Americans to buy cars, boats, radios, and refrigerators on the "buy now, pay later" model. By 1929 consumer borrowing reached $7 billion.

## Working Women in the 1920s

The new consumer-oriented society had a dramatic impact on women, both inside the home and outside. Conveniences like indoor plumbing and electricity as well as new appliances like refrigerators and vacuum cleaners made housework much easier than ever before. Yet in order to keep sales of new cleaning products selling, advertisers kept up steady pressure to women to keep their houses cleaner than ever. Other advertisers hawked beauty supplies, new fashions, and other products aimed directly at the female consumer.

At the same time, women had more disposable income with which to spend on these new products. An increasing number of women worked outside of the home during the early 20th century, particularly in white collar occupations like secretary, bookkeeper, clerk, or telephone operator. At the same time women still faced huge hurdles in the office—it was often assumed, for instance, that single working women would quit their jobs should they become engaged. An office was thought it be a good place for young single women to find a husband, and that the qualities learned on the job—obedience, hard work, and a respect for "superiors"— would make her a good wife. In 1930 women made 57 cents for every dollar made by a man.

Outside of the office women in the 1920s could vote, but they still weren't equal citizens. In most states a woman's services belonged to her husband, meaning a paycheck earned by a woman at an office job belonged not to her to spend, but to her husband. In many other states women could not own property, could not sign legal contracts, and could not serve on juries.

## The Automobile

By far the most important new product of the day was the automobile. Using the assembly line, Henry Ford had reduced the time it took to make a car from 12 hours to about 90 minutes. When it was introduced in 1908, Ford's basic Model T or "tin lizzie," sold for $1000. By 1929 it could be purchased for $260, less than six months income for the average worker. The number of cars on the road jumped from 8.5 million in 1920 to 23 million by 1929.

The car rapidly changed how Americans lived. As Ford had hoped, it gave new freedom to rural Americans. It also allowed people to live farther from their work, and

| Motor Vehicle Registration and Sales, 1900–1930 | | |
| --- | --- | --- |
| Year | Motor Vehicle Registrations | Factory Sales |
| 1900 | 8,000 | 4,100 |
| 1905 | 78,800 | 24,200 |
| 1910 | 468,500 | 181,200 |
| 1915 | 2,490,000 | 895,900 |
| 1920 | 9,239,100 | 1,905,500 |
| 1925 | 20,068,500 | 3,735,100 |
| 1930 | 26,749,800 | 2,787,400 |

thus people could live in the suburbs and drive to jobs in the city. It also allowed shoppers to drive to the store—or even many stores. In 1924, the world's first shopping center arose in Kansas City.

## On the Radio

On November 2, 1920, station KDKA in Pittsburgh went on the air for the first time. The first commercial broadcast covered that year's presidential election.

Soon stations all over the country were broadcasting news, concerts, and popular serials. People gathered around radios to listen to their favorite shows. Unlike Europe, where radio stations were government-owned, in America people listened to privately owned companies like the National Broadcasting Company, or NBC. Not everyone appreciated the radio. "One bad feature of the radio," remarked one schoolteacher, "is that children stay up late at night and are not fit for school in the morning."

Generally speaking, however, the American public—and the American government—applauded the constant array of new consumer products. By 1927 the nation had had nearly a decade of prosperity. The following year, Herbert Hoover, the Secretary of Commerce under both Warren Harding and Calvin Coolidge, declared that America was "nearer to the final triumph of poverty than ever before in the history of any land."

| Women in the Labor Force, 1900–1920 | | | | Percent of Women in Labor Force | | |
| --- | --- | --- | --- | --- | --- | --- |
| Year | Women in Labor Force | Percent of Women in Total Labor Force | Women in Labor Force as Percent of Total Women of Working Age | Single | Married | Widowed/ Divorced |
| 1900 | 4,997,000 | 18.1 | 20.6 | 66.2 | 15.4 | 18.4 |
| 1910* | 7,640,000 | NA | 25.4 | 60.2 | 24.2 | 15.0 |
| 1920 | 8,347,000 | 20.4 | 23.7 | 77.0* | 23.0 | --- |
| 1930 | 10,632,000 | 21.9 | 24.8 | 53.9 | 28.9 | 17.2 |

*Data not comparable with other censuses due to a difference in the basis of enumeration

* Single includes widowed and divorced

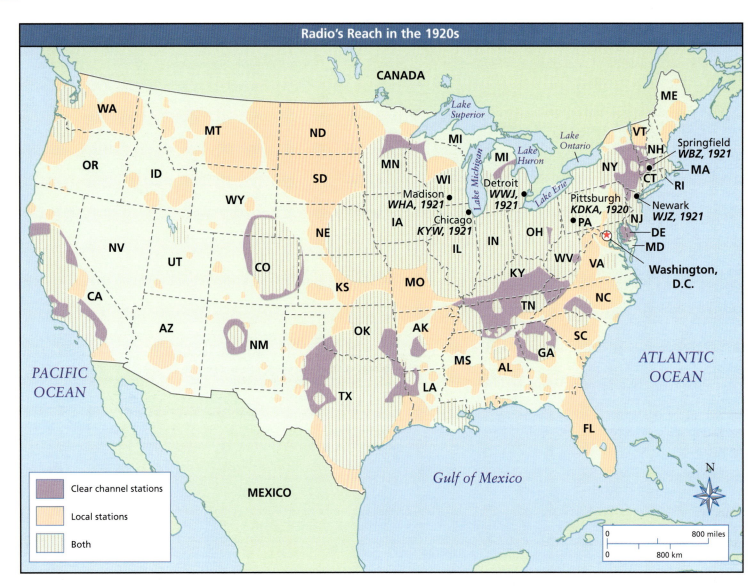

**Radio's Reach in the 1920s**

CANADA

ME

WA

MT    ND    MI    VT

OR    ID         MN    WI    Detroit    NH    Springfield
                      *WWJ,*    NY    *WBZ, 1921*
      WY    SD         Madison    *1921*         MA
                      *WHA, 1921*         CT
NV         NE    IA    Chicago    Pittsburgh    RI
                      *KYW, 1921*    IL    IN    OH    *KDKA, 1920*    Newark
      UT                                  PA    *WJZ, 1921*
CA         CO              WV    VA    DE
                      KS    MO    KY              MD
AZ                              TN    NC    Washington,
      NM    OK    AK                        D.C.
                              SC
            TX    MS    AL    GA
PACIFIC                  LA              ATLANTIC
OCEAN                              OCEAN
                                  FL

Lake Superior
Lake Michigan
Lake Huron
Lake Ontario
Lake Erie

MEXICO    *Gulf of Mexico*

N

Legend:
- Clear channel stations
- Local stations
- Both

0 ——— 800 miles
0 ——— 800 km

**RADIO GOES NATIONWIDE** Beginning in Pittsburgh in 1920 commercial radio spread rapidly during the following decade.

# Changes in Immigration

Between 1910 and 1920 an enormous influx of Mexican immigrants arrived in the United States. Known as the "second wave" of Mexican-American immigrants (the first being the original Californio, Nuevo Mexicano, and Tejano settlers), this group came for a variety of reasons. Many were small farmers who lost their lands in Mexico when the dictatorial government of Porfirio Díaz attempted to privatize lands that had traditionally been considered communal lands, or *ejidos*. Property owners were forced to document their ownership of lands, and those unable to do so were forced from lands they had worked for generations. Confiscated lands were then sold to wealthy domestic and foreign investors, who used the lands in an effort to convert Mexico from a subsistence agricultural economy to an agricultural export economy. This shift caused massive dislocation and alienation among poor Mexican farmworkers. By 1910 this

alienation from the Díaz government exploded into the Mexican Revolution. During the 10-year chaos of the struggle, 1 million Mexicans died and thousands fled northward into the United States.

The violence and chaos of the Mexican Revolution drove Mexicans across the border into the United States in unprecedented numbers. In the decade of 1911–1920, 219,004 Mexicans were recorded as immigrating to the United States—more than four times as many as in the previous decade, when just 49,642 did so. In the following decade (1921–1930), the number of Mexican immigrants to the United States more than doubled, to 459,287. According to the census, the Mexican-born population grew more than 13-fold in 30 years, from about 103,000 in 1900 to 1,400,000 in 1930.

Two distinct waves of Mexican immigration from 1900 to 1930 can be distinguished. The first wave, which lasted from 1900 to 1914, included the many Mexicans who were abandoning Díaz's regime in its last years as well as those leaving Mexico in the first

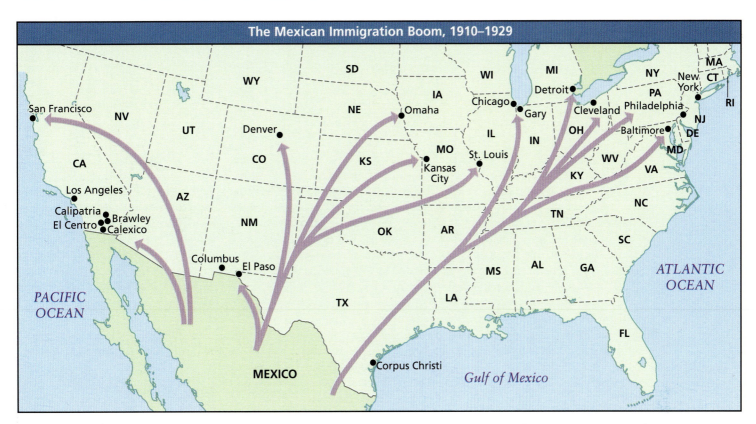

**The Mexican Immigration Boom, 1910–1929**

**EXODUS FROM MEXICO** In the aftermath of the Mexican Revolution, thousands of Mexicans fled violence at home for new lives in the United States.

years of the Revolution. The second, much larger wave, from 1914 to 1929, came as the revolution intensified at home and as World War I and its aftermath created labor shortages and an economic boom in the United States.

The newcomers included many poor people but also well-to-do businessmen and political refugees of various sorts: politicians, army officers, intellectuals, and journalists. Some of the better-educated and better-capitalized immigrants started businesses, including Spanish-language newspapers and bookstores to serve a small but growing Mexican-American middle class. The poorer, unskilled refugees were fortunate to arrive just as commercial agriculture was booming in the West and Southwest.

Several factors fed the agricultural boom. New dams were opening deserts to irrigation and planting. Cattle ranches and small family farms were losing ground to large, mechanized plantations. Refrigerated train cars had been invented, permitting growers to ship fresh produce over long distances to cities with burgeoning populations. Under these circumstances the region's agricultural capitalists needed masses of laborers to pick the crops, preferably laborers who would work for little money. They warmly welcomed the Mexican refugees to fill that role, particularly since many Mexicans were seasonal migrant laborers who would stay long enough to pick the crops and get paid, then return to Mexico.

California's Imperial Valley, where the state's first cotton was planted in 1910, became a favorite destination of Mexican immigrants. By 1918 people of Mexican descent were the largest group of agricultural workers in the valley. In Colorado Mexican Americans picked sugar beets; elsewhere, they picked citrus fruits, grapes, melons, lettuce, spinach, tomatoes, and carrots. They also worked in other industries in the booming region—on

railroads, in copper and coal mines, and in factories. As in the late 19th century, Mexican Americans were aided by laws excluding Asian laborers, including the 1902 Chinese Exclusion Act and the 1907 Gentleman's Agreement with Japan. By 1909 Mexican Americans constituted 98 percent of the work crews employed by the Atchison, Topeka, and Santa Fe Railways west of Albuquerque, New Mexico. By 1928, 75 percent of unskilled construction workers in Texas were Mexican Americans.

Though big business welcomed the labor supply, many Anglo-American and Mexican-American residents of the Southwest reacted with alarm. Some prosperous Mexican-American families that had been in the region since before the Mexican-American War regarded the newcomers with disdain; after all, these refugees were mostly poor and uneducated, without distinguished lineages. To this day the term hispano, which in its broadest sense means simply "Hispanic or Spanish person," is used in New Mexico in a restricted sense to mean people who claim descent from the region's original Spanish settlers, as distinct from all those who have come more recently from Mexico.

Anglo-Americans were even more prone to prejudice against the newcomers from Mexico. Mexican laborers were accused of being communist sympathizers, of being supporters of the outlaw Pancho Villa, of practicing sexual debauchery and thievery, of being unassimilable in American society, and of being charges of the state. U.S. representative S. Parker Frieselle of California put it bluntly in a 1926 debate in which he opposed restriction of Mexican immigration: "We, gentlemen, are just as anxious as you are not to build the civilization of California or any other western district upon a Mexican foundation. We take him [the Mexican immigrant] because there is nothing else available to us."

237

# Chapter 25: The Great Depression

S helters were made of almost every conceivable thing—burlap, canvas, palm branches.... Calves and horses wandered at will about the shelters. There was a huge pile of manure close to the houses.... We found one woman carrying water in large milk pails from the irrigation ditch.... This is evidently all the water which they have in camp. There were no baths." So wrote a visiting minister in a report on conditions in migrant farmer camps in 1929.

## Crisis on the Farm

While the 1920s were a time of prosperity for many Americans, pockets of poverty still existed. This was particularly true in rural America, where a farm crisis had buffeted agricultural workers since the national economic downturn that had followed World War I. While wartime production had boosted farm profits, many farmers continued to produce just as much after the war, even though there was far less demand for their crops. As a result, farm prices plummeted. A bushel of corn that sold for $1.22 in 1919, sold for just 41 cents a year later. The prices of industrial equipment also fell, but not nearly as quickly as farm incomes. Thus the farm machinery that farmers needed became increasingly expensive to purchase. In many cases, farmers took out loans in order to finance their purchases—which only deepened the farm crisis.

Throughout the 1920s, long-term agricultural trends only increased crop production. New agricultural management techniques, the increased use of tractors, and especially the growing use of chemical fertilizers all led to an ever growing surplus of crops. Although the national postwar recession ended in 1923, the farm crisis continued unabated through the decade. As surviving became increasingly difficult, many family farms simply folded. Thirteen million acres of cultivated land were abandoned, and the number of farms declined for the first time in the nation's history.

Farmers pressed for federal aid, but to no avail. In an effort to alleviate the crisis, several farm bills were proposed in Congress. The complex McNary-Haugen bill was designed to restore the balance between agricultural produce and industrial goods by setting up a government corporation to purchase enough of surplus crops to raise farm prices to the level of manufactured goods. Surplus crops would have then been sold overseas, and any loss would have been made up through a small tax on farmers.

Although the bill had the support of his Agriculture Department, President Calvin Coolidge opposed the bill's price-fixing mechanisms as unwarranted government intervention, vetoing it twice in 1927 and 1928.

**HARD TIMES ON THE FARM** An Iowa farmer lifts hay into his barn.

## The Growth of Large-Scale Agribusiness

As the number of U.S. farms fell, another major shift began to occur. While the number of farms fell, the size of those remaining increased. By 1930 half of the farms in the United States produced almost 90 percent of the cash crops. Grain farmers in the Midwest who could afford the land as well as the mechanized machinery to efficiently work it prospered, as did large truck farmers and fruit growers in Florida and California.

Large-scale farms did not rely simply on mechanized equipment for their prosperity. They also needed labor—and to get it as cheaply as possible. During the 1920s, 75 percent of all farm workers in California were migrant Mexican workers who moved from region to region as each crop was ready for harvest. In winter they either returned to Mexico or to the Mexican barrios that had grown up in virtually every city in the Southwest. Whole families worked side by side in the fields with little chance for schooling or relaxation.

By 1929, few Americans were aware of the major shifts on the nation's farms, or of the financial crisis buffeting small farming communities. Most cities and non-farm sectors of the economy were booming. The enormous popularity of the automobile had sparked the steel, rubber, and glass industries, as their products were needed to make cars. State and federal construction projects brought new roads to carry the new cars, as well as new construction and engineering work for workers. Cars also sparked the growth of suburbia, which spurred new home construction, and the manufacture of new, high-ticket items to fill those new homes.

As discussed in Chapter 24, consumers purchased many of these new products on the installment plan. In 1928, for example, fully two-thirds of all furniture, phonographs, and washing machines were bought on credit, as were half of all pianos, sewing machines, and vacuum cleaners. But improved factory production increased the number of consumer goods to such an extent that production exceeded even the growing demand, and the market reached saturation.

## The Crash

Consumer confidence that was reflected in automobile and other high-ticket purchases was also reflected on Wall Street. Throughout the 1920s, individual investors from all walks of life purchased stock, often using minimal upfront cash investments and loans from brokers to cover the costs. Between the end of 1925 and October 1929, the market value of all stocks rose from $27 billion to $87 billion.

### Runaway Stock Speculation

Yet trouble lay on the horizon. With the Coolidge administration pursuing a "hands-off" policy toward Wall Street, banks and securities went largely unregulated, resulting in large-scale credit offerings for stock speculation. Banks began loaning investors money to invest in the market, with borrowers using the stock they intended to purchase as collateral. When Coolidge learned that the regulation of stocks and securities was ultimately the responsibility of the states and not the federal government, he chose not to act. In fact, he could have used his influence to ask the Federal Reserve Bank to tighten regulations. Instead, Coolidge attempted to calm fears by stating that that stocks were "cheap at current prices." As late as January 1928, he argued that he saw nothing wrong with investors using borrowed money to buy shares—a remark that sent trading on the New York Stock Exchange soaring. As consumers were speculating on the stock market, Wall Street firms were also investing widely in stocks, shifting money away from capital improvements and other ventures. The results of this over-investment in stock were artificially high stock prices.

When the economy began to slow in 1928, the Federal Reserve Board lifted interest rates to slow down the rate of investment. Yet despite the warning, stock speculation continued much as it had throughout the decade. Herbert Hoover, Coolidge's Commerce Secretary and eventual successor, was firm in his commitment to laissez-faire economics. As he would later sum up his philosophy, "The sole function of government is to bring about a condition of affairs favorable to the beneficial development of private enterprise."

Despite the administration's limited view of what the government could do about it, national and international forces were coalescing to make economic disaster increasingly possible. Protective U.S. tariffs and war-debt policies had weakened

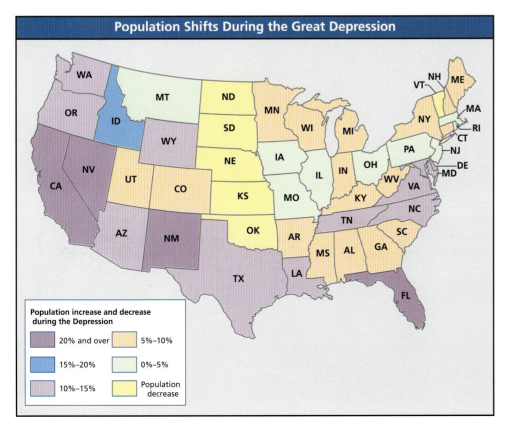

**Population Shifts During the Great Depression**

Population increase and decrease during the Depression

- 20% and over
- 15%–20%
- 10%–15%
- 5%–10%
- 0%–5%
- Population decrease

LEAVING THE PLAINS During the early 1930s, thousands of Americans left their homes in the Great Plains to head west to California, Nevada and New Mexico, among other states, as well as south and east to Florida, North Carolina, Virginia, and Tennessee.

**NEW YORK STOCK EXCHANGE** The floor of the New York Stock Exchange, ca. 1920

foreign economies during the 1920s, particularly in Europe. The European economies, in turn, affected the U.S. economy, particularly farmers. Deteriorating European markets meant a drop in demand for U.S. crops, which meant lower prices on the already weak domestic agricultural market.

### Black Days for Wall Street

On the morning of October 24, 1929, stock prices began to decline, setting off a selling panic on the New York Stock Exchange (NYSE). When trading closed on what became known as "Black Thursday," the Dow Jones Industrial Average had fallen 9 percent and nearly 13 million shares had been sold in the worst day in Wall Street's history.

In response to the crash major New York banks acted quickly to shore up the market. When they purchased $30 million in stock, Hoover confidently announced that a full recovery was expected. Four days later, however, came "Black Tuesday." Sixteen million more shares were sold in a massive sell-off. Thousands of investors were ruined as stock prices declined more than 43 points or 10 percent.

By the end of 1929 the New York Stock Exchange had lost $15 billion, and the impact of the crash on the wider economy was swift and strong. The national economy hurtled into an economic tailspin and a prolonged depression.

Large corporations with investments in the market found themselves with huge losses and halted investment. Factories, banks, and other businesses were shut down, unable to pay their workers. Banks closed because they had no money. Spending on imports fell from almost $4.4 billion in 1929 to just over $1.3 billion by 1932. By 1933 the U.S. gross national product had declined from $103.8 billion to $55.7 billion.

| Selected Stock Prices, October–November 1929 | | |
|---|---|---|
| | **High** | **Low** |
| Stock | 10/3/29 | 11/13/29 |
| | | |
| AT&T | 304 | 197¼ |
| General Electric | 396¼ | 168⅛ |
| General Motors | 72¾ | 36 |
| United States Steel | 261¾ | 150 |
| Westinghouse, E.& M. | 289⅞ | 102⅝ |

# Daily Life in Depression America

As the amount of goods produced by U.S. factories fell, so too did the number of laborers working in them. Although the 1929 unemployment rate had been just 3.2 percent, it rose dramatically over the next four years—to 8.7 percent in 1930, 15.9 percent in 1931, 21.7 percent in 1932, and a peak of 29.9 percent in 1933. The

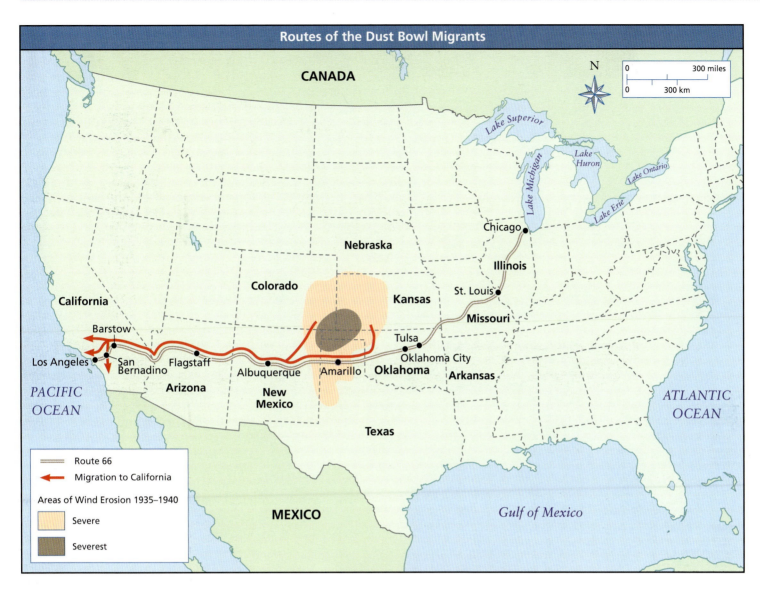

**Routes of the Dust Bowl Migrants**

CANADA

Lake Superior

Lake Michigan

Lake Huron

Lake Erie

Lake Ontario

Chicago

Nebraska

Illinois

Colorado

Kansas

St. Louis

California

Missouri

Barstow

Tulsa

Los Angeles

Oklahoma City

San Bernadino

Flagstaff

Albuquerque

Amarillo

Oklahoma

Arkansas

Arizona

New Mexico

PACIFIC OCEAN

ATLANTIC OCEAN

Texas

Route 66

Migration to California

Areas of Wind Erosion 1935–1940

Severe

Severest

MEXICO

Gulf of Mexico

N

0                    300 miles

0          300 km

rising tide of joblessness became the biggest single crisis in the early years of the Depression.

## The Dust Bowl

While no sector of the economy was unaffected by Depression, the agricultural sector was hit the hardest. As they had done for a decade, when commodity prices tumbled farmers continued to hike production, which caused prices to fall still further. Wheat production, for example, was 35 million bushels higher in 1930 than it was in 1929, causing prices to drop from $1.09 to $0.71 per bushel. By 1930 farm income had fallen to its lowest since the depth of the postwar recession in 1921. Already saddled with debts taken out to purchase the expensive equipment and chemical fertilizers that allowed for increased crop production, farm after farm was forced out of business when banks foreclosed on mortgages for nonpayment.

The farm crisis was especially severe in the Great Plains states. In 1931 a severe drought struck the region, causing crops to die and dust from over-plowed and over-grazed land to blow, creating "black blizzards." Throughout the 1930s, a 150,000 square mile

**MIGRANT MOTHER**
Dorothea Lange, a photographer employed by the Works Progress Administration during the Roosevelt Administration, took this famous photograph of a migrant mother and her children.

**DUST STORM** A father and his children struggle through a dust storm on the Great Plains.

**BONUS ARMY** Members of the Bonus Army at their tent city in Washington D.C. before being evicted by the U.S. Army.

region of the Midwest, known as the Dust Bowl, would continue to suffer from this disastrous combination of drought and soil erosion. In 1932, 14 major duststorms were reported, rising to 38 the following year. By October 1933, desperate farmers had begun to flee the desolate Plains for California, where many sought new work as migrant laborers. Once they arrived they lived in shacks, and moved up and down the state—if they were lucky enough to find work—picking crops on the giant farms of the Central Valley.

By 1934 the drought covered 75 percent of the nation, severely affecting 27 states. That same year, the *Yearbook on Agriculture* reported that "Approximately 35 million acres of formerly cultivated land have essentially been destroyed for crop production. . . . 100 million acres now in crops have now lost all or most of their topsoil; 125 million acres now in crops are rapidly losing topsoil . . ."

### Ill-housed, Ill-clad, and Ill-fed

Statistics only tell part of the story of the Depression. As one historian has said, "Mass unemployment is both a statistic and an empty feeling in the stomach. To fully comprehend it, you have to both see the figures and feel the emptiness."

Very few Americans escaped the fear and hopelessness of the Great Depression. "What is to become of us?" said one Arizona man. "I've lost twelve and a half pounds in the last month, just thinking. You can't sleep, you know? You wake up at 2 A.M. and you lie and think."

The consequences of the Depression were staggering. An army of the unemployed wandered the nation, looking for work and begging for charity. Some—including many children—were unable to receive proper nutrition and healthcare, and actually starved to death. Others committed suicide.

As the Depression continued, people called on President Hoover to act, and blamed him for the nation's economic collapse. Homeless Americans built shacks in city parks, and derisively nicknamed them "Hoovervilles."

Although Hoover was, like Coolidge, philosophically opposed to government intervention in the economy, he did take some action. In 1930, he asked Congress to fund public works projects to put Americans back to work. Congress complied, budgeting $100 million to employ 4.5 million jobless. In 1931 he called on Congress to create the Reconstruction

## The Great Depression: A Statistical Survey

### Major Economic Markers, 1929–1933

|  | 1929 | 1933 |
| --- | --- | --- |
| Banks in operation | 25,568 | 14,771 |
| Prime interest rate | 5.03% | 0.63% |
| Volume of stocks sold (NYSE) | 1.1 billion | 0.65 billion |
| Privately earned income | $45.5 billion | $23.9 billion |
| Personal and corporate savings | $15.3 billion | $2.3 billion |

### Consumer Spending Indicators, 1929–1933

| Type of Goods or Services | 1929 | 1933 |
| --- | --- | --- |
| Food | $19.5 billion | $11.5 billion |
| Housing | $11.5 billion | $7.5 billion |
| Clothing | $11.2 billion | $5.4 billion |
| Automobiles | $2.6 billion | $0.8 billion |
| Medical care | $2.9 billion | $1.9 billion |
| Philanthropy | $1.2 billion | $0.8 billion |
| Value of shares on the New York Stock Exchange | $89.0 billion | $19.0 billion |

### Decline in Economic Indicators, 1929–1933

| Type of goods or services | % Decline |
| --- | --- |
| Construction (overall) | 78% |
| Gross National Product | 29% |
| Manufacturing | 54% |
| Investments | 98% |

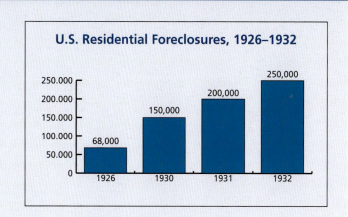

U.S. Residential Foreclosures, 1926–1932

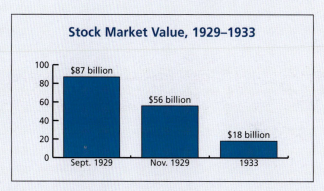

Stock Market Value, 1929–1933

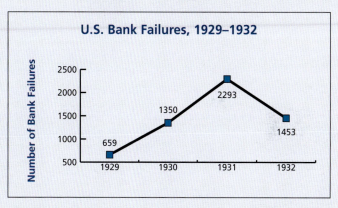

U.S. Bank Failures, 1929–1932

Finance Corporation to provide loans to businesses, farms and banks in danger of collapse. But he also signed the disastrous Smoot-Hawley Tariff Act, which raised tariffs dramatically in an effort to limit competition for domestic goods. Instead of strengthening the domestic economy, the new law sparked an international trade war as other nations passed similar laws increasing their tariffs.

### The Bonus Army

Although reluctantly willing to promote funding for public works programs, Hoover opposed direct federal aid to the poor. In 1932, thousands of World War I veterans and their families, nicknamed the "Bonus Army," marched on Washington to lobby the government. They wanted Hoover to allow them to borrow against military bonuses they had been promised six years earlier, even though they were not due to receive the payments until 1945. For two months Hoover refused to meet with the protest-

ers. Then, in July, he ordered the Army to break up the Bonus Army camps by force. The military, led by Col. Douglas MacArthur, burned the camp to the ground, and rounded up the veterans and their armies with tear gas and armored tanks. Remarking on the events, Hoover said, "Thank God we still have a government . . . that knows how to deal with a mob."

As the nation headed toward the election of 1932, Hoover's popularity was at an all-time low. Unlike Hoover, the Democratic Party's nominee, New York's governor Franklin Delano Roosevelt believed strongly in government intervention in the economy and spending to aid the poor. During the campaign Roosevelt made only vague statements about how he planned to right the economy, but he captured the mood of the times. "The country needs, and unless I mistake its temper, the country demands bold, persistent experimentation," he said. Projecting an attitude of hope and optimism, Roosevelt won over the American people. He defeated Hoover in a landslide.

# Chapter 26: The New Deal

"Dear Mr. President," read the letter from a Depression-weary American. "This is just to tell you that everything is all right now. The man you sent found our house all right, and we went down to the bank with him and the mortgage can go for a while longer. You remember I wrote you about losing the furniture too. Well, your man got it back for us. I never heard of a president like you."

Yet Roosevelt saw his role as far greater that the chief advocate for federal policy. He believed that his job was also to lift the nation's collective spirit, to educate, and to provide vision. As a victim of debilitating polio since the age of thirty-nine, Roosevelt put these ideals into practice, despite enormous pain, by learning how to "walk" with steel braces, supported by aides, so that he might project a strong image to the nation and lead them out of economic turmoil.

## FDR

Franklin Delano Roosevelt, a distant cousin of President Theodore Roosevelt, was a man of great wealth and privilege. His father had been a railroad industry executive and he had grown up in a large estate in New York's Hudson River Valley. A graduate of Harvard, Roosevelt entered politics early. In 1913, he entered the New York legislature, and soon after served as Assistant Secretary of the Navy. In 1920 he was nominated for Vice President. Unlike the Iowa born Herbert Hoover—whose father had been a blacksmith—Roosevelt seemed to have had little in common with Americans who lost their jobs, their homes, and sometimes their hope to the Great Depression.

## The New Deal

Roosevelt also believed it was his duty to act. In his acceptance speech after being nominated as the Democratic party's candidate, Roosevelt declared, " I pledge you, I pledge myself, to a new deal for the American people." Immediately after taking office he began churning out program after "New Deal" program aimed at putting Americans back to work, to stabilize the economy, to increase the money supply. Often these programs were contradictory, and on occasion, even unconstitutional, leaving critics to lambaste him for expanding the scope of the federal government.

**NEW LEADERSHIP** In his first inaugural address in 1933, Franklin Delano Roosevelt promised new government programs as well as a renewed sense of hope, uttering his famous words. "The only thing we have to fear is fear itself" to a Depression-weary nation.

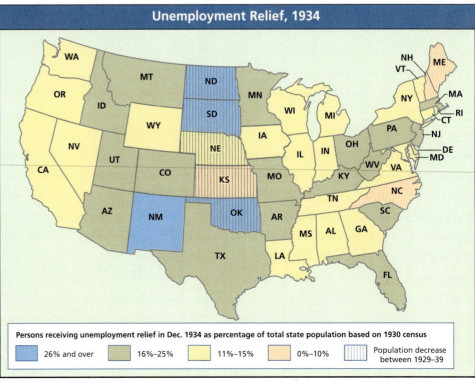

**Unemployment Relief, 1934**

Persons receiving unemployment relief in Dec. 1934 as percentage of total state population based on 1930 census

| | | | | |
|---|---|---|---|---|
| 26% and over | 16%–25% | 11%–15% | 0%–10% | Population decrease between 1929–39 |

**A NATION ON RELIEF** By late 1934, well over 10 percent of the population in most states received some form of unemployment relief from the government.

Even his own allies were alarmed when, in 1937, he tried to pack the Supreme Court with liberal judges. Yet, by and large, the American people loved him.

## One Hundred Days

During the election campaign Roosevelt had promised swift action within the first 100 days of his term. One of his first acts was to declare a national bank "holiday" to halt the public's rush to withdraw money from failing banks. During the bank holiday, which lasted a week, he submitted an Emergency Banking Bill to Congress. The bill gave the president broad powers regarding monetary and foreign exchange transactions, made provisions for the assets of failed banks and imposed strict fines for gold hoarding. The Banking Act (or Glass-Steagell Act) of 1933 followed shortly afterwards, making such enduring changes as the establishment of the Federal Deposit Insurance Corporation (FDIC). On its heels came theFederal Housing Administration (FHA), to insure home-improvement loans for middle-income families.

Also created in 1933 was the Civilian Works Administration (CWA), an unemployment relief program that distributed funds of public works projects. Among the agencies to receive CWA funds was the Civilian Conservation Corps (CCC), which was created at the end of March by the

**Tennessee Valley Authority**

**THE TVA** By harnessing the power of the Tennessee River the Tennessee Valley Authority brought electric power to rural America.

Reforestation Unemployment Act. Through the CCC, single young men lived in work camps and performed tasks such as planting trees, fighting forest fires, and tending to the nation's trails and roads.

To help states and local governments provide relief to their needy, Congress created the Federal Emergency Relief Administration (FERA) with a budget of $500 million.

To address the oversupply of crops on America's farms which was keeping prices for agricultural dangerously low, Roosevelt pushed the Agricultural Adjustment Act (AAA) through Congress. The act restricted the cultivation of certain kinds of crops but provided farmers with cash payments in exchange for their agreement to leave some of their lands fallow.

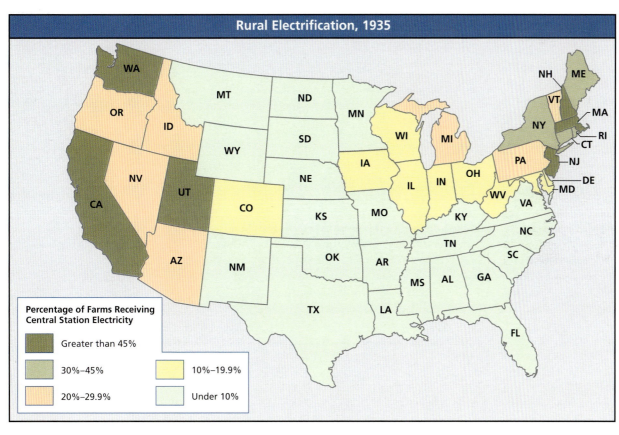

**Rural Electrification, 1935**

**Percentage of Farms Receiving Central Station Electricity**

- Greater than 45%
- 30%–45%
- 20%–29.9%
- 10%–19.9%
- Under 10%

**ELECTRICITY COMES TO THE FARM** Until the New Deal's Rural Electrification Administration brought electrical power to the countryside, very few farms had electricity.

## The Tennessee Valley Authority

One of the most important pieces of emergency legislation Roosevelt signed into law during his first hundred days in office in 1933 was the act creating the Tennessee Valley Authority (TVA). An independent government corporation, the TVA was formed to improve declining natural conditions in the flood-ridden Tennessee River area. Methods to be used included soil conservation programs and development of a system of dams along the Tennessee River.

The original idea for the basin development plan came from Senator George Norris of Nebraska; for years he had wanted to implement it. In honor of his vision the first TVA dam bore his name. Beginning in the 1930s the TVA began constructing a system of dams that created a navigation channel along 650 miles of river ways in Tennessee from Paducah, Kentucky, to Knoxville, Tennessee. By the end of the 1930s the electric power generated from the dams resulted in electrification for nearly 325,000 rural residents in about 100 towns. These rural households, which had never before received regular, low-cost electrical power, used the new power source to increase farm productivity and income many fold. Over the years the increased income resulted in increased federal taxes, which repaid the costs of the initial investment.

Despite these benefits the TVA was, in its early years, denounced by business groups as socialistic. The groups presented their case to the U.S. Supreme Court in the late 1930s, and the Court upheld the constitutionality of the TVA act. Today the TVA continues to operate 50 dams on the Tennessee River and its tributaries, along with more than a dozen power plants (coal-burning steam and nuclear) that generate over 125 billion kilowatt-hours of electricity each year. In addition the TVA has also been central to the preservation of millions of acres of land from erosion.

## The National Industrial Recovery Act

On the day that marked the end of FDR's first hundred days, the National Industrial Recovery Act (NIRA), perhaps the most far-reaching and controversial pieces of New Deal legislation, went into effect. Title II of NIRA created the Federal Emergency Administration of Public Works. Later known as the Public Works Administration (PWA), the agency oversaw the construction of public buildings, roads, subways and bridges.

Another NIRA program, the National Recovery Administration (NRA), was far more controversial. The NRA established a list of fair-business codes, such as the establishment of a minimum wage, maximum work hours, child labor laws, and collective bargaining rights. Businesses that abided by NRA codes were granted national "Blue Eagle" signs by the government. Although the NRA initially served to rally national morale under its motto "We Do Our Part," it drew immediate criticism from both the right and the left for its administrative complexity and for being either too favorable toward business or too lenient toward labor.

**Major Roosevelt-Era Dams**

Grand Coulee Dam 1942
Ft. Peck Dam 1940
Bonneville Dam 1937
Boulder Dam (Hoover Dam) 1936

Dam
1936 Date completed

**DAMMING THE WEST** During the Great Depression a number of large government financed dams were constructed in the West. One of the largest was the Grand Coulee Dam in Washington State, shown above.

# The Second New Deal

In 1935 Roosevelt launched a second phase of the New Deal. In April the Soil Conservation Service (SCS) was founded, and in May the Rural Electrification Administration (REA). In June the Security and Exchange Commission (SEC) was established to regulate the buying and selling of stocks.

That same June day, the Works Progress Administration (WPA), was born. The WPA built streets, highways, and bridges and cleared deteriorated housing. In addition the WPA had a public arts program known as the Federal Theatre, Arts, Music, and Writers Projects. In all 2 million builders, writers and artists were employed by the WPA.

**LABOR CONFRONTATION** Armed guards stand ready outside of Republic Steel in 1937.

| Government Spending and Employment, 1920–1940 | | |
|---|---|---|
| Year | Total Civilian Employees | Federal Spending |
| 1920 | 655,265 | $6.36 billion |
| 1921 | 561,142 | $5.06 billion |
| 1922 | 543,507 | $3.29 billion |
| 1923 | 536,900 | $3.14 billion |
| 1924 | 543,484 | $2.91 billion |
| 1925 | 553,045 | $2.92 billion |
| 1926 | 548,713 | $2.93 billion |
| 1927 | 547,127 | $2.86 billion |
| 1928 | 560,773 | $2.96 billion |
| 1929 | 579.559 | $3.12 billion |
| 1930 | 601,319 | $3.32 billion |
| 1931 | 609,746 | $3.58 billion |
| 1932 | 605,496 | $4.66 billion |
| 1933 | 603,587 | $4.60 billion |
| 1934 | 698,649 | $6.64 billion |
| 1935 | 780,582 | $6.50 billion |
| 1936 | 867,432 | $8.42 billion |
| 1937 | 885,993 | $7.73 billion |
| 1938 | 882,226 | $6.76 billion |
| 1939 | 953,891 | $8.84 billion |
| 1940 | 1,042,420 | $9.01 billion |

Among the many projects paid for and operated by agencies like the PWA, CWA, and WPA were a series of major dam construction projects in the West—not along one connected river system as in the Tennessee Valley, but along many. Examples include the Hoover Dam (known in the 1930s as the Boulder Dam), on the Arizona-Nevada Border; the Fort Peck Dam in Montana, and the Grand Coulee Dam on the Columbia River in Washington State. To promote the Grand Coulee Dam, the federal government even hired a then-little known folksinger named Woody Guthrie to compose songs celebrating the massive construction project. His famous anthem, "Roll On, Columbia" is one such song.

### The Wagner Act and Labor Troubles

In May 1935, the short life of the controversial NRA came to an end. That month the U.S. Supreme Court ruled in *Schechter Poultry Corp. v. United States* that the NRA's code system was unconstitutional since it conferred legislative powers to the executive branch.

With the demise of the NRA all worker protections under its code—minimum wages and hours, child labor restrictions, and the right to collective bargaining—were suddenly invalid. Yet in July Senator Robert F. Wagner of New York sponsored the National Labor Relations Act, or Wagner Act, to regain some of those lost rights.

Roosevelt was wary of giving too much power to unions, but agreed to sign the act into law. The new law created the National Labor Relations Board to help settle disputes. Employers were banned from preventing workers from joining unions or discriminating against union members. The right to collective bargaining was restored as well.

The Wagner Act set off the greatest wave of union organizing in American history. Since its founding the American Federation of Labor (AFL), the nation's largest union, had focused on skilled craftsmen such as carpenters and locomotive engineers. To serve unskilled industrial workers John Lewis, head of the United Mine Workers, decided to form the Congress of Industrial Organizations (CIO).

On December 31, 1936, the CIO began a campaign against General Motors. Instead of striking, which would have allowed strikebreakers to take their jobs, the GM workers sat down in the factories. After 45 days the "sit-down" strikes forced GM to bargain with the United Auto Workers (UAW), a new union affiliated with the CIO.

Next the CIO moved on the steel industry. In 1937 U.S. Steel, the country's largest steel maker, agreed to recognize the Steel Workers Organizing Committee. Other steel companies refused to acknowledge the union. When striking workers held a Memorial Day picnic and rally outside the gates of Republic Steel in Cleveland, violence erupted. Rocks were thrown and police opened fire, killing ten strikers. All 10 were shot in the back. It took four more years before the companies known as "little steel" accepted the union.

### Social Security

On August 14, 1935, Roosevelt resigned the Social Security Act. Republican members of Congress were outraged, arguing that the act would undermine industriousness and the "romance" of life. As originally established, Social Security payments were to be made to workers age 65 and older and were funded by taxing employers and employees; the monthly payments were scaled to one's earnings.

The Social Security Act also established state-sponsored unemployment compensation which, on its inception, ran for a limited number of weeks and was funded by a tax on employees.

In establishing Social Security Roosevelt was reacting to the efforts of Dr. Francis Townsend, a California physician and leading spokesperson for an old-age pension movement. In 1933 Townsend organized Old-Age Revolving Pensions, Inc. to create a program that became popularly known as the Townsend Plan. It called for a pension of $200 a month to be given to any person aged 60 or older if the pensioner was unemployed and spent the entire sum within 30 days of receiving it. The plan, which was to be financed by a 2% federal sales tax, was designed both to provide for the elderly and to stimulate the nation's economy.

Townsend's plan was almost universally criticized by economists, but it was wildly popular with the public. Townsend clubs formed across the country, and the movement's magazine, The Townsend National Weekly, had a circulation of more than 200,000 copies. At the height of its popularity, Old Age Pensions, Inc. had about 2.5 million members and about 10 times that many supporters. However, Congress defeated all bills that proposed the adoption of the plan, and after the Social Security Act's passage, the movement's strength began to fade.

**A PLOT AGAINST FDR?** In 1934, Major General Smedley D. Butler testified in Congress that a group of anti–Roosevelt industrialists had approached him about leading a coup against Franklin Roosevelt.

## Roosevelt's Critics

While Roosevelt won reelection easily in 1936, he faced mounting criticism from both the right and left while in office. Even by the standards of the politically fractious early 21st century the societal divisions of the 1930s, fostered by the Depression, were severe. Many Americans of good will found themselves flirting with extremist movements, from German and Italian fascism on the right to Soviet-style Communism on the left. "It is Communism which desires to save civilization," said a University of Chicago professor in the early 1930s. Communism and socialism seemed the answer for many during the Depression, particularly in the labor movement. In 1932, for instance, Earl Browder of Kansas, candidate of the American Communist Party won over 100,000 votes. Norman Thomas, the nominee of the Socialist Party in every election from 1932 through 1944 and beyond did even better, winning almost 900,000 in 1932. Thomas was supported by the editors of the *Nation* and *New Republic* magazines, as well as theologian Reinhold Niebuhr and poet Stephen Vincent Benet.

The writer Upton Sinclair, who had helped launch the Progressive movement with his meat-packing industry book, *The Jungle*, was also a Socialist, but left the party to form a radical anti-poverty program in California called EPIC (End Poverty in California) within the Democratic Party. Sinclair advocated higher taxes on corporations and the wealthy and the establishment of state-run factories and villages. Enough voters were attracted to the program for Sinclair to win the Democratic nomination for governor of California, though a smear campaign from frightened businesses in the state and lukewarm support from New Deal Democrats cost him the election.

While Sinclair was not an experienced political figure, Senator Huey Long of Louisiana was. A former governor as well, Long was one of the political scene's most

**HUEY LONG** Huey Long, a colorful and thoroughly corrupt Louisiana senator and former governor, proposed a guaranteed minimum income for all Americans. He was shot to death in 1935.

colorful, controversial, and corrupt figures. Playing off the desperation of the down-trodden, Long won a national following with his plans to redistribute wealth and make "Every Man A King." Originally a New Deal supporter, the "Kingfish" as he was known, broke with Roosevelt in 1933, declaring FDR's programs to be bound to bureaucracy and "wealthy plutocrats." Positioning himself as the voice of the common man, he launched a Share-the-Wealth program in 1934, a confiscatory tax program on the rich that would guarantee each American an annual income of $2,500. The ardent, demagogic speaker had a wide following before he was gunned down in Washington by a political opponent's relative in 1935.

On the other side of the political spectrum was the demogoguery of the radio priest, Charles Coughlin. Every Sunday night Coughlin broadcast anti-communist, anti-Roosevelt and anti-semitic tirades over the air. Originally an FDR supporter, he became a celebrity by the middle of the decade by appealing to the worst instincts of the downtrodden public, blaming "Soviet controlled" labor unions, and the "Jew Deal." After he advocated stopping Roosevelt with "the use of bullets," the hierarchy of the Catholic Church ordered him to cease his activities.

Many big business owners were also strongly opposed to Roosevelt's programs. In 1934 members of the DuPont family and other industrialists joined with anti-Roosevelt politicians to found the American Liberty League. The League was a successor to another group, the Association Against the Prohibition Amendment, a lobbying organization that had worked to end Prohibition. Although the AAPA had closed down after Prohibition ended, the Liberty League, using the same offices and employing the same staff, was founded in its wake. For the next six years the League attacked the New Deal and compared Roosevelt to both Hitler and Stalin.

In a little known footnote to history, the Liberty League may have even attempted to overthrow Roosevelt. In 1934 Congress investigated charges made by a Marine general named Smedley D. Butler that a Wall Street bond trader named Gerald MacGuire, representing Grayson Murphy (a wealthy broker who was also the treasurer of the Liberty League), had approached him about leading an army of 500,000 veterans on Washington DC, where they would "protect" Roosevelt from other plotters and install a "secretary of general welfare" to assume the responsibility of running the government in the president's stead. According to Butler's testimony, he quickly realized that the real goal of this effort was a coup to take Roosevelt captive and force the reinstatement of the gold standard, which FDR had recently abandoned. Although Butler also told the committee that Maguire revealed to him that well known figures such as former New York governor and presidential candidate Al Smith, General Hugh Johnson, the head of Roosevelt's NRA, and General Douglas Macarthur all had knowledge of the plot, Butler had no evidence beyond what he said Maguire had told him. The committee investigating agreed with Butler that evidence did exist of a plot against Roosevelt, but after MacGuire's sudden death (apparently from natural causes) a month before the report was released, the Committee took no action to investigate further.

### FDR and the Supreme Court

Although Roosevelt was easily reelected in 1936, and his Democratic party maintained control of both houses of Congress in that election, the president's New Deal agenda faced powerful opponents both outside of the government and within. The greatest threat to FDR's agenda came from the U.S. Supreme Court, which had already ruled the NRA unconstitutional in 1935, and was threatening to do the same with other programs.

In 1937 FDR took steps to solidify power. He announced that for every Supreme Court justice who failed to retire at 70, the president could appoint a new justice—up to a total of six. While the Constitution does not set the number of Supreme Court justices, tradition had put the number at nine. If Roosevelt were able to add six more to the court, he would have assured that all of his New Deal programs would be safe.

Although Roosevelt tried to convince Congress and the public that his plan was merely meant to help justices with their heavy workloads, almost everyone recognized that argument for the sham that it was—what Roosevelt really wanted was a Supreme Court that would bend to his will. Even his then-vice president, John Nance Garner, came out against the plan. Garner, who was 79 years old himself, was insulted by the suggestion that people over 70 needed extra help doing their jobs.

Roosevelt's effort to "pack" the Court was a crucial mistake that played into the hands of the paranoid few who claimed that he had dictatorial aspirations. Although the public still loved him after the episode ended, he would have greater difficulty in pushing his programs through Congress.

Growing divisions in his administration and within the Democratic party were at the core of his problems. In 1935 and 1936 the nation underwent slow but steady economic growth that led some to believe that the worst of the Depression was over. However, in 1937 and 1938 the United States tumbled back into a recession. The collapse in the first months after September 1937 was actually steeper than it had been in the first nine months of the Depression. The administration was divided on how to respond. Henry Morganthau, the Secretary of the Treasury, favored efforts to bring the budget closer to balance, while Harry Hopkins, then head of the WPA, favored an increase in spending. While FDR was initially in favor of the more conservative approach, he reluctantly approved increased spending.

Roosevelt's increased spending helped exacerbate a rift between liberal northern Democrats and the party's more conservative southerners. The southerners were already upset with the administration over the Farm Security Aministration's efforts to assist sharecroppers—many of whom were African-Americans. Southerners also had opposed the Fair Labor Standards Act, which passed in 1938 over their objections. In the 1938 Congressional elections Roosevelt interjected himself into local Democratic state campaigns in hope of seeing conservatives replaced by more liberal opponents. His effort backfired, and after election day Roosevelt suffered huge setbacks—losing seven Senate seats to Republicans and 80 House seats. The defeat marked the end of the most active period of New Deal legislation. In his January 1939 State of the Union, FDR spoke of preserving his reforms rather than creating new programs. What's more, the nation's attention had begun to turn to Europe where Germany had launched a series of invasions upon its neighbors.

# The New Deal's Legacy

Ever since the New Deal, critics of the expansion of the government's role in every day life have been legion. Herbert Hoover, for instance, condemned what he saw as "the growth of executive power and the reduction of the legislative arm." Hoover went on to argue that "[a]s a result of eight years of the New Deal, there was not more but less liberty in America. And . . . we had not ended the Great Depression."

Although many would argue with Hoover's hyperbole, few would disagree with his ultimate point that despite the years of experimentation, the New Deal failed to end the Great Depression. Indeed, critics on the left of the spectrum would rightly point out that race-based benefit restrictions would deny many African Americans, Hispanic Americans, and other poor minorities the benefits received by Caucasian males.

### A Legacy of Activist Government

Nor can anyone argue that Roosevelt had not dramatically increased the size and scope of the federal government in an unprecedented way. Prior to his election in 1932 the center of power in the United States rested in New York, on Wall Street. Afterwards it rested in Washington. Where corporations had held sway at the center of American power in the 1920s and before, Washington politicians and intellectuals were the power during the 1930s. To a great extent, they would remain so until the start of the 21st century.

The New Deal will always be seen through the prism of the individual's political philosophy. The list of New Deal legacies is long—federal insured bank deposits, child labor laws, deficit spending during a recession, Social Security, unemployment insurance, the right of workers to unionize, federal conservation of the environment, aid to farmers, and on and on, and each of these individual program has carried with it benefits or weaknesses, depending on who is making the judgement.

While Republican administrations that followed Roosevelt would generally work to narrow the scope of the federal government and Democratic administrations would not, the expansion of presidential power begun under Roosevelt has crossed party lines. Liberal Democratic and conservative Republicans alike have benefited from the precedent set by Roosevelt, and even those who have professed their desire for limited government have pressed to expand the power of their own offices.

Beyond specific programs and policies, Franklin Roosevelt's greatest legacy to the nation may be that, critics aside, he restored hope to millions of ordinary Americans, hope in the American system of government and its leaders, but more important, hope in themselves and in the strength of the nation. The nation's most successful presidents since Roosevelt, regardless of party, have been those who have been able to use their office to raise the spirits of the citizenry, to offer hope that the future will be brighter than the past. In 1939, as clouds of war darkened the horizons, Roosevelt's continuing ability to offer that hope would be thoroughly tested.

# Chapter 27: World War II

n the early 1930s it looked like democracy was in worldwide retreat. In 1922 fascist leader Benito Mussolini had become Prime Minister of Italy. In 1931 Japanese forces had invaded the Chinese region of Manchuria, and in 1933 Adolf Hitler, the head of Germany's fascist, antisemitic National Socialist (Nazi) Party, had become dictator of Germany. Meanwhile Josef Stalin, a brutal Russian leader, had taken control over the communist Soviet Union.

Shortly after taking power the Nazis pushed legislation known as the Enabling Act through the Reichstag, or parliament. The act gave Hitler total control of the government. Swiftly consolidating his power Hitler dissolved all opposition parties and placed all major businesses, labor unions, publishing houses, and artistic and professional organizations under Nazi control. Opponents were jailed. Hitler's special police, the

Gestapo, then destroyed the anti-Nazi leadership of the German military.

During his first years in power, Hitler was popular with Germans, as the economy had improved from its dire condition following World War I, and because he moved to open government jobs to the lower classes. Meanwhile, Nazi's brutally attacked all those they considered enemies of the state, including Communists, gypsies, gays, and especially Jews. In 1935 the so-called Nuremberg laws stripped Jews of all legal citizenship rights. Three years later the Gestapo burned down the Reichstag building and blamed it on Jews. Hitler then ordered a night of sweeping attacks on all Jewish businesses, homes, and synagogues. The night is remembered as *Kristallnacht*, or "night of broken glass," in German because of the destruction of shops windows in Jewish-owned businesses.

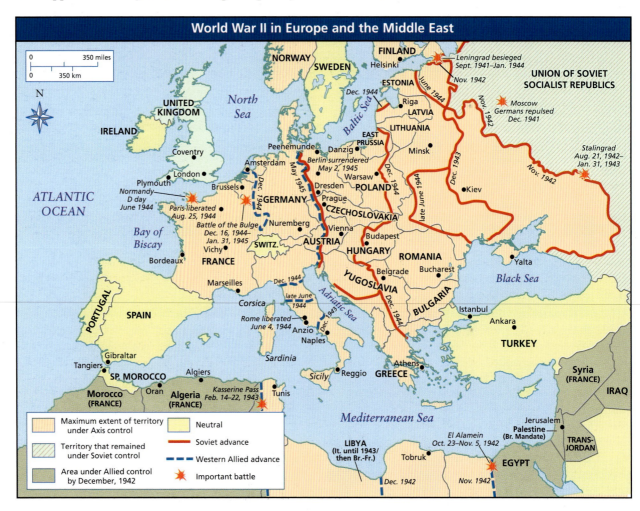

**WORLD WAR II** As 1943 opened, the Axis powers controlled territory stretching from France to Russia, and from Scandanavia to Libya. Yet 1943 marked a turning point, as Italy's fascist government fell and the Soviets repulsed the Nazi advance. Within a year of the Allied invasion of Normandy in June 1944, Germany surrendered.

# Aggression and Appeasement

In 1936 the German army moved into the Rhineland, a border region between France and Germany that was supposed to have no soldiers. The same year fascists in Spain rose up against Spain's republican government. In 1937 Japan invaded the rest of China and Germany captured neighboring Austria without firing a shot.

As German and Japanese forces moved on their neighbors, France, Great Britain and the United States did nothing. None of the former World War I allies came to the aid of the democratic government of Spain, although individuals from each of these countries joined in the fight. A group of Americans who called themselves the Abraham Lincoln Brigade fought the fascists in Spain for three years.

In 1938 Hitler demanded that France and Britain permit him to annex the Sudetenland, a German-speaking part of Czechoslovakia. The French and British prime ministers flew to Germany to meet with Hitler. Czechs were not invited. After agreeing to give Hitler what he demanded, British Prime Minister Neville Chamberlain returned to London and proudly proclaimed that he had obtained. "Peace with honor . . . peace for our time."

Chamberlain's appeasement policy was a direct result of World War I. After suffering enormous losses in that war the British and French desperately wanted to avoid another war. Chamberlain was therefore willing to gamble that with the Sudetenland in his grasp, Hitler would be satisfied. Chamberlain was wrong. In March 1939 the Nazis took the remainder of Czechoslovakia. Still, France and Britain did nothing.

To Germany's east, Soviet premier Josef Stalin, reacting to his fear that the German's would move on his nation next, signed a non-aggression treaty with Hitler. Publicly, the arrangement meant that the two nations would not attack each other. Privately, it also spelled out the terms by which the Germans and Soviets would partition Poland.

With the Soviet Union agreeing not to retaliate, the Nazis were free to invade Poland, which they did in March 1939. In doing so they used a kind of warfare never before seen—*blitzkrieg*, or "lightning war." Two days later France and Britain finally declared war on Germany. World War II had begun.

In the spring of 1940 Hitler turned his sights on Norway, Denmark, Belgium, Holland, and finally France, capturing all of these nations. By June, Great Britain was the only nation in Europe not dominated by foreign forces. That month was the start of a long German bombing campaign, known as the Battle of Britain. For months Nazi bombers attacked London from across the English Channel. London children were evacuated to the relative safety of the countryside. Prime minister Winston Churchill, who had replaced Chamberlain, worked to rally the British people to remain strong in the face of the constant assaults. Churchill felt certain that the bombings were the preliminary stage to a large scale German invasion of Great Britain. Despite the constant bombing the German airforce failed to knock out British air defenses. The German invasion of the British isles never came.

In actuality Hitler had more interest in Russia than in England. In his book *Mein Kampf*, he wrote of giving the German people *Lebensraum* or "living room" by conquering the Slavic peoples of Eastern Europe and Russia, whom he considered inferior. In June 1941 Hitler broke his treaty with Stalin and launched an all-out attack on the Russian front. The German invasion would fail, but millions of Russians would die before 1945.

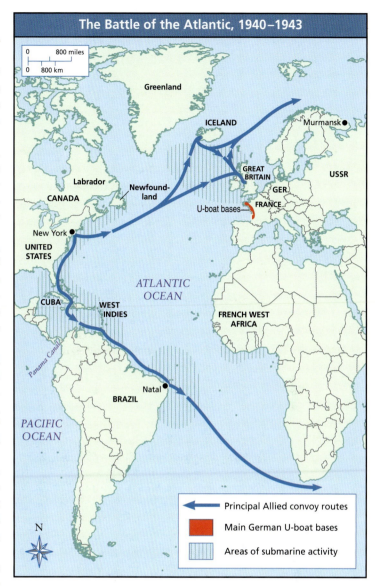

**The Battle of the Atlantic, 1940–1943**

**SUPPLYING THE BRITISH** Before entering the war the United States worked to keep arms flowing to Britain. To do so, American supply ships had to avoid detection by Nazi submarines.

## American Isolationism

Well before the German invasion of Poland in 1938 the American responses to the darkening global scene varied. Many Americans thought that the United States, crippled by the Great Depression at home, should stay out of international affairs.

The isolationist sentiment got a boost in 1934 and 1935 when Senator Gerald Nye and others promoted the so-called "Merchants of Death" idea, suggesting that the nation had only been drawn into World War I to protect the profits of arms manufacturers. In keeping with this sentiment, Congress passed a series of "neutrality laws" outlawing U.S. shipments of arms or financial help to nations at war. A 1935 neutrality law also warned that Americans traveling overseas on ships from warring nations did so at their own risk. In 1936 Congress banned loans to warring nations, adding a stipulation the following year that if a country wanted to buy weapons from the United States, it would have to pay cash and pick the weapons up in its own ships.

In 1939, after Hitler occupied Czechoslovakia and then invaded Poland and the Soviet Union, Congress partially repealed the neutrality laws, permitting belligerent nations to buy war materials from the U.S. if they paid in cash and transported the arms in their own ships, rather than aboard U.S. ships.

Even then most Americans still opposed intervention. Many joined America First, a noninterventionist group whose members included famed pilot Charles Lindbergh. In 1940 Lindbergh expressed the group's sentiment this way: "We are in danger of war today not because Europeans have attempted to interfere with the internal affairs of America but because we American people have attempted to interfere in the internal affairs of Europe . . ."

Others believed that the United States could keep out of the war by beefing up its own defenses. FDR set up committees to prepare the nation for war, or at least to aid the Allies. The Committee to Defend America by Aiding the Allies, for instance, promoted open assistance to Britain, France and other Allies.

A Gallup poll in late 1939 found that 62 percent of Americans favored sending aid to the Allies, although only 29 percent favored sending troops to join the fighting, and even those did so only if it appeared Hitler was "winning."

Roosevelt pursued a middle course—promoting U.S. rearmament and aid to the Allies. In 1940 he brought two Republicans into his Cabinet in an effort to win bipartisan support for his policies. He also agreed to trade 50 World War I-era destroyers to the British in exchange for the use of British bases in the Atlantic. FDR also announced a massive U.S. arms build-up as well as the end to oil and scrap metal exports to Japan. And while he promised during his unprecedented successful campaign for a third presidential term in 1940 that "your boys are not going to be sent into any foreign wars," by October Congress had authorized the first peacetime military draft in U.S. history. Then, on December 29, 1940, Roosevelt addressed the American people by radio, arguing for aid to Great Britain—which was then fighting almost alone against Nazi Germany. America must, said Roosevelt, become "the great arsenal of democracy."

In March 1941 FDR convinced Congress to pass the Lend-Lease Act. The new law gave him the power to "lend, lease, or otherwise dispose of" arms to any country whose defense was important to the interests of the United States. Initially used to assist Great Britain, the Lend-Lease Act also was used to send military supplies to the Soviet Union after its invasion.

To sway the public to support the Lend-Lease program, Roosevelt used the following analogy: "If my neighbor's house is on fire, I don't say to him . . . "Neighbor, my garden hose costs $15; you have to pay me $15 for it. I don't want $15—I want my garden hose back after the fire is over."

Over the next five years America's industry and labor force turned the president's words into reality. Economic mobilization was so successful that by the war's end the output of the nation's factories, mills, plants, and shipyards not only met the needs of the massive U.S. war effort, it also supplied 60 percent of all Allied munitions. In fact, in 1945, U.S. industry accounted for 40 percent of all war materials produced worldwide.

# America Enters the War

By mid-1941 relations between the United States and Japan were reaching a crisis point. Japan's militaristic government, headed by Prime Minister Tojo Hideki, resented American opposition to Japan's war with China. When the United States cut off exports of oil and metal to Japan, hard-liners in the Japanese military demanded action. Throughout the last months of 1941 both nations sought a diplomatic solution to the standoff, but the Japanese government also approved a daring naval operation masterminded by Admiral Yamamoto Isoroku—a surprise attack by carrier-borne warplanes on the U.S. Pacific Fleet base at Pearl Harbor, Oahu, Hawaii. Although U.S. military intelligence suspected the Japanese planned to attack somewhere in the Pacific, warnings arrived too late. When the first wave of Japanese aircraft arrived over Pearl Harbor after dawn on Sunday, December 7, they achieved complete surprise. The devastating two-hour raid left more than 2,400 Americans dead, almost 200 aircraft destroyed, and 18 warships sunk or heavily damaged. Americans responded to the news with shock and anger, instantly ending the long debate between those who wanted to stay out of the war and those who urged intervention. On December 8 a grim President Roosevelt addressed Congress. Calling December 7, 1941, "a date which will live in infamy," he called on Congress to declare war on Japan, which it did within the hour. By then Japanese forces were attacking other United States and European possessions in the Pacific, from Hong Kong to the Philippines. On December 11 Germany and Italy honored their pact with Japan and declared war on the United States, drawing the nation into the wider conflict.

When the United States went to war, it faced enemies on two fronts. The Japanese attack on Peal Harbor was merely part of a much larger Japanese assault on American and European controlled territory in the Pacific. Within weeks of Pearl Harbor, the Japanese had invaded American island territories in Guam and Wake Island, as well as British territory in Hong Kong, Burma and the Malaysian peninsula.

In the Philippines, an American colony since 1898, Japanese forces captured nearly 10,000 American troops, as well as another 50,000 Filipino soldiers serving in the U.S. Army. The captured soldiers were marched through the swampy Bataan Peninsula to a prison camp. En route, thousands of Filipinos and Americans died of starvation, disease and heatstroke. The survivors called the episode the Bataan Death March.

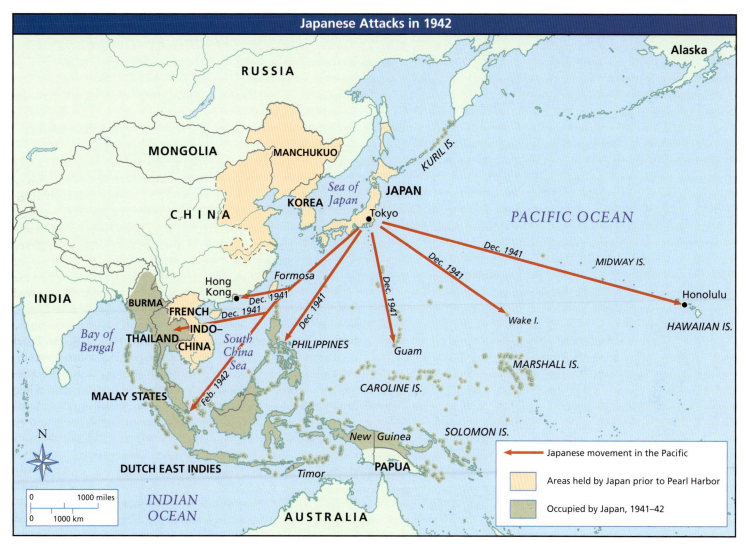

**Japanese Attacks in 1942**

RUSSIA
Alaska
MONGOLIA
MANCHUKUO
Sea of Japan
JAPAN
KOREA
Tokyo
CHINA
KURIL IS.
PACIFIC OCEAN
Dec. 1941
MIDWAY IS.
Formosa
Hong Kong
Dec. 1941
Dec. 1941
Honolulu
INDIA
BURMA
FRENCH
Dec. 1941
Dec. 1941
Wake I.
HAWAIIAN IS.
INDO–
Bay of Bengal
THAILAND
CHINA
South China Sea
PHILIPPINES
Guam
MARSHALL IS.
MALAY STATES
Feb. 1942
CAROLINE IS.
N
SOLOMON IS.
New Guinea
DUTCH EAST INDIES
Timor
PAPUA
0   1000 miles
0   1000 km
INDIAN OCEAN
AUSTRALIA

Japanese movement in the Pacific
Areas held by Japan prior to Pearl Harbor
Occupied by Japan, 1941–42

**JAPAN TAKES THE PACIFIC** On the same day that Japan launched its surprise attack on Pearl Harbor, Hawaii, it also attacked Guam, the Philippines, and Wake Island. Within two months Japan controlled much of the western Pacific.

## The Manhattan Project

Despite the Japanese advances, U.S. military leaders were more concerned about the Nazis in Europe. In 1942 Russian soldiers were dying in huge numbers. If the Soviet Union collapsed, FDR feared, the struggle against Hitler would be far more difficult.

Even more alarming, reports had surfaced of a deadly new weapon under development by the Nazis. In 1939 a group of scientists, including some German Jews who had escaped Nazi Germany, met with Roosevelt to discuss the possibility of building a weapon based on the energy of atomic fission. In response, even before the United States formally entered the war, FDR had created the Office of Scientific Research and Development to study atomic fission.

By the Spring of 1942 scientists at the University of Chicago produced the world's first atomic chain reaction. In June they told Roosevelt that an atomic weapon was therefore possible, although it would take enormous sums of money and manpower to create one. Roosevelt agreed to create such a bomb. The project, called the Manhattan Project, would become the most expensive, most important, and most highly classified secret in American history.

## Japanese-American Internment

The surprise Japanese attack on Pearl Harbor shocked the United States and led to a wave of reaction against Japanese Americans. In spring 1942 the Roosevelt Administration issued an executive order forceably relocating all Japanese-Americans on the West Coast from their homes to inland internment camps. The confinement—organized and operated by a newly authorized government agency called the War Relocation Authority (WRA)—lasted for nearly three years, during which time over 110,000 Japanese (many of whom were American-born U.S. citizens) were moved. When the executive order was challenged in three court cases in 1943 and 1944, the Supreme Court issued narrowly-reasoned decisions without explicitly ruling on the constitutionality of internment. More than 40 years later the government publicly acknowledged that Japanese Americans had been victimized and granted each survivor a payment of $20,000.

## The Tide Turns

For Roosevelt, the possibility of an atomic bomb was welcome news. The war in Europe and North Africa was not going well. Nazi forces had reached the suburbs of Leningrad (present-day St. Petersburg) and Moscow, the two largest cities in the Soviet Union.

## Japanese-American Internment

0 ——— 300 miles
0 ——— 300 km

- Puyallup **WA**
- Portland **OR**
- Kooskia
- Fort Missoula
- **ND**
- Fort Lincoln
- **MN**
- **MT**
- **ID**
- Minidoka
- Heart Mountain
- **SD**
- **WY**
- **WI**
- Tule Lake **CA**
- Marysville
- Sacramento
- Stockton **NV**
- Tanforan
- Turlock
- Merced
- Salinas
- Pinedale
- **UT**
- Topaz
- **CO**
- Grenada
- **KS**
- **IA**
- **NE**
- **IL**
- **MO**
- Fresno
- Tukare
- Santa Anita
- Manzanar
- **AZ**
- Meyer
- Pomona
- Poston
- **NM**
- Santa Fe
- **OK**
- **AR**
- Rohwer
- Gila River
- Fort Stanton
- Jerome
- **MS**
- **TX**
- **LA**
- *PACIFIC OCEAN*
- Crystal City
- Kenedy
- *Gulf of Mexico*

**Legend**
- Military district
- ○ Assembly points
- ▲ WRA* internment camps
- ☐ Justice Department internment camps
- * War Relocation Authority

**JAPANESE–AMERICAN INTERNMENT** The United States imprisoned over 110,000 Japanese-Americans, many born in the United States, during World War II.

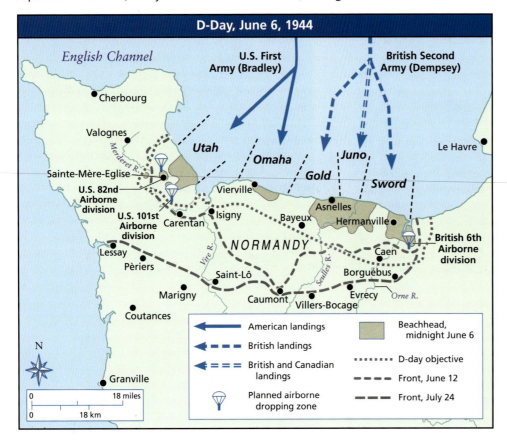

## D-Day, June 6, 1944

*English Channel*

- **U.S. First Army (Bradley)**
- **British Second Army (Dempsey)**
- Cherbourg
- Valognes
- *Merderet R.*
- Sainte-Mère-Eglise
- **U.S. 82nd Airborne division**
- **U.S. 101st Airborne division**
- Carentan
- Lessay
- Pèriers
- Isigny
- *Utah*
- *Omaha*
- Vierville
- *Gold*
- Bayeux
- Asnelles
- *Juno*
- *Sword*
- Hermanville
- Le Havre
- **British 6th Airborne division**
- Caen
- *NORMANDY*
- *Vire R.*
- *Seulles R.*
- Borguébus
- Saint-Lô
- Marigny
- Caumont
- Villers-Bocage
- Evrecy
- *Orne R.*
- Coutances
- Granville

**Legend**
- American landings
- British landings
- British and Canadian landings
- Planned airborne dropping zone
- Beachhead, midnight June 6
- ·········· D-day objective
- – – – Front, June 12
- — — Front, July 24

0 ——— 18 miles
0 ——— 18 km

The Germans were also moving swiftly toward the Soviet Union's Caucasus region, home to huge oilfields that could supply the Nazi war machine for years if captured. What's more, the Nazis had nearly captured Egypt and taken control of the critical Suez Canal. By controlling the Suez the Nazis would be able to stop Allied supplies from reaching the Russian front.

Two great battles turned the tide of the war. In the fall of 1942 British and American forces defeated Germany's brilliant Field Marshall Erwin Rommel at El Alamein, Egypt. By winning the largest tank battle in history, the Allies saved the Suez Canal.

Even more dramatic was the momentous Battle of Stalingrad, which lasted from the fall of 1942 until the following spring.

For six months millions of German and Russian soldiers battled for control of the gateway to the Caucasus—fighting from street to street and from house to house. When the battle was over 300,000 Germans were dead, and hundreds of thousands were taken prisoner. Today Stalingrad remains the single largest battle in human history.

With the Russian victory at Stalingrad, far more Russians had died in fighting the Nazis than had Americans or British. As a result, Stalin pushed to convince FDR and Churchill to attack Germany from the west. Churchill however was unconvinced and argued that the Allies were better off attacking Germany via the southern route through Italy. To ease Stalin's worries, Roosevelt, Churchill and the Russian leader met in 1943 at Casablanca, Morocco. Churchill and Roosevelt agreed that they would not sign separate treaties with Germany, leaving Russia to be the only country to oppose Hitler. Instead, both the United States and Britain would fight to the end—until Germany's unconditional surrender. They also began daily bombings of German munitions factories.

In early 1943, American and British forces invaded Sicily and then Italy. By July the fascist government of Benito Mussolini had fallen. However, the German army quickly moved into Italy, and it would take the Allies another year before they were able to capture the Italian capital of Rome. Meanwhile, Russian forces were pushing

**D-DAY** On June 6, 1944, the Allies launched the largest naval invasion in history. The offensive would help put an end to the war.

the Germans west—back into the Ukraine, and then back into Poland.

## D-Day

Finally, in June 1944, British and American strategists decided they were ready to open the second front. On June 6, known as D-Day, the largest naval invasion force in history landed on the beaches of Normandy, France. By the end of the summer the Allies had retaken Paris. By December 1944 it appeared the war was near its end.

That month, in a counterattack through Belgium known as the Battle of the Bulge, the Nazis pushed the Allies back along a wide front in Western Europe, creating a giant bulge in the Allied front lines. Hitler hoped that the battle would win his scientists enough time to finish their work on the atom bomb, which could then be launched via a V2 rocket, capable of reaching England from behind German lines. After ten days of heavy fighting the Allies pushed the Germans back.

By early 1945 the Americans and British had crossed the Rhine River and entered Germany from the west. Meanwhile, the Russians crossed Poland and invaded Germany from the east. On April 30 Hitler committed suicide in his bunker beneath the ruins of Berlin, his capital city. On May 8 the new German government surrendered unconditionally to the Allies. The war in Europe was over.

## The Holocaust

As Allied troops marched into Germany and Poland they made a horrifying discovery. The Nazis had not only imprisoned millions of Europe's Jews, but they had also attempted to exterminate them. At Dachau, Auschwitz, Buchenwald and dozens of other sites, Allied soldiers discovered Nazi concentration camps where Jews were murdered by the millions, their remains burned in ovens. The Nazis called it the "final solution" to the so-called "Jewish problem."

Historians have since discovered that Roosevelt and other Allied leaders were aware of the concentration camps throughout most of the war, but chose not to try to stop the murders by bombing the camps. Defenders of the Allied strategy have argued however that bombing the camps would not have worked. Hitler was obsessed with destroying the Jews at any cost—even if that goal interfered with military strategy. For instance, even when the German army was desperate for supplies, Hitler refused to allow the trains used to transport Jews to camps for moving military equipment instead. According to

**HOLOCAUST** The Nazis used slave labor and extermination camps to murder millions of Jews, as well as gypsies, homosexuals, and other supposed "undesirables."

### The Holocaust in Europe

**Jews Killed In Europe, 1941–45**

| Country | 1941 Jewish Population | Estimated Number of Jews Killed by 1945 |
|---|---|---|
| Austria | 70,000 | 60,000 |
| Belgium | 85,000 | 28,000 |
| Bulgaria | 48,000 | 40,000 |
| Czechoslovakia | 81,000 | 60,000 |
| Denmark | 6,000 | 100 |
| France | 300,000 | 65,000 |
| Germany | 250,000 | 180,000 |
| Greece | 67,000 | 60,000 |
| Hungary | 710,000 | 200,000 |
| Italy | 120,000 | 9,000 |
| Netherlands | 140,000 | 104,000 |
| Poland | 3,000,000 | 2,600,000 |
| Romania | 1,000,000 | 750,000 |
| Soviet Union | 2,740,000 | 924,000 |
| Yugoslavia | 70,000 | 58,000 |

Legend:
— German border, 1939
← Movement of Einsatzgruppen (Special-Action Groups)
▪ Extermination camp
▼ Concentration camp

Winston Churchill, Great Britain's prime minister, defeating the Nazis as rapidly as possible was the quickest way to end the Holocaust. Even so, it is also known that Allied governments refused to accept Jewish refugees in large numbers, even when it was still possible to get them out of Europe.

Nazi leaders would be put on trial following the war for "crimes against humanity." The Nuremberg trials would end up sending many German leaders to prison and lead to the execution of a few. Israel, created in the wake of the Holocaust, eventually chased down many of the Nazis who had escaped. Adolf Eichmann, the man responsible for running the concentration camp system, became the only man in Israeli history to be put to death.

## War in the Pacific

As it had in Europe and North Africa, the tide of war in the Pacific turned in 1942 and 1943. In May 1942 American forces halted the Japanese advance at the Battle of the Coral Sea, preventing an invasion of Australia. In June, Japan was defeated again as the American and Japanese navies fought the greatest sea battle in history off the Island of Midway. Using aircraft from carriers, it was the first time a sea battle was fought without the ships of the two forces ever firing directly on one another.

In the aftermath of Midway came a series of island invasions at Guadalcanal and Tarawa. On each of these islands, U.S. Marines and other forces fought bloody battles to capture tiny strips of land. At Peleliu an American victory that was expected within days took months as Japanese forces had dug themselves into caves for shelter against attack. When the Japanese refused to surrender American forces used flame-throwers to burn the enemy to death, and then sealed then into the caves. Of the 14,000 Japanese defenders of Peleliu, a mere 100 survived.

In October 1944, General Douglas MacArthur, who as a colonel had led the 1932 assault on the Bonus Army camp in Washington DC, wiped out much of the Japanese navy at the Battle of Leyte Gulf. Then in early 1945 the United States launched two bloody invasions—on Iwo Jima and Okinawa. By capturing these two islands off the coast of Japan, the United States was able to build airbases within striking distance of Japan itself.

By mid-1945 the Japanese military had suffered tremendous losses. A week of firebombing had killed more than 100,000

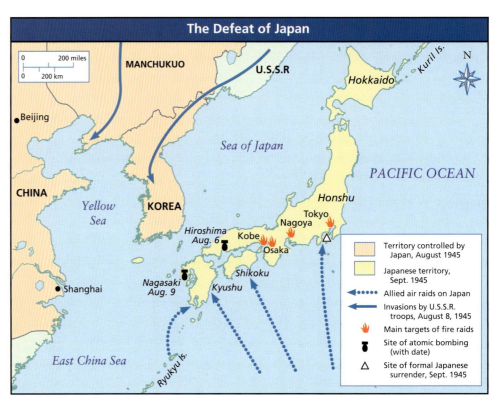

### The Defeat of Japan

**THE EMPIRE FALLS** By Summer 1945 Japanese forces, largely defeated in the air and at sea, were fighting a defensive war to protect Japan itself. Allied firebombing campaigns had killed 100,000 in Tokyo alone. Then in August the Allies dropped atomic bombs on Hiroshima and Nagasaki, forcing Japan to surrender.

people in Tokyo alone. The Japanese had become so desperate that they launched "kamikaze" or suicide attacks, loading planes with explosives and flying them into American ships. In considering a final assault on Japan American planners projected that despite heavy odds in its favor, the U.S. military might lose 100,000 men in a direct assault on Japan.

## The Atomic Bomb

Then in July 1945, scientists working on the Manhattan Project in New Mexico detonated the first atomic blast. President Harry S Truman, who had succeeded Franklin Roosevelt after Roosevelt's sudden death in April 1945, did not hesitate to use the new weapon. On August 6 the crew of the *Enola Gay*, an American B-29 bomber, dropped an atom bomb on the city of Hiroshima. Seventy-five thousand people died instantly. Another 75,000 later died of radiation poisoning. Then, on August 9, the U.S dropped a second bomb on the city of Nagasaki.

Truman's decision to drop the bombs on Hiroshima and Nagasaki have been debated since the mushroom clouds first rose over those two cities. Some have argued that Japan was already preparing to surrender, and that only a negotiation of the

surrender terms were in dispute. Others have argued that while the first bomb may have been justified, the bombing of Nagasaki had less to do with the defeat of Japan than sending a clear warning signal to the Soviet Union. On the other hand, the decision to use the weapons may well have saved 100,000 American lives. In either case, three days after the bombing of Nagasaki, Japan surrendered.

World War II remains the costliest war in human history, with an estimated 60 million people killed worldwide. In the war's aftermath much of Europe and Asia lay in ruins. Meanwhile, most of the United States had remained untouched by attack. While 300,000 Americans had died in the war, that figure paled in comparison to the 20 million Russians killed, many of whom were civilians. Over the next several decades the United States and the Soviet Union, allies of convenience during the war against Hitler, would emerge as the two leading forces in the next world war. While no major battles would be fought directly between the United States and the Soviet Union during the next four decades, the "Cold War" would be fought through both armed and unarmed conflicts taking place in the capitals of Europe, the jungles of Asia and the Americas, and even the halls of the U.S. Congress.

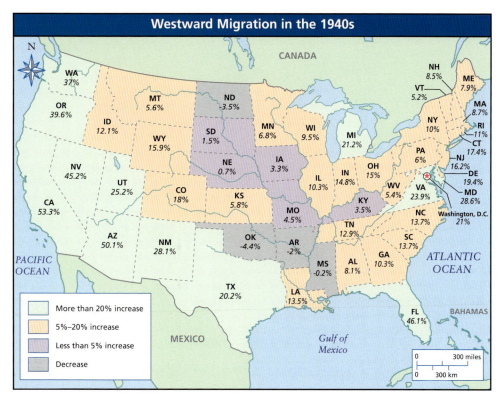

## Westward Migration in the 1940s

N

CANADA

WA 37%
OR 39.6%
MT 5.6%
ND -3.5%
NH 8.5%
VT 5.2%
ME 7.9%
MA 8.7%
ID 12.1%
MN 6.8%
WI 9.5%
MI 21.2%
NY 10%
RI -11%
CT 17.4%
WY 15.9%
SD 1.5%
PA 6%
NJ 16.2%
NV 45.2%
NE 0.7%
IA 3.3%
IL 10.3%
IN 14.8%
OH 15%
DE 19.4%
UT 25.2%
CO 18%
KS 5.8%
MO 4.5%
WV 5.4%
VA 23.9%
MD 28.6%
CA 53.3%
KY 3.5%
Washington, D.C. 21%
AZ 50.1%
NM 28.1%
OK -4.4%
AR -2%
TN 12.9%
NC 13.7%
SC 13.7%
TX 20.2%
MS -0.2%
AL 8.1%
GA 10.3%
LA 13.5%

PACIFIC OCEAN

ATLANTIC OCEAN

FL 46.1%

BAHAMAS

MEXICO

Gulf of Mexico

0 — 300 miles
0 — 300 km

Legend:
- More than 20% increase
- 5%–20% increase
- Less than 5% increase
- Decrease

**AMERICA MOBILIZES** Drawn by jobs in California war production factories, millions of Americans migrated west during World War II.

# Life on the Homefront

When economic mobilization began after war broke out in Europe, the United States was still in the throes of the Great Depression: 9 million Americans remained out of work, and the average factory was in use only 40 hours a week. By mid-1943, when mobilization was deemed completed, unemployment was a memory and most factories were operating 24 hours a day. This achievement occurred without much sacrifice on the part of consumers. Some goods—gasoline, tires, meat—were rationed, but living standards for Americans actually rose during the war years while the inflation rate, which had reached almost 100 percent during World War I, remained relatively low.

## World War II and the American Family

Yet World War II disrupted the daily lives of families in many ways. With several million men away on active duty, families at home were called by the government to contribute to the war effort. In large part this meant adhering to wartime government regulations and suggestions. The most immediate and far-reaching was the rationing of foods and materials essential to the armed forces,

including gas, rubber, fabric, leather, butter, and meat. Growing one's own food was encouraged, and hundreds of thousands of backyard "victory gardens" were begun. Wartime cuisine reflected the need to conserve luxury ingredients, with periodicals offering vegetarian, mock-meat, and low-sugar recipes, many of them using the canned "Spiced Ham," Spam, as a star ingredient. Fats, along with scrap metal and rubber, were routinely collected for reuse by the military. Meanwhile, fashion also pared down for the duration, as skirts were shortened and narrowed to conserve fabric; the tailored lines and wide shoulders bespoke wartime seriousness. From fathers serving in combat to children saving scrap iron, the United States from 1941 to 1945 was engaged in a massive struggle to win the war. Few if any national conditions afterward would so unite the family in a single goal.

The war years were also a time of tremendous movement at home. Troops training for combat were shuttled from base to base. But the greatest migration of civilians during the war took place as 15 million Americans changed or upgraded their jobs in response to soaring labor demand from war production centers. At least 4 million workers crossed state lines seeking better jobs.

Many of the jobs were on the West Coast and in the industrial Midwest and Northeast, with California and Michigan attracting the greatest influx of workers. Some of the war production centers were brand-new cities built for wartime purposes, such as Vanport, Oregon; others were old cities, such as Detroit, Michigan, whose automotive industry shifted to defense production. In either case, people hungry from years of Depression-era employment scarcity migrated eagerly to these locations: from the South, Southwest, Appalachia, and rural areas around the country.

## Women, Minorities and the Defense Industry

Ultimately, the massive war buildup that took place on the homefront could not have occurred without the contributions of women and minorities. Female defense workers totaled 5 million, with many women working out of the home for the first time. Soon the wartime working woman became known as "Rosie the Riveter," representing the defense construction jobs they were now doing.

Blacks were denied jobs in the defense industry. But in 1941, after labor leader A. Philip Randolph threatened a mass march in Washington, D.C., Roosevelt signed Executive Order 8802, banning discrimination in defense industry hiring and creating the Fair Employment and Practices Commission. Blacks were then hired for jobs in Michigan, California, and elsewhere, which fueled the largest migration by blacks from the rural South. Hundreds of thousands of Mexicans also joined the U.S. war effort, brought to the U.S. as part of the U.S.-government sponsored Braceros Program. While many braceros (named for working with their *brazos*, or hands) were employed on farms, many held defense jobs. All minorities faced discrimination: Women were taunted and denied opportunities at skilled jobs, and blacks were subject to "hate" strikes at formerly white auto plants and elsewhere.

Nonetheless, the war helped transform the United States—not only putting it in a position of dominance with the war's end, but also reshaping the nation's domestic forces as well. In the decades to come, African Americans and women would challenge their second class status as American citizens as never before. Ironically, the war against facism overseas would ultimately make the United States more egalitarian as well.

# Chapter 28: The Postwar Boom

Remembering the spectacle of World War I Bonus Army veterans marching around Washington, D.C. in 1932, demanding their bonuses, Franklin Roosevelt devised a plan to pay approximately $4 billion to nearly nine million veterans. Of more lasting effect were the educational, housing, and medical elements of the law. Veterans were offered stipends and living allowances for college or trade school education; they received reduced-rate mortgages that allowed them to purchase their own homes; those that were injured received medical care and vocational rehabilitation through the newly created Veterans Administration (VA).

In later years, the GI Bill would be extended to veterans of the Korean War. By 1956, nearly 10 million veterans had received education and training subsidies through the GI Bill. Although some wartime pundits and historians feared another U.S. depression, even a revolution, after the war the opposite occurred.

## The Economy

The postwar decades were marked by expanding consumer confidence and demand for new goods. The

**Agricultural and Industrial Employment in the United States, 1950**

Major agricultural producing states

Major industrial areas

△ Largest 20 U.S. cities

◉ State capital

**BOOMTOWNS** Following the end of World War II, the United States went through an unparalleled period of economic growth. Los Angeles, a relatively small city just a few decades before, would grow into one of the nation's largest.

boom was spurred by the GI Bill and other federal economic policies, but the successful transition to a peacetime economic boom after World War II was driven by other factors as well. First the advertising industry, boosted by the spread of television, encouraged consumers to purchase items such as furniture, appliances and other goods. Second, breakthroughs in science and technology, often made possible by the war effort, allowed for increased efficiency in American factories as well as the development of new products.

The GI Bill was certainly the most far-reaching domestic economic stimulus package passed during the 1940s and 1950s, but it was not the only one. The New Deal and wartime mobilization had reshaped the relationship between the federal government and the nation's citizens. Even after the crises of economic depression and global war had ended, the legacy of the FDR years lived on. Government offices and systems established during the war eased the transition to peace; for example, the Office of War Mobilization became the Office of War Mobilization and Reconversion. Taking his cue from Roosevelt's New Deal, Harry Truman proposed a raft of large scale federal programs collectively known as the "Fair Deal." While Truman's economic agenda— a higher minimum wage, a national health insurance plan and increased education spending—by and large failed to pass a Republican-dominated Congress, the federal government's role in society in the 1940s and 1950s was still fundamentally different than it had been prior to the FDR era. During the Republican administration of Dwight Eisenhower, for example, a number of major federal projects were initiated. The Housing Act of 1954, for example, set aside federal funds for urban planning grants, encouraged the construction of 35,000 new units of low income urban housing, and required that local housing authorities do a better job enforcing housing codes, all in an effort to prevent the spread of urban blight. Eisenhower personally pushed a major expansion of the federal interstate highway system. In 1956, the Federal Aid Highway Act established a framework for building intercity highways in partnership with the states. The project was even funded by a new federal tax on gasoline.

The new federal highway system would dramatically expand domestic interstate commerce and be a boon to the tourism industry by enabling more and more Americans to drive long distances for vacations. By the end of the twentieth century, the federal highway system had expanded to connect all forty-eight contiguous states, servicing 90 percent of all cities with populations of 50,000 people or more with highways. Today the United States has nearly one-third of the world's roadways, and intercity travel by car is more popular than ever.

## Pockets of Poverty

Despite the growth of the national economy in the postwar years, the period was not without its recessions. A mild recession in 1948–49 was followed by deeper recessions in 1953–54, 1957–58, and 1960–61.

In rural areas, millions of people lost their vocations as miners or farmers as both of those industries became increasingly mechanized. Several million displaced white and black rural workers left the deep South and Appalachia and headed for the cities of the Midwest, Northeast and West. Once there, they joined a new wave of Hispanic immigrants from Puerto Rico, Mexico and elsewhere.

While unempoyment was generally low through much of the 1940s and 1950s, there were not enough jobs for all the newcomers to America's cities. Despite a relatively strong economy as a whole, by 1960, 40 million people—fully 22 percent of the American population—were classified as poor. Most lived in families that made less than $3,000 in a year. Harvard economist John Kenneth Galbraith highlighted this growing gap between rich and poor in his best-selling book, *The Affluent Society* (1958).

# Science and Technology

As interstate commerce was boosted by the growth of the nation's highway system, the makeup of the national economy was also changing. Beginning after World War II, the country began shifting away from a manufacturing based economy toward one based on sales and service.

One key factor in this shift was automation in the workplace. The development of advanced machinery reduced the need for factory laborers, or miners in the field extracting natural resources. During the 1940s and 1950s machines replaced millions of American workers.

While job losses due to workplace automation cost many workers their jobs, scientific and technological breakthroughs ultimately boosted the postwar U.S. economy. Some discoveries were refinements of inventions introduced prior to World War II. The first practical radar system, for example, was invented in 1935 by Scottish physicist Robert Alexander Watson-Watt, but it first became indispensable as a military tracking device during World War II.

Some inventions were prototypes for inventions more fully developed after the war, such as the Colossus calculating device, a precursor to the modern computer developed in Britain to crack

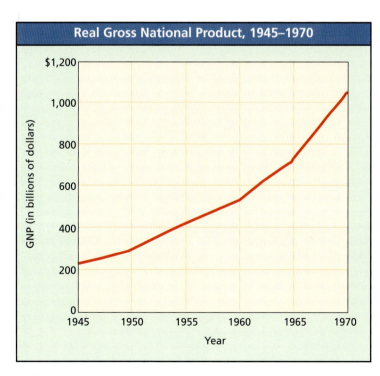

**Real Gross National Product, 1945–1970**

**EXPANDING ECONOMY** The expanded U.S. highway system dramatically boosted production and interstate commerce during the postwar years.

**The Interstate Highway System**

EXPANSION OF THE HIGHWAY SYSTEM  As more Americans left the cities and rural towns for suburbia, new highways sprang up to better serve a nation on the move.

German codes. Others were developed for war but were later turned to peaceful uses, such as the ballistic missile, developed by Germany to bomb Allied cities but later applied to space travel. Closer to Earth, technological improvements in airplanes during the forties and fifties revolutionized aviation. In 1947 test pilot Chuck Yeager broke the sound barrier in a Bell X-1 supersonic aircraft. Just three years later jet fighter technology found its way into a more mundane—and slower—flight as the first international jet passenger flight took place, flying from New York to London. By 1958 the first regular domestic jet service began, flying passengers between New York and Miami.

### Electrifying America

The most fateful advance occurred near war's end, when the United States detonated the first atomic bomb. The device, which compelled Japan to surrender and shaped global politics for decades, led to the postwar development of the atomic power industry. In March 1949 the National Reactor Testing Station opened in Arco,

Idaho, and two years later, the first atomic reactor at that site began to generate electricity. In 1959, the first commercially operated electricity-generating nuclear plant began operating at Shippingport, Pennsylvania.

Even with the advent of atomic energy for commercial use, the vast majority of electricity still came from traditional sources like coal as well as from new sources like hydroelectric power. While most people living in cities already received power from private utilities, those living in rural areas such as farms relied on federal programs such as the Tennessee Valley Authority and the Rural Electrification Administration, both founded during New Deal-days, to bring them electricity. Prior to World War II only about 10 percent of America's farms had electrical power; by the end of the 1950s, almost every community in the nation had electrical access, dramatically improving life for farm families.

### The Growth of Chemical Agriculture

During the 1940s and 1950s, American farms were also impacted by wartime discoveries in other, more contro-

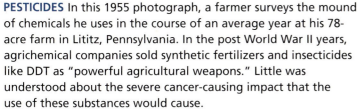

**PESTICIDES** In this 1955 photograph, a farmer surveys the mound of chemicals he uses in the course of an average year at his 78-acre farm in Lititz, Pennsylvania. In the post World War II years, agrichemical companies sold synthetic fertilizers and insecticides like DDT as "powerful agricultural weapons." Little was understood about the severe cancer-causing impact that the use of these substances would cause.

**ELECTRIC POWER** An electrical power generating station.

versial ways. As Allied troops marched into Germany, they uncovered a number of Nazi industrial secrets. For example, at the I.G. Farben plant, they found data from Nazi experiments in nerve gas technology. When American scientists performed relatively simple changes in the molecular structure of these gases, they were able to produce pesticides that were more lethal to insects than to humans. This discovery spurred new pesticide production by the American chemical industry.

These breakthroughs in chemistry would help transform American agriculture particularly when paired with advances in plant genetics. In 1944 a geneticist named Norman Borlaug began working with the Rockefeller Foundation in Mexico and the American Southwest, where he developed high yield, pest-resistant hybrids of wheat. (Borlaug would eventually win the Nobel Peace Prize after introducing high yield wheat to India and Pakistan in the 1960s.)

Borlaug's wheat came with a catch, however. His hybrids required the heavy use of pesticides, chemical fertilizers and irrigation techniques to flourish. Therefore farmers who cultivated these new high yield seeds were required to increase the amount of chemicals applied to their fields. While chemical manufacturers benefited from skyrocketing demand for their products, farmers faced the increased financial cost of greater pesticide application to their fields. In addition, critics charged that the chemicals did long-term damage to both soil and to human health. By the 1960s the health risks associated with many of the strongest chemical pesticides

| Timeline of Health and Medical Breakthroughs, 1948–1959 |
|---|
| **1948** Philip Hench and Edward Kendall are the first to successfully treat arthritic patients with cortisone. |
| **1953** Virginia Apgar (1909-1974), American anesthesiologist, develops the Apgar Score, a uniform method for assessing a newborn's need for resuscitation at one minute and at five minutes after birth. It becomes a standard of medical practice. |
| **1953** John H. Gibbon, American surgeon, is the first to use a mechanical heart and blood purifier in surgery, completely taking over the patient's heart and lung functions for 29 minutes. |
| **1954** Jonas Salk, American physician, develops and successfully tests a polio vaccine that works against all three strains of polio. |
| **1959** Victor Mills, while working for Procter and Gamble, develops the first disposable diaper that is then marketed as Pampers. The first Pampers use safety pins for closure. Tapes are not added until 1971. |
| **1959** Working for Burroughs-Wellcome's pharmaceutical research labs, Gertrude Elion, chemist, is awarded a patent on the first major medicine successful in fighting leukemia. |

**THE FIGHT AGAINST POLIO** A young polio victim confined to an "iron lung" to aid her breathing (above); a button promotes the foundation known today as the March of Dimes.

would gain public attention with the publication of Rachel Carson's book *Silent Spring*, casting a long shadow on the chemical industry's technological "advances."

Many economists argue that the postwar chemical age had dire consequences for traditional small farms. Because the most efficient way to harvest hybrid crops is to grow them on enormous plots of land that were beyond the labor capacity of traditional family farmers, an increasing number of farmers sold out to large-scale agribusinesses that could afford the advanced machinery and costs of industrial agriculture.

### A Cure for Polio

Perhaps the greatest scientific breakthrough of the postwar era was the development of a vaccine against poliomyelitis, the devastating disease that attacked the nervous system, most frequently in children. Adults, including Franklin Roosevelt, had been struck by the disease as well.

For those who were born after the polio vaccine was discovered, the fear caused by the disease is hard to imagine. Because polio epidemics usually struck in summer, many believed that the disease was associated with water and therefore forbade their children from using swimming pools and drinking fountains.

Finally in 1952 Dr. Jonas Salk developed a vaccine—to be joined later by another, introduced by Albert Sabin—ending to polio epidemics in the United States and most of the world. The quest for a vaccine was largely funded by the nonprofit National Foundation for Infantile Paralysis, founded with help from President Roosevelt. The group later became known as the March of Dimes.

### Communications and Broadcasting

The 1940s and 1950s also witnessed dramatic change in the communications and broadcasting fields. In 1941, W47NV became the first FM radio station in the nation, and in 1948 the transistor was invented allowing for the development of pocket sized radios that could go anywhere. Transistor radios became enormously popular, particularly with young people, since they were inexpensive and easy to carry. By the 1950s they were so common that one could walk down the street in New York City on a summer evening and still catch the New York Yankee, Giant or Brooklyn Dodger baseball game on transistor radios carried by passers-by or perched on a neighbor's front steps.

Meanwhile, radio had new powerful competition. In 1941, station W2XBS in New York City became the first television station in the nation with a commercial license. Soon, televisions were everywhere. While just 5,000 households owned televisions in 1946, just five years later, the number had grown to 17 million. In 1951, television began its first coast-to-coast broadcasts, thanks to improvements in transmission cable and amplifying equipment. By 1954 color television had arrived, stimulating even more interest in the new medium, and by 1957 over 41 million Americans tuned in regularly to television fare than ranged from the high-toned live dramas of *Playhouse 90* and *The Alcoa Hour* to the bruising action of *Roller Derby*. What they liked best were the mishaps of Lucy Ricardo (Lucille Ball) on *I Love Lucy*, quiz shows, and westerns like *Wagon Train*. The new medium of television also helped spur a new spirit of religious revival, as Protestant evangelist Billy Graham and Catholic bishop Fulton J. Sheen became stars of the small screen.

# Daily Life in the Forties and Fifties

In 1954 television advertising revenues passed those of radio for the first time. Another postwar factor in the economic boom of the 1940s and 1950s was the growth of the advertising industry. As returning GIs married and purchased new homes, they also needed new furniture, new appliances, new televisions and radios and other new household goods and the advertising industry was ready to influence exactly which goods they planned to purchase.

### The Advertising Age

Even before the end of the war the advertising industry was a fine-tuned machine with great impact on consumers. It spent $2.9 billion on gross expenditures in 1945 alone to make hundreds of items like Jell-O indispensable to everyday life, many sold by celebrities.

**I LOVE LUCY** Lucille Ball and Desi Arnaz starred in the television's most popular program, "I Love Lucy".

**TV TIME** While television was first invented in the 1930s, by the 1950s it had already revolutionized American leisure habits.

Yet despite its success, the advertising industry in 1945 was ready for a lift from Depression-era government consumer advocacy and World War II austerity. It got what it wanted in the consumer demands of the baby boom and the new mass advertising outlet of television. By 1950 gross advertising expenditures had doubled to $5.7 billion. As the economy boomed during the 1950s expensive items like automobiles and televisions became as heavily advertised as low-cost detergent and toothpaste. Postwar television made small-screen personalities into star pitchmen, like their prewar radio compatriots. It also helped sustain both long-lived sales mascots (such as Alka-Seltzer's Speedy), or the short-lived (such as McDonald's Speedee, who would be replaced in 1960 by the better-known Ronald McDonald).

Behind the snappy sales banter and highly visual demonstrations was sophisticated research. Called motivation research it employed psychological testing to determine subconscious desires, then used the findings to devise the product pitch. As advertising became more pervasive during the decade, so did the skepticism of the American public, as witnessed in two bestselling books of the 1950s: Sloan Wilson's *The Man in the Gray Flannel Suit* (1955) and Vance Packard's *The Hidden Persuaders* (1957).

### The Rise of Suburbia

The GI Bill's home loan guarantees, a growing romance with the automobile, and the American dream of home ownership all helped lead to the greatest housing boom in U.S. history in the years after the war.

Prior to the arrival of mass transit in the late 19th and early 20th centuries, most Americans lived in the rural countryside or in cities. As rails, buses, and trollies made the home-to-work commute manageable and the suburbs more desirable, wealthier Americans found suburbs such as Bronxville or Rockville Center, New York attractive and accessible alternatives to the hustle and bustle of city life.

After World War II the U.S. government and private industry built houses in such quantity and at such speed that the suburbs began to attract a wider array of people. The need was great: Millions of veterans were returning home with GI funding to spend, but the depression and the war had slowed home building and many apartment owners did not welcome children.

In 1947 Levittown, New York became the first among the largest mass-produced suburbs in the nation. Builder William Levitt offered families two styles of prefabricated Cape Cod homes to choose from. Veterans looking for affordable houses in a communter-friendly community found Levittown ideal. Other instant suburbs followed Levittown's model, linking new suburbanites not by extended family but by income, age, dependence on cars, and uniformity of the community. (Most suburbs offered racial uniformity as well: the first Levitttown leases were offered to whites only.)

After the Depression and the war, middle-class

**FAST FOOD NATION** The first outlet of McDonald's opened in 1955 in Des Plaines, Illinois. The fast-food restaurant reflected the nation's new automobile-dependant suburban culture.

Americans found hard-won stability in suburbia. For post-war suburbanites, whether in the Northeast, Midwest, or elsewhere, all the necessary retail shops and restaurants could be found conveniently close by. In 1956 the Southdale Center in Edina, Minnesota opened, becoming the first indoor shopping mall in the nation. As new malls were built around the nation, suburban consumers found that they could shop for virtually any items they needed in climate controlled comfort year round.

In the suburban retail environment efficiency became the order of the day. Large suburban department stores and supermarkets were built to anchor roadside strip malls, while offering plentiful parking and a standardized selection of foods and packaged products to appeal to the consumer on the go.

It was with this operating philosophy in mind that the first McDonald's hamburger restaurant opened in Des Plaines, Illinois in 1955. Burgers were 15 cents, fries a nickel. McDonald's also featured drive in service, meaning customers didn't even have to leave their vehicles to get their food. The brilliance of the McDonald's strategy as its one restaurant grew into an army of thousands is that it catered to the suburban lifestyle, serving a consistent menu of items that did not vary from location to location. As more and more retailers and restaurants opened suburban locations across America,

they took care to learn from the McDonald's play-book—quick service and consistent product from one outlet to the next.

At the same time, as many children of the suburbs became young adults, they sometimes questioned their parents traditions and rejected what they saw as suburban conformity. The Baby Boom generation would largely define itself as being from, but not of, the subdivisions that political activist and folksinger Malvina Reynolds called "little boxes made of ticky tacky."

## Pop Culture in the Forties and Fifties

The split between the World War II generation and their children was also reflected in the diversity of popular culture during the forties and fifties.

During World War II, much of American popular culture was, like the rest of the nation, focused on the war effort. Actors Bette Davis and John Garfield founded the Hollywood Canteen, where GIs could chat and dance with the likes of Rita Hayworth and Betty Grable. Bob Hope and others traveled abroad to do dozens of shows for soldiers on the front. Likewise, popular music reflected the war effort as well, as songs such as "Praise the Lord and Pass the Ammunition" and "Boogie Woogie Bugle Boy" raced to the top of the charts.

**ELVIS** Combining the sounds of black rhythm and blues with white country and gospel, Elvis Presley shocked parents and won millions of fans when he emerged in the mid-1950s.

**THE BEAT GENERATION** Poet Allen Ginsberg was one of the main figures of the Beatnik generation of the late 1950s. Together with writers such as Jack Kerouac, Gregory Corso, and Lawrence Ferlinghetti, Ginsberg represented a rejection of 1950s conformity.

With the end of the war, pop culture was marked by both seriousness and frivolity, as well as teen rebellion. The most popular movies reflected popular devotion to novelty and traditional values. *This is Cinerama* touted a new widescreen process, while *The Ten Commandments* combined reverence and spectacle. Yet an increasing number of filmmakers turned inward with realistic films about social concerns, such as union corruption in *On the Waterfront* and teenage alienation in *Rebel Without a Cause.*

Musically, the nation saw great change. Frank Sinatra, who first emerged as a teen hearthrob in the late 1930s, continued to reinvigorate pop standards with "concept" albums such as *Songs For Swinging Lovers* and hit singles such as "All the Way." Yet for many teens of the 1950s new, more rebellious forms of music won their hearts. Rock 'n roll, a musical form based on white country music and black rhythm and blues, exploded onto the charts in 1956 in the form of a one-time truck-driver named Elvis Presley. Through hit songs like "Love Me Tender," "Hound Dog," and "Heartbreak Hotel," the Mississippi-born singer introduced varieties of black or "race" music to mainstream music charts, much to the horror of the older generation.

## The Beat Generation

Other forms of music, art and literature became more abstract and free-form. While jazz music in the early forties had been meant for dancing, by the late forties and into the fifties jazz artists like Charlie Parker, Miles Davis, and Dizzy Gillespie were experimenting with more abstract forms of the music. This new jazz, known as bebop, strongly appealed to a segment of youth culture known as the Beats, or Beatniks.

At the heart of Beat culture was disillusionment with the American dream of a suburban home and a two-car garage. Beatniks believed this dream was shallow. They took the name Beat because they felt that society had beaten down their own hopes for a better world. Beat culture flourished in coffee-houses and cafés. There, jazz and poetry performances intermingled with old socialist songs of workers' rights and human freedom. The "Beat Generation's" notions of personal freedom and rebellion against established culture were spread by their writings. Among the best known figures in Beat culture were novelist Jack Kerouac, author of *On the Road*, and poet Allen Ginsberg, whose best known poem was "Howl."

By the end of the 1950s the Beat culture had been discovered and publicized by the press and television. Its writers and thinkers became familiar names, although they symbolized unconventional morality and lack of ambition. The Beats laid the foundation for the next decade's rebels who would create a counter-culture that would become firmly established in the American mainstream.

# Chapter 29: Cold War and Hot Wars

The League of Nations, formed without American participation after World War I to promote international peace and security, failed to prevent the even greater cataclysm of World War II. Even so, as World War II came to an end, the Allied nations tried again to create an international organization that could maintain peace and security and seek solutions to common problems. The result was the United Nations (UN), chartered in 1945, with 51 original member states, after convening for the first time in London in 1946. The body's permanent headquarters in New York City were completed in 1952. While inheriting much of the structure of the League of Nations, the UN had some important differences. Most notably, it included the United States, now the greatest power in the West. Though not always successful in reducing the climate of global tension that permeated the postwar era, or even at enforcing its security resolutions, the UN would use a U.S.-led military coalition on the Korean Peninsula just a few years after end of World War II. In over six decades in operation, the UN has mediated and supervised peace agreements, and contributed to such causes as global health and education.

## The Cold War in Europe

For most of the postwar period the United Nations' agenda was dominated by the cold war between the capitalist nations of the West and the communist nations of the East. The split was symbolized, in the words of Winston Churchill, by an "iron curtain" between them. The primary cold war combatants on the world stage were the United States and the Soviet Union, but numerous other countries became involved as well, willingly or unwillingly.

### The Marshall Plan

In the immediate aftermath of World War II, the primary battlefield in the cold war was, once again, Europe. In 1945 much of Europe lay in ruins, its productive capacity in desperate straits. In a commencement address at Harvard University on June 5, 1947, U.S. Secretary of State George C. Marshall, with the approval of President Harry S Truman, announced a novel approach to the problem: a program of massive American financial aid to help restore the economies of Europe.

There were a number of reasons for the aid program: first, the United States needed a prosperous Europe as a market for its goods; second, the United States feared that the nations of Europe could turn com-

munist and seek reconstruction aid from the Soviet Union rather than from America; third, with the Soviets already entrenched in East Germany, it was important to rebuild West Germany as a buffer against Soviet expansion while soothing the fears of Germany's neighbors by integrating West Germany back into Europe.

Known as the European Recovery Program, or the Marshall Plan, the U.S. aid program permitted European nations to decide how the aid money would be spent. Although Republican members of Congress opposed the plan initially, that opposition collapsed in February, 1948 when communists took over Czechoslovakia. To the Marshall Plan's backers, the fall of Czechoslovakia underscored the urgency of aiding Europe to forestall further communist revolution.

Beginning in April 1948, participating countries coordinated their efforts through the Organization for European Economic Cooperation (OEEC), with funds distributed by the Economic Cooperation Administration. The Soviet Union was invited to participate in the OEEC, but declined on ideological grounds, and prevented Eastern European countries under its control from participating either.

The Marshall Plan thus contributed to the growing division of Europe between the U.S-supported capitalist West and the Soviet-supported communist East. For those nations that did participate, the Marshall Plan was a spectacular success: By the time it ended in 1952, the United States had dispensed more than $13 billion in U.S. funds and had helped restore prosperity to Western Europe while keeping it out of Soviet hands. Industrial production in Western Europe was 35 percent higher than it had been before the war. Per capita incomes had risen 33 percent between 1947 and 1951.

Although the Marshall Plan helped bring economic and industrial assistance to much of Western Europe, a civil war in Greece and increasingly aggressive behavior by the Soviets in Germany and elsewhere would convince Truman and others that a military alliance was needed.

### The Division of Germany

At the Yalta Conference in February 1945, the United States, United Kingdom, and Soviet Union had agreed to divide Germany into four zones of occupation, each to be supervised by one of these "Big Three" and France. Although Berlin lay within the Soviet sector, it was to be governed by all four nations equally.

However, in 1948, after the three western countries began meeting in secret and subsequently decided to create an independent West Germany, the Soviet Union protested by withdrawing from the partnership and blockading all land routes into Berlin. In June 1948, the

## Nations in the Marshall Plan, 1948

Nations in the Marshall Plan

## NATO and the Warsaw Pact, 1955

NATO countries

Warsaw Pact countries

Neutral countries

**THE IRON CURTAIN** With the creation of the opposing capitalist NATO Alliance and communist Warsaw Pact, Europe remained divided for over forty years.

**MARSHALL PLAN** Following World War II, the United States helped to rebuild the economies of most non-communist European nations.

Soviets responded by establishing a land blockade of the three other zones in order to force the United States, Britain and France to withdraw. thereby leaving an undivided Berlin to East Germany.

In response President Truman set an airlift in motion, and the United States and its allies flew in supplies for the military as well as for civilians in defiance of the blockade. This "Berlin Airlift," as it was termed, continued for 11 months until the land blockade was ended in May 1949.

The split between the Soviet Union and its former allies resulted in the division of Germany into the German Democratic Republic (East Germany) and the Federal Republic of Germany (West Germany). Berlin was also divided, with East Berlin to be controlled by the Soviets and West Berlin by the British, French, and Americans. The city's split was emphasized with the erection of the Berlin Wall in 1961. In 1989, nearly 30 years later, the wall was torn down as the cold war came to an end. Germany became a unified—and democratic—nation in 1990.

### Greece and the Truman Doctrine

Meanwhile in Greece, communism had gained a foothold even before World War II had ended. Thus, a power struggle had been raging since late 1944, when the Nazis had withdrawn. Although the British had supervised the formation of a Greek coalition government, communists briefly overran the country. After a short civil war the communists were defeated by British in January 1945.

Over a year later a general election was held, and a plebiscite in September 1946 restored the Greek king to the throne. However, communist insurgents then began a massive guerrilla war that proved too much for the British to handle.

Consequently, the United States announced the "Truman Doctrine," which vowed that the United States would assist any countries threatened by communist aggression. Under this doctrine the United States sent financial and military aid to Greece and Turkey. With this crucial support the pro-western Greek monarchy succeeded in defeating the rebels. The Greek civil war ended in October 1949.

## NATO and the Warsaw Pact

In the midst of the Berlin and Greek crises, the United States and 11 of its allies created a civil and military alliance known as the North Atlantic Treaty Organization (NATO) to contain the spread of communism. NATO's founding members were Belgium, Canada, Denmark, France, Iceland, Italy, Luxembourg, the Netherlands, Norway, Portugal, the United Kingdom and the United States. Greece and Turkey would both join NATO in 1952, while West Germany was made a member in 1955.

Following the admittance of West Germany to NATO, the Soviet Union responded by forming its own civil and military alliance with most of the communist nations of eastern Europe. Known as the Warsaw Pact, the alliance included Albania, Bulgaria, Czechoslovakia, East Germany, Hungary, Poland, and Romania. With these NATO and the Warsaw Pact countries pitted against each other, the conflict between communism and capitalism would become even more pronounced in the years ahead.

# Red China and the Korean War

In 1949—the same year that the Soviet Union blockaded Germany—a civil war in China that had been raging since the end of World War II came to an end. The victors were Mao Zedong's Communists and the vanquished, former Chinese president Chiang Kai Shek's Nationalists.

In the aftermath of the Communist victory and the creation of the People's Republic of China, the United States lent support to the defeated Nationalists, who evacuated to the island of Formosa (Taiwan), where they established the pro-western Republic of China.

To prevent the Communists from attacking Formosa, President Truman ordered the Seventh Fleet to the China Sea. At the same time, the Americans opposed any actions by the Nationalists against the mainland that might provoke a Communist attack on Taiwan.

This strategy has kept an uneasy peace between the People's Republic and Taiwan to this day. On the other hand, it would not prevent communist China from involvement in the Korean War.

## The Korean War

Historians often say that the Korean War was when the Cold War turned hot. Officially a "police action" rather than a war, the conflict was at one level a fight between the two small south Asian nations of North Korea and South Korea. At another level it embodied the struggle between the communist world—represented by North Korea and its dictator, Kim Il Sung, backed by the Soviet Union and the People's Republic of China—and the non-communist world, with the United States playing the leading role in defending South Korea, backed by a coalition organized by the United Nations.

The roots of the war in Korea date back to the defeat of Japan in August 1945. A few weeks after Japan's surrender, the United States and Soviet Union agreed to divide Korea along the 38th Parallel into American (southern) and Soviet (northern) occupation zones. In August 1948, the Republic of Korea was established

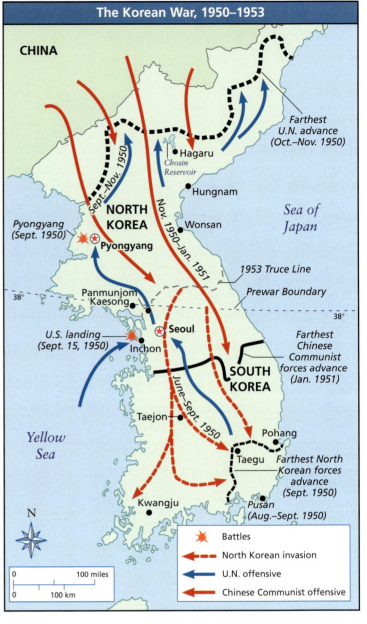

**The Korean War, 1950–1953**

**KOREAN WAR** During the summer of 1950 communist North Korean forces invaded South Korea. A United Nations force, led by the United States came to South Korea's aid, while communist Chinese forces became directly involved after U.N. forces under American General Douglas MacArthur advanced nearly to the Yalu River at the Chinese border. The war ended in a stalemate and Korea remained divided into the twenty-first century.

in the former U.S. occupation zone, with its capital at Seoul. One month later, communist leader Kim Il Sung established the Democratic People's Republic of Korea in the former Soviet occupation zone, with its capital at Pyongyang.

War began with a surprise invasion of South Korea by North Korean forces on June 25, 1950. Almost immediately, President Harry Truman pledged U.S. support for South Korea, and American troops were soon in combat on the Korean peninsula.

To lead the UN coalition Truman chose 70-year old General Douglas MacArthur, who was then overseeing the occupation of Japan. Through the summer of 1950 North Korean forces smashed through the South Korean defenders. The first U.S. units sent to the peninsula—undertrained, inexperienced infantry from the Army of Occupation in Japan—proved unable to stop the advance. By early September the North Koreans had occupied all of South Korea except a pocket around Pusan in the peninsula's southeast corner.

MacArthur gambled on a bold breakout: an amphibious invasion of the port of Inchon 200 miles behind the North Korean lines. The Inchon landing succeeded, and aided by superiority in the air and in the waters around Korea, UN forces went on the offensive. By late fall they had crossed into North Korea itself and were advancing on the Yalu River, the border between Korea and China.

Chinese leaders now warned that they would not tolerate a UN presence so close to their soil, but MacArthur ignored these warnings, along with intelligence reports that Chinese "volunteers" were crossing the Yalu. Then, in late November, a massive Chinese assault caught UN forces by surprise. The advance to the Yalu turned into an epic fighting retreat in freezing winter weather. MacArthur now called for a wider war, including attacks on China itself—counter to President Truman's policies. In April Truman fired MacArthur for insubordination, replacing him with General Matthew Ridgway.

In mid-1951 peace talks began, but fighting continued for two more years while UN and North Korean representatives argued over issues like prisoner exchanges. The election of Dwight Eisenhower as president in 1952 and the death of Soviet dictator Joseph Stalin in 1953 moved the peace talks forward. Finally, on June 27, 1953, an armistice was signed, leaving the peninsula divided between North and South Korea. South Korea's independence was saved, but it was hardly a victory for anyone. The peninsula was devastated, and hundreds of thousands of civilians had been killed. American losses were about 55,000 dead and twice that number wounded. Today U.S. troops continue to keep watch over the "demilitarized zone" along the 38th Parallel.

# U.S. Policy in the Developing World

While the United States led the atomic arms race after it successfully detonated the world's first atomic bomb in 1945, the nation's nuclear monopoly would not last long. On August 29, 1949 the Soviet Union detonated its first atom bomb. By 1955 both countries had created hydrogen bombs, and both had enveloped the world in a cold war that would last for decades and bring it to the brink of nuclear war. Should either side make a first strike with nuclear weapons, the other was capable of retaliating in kind, guaranteeing mutual assured destruction (MAD), if not global annihilation. Nuclear deterrence was therefore necessary, and was achieved by an immense buildup of ever-improving warheads to close the "missile gap" between the two countries.

While the balance of power in Europe between East and West hinged on the fact that each side possessed nuclear weapons, the ensuing Cold War extended well beyond Europe to struggles worldwide. For more than forty years, East and West would compete for primacy in the developing world. On the surface, these crises were ideological clashes between communism and capitalism. Yet they were also strategic, as many developing nations were rich in valuable natural resources that would benefit whichever industrialized country that managed to control them.

For the United States and its allies, the struggles against global communism and for control of natural resources were complicated by the West's long history of colonialism in the developing world. Those in the power centers of America and Europe often have seen third world conflicts as battles between western-style democracy and Soviet-style totalitarianism, but revolutionary leaders in these nations viewed themselves as freedom fighters, working to end the long legacy of outside domination.

## The Middle East

In 1948 the state of Israel was founded after a fierce Jewish guerrilla insurgency against the British managing the protectorate of Palestine, from which Israel sprang. Formed as a permanent homeland for the worldwide Jewish diaspora, Israel had strong backing from the United States, which by the late 1940s had the world's largest population of Jewish citizens.

In addition to acknowledging deep cultural ties to Israel, U.S. support for the Jewish state also served economic and strategic interests. With the developed world's growing need for the Middle East's vast oil reserves, the region became a Cold War tinder box. For example, just as the United States backed Israel against its Arab neighbors, the Soviets aided Egypt, an early opponent of Israel. When the popularly elected government of Iran threatened to nationalize its oil industry in 1953, the American Central Intelligence Agency (CIA) helped overthrow that government. The United States then installed Reza Shah Pahlevi, who established a repressive regime that was propped up for 25 years by United States military and financial aid.

A decade later, the CIA organized the overthrow of Iraq's government. In its place, the Ba'ath Party came to power. Backed by U.S. dollars and weapons, the Ba'ath party's brutal and repressive leaders worked to assure that Iraq—a divided nation made up of clashing national and religious factions—remained stable enough for the country's oil to flow dependably to the United States and elsewhere in the developed world.

U.S. support for repressive regimes in the Mideast and especially for Israel intensified anti-American feelings throughout the Middle East during the post war period. Yet, in at least one occasion, the United States won praise from the Arab world. In 1956 President Eisenhower intervened diplomatically to compel Britain, France, and Israel to withdraw from Egypt, which they had invaded to prevent nationalization of the strategic Suez Canal.

Then in 1958 Marines landed in Lebanon to help protect against a coup in that country. By helping to bring about a truce between warring Lebanese Christians and Muslims, the United States had played the role of peacekeeper.

## U.S. Intervention in Africa and Asia

The Truman Doctrine of halting the spread of communism took the United States to every continent on the globe. During the mid-Fifties, Muslim insurgents known as the Huks rose up in the Philippines, which had been a U.S. colony from 1898 to 1946. Although the United States alleged that the Huks were pro-communist, their roots reached back to the Moro rebellion against the U.S. occupation that began at the turn of the century.

In its efforts to contain communism, the United States frequently ignored the excesses of antidemocratic strongmen that it helped place

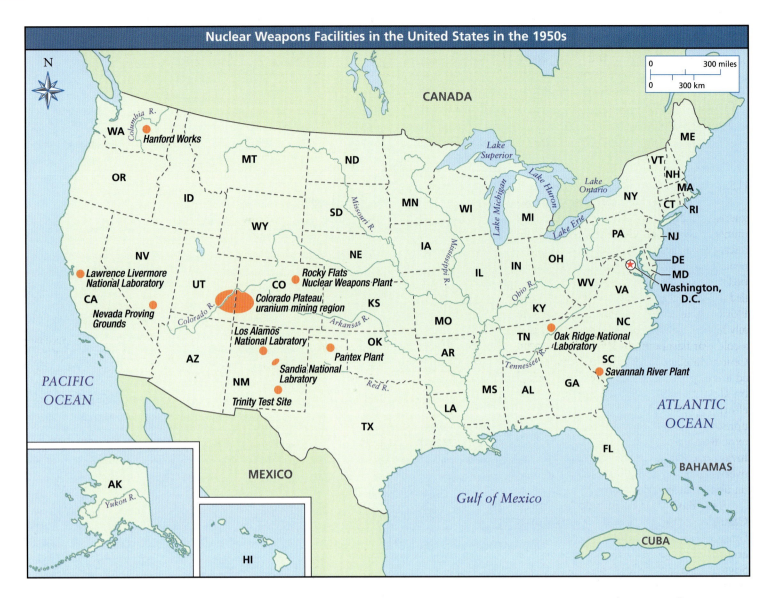

## Nuclear Weapons Facilities in the United States in the 1950s

**AMERICA'S NUCLEAR ARSENAL** By the mid-1950s the United States had established a number of nuclear weapons research and production facilities around the nation. Many Americans built backyard nuclear fallout shelters in preparation for a Soviet attack.

in power. Saddam Hussein, the B'aathist dictator in Iraq, Ferdinand Marcos, the corrupt longtime president of the Philippines, and President Suharto of Indonesia were examples of such men.

In 1965 the CIA helped the Indonesian government prevent a potential coup. To do this the United States backed conservative Indonesian militias, who slaughtered hundreds of thousands. The U.S. embassy in Indonesia provided the names of 5,000 alleged communists, who the militias then summarily killed. For the next thirty years, Haji Mohammad Suharto ruled Indonesia with U.S. support, despite an increasingly repressive hand.

Zaire's Joseph Mobutu was a U.S.-financed dictator. In 1960 the Eisenhower administration opposed Patrice Lumumba, the elected prime minister of the newly independent former Belgian Congo. Lumumba was forced from office by Mobutu, and later assassinated. For more than 30 years Mobutu ruled using U.S. military and economic aid to enrich himself and maintain a hold on his country, which he renamed Zaire. (He also renamed himself Mobutu Sese Seko, or "all-powerful warrior." As a declared anti-communist, Mobutu profited from American military and financial aid throughout his reign.

# Latin America and the Cold War

While the U.S. government worked to prevent the spread of communism in Africa and Asia, it also filtered its policies toward neighboring Latin America through the cold war lens. Franklin Roosevelt's non-interventionist "Good Neighbor Policy" of the 1930s came to an end with the advent of the Cold War.

During the 1950s and 1960s, the United States intervened in countries throughout the region: from Panama, Colombia, Guatemala, Paraguay, and Cuba in the Fifties to the Dominican Republic, El Salvador, Ecuador, Haiti, Honduras, Brazil, Bolivia, and Peru in the 1960s.

### Crisis with Castro's Cuba

As part of the peace treaty that ended the Spanish American War, the United States reserved the right to intervene in Cuban affairs. Beginning in the 1930s, the United States heavily supported the corrupt dictatorship of Fulgencio Batista. In return, Batista allowed

**CONFLICT WITH CUBA** After the United States organized a failed invasion of Cuba in 1961 (top), the Soviet Union placed nuclear missiles on the island. When the United States blockaded Cuba in retaliation (bottom), the Soviets withdrew the missiles in exchange for a U.S. promise not to invade.

U.S. businesses a free hand in Cuba.

When rebel leader Fidel Castro and his guerrilla fighters overthrew Batista, they immediately turned Cuba toward communism. When Castro began ordering his opponents killed or arrested, thousands of refugees fled to the United States. Many of them settled in Miami and surrounding Dade County, Florida. Meanwhile, Castro's decision to ally himself with the Soviets made the island a cold war flashpoint. In 1961 the American Central Intelligence Agency (CIA) supported a group of 1,500 Cuban exiles, backed by an American naval task force, in their effort to land in Cuba and begin a popular uprising that would overthrow Castro. The expedition, known as the Bay of Pigs Invasion, ended in disaster as the exiles were overwhelmed by a 20,000 man Cuban militia upon reaching the shore.

The Bay of Pigs episode convinced Castro to strengthen his ties with the Soviet Union. Within a year 40,000 Soviet troops and advisors were on the island. When the Soviets installed nuclear missiles on Cuba, American President John F. Kennedy faced off against Soviet premier Nikita Khrushchev in what was known as the Cuban Missile Crisis. Kennedy ordered the U.S. Navy to blockade Cuba, stopping Soviet vessels from reaching Cuban ports. Although the move outraged Khrushchev he agreed to withdraw the missiles if the United States agreed not to invade Cuba. The world had stepped back from the brink of nuclear disaster. Although the United States has maintained an embargo against Cuba throughout the forty years that have followed the crisis, Castro remained in power well into the twenty-first century.

While Castro lost the economic support of the Soviet Union in the early 1990s when the communist superpower collapsed, U.S.-Cuban relations remained tense. Although some U.S. business interests have urged an end to the embargo, leaders of the politically conservative Cuban-American exile community, backed by allies in Congress, rejected any talk of compromise with Castro's regime.

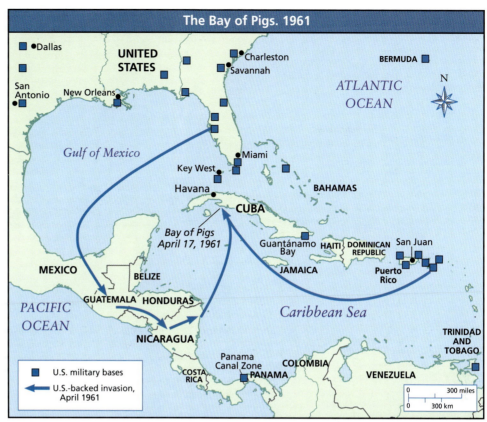

**MARINES IN ACTION** U.S. Marines patrol the streets of Hue, South Vietnam.

# The Vietnam War

Even as the Cuban missile crisis was coming to a peaceful resolution, a more prolonged Cold War crisis was stirring in Southeast Asia. During World War II territory that had been the colony of French Indochina fell under Japanese control. With Japan's defeat, France waged a losing battle against Ho Chi Minh's nationalist and communist guerrillas to reclaim control of the territory. At last, in 1954, France agreed to withdraw. According to the terms of the peace treaty, the new nation of Vietnam would be temporarily divided between a communist-controlled north and a capitalist south, pending elections to be held in 1956.

To U.S. policymakers the possibility that the former French Indochina could become communist was unacceptable. The risk, according to the prevailing "domino theory" of the time was that if Indochina became communist—even by a fair election—adjacent nations would follow, one by one. In 1955 the U.S.-backed Ngo Dinh Diem declared the south to be the Republic of Vietnam and refused to participate in elections to determine a unified Vietnamese government. This was a clear violation of the peace treaty terms. Diem, a Catholic in a mostly Buddhist nation, made matters worse by attacking Buddhists and anyone else who criticized him. His actions set off an open rebellion against Diem's government in South Vietnam. Armed with weapons supplied by the North Vietnamese communists, the anti-Diem forces took to the jungles to wage war on their U.S.-backed government.

## An Escalating Commitment

After John F. Kennedy succeeded Eisenhower in 1961 as president, he sent 17,000 American military advisors to South Vietnam to prevent its fall to communism. He also ordered a plan to assassinate Diem in favor of a less difficult Vietnamese leader. Less than three weeks after Diem's assassination, Kennedy was also gunned down.

After taking office Lyndon Baines Johnson, Kennedy's vice-president, expanded the number of U.S. advisors in Vietnam. Then, in August 1964, he appeared to television to announce that U.S. warships had been fired on by Vietnamese communist forces in the international waters of the Gulf of Tonkin. Johnson asked that the U.S. Senate pass the Gulf of Tonkin Resolution, authorizing him to take all neccessary measures to prevent further attacks on U.S. forces. By a vote of 98–2 the Senate approved the resolution. Only later was it learned that no attack had taken place.

Following the Senate vote Johnson sent Marines to Vietnam to protect U.S. bases. When those Marines were attacked, Johnson and his advisors decided to take offensive measures. By the end of 1965 the United States had 150,000 soldiers in Vietnam.

Over the next few years, U.S. generals repeatedly asked Johnson for more troops to turn the tide of war, and repeatedly, Johnson sent them. But Vietnam differed from all previous wars the U.S. military had fought. The Viet Cong, as the South Vietnamese guerrillas were called, rarely engaged in open battle. Instead they used hit and run attacks, attacking quickly and then retreating into the jungle.

The United States responded by dropping millions of gallons of a toxic chemical herbicide known as Agent Orange on Vietnam's jungles. By the war's end Agent Orange had destroyed 10 percent of all jungles in Vietnam, causing cancer both to U.S. troops and to Vietnamese soldiers and civilians alike.

By 1966 U.S. strategy shifted toward a series of major bombing campaigns against North Vietnamese port cities in order to halt the flow or arms to the South. The United States offered North Vietnam economic aid in exchange for peace, but the offer was rejected.

In the end the bombing strategy failed, and helped cost Americans the support of Vietnamese villagers. The heavy bombing and the use of napalm, a gasoline that burned its victims alive, outraged many ordinary Vietnamese.

As the war dragged on, more and more villagers came to support the Viet Cong, often hiding weapons in their homes in support of them. For U.S. troops this made it nearly impossible to know who their enemy was. In 1968 a group of U.S. soldiers commanded by Lieutenant William Calley murdered hundreds of Vietnamese civilians while searching for Viet Cong. Calley, who claimed to have been following direct orders, was the only officer found guilty of any war crimes. He received a life sentence, later reduced to 10 years, but President Nixon pardoned him in 1974.

## The Anti-War Movement

As 1968 began most Americans supported the war. The protests against the war were generally limited to college campuses such as Berkeley in California or Columbia in New York. Then in late January the Viet Cong used the Vietnamese New Year's celebration, Tet, to launch their greatest offensive of the war. Attacking major cities across the country, they even temporarily captured the U.S. embassy in the South Vietnamese capital of Saigon.

Although the Viet Cong were eventually pushed back, the Tet Offensive proved to be a turning point in American public opinion. Despite official predictions that there was "a light at the end of the tunnel," more and more Americans began to feel that the war could never be won. After news of the My Lai massacre spread later that year, Americans also began to feel that the war wasn't just unwinnable, but that it was also unjust. Throughout 1968 demonstrations spread across the country, tearing at the fabric of the nation. After Johnson only narrowly defeated the antiwar Senator Eugene McCarthy in the New Hampshire primary at the start of his reelection campaign the president announced that he would no longer be a candidate for reelection. As vice president Hubert Humphrey accepted the Democratic nomination that August in Chicago, the nation watched on television as police attacked young protesters with clubs and tear gas in Chicago's Grant Park.

## The War Winds Down

The violence in Chicago helped turn the election in favor of Richard Nixon, the vice president under Eisenhower. Nixon had campaigned on the promise that he had a secret plan to end the war.

Nixon's plan was known as "Vietnamization," which meant giving the South Vietnamese army more and more responsibility for the war as the United States gradually withdrew troops. At the same time, Nixon and his national security advisor, Henry Kissinger, devised a new strategy for preventing North Vietnamese weapons from reaching the Viet Cong. Because many of these weapons reached the South through the neighboring country of Cambodia, Nixon secretly ordered that the United States invade Cambodia.

The Cambodia invasion sparked new protests, including college protests at Kent State in Ohio and Jackson State in Mississippi in which National Guard troops fired on and killed students.

Meanwhile peace talks began between the United States, South Vietnam, and North Vietnam. By late 1972, a deal began to emerge: the Viet Cong and North Vietnamese would be allowed to stay where they were, but there would be no further fighting. The North Vietnamese, who continued to press for a united Vietnam, hesitated. As they did, the United States unleashed a massive Christmas bombing campaign, dropping the equivalent firepower of several Hiroshima atom bombs on on port cities of North Vietnam. This devastating assault shattered

**The Vietnam War**

*Legend:*
- ✈ U.S. Air Force bases
- Ho Chi Minh Trail (North Vietnamese supply route)
- **U.S. and South Vietnamese offensives**
  - ◄····· Invasion of Cambodia, April–June 1970
  - ◄── Invasion of Laos, February–March 1971
- **North Vietnamese offensives**
  - ◄── Easter offensive, March–April 1975

**A REGIONAL WAR** The conflict in Vietnam impacted all of Southeast Asia, and the United States and South Vietnam invaded neighboring Laos and Cambodia in unsuccessful attempts to stop the enemy from launching offensives from those countries. The United States withdrew from Vietnam in 1973, and two years later South Vietnam fell to the communists.

North Vietnam's air defenses and fighter force. Now North Vietnam was persuaded to accept the Paris Peace Agreement. Thousands of American prisoners of war were released, and the longest war in American history was over. In early 1975, the truce between the North Vietnamese and South Vietnamese collapsed. The Viet Cong captured Saigon so rapidly that people had to flee the American embassy by rooftop helicopter. On July 30, 1975, North Vietnamese tanks rolled into Saigon, which was prompt-ly renamed Ho Chi Minh City. North and South Vietnam were united as one nation under communist rule.

The war had cost approximately 57,700 American lives, with another 153,329 seriously wounded. The American defeat in Southeast Asia shook the nation's self-confidence. For decades to come, the role of the United States as policeman of the world would remain under a cloud of uncertainty and self-doubt.

# Chapter 30: The Civil Rights Movement

*"I'm not concerned with your liking or disliking me . . . All I ask is that you respect me as a human being."*

—JACKIE ROBINSON

One of the great ironies of American history is that even the nation's most traumatic wars—the Civil War and World War II—dramatically reshape the lives of American minorities for the better. The Civil War ended slavery and set the stage for the civil rights program of the Reconstruction era; the Second World War ushered in the modern African American civil rights era, which in turn gave momentum to the causes of Hispanic–American, Asian–American, and Native–American civil rights as well. In both wars the need for soldiers helped break down some of the institutional barriers to full legal equality within the armed forces themselves. In addition, minority valor on the battlefield won respect from all but the most prejudiced whites. Both wars were also fought—at least in part—in the name of freedom and human rights and against the forces of slavery and totalitarianism. A crusade abroad for basic human rights could not help but affect the cause of human rights at home. World War II—with its enormous demand for manpower, as well as its upward effect on the value of agricultural commodities—offered unprecedented prosperity for civilian African Americans, both for those who sought work in northern factories and those who remained on southern farms. The confidence engendered by this economic bounty—as well as the ideals for which the war was fought—combined to set in motion the most powerful social struggle in 20th-century American history: the civil rights movement.

## Jackie Robinson and the Integration of Baseball

It is impossible to find a single date to mark the onset of something as profound as the civil rights movement. A. Philip Randolph's 1941 threat of a mass march on Washington to protest the the lack of opportunity for African-American workers in the

nation's war production industry—which convinced Franklin Roosevelt to create the Fair Employment Practices Committee in 1941 is one possibility. Yet another event just a few years later had a far more sweeping impact, not on the nation's laws, but on its national consciousness.

Since the turn of the 20th century, professional baseball in America was segregated; whites and blacks played in separate leagues. Yet the World War II fight against Nazism forced America to think about its own racial practices. Some baseball owners also realized that desegregation might benefit them financially.

The Negro Leagues—boosted by national stars like pitching sensation Satchel Paige and home-run hitting king Josh Gibson—had proven their ability to draw African-American fans. At a time when many of baseball's most talented players were only just returning from military service, the all-white major leagues were in desperate need of new talent. In addition, black fans in big-league parks meant new ticket sales.

The first major league executive to desegregate his team was Branch Rickey, general manager of the Brooklyn Dodgers. In 1946 he began looking for an Negro League player tough enough mentally to ignore the taunts of racists that were sure to come. He found that—and more—in Jackie Robinson.

Robinson was born to sharecropping parents in rural Georgia but was raised in Pasedena, California. He attended UCLA, where he lettered in four sports. Upon graduation, he accepted a position as an athletic director with the National Youth Administration, a New Deal agency that offered employment and educational opportunities for young people. In 1942 Robinson was drafted into the military and court-martialed for refusing to sit in the back of an army bus at Fort Hood, Texas.

To Branch Rickey, Robinson's resume made him the ideal candidate to desegregate the National Pastime. Not only was Robinson a talented athlete, but he was also a man of upstanding character and fortitude, essential attributes in challenging the

**JACKIE ROBINSON**

prejudice of white owners, players, and fans.

At a secret 1945 meeting held to discuss the subject, Rickey's request to bring Robinson to Brooklyn (where the Dodgers played until their move to Los Angeles in 1958) was voted down unanimously by the owners. Rickey decided to challenge their decision, hiring Robinson to play for the Montreal Royals, a Dodger farm team, in 1946. His exceptional stats there—.349 batting average and 112 runs scored—convinced Rickey that Robinson was professionally ready for the majors, even if the majors were not ready for him.

In April 1947, "baseball's great experiment" began. Despite jeers from opposing players and fans, Robinson proved an exceptional ballplayer, winning Rookie of the Year honors that season and the National League Most Valuable Player award in 1949. Other Negro League stars soon joined Robinson, including Willie Mays, Hank Aaron, and Larry Doby. Robinson finished his career in 1956, retiring with a lifetime batting average of .311. In 1962 he became the first African American elected to the Baseball Hall of Fame.

## Integration of the Nation's Military

During World War II the Army Air Force's all-black Ninety-ninth Pursuit Squadron, or Tuskegee Airmen, escorted bombers deep into Italy and Germany, never losing a single plane while doing so. The all-Japanese American 442nd Regimental Combat Team/100th Battalion became the most decorated U.S. military unit in the war—even though a number of the soldier's in the unit had parents, wives and children interned back in the United States as potential security risks. Although the all-Puerto Rican 65th Infantry Regiment was the only segregated Hispanic unit, as many as 500,000 Hispanic Americans served in the war.

Despite proving their valor on the battlefield, most American minorities remained in segregated units after the end of the war. Military leaders feared that integration would stir resentment among white soldiers and undermine combat readiness, a crucial consideration during a time of heightened cold war tensions. But in 1948, under pressure from the NAACP and other civil rights organizations, Harry Truman issued an executive order requiring integration of all branches of the military.

Resistance was stiff at first, but the onset of the Korean War in 1950 accelerated the process. For instance, by war's end,

**MILITARY DESEGREGATION** Desegregated American troops in Korea.

more than 90 percent of all black troops were serving in integrated units. By the Vietnam era of the 1960s, the ranks of enlisted men were fully integrated and, while the officer corps lagged behind, even there significant progress had been made.

Nonetheless, the Vietnam War offered up a different kind of civil rights problem. While blacks represented roughly 11 percent of the total military force in the war zone, they accounted for fully 20 percent of all battlefield casualties. It was, one African-American soldier remarked, "the kind of integration that could kill you." Many civil rights leaders, including Martin Luther King Jr., employed such statistics to bolster their arguments in favor of ending American involvement in the war. King and critics of the war also criticized American policy in Vietnam as an armed attack on a poor, nonwhite population—the Vietnamese—and as a drain on government financial resources that should have been spent on antipoverty programs.

The military's transition to an all-volunteer force after Vietnam served to increase the percentage of minorities in uniform. With higher unemployment levels, continued discrimination against them in private industry, and fewer economic opportunities in the rural South and inner-city North, blacks and Hispanics joined the military in far greater numbers than did whites. As a result minority soldiers were able to rise through the ranks, eventually reaching the officer corps of the various branches of the service. During the early 1990s General Colin Powell, the son of West Indian immi-

grants of African heritage, became chairman of the Joint Chiefs of Staff—the military's highest uniformed position. As Powell himself noted, "The Army was living the democratic idea ahead of the rest of America. Beginning in the fifties, less discrimination, a truer merit system, and leveler playing fields existed inside the gates of our military posts than in any southern city hall or northern corporation."

## Integration of the Nation's Schools

In marked contrast to the military, the integration of the nation's schools proved to be one of the slowest, most difficult, and most controversial civil rights efforts in U.S. history. Since Reconstruction times southern schools had been kept strictly segregated, a fact of life legally enshrined by the 1896 *Plessy v. Ferguson* Supreme Court decision. The decision allowed for "separate but equal" educational facilities, even as most local school systems made little effort to provide equal facilities to blacks. Alabama, for example, spent $36 per white pupil but just $10 per black in 1929. While Maryland, Missouri and Oklahoma were forced to open up their graduate schools to blacks, segregation remained strictly enforced at the primary, secondary, and college levels.

In 1948 the NAACP decided to challenge this policy. In order to challenge directly the "separate" part of the Plessy decision, the NAACP sued the Board of Education in Topeka, Kansas, where spending was roughly equal between black and white schools. Thus, in 1952 the most important challenge to school segregation in U.S. history was put in front of the Supreme Court as *Brown v. Board of Education* (of Topeka).

NAACP lawyer Thurgood Marshall argued that segregation was inherently unequal even if the facilities for blacks and whites were identical down to the last nail. And because they were unequal, they were in violation of the equal protection clause of the 14th Amendment to the Constitution, the amendment ratified in the late 1860s to protect the rights of former slaves.

To illustrate their point, Marshall used the research of Harvard University sociologist Kenneth B. Clarke. Using two sets of dolls—one set with white features and one with black ones—Clarke asked black children to state their preferences. Virtually all chose the white dolls, which Clarke said indicated how segregated education lowers the self-esteem of black children, even when facilities at their schools matched those of whites. That study—and Marshall's reasoned arguments—swayed the Court. Writing for the majority, Chief Justice Earl Warren argued that segregation "generates [in black children] a feeling of inferiority as to their status in the community that may affect their hearts and minds in a way unlikely to ever be undone." A year later, in a follow-up decision to the case commonly known as Brown II, the Court set out guidelines for dismantling segregated education in America.

But its choice of words—"with all deliberate speed"—was interpreted by many southern governments to mean "as slowly as possible." In 1956, more than 100 southern congressmen issued the "Southern Manifesto" denouncing *Brown* and urging their constituents to defy it. Only three senators from southern states—Estes Kefauver and Albert Gore of Tennessee and Lyndon Baines Johnson of Texas—refused to sign the manifesto. By early 1957

THE LITTLE ROCK NINE

**LITTLE ROCK NINE** Nine African-American teens desegregated Central High in Little Rock, Arkansas in 1957.

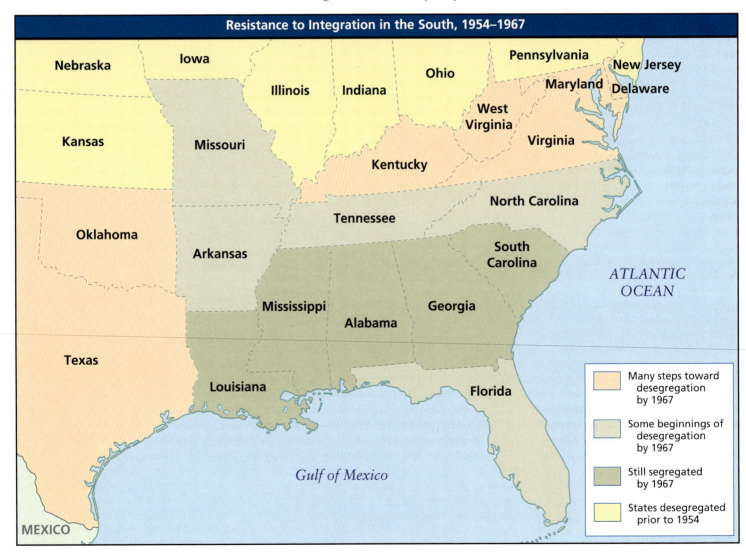

### Resistance to Integration in the South, 1954–1967

Legend:
- Many steps toward desegregation by 1967
- Some beginnings of desegregation by 1967
- Still segregated by 1967
- States desegregated prior to 1954

**RESISTANCE TO INTEGRATION** Throughout the 1960s, segregationist governments in the deep South continued to ignore the Supreme Court's *Brown v. Board of Education* decision of 1954.

more than half a million southern whites had formed White Citizens' Councils, organizations bent on blocking the implementation of civil rights measures. More extremist southerners flocked to the Ku Klux Klan, swelling its numbers to the highest level since the 1920s. As the 1957–1958 school year loomed, civil rights organizations and pro-segregation groups readied for confrontation.

In September 1957 the Little Rock, Arkansas, school board attempted to integrate nine black students in Little Rock's Central High School, an all-white institution. The nine students were met by crowds of jeering, stone-throwing white students and parents. Meanwhile, Governor Orval Faubus called in the National Guard to bar the students from the school. Faubus's challenge to federal authority forced a reluctant President Dwight Eisenhower to act. He nationalized the National Guard so that Faubus could no longer use them to block access to the school. Eisenhower, the former commander of Allied forces in Europe, then sent in 1,000 paratroopers from the 101st Airborne to force the integration of the school. The paratroopers stayed through the school year. The struggle did not end there, however, as Faubus ordered Central High closed entirely for the 1958 school year rather than allow it to educate blacks. Thus, despite the *Brown* decision, the road to school desegregation would remain a long and arduous one. As late as 1960 less than 1 percent of southern blacks were attending integrated schools.

# Civil Rights Protests

Important as they were, the integration of baseball, the *Brown* decision, and the events in Little Rock were events spearheaded by forces outside of the Deep South—whether they be a courageous though calculated move by a baseball executive, the brilliance of the NAACP's legal team or the executive decisions of a president in Washington forced into action. Yet the most important advances in the civil rights movement of the 1950s and 1960s originated among the black citizenry of the South. First among these events was a simple but powerful act of of defiance that took place on a city bus in Montgomery, Alabama on December 2, 1955.

**PARKS UNDER ARREST** Rosa Parks is fingerprinted after her arrest.

## Montgomery Bus Boycott

Rosa Parks—a Montgomery, Alabama seamstress and a member of the local NAACP chapter—was coming home from work on the bus one evening when she was asked to give up her seat to a white man, as per bus company rules and southern custom and law. Segregation of public facilities had been widespread throughout the South since the late 19th century and represented a daily reminder to African Americans of their second-class status in society. This time, however, Parks refused to surrender her seat. While it is true that Parks's act of resistance was spontaneous, it was equally the case that local black civil rights activists—of whom Parks was one—were looking for an opportunity to challenge Montgomery's segregation laws. Thus, the day after Parks's arrest for "disorderly conduct," local black civil rights and religious leaders formed the Montgomery Improvement Association (MIA), and called for a one-day bus boycott to begin on December 5, the day of Parks's trial. The group chose Reverend Ralph Abernathy of the First Baptist Church to lead negotiations with the city and Dr. Martin Luther King Jr. of the Dexter Avenue Baptist Church to head the MIA. Meanwhile the Women's Political Council, a local black women's civic group, distributed 52,000 fliers to homes in black neighborhoods and black ministers throughout the city urged their parishioners to support the boycott.

On December 5 the city's buses—usually full of black workers on their way to jobs in factories and white homes—ran almost entirely empty. White officials—convinced "Negro goon squads" were intimidating black riders—dispatched police to restore order. But there were no goon squads; the boycott had the support of the vast majority of Montgomery's black community. When Parks was found guilty of violating the city's segregation ordinances, the boycott leaders called for a continuing boycott to force an end to segregation on city buses. "There comes a time," King told an audience of 7,000 at the Holt Street Baptist Church, "when people get tired of being trampled over by the iron feet of oppression." For the next 381 days Montgomery's African-American community refused to ride buses, choosing to drive, hitchhike carpool and walk instead.

King's nonviolent philosophy was adopted from the teachings of Mohandas K. Gandhi, leader of the anticolonial movement in India. Even when a bomb exploded on the front porch of King's home just shy of two months into the boycott, King addressed an angry crowd of supporters by saying, "We must meet violence with nonviolence."

By the summer of 1956 the boycott had become a nationwide newspaper story, and King had appeared on the cover of *Time* and the *New York Times Magazine*. In June a federal court ruled that segregated seating was unconstitutional, and although the case was appealed to the U.S. Supreme Court, the high court voted on December 20, 1956 to support the lower court's decision. Parks, Abernathy, King, the MIA, and the black community of Montgomery had won. The implications of the boycott were enormous—for the African-American community, the South, and the nation as a whole. "We have gained a new sense of dignity and destiny," King wrote. "We have discovered a new and powerful weapon—nonviolent resistance."

### Sit-ins and Freedom Rides

During the decade that followed the Montgomery bus boycott victory, nonviolent resistance served as the central strategy in the fight against segregation. On February 1, 1960 four students from North Carolina AT&T College sat down at the all-white lunch counter at Woolworth's store. Although they were refused service they would not leave, remaining seated for over an hour. Rather than serve them the store closed the counter for the day. Although the first "sit-in" of this kind occurred in 1942, it was not until this incident in 1960 that the sit-in movement received national attention.

Within days of the Greensboro sit-in, 100 college students staged a similar protest in Montgomery, Alabama. Similar protests were held at segregated churches, and wade-ins were held at whites-only swimming pools.

Another target of desegregation efforts was interstate buses. Although the Supreme Court outlawed segregation on interstate buses and trains (and in bus and train stations as well) in 1946, segregation on interstate buses and trains still existed throughout the South as the nation moved into the 1960s. In 1961 James Farmer, head of the Congress of Racial Equality (CORE), organized a campaign to bring attention to the situation. Dozens of black and white young people—nicknamed Freedom Riders—would ride through the Deep South together, attempting to integrate the buses as well as bus station lunchcounters, rest rooms and waiting rooms. Their destination would be New Orleans, Louisiana, where they would join in a celebration marking the the seventh anniversary of the *Brown v. Board of Education* school desegregation decision.

Once the journey began the Freedom Riders faced arrests, and particularly in Alabama, brutal violence. Although the first group of Riders were forced to end their bus campaign in Birmingham, Alabama, and fly the final leg of the journey to New Orleans, a second group, organized by Diane Nash of the Student Nonviolent Coordinating Committee (SNCC), attempted to continue the journey. That attempt ended when Mississippi officials arrested the riders in Jackson, Mississippi. Although neither of the original two groups of freedom riders reached their destination by bus, their story gained international attention for their cause and helped force the federal government into action.

On May 29, 1961 President John F. Kennedy sent federal authorities to guard the riders and ordered the Interstate Commerce Commission to enforce regulations against segregation in transportation facilities. With the weight of the federal government coming down on their shoulders, most southern municipalities accepted the orders and quietly integrated interstate bus and rail stations.

### James Meredith and the University of Mississippi

A few months after the Freedom Rides ended, the Kennedy Administration was forced to act again to enforce federal law. After serving in the U.S. Air Force from 1951 to 1960, Kosciusko, Mississippi native James Meredith decided to apply to the all-white University of Mississippi ("Ole Miss"). Meredith's personal struggle became a national event when Governor Ross Barnett defied court orders and physically stopped Meredith from entering the school. President John F. Kennedy sent in federal troops to defend Meredith's right to an equal education. The riot that followed left two people dead and hundreds injured, but Meredith was finally admitted, and graduated in 1963. In 1966, he began a solo voter registration march in Mississippi, during which he was wounded by gunfire, but survived.

### Bloody Birmingham, 1963

In January 1963, Martin Luther King, Jr. announced that the Southern Christian Leadership Conference (SCLC) would launch "Project C"—a campaign to integrate Birmingham, Alabama's public facilities and department stores. Although the "C" stood for confrontation King's tactics, which included sit-ins and boycotts, were based on the same non violent approach that he had advocated ever since the Montgomery bus boycott eight years earlier. Nonetheless, American TV viewers watched in horror as Eugene "Bull" Connor, Birmingham's public safety commissioner, launched a ruthless clampdown on the protesters. Police unleashed attack dogs on children, and knocked crowds to the sidewalks with powerful fire hoses. Thousands, including King himself, were arrested. When white clergymen wrote to King to complain that his tactics broke local laws and were ill-advised, he responded by penning his eloquent "Letter from a Birmingham Jail." Although the SCLC protests led to a temporary settlement by late May, violence continued to mar the progress. In September 1963 four black girls were killed by a bomb during services at the Sixteenth Street Baptist Church.

### March on Washington

Meanwhile, a century after the Emancipation Proclamation, it had become increasingly clear that only federal action could bring African Americans equality under the law. On June 11, 1963, President Kennedy asked the nation on national television, "Are we to say to the world and much more importantly, to each other that this is is the land of the free, except for Negroes; that we have no second-class citizens, except for Negroes, that we have no class or caste system, no ghettoes, no master race except with respect to Negroes?" The very same night that Kennedy delivered his address, Medger Evers, the head of the NAACP in Mississippi, was killed outside of his home. One week later Kennedy sent a new civil rights bill to Congress. Although it was not as strong as some hoped, it went further than any civil rights bill before it.

Much to Kennedy's annoyance A. Philip Randolph, the labor leader who had threatened to lead a march on Washington in 1941

**MARCH ON WASHINGTON** Dr. King, seen second from left in front row, and fellow marchers during the 1963 March on Washington.

to protest unfair hiring practices in the defense industry, devised a plan to pressure Congress to pass the bill. Kennedy feared that a large march would cause a backlash in Congress that would sink his bill.

Nonetheless, planning for the march moved forward. Much of the credit belongs to Bayard Rustin, one of the unsung heroes of the civil rights movement. Rustin was instrumental in shaping the march's message. As a labor leader, Randolph wanted to focus on jobs but Rustin suggested the broader theme of "freedom." It was also Rustin who brought the diverse—and often divided—coalition of civil rights groups to the march. Before agreeing to participate, older, more conservative groups like the National Urban League and the NAACP insisted on a nonconfrontational, nonvio-

lent march while younger organizations such as SNCC preferred a march that left open the possibility of nonviolent resistance. In June, King and the SCLC agreed to participate, and King sided with the more conservative groups. Following King's lead, liberal white religious organizations—like the National Council of Churches, the Unitarian Universalist Association, the National Conference of Catholics for Interracial Justice, and the American Jewish Congress—also agreed come on board.

In the days leading up to August 28, tens of thousands of people poured into Washington by car, rail, and plane. One man even roller-skated there from Chicago. The sheer size of the crowd—some 250,000 persons attended—as well as its ethnic and religious diversity was perhaps the

best demonstration of the widespread support the civil rights movement enjoyed across America. The audience listened as Rustin read the march leaders' ten demands, which included an end to housing and school desegregation, more job training, and a raise in the minimum wage. Later, organizers met with a supportive President Kennedy.

But if the 1963 March on Washington is remembered for one thing, it is the stirring words of King. "I have a dream," he told the assembled thousands, "that one day on the red hills of Georgia the sons of former slaves and the sons of former slave-owners will be able to sit down together at the table of brotherhood. I have a dream that one day even the state of Mississippi, a state sweltering with the heat of injustice and oppression, will be transformed into an oasis of freedom and justice. I have a dream that my four little children will one day live in a nation where they will not be judged by the color of their skin but by the content of their character." Then he ended the speech with the words of an old Negro spiritual, "Free at last! Free at last! Thank God almighty, we are free at last!"

While King's eloquence had long been familiar to civil rights activists in the field, this was the first time many ordinary Americans—both black and white—had had a chance to hear him. The speech established King as one of the towering figures in 20th century U.S. history.

The march demonstrated through a peaceful gathering of hundreds of thousands of white and black Americans the power of nonviolent protest. Sadly that concept would soon be tested. Just three weeks after the March, a bomb was set off at the Sixteenth Street Baptist Church in Birmingham, killing four young African-American girls. Two months after that, on November 22, 1963, President Kennedy was assassinated in Dallas.

## Civil Rights Act of 1964

The rise to the presidency of Vice President Lyndon Baines Johnson alarmed civil rights leaders. Johnson was a southerner from Texas, and had shown little commitment to black issues in his long political career in the House and Senate. But perhaps the African-American community should not have been surprised that Johnson would put civil rights high on his agenda—he had been one of only three southern senators to reject the racist "Southern Manfesto" against school desegregation in 1956. Just days after Kennedy's death, Johnson told Congress that passage of the Civil Rights Act would serve as a memorial to the slain president. In June 1964 Congress passed and Johnson signed the Civil Rights Act, the first major civil rights bill since Reconstruction times. The act's key provision is Title VII, which outlawed segregation in public accommodations and job discrimination on the basis of race, national origin, religion, or sex. The legislation also allowed the U.S. Attorney General to withhold federal funds from any state program that practiced discrimination and permitted aggrieved persons to petition the federal Equal Employment Opportunity Commission—an agency that President Kennedy had authorized—for redress.

## Johnson's Great Society

Although Johnson should be credited with keeping his vow to see the Civil Rights Act passed as a memorial to Kennedy, the truth is that the Texan president deserves more credit than Kennedy for working to improve the lives of Black Americans and Americans in poverty that Kennedy does. In a May 1964 commencement address at the University of Michigan, Johnson said: "The Great Society rests on abundance and liberty for all. It demands an end to poverty and injustice, to which we are totally committed in our time."

Central to his Great Society plan is his "War on Poverty," which will lead to the passage of several social services laws. By the end of summer, he had pushed the Economic Opportunity Act through Congress, authorizing nearly $950 million for such programs as Volunteers in Service to America (VISTA), the Job Corps, Head Start, and Legal Services.

Johnson's wide popular support helped him handily defeat the conservative Arizona senator Barry Goldwater in the 1964 presidential election, and initiate a burst of social programs unheard of since the New Deal era. In April 1964 he guided the Elementary

**MISSING** An FBI poster released after the disappearance of civil rights workers Andrew Goodman, James Chaney, and Michael Schwerner.

and Secondary Education Act through Congress. The bill allocated funds for schools that serve children of low-income families. In July he signed the landmark Medicare and Medicaid programs into law as amendments to the Social Security Act of 1935. Medicare provides for hospital care and supplemental insurance for people over 65. Medicaid provides medical care to low-income patients. Later in the year Congress passed the Higher Education Act funding many education programs including the Guaranteed Student Loan program, and established the Department of Housing and Urban Development to oversee national policies and programs regarding housing issues for low- and moderate-income families.

## Freedom Summer

Despite the many improvements brought on by Johnson's Great Society Programs, many civil rights leaders recognized that African-Americans would never gain true equality if they were prevented from exercising their right to vote. Since the late 19th century qualified black voters had been disenfranchised by measures like poll taxes and literacy tests, which were rigorously enforced in areas with large numbers of African Americans and laxly enforced where poor and uneducated whites lived.

In the summer of 1964 CORE and SNCC launched a campaign to register African-American voters in Mississippi, the state with the South's lowest level of black voter registration. Hundreds of local blacks, as well as black and white workers from the North, would participate. To prepare for what would be called Freedom Summer, organizers were sent to Mississippi early in the year. One of these was Michael Schwerner, a 24 year-old white social worker from Brooklyn, New York. Schwerner helped establish a CORE office with James Chaney, a 21 year-old black from the area. On June 20, hundreds of volunteers descended on Mississippi, including Andrew Goodman, a 20 year-old white anthropology student at City College, New York. All three were murdered the next day by local Ku Klux Klansmen and law enforcement officers.

The murders—as well as dissension in the ranks as local blacks complained that the white volunteers were usurping leadership positions—failed to stop the drive. Nor did the more than one thousand arrests, 80 beatings by white mobs, and 67 bombings of black homes and churches. Despite fear of white reprisals, more than 80,000 black Mississippians registered to join the Mississippi Freedom Democratic Party (MFDP). At that year's Democratic convention in Atlantic City, New Jersey, however, party officials refused to recognize the MFDP's delegation, choosing the all-white regular Mississippi Democratic Party to represent the state. But MFDP delegation leader Fannie Lou Hamer—who had been evicted from the farm she had sharecropped for 18 years for her organizing efforts—won a ban against racially discriminatory delegations at future conventions.

Meanwhile, in Mississippi, the Freedom Summer volunteers set up 30 Freedom Schools throughout the state. The schools had a dual purpose: first, to highlight the gross inequalities between the state's white and black schools; and second, to provide classes for the children of impoverished black Mississippians. Again, using local black volunteers and white college students from the North as teachers, the schools offered courses in civil rights, black history, and leadership development, as well as more basic instruction in reading, writing, and arithmetic. Expecting about a thousand students, the Freedom Schools eventually enrolled more than 3,000. Beyond educating and registering thousands of Mississippi's African Americans, Freedom Summer—as well as the Selma-Montgomery (Alabama) march of the following year—paved the way for perhaps the greatest political accomplishment of the civil rights era, the Voting Rights Act of 1965.

## The Selma March and the Voting Rights Act of 1965

In February 1965, black voting-rights advocate Jimmy Lee Jackson was murdered by sheriff's deputies in Selma, Alabama while leaving a protest rally at a local church. National civil rights leaders therefore decided to focus their voter registration efforts on the town of 30,000, divided equally between blacks and whites. On March 3 Martin Luther King, who had arrived in Selma two months earlier to assist in the registration drive, came to speak at Jackson's funeral and, in one of his first public criticisms of President Johnson, asked why the government could spend millions defending the South Vietnamese but could not protect one of its own citizens on American soil. King and other civil rights leaders felt that a dramatic gesture was needed to prod the federal government on voting rights legislation. A series of marches—designed to draw media attention to the violence and discrimination that barred black political participation—had met with violence from white mobs and police. On March 7, just four days after Jackson's funeral, a four-day march was organized from Selma to Montgomery—some 50 miles to the east—to petition Governor Wallace directly. On Sunday, March 7, state troopers attacked the marchers as they crossed Selma's Edmund Pettus Bridge at the start of a planned 54-mile march to Montgomery. Labeled "Bloody Sunday," the event helped spur President Lyndon B. Johnson to push for the Voting Rights Act of 1965. On March 15, Johnson went on national TV to announce that he was submitting a comprehensive voting rights bill to Congress. "Their cause," he said of the marchers, "must be our cause, too. Because it's not just Negroes, but it's really all of us who must overcome the crippling legacy of bigotry and injustice." Appearing to speak to Wallace and other white Alabamans, he insisted, "It is wrong—deadly wrong, to deny any of your fellow Americans the right to vote in this country." Then, borrowing the rallying cry of the movement, he ended his speech, "And, we shall overcome." Never before had a president identified himself so closely and unapologetically with the cause of civil rights. King, it was said, cried as he listened to the speech. On March 21 another group of marchers—this time protected by federal troops—completed the 54 miles to the capital of Montgomery.

The Voting Rights Act, signed into law on August 6, 1965, was last major piece of legislation of the civil rights era. It was a sweeping and powerful bill that banned literacy tests and put Washington in the business of voter registration for the first time, by sending federal examiners to register voters in any county where more than 50 percent of the voting age population failed to show up on the registration lists. Together with the 24th Amendment of 1964, which banned poll taxes, the act ended all the legal tricks that southern states had employed since the late 19th century to stop blacks from voting.

The Voting Rights Act of 1965 and the Civil Rights Act of 1964 fulfilled the promises of equal protection made by the 14th Amendment during Reconstruction. They reversed nearly a century of Jim Crow laws, though it would take another decade or so to finally end the practice of southern segregation. But just as these bills represented a landmark of civil rights legislation, so too the Selma-Montgomery march marked the culmination of nonviolent protest as the centerpiece of the civil rights struggle.

The Voting Rights Act was the high water mark of the African-American civil rights movement. Less than six months later, a city far from Alabama and Mississippi would explode in violence. The Watts riot, named after the African-American neighborhood in Los Angeles where it took place, would also be the first of more than 100 riots that would erupt in American cities over the next three summers. The riot devastated President Johnson, who bitterly asked:

> How is it possible, after all we've accomplished?. . . God knows how little we've really moved on this issue despite the fanfare. As I see it, I've moved the Negro from D+ to C-. He's still nowhere. He knows it. And that's why he's out in the streets.

The riots struck right at the heart of Johnson's Great Society programs, seemingly tearing down everything he had worked to build up. It would also signal a new and more violent phase of black unrest that would polarize the civil rights community and spur a backlash among some whites who felt that African Americans were receiving too much attention from the government.

# Malcolm X and the Rise of Black Nationalism

Throughout the 20th century, two conflicting tendencies have permeated African-American political thought. One traces back to the writings of W. E. B. DuBois and the founding ideals of the NAACP: an integrated, multiracial United States, free of prejudice and discrimination, where African Americans enjoy equality of economic opportunity and full political participation. The integrationist tendency, as it has been called, reached its highest peak in the civil rights movement of the 1950s and early 1960s and found its greatest leader in the Reverend Martin Luther King Jr.

But there has been another school of thought and action among black activists in this century, one that traces back to Marcus Garvey and his Universal Negro Improvement Association. While the integrationist approach to freedom and equality was premised on the idea that white America could be changed and redeemed, the separatist approach—as it is sometimes referred to—condemned white America as unalterably hostile to the aspirations of blacks. This separatist tendency achieved its own peak—in the Black Power movement of the late 1960s and early 1970s—and found its greatest leader—and martyr—in Malcolm X.

Malcolm X—the self-proclaimed "angriest black man in America"—was one of the most important advocates for black liberation in American history. Born Malcolm Little in 1925, he led an early life of crime, but converted to the Nation of Islam in prison. Following his release he recruited thousands of blacks to the organization before eventually breaking with the group altogether. Although he enjoyed a warm personal relationship with Martin Luther King Jr., the two men represented two factions of the struggle for equality and freedom. On the one hand, King preached nonviolent resistance and saw integration as a major goal. Malcolm, on the other hand, viewed black self-sufficiency and self-awareness as a greater goal—one for which blacks should strive to achieve "by any means necessary."

Black integrationist and separatist leaders like King on the one hand and Malcolm on the other differed in more than just strategy. The movements were fundamentally different. Where the civil rights movement came out of the rural (and urban) South, the separatists were largely a northern and urban phenomenon. And where the integrationists placed their faith in a Christian god, separatists often looked to Allah and Islam, which—along with Marcus Garvey's Back-to-Africa movement of the 1920s—is where the history of 20th-century black nationalism begins.

## The Nation of Islam

Although most of the first generations of Africans brought to the Americas as slaves in the 17th and 18th centuries practiced local indiginous faiths—and to a lesser extent Islam—most enslaved African-Americans soon melded traditional beliefs of their ancestors to Christianity. For hundreds of years African Americans used the Christian faith to sustain their spirit and hopes for a better life in the next world, even as they developed Christian institutions that served as centers of cultural, political, and social life in this one.

But to Wallace Fard, a door-to-door silk salesperson in early 1930s Detroit, Christianity was the faith of the oppressor, and its worship by African-Americans a symbol of their servitude. To address his concern Fard created a new religion, called the

**MALCOLM X**

Nation of Islam, which fused some of the rites of Christianity with Islam. In 1931 Fard and his assistant, Elijah Poole—who would change his name to Elijah Muhammad—opened the first Nation of Islam temple in Detroit.

In 1934 Elijah Muhammad took control of the Nation of Islam after Fard disappeared. Over the next few years he moved the Nation of Islam headquarters to Chicago where he opened Temple Number 2, and began preaching that Fard was Allah and that he, Muhammed, was his messenger. Even as Muhammed was jailed during World War II for speaking out in support of Japan (because the Japanese were not white), the Nation of Islam's membership roles swelled, particularly among northern, urban poor and the prison community.

## Malcolm X

In 1947 the Nation of Islam recruited its most famous convert—an imprisoned former drug dealer and petty thief named Malcolm Little. After joining the Nation of Islam Little changed his name to Malcolm X. When he was released from prison in 1952, Malcolm began working to expand the movement. After organizing his first temple in Boston and then spending a year as its minister, Malcolm

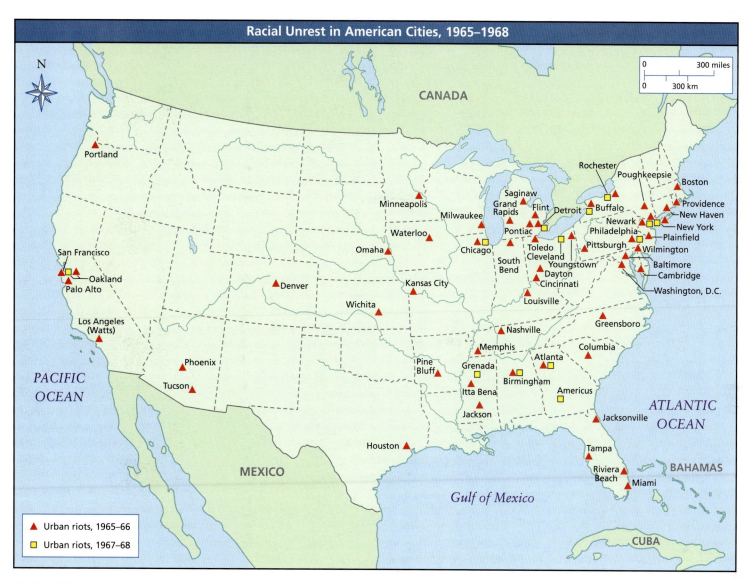

**Racial Unrest in American Cities, 1965–1968**

Legend:
- ▲ Urban riots, 1965–66
- ▢ Urban riots, 1967–68

**RACE RIOTS** Many of America's major cities experienced racial unrest during the 1960s.

became minister of Temple Number 7 in New York's Harlem. From that post he gained wide attention and legions of new followers for the movement.

By 1962, Elijah Muhammad had appointed Malcolm national minister and official spokesperson of the Nation of Islam. But he also may have felt overshadowed by Malcolm's popularity. He also resented what he viewed as Malcolm's independence: as early as the late 1950s, Malcolm had begun openly questioning Muhammad's belief that all white people were "devils."

In 1963 Muhammad found an opportunity to assert his authority. When Malcolm remarked that Kennedy's assassination was an example of "the chickens come home to roost," or American society's violence turning back on itself, Muhammed censured him, and ordered him to cease preaching. This move—com-

bined with revelations that Muhammad had fathered several illegitimate children—led Malcolm to resign from the Nation of Islam. On March 8, 1964, he announced the founding of a new Islamic movement—the Muslim Mosque, Inc.—which would commit itself to political activism and cooperation with civil rights leaders.

Malcolm also took time off to make a pilgrimage to Mecca, a requirement of all able-bodied Muslims, and to several newly independent African countries. The trip had a profound impact on the last remaining year of his life and led to his formation of the Organization of Afro-American Unity, which advocated both independent black institutions and black participation in electoral politics. The impact that the new organization might have had can never be known, however. On February 21, 1965, while speaking at Harlem's Audubon ballroom, Malcolm was assas-

sinated, allegedly by members of the Nation of Islam.

Like King's, Malcolm X's legacy is profound. His warnings that African-American frustration would turn to anger and violence was born out within months of his death, in the rioting in the Watts section of Los Angeles. His rhetoric of black militancy and self-defense was picked up by radical groups like the Black Panthers and his calls for African-American self-dignity bore fruit in the "black is beautiful" movement of the late 1960s. His autobiography—dictated to *Roots* author Alex Haley—was read by millions of young blacks and whites as both a paean to self-improvement and as a primer in radical political education.

**The Black Power Movement**

Nowhere was Malcolm X's legacy more immediately and more powerfully felt than in the Black Power movement of the mid-to-late-1960s. With the passage of the Civil Rights Act of 1964 and the Voting Rights Act of 1965, segregation rules and discriminatory statutes had virtually been wiped from the legal record, thanks to the activism of CORE, SNCC, and the SCLC and the legal strategies of the NAACP and other civil rights groups. Yet despite these hard-fought successes, discrimination remained very much a part of the American way of life.

In early 1966 Stokely Carmichael (later Kwame Turé), a black Trinidadian immigrant raised in the Bronx, New York, led a radical coalition to power within SNCC. As one of his first moves he ousted whites from the organization. In June 1966 SNCC joined a march to protest the shooting of James Meredith, the University of Mississippi's first African-American student. While marching Carmichael and other SNCC members took up the call-and-response chant: "What do you want? . . . Black Power!" The media immediately focused on this militancy as a new angle on the civil rights movement story.

While more conservative black leaders like King applauded the call to black pride, Carmichael's militancy alarmed them. He not only called for separatism, but also vengeance against the "honky," in time arguing that "we must become the executioners of our executioners." King condemned this new militancy by writing, "In advocating violence, it is imitating the worst, the most brutal, and the most uncivilized value of human life. . . . There is no salvation for the Negro through isolation . . . the black man needs the white man and the white man needs the black man."

Yet the spirit behind the Black Power ideology predated Stokely Carmichael's aggressive political sloganeering, and it involved far more than politics. It also had cultural aspects: from the poetry of Amiri Baraka (LeRoi Jones) and the establishment of Black Studies programs at universities to the creation of Kwanzaa, a new Afrocentric cultural holiday that lasted seven days in December to honor what Professor Maulana Karenga, the holiday's founder, called the "Seven Principles" or African-American values.

During the 1960s, many white Americans were oblivious to the intellectual undercurrents behind the Black Power movement. Yet as cultural movements often will, the Black Power movement adopted its own recognizable fashions that did enter the mass consciousness of American culture: ordinary African Americans expressed a political message by sporting the Afro hairstyle, and by wearing dashikis, a billowing and colorful West African upper garment.

### The Black Panthers

The Black Panther Party, established in Oakland, California, on October, 1966, was organized by Huey Newton and Bobby Seale—young African Americans who were impatient with Martin Luther King Jr.'s nonviolent approach. Angered by police violence against members of the black community, the Panthers advocated armed self-defense. Seale, Newton, and Panther "Minister of Information" Eldridge Cleaver drafted a 10-point program for economic, social and political development in black neighborhoods.

The Panthers took a cue from both Malcolm X and Carmichael. In fact Carmichael formally joined the Panthers in 1967. When Betty Shabazz, Malcolm's widow, visited San Francisco the same year the Panthers provided her with armed security. When they were stopped by police, the Panthers cited their right to bear arms and were not arrested. In May 1967 the Panthers showed up in the state capital of Sacramento bearing arms; they read a statement proclaiming their right to bear arms.

Perhaps not surprisingly, provocative actions such as this made the groups a target by law enforcement agencies. FBI Director J. Edgar Hoover called the Panthers "the greatest threat to internal security in the country."

In October, as Huey Newton was returning home from a party, he was stopped by police; a shootout erupted and a police officer was killed. Newton was wounded and charged with murder. Though no gun was found on him Newton was convicted of murder. Because Newton received a sentence of 2–15 years rather than a life sentence, outraged Oakland police shot out the windows of Panther headquarters. In 1969, Chicago policemen killed two Panthers in an unprovoked attack, spurring nationwide anger among African-Americans and leading to unfounded conspiracy theories of a national police campaign to kill the groups members.

As there had been in 1965 and 1966, urban riots continued into the summers of 1967 and 1968. Lyndon Johnson, increasingly isolated by growing opposition to the Vietnam War, and frustrated by the simmering tensions in the inner cities, continued to fight for civil rights legislation. Following the riots of 1967, he created the National Advisory Commission in Civic Disorder, or the Kerner Commission, after its leader, Governor Otto Kerner of Ohio. After studying 164 civil disturbances, the Kerner Commission released its findings, stating:

> This is our basic conclusion: our nation is moving toward two societies, one black, one white—separate, but unequal . . .This deepening racial division is not inevitable. The movement apart can be reversed. Choice is still possible. Our principal task is to define that choice and to press for a national solution.

A few weeks later, Martin Luther King was assassinated in Memphis. Although the Black Panthers joined mainstream civil rights leaders in pleading for peace, riots broke out in 172 cities, resulting in 43 deaths, 3,500 injuries and 27,000 arrests. With the murder of Robert F. Kennedy two months later, many blacks felt a deep hopelessness. Yet despite the mood of despair and continued poverty in many black communities in 1968, the past dozen years had brought sweeping changes to race relations in American life. The civil rights movement had won major victories with the passage of the Civil Rights Act of 1964 and the Voting Rights Act of 1965. While the more aggressive stances of Malcolm X, Stokely Carmichael and the Black Panthers had frightened some potential white allies and others, these more radical voices had brought a powerful sense of positive identity to a younger generations of African Americans.

# The Hispanic-, Asian- and Native-American Rights Movements

As the African-American civil rights movement took center stage during the 1950s and 1960s, the victories won and tactics used in winning them inspired similar action among other American minority groups, as well as among women. At the same time each of these movements took its own distinctive shape, whether the more radical "Red Power" movement led by the militant American Indian Movement (AIM), the diverse array of Hispanic-American

## Migrant Farm Worker Migration

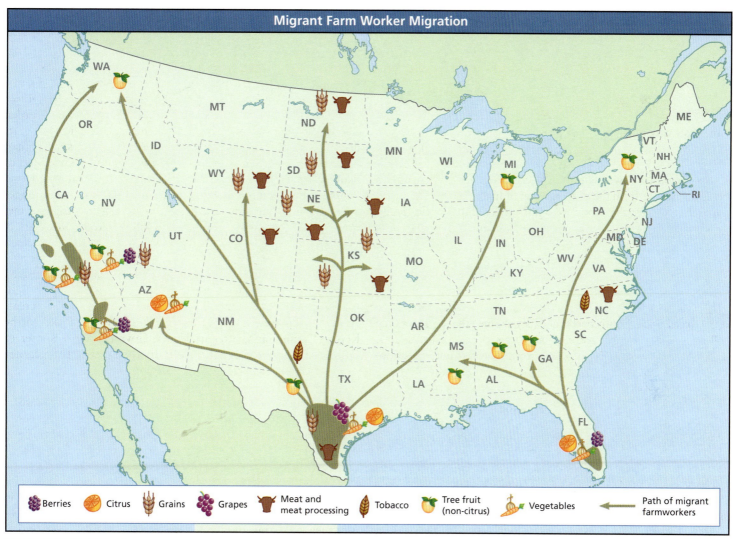

Legend:
- Berries
- Citrus
- Grains
- Grapes
- Meat and meat processing
- Tobacco
- Tree fruit (non-citrus)
- Vegetables
- Path of migrant farmworkers

**THE MIGRANT LIFE** Migrant farmworkers moved north with the growing season, living and working in difficult conditions. In 1965 field hands in Delano, California were making well under poverty-level wages. Most lived in housing with no running water.

rights efforts from the nonviolent struggle for Mexican-American farmworker rights led by labor leader César Chávez, to the Mexican-American civil rights movement, the generally peaceful student-led "Yellow Power" movement among Asian Americans. Behind all the activism lay a growing sense of ethnic identity.

### Mexican-American Civil Rights

To a large degree, the Mexican-American civil rights movement began in 1954, with the Supreme Court's *Hernandez v. Texas* decision. The decision was rendered by Chief Justice Earl Warren who had also overturned racial segregation in schools the same year with the landmark *Brown* decision. A 1944 Texas law known as the Caucasian Race Resolution had declared all Mexican Americans to be white, and thereby due the same protections as all white Texans. At the same time Texas remained

a highly segregated society, not just for African Americans, but for the state's large Hispanic population as well. The race resolution made it more difficult for Hispanics to sue for discrimination, since Hispanics were not considered a legally distinct group of people. Pete Hernandez had been convicted of murder by an all-white and non-Hispanic jury in Jackson County, Texas, where no Hispanic had been permitted to serve on a jury for the previous 25 years. When the Supreme Court overturned the conviction using the Equal Protection clause of the 14th Amendment to the U.S. Constitution, it recognized Hispanics as a special class of citizen who had suffered discrimination because of their ethnic background. It was the first time in American history that a minority group other than African Americans was recognized as being equally protected under the Constitution. This paved the way for Hispanics to use the courts to fight discrimination.

For Mexican Americans, who made up the largest Hispanic American nationality in the United States, many of the most significant gains in civil rights came through the collective action of individuals rather than through the courts. Many of the most significant of these gains centered around the labor rights of the nation's large migrant farmworker population

Because of the nature of their work, migrant farmworkers have always lived on the move. Traditionally they have followed one of three streams of migration through the growing season from late spring to early fall. One stream of migration is based in the Central, Imperial, and Salinas valleys of Southern California and heads up to Washington state. A second emerges from South Texas and works northward through the Great Plains and Midwest. A third branch moves up the east coast from Florida to New York or branches west to Georgia, Alabama, and Mississippi.

**BRACEROS** These Latino fieldworkers are on their way to the Midwest to harvest beets.

When World War II began, the rush to enlist drew thousands of men away from factories and fields. To head off a farm labor shortage, the U.S. government created the Braceros program with the Mexican government. Workers known as *braceros*, (whose name derives from the Spanish word *brazo*, or arm), were hired Mexican laborers brought to the United States on a seasonal basis to harvest crops. Once crops were in, the braceros were sent back to Mexico.

This practice had actually existed informally since World War I, but the Mexican government had consistently complained about the harsh treatment of its citizens in the United States. Because these migrants are constantly on the move, they have often faced greater hardships than workers who remain in one place. For example, many of their children were unable to stay in the same school for any length of time. To the Mexican government the Bracero program was a chance to win promises of better treatment from the U.S. government. However, as the program started the abuses continued, with landowners commonly withholding wages, physically abusing workers, and forcing them to live in little more than shacks. Particularly as smaller farms owned by generations of individual families gave way to large scale corporate agribusinesses, the number of illnesses due to exposure to toxic pesticides and fertilizers increased. Workers were offered little protection from crop-dusting planes, for instance, and when workers and their children (who often also worked) fell ill, they lost their pay.

Not until after 1962, when the National Farm Workers Association (NFWA) was founded would conditions improve for migrant workers. Two years after the group's founding, the Bracero program came to an end. In part, mechanization of farm equipment had helped ease the demand for labor. But it also came from pressure from the NFWA. Founded by César Chávez and Delores Huerta, the group became known as the United Farm Workers Association in 1966. In 1965, the group joined with a Filipino farmworkers

union to launch a strike against California table grape growers. Using tactics such as boycotts and nonviolent civil disobedience inspired by the African-American civil rights movement, the NFWA and its supporters braved intimidation, arrest and violence before eventually winning concessions from the growers. After

**CÉSAR CHÁVEZ** Chávez brought national attention to the plight of migrant farm workers.

**WOUNDED KNEE** Native American activists during the occupation of Wounded Knee in 1973.

Senator Robert F. Kennedy announced his support for the strike, and the boycott captured wide attention of the American public and inspired *La Causa*, the popular name for the Hispanic civil rights movement. In addition to calling for improved pay and working conditions, Chávez had stressed the importance of cultural pride and a greater sense of heritage. Young Mexican Americans took up Chávez's call with vigor, adopting the term Chicano to describe themselves, even though previous generations had used that term as derisive slang for uneducated laborers.

In fact, many Hispanic Americans first became active in American politics when Kennedy's older brother had run for president. Among the organizations that helped John F. Kennedy win election was the Mexican American Political Association (MAPA). As had been the case in the African American civil rights movement, by the late 1960s many Chicanos had moved away from groups like MAPA, which they considered too mainstream, to form their own political organizations. Among these groups were the Brown Berets, La Raza Unida, the Chicano War Moratorium, and United Mexican American Students.

## Puerto Ricans and Cubans

When the United States defeated Spain, the former Spanish colonies of Puerto Rico and Cuba became free from Spanish control. That is not to say that they were free from foreign intervention, however, as the United States exercised strong control over both, though in different ways. Cuba remained independent, though its economy was largely centered around U.S. sugar and

other businesses interests in the United States until Fidel Castro's communist revolution in 1959. Puerto Rico, on the other hand, remained a U.S. territory—a status which caused considerable debate—and occasional violence—over the years. Despite these differences the Cuban and Puerto Rican communities have both become politically powerful and culturally vibrant forces in American life.

A turning point in Puerto Rico's unique relationship with the rest of the United States came in 1948, when Luis Muñoz Marín became the first popularly elected governor. Muñoz Marín objected to Puerto Rico's status as a colony with little control over its internal affairs. Rather than seek full independence from the United States, he promoted a policy of *autonomismo*, or self-government, in free association with the United States. For many decades the ties between the United States mainland and Puerto Rico had been highlighted by the back-and-forth pattern of migration by Puerto Ricans between the island and New York City. Some critics felt that anything less than independence was inadequate, but the independence cause was hurt by the terrorist activities of the radical Nationalist Party. In 1950 members of the Nationalist Party attempted to assassinate Muñoz Marín, and then attempted to kill Harry Truman by shooting their way into Blair House, where the president was living during a White House renovation. Two years later Congress approved a constitution under which Puerto Ricans are given control over virtually all of their internal affairs. Although several Nationalists assaulted a session of the U.S. Congress in 1954, wounding four

Congressmen on the floor of the U.S. House of Representatives, Puerto Rico's status has not changed. A majority of Puerto Ricans favor remaining a commonwealth of the United States rather than seeking independence.

In the aftermath of the Cuban Revolution a dramatic exodus of refugees left the island, many of them settling in Miami, Florida. The neighborhood where Cubans initially settled and remain most highly concentrated is known as Little Havana, and it has become the cultural hub of Cuban life in the United States.

Although the demographics of Little Havana would later change somewhat, the first generation of Cuban exiles tended to be from among the wealthy and middle class segments of Cuban society. Politically conservative and strongly anti-Communist, Miami's Cuban-American community has been a major power center in American political life.

### Yellow and Red Power

The African-American civil rights movement also inspired many young Asian-Americans—primarily Chinese and Japanese—to take up the banner of protest. Many participated in the anti-Vietnam War movement, strongly influenced by a sense of solidarity with the Vietnamese. Many also identified with the Black Power movement, in which African-American leaders like Malcolm X and Stokely Carmichael encouraged blacks to find empowerment through increased knowledge of their own history. As a result Asian-American students fought for and won the inclusion of Asian-American studies into university curricula. The era also witnessed a new emphasis on Asian arts, film, and literature.

At the same time young American Indians, among the poorest of the poor in the United States, took a more radical approach. In the 1950s President Eisenhower initiated a policy known as "termination," which turned over all federal decisions involving Native Americans to the states. In most cases, however, states did little to provide health, education and welfare services that Indians needed. What's more, the Eisenhower administration made matters even worse with a new relocation policy that was a disaster. Although many urban Indians had higher incomes that those remaining on reservations, many felt displaced and disconnected from their heritage.

Although Congress voted to spend $510 million for new Indian aid programs at Lyndon Johnson's request, a new generation of Indian activists took up militant action to call attention to their demands. In 1969 a group of Indians occupied the abandoned Alcatraz Island prison complex in San Francisco Bay and demanded that it be turned into a cultural center. They were not evicted by U.S. marshals until 1971.

In 1972 an organization known as the American Indian Movement (AIM) occupied the offices of the federal Bureau of Indian Affairs (BIA) in Washington, demanding all rights and property that they said had been guaranteed to the Indians over many years.

After a week of talks and roughly $2.2 million in damage to the building, the AIM members left.

Then, on February 23, 1973, AIM members congregated at the site of the Wounded Knee massacre in South Dakota to demonstrate against the corruption at the Pine Ridge reservation. Tensions between the AIM activists and officials rose until the situation developed into a siege of the town, which drew two thousand Indians from around the area and lasted seventy days. They were surrounded by three hundred armed federal marshals and FBI agents equipped with armored vehicles. In March AIM declared Pine Ridge sovereign territory in keeping with the terms of the Laramie Treaty of 1868 which recognized the Sioux as an independent nation. The siege finally ended when two Indians were shot and killed, but it served to call national attention to the Native American civil rights movement.

The movement, sometimes referred to as the Red Power movement, also had considerable sympathy from the general public. The film *Little Big Man* (1969) and Indian author Dee Brown's book *Bury My Heart At Wounded Knee* both had wide audiences. The same year as the AIM occupation of the BIA, the Nixon Administration agreed to end the termination policy. Nixon proposed that federal programs that had been run on Indian reservations be turned over to the Indians themselves to run. He also appointed Indians to twenty top posts at the BIA, and after a two-year study by the Office of Education, recommended that tribal history, culture, and languages be stressed in Indian education.

# The Women's Movement

The other major civil rights movement that grew out of the 1960s was the Women's Liberation Movement. After World War II women were encouraged to leave their wartime jobs and raise families. In large part they did, but for many there was a cost. The emotional void many felt was crystallized by New York housewife and mother Betty Friedan. While researching her classmates' experiences for an upcoming school reunion, she uncovered feelings of disillusionment and entrapment in the roles of housewife and mother, and estrangement from the larger world. Her findings led to her 1963 bestselling book *The Feminine Mystique*, which defined for middle-class women "the problem with no name." The book made her a headline spokesperson for a growing feminist or women's liberation movement. When she and other activists noted that the sex-discrimination guidelines of the Civil Rights Act of 1964 were not being enforced, they founded the National Organization for Women (NOW) in 1966. Friedan served as the organization's president until 1970.

Friedan was joined in her work by Gloria Steinem, a former magazine writer who came face to face with sexual inequality while posing as a Playboy bunny for a magazine exposé. A nearly all-male commission in New York that was created to investigate abortion further solidified her commitment to women's rights, and in 1971 she founded the Women's Political Caucus and the Women's Action network. In 1972 Steinem also founded *Ms.* magazine, serving as its editor until 1987.

The 1973 Supreme Court ruling in *Roe v. Wade* made abortion legal and, along with the development of the Pill oral contraceptive in 1960, helped to assure women's sexual rights. Women's athletic programs were funded more equitably with the 1973 passage of Title IX of the Educational Amendments. Women also gained representation in politics, with numerous female U.S. congresswomen and senators elected; one politician, Geraldine Ferraro, was the 1984 Democratic vice-presidential candidate. While the Equal Rights Amendment failed to be ratified for passage by 1982, important legislation at the end of the century included the Family and Medical Leave Act (FMLA) in 1993, which assisted working families. Financially, however, women still have far to go: As of 1999, women's median weekly earnings were only 76.5 percent of men's earnings, a gap that has persisted for the past 50 years.

**BETTY FRIEDAN** Betty Friedan's *The Feminine Mystique* helped launch the modern women's movement.

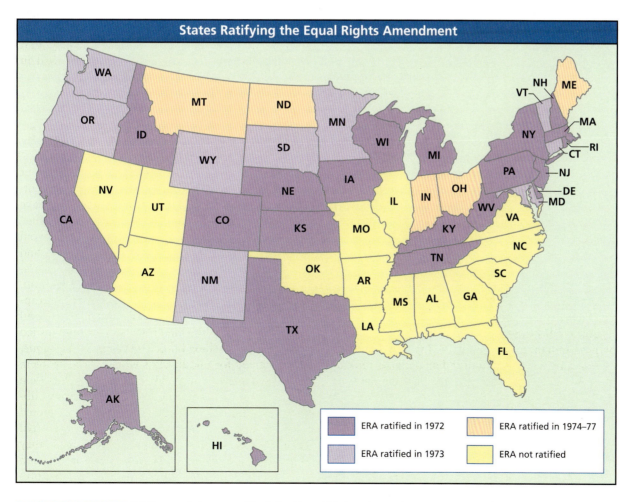

**States Ratifying the Equal Rights Amendment**

Legend:
- ERA ratified in 1972
- ERA ratified in 1973
- ERA ratified in 1974–77
- ERA not ratified

**A NARROW DEFEAT** While most states ratified the Equal Rights Amendment, most southern states rejected it, and it failed to win ratification.

# Chapter 31: Domestic and Foreign Policy Since 1968

n August 1968 a badly fractured Democratic party met in Chicago for their presidential nominating convention. Lyndon Johnson, the incumbent, had announced that spring he would not seek reelection. Senator Robert F. Kennedy, who had entered the race after Johnson's withdrawal, had been assassinated in June just moments after winning the California primary. Hubert H. Humphrey, Johnson's vice-president, seemed the certain nominee of the party. Yet the party was still badly divided, particularly over the Vietnam War. Kennedy and Senator Eugene McCarthy, who had both run as opponents of Johnson's Vietnam policy, both supported a strong anti-war statement in the party's platform. Humphrey, on the other hand, favored opening of peace talks with the North Vietnamese, but not outright withdrawal. When a motion to add the anti-war statement to the platform failed to pass, anti-war delegates put black arm-

bands on and began to sing the African-American civil rights anthem, "We Shall Overcome."

Outside in the streets the situation was even more tense, as thousands of anti-war protesters had converged on Chicago. In response Chicago's strong-armed mayor Richard Daley had called out the National Guard and put his entire police force on 12-hour shifts. Although isolated skirmishes between police and protesters occurred in the convention's opening days, on August 28—"Bloody Wednesday"—the situation deteriorated into an all-out riot, as police and guardsmen began indiscriminately clubbing and teargassing protesters, bystanders, and reporters. A stunned nation watched on national television, just as Humphrey was accepting his party's nomination. Many blamed the police for the violence, while many others blamed the protesters for inciting them. Humphrey decried the police violence while also calling for law and order, but his

campaign would remain linked to those images of the teargas and blood-stained streets of Chicago.

A week later Richard M. Nixon, former senator from California and vice-president under Eisenhower, accepted the Republican Party's nomination in Miami Beach, Florida. Unlike the Democratic Convention there was little drama, save for a last minute but unsuccessful challenge for the nomination by the conservative governor of California, Ronald Reagan. In accepting the nomination Nixon alluded to the trouble in Chicago, turmoil over civil rights, and protests over the war, saying:

As we look at America, we see cities enveloped in smoke and flame. We hear sirens in the night. We see Americans dying on distant battlefields abroad. We see Americans hating each other; fighting each other; killing each other at home. And as we see and hear these things, millions of Americans cry out in anguish. . . Did we come all this way for this? . . . Listen to the answer to those questions. It is another voice. It is the quiet voice in the tumult and the shouting. It is the voice of the great majority of Americans, the forgotten Americans — the non-shouters; the non-demonstrators. They are not racists or sick . . . They are black and they are white — they're native born and foreign born — they're young and they're old. . . . They are good people, they are decent people; they work, and they save, and they pay their taxes, and they care.

Nixon's address appealed to what his campaign called the "silent majority" of Americans, those who rejected the rebellion and conflict in America's cities and on its college campuses, those who trusted the government as long as its role in American life was limited, and those who supported the war effort, or at least a peace settlement that preserved American honor and dignity. In many ways Nixon was promising a return to the spirit of the 1950s—or at least an idyllic version of the fifties that was free of conflict. Nixon even began his speech by invoking the spirit of the then-ailing

**BLOOD IN THE STREETS** During the Democratic Presidential Convention in 1968, Chicago police attacked anti-war protesters as well as innocent bystanders. Inside the convention center party delegates chose Vice-President Hubert Humphrey as their nominee.

General Eisenhower, who would die the following spring after a long illness:

> General Eisenhower, as you know, lies critically ill in the Walter Read Hospital tonight. I have talked, however, to Mrs. Eisenhower on the telephone and she tells me that his heart is with us. And she says there is nothing that he lives for more and there is nothing that would lift him more that for us to win in November.

During the campaign Nixon made the Supreme Court and some of its recent decisions an issue. Although Eisenhower had appointed Chief Justice Earl Warren to the Court, Warren led one of the most liberal courts in American history. Conservatives believed that under Warren the Court had constantly and illegally been interfering with states' rights. Whether it was the 1954 *Brown v. Board* decision desegregating public schools, or a 1962 decision banning a prayer written for classroom use by the New York Board of Regents on the grounds that it violated protections against the establishment of religion, or the 1966 *Miranda v. Arizona* decision, which stated that criminal convictions could not stand unless police had first informed the suspect of his or her rights to remain silent and to have an attorney present when questioned—each of these cases, thought conservatives, seemed to weaken traditional values and overstep the limits of judicial power in public life. Nixon vowed that if he were elected president, he would end these sorts of decisions by only appointing "strict constructionists," or those who would interpret the Constitution strictly, to the Court.

### The Counterculture Backlash

In many ways Nixon was campaigning against the counterculture spirit of the 1960s as much as he was against liberal judges or Hubert Humphrey. The counterculture that emerged in the 1960s was, after all, a response to the conservatism and conformity of mainstream culture in the 1950s. As they came of age, the "baby-boom" generation—children born between the end of World War II and the early 1960s—had begun to question society's norms, creating a "generation gap" by distancing themselves from the values and beliefs of their parents. Those in the counterculture were linked by their nonconformist tendencies in clothing, music, art, and literature; and by certain ideals such as mind-altering drug use, sexual liberation, and communal living.

As in the various civil rights movements of the same time, there was tension among various members of the counterculture between those who advocated violent protest and those who practiced nonviolent civil disobedience. There was also a separation between the New Left—college activists and intellectuals working for radical social change—and the "hippies," who were considered less politically motivated.

Ultimately the 1960s counterculture paved the way for future activist movements, including women's liberation, gay pride, abortion rights, and environmental protection. Even today the 1960s counterculture has left an impact on how Americans dress and live and how they think about everything from politics to sex to drugs. But in the tumultuous year of 1968, Richard Nixon was able to harness the support of those that rejected these cultural and political shifts in favor of stability and a desire to return to traditional ideals. In the end it was not a "silent majority" that elected Nixon president, but a minority, since he won just over 41 percent of the total vote with roughly 31.7 million votes to 31.2

for Humphrey, and almost 10 million for the third party candidacy of Alabama's segregationist governor, George Wallace.

# Domestic Policy from Nixon to Reagan

As president, Nixon proved to be far less ideological than the conservative wing of his party that had briefly supported Ronald Reagan at the Republican convention. Rather, he would be a political pragmatist, whose civil rights policies, judicial appointments, and failed attempts to place Southern conservatives on the Supreme Court were done more to pacify the right wing of his party than out of philosophical commitment.

At the same time, Nixon was forced to work with a Congress that was still controlled by the Democrats. Rather than block legislation, he willingly signed laws that appealed to liberals, including the landmark Clean Air Act, which gave automobile manufacturers six years to develop a pollution-free vehicle and to set air quality standards regarding major pollutants; the Federal Consumer Product Safety Act, which instituted standards for potentially hazardous products; the Twenty-sixth Amendment to the Constitution, which lowered the voting age from twenty-one to eighteen; and the Civil Rights Act of 1972, which extended the landmark 1964 law forbidding employment discrimination on the basis of race, color, religion, sex, or national origin to include educational institutions. In his economic policies he introduced a series of unorthodox and innovative measures, including a ninety-day wage, price, and rent freeze, and a "floating" dollar, no longer tied to gold, in order to stabilize a weakening economy. In foreign affairs Nixon's controversial authorization of secret bombing raids in Cambodia caused an enormous public outcry, but his opening of diplomatic relations with China was an historic achievement.

### Watergate

Regardless of his legislative and diplomatic accomplishments, Nixon's personal and political legacy will always be clouded by the Watergate scandal, named after the burglary at the Democratic National Committee's (DNC) headquarters in the Watergate office complex in Washington, D.C. during Nixon's reelection campaign in 1972. In the wake of the break-in the news media, led by *Washington Post* reporters Carl Bernstein Bob Woodward, began to uncover a pattern of covert and illegal activities committed by Nixon aides and members of his reelection committee. It also became clear that the Nixon administration was working to cover up its activities, but by early in 1973 the Senate had launched a full scale investigation into the affair.

Although Nixon announced the resignations of Attorney General Richard Kleindienst and senior aides John Ehrlichman and H.R. Haldeman, and the firing of counsel John Dean for their connections to the scandal in order to quell the crisis, the investigations took a dramatic turn when Congress appointed a special prosecutor to examine the affair. In June the nation learned that Nixon had secretly recorded all discussions and phone conversations in his office, and Congressional efforts to force Nixon to release the tapes to investigators then became the focus of the affair. Making matters worse for Nixon, Vice President Spiro T. Agnew was forced to resign after the disclosure of a bribery scandal that occurred when he was gov-

**WATERGATE** Protesters outside the White House call for Richard Nixon's impeachment.

ernor of Maryland. Nixon selected Representative Gerald Ford, an uncontroversial congressman from Michigan, to replace Agnew.

By early 1974 the House of Representatives began hearings on whether to impeach the president, and by late July the House Judiciary Committee recommended that Nixon be charged with three impeachable offenses: obstruction of justice, abuse of executive power and contempt of Congress. At the same time, the U.S. Supreme Court ruled in the case of *U.S. v. Richard Nixon* that Nixon be obliged to turn over the presidential tapes and all documents relating to the investigation. Once they were released, the tapes revealed that Nixon had ordered the FBI not to investigate the Watergate break-in. In the wake of this disclosure Nixon at last resigned from office, the only president in U.S. history to do so.

Watergate shook the public's confidence in the government in a manner that still reverberates today. Already weary from the protests and unrest prevalent during the 1960s and early 1970s, Americans felt betrayed by the depth of the scandal, which involved high-level officials and ultimately was recognized as a massive web of corruption that included sabotage, espionage, hush money, and illegal campaign contributions. In addition, Watergate helped bring about a victory by the Democrats in the next presidential election. Perhaps most significantly, it set a

new standard for inquiry into presidential and government activities, greatly affecting the presidencies of Ronald Reagan, George H. W. Bush, and Bill Clinton. These new standards would result in new checks and balances on presidential power that would last, arguably, to the present day. Watergate also directly or indirectly resulted in election and campaign contribution reforms, and, for a time, greater public access to classified documents. In the fallout from Watergate many officials in the Nixon administration and the Committee to Reelect the President (which gained the acronym CREEP) were convicted of a variety of conspiracy-related crimes.

### The Ford and Carter Presidencies

Republican president Gerald Ford, who became president upon Nixon's resignation, and his successor, Democrat Jimmy Carter, inherited the daunting task of leading a country torn apart for years by the Vietnam War, civil rights demonstrations, student uprisings, and Watergate. Ford, who assumed the presidency in August 1974, lost much of his public support that September when he pardoned Nixon of all criminal offenses related to Watergate and his term of office. He was further embarrassed when Congress passed the Freedom of Information Act over his veto, allowing the public greater access to government files. While Ford played no role in Watergate itself, the public outrage over his pardon of Nixon marred his popularity and

ability to accomplish his program.

Ultimately, the state of the economy was Ford's greatest challenge. He inherited a fractured economy marred by an energy shortage, high unemployment rates, and rising inflation. A long period of "stagflation"— or inflation occurring during a stagnant business climate when unemployment was rising—had begun in 1970. Increasing global competition and a 1973 embargo on oil sales to the United States by Arab oil-producing states following Egypt's defeat in the Yom Kippur War by Israel deepened the crisis. Rather than continue Nixon's wage, rent, and price freezes, Ford adopted a voluntary program, Whip Inflation Now (WIN).

At the Republican convention of 1976, Ford was challenged for his party's nomination by Ronald Reagan, who had mounted the last-minute challenge to Nixon in 1968. This time Reagan made a stronger showing, rallying millions of conservatives to his side by calling for an end to government regulation of the economy, dramatic cuts in social programs and a more vigorous challenge to the Soviet Union. Ford narrowly won the nomination and thus an opportunity to be elected president in his own right. The Democrats nominated Jimmy Carter, the former governor of Georgia, who had based his campaign largely on his status as a Washington outsider and his own personal integrity. In a close contest, Carter swept his home territory in the South and won enough of the traditional Democratic northeast to be elected the nation's thirty-ninth president.

Carter entered office with a variety of ambitious goals, including an energy program, tax reform, electoral reform, a balanced budget by 1980, a strong environmental program, a new welfare system, and more. But like Ford, Carter inherited a feeble economy and was unable to improve it. To address the situation Carter also opted for voluntary measures and deregulation, as well as cuts to the number of federal employees in order to restore the economy. Yet continued instability in oil prices hampered his efforts. In 1977, for example, the national trade deficit reached record levels.

Carter's greatest handicap as president may have been his inexperience as a politician. His status as a "Washington outsider" appealed on the campaign trail but made it difficult for him to push his program through Congress. Most of Carter's aides were far younger and even more inexperienced than he was and had little understanding of the ways of Washington. Despite a Congress that was controlled by his own party, Carter was unable or unwilling to establish a close working relationship with Democratic leaders. Part of the problem was that Carter proposed a wide range of programs, but often changed his mind about them without informing his potential allies in Congress.

### The Energy Crisis

As Carter's policy priorities shifted, he began to have greater and greater difficulty communicating with the American people. His handling of American energy policy illustrates this point.

Because the high cost of petroleum and natural gas impacted the entire economy, one of Carter's top goals was to reduce American dependence on foreign energy sources. To accomplish this he pressed for conservation and the development of alternative sources of energy. In his first year in office he created the Cabinet-level Department of Energy to oversee American energy policy. Carter also appealed to the public, calling on Americans to drive their cars less, to turn down their thermostats and wear sweaters at home, and to otherwise work to conserve fuel in any way they could. He asked Americans to consider these conservation efforts "the moral equivalent of war." Carter also called for the government to lift price limits on natural gas in the hope that rising prices would convince Americans to conserve even more. In 1978 Congress passed the Natural Energy Act, easing, but not lifting, energy price controls and granting tax credits to those who installed energy saving devices in their homes and businesses. To many Americans Carter's warnings were not convincing. Rather than accepting limits and sacrifice, Americans were looking for a future of expanding opportunity. Instead of driving less or wearing sweaters indoors, most people did nothing.

In 1979 the Organization of Petroleum Exporting Countries (OPEC) announced a dramatic 60 percent increase in oil prices. The increase impacted the entire U.S. economy—heating homes, offices, schools, and stores cost more money, as did flying planes, driving trucks, and running factories. The cost of living skyrocketed. By June gasoline shortages led to nationwide rationing, fistfights at the gas pumps, and even shootings.

On March 30, 1979 the dangers of the nation's huge appetite for and dependence on energy was clearly outlined when a valve in a nuclear power plant on Three Mile Island, near Harrisburg, Pennsylvania, became stuck, causing the plant's reactor to overheat and threaten to melt its nuclear core. Thankfully, only a partial meltdown occurred, but it still took weeks to bring the plant back into control.

The accident at Three Mile Island helped to galvanize the opposition to nuclear power. A once small but vocal group of antinuclear activists grew with public alarm over the accident. As public support for the construction of new nuclear plants waned, the need for greater conservation efforts and new, safer energy sources became even clearer.

During the summer of 1979, as the energy crisis deepened, President Carter planned to address the nation about the situation. However, after inviting more than 100 advisors to speak to him about the issues facing the country, he decided to cancel the energy speech. Instead, he decided to address what he described as a "crisis of the American spirit."

In his speech Carter argued that over the previous twenty years the nation had lost its "unity of purpose." The deaths of the Kennedys and Martin Luther King, Jr., the defeat in Vietnam, the scandal of Watergate, the weakness of the economy, the shortage in energy—all of these, said Carter, had left deep scars on the American psyche.

In many ways Carter was exactly right. But telling the American people exactly what they do not want to hear does not make for a successful political strategy. Many of Carter's critics argued that he was blaming the American people for crises that he had caused. That October, when student radicals took 53 Americans hostage at the American embassy in Tehran (see page 298), many Americans began to feel that under Carter's leadership the United States was simply lurching from crisis to crisis. As the 1980 election approached, Carter's presidency appeared doomed.

# The Reagan Revolution and its Aftermath

In 1980 a battered and bruised Jimmy Carter was forced to head off a nomination challenge from Senator Edward Kennedy of Massachusetts, the younger brother of President Kennedy and Robert F. Kennedy. In the general election Carter faced Ronald Reagan, who after failing to secure the Republican nomination in 1968 and 1976, had defeated a field of Republican hopefuls during the primary season. The Reagan of 1980 was, by and large, the Reagan of 1968—and 1954, for that matter. In that year, the then-Hollywood actor had been hired by the General Electric Corporation to boost the morale of its workers. In that capacity, Reagan had traveled the nation speaking out against New Deal-style government economic intervention and government social programs, and in favor of a strong national defense and an aggressive response to communism.

As governor of California during the tumultuous 1960s, Reagan's strong law-and-order approach appealed to conservatives who felt that traditional values had been abandoned in favor of the free-wheeling, anti-establishment youth culture.

Reagan's own story added to his appeal. He had grown up in the small town of Tampico, Illinois, and, after graduating from Eureka College, had begun a career as a radio sports announcer. By 1937 he had launched his movie career.

Throughout his successful film career Reagan had been politically active—though as a liberal Democrat. However, over time

**THE CONSERVATIVE REVOLUTION** Ronald Reagan's election in 1980 symbolized the triumph of the conservative wing of the Republican Party. Two decades later national policy debates would still be shaped by his legacy.

he moved steadily to the right, particularly during the Cold War, when he became an outspoken anticommunist.

Reagan's small town roots and sunny optimism appealed not just to conservatives but to many working-class Americans, who had traditionally voted Democratic. So did his simple question, put to voters during one of the televised debates with Carter: "Are you better off today than you were four years ago?" On election day, the nation answered with a resounding "No." Reagan handily defeated Carter, winning by 8 million votes.

Reagan's impressive victory came at the expense of the long-standing Democratic coalition of Northeastern liberals, minorities, conservative Southerners and Midwestern working-class labor union members. Southerners abandoned Carter in droves. So did white union members, who political analysts began referring to as "Reagan Democrats." A new Republican coalition of economic and social conservatives—the New Right—was born. It would remain a dominant force in American life well into the twenty-first century.

## Reaganomics

Upon taking office Reagan embraced supply-side economics, holding that tax cuts, spending cuts and deregulation, combined with efforts to cap wages paid to union workers, would stimulate the economy. Although critics condemned these policies as "trickle-down" economics (in which tax cuts heaped upon the wealthiest Americans would "trickle down" to the less fortunate), Congress passed many of the sweeping economic changes endorsed by the administration. Congress passed a $750 billion tax cut and slashed social programs by $500 billion. About nine million poor people were cut from food

stamp programs, and another million from the welfare and Medicaid rolls. In many cases the administration saved money by reinterpreting laws. For example, to reduce spending on school nutrition programs, the administration loosened requirements that vegetables be included in school lunches by defining ketchup as a vegetable. Likewise, the Environmental Protection Agency began giving polluters broad leeway in the way they met standards set by the Clean Air and Clean Water Acts and other environmental laws.

In August 1981, Reagan signaled his willingness to take on labor unions when the 15,000 member Professional Air Traffic Controllers Union went on strike, bringing air traffic to a standstill. Reagan gave the strikers forty-eight hours to return to work and then fired all workers who stayed at home.

One of Reagan's stated priorities was cutting the budget deficit. Federal deficit spending had meant that more and more money was needed just to pay interest on the federal debt, which as of 1981 stood at $1 trillion. Yet despite the cuts to social programs, the federal deficit climbed dramatically during Reagan's time in office since huge increases in defense spending, paired with large tax cuts, far outweighed savings in other areas of the budget.

Despite the dramatic change in economic policy, the federal economy failed to improve during Reagan's first years in office. In fact, from July 1981 to December 1982, the nation underwent the longest and worst economic downturn since the Great Depression. Across the Midwest and Northeast, factory towns like Flint, Michigan, Beloit, Wisconsin, and Allentown, Pennsylvania lost workers as local factories laid off crews or shut down altogether. By mid-1982, one out of every five blue-collar workers was out of work across America.

By 1983 the recession had come to an end. Oil discoveries in Mexico and the completion of an enormous oil pipeline in Alaska increased the oil supply, causing oil prices to finally come down. As oil prices fell the overall inflation rate also dropped. Unemployment rates came down; consumer spending went up.

As Reagan's 1984 re-election campaign began, he was able to claim credit for turning the economy around. In fact, what actually turned the economy around was massive government spending, particularly on national defense. Federal spending on expensive new weapons programs meant new jobs in the nation's defense plants.

Regardless of how the economy turned around, what mattered to American voters in 1984 was that it *had* turned around. While Democratic nominee Walter Mondale—a former Minnesota senator and Carter's vice-president—stated that he would raise taxes in order to close the budget deficit, which had risen to during Reagan's first term to $2.7 billion. The higher the budget deficit, the more the government had to spend each year just to pay interest on the debt. By bringing down the federal deficit, Mondale argued, the nation would have more money left over to restore some of the social programs that Reagan had eliminated.

Mondale's otherwise lackluster campaign was notable for his choice of the vice-presidential nominee, Geraldine Ferraro of New York—the first time a woman had run for this office on the ticket of one of the major parties. But Mondale and Ferraro were no match for the Reagan juggernaut. As the election approached, the president's popularity was riding high, and he swept to reelection in a landslide.

Although oil prices continued to fall in the first years of Reagan's second term, by 1987 rising oil consumption and political instability in the Middle East began to force prices back up. Oil that had cost under $9 a barrel in 1986, reached $22 a barrel in 1987. Although unemployment remained low, that was only because of the extraordinary budget deficits that had built up during the Reagan years. Even David Stockman, Reagan's budget chief during the first term, condemned the deep red ink, accusing the Administration of committing "fiscal carnage."

Meanwhile on Wall Street the stock exchanges were booming. Throughout the first half of the year, the Dow Jones Industrial Average reached one all-time high after another. But on October 17, 1987, the New York Stock Exchange lost a whopping 508 points—the worst day for the market since the Crash of 1929. In just seven hours, prices fell 22.6 percent. When the following day's market opened up with a massive sell-off, banks refused to extend credit and the Federal Reserve was forced to stepped in to flood the market with dollars. With money once again available, corporations began buying up shares of their own stock, helping to stabilize the market. By the end of the day, the New York Stock Exchange had regained more than 100 points. The next day, it gained back 187 more. A complete financial meltdown had been averted, but the crash had sent a clear warning—the massive deficit was damaging the nation's economy.

## George H.W. Bush

During the Republican presidential primaries of 1980, one of Ronald Reagan's most competitive opponents for the nomination had been George H. W. Bush, a one-time U.S. representative from Texas who had gone on to a long career in international diplomacy. Among his assignments had been U.S Representative to the United Nations, Special Envoy to China, and Director of the Central Intelligence Agency. Although Bush's business career had been in the Texas oil industry, his roots were in the Northeast. He had been born in Massachusetts and raised in Connecticut. His father, Prescott Bush, had served as a U.S. Senator from that state.

Educated at an elite private prep school and Yale University, Bush's background was quite different than Reagan's. In many respects, his political philosophy was also a far more cautious brand of conservatism: during the fight for the 1980 nomination, he had called Reagan's supply-side economic proposals "voodoo economics." Yet Bush possessed all of the foreign policy experience that Reagan did not. When Reagan won his party's nomination his campaign shrewdly picked Bush, his former rival, as his running mate. By 1988, Bush would be seen as Reagan's heir.

Despite the October 1987 crash on Wall Street, the nation entered the election year of 1988 with a strong economy. In accepting his party's nomination Bush pledged to honor the Reagan legacy by promising never to raise taxes. In November Bush overwhelmed the Democratic candidate Governor Michael Dukakis of Massachusetts to become the nation's forty-first president.

Much of Bush's presidency would be dominated by foreign affairs. During his tenure the Cold War ended with the collapse of the Soviet Union. Bush would also skillfully oversee the building of a multinational military coalition that would force Iraq to retreat after its 1990 invasion of neighboring Kuwait.

In domestic affairs, however, Bush would have trouble maintaining his footing. Faced with the large burden of debt and a Democratic-controlled Congress, Bush's domestic agenda was by and large stalled. Nonetheless, the Bush Administration and the Congress were able to agree on two major pieces of legislation—the Americans with Disabilities Act, which required businesses to make their facilities more accessible to disabled Americans, and the Clean Air Act of 1990, a compromise measure between business groups and environmentalists that updated prior air pollution laws and imposed stricter standards for the first time in 12 years.

By 1991 the economic boom that had begun in 1983 at last began to stall. Caught between the need to reduce the deficit and increase military spending due to the 1991 Gulf War, Bush agreed to compromise with Congress, authorizing an increase in taxes, despite his campaign promise never to do so.

## The Clinton Presidency

Bush's reversal on his tax pledge deeply wounded his chances of reelection in 1992. What's more, he faced a far more formidable opponent than he had in 1988. While neither Bush nor Dukakis had the personal charisma or communication skills of Ronald Reagan, Bush's 1992 opponent did. Governor Bill Clinton of Arkansas, who was just 46 when he won his party's nomination, was a man of enormous energy and personal charm. As a young man Clinton had idolized John F. Kennedy and brought with him a similar idealistic spirit of change. Campaigning as a "different kind of Democrat," he pushed a "new covenant" that emphasized community service and individual responsibility.

On Election Day Clinton also benefited from the surprisingly strong third party candidacy of Texas businessman H. Ross Perot. Perot, whose unorthodox manner and sarcasm-tinged, political spin-free honesty appealed to many voters, won 19 million votes, more than any third party candidate in history.

Clinton was elected with just over 40 percent of the vote and would become the first Democrat to be elected president since

Jimmy Carter in 1976 and the first Democrat to serve two complete terms since Franklin D. Roosevelt. More moderate than liberal, he had campaigned on the struggling U.S. economy, advocating the reduction of the deficit—which was eliminated during his tenure—and reform of the welfare system.

He failed, however, to realize one of his major goals: a national health-care system. In a controversial move he appointed his wife, Hillary Rodham Clinton to head the reform effort. An advocate for children and a skilled lawyer, Mrs. Clinton nonetheless became a lightening rod for the opposition. Her commission's proposed overhaul went down in resounding defeat. To make matters worse, a federal assault on a Waco, Texas religious cult ended in a fiasco.

What's more, accusations surfaced early in Clinton's first term that he and his wife had illegally profited from a phony Arkansas land deal known as Whitewater. By 1994, Clinton's popularity had plummeted, and the Democrats had lost control of Congress for the first time since the Truman administration.

It has been said that Bill Clinton possessed the sharpest political skills of his era. Following the humiliating midterm election in 1994, Clinton outmaneuvered the Republican-led Congress when they threatened to shut down the government unless he cut the Medicaid and Medicare programs. When he refused, the Republicans made good on their threat, and found that the public blamed them instead of Clinton for the impasse.

With his momentum regained and the economy now booming once again, Clinton called for and won increases in the minimum wage and a program of student loans in exchange for community service. He also approved a major overhaul of the federal welfare system.

In 1996 Bill Clinton became the first Democrat to be reelected to office since FDR. But the turnaround was not to last. In 1997, the Supreme Court ruled that Paula Jones, a former Arkansas government employee, could proceed with a sexual harassment lawsuit against the president. During that trial, allegations surfaced that Clinton had had an affair with a young White House intern. When he denied it the House launched impeachment hearings against him, and for only the second time in history, issued formal charges of perjury and obstruction of justice against him to the Senate. Although he was eventually forced

**A NEW DEMOCRAT** Bill Clinton, the youngest man elected president since John F. Kennedy, was elected as a centrist Southern Democrat. During his first term he moved to the left, proposing a national health care plan that was widely criticised by conservatives. In 1994 the Republicans took control of Congress, thanks in large part to the efforts of Representative Newt Gingrich, seen at right. By 1996, however, Clinton had moved back to the center, and handily won reelection.

to admit to the nation and his family that the affair had taken place, the Senate voted to acquit him of the charges, which were not considered to rise to the level of impeachable offenses.

Much to the chagrin of his Republican rivals, Clinton's personal approval rating—even after having been impeached—reached as high as 60 percent in his final years in office. Whatever his personal failings, he had presided over the longest period of peace and prosperity in the nation's history. Ultimately, however, Clinton's reputation will always be marred, and he will be remembered for the personal flaws that prevented him from reaching even greater success.

## Back to the Bushes

Clinton's mixed legacy had left the nation bitterly divided. Democrats by and large still fully supported Clinton's policies. Yet Republicans, and some independents, were desperate for change. Heading into the 2000 election season, Governor George W. Bush of Texas, the son of the former president, promised to bring that change. Arguing that he would be a "uniter, not a divider" and a "compassionate conservative" who would "change the tone" in Washington, Bush faced off against Clinton's vice president, Albert Gore. Gore

found himself in the uncomfortable position of running on the Clinton administration's record of economic prosperity while also distancing himself from his boss's personal scandals.

On election day Gore won the popular vote. However, the electoral vote for the state of Florida, where Bush's younger brother Jeb was governor, was contested due to the astoundingly close vote tally of a few hundred votes out of millions cast. For six weeks the two campaigns sued and countersued over recounting votes until at last the U.S. Supreme Court voted 5-4 to halt the recount, awarding Bush the presidency. In making the case for the majority decision, Justice Antonin Scalia argued that stopping the vote recount was necessary since continuing to count the votes might cast doubt on the legitimacy of Bush's election. Rather than quell the controversy, Scalia's argument only opened the Court's decision to charges of political bias.

Despite the cloud over his election, when Bush took office he persuaded Congress to approve the largest tax cut since the Reagan years. Two years later, faced with a lagging recession, he pushed through an even larger tax cut. He also moved quickly to shape the agenda on education reform by imposing annual standardized testing for students. Proving to be more of a political heir to Ronald Reagan than to his father, Bush also moved to reduce government regulation on business—proposing relaxed standards on the amount of arsenic in drinking water, and working to make it more difficult for individuals to sue corporations for damages.

In foreign affairs Bush proved as distrustful of international treaties that he viewed as counter to U.S. interests as he was to domestic regulations. Two months after taking office he rejected the U.S. commitment to the Kyoto Protocols, a global pact to fight global warming. The administration argued that the issue of global warming needed further study, and since China and India, two of the world's largest nations were not party to the treaty, it was against U.S. interests to sign the document. Further, the administration also took the controversial position that no conclusive evidence existed linking human made pollution to the heating of the Earth's atmosphere.

### Energy Policy and the Bush Administration

Critics accused the administration of setting back the fight against global warming for years with their action. Some also suggested that Bush was unduly biased in favor of energy interests. As with his father, George H.W. Bush, much of George W. Bush's professional career had been in the Texas oil and gas industry. When it was discovered that management at the Houston-based Enron Corporation, one of the world's largest energy companies and a major financial supporter of the president, had cheated investors—and its own employees—by falsifying its financial reports, the company's close ties to the president became a politically inconvenient association. Likewise, when Halliburton Corporation's Brown and Root Engineering subsidiary was given a string of multibillion dollar contracts in Iraq without having to bid against other companies for the work, eyebrows were raised once more, particularly since Vice President Dick Cheney had been Halliburton's chief operating officer until he left that post to join Bush's 2000 campaign.

In the aftermath of the September 11, 2001 attacks, Bush had placed increased emphasis on the goal of American energy independence. Rather than ask Americans to drive less or to wear sweaters indoors as Jimmy Carter had done years before, Bush emphasized new exploration, particularly

for oil and gas. Of particular interest to the administration was the Arctic National Wildlife Reserve (ANWR), a pristine stretch of Alaskan coastland on the Arctic Circle that had been named a wildlife preserve and closed to oil exploration by President Eisenhower. The plan faces considerable opposition from environmentalists and many Democrats in Congress, and by the summer of 2006 has not been approved.

### The War on Terror at Home

What kind of president Bush would have ultimately been had the events of September 11, 2001 not taken place is mere speculation. But on that day, when terrorists flew passenger jets into the two towers of the World Trade Center in New York City and into the Pentagon in Washington DC, killing over 3,000 Americans, everything changed—for the administration and for the nation. Since that date, all other issues—whether education, energy, economic policy, or anything else—have ultimately become secondary to the administration's efforts to combat international terrorism and to protect the United States from another attack. In addition to launching wars in Afghanistan and Iraq, Bush authorized the USA Patriot Act, a controversial anti-terrorism bill authorizing law enforcement agencies to investigate terrorism suspects, obtain the public library and video store rental records of any American, and carry out wiretap and surveillance activities that had been banned since Watergate. The following June, Bush proposed the creation of the Department of Homeland Security, a new Cabinet-level department that would merge government agencies to better coordinate domestic protection against terrorism. The following November Congress passed the bill.

As a wartime president, Bush has by and large had the support of a majority of the American public. During the 2004 election, he was able to fight off a challenge from Senator John Kerry of Massachusetts, a decorated Vietnam veteran who had returned home as a young man to lead veterans in opposition to the war. Kerry's vocal opposition to the Vietnam war in the early 1970s still angered some veteran groups—a fact that the Bush campaign successfully used to its benefit. Likewise, Kerry had initially voted in favor of authorizing President Bush to go to war against Iraq, a vote that frustrated many liberal Democrats. In the end, Bush defeated Kerry in a close election to win a second term.

## Foreign Policy in the 1970s

In 1972 Richard Nixon made a startling move that may be his greatest legacy: he traveled to the People's Republic of China and reopened diplomatic doors closed to the West since Mao Zedong led the communist takeover in 1949. Though China was allied with the United States during World War II, once the communists took over and exiled the Nationalist government to Taiwan, the People's Republic of China isolated itself from the Western world.

Decades later, Nixon made secret plans to reestablish America's ties with China. In July 1971 Nixon sent Secretary of State Henry Kissinger to a secret meeting to lay the groundwork for his own visit. Upon Kissinger's return, Nixon made a television announcement that stunned the nation: He would be the first president in 23 years to engage in formal diplomatic relations with the communist Chinese regime.

On February 17, 1972, Nixon traveled to Beijing for one week. He met with Chinese premier Chou En-Lai and with the now aged Mao Zedong and successfully began the process of normalizing relations between the United States and China.

Because Nixon had made his career in the Senate as a strong anti-communist during the 1940s and early 1950s the China initiative came as a surprise to many, particularly since the United States was still at war with communist North Vietnam when the trip occurred. Yet again Nixon was more pragmatist than ideologue. He may have had several motivations for his trip, ranging from gaining China as an ally against the Soviet Union, to stopping China from supplying the North Vietnamese Army, and acquiring a lucrative trading partner.

While working to ease tensions with China, Nixon did the same with the Soviet Union by pursuing a policy of détente, or relaxation of tensions. Again, Nixon hoped to open up new trading markets for American technology and surplus agricultural products. Thus he followed his trip to China with a visit to Russia in a few months later.

Although many hardline anti-communists felt that Nixon had made too many concessions to the Soviet Union to achieve détente, the warming relations led to a series of major nuclear weapons treaties. In 1972 both the United States and Soviet

Union signed the Strategic Arms Limitation Talks (SALT) Treaty, followed the next year by a nuclear non-aggression pact, as well as a series of cultural, transportation, and scientific agreements. By 1975 the United States and Soviet Union had cooperated in a joint mission in outer space when an American Apollo spacecraft docked in space with a Soviet Soyuz craft. In addition, the Soviet Union purchased U.S. grain.

## The Yom Kippur War and its Aftermath

The United States and Soviet Union did continue to compete for the allegiances of other nations around the world, particularly in the oil-rich Middle East. As discussed earlier, the U.S. economy has long been affected by fluctuation in global energy prices. During the 1970s, turbulence in the Middle East helped lead to sometimes wildly fluctuating oil prices. OPEC, the Organization of Petroleum Exporting Countries, was created in September 1960 by some of the world's top oil-producing countries, most of them Arab, with the goal of coordinating oil policies and providing member states with financial aid.

To the United States, maintaining solid alliances with members of OPEC was a crucial component to guaranteeing a continuous and stable flow of oil from the Middle East. In pursuing this strategy, the United States had long sent financial and military aid to the region.

Yet guaranteeing stable relations with the nations of the Middle East has been a difficult balancing act, particularly since 1947, when the state of Israel was founded. The original homeland of the Jewish people, Israel had been rebuilt beginning in the nineteenth century, by Jews fleeing oppression in Europe. After World War II, Israel became a safe haven for survivors of the Nazi holocaust and for those Jews who had been denied entry into the United States or other nations. In 1947 the United Nations had officially recognized Israel and divided what had been the British mandate of Palestine since World War I into two states—Israel, a small Jewish state along the coast of the Mediterranean, and Palestine, a larger Arab state to the east.

Yet Arab nations had refused to recognize Israel. In May 1948, they attacked the new state, but were repelled by the Israelis. Israel then extended its borders along the cease-fire lines. Meanwhile, Jordan annexed the land that had been set aside as the new Palestinian state.

In 1967 a new Arab-Israeli War ended with another Israeli victory—and the occupation of more Arab land. Then, in October 1973 as Israelis were celebrating Yom Kippur one of the holiest days on the Jewish calendar, Arab states made a third attempt to defeat Israel. Backed by weapons obtained from the Soviet Union, Egypt and Syria delivered a powerful blow to Israel. Despite initial losses, the Israelis again beat off their attackers in what is known as the Yom Kippur War. When Israel moved to go on the offensive, the Soviet Union threatened to enter the war on the Egyptian side. In response Nixon placed the U.S. military on high alert, and began sending shipments of supplies to Israel. At last the Soviet Union backed down from its threat of intervention and agreed to send a United Nations force to the region to keep the peace.

While the threat of a wider war had been contained, the United States' support for Israel did not sit well with the Arab members of OPEC. As discussed earlier, to punish the United States and other nations that had aided the Israelis, OPEC raised oil prices and limited its oil supply—thereby setting off the 1970s energy crisis.

## Carter and Foreign Affairs

When Jimmy Carter took office in 1977, he brought a new approach to foreign affairs by stressing the human rights record of foreign governments when determining which alliances to form. Although many applauded Carter's emphasis on human rights, others felt it was naive. Worse, Carter appeared to apply human rights standards inconsistently. While he did not hesitate to condemn strategically unimportant nations like Uruguay, he did not hold others, such as the Philippines under Ferdinand Marcos or Iran under Shah Mohammed Reza Pahlavi, to the same standards.

In regard to the Soviet Union, Carter argued that the time for "inordinate fear" of the Soviet Union had passed, and that rather than challenge the Soviets, the United States should exhibit its good will. In keeping with that policy, Carter halted a number of arms programs that he felt would speed up the arms race. He then moved ahead in the area of arms control, signing the SALT II agreement with the Soviets in 1979. The new treaty added further restrictions to the number of new nuclear weapons each super power possessed. This policy infuriated conservatives who believed Carter was showing weakness at a time that the Soviet threat was as strong as ever.

Carter also angered his conservative critics when he signed a treaty agreeing to turn over the Panama Canal Zone to Panama by the year 2000. But Carter's natural instinct as president was negotiation rather than confrontation. In 1978 he achieved his greatest foreign policy victory by mediating an historic peace settlement between Israel and Egypt.

In the 1973 Yom Kippur War, Egypt's military had been one of the main forces to attack Israel. The Egyptians had also purchased significant supplies of Soviet weaponry. Yet under president Anwar el-Sadat, Egypt moved towards warmer relations with the United States. Recognizing that his nation was suffering from severe economic problems, Sadat then decided that turning his nation's economy around was a higher priority than destroying Israel. When Israeli intelligence warned Sadat that Libyan strongman Muammar Qaddafi had ordered assassins to kill him, thereby saving his life, President Carter realized that he might have an opportunity to bring peace to the two former enemies. After 13 days of difficult negotiations at the presidential retreat at Camp David, Maryland, Sadat and Israeli prime minister Menachem Begin signed an historic accord. In the treaty Begin agreed that Israel would return Egyptian land captured by Israel in the 1973 war.

## The Iran Hostage Crisis

Despite the success of the Camp David Accords, relationships with most Arab states in the Middle East remained strained as 1978 came to a close. Since 1953, however, the United States had been on relatively good terms with Iran, one of OPEC's founding members. Although most Iranians, like their Arab neighbors, were Muslims, Iranians were of Persian, not Arab descent. In addition, their country was considerably more westernized than other Middle Eastern states. One reason for this was that in 1953 the CIA had overthrown a communist-backed Iranian political party and reinstalled the deposed Shah Mohammed Reza Pahlavi to the throne. To the United States the Shah was a valuable ally, as he kept Iranian oil flowing to the West. In addition, because Iran bordered the Soviet Union, it was an important strategic U.S. ally in the Cold War. The Nixon Administration therefore encouraged the Shah in his desire to become a major world power by selling him vast amounts of military and industrial equipment.

The Shah of Iran may have been a valuable U.S. ally, but he was also a brutal dictator who became increasingly out of touch with his people. He may have desired to see Iran become a major player on the world stage, but his growing arsenal of U.S.-made fighter planes did not mask the dire poverty that many Iranians suffered. What's more, his efforts to westernize Iranian society—by allowing women to be educated and to wear western style clothing, for example—was offensive to the nation's powerful Islamic clerics.

Rather than work to resolve these conflicts, the Shah used his notorious secret police to terrorize and torture his opponents. By 1978 the Shah's government was on the brink of collapse. In early 1979 he was forced to flee the country.

Although he recognized the Shah's brutality, during the summer of 1979 President Carter agreed to allow the Shah to come to New York for medical treatment. Carter's move sparked violent protests against the United States, culminating on November 4, 1979 with the capture of 66 Americans working at the U.S. Embassy in Tehran by radical student followers of the Islamic clergymen Ayatollah Ruhollah Khomeini, who had recently returned to Iran after being exiled in 1963. Although Khomeini ordered the release of all women and African Americans, the Iranians continued to hold the remaining fifty-two hostages for 444 days.

The crisis created a deep sense of frustration in the American public. Each night Americans watched on television as the news media counted up the mounting total of days that the hostages remained in captivity. For Carter, the low point came in April 1980 when he ordered a special force to launch a surprise rescue mission to free the hostages. The mission ended in disaster when eight servicemen were killed as a helicopter collided with a transport plane in the Iranian desert.

### The Soviet Invasion of Afghanistan

In December 1979, just weeks after the start of the Iran hostage crisis, the Soviet Union launched an all-out invasion of Afghanistan, just to Iran's east. The purpose of the invasion was to prop up a weak communist government that had come to power the year before. In response President Carter took a number of actions to punish the Soviets for the invasion. First he withdrew the SALT II nuclear arms treaty from the Senate's consideration, while also announcing an embargo on the transfer of American technology and a sharp reduction in grain sales to the Soviets. He then announced that the United States would boycott the 1980 Olympic Games scheduled for that summer in Moscow. Ultimately forty-four other nations joined the boycott. Although the boycott meant that the Moscow Games were ultimately held without the participation of many of the world's greatest athletes, it had no effect on the Soviet Union's actions in Afghanistan. To many Americans, the Olympic boycott was simply one more failed Carter administration policy that made the United States look weak rather than strong. Coming on top of the energy shortage, skyrocketing inflation, the Three Mile Island nuclear accident and most of all the Iran hostage crisis, Americans were ready for change.

**THE IRAN HOSTAGE CRISIS** In 1979 radical Iranian students seized the American embassy in Tehran, Iran, and took fifty-two Americans hostage. The Americans remained in captivity for 444 days and helped destroy Jimmy Carter's chances for reelection in 1980.

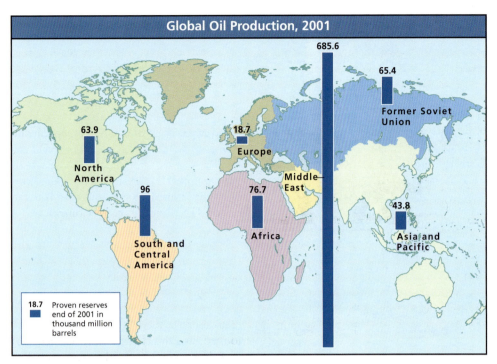

## Global Oil Production, 2001

685.6

65.4

**Former Soviet Union**

63.9

**North America**

18.7

**Europe**

Middle East

96

**South and Central America**

76.7

**Africa**

43.8

**Asia and Pacific**

18.7 Proven reserves end of 2001 in thousand million barrels

**THE POLITICS OF OIL** U.S. foreign policy has been closely tied to energy policy. For example, the United States has worked to maintain close relations with undemocratic governments in the Middle East, while also maintaining strong support for Israel.

# Foreign Policy in the Reagan Years

After his defeat by Ronald Reagan in November, 1980, Jimmy Carter spent the last two and one half months of his presidency working tirelessly to secure the release of the Iranian hostages. At last, on January 18, 1981, American and Iranian negotiators reached a final agreement. Iran would release the hostages in exchange for the release of billions of dollars in frozen Iranian assets in the United States. Yet Carter would be forced to bear a final indignity at the hands of Iran when the actual release of the hostages was delayed for two days. Not until January 20—just hours after Ronald Reagan was sworn in as president—were the hostages actually freed.

## Hot Spots in the Global Cold War

To Reagan's supporters, the fact that the hostages were released just as the new president's watch began seemed to symbolize the restoration of the nation's global might after four years of frustration. With the hostages free, the new administration felt free to focus on combating Soviet expansion. In his first federal budget, Reagan proposed an enormous expansion of the defense budget, including the construction of a

space-based missile-defense system, officially called the Strategic Defense Initiative or SDI, but dubbed "Star Wars" by critics, after the science fiction fantasy films of the same name.

In his public speeches on Soviet relations Reagan was equally forceful. Condemning the Soviets for their support of communist insurgencies in the developing world, as well as their continuing presence in Afghanistan, the president characterized the Soviets in 1983 as "an evil empire." The next year, the Soviet Union retaliated for the boycott of the 1980 Moscow Olympics by boycotting the 1984 games in Los Angeles.

The invasion of Afghanistan provided Reagan with one of his first opportunities to challenge Soviet expansion. Following the invasion, a powerful resistance, known as the Mujihadin, or "holy warriors," had taken up arms against the Soviet army. Before long the fight would also attract volunteer fighters from throughout the Muslim world. For the Mujihadin and their allies from Egypt, Saudi Arabia and other Arab countries, turning back the Soviets in Afghanistan became a *jihad*, or holy war, for the future of Islam.

To American military planners, on the other hand, Islamic fundamentalism was a weapon to be used in the cold war battle against Soviet expansion. In fact, in 1978, well before the Soviets moved into Afghanistan to prop up its communist-lean-

ing government, President Carter's National Security Advisor Zbigniew Brzezinski convinced Carter to authorize $500 million to help fund covert anti-government activity in Afghanistan. During the 1980s, Reagan's CIA chief, William Casey, followed Brzezinski's lead by sending billions of dollars in aid to the Mujihadin through Pakistan's intelligence agency, the Inter-Services Intelligence Agency (ISI). By 1988, the Soviets were forced to withdraw their forces from Afghanistan.

Although the U.S. government has continued to deny any direct connection between its covert activities in Afghanistan and the growth of international terrorism, the ISI is known to have supported fundamentalist Arabs converging on Afghanistan from elsewhere in the Muslim world, including Maktab al-Khidamar, or the MAK, which in turn sent money, arms and fighters to Afghanistan. By 1984 the MAK was headed by a young Saudi Arabian extremist named Osama bin Laden. Three years later, Bin Laden split with the MAK to form al-Qaeda, the global terrorist group that would be responsible for the destruction on September 11, 2001.

### Lebanon and Libya

While al-Qaida would remain an obscure organization that few Americans could identify during the 1980s, terrorism became increasingly common during that decade. Much of the threat centered around the continuing Israeli-Palestinian conflict.

In 1982 Israel invaded Lebanon to its north to force the Palestinian Liberation Organization (PLO) from the capital city of Beirut. After fierce fighting that cost many Lebanese civilians their lives, the PLO was forced to evacuate Beriut by sea to the Libyan city of Tripoli.

Israel's invasion was widely condemned, particularly when Israeli general Ariel Sharon granted a Lebanese militia group access to a Palestinian refugee camp, after which the militia group massacred more than 600 people, including women and children. Although Israel began to remove its troops by the end of 1982, violence between various Lebanese factions led to the arrival of a multinational peacekeeping force, including a number of U.S. Marines, to restore order.

Despite the presence of the peacekeepers, violence continued throughout 1983. Then on October 23, a truck loaded with explosives crashed into the main Marine barracks in Beirut and blew up. Two hundred and forty-one Marines died in the explosion.

After widespread condemnation of the U.S. mission in Lebanon in the aftermath of the terrorist tragedy, Reagan decided to withdraw the remaining U.S. troops from Lebanon in early 1984.

Even after the Marine withdrawal from Beirut, terrorism continued to increase. Egyptian president Anwar el-Sadat and Swedish Prime Minister Olaf Palme both died at the hands of assassins, and Pope John Paul II was wounded by a gunman. In June 1985, a TWA airliner was hijacked on its way to Rome and forced to land in Beirut. Once on the ground the Palestinian hijackers killed a U.S. Navy diver who was on board and held the crew and remaining passengers hostage for 17 days. In October another group of terrorists hijacked the *Achille Lauro*, a cruise ship on the Mediterranean and murdered a wheelchair-bound Jewish-American passenger. In response to this brutal murder, Reagan ordered U.S. Navy fighter planes to force down the plane carrying the highjackers to safety. Then, on Christmas Day, twenty people were killed in bombings in the Vienna and Rome airports and two American soldiers were killed by a bomb that exploded in a Berlin discotheque. After evidence was found linking Libya's government to the Berlin bombing, Reagan ordered U.S. bombers to bomb the Libyan cities of Beghazi and Tripoli in April 1986, and to specifically target Libyan dictator Muammar Qaddafi. Although his home and members of his family were killed, Qaddafi escaped unharmed.

## Central American Conflicts of the 1980s

Clearly, as the 1980s progressed Reagan's goal of defeating global communism was complicated by the necessity of combatting the growing threat of terrorism. Maintaining multiple alliances in the critical Middle East—with Israel, with Jordan, with Egypt, with Saudi Arabia and the Arab Emirates on the Saudi peninsula—was by definition a tricky balancing act, on occasion leading the United States into partnerships with unsavory and certainly undemocratic factions in the name of competing with the Soviets for supremacy. For instance, throughout the 1980s Iran and Iraq waged one of the bloodiest wars of the twentieth century. While the United States remained nominally neutral, by the time the 1980s had ended the U.S. government was sending conventional and chemical weapons to Saddam Hussein, Iraq's despotic strongman. In addition to using

**PEACEKEEPERS** U.S. Marines were stationed in Beirut, Lebanon in the early 1980s, but were withdrawn following a terrorist attack on Marine headquarters that left two hundred and forty-one Americans dead.

these weapons on Iranian soldiers, Hussein would in time also use them on his own people to quell a revolt after the 1991 Gulf War. In 1986 the nation would also learn that the United States had also illegally sold weapons to Iran as part of the Iran-Contra Scandal.

From the start of Reagan's first term Latin America posed a similar challenge to American policymakers. On the one hand pro-Marxist insurgents were active in El Salvador and Guatemala, and had actually overthrown the U.S. backed dictatorship in Nicaragua. On the other hand, all three Central American nations were also being terrorized by right wing groups. In El Salvador and Guatemala the United States supported right-wing governments and did little to object when "death squads" terrorized people throughout the countrysides and cities of their nations.

More troubling to the Reagan Administration was the 1979 victory by the Marxist Sandinista rebels in Nicaragua over that nation's U.S.-supported Samoza dictatorship. Reagan vowed to do all he could to topple the Sandinista government, which received substantial aid from the Soviet Union—short of committing U.S.

troops to Nicaragua. Instead, his administration offered support to the "Contras" a mix of former Samoza officials and other anti-Sandinista rebels. While Reagan hailed the Contras as "the moral equal of our founding fathers," Democrats and a large segment of the American public were outraged by evidence of Contra corruption and atrocities. In 1984, shortly after the Central Intelligence Agency admitted that it had illegally planted mines in Nicaragua's harbors, the House of Representatives voted to cut off U.S. funding to the Contras.

### The Iran-Contra Scandal

In 1986, the Reagan administration would face its greatest political crisis when charges surfaced that the White House National Security (NSC) staff had secretly sold weapons to Iran. When investigators looked into the charges they learned that high level members of the NSC staff had tried to win the release of American hostages held in Lebanon by selling arms to Iran and then using the money to illegally circumvent Congress's ban on aid to the Nicaraguan contras. The key player in the affair, Colonel Oliver North, became a national celebrity when he testified about the plan, arguing that although he had knowingly broken federal laws, that he was bound to obey a "higher law" that justified his actions. Throughout the summer of 1987, various high officials in the Reagan administration gave conflicting accounts of how the affair had unfolded and who had authorized it. CIA director William Casey, who it was discovered had facilitated the transfer of funds to the Contras, died before testifying. For his part, Reagan first denied knowledge of the affair but finally admitted that he had approved the sale of arms to Iran, but said that he never knew about the channeling of funds to the Contras. Ultimately, six members of his administration were convicted of conspiracy for their roles in the affair. All six later received full pardons in 1992 by President George H. W. Bush. In 1994, a final report on the affair was released by Special Prosecutor Lawrence Walsh criticising both Reagan and Bush for overlooking the crimes being committed by members of their staffs.

### Reagan and Gorbachev

Despite the frosty state of U.S.–Soviet relations when Reagan entered office, by his second term relations with the Soviets underwent a program of *glasnost*, or open-

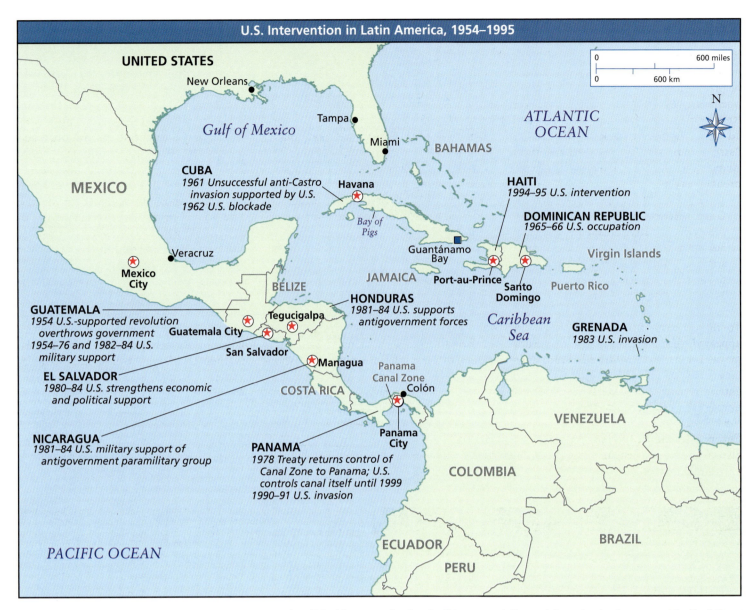

## U.S. Intervention in Latin America, 1954–1995

**UNITED STATES**

New Orleans

*Gulf of Mexico*

Tampa

Miami

**BAHAMAS**

**ATLANTIC OCEAN**

N

**MEXICO**

**CUBA**
1961 Unsuccessful anti-Castro invasion supported by U.S.
1962 U.S. blockade

Havana

*Bay of Pigs*

**HAITI**
1994–95 U.S. intervention

**DOMINICAN REPUBLIC**
1965–66 U.S. occupation

Veracruz

Mexico City

**BELIZE**

Guantánamo Bay

**JAMAICA**

Port-au-Prince

Santo Domingo

*Virgin Islands*

Puerto Rico

**GUATEMALA**
1954 U.S.-supported revolution overthrows government
1954–76 and 1982–84 U.S. military support

Tegucigalpa

Guatemala City

**HONDURAS**
1981–84 U.S. supports antigovernment forces

*Caribbean Sea*

**GRENADA**
1983 U.S. invasion

San Salvador

Managua

**EL SALVADOR**
1980–84 U.S. strengthens economic and political support

**COSTA RICA**

Panama Canal Zone

Colón

**NICARAGUA**
1981–84 U.S. military support of antigovernment paramilitary group

**PANAMA**
1978 Treaty returns control of Canal Zone to Panama; U.S. controls canal itself until 1999
1990–91 U.S. invasion

Panama City

**VENEZUELA**

**COLOMBIA**

**PACIFIC OCEAN**

**ECUADOR**

**PERU**

**BRAZIL**

0          600 miles
0     600 km

**SPHERE OF INFLUENCE** United States economic and political interests in the Caribbean and Central America in the second half of the twentieth century were backed up by military interventions. In some cases, secret CIA operations affected events but went unpublicized for years.

ness and economic and democratic reforms. The architect of *glasnost* was Soviet premier Mikhail Gorbachev, who entered office in 1985. Unlike his predecessors, Gorbachev invited the United States to reopen discussions on arms control and other issues for the first time since the SALT II Treaty had been abandoned.

Although some conservatives remained deeply wary of Gorbachev's motives, public opinion was strongly in favor of renewed arms control negotiations. In November 1985, Reagan and Gorbachev met in Geneva, Switzerland and agreed to discuss a 50 percent reduction in nuclear arms in a future negotiation.

That discussion took place at Reykjavik, Iceland the following October. After initial progress, the talks stalled over the Strategic Defense initiative, or "Star Wars" program. Despite the fact that a workable SDI program was still a theoretical concept many years from completion, the idea of a space-based technology that could shield the United States from nuclear attack had great personal appeal to Reagan, and he refused to compromise.

Despite the failure to reach an agreement at Reykjavik, Reagan and Gorbachev met a third time in Washington in December, 1987. At that meeting the two leaders signed the Intermediate Nuclear Forces (INF) treaty, which called for a reduction of medium range missiles in Europe and for the verification of missile sites in the Soviet Union, the United States and in Europe. While critics on the right complained that the agreement weakened America's deterrent force and critics on the left complained it didn't go far enough, the agreement marked the culmination of a surprisingly cordial relationship between America's anti-communist president and his Soviet counterpart.

### The Collapse of the Soviet Empire

On June 12, 1987, President Reagan visited the divided city of Berlin in East Germany and spoke to the German people. Despite his cordial relationship with Mikhail Gorbachev, he had never wavered in his strong opposition to communism. That day, using an amplifying system that could be heard on the communist-controlled eastern side of the Berlin Wall, he gave what may be his best-remembered speech. He argued that the Soviet system of central planning had failed, that "we see failure, technological backwardness, declining standards of health, even want of the most basic kind: too little food." Although he praised the Soviet Union for its increased openness and reforms under Gorbachev, Reagan asked whether Gorbachav intended real change or token gestures to "strengthen the Soviet system without changing it." He then challenged the Soviet premier, saying:

General Secretary Gorbachev, if you seek peace, if you seek prosperity for the Soviet Union and Eastern Europe, if you seek liberalization: Come here and open this gate! Mr. Gorbachev, open this gate! Mr. Gorbachev, tear down this wall!

To many, Reagan's dramatic statement appeared to be prescient in light of the dramatic events that followed. Gorbachev may not have opened the Brandenburg gate at Reagan's request, but his reforms opened the floodgates of change both in the Soviet Union and throughout Eastern Europe. Ronald Reagan's supporters have also argued that Reagan's rapid defense build-up of the 1980s ultimately bankrupted the Soviet Union and led to its collapse. Whatever the cause, when the collapse of the entire Soviet bloc came, it came suddenly and perhaps most surprisingly of all, generally peacefully.

One of the earliest members of the Soviet bloc to transform itself was Poland. In 1989 the communist government was voted out of power through peaceful elections. Coming to power in its place were members of Solidarity, a trade union that had been banned for nine years by the communists.

After the transformation of Poland, one country after the next followed suit. Late in 1989 massive demonstrations in East Germany demanding new leadership, led to one of the most dramatic events of the twentieth century—and the fulfilment of Ronald Reagan's demand two years earlier. In a last ditch effort to quell national unrest, the communist government of East Germany allowed its citizens to move freely from East Berlin to West Berlin. As camera's recorded the amazing sight, the citizens of a united Berlin took sledgehammers to the wall and tore it down.

At virtually the same time, the citizens of Hungary, Czechoslovakia and Bulgaria elected reformist governments. Only in isolated and poverty stricken Romania did serious violence occur, when security forces of the despot Nicolae Ceausescu fired on demonstrators. Yet the episode would mark the leader's downfall, as an outraged Romanian military then joined the citizenry in overthrowing the tyrannical despot.

Between 1990 and 1991 Eastern Europeans, most voting freely for the first time, voted communist governments out of power. The Soviet Union's Baltic republics (Lithuania, Latvia, and Estonia) joined the republic of Georgia in declaring independence from the Soviet Union. In August 1991, when the Soviet Union appeared to be crumbling, communist officials attempted to overthrow Gorbachev, but were halted by Russian president Boris Yeltsin. By then the Soviet Union had virtually ceased to function as a state. In December Gorbachev resigned his leadership of the Soviet Union. The nation then split into 15 independent, though allied, nations known as the Commonwealth of Independent States, or CIS.

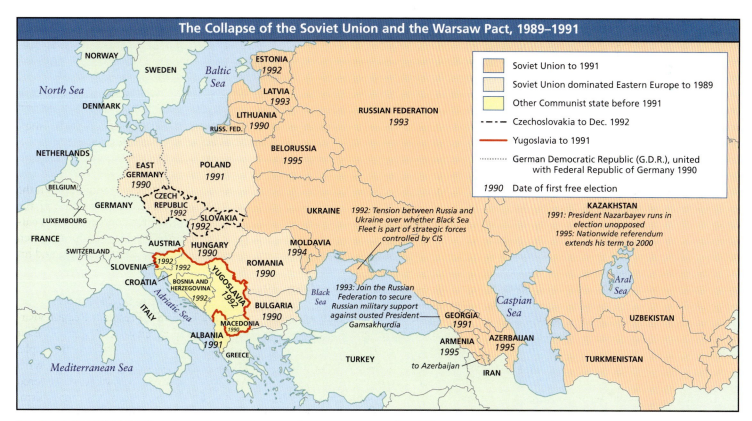

**The Collapse of the Soviet Union and the Warsaw Pact, 1989–1991**

Legend:
- Soviet Union to 1991
- Soviet Union dominated Eastern Europe to 1989
- Other Communist state before 1991
- Czechoslovakia to Dec. 1992
- Yugoslavia to 1991
- German Democratic Republic (G.D.R.), united with Federal Republic of Germany 1990
- *1990* Date of first free election

**COMMUNISM CRUMBLES** In 1989, East Berliners pulled down the Berlin Wall, defying communist leaders. Nationalist and anti-Russian feelings brought calls for greater independence in the Soviet Union's fifteen republics, and by early 1990 many were establishing their own laws. Meanwhile democratic and nationalist movements also toppled communist dictatorships in Poland, Czechoslovakia, Hungary, Romania, and Bulgaria. On December 31, 1991, the Soviet government officially dissolved.

# Foreign Policy in the Post-Cold War Era

George H. W. Bush took office as Ronald Reagan's successor just as the Soviet bloc began its collapse. Not all communist powers had fallen in the face of western style reforms, as China proved in 1989 when the Chinese government brutally crushed student-led pro-democracy demonstrations in Beijing's Tiananmen Square, but when Bush's term ended the United States stood as the world's sole remaining superpower.

In general Bush maintained many of his predecessor's forceful policies. In December 1989 he sent 25,000 troops to Panama to overthrow Manuel Noriega, a drug dealing dictator whom had once been on the payroll of the CIA.

Bush's greatest foreign policy challenge, and greatest achievement, came after Iraq invaded and occupied its tiny, oil-rich neighbor Kuwait. Declaring that the invasion "will not stand," Bush quickly ordered air, naval, and ground forces to Saudi Arabia, a military buildup known as Operation Desert Shield. Eventually thirty-two nations, including several Arab states, joined the U.S.-led coalition committed to liberating Kuwait. Negotiations between U.S. Secretary of State James Baker and Iraqi Foreign Minister Tariq Aziz broke down, and with the support of both Congress and the United Nations the Allied forces began their offensive—launching Operation Desert Storm on January 17, 1991 from a command and control center in Saudi Arabia.

Many feared a long and costly conflict—Iraq had more than a million troops and possessed chemical weapons—but after five weeks of bombardment from the air and a 100-hour ground assault, Iraqi troops withdrew from Kuwait. Allied casualties were amazingly low, particularly after President Bush opted not to invade the Iraqi capital of Baghdad in an effort to capture Saddam Hussein for fear of bogging the United States down in a protracted war. Thus, the lightning victory was joyfully celebrated by many in the United States as a triumph of American-led military might.

Despite the unquestionable victory, Saddam Hussein would remain for another dozen years. And the Saudi Arabian government's decision to allow the U.S. military to use its soil to launch an attack on another Muslim state would be seen as

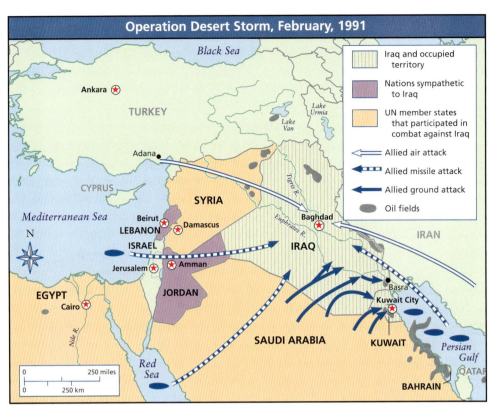

**Operation Desert Storm, February, 1991**

**THE GULF WAR** In 1991 President George H.W. Bush oversaw the successful invasion of Iraq after Iraq invaded neighboring Kuwait. Once Saddam Hussein agreed to withdraw his forces from Kuwait, the U.S.-led coalition withdrew from Iraq.

a blasphemous act by the growing number of radical Islamic fundamentalists in the Middle East.

## Clinton's Foreign Policy

Despite Bush's successful leadership in the Gulf War, he lost his bid for reelection to Arkansas governor Bill Clinton in 1992. Initially, Clinton's lack of foreign policy experience showed: he alienated many members of the military with his clumsy "don't ask don't tell policy" that was meant to resolve a ban on openly homosexual or lesbian soldiers serving in the Armed Forces. He also mismanaged a peacekeeping mission in the East African nation of Somalia, leading to a disastrous ambush of American soldiers. Yet by 1994, he appeared to have gained his foreign policy footing when he successfully forced Haitian military leaders to step down and allow the democratically elected president of that country to return from exile. The following year he agreed to send U.S. troops to help keep the peace in the former Yugoslav republic of Bosnia which had been engaged in a bloody civil war, and during his second term he authorized the U.S. Air Force to bomb Serbia in an effort to halt the "ethnic cleansing" of Muslims in the Yugoslav territory of Kosovo. In

1994 he was also instrumental in convincing Israel and the Palestinian Authority to reopen peace talks, although a last ditch effort to bring a negotiated settlement between Israel and the Palestinians in the winter of 2000 ended in failure.

Another major foreign policy concern for the Clinton Administration was terrorism. In February 1993 Islamic fundamentalists living in the United States detonated a bomb in the basement of one of the World Trade Center towers in New York City. Six people were killed and over 1,000 were injured. Several people, including an Egyptian cleric named Sheikh Omar Abdel-Rahman, were convicted of the crime as well as for conspiring to blow up several other New York landmarks.

During Clinton's two terms terrorist incidents targeting Americans overseas also continued. In 1993 he ordered 23 Tomahawk missiles to be fired at the building housing the Iraqi Intelligence Service when it was learned that the Iraqi government had plotted to assassinate former president Bush during a Bush visit to Kuwait after he left office. (Clinton also ordered U.S. warplanes to attack Iraqi military installations several times in the 1990s when Iraq violated terms of the 1991 Gulf War cease-fire agreement.)

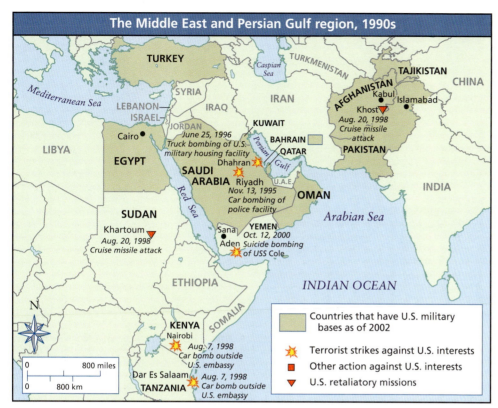

### The Middle East and Persian Gulf region, 1990s

**ANTI-U.S. TERRORISM** Africa and the Middle East saw a steady rise in major violence against U.S. interests. Terrorist attacks brought U.S. counterattacks.

By the mid-1990s, al-Qaeda, founded by Saudi-born fundamentalist Osama bin Laden, had grown strong enough to carry out a series of attacks on U.S. targets overseas. In 1996 al-Qaeda operatives sent a truck bomb into a U.S. military barracks in Saudi Arabia, killing 19 American servicemen. Two years later Bin Laden's group masterminded bombings of U.S. embassies in Kenya and Tanzania, killing 190. In response Clinton launched cruise missile strikes at Bin Laden's bases in Sudan and Afghanistan.

Afghanistan posed a special problem for the American government. Following the withdrawal of the Soviet Union in the late 1980s the country had fallen into chaos, with warring regional factions squaring off against each other. In 1996 a radical fundamentalist group known as the Taliban came to power. The Taliban ruled with an iron hand, severely restricting women's rights and attempting to wipe their nation clean of any foreign, non-Muslim influence. In one particularly attention-grabbing episode that provoked worldwide outrage, the Taliban destroyed two gigantic Buddhist figures that had stood carved into a Afghan hillside for almost two thousand years.

Nonetheless, the Clinton administration recognized that if they wanted direct negotiations with the Afghan government, they would have to deal with the Taliban. The administration hoped to achieve two aims in this way. First, they hoped to arrange permission for Unocal, a U.S. energy company, to build an pipeline from the rich oilfields of the Caucusus to the north. Second, they wanted the Taliban to turn over Osama bin Laden, whom they had granted safe haven to after he had been expelled from Sudan. In December 1997 a Taliban delegation visited Washington to open talks on the subject and then traveled to Sugar Land, Texas to meet with executives of Unocal.

Ultimately, these talks and others held between the Clinton administration and the Taliban failed to garner either a pipeline deal, or cooperation in capturing Osama bin Laden. On October 17, 2000—two weeks before the disputed U.S. election of that year was to take place—seventeen American sailors onboard the U.S. navy destroyer U.S.S. *Cole* were killed by another attack orchestrated by Bin Laden.

### The War on Terror Begins

On October 11, 2000, during a televised debate with Democrat Albert Gore, Governor George W. Bush of Texas, the son of the former president and the Republican nominee for president, was asked about the appropriate use of American power in the world, particularly since the United States

was the only remaining superpower. While Bush generally agreed with most of the global troop commitments made by the Clinton Administration, he argued that a Bush administration would take a more limited view of when it was appropriate to exercise U.S. military power. "I'm not sure the role of the United States is to go around the world and say this is the way it's got to be," he remarked. "We can help. I mean I want to empower people. I want to help people help themselves, not have the government tell people what to do. I just don't think its the role of the United States to walk into a country and say, we do it this way, so should you."

Unlike his father, George W. Bush had little foreign policy experience when he entered the White House. While many members of his administration, such as Defense Secretary Donald Rumsfeld and Vice President Dick Cheney, had worked in previous Republican administrations dating back to the Nixon era, Bush's focus when he entered office in January 2001 appeared to be on domestic issues.

In the administration's first months, much of its foreign affairs efforts focused on extracting the United States from diplomatic efforts that it deemed to be counter to U.S. interests, such as the Kyoto Accords on Global Warming, or the Antiballistic Missile Treaty with the former Soviet Union. Other discussions centered on global energy policy, as Vice President Cheney led a series of strategy sessions with oil industry executives in order to formulate a comprehensive strategy. Among the topics included in the discussion were the potential use of Iraq's rich oil resources and the hopes for a pipeline through Afghanistan. To reopen negotiations on the pipeline, the Administration invited a Taliban representative to visit Washington in March 2001. Again the visit failed to make progress on the issue. Six months later, on September 11, 2001, hijackers destroyed the World Trade Center in New York City and damaged the Pentagon in Washington, DC, leaving more than 3,000 people dead.

In minutes, the focus of George W. Bush's administration changed from domestic issues to the need to protect the United States from further attacks. On September 14, in what may have been the most dramatic speech of his presidency, visited the site of the collapsed World Trade towers, and grabbing a bullhorn, spoke to the cheering crowd of firefighters and rescue personnel who had been working nonstop to find survivors for three days: "I can hear you," he said firmly. "The rest of the world hears you. And the people who knocked down these buildings will hear from us soon." In a speech to the nation on September 20, Bush declared a war on terror, one that aimed to put a stop to all terrorist organizations with global reach.

He began the war by targeting al-Qaeda's strongholds in Afghanistan. On October 7, 2001, he ordered bombing of Afghanistan to begin. By December anti-Taliban forces in Afghanistan, known as the Northern Alliance, defeated the last major pocket of Taliban resistance in the mountainous Tora Bora region bordering Pakistan. Although the United States had evidence that Bin Laden had been holed up in Tora Bora, he managed to escape.

As it had since the Soviet occupation of Afghanistan, the United States worked with the assistance of Pakistan's Inter-Services Intelligence Agency (ISI) to achieve its goals. However, the Pakistan-Afghanistan border region is a notoriously lawless area, largely controlled by various tribal chieftains rather than the Pakistani or Afghani federal governments. Even Pakistan's capital city of Karachi remained a locus of terrorism, as was proved when a *Wall Street Journal* reporter was kidnapped and executed by Pakistani terrorists in January, 2002.

## The March to War

In President Bush's 2002 State of the Union address, he described an "axis of evil" between Iran, Iraq, and North Korea, the deeply repressive communist state that had begun a nuclear weapons program. The mention of Iraq was one of the first public charges by the President to imply that since the Iraq War, Iraq had come to possess significant quantities of "weapons of mass destruction" (WMD), and that it was connected to the September 11 tragedy. In the following months, other members of his administration would do the same, shifting the focus away from Osama bin Laden to Iraqi dictator Saddam Hussein. In March, CIA director George Tenet told the Senate Intelligence Committee that, "[t]here is no doubt that there have been (Iraqi) contacts and linkages to the al-Qaeda organization," and that "it would be a mistake to dismiss the possibility of state sponsorship [of the September 11th plot] whether Iranian or Iraqi..." In a June speech to the graduates at West Point, Bush announced that for the first time in U.S. history, the United States would take preemptive military action

SEPTEMBER 11 On September 11, 2001, terrorists hijacked four passenger planes. Two crashed into the twin towers of the World Trade Center in New York City, a third struck the Pentagon outside Washington DC, and a fourth, crashed in rural Pennsylvania, reportedly en route for the White House.

**Flight Paths of Hijacked Airliners on September 11, 2001**

American Airlines flight 11

United Airlines flight 175

United Airlines flight 93

American Airlines flight 77

against other countries if it was deemed to be in the national interest.

As the administration's rhetoric began to heat up during the Summer of 2002, investigations into what went wrong on the morning of September 11 made it clear than the communications between the FBI and CIA had suffered a major breakdown in the months leading up to September. At the same time, intelligence sources also began to question both Iraq's connection to September 11 and its possession of WMD. Vehemently asserting that intelligence proved that Iraq had such weapons and that Iraq was "hosting, supporting, or sponsoring" al-Qaeda in Iraq, Defense Secretary Donald Rumsfeld nonetheless refused to disclose the nature of this intelligence. By September the administration was charging that Iraq possessed aluminum tubes that were clearly, it believed, to be used to develop a nuclear weapons program. By the end of the month, the British government released a report that stated that Saddam Hussein had attempted to obtain uranium from the African nation of Niger. Several weeks later, Congress approved a resolution to authorize the president to use military force against Iraq.

Even as preparations for a U.S. war on Iraq mounted, doubts about Saddam's true capabilities continued to surface. When former ambassador Joseph Wilson reported that he had been dispatched to Niger by the CIA to investigate the British claim of Iraqi uranium purchases, and that he had found no evidence of any such Iraqi con-

tact, he reported his doubts to the CIA. And when UN inspectors arrived in Iraq to search for WMDs in November, they found no traces of their existence. Nonetheless, in December, Bush approved the deployment of U.S. troops to the Gulf region in preparation for war, and argued in his 2003 State of the Union address that he was ready to attack Iraq with or without a UN mandate.

Although popular opinion in the United States was divided on the issue of Iraq, the administration's stance caused widespread popular protest around the world. On February 15, 2003, millions of people in the United States and around the world participated in peaceful protests against the impending war. At the same time, the governments of France and Germany declared their firm opposition to the U.S. course and pledged to work against the war. In this climate the United States failed to win UN Security Council support for a war resolution, winning only the support of Great Britain, Spain, and Bulgaria. Rather than calling for a vote on the resolution, the United States decided to halt all diplomatic efforts, and on March 19, 2003, launched war on Iraq.

Beginning with a campaign of heavy aerial attack dubbed "shock and awe," U.S. forces quickly advanced on Baghdad, taking control of it on April 9, while British forces captured the southern city of Basra. On May 1, President Bush, dressed in a Navy fighter flight suit, declared from the deck of the carrier U.S.S. *Lincoln* that "major combat operations" in Iraq were over.

## Continuing Insurgency, Continuing Controversy

In the years since Bush's declaration, the U.S. military has remained in Iraq. By May 2006, American combat deaths in Iraq had reached nearly 2,005, with official estimates of the wounded ranging from roughly 18,000.

While Saddam Hussein's army had quickly dissolved in the face of the initial U.S. assault, U.S. and other coalition forces have faced virtually daily attacks from insurgents in Baghdad, and other major cities. Critics of administration strategy have argued that American military planners prepared for the initial military operation, but were caught by surprise by the insurgency that followed.

First and foremost, say the critics, the United States vastly underestimated the number of American troops that would be required to contain Iraq once Saddam had fallen. In fact, the war had placed such great demands on the regular armed forces that the Administration came to rely on the National Guard that normally remain stationed in the United States, tending to natural disasters and other domestic emergencies. Such was the case in September 2005, when the largest hurricane to hit the Gulf Atlantic coast struck New Orleans and the surrounding region in Louisiana, Mississippi, and Alabama. All three states found their National Guard contingents depleted because many of the Guard were stationed in Iraq.

Complicating matters is the fact that in the early weeks of the war, American authorities dissolved the Iraqi Army, often without disarming its soldiers first. Therefore, say critics, Iraqis loyal to the deposed Saddam Hussein—who U.S. forces captured in an underground bunker in December 2003—were free to disappear and then regroup to launch hit and run attacks on U.S. troops.

Critics of the Bush administration's conduct of the war have also charged that while Iraq may not have actually been the nexus of global terrorism before the war, it has become so since the war began. They argue that the American invasion has incited radical fundamentalists to travel into Iraq and take up arms against the United States, just as another generation of Islamists had done against the Soviet Union in Afghanistan twenty-five years ago. Revelations in April 2004 that U.S. forces in charge of a prison camp at Abu Ghraib, Iraq had physically and and sexually abused Iraqi prisoners only added to anti-U.S. outrage around world.

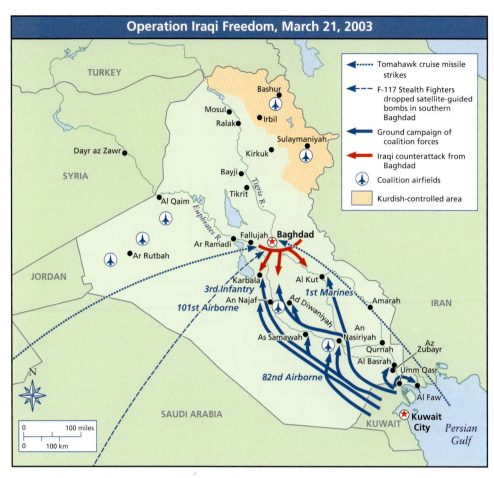

**Operation Iraqi Freedom, March 21, 2003**

**THE IRAQ WAR BEGINS** In 2003, the Bush Administration launched the first preemptive U.S. attack on another nation when U.S. forces invaded Iraq and toppled the regime of Saddam Hussein. Three years later, U.S. forces remained in Iraq, as rival Shi'ite and Sunni Muslims and radicals drawn to Iraq by the U.S. invasion battled for supremacy.

In January 2004, David Kay, the former chief UN weapons inspector for Iraq, reported to the Senate that no weapons of mass destruction had been found in Iraq and that prewar intelligence had been "almost all wrong" about Saddam's arsenal. Thus, the main public rationale for entry into the war had been shown to be based on faulty—or as some critics charged falsified—intelligence. (British documents released in Spring 2005 reported that as early as 2002 American officials had adjusted intelligence to fit their predetermined policy.)

With the release of the Kay Report, however, the administration shifted its focus away from the existence of WMDs to the desire to bring a stable democratic government to Iraq. On June 28, 2004, the United States transferred governing power to an interim Iraqi governing council, and plans were soon made for the first free elections in Iraqi history to take place in January 2005. The image of Iraqi citizens standing in long lines enthusiastically embracing their right to vote gave Americans some of the first positive news on Iraq in some time. Yet the election underscored the deep ethnic rivalries that split the Iraqi people. Sunni Muslims, who under Saddam had been the dominant political force in the country even though they were a religious minority, largely boycotted the elections and then were left out of the Summer 2005 agreement on the new Iraqi constitution that the Shi'ite majority and Kurdish minority reached without them. That constitution disappointed many when it was learned that it would deprive Iraqi women of many of their rights and would be based not on democratic principles but on Islamic law.

As of 2006 U.S. forces remained in Iraq. Yet the Iraqi government appeared further than ever from forming a workable democratic government. Although the United States emerged from the Cold War as the world's lone superpower, the Iraq War seemed to underscore that America's ability to reshape the world to suit its interests still had dangerous limitations.

# Chapter 32: Economic, Social and Cultural Changes

Comprising fifteen southern and western states that stretch from Virginia to Florida in the East and from the Southeast to the Southern California in the West, America's Sunbelt region underwent unprecedented growth between 1968 and 2000. Companies initially were drawn to the Sunbelt by its cheap land, low taxes, and low-wage, largely non-union, labor pool. In addition to a vast number of job opportunities in thriving industries, the Sunbelt also offered migrants mild climates, year-round recreational opportunities, and inexpensive housing. With abundant national resources the Sunbelt became a hotbed of research and high tech opportunity in the late twentieth century, particularly in aerospace, electronics, and pharmaceuticals.

The gains of the Sunbelt came at the expense of the northeastern and north central states from Maine to Minnesota. To many, this area became known as the Frostbelt for its colder climate, or the Rustbelt for its declining heavy manufacturing sector. Traditional industries in those states, such as steel, textiles and automobiles floundered due to globalization, as foreign companies proved capable of producing comparable goods more cheaply than American companies. Automation brought about by the computer revolution put even more workers on the unemployment lines, and sped the influx of people to the Sunbelt.

As the U.S. population shifted south and west, so too did the national political power of those regions, as the South and West gained greater representation in the House of Representatives. This shift in regional political power would be a major factor in the rise of the conservative movement in the late twentieth century. Likewise the rising economic power of the Sunbelt, as jobs moved from the East and Midwest to the South and Southwest, would also have repercussions.

## Changes in the Workplace

From roughly the 1860s to the 1960s, the U.S. economy was dependent on manufacturing. But since 1968 vast changes have occurred in the workplace, resulting in the development of a service economy. Today those services range from health care to fast-food restaurants to financial analysts to housekeepers. American manufacturing was greatly affected by globalization—the ability of foreign markets to provide cheaper goods and produce them more efficiently—resulting in massive layoffs in the automotive manufacturing, steel and clothing and textiles industries. The cheap labor costs in foreign countries also lured away many American manufacturers. The number of steelworkers, for example, fell from 457,000 in 1975 to 164,000 in 1990.

The recession of 1979–82 was a particularly hard one for American industry. During this downturn one third of all American industrial facilities were idle. As more and more factories became idle, labor unions saw a decrease in membership. In 1978, 20.2 million Americans were members of labor unions. The number decreased to 17.7 million in 1985 and to 16.3 million in 1999.

### The Computer Age

Industry was also revolutionized by computerized, automated systems that reduced the number of employees needed in factories. Automated systems also allowed corporate offices to cut staff by streamlining such areas as payroll services, accounting and sales analysis. Meanwhile, the rise of computers led to the development of new careers in software development, computer programming, and systems analysis.

During the 1990s computer related service jobs became one of the fastest growing area of employment, rising from just 106,700 jobs in 1972 and 2.1 million jobs in 2000. New positions were created, ranging from the development of hardware and systems which required specific education and training, to e-com-

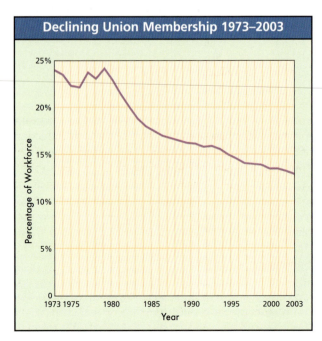

**Declining Union Membership 1973–2003**

*Percentage of Workforce vs. Year*

**HARD TIMES FOR UNIONS** Labor union membership has been declining since the 1970s.

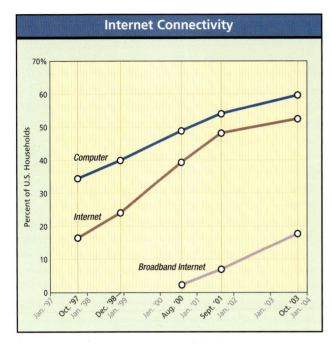

**Internet Connectivity**

Percent of U.S. Households

Computer

Internet

Broadband Internet

70%
60
50
40
30
20
10
0

Jan. '97  Oct. '97  Jan. '98  Dec. '98  Jan. '99  Jan. '00  Aug. '00  Jan. '01  Sept. '01  Jan. '02  Jan. '03  Oct. '03  Jan. '04

**A TRANSFORMATIVE TECHNOLOGY** Personal computers and high-speed Internet connectivity have transformed the world of work and the private lives of millions of Americans.

merce, a brand new industry developed to sell good and services over the Internet.

The technology revolution of the late twentieth century didn't merely create jobs. It changed the way Americans got their information and how they communicated with each other. In 1991 computer scientists developed the software that led to the development of the World Wide Web. Two years later software known as MOSAIC (later called Netscape) gave users a graphical interface—or visual means of viewing text and pictures on the Internet. Combined with electronic mail or e-mail that allowed users to send text (and eventually sound and images) anywhere in the world, the Internet changed the way that people worldwide processed and shared information.

Other forms of technology, such as facsimile (fax) machines, portable cellular phones, and pagers also allowed people to keep in constant touch. Websites, radio phone-in shows, and television town meetings were just some of the ways people communicated with each other.

## Fast Food and Shopping Malls

Although the trend toward chain retailing had begun with the post-World War II rise of suburbia, during the last quarter of the twentieth century it accelerated. Increasingly local stores in America's downtown shopping districts gave way to shopping malls and stand-alone superstores on the outskirts of town, and to chain restaurants in virtually every neighborhood. Fast food restaurants—McDonald's, Burger King, Taco Bell, and their numerous counterparts—expanded dramatically during this era, and by the end of the 1990s more that 2.3 million workers were collecting their $6 or $7 an hour pay from these establishments. While many of these chains began to offer benefits and other perks to their staff by the late 1990s, low wages still led to rapid turnover from a largely unskilled workstaff made up of high school students and recent immigrants.

In the malls of America, chain stores like the Gap, Victoria's Secret and the Limited offered shoppers convenience and consistency from Alaska to Florida. Discount departments stores also underwent changes, as local stores and older downtown chains like F.W. Woolworth's were supplanted by Wal-Mart and similar superstores. Wal-Mart, founded with one store in Bentonville, Arkansas in the 1960s, grew to 3,600 outlets by 2001. Meanwhile, the total number of retail jobs in America also rose, growing from 10.3 million in 1968 to 23.3 million in 2000.

## Women and Minorities in the Workforce

Between 1970 and 2000, the minority share of the labor force increased from 11.1 percent to 15.5 percent. Despite great strides being made by people of color, as well as by women, white men still dominated the corporate world in the early twenty-first century. Although an increasing number of women assumed traditionally male roles in the workplace, they were still paid an average of 30 percent less than their male peers and rarely held upper management positions.

Yet many women took alternate routes by opening their own businesses. In fact the 9.1 million women-owned small businesses accounted for 33 person of all small businesses by 1999. Meanwhile, government statistics show that as of 1997, African-American and Hispanic-American men were still paid less than their white male counterparts.

## Changes in Health Care

The American healthcare system experienced extraordinary changes in the last quarter of the twentieth century, due to technological and scientific breakthroughs, an aging population, and new methods for delivering care. Medical breakthroughs included the first human heart transplant in 1967, and the first mechanical heart transplant in 1982. By the end of the 1970s other organ transplants, such as kidneys and livers, had become increasingly common.

A doctor's ability to diagnose patients has also leapt forward in the past few decades. The 1972 introduction of the CAT scan (CAT is short for Computerized Axial Tomography) gave physicians the ability to see a cross-section of a patient's interior, thus reducing the need for invasive, exploratory surgery. Ultrasound devices, using high frequency sound waves to create images of the interior of the body, also came into being in a manner far safer than tests that use radiation. In 1977 the first "balloon angioplasty" was performed in San Francisco to treat collapsed arteries. Small "balloons" were inserted into collapsed arteries and then inflated to clear blockage.

Beginning in the 1980s laser technology began to find medical applications. Lasers could break off material

## The Growth of the Service Economy, 1990–2005

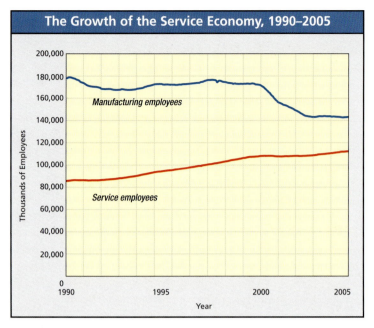

## Women Working Outside the Home, 1955–2005

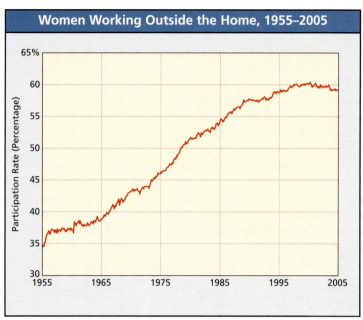

**THE SERVICE ECONOMY** While many American manufacturing jobs have moved overseas, the number of service jobs has increased.

**WORKING WOMEN** The number of working women has increased dramatically since the 1950s.

that clogged arteries, could destroy cancerous tumors and could fix vision problems. Fiber optics also had medical uses. Fiber optic cables could be inserted into a patient's body, bending to follow the throat or even blood vessels. By connecting the fiber optic cables to video screens, doctors could see inside a person's internal organs without surgery. What's more, when surgery was required, doctors could attach tools to the cables and then perform far less invasive and dangerous surgery.

While new technology had allowed doctors to diagnose and treat patients more effectively during this period, these new tools were expensive — often too expensive for smaller, rural hospitals. By the early 1980s many small hospitals teetered on the brink of bankruptcy. In response many nonprofits moved to for profit status, which usually spelled higher medical costs for consumers.

Beginning in the 1970s the care of the mentally ill changed drastically as well. In the 1960s only half the hospital beds that were needed were available for the mentally ill. Until that time most care of mentally disabled patients was conducted at the state and local level with no federal support. Beginning in the 1970s federal funds were made available for the first time to local clinics that treated mental disorders.

During the 1970s the federal government also became more actively engaged in warning about the dangers of tobacco. The Surgeon General had first determined that cigarettes were hazardous to health in 1964, and by 1967 his report first explicitly linked tobacco to lung cancer and heart disease. Three years later, in an effort to halt the rise of smoking among young people, Congress banned all cigarette advertising on television and radio. In 1972 an updated Surgeon General's report linked second hand smoke to increased health risks as well.

In response to federal government action to regulate smoking, tobacco companies argued that the health risks of their products were not proven. In the decades to come, however, not only would the risks be confirmed—leading to further federal and local bans on smoking in airplanes, restaurants, bars and other public places—but it would be discovered that top executives of the nation's largest tobacco companies had known the risks themselves and had systematically covered up the dangers. By the late 1990s tobacco companies found themselves sued by former smokers for the illnesses and deaths caused by their products. Ultimately, the government arranged for the tobacco industry to pay a multi-billion dollar settlement for damages in exchange for protection against further lawsuits.

### The AIDS Crisis

During the early 1980s a devastating new disease identified as Acquired Immune Deficiency Syndrome, or AIDS, appeared. AIDS is caused by the HIV virus that attacks the body's ability to fight off infections, and is spread through contact with infected blood or semen. However, because many of the first patients were homosexuals who had obtained the virus through unprotected sexual activity, or intravenous drug users, the search for a cure was handicapped by the stigma associated with it. Throughout much of the 1980s AIDS was thought to be a "gay plague," rather than a national heath crisis impacting all Americans. The socially conservative Reagan administration largely ignored the epidemic and resisted pleas for federally funded research for a cure. By the end of the 1980s hundreds of thousands of Americans had become infected with HIV. Although no cure had been found, public health officials mounted massive public information campaigns to curb the spread of the disease.

During the 1990s AIDS researchers were finally able to find new ways of treating the disease that were able to halt many HIV infections from developing into full-blown AIDS. Although an actual cure had not been found, the number of AIDS deaths in the United States plummeted during the mid-1990s, from nearly 50,000 a year in 1994 to under 14,000 in 1998. Despite this positive news, health officials have grown concerned that that while the total number of deaths had fallen, prevention efforts had been less successful in poor and uneducated communities. What's more, as a new generation of young people grew to sexual maturity,

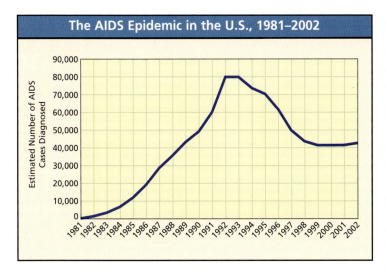

### The AIDS Epidemic in the U.S., 1981–2002

**PROGRESS AGAINST AIDS** Education and advances in treatment halted the rise in AIDS cases during the 1990s, although by decade's end, the number of cases had begun to increase again.

many falsely believed that an AIDS cure had been found, leading to an early twenty-first century rise in both unprotected sex and new HIV cases. Even more ominous has been the spread of AIDS globally. By 2000, HIV infection rates in some sub-Saharan African nations had reached as high as one-third of the adult population.

# The New American Immigrants

When Congress passed the Immigration Act of 1924 immigration from Asia, as well as from southern and eastern Europe, to the United States virtually ended. The law used a quota system that favored immigrants from northern and western Europe. Yet in 1965 a new law, known as the Hart-Celler Act, reformed American immigration law, opening the country to wide-scale Asian immigration for the first time in forty years. Under Hart-Celler, the use of quotas based on national origins ceased. The new system allowed an annual admission of 170,000 immigrants from the Eastern Hemisphere (with a maximum of 20,000 per country) and 120,000 from the Western Hemisphere.

In the mid-1960s Asian Americans totalled less than 1 percent of the U.S. population. The architects of Hart-Celler believed that Europeans would continue to take up most immigration slots and that the number of immigrants from Asia would remain small. This proved grossly inaccurate, and millions of immigrants from the Philippines, China, India, and South Korea, and Southeast Asia have arrived in the United States to establish new lives since 1965.

Although immigrants from Latin America had been exempted from the 1920s immigration restrictions, the last several decades of the twentieth century also witnessed a dramatic rise in the number of Mexican, Central American, Cuban, Dominican and South American immigrants. By 1980 the Latino population of the United States accounted for roughly 6.4 percent of the total U.S. population; by 2000 the proportion had almost doubled, making Hispanic-Americans the single largest minority in the United States, outnumbering African Americans for the first time.

## Asian Immigrants

No single identity defines the new American immigrant. For example, many of the Asian Indian and Filipino immigrants who began arriving in the United States in the late 1960s and 1970s differed from earlier Asian immigrants in that they were often highly educated, English-speaking urban professionals, who had left India and the Philippines due to lack of opportunities at home.

Today Indians occupy more managerial and professional positions than any other Asian American group. Yet of the nearly 900,000 Filipino immigrants to the United States between 1970 and 1990, fully two-thirds were educated professionals, with many concentrated in the medical professions. Many first generation Korean Americans were doctors, skilled laborers, engineers, accountants, chemists, technicians, and other professionals. At the same time many Asian immigrants established themselves as entrepreneurs. Many Indians, for example, have found success in the hotel business. And by 1983 three-quarters of all green groceries in New York City were Korean-owned.

Chinese Americans refer to post-1965 immigrants from mainland China as *san yi man* ("new immigrants"). The Chinese *san yi man* range in background from blue collar laborers to white collar professionals. Well-educated, professional-level Chinese have assimilated quickly into mainstream America and live in middle- and upper-middle-class suburban communities. Meanwhile, blue-collar *san yi man* have settled in urban Chinatowns. Like their predecessors, they have tended to hold menial and low-paying jobs, often in family owned retail businesses. Lack of education and English language skills have compounded their economic problems. Many lived below the poverty line in substandard housing, even though they worked long hours.

Among the poorest of Asian immigrants to the United States since the 1970s were the more than one million Vietnamese, Cambodians, and Laotians who began arriving in the United States after the Vietnam War. Arriving as wartime refugees rather than immigrants for economic reasons, few brought with them the qualifications or means to easily become acculturated into American society. Yet the long U.S. involvement in Vietnam created close ties to America. When South Vietnam fell to the communist north, the United State agreed to accept roughly 140,000 refugees fleeing persecution. In much the same way, the United States also accepted a smaller number of Cambodians after that nation fell to the communist Khmer Rouge.

The first wave of Indochinese refugees tended to be those with the closest ties to the United States—Vietnamese who had worked closely with Americans during the war, for instance. In 1978 internal crisis in Vietnam and the Vietnamese invasion of Cambodia led to a second, much larger wave of refugees. Joined by additional refugees from the neighboring nation of Laos, this second wave became known as "boat people," due to their practice of setting off in small, and often only marginally seaworthy, boats. Thousands of boat people died at sea or were preyed upon by pirates. Survivors ended up in refugee camps across Southeast Asia. Roughly half a million additional refugees were admitted to the United States during the 1980s until the camps were emptied. During the 1990s, warmer relations between the United States and Vietnam led to a continued immigration flow from Vietnam.

Most Southeast Asian refugees have struggled in America. Many came from rural communities and were thus unready for life in a modern urban society. Despite government efforts to

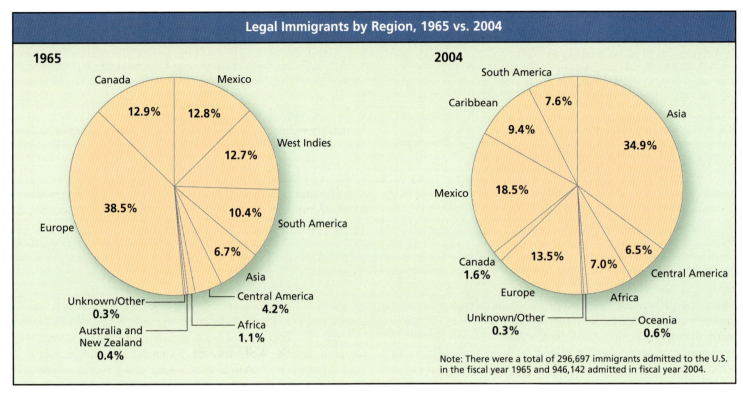

**Legal Immigrants by Region, 1965 vs. 2004**

**1965**

Canada 12.9%
Mexico 12.8%
West Indies 12.7%
South America 10.4%
Asia 6.7%
Central America 4.2%
Africa 1.1%
Australia and New Zealand 0.4%
Unknown/Other 0.3%
Europe 38.5%

**2004**

South America 7.6%
Caribbean 9.4%
Asia 34.9%
Mexico 18.5%
Central America 6.5%
Africa 7.0%
Oceania 0.6%
Europe 13.5%
Canada 1.6%
Unknown/Other 0.3%

Note: There were a total of 296,697 immigrants admitted to the U.S. in the fiscal year 1965 and 946,142 admitted in fiscal year 2004.

**MULTICULTURAL AMERICA** Since 1965 the percentage of immigrants to the United States from Asia and Latin America has increased, while the percentage of immigrants from Europe has fallen.

disperse former refugees throughout the nation, many have, like immigrant groups before them, maintained tightly knit and insular communities in California, Minnesota, and the Gulf Coast of Mississippi, Louisiana and Texas.

## Hispanic Immigration

While the Asian-American population in the United States has grown faster than any other minority group, the Hispanic-American population has become America's largest minority group over the past three decades. Of that diverse groups representing people from the Caribbean Islands to the southern tip of South America, immigrants from Mexico—both legal and illegal—accounted for far and away the largest percentage.

The Mexican American community of the late twentieth century had many faces. There were the Mexican Americans who had migrated from the Southwest to other parts of the country. There were those who stayed in the border region, creating a culture with strong ties to northern Mexico. There were the second- and third-generation Mexican Americans, likely to assimilate as other immigrant groups before them had. But there were also millions of newcomers from Mexico, many coming with the required immigration documents, many without them.

Problems facing Mexican Americans remain substantial. As of the late 1990s, 28 percent of Mexican Americans lived in poverty, a greater proportion than the 23.5 percent of 1981. The high school dropout rate among Mexican-Americans was 50 percent. Many Mexican Americans are recent immigrants, enduring the hard times often faced by new arrivals, perhaps with well-founded hopes of bettering their condition in the future. But many Mexican Americans born in the United States inherit the poverty of their parents and seem unable to change it. The children of migrant worker families, for example, are still unlikely to receive adequate education and health care, despite the advances wrought by the farmworkers movement of the 1960s and 1970s.

As it had been for most of the twentieth century, the United States at the century's end continued to be a magnet for Mexicans in search of a better life. Yet by the late 1970s, with the United States facing an economic downturn, the flow of illegal aliens from Mexico became a major issue in domestic politics and in U.S.-Mexico relations. In 1976 Congress extended the immigration ceiling to cover Western Hemisphere countries. Likewise when a deep U.S. recession intensified U.S. anti-immigrant sentiment in the early 1980s and more Americans began accusing "foreigners" of taking away jobs, Congress again responded by passing the Immigration Reform and Control Act (IRCA) of 1986.

IRCA took aim at the growing flow of illegal immigration by beefing up the U.S. Border Patrol and making it unlawful to knowingly employ undocumented aliens. Nonetheless, the act also conceded the impossibility of deporting all those who had ever entered illegally by offering amnesty and legal status to undocumented immigrants who had entered the United States before 1982 and remained there since, as well as to immigrants who could demonstrate that they had engaged in farmwork for a sufficiently long period in more recent years.

IRCA had some impact in reducing illegal immigration, but undocumented workers often could obtain counterfeit documents "proving" their legal status to employers. The act also resulted in some cases of discrimination against all Hispanics, as employers decided the best way to avoid prosecution was not to hire Hispanics. Congress enacted another immigration law in 1996 that included penalties for undocumented aliens who try to legalize their status by marrying a U.S. citizen. But Mexicans continued to flow into the country illegally despite all such efforts.

While Mexico has remained the largest source of immigrants to the United States, the Dominican Republic, El Salvador, Puerto Rico and Cuba continued to be major sources of migration to the United States. As of 2000 the Dominican American community was among the most recently developed Hispanic American groups. Mostly poor and living in urban areas, Dominican Americans were facing socioeconomic problems similar to those Puerto Ricans have historically faced.

Migration from Puerto Rico to the mainland United States slowed after the heyday of the 1950s and 1960s but continued. As of 1997 about 2.7 million people of Puerto Rican ancestry were living on the U.S. mainland, a number equal to 71 percent of the 3.8 million living in Puerto Rico. If current trends continue, people of Puerto Rican ancestry living on the mainland United States will soon outnumber those remaining on the island.

The majority of Puerto Ricans were blue-collar workers. Like Dominican Americans, they were hurt by the flight of manufacturing jobs from New York City in the late twentieth century. Many Puerto Ricans continued to endure poverty and its related problems, including broken families, low educational attainment, drugs, and crime. As of the late 1990s Puerto Rican families were more likely to be headed by a single parent, usually a female, than families in any other Hispanic-American group.

The story of the Cuban American community since the 1970s has been intertwined with the political relationship between the United States and Cuba—just as it had in the years immediately following Fidel Castro's takeover in 1959. In 1980 the dictator temporarily lifted a ban on immigration to the United States, allowing about 125,000 to leave by boat from the port of Mariel. The people in the Mariel boatlift were unlike previous Cuban immigrants, who had largely been well-educated, middle class, and white. Most Marielitos, as they were known, were poor, less educated, and of African descent. A small percentage were criminals or mentally ill, though many sensationalist news reports in the United States made it seem like most of them were sick or criminals. Many Americans thus gave the Marielitos a cold reception. With the boatlift coming at the height of an economic recession, Americans feared the Cubans would compete for scarce jobs.

The collapse of the Soviet Union in 1991 ended the cold war and put Cuba in a difficult position. Banned from trading with the United States and now bereft of Soviet aid, Cuba suffered economic deterioration. But Castro retained his grip on power, with cold war tensions persisting. In 1996 Castro launched a crackdown on dissidents and shot down two private planes operating out of the United States. The United States reacted by tightening its economic embargo, adding penalties for foreigners investing in Cuba. Any discussion of easing sanctions on Cuba or normalizing diplomatic relations with the island has been strongly opposed by the politically powerful Cuban American exile community in Miami.

In the 1980s the flow of immigrants from Central America took a sharp upturn in the 1980s, driven by civil wars that wracked the region. During the decade 425,000 Central Americans immigrated legally to the United States, and many more have come illegally. The largest number of legal immigrants came from El Salvador, while many others came from Guatemala and Nicaragua.

Even though many of the Central Americans who made their way to the United States were fleeing oppressive, violent governments, they had a hard time proving to U.S. officials that they were political refugees. Under U.S. immigration law, political refugees received special consideration and were not subject to the same restrictions as other immigrants. But because the United States was publicly aiding the governments of El Salvador and Guatemala, U.S. officials were not inclined to acknowledge that the hundreds of thousands of Salvadorans and Guatemalans begging for political asylum had really been politically persecuted by those governments. Instead, newcomers who entered without the proper immigration visas were regarded as illegal immigrants and subject to deportation as such, unless they could prove a "well-founded fear of persecution"—which in most cases was impossible to prove.

The cause of the refugees was aided by the sanctuary movement, operated by a national network of churches and synagogues that sheltered undocumented Central American refugees for moral and religious reasons, despite the threat of fines and imprisonment. The U.S. government successfully prosecuted some leaders of the sanctuary movement but, due to public opposition to U.S. policy in Central America, found it politically inadvisable to punish them to the full extent of the law or to prosecute all the cases it might have.

The end of the civil wars in the 1990s brought a decrease in the number of new refugees from Central America but made it more difficult for Central American refugees whose cases were still pending to win political asylum. According to the Illegal Immigration Reform and Immigrant Responsibility Act of 1996, a maximum of 1,000 aliens per fiscal year could be granted asylum by the United States or admitted as refugees. The law also provided for a new category of immigration status known as "withholding of removal," available to refugees in the United States who could show a likelihood that their lives or freedom would be threatened if they were returned to their country of origin. However, the rules governing withholding of removal required applicants to prove that it was more likely than not that they would be persecuted—again, a difficult or impossible condition to prove. Therefore, the ultimate legal status of many refugees of Central America's civil wars remained uncertain by the close of the twentieth century.

Finally, South Americans also immigrated to the United States in great numbers in the last quarter of the twentieth century. In the 1980s alone 462,000 South Americans were legally admitted to the United States, and an unknown number came illegally. The most came from Colombia, although many others came from Ecuador. Substantially fewer immigrants came from other South American countries. By the end of the 20th century the diverse South American population in the United States probably comprised close to 1 million people. Because they usually arrived in the United States with fairly high levels of education and skills, South American immigrants have generally prospered more than those from Mexico and Puerto Rico, though not so much as those from Cuba.

## Language and Education

The unparalled growth in the number of immigrants arriving in the United States in the late twentieth century had a major impact on U.S. society. As many have noted, the American "melting pot" of diversity has often more closely resembled a stew, as immigrants have arrived in the United States but still maintained their sense of cultural identity and tradition. To some conservatives, this trend has led to a deeper fragmentation of society, pulling the nation's population away from any sense of shared "American-ness."

Much of the anger on the part of conservatives has crystalized around the issue of bilingual education. Ever since the U.S. Supreme Court ruled in the 1974 case of *Lau v. Nichols* that public schools should be in effect required to provide bilingual education programs for students who needed them, some have argued that bilingual education programs are a subversive force undermining national unity. In the late 1970s, an English Only movement emerged, calling for the "defense" of the English language. The movement spawned a Washington, D.C.–based organization called U.S. English, which prodded states to approve legislation making English the official language.

In some instances tensions have boiled over into violence, as in the early 1980s when a young Chinese man named Vincent Chin was beaten to death in Detroit by out-of-work white autoworkers who believed he was Japanese and somehow to blame for the rise in imported Japanese automobiles, or in the burning and looting of Korean stores in 1992 Los Angeles race riots.

# Religious Fundamentalism, Religious Pluralism

As immigration to the United States grew in the late twentieth century, the new immigrants brought with them cultural practices and traditions that were sometimes new to America. For example, Asian immigration has boosted the presence of Islam, Buddhism, and Hinduism in the United States. Other faith traditions have had to adapt: most Hispanic Americans who arrived in the United States over the past quarter century, for example, are Catholics. Because many do not speak English, a growing number of Catholic churches conduct services in Spanish.

During the 1980s and 1990s, American spiritual life underwent other major changes. One of the most significant was a drop in the percentage of Americans who said they regularly attended church. By the end of the 1990s, the percentage had fallen to about 40 percent, down from nearly 50 percent in 1958. Within Protestant Christianity some older denominations, especially those drawing congregants from the Northeast and Midwest such as Methodists, Lutherans, Presbyterians, and Episcopalians, saw their attendance drop. As a result some denominations that had been split into smaller groups reunited. During the 1980s three Lutheran churches merged, as did two Presbyterian groups. On the other hand Baptists, who drew strength from their strong base in the South, remained divided on many issues and have branched out into several denominations as a result.

American Judaism also found itself divided. American Jews were divided into three main groups—Orthodox, Conservative, and Reform. The openness of the Reform movement to change led some Orthodox leaders to push for stronger adherence to traditional beliefs and practices, which angered some Reform Jews who felt that their faith was being challenged. On the other hand, many Orthodox and Conservative Jews were alarmed by the number of Jews marrying outside of their faith. According to a 1990 Jewish Population Survey, 28 percent of the 2.6 million married Jews in the United States were married to non-Jews.

The fastest growing religion in America at the end of the twentieth century was the Church of Jesus Christ of Latter Day Saints, or the Mormons. Although the Mormons drew criticism for the fact that few of its members were African-American and that it made little effort to reach out to the black community, Mormons made vigorous efforts to recruit new members in other countries.

While most Americans were Protestants, the single largest faith was Catholicism. More than 60 million Americans were Catholics, and generally speaking, Catholics were the most religiously active of all Americans. Catholics were united by their reverence for Pope John Paul II, who served from 1978 until his death in 2005. During the 1980s, the Polish pontiff spoke out against Communist oppression and for human liberty. At the same time, many American Catholics broke with their Church on some issues. For instance, many American Catholics accepted birth control and some supported abortion rights, which John Paul condemned.

During the 1990s and 2000s, lay Catholics and clergy were shaken by sex abuse by priests and cover-ups of the abuse by Catholic hierarchy. The early years of the twenty-first century were marked by demands that those responsible for the abuse, and those who worked to keep it hidden be held accountable for their actions. According to a study done by John Jay College of Criminal Justice, 4 percent of all American priests, or 4,392 clergymen, were accused of abusing 10,667 people, with 75 percent of the incidents taking place between 1960 and 1984.

## The Evangelicals

Perhaps the most significant trend in recent American religion is the rise of evangelical, or "born-again" Christianity. Called "born-again" because they believed that they had received a spiritual rebirth through an intense religious experience, which had allowed them to develop what they saw as a personal relationship with God. Although estimates vary, roughly 20 to 40 percent of all Americans considered themselves evangelical Christians who were obligated to God to share their faith with others.

Some born-again Christians, including roughly 20 percent of all Catholics, practiced their faith within traditional denominations. Many others formed or joined newer evangelical churches. Some evangelical churches were massive—known as "mega-churches." A few, such as Willow Creek Community Church in Illinois, drew an astounding 20,000 people to weekend services. Robert Schuller's Crystal Cathedral in Southern California could hold 3,000 people in a single worship service.

Some evangelicals also considered themselves Fundamentalist Christians. As Fundamentalists they believe every word in the Bible's Old and New Testament to be literally true, and that Jesus Christ would return to Earth to gather the faithful around him to ascend to Heaven while nonbelievers would be left behind to eternal damnation. Fundamentalists have also been extremely active in politics, condemning what they saw as the moral decay of traditional values. Fundamentalists strongly reject abortion rights and civil liberties for homosexuals and lesbians.

Beginning in the 1980s Fundamentalists worked to spread their beliefs out from their houses of worship and into the public arena. One target of this political activity was their focus on local school systems. Arguing against court-ordered bans on prayer in the public school classroom, Fundamentalists have lobbied to allow schools to set aside time out of each day for prayer. They have also worked to keep sex education information out of curricula and mounted challenges to textbooks that they believed promoted "secular humanism," a philosophy that promotes values based on human reasoning rather than on strict adherence to Biblical doctrine. In keeping with this view, they favor the

## Christian Denominations in the U.S., 2000

*The 2005 Yearbook of American and Canadian Churches reported the following figures, based primarily on 2003 denominational reporting data:*

1. Roman Catholic Church: 67.2 million.
2. Southern Baptist Convention: 16.4 million.
3. United Methodist Church: 8.2 million.
4. Church of Jesus Christ of Latter-day Saints: 5.5 million.
5. Church of God in Christ: 5.4 million.
6. National Baptist Convention USA: 5 million.
7. Evangelical Lutheran Church in America: 4.9 million.
8. National Baptist Convention of America: 3.5 million.
9. Presbyterian Church (U.S.A.): 3.2 million.
10. Assemblies of God: 2.7 million.

teaching of creationism or "intelligent design" in the schools to explain Earth's origins, alongside Darwin's theory of evolution. Although some school systems attempted to ban the teaching of evolution and require the teaching of creationism, by the late 1990s the U.S. Supreme Court ruled that such laws violated the constitutional separation of church and state. As the twenty-first century opened, an increasing number of Fundamentalist parents were opting to withdraw their children from public school to give them a conservative Christianity-centered education at home.

Fundamentalist influence was also strongly felt outside of the classroom, and some fundamentalist leaders became very influential in promoting the the conservative Christian philosophy. In the early 1980s Jerry Falwell used his platform as the host of a religious television show to form a national political organization called the Moral Majority. The group, which entered national politics by supporting Ronald Reagan's 1980 run for the presidency, also created "moral report cards" on members of Congress, rating their stances on issues such as abortion, school prayer, and gay rights. By the middle of the 1980s Jerry Falwell was joined by another television evangelist, Pat Robertson. In 1988 Robertson ran for the Republican nomination for president and although he was defeated by then Vice President George Bush, he continued to be involved in politics into the twenty-first century. During the 1990s other Fundamentalist leaders also grew to national prominence. A number of these leaders, such as Tony Perkins of the Holland, Michigan-based Family Research Council, James Dobson of Focus on the Family, in Colorado Springs, or Ted Haggard, Pastor of New Life Church, also in Colorado Springs, gained particular prominence during the administration of George W. Bush, a born-again Christian himself, whose election hopes were bolstered by major get-out-the-vote drives among Christian fundamentalist voters. Throughout his presidency, Bush held weekly conference calls or in-person meetings with Fundamentalist leaders.

# Contemporary Culture

The 2000 and 2004 presidential elections, both won by George W. Bush, highlighted deep divisions in American society, not just in terms of political opinions but in social attitudes as well. Electoral maps from both of those elections show much of the heavily populated coastal United States colored blue for Democratic voters and a huge swath of the South, Central Plains, and Rocky Mountain region colored red for Republican. Commentators spoke of "Red States" and "Blue States" as if the nation were divided into two homogeneous but separate and warring parties.

The truth, as it usually is, is more complex. To be sure, the shift of America's population toward the South and West have helped to give rise to conservative social and political movements that condemned what they felt were declining values in American culture. During the election of 2004 conservatives raised the issue of same-sex marriage rights for gays and lesbians, and President Bush vowed to support a constitutional definition of marriage as being between a man and a woman. Many analysts believe that the same-sex marriage debate helped Bush win the state of Ohio, and therefore re-election.

### The Abortion Debate

Not all divisions between conservatives and liberals can be attributed to regional differences. For instance, the debate over abortion rights has divided much of the nation, regardless of geography, since the U.S. Supreme Court legalized it with its 1973 *Roe v. Wade* decision. In that ruling, the Court stated that during the first three months of a pregnancy, decisions regarding abortion must be left to a woman and her doctor. The decision struck down many state laws banning abortion, and years later controversy still exists over whether the decision to have an abortion is a woman's right. Opponents argue that aborting a fetus is the murder of an unborn child. Proponents of abortion rights, who refer to their philosophy as "pro-choice," contend that a fetus is not a human being and therefore abortion is not murder. Rather than being simply regional, the national split over the abortion is in part religious, as many Catholics join with Evangelical Christians and other social conservatives to oppose abortion.

### Pop Culture and Family Values

Because national television and film studios are located in California and New York rather than in the American heartland, some social conservatives have come to view Hollywood and New York City as modern-day equivalents of the Biblical Sodom and Gomorrah. As cable television had opened the airwaves to hundreds of new, specialized channels that show R and even X-rated movies, broadcast television airs lowest-common denominator talk shows that feature dysfunctional families as a form of entertainment, and many of the modern pop, rock and hip-hop music artists hawk sex and violence-drenched lyrics to younger and younger shoppers.

Conservative and liberal parents alike, from Nebraska to New York, have expressed concern. During the late 1980s a group of concerned parents led by Tipper Gore, the wife of the future vice-president and presidential candidate Albert Gore, formed the Parental Music Resource Center (PMRC) in an effort to pressure the music industry to apply ratings to their products. The idea was to give parents information that could be used to filter out messages they deemed harmful. By the end of the decade, record companies reluctantly agreed to add content warnings to some of their products. With the rise of the Internet, e-mail, and instant messaging during the 1990s and early 2000s as a major form of communication, information, and entertainment, parents faced new challenges.

## Racial and Economic Divides

On the evening of March 3, 1991, a black motorist in Los Angeles named Rodney King was pulled over for speeding. A nearby amateur video cameraman then captured on film four police officers striking and kicking King fifty-six times, as well as administering several shocks from their stun guns, even after King appeared to be lying helpless on the ground. Broadcast on national television, the video outraged both black and white citizens and led to the trial of the four officers. Yet when the officers were acquitted in April 1992 by an all-white suburban jury, African Americans in South Central Los Angeles lashed out in a fury. In the nation's worst rioting since the 1863 New York draft riots, more than fifty people were killed and nearly 400 injured. Fires and looting spread across the city, causing more than $1 billion in property damage. Particularly distressing to the city's many new immigrants were the open clashes between Korean businesspeople and black protesters. In the end, it took 4,500 U.S. Army troops and 17,000 arrests—many of which did not lead to trials or convictions—to end the three days of violence.

Two years later in June 1994, O. J. Simpson, one of the most successful running backs in professional football history, was charged with the murders of his former wife, Nicole Brown Simpson, and Ronald Goldman, a friend of hers, after the two victims were found stabbed to death outside Nicole Simpson's Los Angeles condominium. Although no witnesses to the crime came forward, prosecutors presented blood evidence found at the crime scene, in Simpson's car, and at his home, and used these samples to argue for Simpson's guilt. Simpson's lawyers argued that the evidence had been planted by police, and they buttressed their case by producing witnesses and a taped interview that showed police detective Mark Fuhrman had lied about his racist beliefs on the witness stand. On the night of the murder, Fuhrman had scaled a wall at Simpson's estate and found a bloody glove that was at the center of the prosecution's case. Prosecutors claimed that hair, fiber, footprints, and other circumstantial evidence all proved Simpson's guilt. Simpson's defense team maintained that this evidence had been contaminated by sloppy police procedure and was therefore unreliable. At the end of the sensational, racially charged nine-month trial, the jury deliberated for just three hours before acquitting Simpson.

The verdict was celebrated by a majority of African Americans, many of whom viewed the acquittal as an indictment against a U.S. justice system that in their view discriminated against African Americans. Most white Americans, however, saw Simpson as clearly guilty and were stunned by the verdict. To some, the trial thus revealed the deep schism between white and black views of the basic fairness of the U.S. justice system.

To others it was not so much a racial schism that was revealed as an economic one. Without the best lawyers in the land that only a celebrity athlete could afford, went this argument, Simpson would have been convicted. As they have so often throughout American history, the interrelated topics of race and class divisions remained just below the surface of American society at the end of the twentieth century.

Few can argue that with the fact that after nearly 400 years on the North American continent—two-thirds of that time in bondage and much of the rest as second-class citizens—black Americans achieved much in the late twentieth century. Facing extraordinary violence and intimidation, African-Americans in the South tore down all of the legal restrictions that kept them from voting, exercising their civil rights, and fully sharing in the public accommodations that their tax and consumer dollars helped to pay for. Pushing through the barriers to educational and economic opportunity, African Americans throughout the country have gone to college in unprecedented numbers; excelled in the arts, entertainment, and sports—arguably the most merit-based sectors of U.S. society—won high political office; and achieved virtual parity with whites in the military. And yet, for all of these noteworthy accomplishments, African-Americans lag behind white Americans in virtually every education, health, income, and social index.

No single statistic can explain why people of African descent enjoy a lower quality of life in this country than people of European descent. Lower incomes and less steady employment, for example, mean that fewer African Americans can send their children to college, while lower college attendance records contribute to lower incomes. Still, as education largely applies to the young, it offers perhaps the best place to begin the assessment of modern black America.

To start, there has been progress. In 1980, for example, just 51 percent of all African Americans over the age of twenty-five had a high school diploma, versus 69 percent for the U.S. population as a whole. By 1999, the black high school graduation percentage was 77 percent, versus 83 percent for the population as a whole, meaning that African Americans had closed the gap by half. College graduation rates show similar gains. While just 8 percent of blacks over the age of twenty-five had college diplomas in 1980, that figure had more than doubled to over 16 percent by 1999.

Still, while the gap between white and black educational levels has been closing, the same cannot be said of the health gap, particularly for African American males. For example, a black male child born in the year 2000 is likely to live just 64.6 years, while a white male can expect to make it to his seventy-third birthday, nearly a decade longer. For females the racial health gap is not as large. Black females born in 2000 can expect to live to be nearly seventy-five, while white females will live to be about eighty, a gap of just half a decade.

In other health-related areas the racial gap is even wider. For example, infant mortality rates among blacks in the mid-1990s were 16.5 per 100,000 live births versus just 6.8 for whites, or about 140 percent higher. Similarly, low birthweight babies were more prevalent in the black population (13.2 percent) than among whites (6.1 percent). In virtually every other category the picture remains the same. Blacks had a rate of death from cardiovascular disease 50 percent higher than whites and they were nearly twice as likely to die from stroke. The most glaring discrepancies, however, emerged in the areas of violence and sexually transmitted disease. At 40.9 per 100,000 persons, blacks were nearly seven times more likely to be murdered than whites. And with a rate of 93.3 per 100,000, African-Americans were more than six times more likely to be suffering from AIDS.

A number of factors help explain why African-American health indices lag so badly behind those of whites. First, and

## The Growing Income Gap, 1980–2004

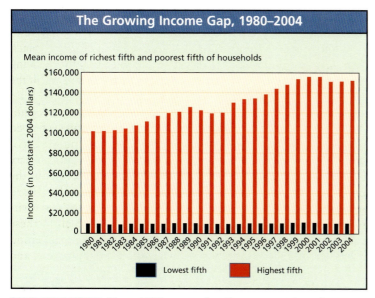

Mean income of richest fifth and poorest fifth of households

Income (in constant 2004 dollars)

Lowest fifth     Highest fifth

**RICH AND POOR** Since 1980 wages for the poorest Americans have remained stagnant while incomes for the wealthiest Americans climbed rapidly, particularly during the 1990s.

## Life Expectancy of White and Black Americans, 1900–2002

| | WHITE | | BLACK | |
| | Male | Female | Male | Female |
| --- | --- | --- | --- | --- |
| 1900–02: | 48.2 | 51.1 | 32.5 | 35.0 |
| 1909–11: | 50.2 | 53.6 | 34.0 | 37.7 |
| 1919–21: | 56.3 | 58.5 | 47.1 | 46.9 |
| 1929–31: | 59.1 | 62.7 | 47.5 | 49.5 |
| 1939–41: | 62.8 | 67.2 | 52.3 | 55.6 |
| 1949–51: | 66.3 | 72.0 | 58.9 | 63.7 |
| 1959–61: | 67.5 | 74.2 | 61.5 | 66.5 |
| 1969–71: | 67.9 | 75.5 | 60.0 | 68.3 |
| 1979–81: | 70.8 | 78.2 | 64.1 | 72.9 |
| 1989–91 | 72.7 | 79.4 | 64.5 | 73.7 |
| 2002: | 75.1 | 80.3 | 68.8 | 75.6 |

**LONGER LIVES** Advances in health care have led to longer lives for most Americans.

perhaps foremost, is poverty. While less than 17 percent of white children under the age of eighteen lived in poverty, the rate for black youths was nearly 44 percent in the mid-1990s. Poverty and lack of steady employment also means less health care coverage. White children were 50 percent less likely to be without health insurance than black children in 1996.

Ultimately much of the gap between whites and blacks in educational levels and particularly health comes down to income and employment. Just as the average wage-earner of all races saw little income gain during the last two decades of the 20th century, so average black mean income continued to lag behind average white mean income. For example, in 1980 average black mean income averaged $15,749, or 70 percent of average white mean income. By 1998 black mean incomes had climbed to $20,609. At the same time average white mean incomes had risen to $29,314. Thus, by the late 1990s, black mean incomes were still only slightly higher than 70 percent of white household incomes.

Income distribution is directly related to job skills and education. Not surprisingly, lower black income levels can be directly traced to the kinds of jobs African-Americans perform. While 29 percent of the total population was engaged in managerial or professional work in 1997, the rate for blacks was just 7.3 percent, or about one-fourth that of the population as a whole. Looking to the other end of the job ladder, blacks were nearly a third more likely to be working in low-paying, low skill service jobs than whites.

Meanwhile, while poverty rates for black families remained much higher than those for whites, the gap closed somewhat over the last two decades of the 20th century. At the same time, while income levels rose modestly for both blacks and whites, employment rates climbed significantly. While blacks experienced double-digit unemployment rates throughout the 1980s and early 1990s, by the year 2000, they had fallen to around 8 percent. White unemployment levels fell as well, to around half that of blacks by 2000.

The statistical gulf between black and white standards of living is not something that has an impact on everyday lives. Yet in late August and early September 2005, the disparity became

## Growing Home Ownership, 1960–2000

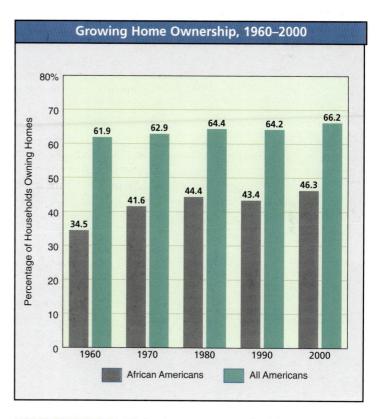

Percentage of Households Owning Homes

African Americans     All Americans

**HOME OWNERSHIP** While the percentage of African-Americans who own their own homes has risen since 1960, the percentage has been relatively stagnant since 1980.

clearly visible on television screens across the nation. On August 31 the worst hurricane to hit a major U.S. city in 100 years swept through New Orleans, Louisiana and along the Gulf Coast region. After Hurricane Katrina passed, two sections of the New Orleans levee system gave way, flooding 90 percent of the historic city. Before the hurricane made landfall, most people with cars had already evacuated the below-sea level city. Those remaining were the elderly, the poor, and their family members who stayed to care for them. At press time, more than 1,600 had died—many due to heat and dehydration when the local and state emergency plans were overwhelmed and the federal government failed to act in a timely manner. Many Americans were outraged that many of society's poorest and most vulnerable seemed, in the days immediately after the crisis, to have been abandoned by its government. Two weeks after Katrina hit, President Bush pledged that his administration would oversee a massive rebuilding program that would not only rebuild lost property, but also create new job training programs and other anti-poverty efforts. In this way, he argued, he would help to close the economic gap between the Crescent City's haves and have-nots.

At the close of 2005, however, few promised programs had actually been passed by Congress, as many questions remained about the government's response and long-term plans for New Orleans. First among them was how to pay for the effort. Analysts estimated that at least $200 billion would be needed to rebuild the city at a time that the nation had already spent that much invading and occupying Iraq and fighting insurgents there and in Afghanistan. Members of President Bush's own party, already alarmed by surging federal spending under a Republican president, and Congress began to insist that deep cuts in other areas of the federal budget would have to be made to pay for the costs of New Orleans construction.

Other questions remained. What kind of city would the "new" New Orleans be. Would it retain its multicultural flavor that reflected its French, Spanish, English, African, Irish and assorted other influences? What lessons from New Orleans' past would be relearned, what treasures from its rich cultural history restored?

In 1992 America celebrated the 500-year anniversary of Columbus's landing in the Caribbean. Over 230 years have passed since the assembled patriots in 1776 gathered in Philadelphia to declare their independence from Britain, beginning the individual and common pursuit of life, liberty and happiness.

The pursuit has been a complex and often contradictory one, as the pursuit of one person's happiness has sometimes come at the expense of another's liberty. In many ways, American history has been the the struggle that individuals and communities have undertaken to live up to the promise spelled out by the Declaration of Independence. As the United States moves further into the twenty-first century, the nation will, like the people of New Orleans, build from the old by maintaining its traditions while also endeavouring to include all of its citizens in the pursuit.

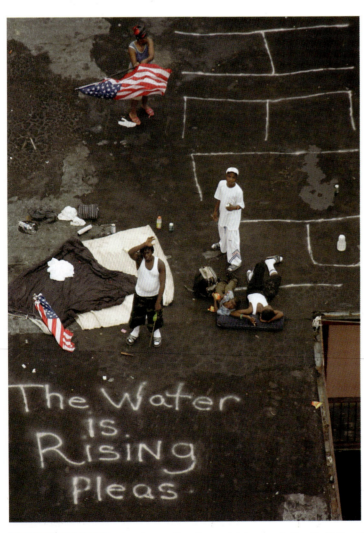

**KATRINA'S WRATH** Hurricane Katrina, which struck the Gulf Coast in late August 2005, flooded large portions of New Orleans. As federal, state and local officials blamed each other for the slow governmental response, poor and elderly residents of the Crescent City found themselves stranded. At left, residents call for rescue from a rooftop, while at right an elderly citizen waits to be evacuated.

# BIBLIOGRAPHY

Allen, Frederick Lewis. *Only Yesterday: An Informal History of the 1920's*. New York: Harper & Row, 1931.

Ambrose, Stephen E. *Undaunted Courage: Meriwether Lewis, Thomas Jefferson, and the Opening of the American West*. New York: Simon & Schuster, 1996.

American Social History Project. *Who Built America? Working People & the Nation's Economy, Politics, Culture & Society*. New York: Pantheon Books, 1992.

Anderson, Terry H. *The Movement and the Sixties: Protest in America from Greensboro to Wounded Knee*. Oxford: Oxford University Press, 1995.

Andrew, John A. *Lyndon Johnson and the Great Society*. Chicago: Ivan R. Dee, 1968.

Berlin, Ira. *Many Thousands Gone: The First Two Centuries of Slavery in North America*. Cambridge, MA: Harvard University Press, 1998.

Beschloss, Michael, ed. *American Heritage Illustrated History of the Presidents*. New York: Crown, 2000.

Blow, Michael, ed. *The American Heritage History of the Thirteen Colonies*. New York: American Heritage, 1967.

Blum, John M., ed. *The National Experience: A History of the United States*. San Diego: Harcourt Brace Jovanovich, 1989.

Burg, David F. *The Great Depression: An Eyewitness History*. New York: Facts On File, 1995.

Ciment, James. *Atlas of African-American History*. New York: Facts On File, 2001.

Clarke, Clorinda. *The American Revolution 1775-83: A British View*. New York: McGraw-Hill, 1964.

Cowley, Robert, and Geoffrey Parker, eds. *The Reader's Companion to Military History*. Boston: Houghton Mifflin, 1996.

Dear, I.C.B., ed. *The Oxford Companion to World War II*. Oxford: Oxford University Press, 1995.

Deighton, Len. *Blood, Tears and Folly: An Objective Look at World War II*. New York: HarperCollins, 1993.

Faragher, John Mack, ed. *The American Heritage Encyclopedia of American History*. New York: Holt, 1998.

Finkelstein, Joseph. *The American Economy*. Arlington Heights, IL: Harlan Davidson, 1992.

Flanders, Stephen A. *Atlas of American Migration*. New York: Facts On File, 1998.

Fleming, Thomas. *Liberty!: The American Revolution*. New York: Viking, 1997.

Fogel, Robert William. *Without Consent or Contract: The Rise and Fall of American Slavery*. New York: W.W. Norton & Co., 1989.

Foner, Eric, and John A. Garraty, eds. *The Reader's Companion to American History*. Boston: Houghton Mifflin, 1991.

French, Michael. *U.S. Economic History Since 1945*. Manchester: Manchester University Press, 1997.

Genovese, Eugene. *Roll, Jordan, Roll: The World the Slaves Made*. New York: Random House, 1972.

Gitlin, Todd. *The Sixties: Years of Hope, Days of Rage*. New York: Bantam Books, 1987.

Glaab, Charles. *A History of Urban America*. New York: MacMillan, 1976.

Harrington, Michael A. *The Other America*. New York: Collier Books, 1962.

Herring, George C. *America's Longest War: The United States and Vietnam 1950-75*. New York: Alfred A. Knopf, 1979.

Hirschfelder, Arlene. *The Native Americans: A History*. New York: DK Publishing, 2000.

Hofstadter, Richard. *America at 1750: A Social Portrait*. New York: Alfred A. Knopf, 1971.

Holliday, J.S. *The World Rushed In: An Eyewitness Account of a Nation Heading West*. New York: Simon & Schuster, 1981.

Hutson, James A. *Religion and the Founding of the American Republic*. Washington, DC: Library of Congress, 1998.

Ingraham, Leonard W. *An Album of Colonial America*. New York: Franklin Watts, 1969.

Jackson, Kenneth T. *Crabgrass Frontier: The Suburbanization of the United States*. New York: Oxford University Press, 1985.

Johnson, Darv. *The Reagan Years*. San Diego: Lucent Books, 2000.

Josephy, Alvin M., Jr. *The Indian Heritage of America*. New York: Alfred A. Knopf, 1968.

Josephy, Alvin M., Jr., ed. *The American Heritage Book of American Indians*. New York, American Heritage, 1961.

Keegan, John. *The Second World War*. New York: Penguin, 1989.

Kennedy, David. *Freedom from Fear: The American People in Depression and War, 1929-1945*. New York: Oxford University Press, 1999.

Kort, Michael. *The Columbia Guide to the Cold War*. New York: Columbia University Press, 1998.

Langdon, William Chauncy. *Everyday Things in American Life: 1776–1876*. New York: Charles Scribner's Sons, 1941.

Leckie, Robert. *The Wars of America*. New York: HarperCollins, 1992.

Levy, Leonard W. *Original Intent and the Framers' Constitution*. New York: Macmillan, 1988.

McElvaine, Robert S. *The Depression and New Deal: A History in Documents*. New York: Oxford University Press, 2000.

McPherson, James M. *The Battle Cry of Freedom: America in the Civil War Era*. New York: Oxford University Press, 1988.

Manchester, William. *The Glory and the Dream: A Narrative History of America, 1932-1972*. New York: Bantam Books, 1975.

Marty, Martin E. *Pilgrims in Their Own Land: 500 Years of Religion in America*. New York, Penguin Books, 1985.

Miller, James. *Democracy is in the Streets*. New York: Simon & Schuster, 1987.

Morison, Samuel Eliot. *The Oxford History of the American People*. New York: Oxford University Press, 1965.

Morison, Samuel Eliot, Henry Steele Commager, and William E. Leuchtenberg. *A Concise History of the American Republic*. 2nd ed. New York: Oxford University Press, 1983.

Nash, Gary B. *Red, White and Black: The Peoples of Early North America*, 5th ed. Upper Saddle River, N.J.: Pearson Prentice Hall, 2006.

Nash, Gary B., general editor. *Encyclopedia of American History*. New York: Facts on File, 2003.

Morris, Jeffrey B., and Richard B. Morris, eds. *Encyclopedia of American History*, 7th ed. New York: HarperCollins, 1996.

Ochoa, George. *Atlas of Hispanic-American History*. New York: Facts On File, 2001.

*The Old West: The Pioneers*. Alexandria, VA.: Time-Life Books, 1974.

Posner, Gerald. *Killing the Dream: James Earl Ray and the Assassination of Martin Luther King, Jr*. New York: Random House, 1998.

Prange, Gordon W. *December 7, 1941: The Day the Japanese Attacked Pearl Harbor*. New York: Warner Books, 1988.

Ravitch, Diane, ed. *The American Reader: Words That Moved a Nation*. New York: HarperPerennial, 1991.

Resnick, Abraham. *The Holocaust*. San Diego, CA: Lucent Books, 1991.

Rice, Eugene F., Jr. *The Foundations of Early Modern Europe, 1460–1559*. New York, W.W. Norton & Co., 1970.

Schlesinger, Arthur Meier, Jr. *The Age of Jackson*. Boston: Little, Brown, 1988.

Silcox-Jarrett, Diane. *Heroines of the American Revolution: America's Founding Mothers*. Scholastic, 1998.

Small, Melvin. *The Presidency of Richard Nixon*. Kansas: University Press of Kansas, 1999.

Smith, Carter, ed. *Daily Life: A Sourcebook on Colonial America*. Brookfield, CT: Millbrook Press, 1991.

_____. *Governing and Teaching: A Sourcebook on Colonial America*. Brookfield, CT: Millbrook Press, 1991

Smith, Jean Edward. *John Marshall: Definer of a Nation*. New York: Holt, 1996.

Spangenburg, Ray, and Diane K. Moser. *The Story of America's Railroads*. New York: Facts On File, 1991.

Speare, Elizabeth George. *Life in Colonial America*. New York: Random House, 1963.

Terkel, Studs. "The Good War": *An Oral History of World War Two*. New York: Ballantine Books, 1985.

Thomas: Legislative Information on the Internet. Available online. URL: http://memory.loc.gov. Downloaded March 16, 2006.

Toropov, Brandon. *Encyclopedia of Cold War Politics*. New York: Facts On File, 2000.

Urdang, Laurence. *The Timetables of American History*. New York: Simon & Schuster, 1996.

Van Every, Dale. *Disinherited: The Lost Birthright of the American Indian*. New York: Morrow, 1966.

Waldman, Carl. *Atlas of the North American Indian*, rev. ed. New York: Facts On File, 2000.

Zinn, Howard. *A People's History of the United States*. New York: Harper & Row, 1980.

# INDEX

## A

Abercrombie, James 61
Abernathy, Ralph 277, 278
abolitionist movement 134–136
abortion 289, 315
Abraham Lincoln Brigade 251
Acheson, Edward Goodrich 173
*Achille Lauro* hijacking 301
Acoma people 33
Adams, John 49, 65, 84, 85, 86
Adams, John Quincy 124
Adams, Samuel 63, 64, 65, 67, 81, 83
Adams-Onis Treaty 97, 98
Adena Culture 4
advertising 234, 259, 262–263
Afghanistan
    defeat of Taliban 306
    Soviet invasion of 299, 300
    Taliban rule of 305
Africa. *See* also slave trade
    colonization movement in 133, 134
    European settlements in 19–20
    exploration of 11, 20
    Islamic expansion in 15
    kingdoms of 14, 16–17
    slavery in 16–17, 18
African Americans. *See* also civil rights;
    integration; slavery; slave trade
    abolitionists 135–136
    in armed forces 275
    "Back to Africa" movement 233–234
    in civil rights movement 277–281
    colleges of 185–186
    colonization movement 133–134
    education levels of 316
    free blacks 59, 73, 89, 134
    Harlem Renaissance 233, 234
    health of 316–317
    income levels of 317
    in labor force 257, 309, 317
    loyalists 73
    lynching of 184, 228, 232
    in New Orleans flood 317–318
    northern migration of, 224, 257
    in race riots, 156, 228, 316
    in Reconstruction governments 167
    segregation of 184–185
    in Seminole Wars 102–103, 104
    sharecroppers 168, 171, 194–195, 249
    in Union Army 153, 154–156
    westward migration of 89

Agent Orange 272
Agnew, Spiro T. 291–292
Agricultural Adjustment Act (AAA) of 1933
    245–246
Agriculture. *See* plantation system
    in Africa 14
    Columbian Exchange and 23
    decline of family farm 238
    drought 241
    Dust Bowl 242
    in English colonies 55
    during Great Depression 241–242
    large-scale farms 239
    Mexican labor in 237
    migrant workers in 257, 285–286
    organizations 192–193
    pesticide development for 260–261
    plant genetics in 261
    Populist Party and 193–196
    pre-Columbian Indian 4, 5
    sharecropping 168, 171, 194–195
    Shay's Rebellion 80
    technology 193
Aguinaldo, Emilio 208, 209
AIDS (Acquired Immune Deficiency
    Syndrome) 310–311
Alamo 106, 107
Alaska, land bridge to (Beringia) 2, 6
alcohol consumption 128
    bootlegging 231
    Prohibition 128, 211–212, 230, 231
    temperance movement 128, 210–211
Alexander VI, Pope 20, 24
Alta California 34–35
American Anti-Slavery Society 134, 135
American Civil Liberties Union (ACLU) 233
American Colonization Society (ACS) 134
American Communist Party 248
American Federation of Labor (AFL)
    190–191, 228, 247
American Indian Movement (AIM)
    284–285, 288
American Revolution. *See* Revolutionary
    War
Americans with Disabilities Act 295
American Temperance Society 128
American Woman's Suffrage Association
    (AWSA) 186, 216
Americas. *See* also North America
    Columbus's voyages to 22–23
    Portuguese colony in 24
    Spanish colonial system in 24–25

**JOHN ADAMS**

Americas, *cont.*
   Spanish conquest of 28–29
Amherst, Jeffrey 61
Ampudia, Pedro de 109
amusement parks 178, 183
Anaconda Plan 144
Anasazi Culture 5
Anderson, Robert 143
Anglican Church 12–13, 45, 48, 49
Annapolis Convention 80
Anthony, Susan B. 130, 186, 187
Antifederalist party 82–83, 85
Anti-Saloon League 211
anti-slavery movement
      abolitionists 134–136
      African colonization and 133–134
      slave rebellions and 130–132
      underground railroad 132–133
anti-Vietnam War movement 272–273, 288,
      290
Apache 2, 5, 204
Apgar, Virginia 261
appeasement policy 251
Arab-Israeli War 298
Arawak 22–23, 25
Arctic National Wildlife Reserve (ANWR)
      297
Arianism 126
Arkwright spinning frame 114
Armat, Thomas 173
armed forces. *See* battles; Navy; Union
      Army
      homosexuals in 304
      in Indian wars 200, 201–205
      integration of 275
      in Korean War 268–269
      in Philippine-American War 208–209
      in Spanish-American War 207–208
      in Vietnam War 272
      in World War I 224, 225, 227
      in World War II 252, 254–255
Armijo, Manuel 109
Army of the Cumberland 150
Army of Northern Virginia 150, 150–151
Army of the Potomac 149, 150–151
Arnold, Benedict 67
Aroostook War of 1839 113
Arthur, Chester A. 176
Articles of Confederation 74, 81
artisans, colonial 55
Asian Americans 288, 311–312
asylum reform 128–129
atomic bomb 253, 255, 256, 269
atomic power industry 260
Attucks, Crispus 63

Austin, Moses 106
Austin, Stephen 106
automobile industry, labor relations in 247
automobile travel 230, 235, 239
aviation technology 259–260
Avilés, Pedro Menendez de 30
Aziz, Tariq 304
Aztecs 28

# B

Ba'ath Party 269, 270
"baby-boom" generation 291
"Back to Africa" movement 233–234, 282
Bacon's rebellion 58
Baffin, William 27
Baker, James, 304
Baldwin, Roger 233
bank holiday 245
Banking Act of 1933 (Glass-Steagall) 245
Banks, Nathaniel 161
Bank of the United States 125
Baptist Church 45, 49, 128
Baraka, Amiri (LeRoi Jones) 284
Barbados 56
Barnett, Ross 278
Baruch, Bernard 224
baseball 178, 274–275
Basket Maker period 5
Bataan Death March 252
Batista, Fulgencio 271
battles
      Alamo 107
      Antietam 150
      Argonne Forest 227
      Bad Axe 100
      Belleau Wood 225
      Bloody Swamp 41
      Buena Vista 111
      Bulge 255
      Bull Run 149
      Cedar Creek 203
      Chancellorsville 150
      Chapultepec 111
      Chickamauga 152
      of Civil War 149–153, 157, 158
      Concord and Lexington 65–66
      Coral Sea 256
      D-Day 254, 255
      El Alamein 254
      Fallen Timbers 99
      Fredericksburg 150
      Gettysburg 150–151
      Iwo Jima 256

*Atomic bomb over Nagasaki, Japan*

Lake Erie 94
Lake George 60
Leyte Gulf 256
Manila Bay 207, 209
Marne 225
Midway 256
Mobile Bay 157
Molina del Rey 111
Murfreesboro 150
New Orleans 94, 124
Okinawa 256
Peleliu 256
Petersburg 157
Port Hudson 153
of Revolutionary War 67, 68–70
San Jacinto 107
San Juan Hill 207–208
Shiloh 149
Slim Buttes 203
Somme 222
Stalingrad 254
Thames 94, 101
Veracruz 111
Vicksburg 151–153
White Plains 68
Wisconsin Heights 100
Wounded Knee Massacre 205
York 94
Yorktown 69, 70
Beard, Charles 36
Bear Flag Revolt 110
Beat culture 265
Beauregard P.G.T., 111, 143
Beckwourth, James 93
Beecher, Catharine 129
Beecher, Lyman 128, 129
Bell, Alexander Graham 173, 174
Bell, John 141
Bellamy, Edward 188
Benin, Kingdom of 18
Beringia 2
Berkeley, John 38
Berkeley, William 39, 58
Berkman, Alexander 191
Berlin, Irving 224
Berlin Airlift 267
Berlin Blockade 266–267
Berlin Wall 267, 303
Bernstein, Carl 291
Beveridge, Albert J. 209
Bickerdyke, Mary Ann "Mother" 148
Biddle, Nicholas 125
Big Foot 205
bilingual education 314
Bill of Rights 82, 83

Bin Laden, Osama 300, 305, 306
Birmingham (Alabama), civil rights protests in 278
birthrates 186, 187
bison hunting 198–199
Bissell, George 174–175
black codes 163
Black Hawk War 100
Black Kettle 200, 201
Black Panther Party 285
Black Power movement 282, 283–284, 288
Blacks. *See* African Americans; Slavery; Slave trade
Blackstone, William 81
"Black Thursday" 240
Blackwell, Elizabeth 148
Bleeding Kansas 139
Bliss, William Dwight Porter 210
blockade runners, Confederate 144–145, 146
Bolshevik Revolution 225
Bontemps, Arna 233
Bonus Army 242, 243
Boone, Daniel 72, 88
bootlegging 231
borders
  49th parallel 113
  Mexican 112, 113
  Pinckney's Treaty 79
  Treaty of Paris (1783) 73, 113
Borlaug, Norman 261
Bosnian civil war 304
Boston (Massachusetts)
  "Boston Massacre" 63
  Boston Tea Party 64
  Stamp Act protests in 63
  Boston Port Act of 1774 64
Bowie, James 107
Boxer Rebellion 218
Bozeman Trail 200, 201
Braceros Program 257, 286
Braddock, Edward 60
Bradley, Joseph 170
Brandeis, Louis D. 214
Brant, Joseph (Thayendanekea) 70
Brazil, Portuguese colony of 24, 52
Breckinridge, John 141
Bridger, Jim 93
Britain. *See* English colonies
  abolition of slavery 21, 139
  appeasement of Hitler 251
  explorers and exploration 26, 27, 33, 35, 36
  in Napoleonic Wars 96
  Protestant Reformation in 12–13

The "Bonus Army" camp in Washington D.C.

**RACHEL CARSON**

Britain, *cont.*
   Puritans in 37
   in Revolutionary War 68–70
   in World War I 222, 223
   in World War II 251, 252
Britain-U.S. relations
   border disputes 113
   during Civil War 146–147
   Jay's Treaty 79, 85–86
   Lend Lease 252
   War of 1812 94, 100
British East India Company 64
broadcasting technology 262
Brook Farm 127
Brooklyn Bridge 173, 179
Brooklyn Dodgers, integration of 274–275
Brooks, Preston 139
Browder, Earl 248
Brown, Dee 288
Brown, John 136, 139, 140–141
*Brown* v. *Board of Education* 275–276, 291
Bryan, William Jennings 196, 197, 210, 215, 233
Brzezinski, Zbigniew 300
Buchanan, James 139, 141
Bull Moose Party 215
Burgoyne, John 69, 70
Burkitt, Frank 196
Burnside, Ambrose 148, 150
Burr, Aaron 87
Burroughs, John 215
Bush, George H.W. 295, 304
Bush, George W.
   domestic policy of 296–297
   election of 2000 296
   Fundamentalists and 315
   Iraq war and 306–307
   War on Terror 297, 305–306
Bustamante, Carlos María 96–97
Butler, Andrew 139
Butler, Benjamin 149, 153
Butler, John Washington 233
Butler, Smedley D. 248–249
Button, Thomas 27

# C

Cabeza de Vaca, Alvar Núñez 30, 31
Cabot, John 26, 36
Cabot, Sebastian 26
Cabral, Pedro Alvares 24
Cahokia, mound culture at 5
Calhoun, John C. 94, 137

California
   Bear Flag Revolt 110
   Chinese immigrants in 180–181
   exploration of 33, 34–35
   as free state 137
   Gold Rush 123, 137, 174, 180
   Indian culture areas 7
   Los Angeles race riots 281, 316
   Mexican immigrants in 237
   under Mexico 105, 107–108, 110
   overland route to 93
   under Spain 31, 35
   U.S. annexation of 110, 112, 123
Calley, William 272
Calvert, George 37
Calvinism 32, 126
Calvin, John 13, 32
Cambodia 273
Cameron, Simon 148
Canada
   African American loyalists in 73
   Aroostook War 113
   New France 32, 33, 61
   during Revolutionary War 66–67, 69
   Treaty of Paris (1783) 73
   in War of 1812, 94
canals 89–90, 115, 116
Canary Islands 22
Cape of Good Hope 11, 20
Capone, Al 231
Caribbean
   immigration from 313
   plantation system in 56
   slavery in 52, 56–57
   Spanish-American War 206–209
   Spanish colonization of 23, 24–25
   Spanish conquest of 28
   Spanish exploration of 22–23
   U.S. intervention in 219–220
Carmel mission 35
Carmichael, Stokely (Kwame Turé) 284, 288
Carnegie, Andrew 174, 176–178
Carolina colony 39, 42, 58–59
carpetbaggers 167
Carranza, Venustiano 222
Carson, Kit 93, 202
Carson, Rachel 261
Carter, Jimmy 292–293, 298, 299–300
Carteret, George 38
Cartier, Jacques 27
Casey, William 300, 301
Castro, Fidel 270–271, 288, 313
Catholic Church
   in English colonies 37, 45

Papal Line of Demarcation 24
Protestant Reformation and 12
sexual abuse scandals in 314
Spanish missions 33–34, 35
CAT scan 309
Catt, Carrie Chapman 216
cattle drives 200–201
cattle ranching 35
Ceausescu, Nicolae 303
Centennial Exposition, Philadelphia 172, 173
Central Intelligence Agency (CIA) 269, 271, 298–299, 300, 306
Cervera y Topete, Pascual 207, 208
Chamberlain, Neville 251
Champlain, Samuel de 32
Chaney, James 280, 281
Channing, William Ellery 126, 127
Charbonneau, Toussaint 92
Charles I, King of England 37, 50
Charles II, King of England 38
Charleston (South Carolina) 41, 67
Fort Sumter 141, 142, 143
slave rebellions 130–131
Charles V, Holy Roman Emperor 12
charter colonies 42
Chase, Salmon P. 157
Chauncy, Charles 49
Chávez, César 286, 287
checks and balances 81, 84, 86
Cheney, Dick 297, 305
Cherokee 102, 103, 104, 148, 198
*Chesapeake* 94
Cheyenne 200, 201–202
Chiang Kai Shek 269
Chicago (Illinois)
anti-Vietnam War protest 273, 290
Haymarket Riots 190
Pullman strike 191
World's Columbian Exposition 173, 205
Chickasaw 102, 103, 104, 148, 198
child labor 212, 213, 214, 217
Children's Bureau Act of 1912, 212
China
communist victory in 268
in Korean War 268, 269
Nixon in 297
Open Door Policy 218–219
Chinese Americans
anti-Chinese movement and 181–182
post-1965 immigrants 311
in West 180–182
Chinese Exclusion Act 181, 182, 237
Chivington, John 200
Choctaw 102, 103, 104, 148, 198

Chou En-Lai 297
Churchill, Winston 251, 254, 255, 266
Church of Jesus Christ of the Latter Day Saints 122–123, 314
cigarette smoking, health risks of 310
cities
Chinatowns in 181, 311
class differences in 179
in English colonies 46, 47–48
immigrants in 117, 179, 183, 231
industrialization and 116
labor migration to 259
population 118
Progressive reform in 213–214
public health in 118–119
Civilian Conservation Corps (CCC) 245
Civilian Works Administration (CWA) 245
civil rights. *See* also integration
black nationalism and 282–284
demonstrations and protests 277–281
Franklin Roosevelt and 257, 274
integrationist vs separatist approach to 282
Jim Crow laws and 184–185, 275
for Mexican Americans 285–287
during Reconstruction 161–162, 163, 164, 166, 170
Supreme Court and 185, 275–276
voter registration drive 280–281
Woodrow Wilson and 215–216
Civil Rights Acts
of 1866 164
of 1964 280, 281
of 1972 291
Civil War
African-American soldiers in 152–156
battles of 148–152, 156, 158
casualties in 144, 152, 159
Confederate home front 142, 143, 144–147
Emancipation Proclamation 153–154
events leading to 138–141
firing on Fort Sumter 143
legacy of 159
New York draft riots during 156
Reconstruction during 160–162
secession crisis 141–142, 147–148
surrender of Confederate army 158
Union home front 147–148
weapons in 149, 150
Clark, George Rogers 71, 91
Clark, William 91, 92
Clarke, Kenneth B. 276
Clay, Henry 94, 98, 124, 125, 133, 134
Clean Air Act 291, 294, 295

*Bill Clinton and Albert Gore on the 1992 campaign trail*

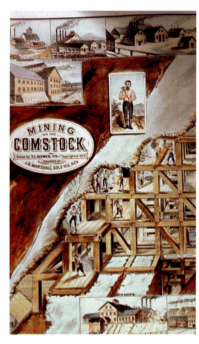

An advertisement for the Comstock Lode in Nevada

Cleaver, Eldridge 284
Clement VII, Pope 12
*Clermont* 115
Cleveland, Grover 191, 196, 197
cliff dwellers 5
Clinton, Bill 295–296, 304
Clinton, Hillary Rodham 296
Clinton, James 71
Clovis Culture 3
Coercive (Intolerable) Acts of 1774 64
*Cohens* v. *Virginia* 87
Colden, Cadwallader 63
Cold War
    in Developing World 269–270
    end of 295, 302–303
    in Europe 266–268
    Korean War 268–269
    in Latin America 270–271
    nuclear deterrence and 269, 270
    Reagan's policy and 300
    Vietnam War 272–273
*Cole, USS* 305
Colfax, Schuyler 176
colleges and universities
    African American 185–186
    coeducational 128
    colonial 48, 49
    GI Bill 258
    integration of 278
    land grant 185
    women's 187
colonization of Africa 19–20
colonization of Americas. *See* English
    colonies; French colonies; Spanish
    colonies
    Dutch 30, 38, 39, 40
    Portuguese 24
    Swedish 38
Colored Farmers' Alliance 195
Colter, John 93
Columbian Exchange 23
Columbus, Christopher 22–23, 318
Commonwealth of Independent States (CIS)
    303
Compromise of 1850 136–137
Compromise of 1877 170–171
computers 308–309
Comstock Lode 123
Concord, Battle of 65–66
Confederate Army 143, 145, 149–153, 157,
    158
Confederate States of America 142, 143,
    144–147
Congregational Church 45, 48, 49, 126
Congress

business regulation bills in 196
during Civil War 147–148
energy bill in 297
immigration bills in 181, 231, 311, 312
isolationism in 251–252
Johnson's impeachment in 165
Missouri Compromise 98
New Deal legislation in 245, 247, 248
powers of 84
Reconstruction and 161–162, 163–164,
    165, 170–171
representation in 81
Congress of Industrial Workers (CIO) 247
Congress of Racial Equality (CORE) 278,
    281
Connecticut colony 37, 42
Connor, Eugene "Bull" 278
conquistadors 24, 28–29
conservation movement 214–215
Constitution U.S.
    Amendments
        Thirteenth 163
        Fourteenth 164, 178, 185, 276
        Fifteenth 166
        Eighteenth 212, 231
        Nineteenth 216
        Twenty-fourth 281
        Twenty-sixth 291
    Bill of Rights 82, 83
    checks and balances in 81
    congressional powers in 84
    executive powers in 84–85
    Great Compromise 81
    judicial powers in 86
    ratification debate 82–83
    slavery and 81, 97–98, 135
    suffrage and 124
Constitutional Convention 80–81
constitutions, state 76–77
consumerism
    advertising and 234, 259, 263
    credit and 239
    shopping malls 264, 309
    women and 234–235
Consumer Product Safety Act 291
Continental Army 66, 68–70
Continental Congress 65, 66, 74, 75
Coolidge, Calvin 216, 228, 235, 238, 239
Cooper, James Fenimore 215
Cooper, Peter 115
Copperheads (Peace Democrats) 148
Cornwallis, Charles 68, 69, 70
Coronado, Francisco 30
corporations. *See* industry
Corps of Discovery 91–92

Cortés, Hernán 28 111
Cotton, John 37, 45
Cotton Club 233
cotton gin 97, 114
cotton mills 114
cotton production 97, 102, 114, 119, 143
Coughlin, Charles 248
counterculture 291
Coxey's Army 192
Crawford, William 124
Crazy Horse 200, 202–203
creationism 233, 315
credit 239
Credit Mobilier scandal 176
Creek 102, 103, 104, 149, 198
Creek War 101, 102
Crittenden, John J. 141
Crockett, Davy 107
Cromwell, Oliver 37
Crook, George 202, 203, 204
crown colonies 42–43
Cuba
    Bay of Pigs invasion 270–271
    Columbus's voyage to 23
    Mariel boatlift from 313
    plantation agriculture in 56
    Spanish-American War in 206–208
    Spanish colonization of 25, 28
    U.S. policy 219–220, 313
Cuban Americans 288, 313
Cuban Missile Crisis 271
Cuffe, Paul 133
Cullen, Countee 233
Cumberland 149
currency
    Confederate 146
    of Continental Congress 74, 75
    greenbacks 148, 196
    silver-backed 196, 197
Custer, George Armstrong 201, 202, 203
Cuzco (Peru) 29
Czologosz, Leon 210

# D

Daley, Richard 290
dam construction, New Deal 246, 247
Darrow, Clarence 233
Davies, Samuel 49
Davis, David 170
Davis, Jefferson 142, 143, 145, 146, 158
Dawes, William 65
D-Day 254, 255

Dean, John 291
Debs, Eugene V. 191, 225
Declaration of Independence 67
defense industry 257
Deism 126
Delaware
    constitution of 76
    Swedish colony in 38
De la Warr, Lord 36
Democratic Party. *See also* presidential
    elections
    Copperheads (Peace Democrats) 148
    northern/southern factions of 249
    Populists and 196
    slavery issue and 138, 141
    in South 165, 170, 185, 195
Democratic-Republican party 85, 130
desegregation. *See* integration
De Soto, Hernando 30
Dewey, George 207
Dias, Bartolomeu 20
Diaz, Bernal 11
Díaz, Porfirio 221–222, 236
Dickinson, John 65
Diem, Ngo Dinh 272
disease
    in Africa 19
    AIDS epidemic 310–311
    in cities 118–119
    Columbian Exchange and 23
    European, among Indians 23, 25, 50
    influenza epidemic of 1918, 226
    medical breakthroughs and 261, 262,
     309–310
    racial gap in 316–317
    smallpox epidemic of 1775–1782, 72
    tobacco-related 310
Dix, Dorothea 129, 148
Dobson, James 315
dollar diplomacy 220–221
Dominican Republic, 96, 220–221,
    *See also* Hispaniola
domino theory 272
Doniphan, Alexander 111
Douglas, Stephen 138
Douglass, Frederick 130, 133, 135, 141
Drake, Edwin 175
Drake, Francis 30, 33, 35
Dred Scott case 139
Drouillard, George 93
Du Bois, W.E.B. 215, 233, 282
Dukakis, Michael 295
Dunbar, William 92
Durant, Thomas 180
Dust Bowl 242

**SIR FRANCIS DRAKE**

Dutch colony and exploration 27, 30, 38, 39, 40
Dutch East India Company 20, 38
Dutch Reformed Church 45, 49
Dutch West India Company 38

# E

Early, Jubal 158
economy
    during Civil War 148
    of Confederacy 146
    of English colonies 54–56, 74–75
    during Great Depression 240–242, 243, 249
    industrialization of 114–115, 116
    mercantalism and 10, 11
    Panic of 1819, 115
    postwar 258–259
    pre-Columbian Indian 9
    Reagan's economic policy and 294–295
    recession 294–295, 308, 312
    during Revolutionary War, 74, 75, 80
    service 259, 308, 310
    of South 143
    "stagflation" 292
    Wall St. crash 239–240
    during World War II, 257
Edison, Thomas Alva 173–174
Education. See colleges and universities
    bilingual 314
    evolution vs creationism 233, 315
    Freedom Schools 281
    government funding for 280
    integration of schools 275–277
    Progressive reforms in 212, 213
    reform 296–297
    segregated schools 185
    of women 129, 187
    education levels, racial gap in 316
Edwards, Jonathan 48, 126
Egypt 269, 292, 298
Ehrlichman, John 291
Eichmann, Adolf 256
Eisenhower, Dwight 259, 269, 277, 288, 291
electrification
    rural 245, 246, 260
    sources for 260, 261
Elementary and Secondary Education Act 280
Elion, Gertrude 261
Ellington, Duke 233

Ellsworth, Oliver 81
El Salvador 301, 313
Emancipation Proclamation 153–154
Embargo Act of 1807 94
Emerson, Ralph Waldo 127
employment. See labor force
encomienda system 24, 50
energy policy 293, 297, 305
England. See Britain
English colonies. See also Revolutionary War
    Carolinas 39
    colleges in 48, 49
    Dutch War 40
    economy of 54–56, 74
    in French and Indian War 60–61
    French wars 40–41
    Georgia 39
    government of 42–43
    immigration to 47
    Jamestown 36–37
    Maryland 37
    population of 46, 46–47
    Puritan separatists 37, 39, 44–45
    Quaker Pennsylvania 39, 45
    religion in 37, 38, 39, 44–46
    Roanoke 36
    slavery in 47, 56, 58–59
    Stamp Act protests 62–64
    taxation of 61, 62–63, 64
    trade of 54–55, 75
    urban growth in 46, 47–48
    western expansion ban 62, 72
    western expansion of 47, 71–72
Enola Gay 256
Enron Corporation 297
environmental policy
    under Bush (George W.) 297
    conservation movement and 214–215
    under Nixon 291
    under Reagan 294
EPIC (End Poverty in California) 248
Equal Employment Opportunity Commission 280
Equal Rights Amendment (ERA) 289
Eric the Red 9
Erie Canal 89–90, 116
Europe. See also colonization of Americas; explorers and exploration; slave trade
    in Africa 19–20
    collapse of communism 302–303
    Marshall Plan 266, 267
    mercantilism in 10, 11
    nation states, rise of 10, 11
    Protestant Reformation 12–13

**EDWARD "DUKE" ELLINGTON**

Renaissance 10
World War I 222–228
in World War II 250, 251, 253–255
evangelical Christianity 314–315
Evers, Medgar 278
evolution, teaching of 233, 315
explorers and exploration
Columbus's voyages 22–23
Dutch 27
English 26, 27, 33, 35, 36
French 27, 32, 33
Norse 10
Portuguese 10–11, 20, 24
Spanish 12, 22–23, 26, 30–31, 34–35
western 91–94

# F

Fair Employment and Practices Commission
257, 274
Fair Labor Standards Act of 1938 249
Falwell, Jerry 315
Fard, Wallace 282
Farmer, James 278
Farmer's Alliances 193–194
farming. *See* agriculture
Farragut, David 150, 157
fashion 257
fast food 264, 309
Faubus, Orval 277
Federal Deposit Insurance Corporation
(FDIC) 245
Federal Emergency Relief Administration
(FERA) 245
Federal Housing Administration (FHA) 245
Federalist Papers 82
Federalist party 82, 85, 94
Federal Reserve Board 239
Federal Theatre, Arts, Music, and
Writers Projects 246
Ferdinand and Isabella of Spain 22, 23, 24
Ferraro, Geraldine 289, 295
Fessenden, William 163
Fetterman, William 200
feudalism 10, 11
Finney, Charles G. 128
Firestone, Harvey Samuel 173
Fitzpatrick, Thomas 199
Five Civilized Tribes 102, 103, 149
Flores, José Maria 110
Florida
ceded to U.S. 96, 97
French settlement in 32

Seminole Wars in 96, 102–104
under Spain 30, 79, 96
Folsom culture 3
food
fast food 264, 309
wartime rationing 257
Ford, Gerald 292
foreign policy. *See also* Cold War
Adams-Onis Treaty of 1819 97
in Africa 270
in Asia 269–270
in China 268, 297
détente 297–298
dollar diplomacy 220–221
isolationism 251–252
Jay's Treaty 79, 85–86
in Latin America 219–222, 270–271,
301
in Middle East 269, 298–299, 300–301,
304
Monroe Doctrine 219
Open Door 218–219
post-Cold War 304–307
Roosevelt Corollary 220
terrorism and 297, 300, 301, 304,
305–306
Truman Doctrine 267, 269
War of 1812 and 94
Formative Period 4
Forrest, Nathan Bedford 169
Fort Laramie Treaty 199, 201, 202
forts
Christina 38
Custer 203
Donelson 149
Duquesne 60
Frontenac 61
Henry 149
in Indian country 99
Jay's Treaty on 79
Louisbourg 41
Mandan 92
Oswego 61
Phil Kearney 200, 201
Sackville 71
Spanish forts 35
Sumter 141, 142, 143
Ticonderoga (Carillon) 61, 66, 67
Washington 68
William Henry 61
49th parallel 113
"Forty–Niners" 123
"Fountain of Youth" 30
Fourteen Points 227, 228
Fourteenth Amendment 164, 178, 185, 276

**BENJAMIN FRANKLIN**

**HORACE GREELEY**

France. *See also* French colonies
    abolition of slavery 139
    appeasement of Hitler 251
    Civil War and 147
    explorers and exploration 27, 32, 33
    Huguenots in 32
    in Indochina 272
    Louisiana Purchase of 1803 34, 88, 90
    in Revolutionary War 69, 70
    in World War I 222, 223, 224, 225
Franklin, Benjamin 48, 55, 67, 73, 81
Franz Ferdinand, Archduke of Austria 222
free blacks 59, 73, 89, 134
Freedmen's Bureau 162, 163, 164
Freedom Riders 278
Freedom Schools 281
Freedom Summer 280
Free Soil Party 135
Frelinghuysen, Theodorus 48
Frémont, John C. 93, 110, 138–139, 157
French colonies
    in Canada 32, 33, 61
    fall of New France 61
    French and Indian War 60–61
    Huguenot settlement 32
    King George's War 41
    King William's War 40–41
    Louisiana Territory 34
    in Mississippi River Basin 33
    Queen Anne's War 41, 47
    slavery in 50
French and Indian War 60–61
French Revolution 96, 126
Frick, Henry Clay 191
Friedan, Betty 288–289
Frieselle, S. Parker 237
Frobisher, Martin 27
Frontenac, Louis de Baude, Comte de 40
frontier thesis, Turner's 205–206
Fugitive Slave Act of 1850 136, 137
fugitive slaves. *See* runaway slaves
Fulton, Robert 114–115
Fundamentalist Christianity 232–233,
    314–315
Funston, Frederick 209
fur trade 33, 38, 93
fur trappers 93–94

# G

Gabriel's rebellion 130
Gadsden Purchase 113
Gage, Thomas 65

Galbraith, John Kenneth 259
Galloway, Joseph 65
Gálvez, Bernardo de 70
Gama, Vasco da 11, 20
Garfield, James 176
Garner, John Nance 249
Garrison, William Lloyd 134, 135
Garvey, Marcus 233–234, 282
*Gaspee* affair 64
Gates, Horatio 69
Geary Act of 1892 181
General Motors 247
George III, King of England 66, 67
Georgia colony 39, 42, 43, 59
German Americans
    during World War I 224
    immigration of 45, 47, 117
Germany
    collapse of communism 303
    division of 266–267
    Holocaust and 255–256
    Nazi regime 250, 260–261
    in World War I 222–223, 225, 228
    in World War II 251, 253–255
Geronimo 204
Gerry, Elbridge 83
Ghana, Kingdom of 15, 16, 17
"Ghost Dance" 204–205
Gibbon, John H. 261
*Gibbons v. Ogden* 87
GI Bill 258, 259, 263
Gilded Age 170, 206
Ginsberg Allen 265
glasnost 302
Glass-Steagall Act of 1933 245
Glidden, Joseph Farwell 173
global warming 297, 305
Goldman, Emma 191
Gold Rush, California 123, 137, 174, 180
Goldwater, Barry 280
Gompers, Samuel 190
Goodman, Andrew 280, 281
Good Neighbor Policy 270
Gorbachev, Mikhail 302, 303
Gore, Albert (senator) 276
Gore, Albert (vice president) 296, 305
Gore, Tipper 315
Gosnold, Bartholemew 36
Government. *See also* Congress;
    Constitution, U.S.
    in Articles of Confederation 74, 81
    during Civil War 147–149
    of Confederacy 145–146
    in English colonies 42–43
    of Northwest Territory 77–78

pre-Columbian Indian 8, 9
Progressives in 212–216
in Reconstruction South 167–168
during Revolutionary War 65, 66
regulation 193
Grand Coulee Dam 246, 247
Granges 192–193
Grant, Ulysses S.
    in Civil War 149, 150, 151, 152, 158
    in Mexican-American War 111
    presidency of 165–166, 170, 172,
        196, 201
Great Awakening
    First 48–49
    Second 128–129
Great Compromise 81
Great Depression 239–243
Great Serpent Mound 4
Great Society 280
Greece, civil war in 267
Greeley, Horace 147
Greenback Party 196
greenbacks 148, 196
Green Corn Rebellion 225
Greene, Nathanael 68, 69
Greenland, Norse settlement in 10
Guadalupe Hidalgo, Treaty of 112–113
Guatemala 301, 313
Guerrero, Vincente 105
Gulf of Tonkin Resolution 272

# H

Haiti 96, 304. *See also* Hispaniola
Haldeman, H.R. 291
*Half Moon*, The 27
Halliburton Corporation 297
Hamer, Fannie Lou 281
Hamilton, Alexander 75, 80, 82, 85, 86,
    90, 114
Hampton Institute 186
Hancock, John 65, 81, 83
Hancock, Winfield Scott 201
Hanna, Mark 197, 210, 214
Harding, Warren 225, 230, 231
Harlem Renaissance 233, 234
Harmer, Joseph 99
Harper's Ferry, raid on 140
Harrington, James 81
Harrison, William Henry 100
Hart-Celler Act of 1965 311
Harvard College 48
Hawthorne, Nathaniel 127

Hay, John M. 208, 218
Hay-Bunau-Varilla Treaty 220
Hayes, Rutherford B. 170–171, 190
Haymarket Riots 190
Hay-Pauncefote Treaty 220
health care. *See also* disease
    Clinton plan 296
    medical breakthroughs 261, 262,
        309–310
    for mentally ill 128–129, 310
Hench, Philip 261
Hennepin, Louis 33
Henry, Patrick 62, 65, 81, 83
Henry IV, King of France 32
Henry VIII, King of England 12–13
Henry the Navigator, Prince 10–11, 20
*Hernandez* v. *Texas* 285
Hessians, in Revolutionary War 69
Hidalgo y Costilla, Miguel 105
Higginson, Thomas 154
highway system, federal 259, 260
Hill, A.P. 150
Hiroshima, bombing of 256
Hispanic-Americans 311, 312–313.
        *See also* Mexican Americans
Hispaniola 23, 24, 25, 28, 50, 56, 96
Hitchcock, Ethan Allen 109
Hitler, Adolf 250, 251, 255
HIV virus 310, 311
Ho Chi Minh 272
Hoe, Richard 173
Hohokam people 5
Hollerith, Herman 173
Holmes, Oliver Wendell 228
Holocaust 255–256
Holy Roman Empire 12
Homeland Security Department 297
Homestead Act of 1862 148
Homestead strike 191
homosexuals
    AIDS epidemic 310
    in military 304
    same-sex marriage and 315
Hooker, Thomas 37, 45
Hoover, Herbert 224, 231, 235, 239,
        242–243, 249
Hoover, J. Edgar 284
Hoover Dam 246
Hoovervilles 242
Hopewell Mound Culture 4
Hopi 33
Hopkins, Harry 249
horses, wild 34
housing
    GI Bill loans 258, 263

**OLIVER WENDELL HOLMES**

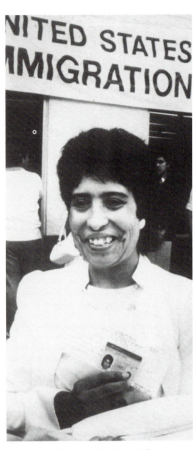

A new immigrant to the United States

housing, *cont.*
  Native American 9
  social class and 179
  suburban 263
  tenements 179, 183
Housing Act of 1954 259
Houston, Sam 107
Howard, Oliver 163
Howe, Richard 68
Howe, William 68, 69
Hudson, Henry 27, 38
Hudson's Bay 27
Huerta, Delores 286
Huerta, Victoriano 222
Hughes, Langston 233, 234
Huguenots 30, 32
Humphrey Hubert, 273, 290, 291
Hunter, George 92
hunter-gatherers 4, 6
Huron 32
Hurricane Katrina 307, 317–318
Huss, Jan 12
Hussein, Saddam 270, 301, 304, 307
Hutchinson, Thomas 63, 64

# I

"I have a dream" speech 279–280
Illegal Immigration Reform and Immigrant
    Responsibility Act of 1996 313
Illinois, statehood of 78
*I Love Lucy* 262, 263
immigrants and immigration. *See also*
    westward expansion
  bilingual education and 314
  Chinese 180–182
  in cities 117, 179, 183
  in English colonies 47
  from Europe 182–183
  geographical distribution of 182
  of illegal aliens 312, 313
  laws 311
  Mexican 231, 236–237
  "Palmer Raids" on 228–229
  post-1965 311–313
  restriction 181, 231, 311
  Sacco and Vanzetti case 229
Immigration Reform and Control Act
    (IRCA) of 1986 312
Inca Empire 29
income distribution 317
indentured servants 44, 47, 55–56
Indiana, statehood of, 78

Indian Americans (Asian) 311
Indiana Territory 100
Indian Removal Act of 1830 103
Indians. *See also* Indians, pre-Columbian;
    Indian wars
  American Indian Movement (AIM)
    284–285, 288
  attacks on settlers 148, 200, 201–202
  bison hunting 198–199
  in English colonies 44
  in English-French wars 40, 41, 60–61
  European diseases and 23, 25, 50
  French colonies and 32, 50
  "Ghost Dance" 204–205
  Grant's policy toward 201
  horses of 34
  land ceded in treaties with 79, 99, 100,
    101, 199–200, 202
  New Amsterdam and 38
  Pontiac's Rebellion 62
  Powhatan Confederacy 36
  Red Power movement 284–285, 287,
    288
  removal of 99–104, 198
  Revolutionary War and 70, 71
  slaves 50
  termination policy and 288
  under Spanish colonization 24–25, 33
  in War of 1812 100
Indians, pre-Columbian
  agriculture 4, 5
  cliff dwellers 5
  culture areas 6, 7
  mound builders 4–5
Indians, pre-Columbian, cont.
  nomadic migration to North America
    2–3
  tool use 3, 4
  trade between 6
  women 8
  worldview of 8–9
Indian wars
  Black Hawk War 100
  Creek (Red Stick) War 101, 102
  Seminole Wars 96, 102–104
  Tecumseh confederacy 99–100, 101
  of West 199–205
Indonesia 270
industry
  during Civil War 142, 148
  globalization and 308
  government regulation of 196, 214, 216
  post-bellum era 172–178
  technology and 114–115, 172–173
  urban growth and 116

Wall St. crash and 240
during World War II 252, 257
infant mortality 316
influenza epidemic of 1918, 226
*In re Debs* 191
integration
of armed forces 275
of baseball 274–275
bus, city 277–278
bus, interstate 278
school 275–277
university 278
Intermediate Nuclear Forces (INF) treaty 302
Internal Revenue Act of 1862 148
International Workers of the World (IWW) 224–225
Internet 309
Interstate Commerce Commission 193
Intolerable (Coercive) Acts of 1774 64
inventors and inventions 173–174, 259–260
Iran 269, 298–299, 300
Iran-Contra scandal 301
Iran hostage crisis 299, 300
Iran-Iraq War 301
Iraq 269, 270
Gulf War of 1991 304
Iran War 301
U.S. war on 306–307
Irish immigrants 117, 118
ironclads 150
"iron curtain" 266, 267
Iroquois 32, 38, 40, 70, 71, 79
Islam
in Africa 14, 15
Fundamentalism 300, 304, 307
in Iberian peninsula 11
Nation of Islam 282–283
isolationism 251–252
Israel 269, 292, 298, 300–301, 304
Italy
Renaissance in 10
in World War II 254–255
Iturbide, Agustín de 105

# J

Jackson, Andrew
African colonization and 133
in Indian wars 96, 101, 102
presidency of 87, 108, 124–126
in War of 1812 94
Jacksonian Democracy 124, 126

Jackson, Jimmy Lee 281
Jackson, Thomas "Stonewall" 111, 149, 150
Jamaica 25, 57
James I, King of England 36, 37
James, Duke of York 38–39
Jamestown colony 36–37, 58
Japan, in World War II 252, 256
Japanese Americans
in armed forces 275
internment of 253, 254
Jay, John 79, 82, 85–86
Jay's Treaty 79, 85–86
jazz 233, 265
Jefferson, Thomas 49
on African American colonization 133
in Antifederalist party 85
Burr and 87
Declaration of Independence 67
on economy 114
at First Continental Congress 65
foreign policy of 94
on Missouri Compromise 98
at Second Continental Congress 55
slavery and 67, 81
western exploration and 91, 92
western lands and 77, 78, 90–91
Jenkins, Charles Francis 173
Jenney, William LeBaron 173
Jesup, Thomas 103
Jews
in English colonies 45
Holocaust 255–256
immigration of 182
in Nazi Germany 250
religious divisions among 314
Jim Crow laws 184–185
João III, King of Portugal 18
Joffre, Joseph 224
John Paul II, Pope 301
Johnson, Andrew 157, 159, 163, 164–165
Johnson, Hugh 248
Johnson, James Weldon 233
Johnson, Lyndon Baines 288
and civil rights 276, 280, 281, 284
Vietnam War policy of 272, 273
"War on Poverty" 280
Johnston, Joseph 152
Joliet, Louis 33
Jones, Samuel "Golden Rule" 214
Jones, Thomas Catesby 107
Joseph (Chief) 204
judiciary, powers of 86
*Jungle, The* (Sinclair) 211, 248

*John F. Kennedy and Robert Kennedy*

# K

Kalm, Peter 61
Kansas-Nebraska Act of 1854 138–139
Kansas Territory, civil war in 139
Karenga, Maulana 284
Kay, David 307
Kearny, Denis 181
Kearny, Stephen Watts 109, 110
Keating-Owens Act of 1916 212, 214
Kefauver, Estes 276
Kelley, Oliver 192
Kendall, Edward 261
Kennedy, Edward 293
Kennedy, John F. 271, 272, 278–279, 280, 295
Kennedy, Robert F. 284, 287, 290, 293
Kentucky, statehood of 88
Keokuk 100
Kerner Commission 284
Kerouac, Jack 265
Kerry, John 297
Key, Francis Scott 133–134
Khomeini, Ayatollah Ruhollah 299
Kim Il Sung 268
King, Martin Luther, Jr.
    assassination of 284
    on Black Power movement 284
    in civil rights protests 277–278, 281
    "I have a dream" speech 279–280
    Malcolm X and 282
    opposition to Vietnam War 275
King George's War 41
King, Rodney 316
King Philip 103
King William's War 40–41
Kino, Eusebio 33
Kiowa 201–202
Kissinger, Henry 273, 297
Kleindienst, Richard 291
Knights of Labor 190
Knox, Henry 67
Kongo, Kingdom of 18
Korean Americans 311, 316
Korean War 268–269, 275
Ku Klux Klan 168–170, 231–232, 277, 281
Kuwait 304
Kwanzaa 284
Kyoto Accords 297, 305

# L

labor force. See also occupations; slavery; strikes
    African Americans in 257, 309, 317
    automation and 259, 308
    child labor 212, 213, 214, 217
    Coxey's Army 192
    encomienda system 24, 50
    factory workers 142
    during Great Depression 240–241
    immigrant 180, 237, 257
    indentured servants 44, 47, 55–56
    migrant workers 257, 285–286
    migration of 257, 259
    Progressive reform and 212–213, 214, 217
    unemployment 240–241, 242, 259, 317
    wages 192, 309, 317
    women in 187, 190, 212, 213, 235, 257, 309, 310
    during World War II 257
labor unions 188–191, 228, 247, 308
LaFollette, Robert 212
laissez-faire economics 239
Lamar, Mirabeau Bonaparte 107
Lancaster Turnpike 88
land
    ceded by Indians 79, 99, 100, 101, 105, 199–200, 202
    Gadsden Purchase 113
    Homestead Act of 1862 148
    Indian view of 8
    Louisiana Purchase 34, 88, 90
    in Northwest Territory 77–78
    during Reconstruction 163, 164, 167
La Salle, René Robert Cavelier, sieur de 32, 33
Las Casas, Bartolomé de 25, 50
laser technology 309–310
Latin America
    immigration from 313
    U.S. policy in 219–222, 270–271
Laudonniere, René de 32
Lawrence (Kansas), proslavery raid on 139
League of Augsburg 40
League of Nations 228, 266
Lease, Mary Elizabeth 194
Lebanon 269, 300–301
Lee, Richard Henry 67, 81, 83
Lee, Robert E. 111, 140, 146, 149, 150–152, 156, 158
leisure time 178
Lenape 38
Lend-Lease Act of 1941 252
Levittown 263
Lewis, John 247
Lewis, Meriwether 91, 92
Lewis and Clark expedition 91–92
Lexington, Battle of 65–66

**ABRAHAM LINCOLN**

*Liberator, The* 134, 135
Liberia, colonization movement in 134
Liberty Bonds 224
Liberty League 248
Liberty Party 135
Libya 301
life expectancy, racial gap in 316, 317
Lincoln, Abraham
    assassination of 158
    background of 143
    cabinet of 147
    election of 1860 141
    election of 1864 157–158
    Emancipation Proclamation 153–154
    Indian policy of 148
    Reconstruction plan of 159, 162
    as war leader 144, 149, 150, 151
Lisa, Manuel 93
literature 233, 265
Lithic (Stone) Age 3
Little Rock (Arkansas), school integration
    in 276, 277
Little Turtle (Mishikinakwa) 99
Livingston, Robert 115
Locke, Alain 233
Locke, John 39, 81
Long, Huey 248
Longstreet, James 151
Los Angeles (California), race riots in 281,
    316
Louisiana Purchase of 1803 34, 88, 90
Louisiana Territory 34
Low, Seth 214
Loyalists (Tories) 68
Lumumba, Patrice 270
lunch counter sit-ins 278
*Lusitania RMS* 223
Luther, Martin 12, 13
Lyman, William 173
lynchings 184, 228, 232
Lyons, Mary 187

# M

MacArthur, Arthur 209
MacArthur, Douglas 243, 248, 268, 269
Mackenzie, Ranald 203
Madero, Francisco 222
Madison, James 81, 82, 83, 94
Magellan, Ferdinand 26
Maguire, Gerald 248–249
*Maine, USS* sinking of, 206
Maktab al-Khidamar (MAK) 300
Malcolm X (Malcolm Little) 282–283, 288

Mali, kingdom of 14, 16, 17
Mande-speaking people 14
Manhattan Project 253, 256
"Manifest Destiny" 109, 142
Manning, Patrick 19
Mao Zedong, 268 297
*Marbury* v. *Madison* 86–87
March on Washington 278–280
Mariel boatlift 313
maroons 57
Marquette, Jacques 33
Marshall, George C. 266
Marshall, John 86–87
Marshall, Thurgood 276
Marshall Plan 266, 267
Maryland
    Annapolis Convention 80
    Catholic founders of 37, 45
    Civil War battles in 150
    colonial government 42, 43
Mary Mount colony 44
Mason, George 83
Massachusetts. *See also* Boston
    (Massachusetts)
    colonial government of 42, 43
    Concord and Lexington, Battles of 65
    constitution of 76
    Great Awakening in 48–49
    Intolerable Acts in 64
    Puritan colony in 37, 44–45
    Shay's Rebellion 80
Massachusetts 54th Regiment 154–155
Mayflower 37
Mayflower Compact 37
Mbemba, Nzinga (King of Kongo) 18
McCarthy, Eugene 273, 290
McClellan, George 111, 149, 150, 157, 158
*McClure's Magazine* 211
McCrea, Jane 70
*McCulloch* v. *Maryland* 87
McDonald's 264
McKinley, William 197, 210
Meade, George 151
Meadowcraft Rock Shelter 3
medical breakthroughs 261, 262, 309–310
Medicare and Medicaid programs 280, 296
Melville, Herman 127
Memminger, Charles 146
mentally ill, care of 128–129, 310
mercantilism 10, 11, 54–55, 75
Meredith, James 278, 284
Mergenthaler, Ottmar 173
*Merrimack USS* 149
Methodist Church 45, 128
Mexican American Political Association
    (MAPA) 287

*The U.S.S. Maine*

**PETER MINUIT**

Mexican Americans
   civil rights movement 285–287
   illegal immigrants 312
   immigration of 231, 236–237, 257
   in labor force 237, 285–286
Mexican Revolution 221–222, 236
Mexico
   independence of 105–106
   northern territories of 105–110
   Spanish conquest of 28
   Texas independence and 106–107
Mexican-American War 107–113, 136
Michigan, statehood of 78
middle passage 52–53
migrant workers 257, 285–286
migration. *See also* immigrants and
   immigration; westward expansion
   of African Americans 224
   during Great Depression 239, 241
   Indian removal 99–104, 198
   labor force 257, 259
migration, cont.
   nomadic, from Asia 2–3
   to Sunbelt region 308
Miles, Nelson 203, 204, 207
Mills, Victor 261
mining industry 174–175, 190, 191
Minnesota, statehood of 78
Minuit, Peter 38
Minutemen 65, 66
*Miranda* v. *Arizona* 291
missions, Spanish 33–34, 35
Mississippian Culture 4–5
Mississippi Freedom Democratic Party
   (MFDP) 281
Mississippi River
   exploration of 33
   as western boundary 73, 79, 88–89
Missouri Compromise of 1820 98, 99,
   130
Mobutu Sese Seko 270
Model T 230, 235
Modoc War 202
Mogollan people 5
Mohawk 38
Molasses Act of 1733 54
"Molly Maguires" 190
Mondale, Walter 295
*Monitor* USS 149
Monroe, James 83, 219
Monroe Doctrine 219
   Roosevelt Corollary to 220
Montcalm, Marquis de 61
Montesquieu 81
Montezuma II 28

Montgomery, Richard 66–67
Montgomery (Alabama), bus boycott in
   277–278
Montreal (Canada) 61, 66
Moral Majority 315
Morgan, J.P, 196, 228, 229
Morgenthau, Henry 249
Mormons 122–123, 314
Morrill Land Grant Act of 1862 185
Morris, Gouverneur 81
Morris, Robert 75
Morton, Thomas 44
Mott, Lucretia 130
mound builders 4–5
movies 178, 231, 265
muckrakers 211
Muhammad, Elijah (Elijah Poole) 282, 283
Muir, John 215
*Muller* v. *Oregon* 214
*Munn* v. *Illinois* 193
Muñoz Marin, Luis 287
Murphy, Grayson 248
Musa, Mansa (King of Mali) 14, 16
music 233, 264, 265, 315–316
Muslims. *See* Islam
Mussolini, Benito 250, 254
mutual assured destruction (MAD) 269

# N

Nagasaki, bombing of 256
Napoleon Bonaparte 94, 96, 104
Napoleon III 146
Narváez, Pánfilo de 30
Nash, Diane 278
Nash, Gary 8
Nation, Carrie 210–211
National American Woman Suffrage
   Association (NAWSA) 216
National Association for the Advancement
   of Colored People (NAACP) 275–276,
   279, 282
National Farm Workers Association
   (NFWA) 286
National Guard, in Iraq war 307
National Industrial Recovery Act (NIRA) 246
National Labor Relations Act 247
National Labor Relations Board 247
National Organization for Women (NOW)
   288
national park system 213, 214, 215
National Recovery Administration (NRA)
   246, 247, 249

National Road 88
National Union Party 157
National Woman's Party 216
National Woman's Suffrage Association
    (NWSA) 130, 186, 187, 216
National Women's Rights Convention 130
Nation of Islam 282–283
nation states, rise of 10, 11
Native Americans. See Indians
Navajo War 202
Navigation Acts 54, 55
Navy
    in Civil War 149, 157
    Pearl Harbor attack 252
    in Spanish-American War 207, 209
    in World War II 254, 255, 256
Negro Leagues 274
New Amsterdam 30, 38, 40
New Deal, 244–249
New France. See French colonies
New Jersey colony 39, 42, 43
New Jersey Plan 81
New Light Congregationalists 49
New Mexico
    Indian Wars in 202
    in Mexican-American War 109–110
    under Spain 31, 33–34
New Netherland 38, 39, 45
New Orleans (Louisiana)
    in Civil War 149
    Hurricane Katrina 307, 317–318
    public health in 118–119
Newport, Christopher 36
New Spain. See Spanish colonies
newspapers 126
Newton, Huey 284
New York
    Brooklyn Bridge 173, 179
    colonial government of 38–39, 42, 43
    constitution of 76–77
    draft riots of 1863 156
    Erie Canal 89–90, 116
    free blacks in 59
    Harlem Renaissance 233
    New Amsterdam 30, 38
    Revolutionary War battles in 68–69
    Stamp Act protests in 63
    Triangle Shirtwaist fire in 213
    New York Plan 81
    New York Stock Exchange (NYSE) 239,
        240, 295
Nez Percé 204
Nicaragua 301
Nina 22, 23
Nixon, Richard

domestic policy of 288, 291
election of 1868 290–291
foreign policy of 297–298, 299
Vietnam War policy of 272, 273
Watergate scandal 291–292
nonviolence, in civil rights movement
    277–278, 279
Noriega, Manuel 304
Norris, George 246
Norse settlements 10
North America. See also English colonies;
        French colonies
    Dutch colony 30, 38, 39, 40
    exploration of 27, 30–31, 33, 36
    Indian migration to 2–3
    Norse settlement 10
    Spanish colonies 30–31, 33–35
    Swedish colony 38
North, Oliver 301
North Atlantic Treaty Organization (NATO)
    268
North Carolina colony 39
Northwest Ordinance (Ordinance of 1787)
    77, 90, 97
Northwest Passage 26, 27
Northwest Territory 77–78
Nova Scotia
    African American loyalists in 73
    Fort Louisbourg 41
nuclear arms treaties 298, 299, 302
nuclear arsenal 269, 270
nuclear power 260, 293
Nye, Gerald 251

# O

O'Banion, Dion 231
Oberlin College 128
occupations
    computer-related 308–309
    in English colonies 55–56
    industrialization and 172–173
    for women 190
Office of War Mobilization and
    Reconversion, 259
Oglethorpe, James 39
Ohio, statehood of 78
Ohio River, westward expansion on 88–89
oil industry 174–175, 176, 297, 305
oil prices 293, 295, 298
Oklahoma Territory 198
Old Light Congregationalists 49, 126
Olive Branch Petition 66

**LUCRETIA MOTT**

Oliver, Andrew 63
Olympic Games boycotts 299, 300
Oñate, Juan de 33
One Hundred Days 245
Open Door Policy 218–219
Operation Desert Shield 304
Ordinance of 1784 77
Ordinance of 1785 77
Ordinance of 1787 (Northwest Ordinance) 77, 90, 97
Oregon Territory 97, 113
Oregon Trail 93–94, 122
Organization of Afro-American Unity 283
Organization for European Economic Cooperation (OEEC) 266
Organization of Petroleum Exporting Countries (OPEC) 293, 298
Osceola 103
O'Sullivan, John L. 109
Otis, Ewell S. 209
Oyo, Kingdom of 18

# P

Pahlevi, Reza Shah 269, 299
Paine, Thomas 86, 126
Paleolithic age 2
Palestine Liberation Organization (PLO) 300–301
Palme, Olaf 301
Palmer, A. Mitchell 228
Palmerston, Lord 146
Panama 304
Panama Canal 220, 298
Panic of 1819 115
Panic of 1837 196
Papal Line of Demarcation 24
Paredes, Mariano 109
Paris, Treaty of (1783) 72–73, 79, 113
Parker, Ely 148, 201, 202
Parks, Rosa 277, 278
Patriot Act 297
Patrons of Husbandry 192–193
patroonships 38
Patterson, William 81
Paul, Alice 216
Pearl Harbor, attack on 252
Pendelton, George 157
Peninsular War 96
Penn, William 39
Pennsylvania. See also Philadelphia (Pennsylvania)
    Battle of Gettysburg 150–151

    colonial government of 42, 43
    constitution of 76
    German immigration to 47
    Homestead strike 191
    Quaker settlement in 39, 45
    in Revolutionary War 69–70
Peralta, Pedro de 33
Perkins, Tony 315
Perot, H. Ross 295
Pershing, John 221, 222, 223–224, 225
pesticides, chemical 260–261
Philadelphia (Pennsylvania)
    Centennial Exposition in 172, 173
    colonial 48
    Constitutional Convention in 80–81
    Continental Congresses in 65, 66
Philippines 208–209, 252, 269, 270
Pickett, George 150–151
Pike, Zebulon 92–93
Pilgrims 37
Pinckney, Charles C. 94
Pinckney's Treaty 79
Pine Ridge reservation 288
Pingree, Hazen 214
Pinta 22, 23
Pinzón, Martin Alonzo 22
Pinzón, Vicente Yáñez 22, 24
Pizarro, Francisco 29
Plano Culture 3
plantation system
    in Caribbean 56–57, 219
    cotton 97, 102, 119, 120
    financing of 120–121
    rice 59
    sugar 56, 57, 119
    tobacco 36–37
Platt Amendment 219
Plessy v. Ferguson 185, 275
Plymouth colony 37, 42, 44–45
Poland, collapse of communism 303
polio vaccine 261, 262
political parties
    abolitionist 135
    on left 248
    Populist 193–196
    Progressive 215
    rise of 85
Polk, James K. 109, 111, 113, 136
Polo, Marco 10
Ponce de León, Juan 30
Pontiac's Rebellion 62
Popé 33
popular culture
    in 1920s 230–231
    contemporary 315–316

**GEORGE PICKETT**

in 1940s and 1950s 264–265
in nineteenth century 178, 183
population. *See also* migration
    of English colonies 46
    immigrant 117, 182
    in slavery 47
    urban 179
    U.S. 108, 116–117
Populist Party 193–196
Porter, David 152
Portugal
    in Africa 18, 20
    in African slave trade 19
    Brazil colony of 24, 52
    explorers and exploration 10–11, 20, 24
    Treaty of Tordesillas 20, 24, 25
Post, Louis F. 229
Pottawatomie Creek massacre 139
poverty
    during Great Depression 240–242
    among Mexican Americans 312
    postwar 259
    race and 317
    "War on Poverty" 280
Powderly, Terrence V. 190
Powell, Colin 275
Powhatan Confederacy 36
Presbyterian Church 45, 49, 128
Prescott, Samuel 65
presidency, powers of 84–85
presidential elections
    1824 124
    1860 141
    1864 157–158
    1868 165, 273
    1876 170–171
    1896 196, 197
    1900 210
    1904 215
    1912 215
    1920 230
    1932 243, 248
    1964 280
    1968 273, 290–291
    1976 292–293
    1984 295
    1988 295
    1992 295–296
    2000 296
    2004 297, 315
Presley, Elvis 265
prison reform 128–129
Proclamation of 1763 62, 72
Progressive reform
    in city government 213–214

legacy of 216–217
    in state government 212–213
    under Theodore Roosevelt 214–215
    under Woodrow Wilson 215–216
Prohibition 128, 211–212, 230, 231
proportional representation 81
proprietary colonies 42
Protestantism. *See* Religion
public health system 118–119
Public Works Administration (PWA) 246
Pueblo Revolt 33
pueblos, Anasazi 5
Puerto Rican Americans 313
Puerto Rico
    migration from 313
    plantation agriculture in 56
    self-government of 287–288
    in Spanish-American War 208
    Spanish colonization of 25, 28, 30
    as U.S. territory 219, 287
Pullman strike 191, 192
Puritans 37, 39, 44–45

## Q

al-Qaeda 300, 305, 306
Quaddafi, Muammar el- 298, 301
Quakers 38, 39, 45
Quebec 32, 40, 41, 67
Quebec Act of 1774 64
Queen Anne's War 41, 47

## R

race riots 156, 228, 281, 316
radio broadcasting 235, 236, 262
Rahman, Omar Abdel- 304
railroads
    in Civil War 150
    government regulation of 193
    immigrant construction workers 180, 237
    on Indian land 199, 200
    steam power and 115–116
    strikes 190, 191
    transcontinental 175–176, 180
Raleigh, Walter 36
Randolph, A. Philip 257, 274, 278–279
Rauschenbush, Walter 210
Reagan, Ronald 290, 292
    background of 293–294

*Great steam engines like this one helped link the nation from east to west.*

Reagan, Ronald, *cont.*
    economic policy of 294–295
    foreign policy of 300–303
Reconstruction
    black codes and 163
    Congressional 163–166
    end of 170–171
    Lincoln's plan for 159, 162
    social 166–170
    wartime 160–162
Reconstruction Act of 1867 165
Red Cloud 200, 201, 202
Red Eagle (William Weatherford) 101, 102
Red Power movement 284–285, 287, 288
Reforestation Unemployment Act of 1933
    245
Reformation 12–13
reform movements. *See also* Progressive
    reform
    prisons and asylums 128–129
    Social Gospel 210
    suffrage 129–130
    temperance 128, 210–212
    women in 187
religion. *See also* Catholic Church; Islam
    abolitionist movement and 134
    Calvinism 32, 126
    denominations 45–46, 49, 128, 314, 315
    of European immigrants 182–183
    Fundamentalist Christianity 232–233,
        314–315
    "Ghost Dance" 204–205
    Great Awakening, First 48–49
    Great Awakening, Second 128–129
    Huguenots 30, 32
    Judaism 314
    liberal theology in 126–128
    Mormons 122–123
    pre-Columbian Indian 9
    Protestant Reformation 12–13
    Puritans 37, 39, 44–45, 49
    Quakers 38, 39, 45
    revival meetings 128
    sanctuary movement 313
    Social Gospel movement 210
    televangelists 262
Renaissance 10, 12
repartimento, 24
Republican Party. *See also* presidential
    elections
    abolition movement and, 135, 138–139
    Emancipation and, 153
    New Right, 294
    Reconstruction policy and, 163–165
    in Reconstruction South, 167–168

reservations, Indian, 79, 204
Revels, Hiram, 167
Revere, Paul, 63, 65
revival meetings, 128
Revolutionary War
    Articles of Confederaton 74
    battles of 67, 68–70
    Concord and Lexington 65–66
    Continental Congress, First 65
    Continental Congress, Second 66
    Declaration of Independence 67
    economic problems during 74, 75, 80
    events leading to 61–64
    Indians and 70, 71
    Patriots and Loyalists in 67–68
    smallpox epidemic during 72
    Treaty of Paris 72–73
    in West, 71–72
Rhode Island
    colony 37, 42
    Constitutional Convention and 80, 82
rice plantations 59
Rickey, Branch 274–275
Ridgway, Matthew 269
river transportation 88–89
roads and highways 72, 88, 230, 259, 260
Roanoke colony 36
Robertson, Pat 315
Roberval, sieur de 32
Robidoux, Louis 108
Robinson, Jackie 274–275
Rockefeller, John D. 176, 178, 196, 228
Rodríguez Cabrillo Juan, 34–35
Roebling, John Augustus 173
*Roe* v. *Wade* 289, 315
Rolfe, John 36
Rommel, Erwin 254
Roosevelt, Franklin Delano
    background of 244
    civil rights and 257, 274
    election of 1932 243
    GI Bill of 258, 259
    Lend-Lease program of 252
    New Deal programs of 244–249
    as polio victim 262
    Supreme Court and 249
    wartime leadership of 252, 253, 254,
        255
Roosevelt, Theodore
    Bull Moose Party candidacy of 215
    foreign policy of 219–221
    Progressive reform of 214–215
    in Spanish-American War 207–208
    as vice president 210
Roosevelt Corollary 220

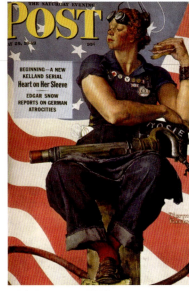

**ROSIE THE RIVETER**

Rosecrans, William S. 149
"Rosie the Riveter" 257
Rough Riders 207–208
Rumsfeld, Donald 305, 306
runaway slaves
    with Seminole 102–103
    in underground railroad 132–133
    with Union Army 153
Rural Electrification Administration (REA)
    245, 246, 260
Russia. *See also* Soviet Union
    Bolshevik Revolution 225
    Civil War (U.S.) and 147
Rustin, Bayard 279

# S

Sacagawea 92
Sacco, Nicola 229
Sadat, Anwar el- 298, 301
Saint Domingue 96, 130
Salk, Jonas 261, 262
SALT II agreement 298, 299
Sampson, William T. 207
San Antonio (Texas) 31, 34
sanctuary movement 313
Sand Creek Massacre 200
Sandia Culture 3
Sandinistas, in Nicaragua 301
San Salvador 22
Santa Anna, Antonio Lopéz de 105, 107,
    111, 112, 113
*Santa Clara County* v. *The Southern Pacific
    Railroad* 178
Santa Fe (New Mexico) 31, 33, 106, 107,
    122
Santa Fe Trail 93, 106, 109
Santa Maria 22, 23
Santo Domingo 23, 96
Satanta 201–202
Scalawags 167
Scalia, Antonin 296
*Schechter Poultry Corp.* v. *United States*
    247
schools. *See* education
Schwerner, Michael 280, 281
scientific research
    medical 261, 262, 309–310
    pesticide development 260–261, 262
    in plant genetics 261
Scopes trial 233
Scots-Irish immigrants 45, 47
Scott, Winfield 111, 112, 144, 149

Sea Islands, Reconstruction in 160–161,
    163
Seale, Bobby 284
secession crisis 141–142, 147–148
Security and Exchange Commission (SEC)
    246
Segregation. *See also* integration
    Jim Crow laws and 184–185
Selma-Montgomery march (Alabama) 281
Seminole 149, 198
Seminole War 96, 102–104
Seneca Falls Convention 130, 134
"separate but equal" 185, 275
September 11 attacks 297, 305–306
Serra, Junípera 35
service economy 259, 308, 310
Seven Cities of Cibola 31
Seward, William 147
Shabazz, Betty 284
Shafter, William R. 207
sharecroppers 168, 171, 194–195, 249
Share-the-Wealth program 248
Shaw, Robert Gould 154–155
Shay's Rebellion 80
Sheppard-Towner Maternity Act of 1921
    212
Sheridan, Philip 158
Sherman, John 196
Sherman, Roger 67, 81
Sherman, William Tecumseh 157, 158, 202
Sherman Antitrust Act of 1890 196, 214
Sherman Silver Act of 1890 196
Shope, Richard 226
shopping malls 264, 309
Sickles, Dan 150
Sierra Leone, colonization movement in
    133, 134
"silent majority" 290
Silliman, Benjamin, Jr. 174–175
silver-backed currency 196, 197
Simpson, O.J. 316
Sinclair, Upton 211, 248
Sioux 148, 199, 200, 201, 202–203, 205
sit-ins 278
Sitting Bull 205
Slater, Samuel 114
slave narratives 135
slavery. *See also* anti-slavery movement;
    runaway slaves; slavery, expansion of
    in Africa 16–17, 18
    in Caribbean 52, 56–57
    Columbian Exchange and 23
    Constitution and 81, 97–98
    cotton production and 97, 119, 120
    Emancipation Proclamation 153–155

**SITTING BULL**

**PETER STUYVESANT**

slavery, *cont.*
  in English colonies 47, 56, 58–59
  in French colonies 50
  Jefferson and 67, 81
  maroons 57
  rebellions 96, 130–132, 134
  during Revolutionary War 73
  resistance to 102
  sales of slaves 121–122
  in Spanish colonies 50
slavery, expansion of
  Compromise of 1850 136–137
  Kansas-Nebraska Act 138–139
  Missouri Compromise of 1820 98, 99, 130
  in western territories 90, 97–98
slave trade
  abolition of 21, 121
  expansion of 18–19, 50
  middle passage 52–53
  routes of 53
Slidell, John 109
Sloat, John D. 110
smallpox 23, 72
Smalls, Robert 167
Smith, Jedediah 93
Smith, John 36, 37
Smith, Joseph, Jr. 122–123
Smith-Hughes Act of 1917 212
Smoot-Hawley Tariff Act 243
social class
  in cities 179
  industrialization and 172–173
  Jacksonian Democracy and 124, 126
  pre-Columbian cultures and 9
Social Darwinism 178
Social Gospel movement 210
Socialist Party 248
social reform. *See* reform movements
Social Security Act of 1935 247–248, 280
Songhai Empire 16, 17
Sons of Liberty 62–63
South Carolina
  colonial government in 39, 42
  Fort Sumter 141, 142, 143
  secession of 141, 142
  slave rebellion in 59, 130–131
  slavery in 59
Southeast Asian refugees 311–312
Southern Alliance 195
Southern Christian Leadership Conference (SCLC) 278, 279
"Southern Manifesto" 276, 280
Soviet Union. *See also* Cold War
  Afghanistan invasion of 299, 300

  Arab-Israeli War and 298
  collapse of 302
  in Cuban Missile Crisis 271
  détente with 297–298
  formation of 225
  glasnost 302
  in nuclear arms treaties 298, 299, 302
  and Warsaw Pact 268
  in World War II 251, 253–254
space program 298
Spain. *See also* Spanish colonies
  Adams-Onis Treaty of 1819 97
  Bonaparte rule in 96, 104–105
  Catholic church in 12
  civil war in 251
  Columbus's voyages for 22–23
  explorers and exploration 22–23, 26, 30, 31
  in Peninsular War 96
  in Revolutionary War 70
  Treaty of Tordesillas 20, 24, 25
  Spanish-American War 206–209
  Spanish Armada 36
Spanish colonies
  conquistadores 28–29
  encomienda system 24, 50
  independence movements in 96–97, 105–107
  Indians and 24–25, 33
  missions 33–34, 35
  in North America 30–31, 33–35
  Pinckney's Treaty 79
  slavery in 50
  trade and 29, 34
  U.S. annexation of Florida 96, 97
  War of Jenkins' Ear 41
spearpoints 2, 3
Spencer, Herbert 178
sports 178
Spotswood, Alexander 47
Stalin, Joseph 250, 251, 269
Stamp Act of 1765 62
Stamp Act protests 62–64
Standard Oil Company 176, 196, 211
Standish, Miles 44
Stanford, Leland 180
Stanley, William 173
Stanton, Edwin 147, 165
Stanton, Elizabeth Cady 130
*Star of the West* 141
states
  constitutions 76–77
  from Northwest Territory lands 78
  populous (1790–1840) 118
  Progressive governments in 212–213

secessionist 141
   voting rights in 124
St. Augustine (Florida) 32, 40, 41
St. Clair, Arthur 99
steam engine 172
steam locomotive 115–116
steamships 115
steel strikes 228, 247
Steffens, Lincoln 211
Steinem, Gloria 289
Stephens, Alexander 146
Steuben, Wilhelm von 70
Stevens, Thaddeus 163
St. Lawrence River 27, 32, 33, 41, 61
stock exchange 239–240, 295
Stockton, Robert E. 110
Stone (Lithic) Age 3
Stono Rebellion 59
Stowe, Harriet Beecher 129, 140
Strategic Defense Initiative (SDI) 300, 302
strikes
   air traffic controllers 294
   farm workers 286–287
   in nineteenth century 189, 190, 191
   steel workers 228, 247
   Theodore Roosevelt and 214
Student Nonviolent Coordinating
      Committee (SNCC) 278, 279, 281, 284
Stuyvesant, Peter 38, 39
suburbs, growth of 235, 239, 263–264
suffrage
   African American 162, 164, 170, 184
   expansion of 124, 125
   restrictive measures 166
   Voting Rights Act of 1965 281
   women's 129–130, 186–187, 216, 217
   sugar plantations 56, 57, 119, 219
Sullivan, John 71
Sumner, Charles 139, 163
Sumner, William Graham 178
Sunbelt region, migration to 308
supply-side economics 294, 295
Supreme Court, U.S.
   abortion in, 289 315
   business regulation in 178, 193, 214
   civil rights cases in 185, 275–276, 285
   Dred Scott case 139
   greenback currency in 196
   Japanese-American internment in 253
   labor relations in 191
   under Marshall 86–87
   New Deal programs in 246, 247, 249
   Nixon tapes and, 292
   progressive reform in 214
   Roosevelt's plan to "pack" 249

2000 election recount in 296
   under Warren 291
Sutter, John Augustus 108, 123
Swedish colony 38
syphilis 23

# T

Taft, William Howard, 215, 221
Taiwan, 268
Taliban, 305
Taney, Roger, 139, 160
Tappan, Arthur and Lewis, 134
Tarbell, Ida 211
taxes
   during Civil War 148
   colonial 61, 62–63
   cuts in 294
   in Reconstruction South 167–168
Taylor, Zachary 109, 110–111
Tea Act of 1773 64
Technology. See also scientific research
   agricultural 193
   broadcasting 262
   computer 308–309
   cotton gin 97, 114
   industrial development and 114–115,
      172–173
   inventors and inventions 173–174,
      259–260
   pre-Columbian Indian 9
   workplace automation 259
Tecumseh 100, 101
television broadcasting 262, 263, 315
temperance movement 128, 210–211
tenements 179, 183
Tenet, George 306
Tennent, Gilbert 48
Tennent, William 48
Tennessee, statehood of 88
Tennessee Valley Authority (TVA) 245, 246,
      260
Tenochtitlán 28
Tenskwatawa 100
territorial expansion. See westward
      expansion
terrorism, international 297, 300, 301, 304,
      305–306
Tesla, Nicolai 174
Tet Offensive 272–273
Texas
   annexation of 109
   independence of 106–107, 108

**ZACHARY TAYLOR**

**SOJOURNER TRUTH**

Texas, *cont.*
    as slave state 107, 136
    under Mexico 105, 106
    under Spain 31, 34
    textile industry 114, 116, 174
Thomas, Norman 248
Thoreau, Henry David 127–128
Three Mile Island accident 293
Tilden, Samuel J. 170
tobacco, health risks of 310
tobacco plantations 36–37
Tompkins, Sally 147
*Tom Thumb* (steam locomotive) 115–116
Toombs, Robert 145
Tordesillas, Treaty of 20, 24, 25
Townsend, Francis 247–248
Townshend Act of 1767 64
Trade. *See also* slave trade
    in African colonization 20
    with California 108
    in English colonies 54–55, 75
    fur trade 33, 38
    medieval European 10
    mercantilism and 11, 54
    pre-Columbian Indian 6
    restrictions 94
    Spanish colonial 27, 29, 34
    tobacco 37
trans-Saharan 15, 18
Trail of Tears 103
transcendentalists 127
transplant surgery 309
transportation. *See also* railroads
    automobile 230, 235, 239
    canals 89–90, 115, 116
    river and lake 88–89
    roads and highways 72, 88, 230,
      259, 260
    speed of 118
    steamship 115
    suburban development and 263
Travis, William 107
treaties
    Adams-Onis 97, 98
    of Brest-Litovsk 225
    of Fort Jackson,101
    Fort Laramie 199, 201, 202
    of Fort Stanwix 79
    of Fort Wayne 100
    of Greenville 99
    of Guadalupe Hidalgo 112–113
    Hay-Bunau-Varilla 220
    Hay-Pauncefote 220
    with Indians 79, 99, 100, 101, 199–200,
      202

Jay's Treaty 79, 85–86
    nuclear arms limitation 298, 299, 302
    Oregon 113
    of Paris (1783) 72–73, 79, 113
    of San Lorenzo (Pinckney's Treaty), 79
    of Tordesillas 20, 24, 25
    of Versailles 227–228
Triana, Rodrigo de 22
Triangle Shirtwaist fire 213
Trollope, Frances 128
Trotter, William Monroe 215
Truman, Harry S. 256, 259, 267, 268, 269,
    287
Truman Doctrine 267, 269
Trumbull, Lyman 163
Truth, Sojourner 130
Tubman, Harriet 133
Turner, Frederick Jackson 78, 205–206
Turner, Nat, Rebellion of 131–132, 134
Tuskegee Airmen 275
Tuskegee Institute 185, 186
Twain, Mark 170, 180
Tweed, William Marcy "Boss" 176
Tyler, John 108

## U

*Uncle Tom's Cabin* (Stowe) 129, 140
underground railroad 132–133
unemployment 240–241, 242, 259, 317
unemployment compensation 247
Union Army
    African-American soldiers in 153–155
    battles 149–153, 156, 157, 158
    runaway slaves with 153
Union Navy 149, 157
Unitarianism 49, 126–127
United Auto Workers (UAW) 247
United Farm Workers Association 286
United Nations (UN) 266, 298
United States Sanitary Commission 148
Universal Negro Improvement Association
    233, 282
universities. *See* colleges and universities
University of Mississippi, integration of 278

## V

Vallandigham, Clement 148, 157
Vallejo, Mariano 110
Van Buren, Martin 135

Van Rensselaer, Kiliaen 38
Vanzetti, Bartolomeo 229
Vásquez de Ayllón, Lucas 30
Verrazano, Giovanni da 27
Versailles, Treaty of 227–228
Vesey, Denmark 130–131
Vespucci, Amerigo 26
veterans
    in Bonus Army 243
    GI Bill 258, 259, 263
Veterans Administration (VA), 258
Viet Cong 272, 273
Vietnam War 272–273, 275
Vietnam War protests 272, 273, 288, 290
Villa, Pancho 221
Vineland 10
Virginia
    Civil War battles in 149
    colonial government of 42, 43, 44
    constitution of 76
    Jamestown colony 36–37, 58
    slave rebellions in 130, 131–132
    slavery in 58
    western expansion of 47
Virginia Company 36, 37
Virginia Declaration of Rights 83
Virginia (Merrimack USS) 149
Virginia Plan 81
Virginia Resolves 62
Volstead Act 231
voter registration campaign 280–281
voting rights. See suffrage
Voting Rights Act of 1965 281

# W

Wabash, St. Louis, and the Pacific Railway
    Company 193
wages 192, 309, 317
Wagner, Robert F. 247
Wagner Act 247
Walker, David 134
Walker, Joseph 93
Wallace, George 281, 291
Walla Walla Council, 200
Wall St. crash, 239–240
Wal-Mart 309
Walsh, Lawrence 301
Wanamaker, John 179
War of 1812 94, 95, 100
War of the Austrian Succession 41
War for Independence.
    See Revolutionary War

War Industries Board 224
War of Jenkins' Ear 41
War of the League of Augsburg 40
Warmouth, Henry 176
"War on Poverty," 280
War Relocation Authority (WRA) 253
Warren, Earl, 276 285
Warsaw Pact 268, 302–303
War of the Spanish Succession 41
War on Terror 297, 305–306
Washington, Booker T. 185, 186, 215
Washington, Bushrod 134
Washington, George
    at Constitutional Convention 81
    in French and Indian War 60
    presidency of 84–86, 114
    in Revolutionary War 66, 68, 69–70,
        71, 72
Watergate scandal 291–292
Watson, Tom 195
Watson-Watt, Robert Alexander 259
Watts riot 281
Wayne, Anthony 99
weapons
    atomic bomb 253, 255, 256
    in Civil War 149, 150
    nuclear 269, 270
    in World War I 222
    "weapons of mass destruction" (WMD)
        306, 307
Weatherford, William (Red Eagle) 101, 102
Weaver, James 195, 196
Weld, Theodore Dwight 128, 134
Wells-Barnett, Ida 233
Westinghouse, George 174
westward expansion
    annexation of Mexican territories 109,
        110, 112–113
    of English colonies 47, 71–72
    exploration for 91–94
    frontier thesis of 205–206
    Indian attacks on settlers 148–149, 200
    Jefferson and 77, 78, 90–91
    "Manifest Destiny" in 109, 142
    Mormons in 122–123
    in Northwest Territory 55–79
    Proclamation of 1763 ban on 62, 72
    routes in 93–94, 122
slavery and. See slavery, expansion of
    transportation methods for 88–90
Whig Party 138
White Citizens' Councils 277
Whitefield, George 48, 49
White Sticks 101
Whitney, Eli 97, 114, 119

**WOODROW WILSON**

**BRIGHAM YOUNG**

Wild Cat 103

Wilderness Road 72, 88

William III, King of England (William of Orange) 40

William and Mary College 48

Williams, Ezekial 93

Williams, Roger 37, 45

Wilmot, David 136

Wilson, Joseph 306

Wilson, Woodrow

    civil rights policy of 215–216

    Fourteen Points 227, 228

    women's suffrage and 216

    World War I and 223, 224

Winthrop, John 37

Wisconsin

    Progressive Movement in 212

    statehood of 78

Wolfe, James 61

Wollaston, Captain 44

women

    in abolitionist movement 134

    during Civil War 147, 148

    in consumer society 234–235

    education of 129, 187

    Equal Rights Amendment 289

    factory workers 116

    in labor force 187, 190, 212, 213, 235, 257, 309, 310

    married women's rights 129, 130, 167

    pre-Columbian Indian 8

women, *continued*

    suffrage movement 129–130, 186–187, 216, 217

    in temperance movement 210–211

Women's Christian Temperance Union (WCTU) 211

Women's Liberation Movement 288–289

Woodhull, Victoria 187

Woodward, Bob 291

workforce. *See* labor force

Works Progress Administration (WPA) 246

World's Columbian Exposition 173, 205

World Trade Center

    bombing of 304

    September 11 attack on 297, 305–306

World War I 222–228

World War II

    atomic bomb 253, 255, 256

    casualties 256

    in Europe and Middle East 250, 251, 253–255

    home front during 257

    Japanese-American internment during 253, 254

    in Pacific 252, 256

    segregated troops in 275

    U.S. entry 252

    U.S. isolationism and 251–252

    veterans benefits program 258

World Wide Web 309

Wounded Knee, AIM occupation of 287, 288

Wounded Knee Massacre 205

Wycliffe, John 12

## Y

Yale College 48

Yeager, Chuck 260

Yeltsin, Boris 303

Yom Kippur War 298

Young, Brigham 123

## Z

Zaire 270

Zimmerman Note 223

Zuni 31, 33

Zwingli, Ulrich 13

# PICTURE SOURCES